Symbol of Courage

Also by Max Arthur

Above All, Courage: First-hand Accounts from the Falklands Front Line

Northern Ireland: Soldiers Talking

Men of the Red Beret: Airborne Forces 1940–1990

There Shall be Wings – The RAF: 1918 to the Present

The True Glory: The Royal Navy, 1914–1939

The Navy: 1939 to the Present Day

The Busby Babes: Men of Magic

When This Bloody War Is Over: Soldiers' Songs of the First World War

Forgotten Voices of the Great War

MAX ARTHUR

Symbol of Courage

A HISTORY OF THE VICTORIA CROSS

SIDGWICK & JACKSON

First published 2004 by Sidgwick & Jackson
an imprint of Pan Macmillan Ltd
Pan Macmillan, 20 New Wharf Road, London N1 9RR
Basingstoke and Oxford
Associated companies throughout the world
www.panmacmillan.com

ISBN 0 283 07351 9

1 3 5 7 9 8 6 4 2

A CIP catalogue record for this book is available from
the British Library.

Typeset by SetSystems Ltd, Saffron Walden, Essex
Printed and bound in Great Britain by
Mackays of Chatham plc, Chatham, Kent

To David Harvey,
who devoted his life to locating
the final resting places of all holders of
the Victoria Cross

Picture Credits

Acknowledgements

My initial thanks are to William Armstrong, who commissioned me to write this book as he did with my first, *Above All, Courage*. I am indebted to my editor, Ingrid Connell, who has over the last two years lived with the various changes of format and drafts and dealt with all of them with skill, humour and patience. Nicholas Blake, senior desk editor, has also diligently and patiently carried out his task, and given sound advice. I would also like to thank Penny Price, assistant editor, for her photographic research for the book, and Becky Folkard-Ward, my more than helpful production assistant.

Throughout the writing of this book, I have had the remarkable assistance of two very fine researchers: Vicky Thomas and Joshua Levine. Their contribution to this book is inestimable and I profoundly thank them.

I owe a great debt to the late David Harvey, whose work *Monuments to Courage* showed all the hallmarks of his own courage and determination.

Brian Best of the Victoria Cross Society gave me advice throughout and kindly read the proofs and made a number of suggestions, all of which I incorporated. Tom Johnson BEM supplied all the information for the citations in the appendices as well as personal details to each of the biographies and the *London Gazette* details. His research throughout this book has been of the highest calibre and his support has been vital. I would also like to thank John Mulholland for his expertise on the subject and James W. Bancroft for his contribution to the Boer War and the Zulu Campaigns. My thanks must also go to Steve Snelling, who kindly read through drafts of the First World War and advised changes that I was happy to incorporate. I must thank my brother Adrian, a recognized expert on the Victorian army, who has never ceased to amaze me with his detailed knowledge of British regiments. Allan Percival kindly allowed me access to his considerable research on the Victorian wars.

Three websites have proved to be invaluable, Brian Best's at www.victoria crosssociety.com, Mike Chapman's at www.victoriacross.net and Iain Stewart's at www.victoriacross.org.uk/vcross.htm, and I am most grateful to them all. I am also most grateful to the Photographic Department of the Imperial War Museum, who kindly gave me permission to use many of the photographs in this book.

Throughout the writing of this book I have had the support of my friend Sir Martin Gilbert, whose advice I have sought on various occasions as well as receiving innumerable insights into individual holders of the Victoria Cross. I profoundly thank him.

My close friend Ruth Cowen has been an enormous source of encouragement throughout the writing of the book and travelled with me to the Crimea, where we walked the battlefields of the war, not only for this book, but for her own biography on the French chef Alexis Soyer, whose camp stove helped to save the lives of so many soldiers.

My thanks are also due to the writer and broadcaster Susan Jeffreys for her great support and sound advice. I particularly want to thank Maurice Horhut, who organized the book on the computer and spent many hours researching the campaigns. He also plays a mean piano. Don and Liz McClen have given great support throughout the writing of all my books and I thank them.

Finally, I would like to thank Cathy Waterhouse, for enriching the last few months of the book with her love and laughter.

Contents

Introduction

For Valour

During the past twenty years it has been my privilege to meet a number of Victoria Cross holders. The one characteristic that immediately struck me was their modesty. They did not want to be singled out from ordinary people, just because of one particular moment in their life.

Field Marshal Sir William Slim, whose own personal courage was never in doubt, and who was no mean judge of character, thought that those who perform individual acts of the highest physical courage are usually drawn from one of two categories: those with quick intelligence and vivid imagination, or those without imagination. One type suddenly sees the crisis, his imagination flashes the opportunity and he acts. The other meets the situation without finding it so very unusual and deals with it in a matter-of-fact way. As you read the individual accounts, I think you will see both categories emerge, and perhaps others.

There is no doubt that courage inspires, for it is contagious. When brave men go forward under fire others follow. But equally it takes courage to crawl forward under fire to recover a wounded comrade or supply those around you with ammunition, or when your aircraft is shot to pieces to still fly it to the intended target, or turn your stricken ship towards the enemy to ram it, knowing that the outcome will undoubtedly be death or injury.

The Origin of the Medal

It was the young Queen Victoria who recognized that the bravery of her soldiers and sailors had, apart from the officers, gone unrewarded. She wanted a new medal to be struck for all ranks who conducted themselves with unusual bravery. The initial Royal Warrant of 1856 stipulated 'that the cross shall only be awarded for most conspicuous bravery, or some daring or pre-eminent act of valour or self-sacrifice or extreme devotion to duty in the presence of the enemy' and was made retrospective to June 1854 to cover the recent war against Russia.

The medal is in the shape of a Cross Patté (from the French for 'with feet' or 'paws' and referring, in the case of a cross, to the spreading ends) –

rather than a Maltese Cross, as described in the original warrant. It measures 1.375 inches across and, with the suspender bar and link, weighs around 0.87 ounces. It's dull in colour, made as it is from gunmetal – specifically, at first, from the cascabels of two cannon captured from the Russians at Sebastopol in the Crimea, although later in the First World War it's probable that other gunmetal was used. The cascabel is the large knob at the rear of a cannon which holds the rope for transporting it – and the two original cannon from Sebastopol stand outside the Officers' Mess in Woolwich.

The Cross is cast, then chased and finished by hand, then the award, suspender bar and link are treated chemically to give an overall dull brown appearance, which is darker in some issues than in others.

Although all VCs are cast and finished by the London jewellers Messrs Hancocks (now Hancocks and Co.), and always have been, the chunk of gunmetal from which they are made is kept in a vault tended by the Royal Logistic Corps in Donnington, and is rarely seen.

On the front of the cross is simply inscribed 'For Valour' – the other details of the recipient are on the reverse. The suspender bar is decorated with laurel leaves (the traditional Roman award to a hero was a wreath of laurel) and on the reverse is inscribed the name, rank and regiment of the recipient, along with the date of the deed engraved on the central circle. In the unlikely event of a Bar being awarded to the VC – there have been just three – the bar is designed like the suspender bar, but without the V-shaped lug for hanging the cross itself. The ribbon, referred to as 'red' in the original warrant, is more properly crimson, although it was first ordained to be dark blue for the Royal Navy and crimson for the army. Shortly before the formation of the Royal Air Force on 1 April 1918, the King approved the use of crimson for all future awards.

The first presentation of the award was made in Hyde Park, London, on 26 June 1857 when Queen Victoria decorated 62 officers and men for their actions in the Crimea.

The crowd of about a hundred thousand people began gathering at 7 a.m. – and they were witnesses to a massive spectacle of nine thousand troops assembled before the specially built pavilion. With the military dignitaries assembled, at 9.55 a.m. a flash from the field batteries and a heavy boom announced the approach of the Queen's cortege through the Hyde Park Corner gate. Queen Victoria rode between Prince Albert and her future son-in-law, Prince Frederick William of Prussia. With precision timing, as the royal party approached, the whole assembled force presented arms as the Queen inspected her troops.

The sixty-two newly made Victoria Crosses were laid out on a scarlet-covered table, in front of the Queen, who, unexpectedly, decided to remain on horseback throughout the investiture. As each name was called, the man stepped forward, the army recipients saluting and the naval men removing their hats. Lord Panmure passed the medals to the Queen as she pinned them on to the specially provided loop of cord which each man wore to make the fixing easier. In ten minutes it was done. The royal party was back at Buckingham Palace before noon.

Writing in her diary, the Queen considered – 'It was indeed a most proud, gratifying day.'

Changes to the Warrant

Since the inception of the Victoria Cross there have been a number of changes within the warrant. In October 1857 it was extended to include the Honourable East India Company. This, however, did not include native soldiers. From 1858 to 1881 there was an extension granted for cases of conspicuous courage and bravery displayed under circumstances of danger, but not before the enemy (six awards were made). In January 1867 there was an extension to local forces in New Zealand and in the colonies and their dependencies, and as late as 1911 the warrant was extended to include native officers, NCOs and men of the Indian Army.

Surprisingly, it was not until 1920 that an official amendment was instituted allowing the VC to be awarded posthumously, reflecting the experience of the First World War. The original warrant made no mention of posthumous awards and it had been decided that the VC would not be given for an act in which the intended recipient had been killed or where he had died shortly afterwards. However, in 1900 the VC was awarded to Frederick Roberts for his action at the Battle of Colenso, although he died a day later. Two years later a further six VCs were awarded posthumously and in 1907 six others dating between 1859 and 1897 were also awarded. In all, 298 VCs have been awarded posthumously.

Until 1920 the award could be forfeited for discreditable acts; the VC holder also lost his pension. In the history of the award this occurred eight times, for desertion, assault, theft, and bigamy. The eight men who lost the award were Edward Daniel, James McGuire, Valentine Bambrick, Michael Murphy, Thomas Lane, Frederick Corbett, James Collis and George Ravenhill. George V revoked this clause in response to a letter from James Collis's widow, declaring: 'Even were a VC to be sentenced to be hanged for murder, he should be allowed to wear the VC on the scaffold.' The names of all eight men were restored to the register.

Originally the recommendation for the award was to be made by a superior officer, but this too was changed by Royal Warrant, which allowed for a VC to be awarded on the result of a ballot by the man's peers in order to recognize the bravery of a larger group of men through one elected representative. Forty-six VCs have been awarded this way.

These days, it is necessary for three witnesses to the act of bravery to make a sworn statement in order for a VC to be awarded – it seems that it is becoming harder and harder to earn such an award. Controversy has often surrounded the award of this most prestigious honour, since it is often difficult to define what represents an act of selfless bravery as opposed to the instinctive response of a man to preserve his own life – and those of his comrades around him.

What was most important, from the very first, was that any man or boy (or woman – but none has been awarded yet), whatever their rank, was eligible for the award. The final word on the award would rest with the monarch who, wherever possible, would present the medal in person.

The Life of the Medal

Since its inception, fourteen men not born in Britain or the Commonwealth have received the award – five Americans, one Belgian, two Germans, three Danes, one Swiss, one Swede and one Ukrainian.

The most VCs won in one day was twenty-four, in the second relief of Lucknow on 16 November 1857, during the Indian Mutiny.

The highest tally of awards for a single action (which lasted overnight on 22/33 January 1879) was eleven, for the defence of Rorke's Drift during the Zulu War

The first VC awards allowed a special pension of £10 a year payable to non-commissioned ranks. From 1898 this could be increased, at discretion, to £50, then later £75. Only in 1959 was the pension granted irrespective of rank and raised to £100. When, in 1995 it was increased to £1,300, there were just 33 recipients alive. At the time of writing, April 2004, just fifteen VC holders survive.

The army unit with the most VC awards made is the Royal Artillery, with fifty-one recipients, followed by the Royal Engineers with forty-one, and the Royal Army Medical Corps and Rifle Brigade with twenty-seven apiece.

Over 75 per cent of VC awards have been made to a man who has grown up as the responsible child of an early-widowed mother or the eldest child in a large family.

Only three men have won a bar to the VC – Arthur Martin-Leake, Noel Chavasse and Charles Upham.

Four pairs of brothers have been awarded the VC – George and Roland Bradford, Charles and Hugh Gough, Euston and Reginald Sartorius and Alexander and Victor Turner. On two occasions the award has been made to a man for saving his brother's life.

Three father and son pairs have been awarded the VC – Frederick S. and Frederick H. S. Roberts, Walter and William Congreve and Charles and John Gough. The Gough family is the only one in which a father/son/uncle trio have received the VC.

Although a military award, the VC has been given to five civilians who were acting under military command – James Adams, George Chicken, Thomas Kavanagh, William McDonell and Ross Mangles.

The youngest winners of the VC were just fifteen years old – Andrew Fitzgibbon and Thomas Flinn – and the oldest, William Raynor, was sixty-one.

Three men from one street in Winnipeg, Manitoba, Canada – Pine Street – have been awarded the VC: Fred Hall, Leo Clarke and Robert Shankland. This street has since been renamed Valour Road.

Notable firsts – the first man to receive his award from Queen Victoria was Henry Raby, but the first nomination was to Charles Lucas and the first gazetted VC was for Cecil Buckley.

The first airman to receive the VC was William Rhodes-Moorhouse for an action in April 1915.

Of all VC winners, William McBean, uniquely, held every rank from private to major general during his career.

The naval services hold a total of 119 VCs, the British army 837 (including two bars) and the air services (except the Fleet Air Arm) 32. The most awards outside these services are to the Indian Army (including the Honourable East India Company), with 137.

The only ungazetted award was made to the American Unknown Soldier of the First World War, buried at Arlington National Cemetery.

The last awarded VCs were in 1982 during the Falklands campaign. Since the end of the Second World War the VC has only been awarded eleven times. With the nature of warfare becoming more technological there has been fewer opportunities to 'close with the enemy' but no one can dispute the courage of today's servicemen nor of their inheritance of courage.

Winston Churchill wrote in 1897: 'I am more ambitious for a reputation for personal courage than for anything else in the world.'

A Note on the Text

Throughout the book there is a brief outline of the campaign or action in which the Victoria Cross was awarded. I have wherever possible mentioned the location of the action in which the deed was carried out. Each deed which merited the award is described in detail. These details have been adapted from the original citation issued in *The London Gazette*. However, from 1939 onwards, each recipient's citation is given in full, though in some cases they have been edited for greater clarity or for length.

In the Biographical Index the reader will find each recipient's place and date of birth and, where known, the location of his death and place of burial. In order to read the full citation of every recipient, I have given in the Appendix the *London Gazette* number and where necessary, any supplement.

I have become increasingly aware as I have compiled this book that errors are bound to creep in. Every effort has been made to check each entry, and should there be any errors, the responsibility is entirely mine. However, should you find one, or can enrich any of the 1,354 accounts, I would be most grateful if you would contact me at the publisher's address. The same applies to the copyright of the photographs, sketches and paintings contained in the book. Every effort has been made to ascertain the copyright holder and request their permission for use, but in some cases the mist of time has descended and the trail to the original holder has disappeared. Again, please contact me at the publisher's should you wish to raise a point on copyright.

Max Arthur

London, 2004

Maps

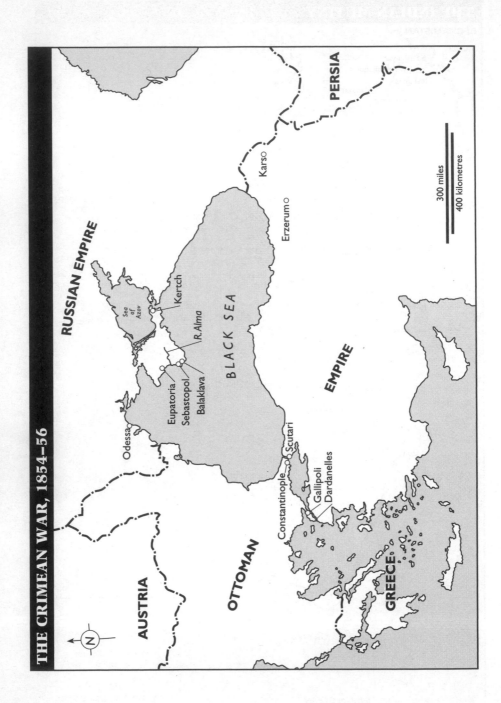

THE CRIMEAN WAR, 1854–56

N

AUSTRIA

RUSSIAN EMPIRE

Odessa

Sea of Azov

Kertch

R. Alma

Eupatoria
Sebastopol
Balaklava

BLACK SEA

OTTOMAN

Constantinople
Scutari
Gallipoli
Dardanelles

GREECE

EMPIRE

Erzerum

Kars

PERSIA

300 miles
400 kilometres

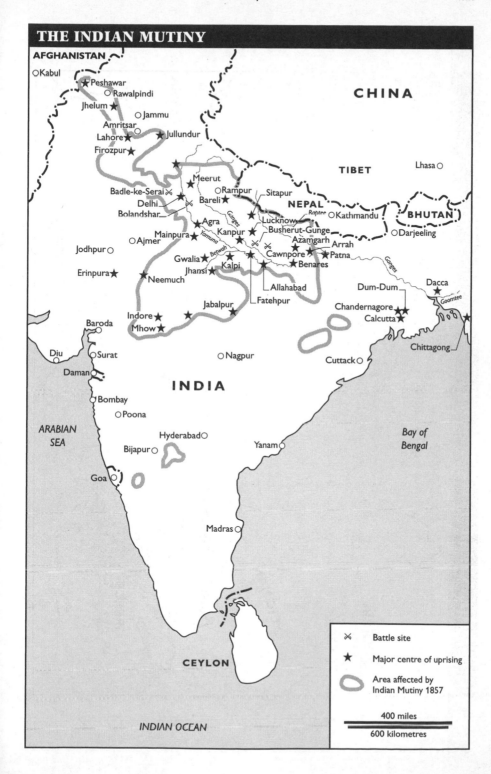

THE INDIAN MUTINY

AFGHANISTAN

CHINA

○ Kabul

★ Peshawar
○ Rawalpindi

Jhelum ★
○ Jammu

Amritsar
Lahore ★ ★ Jullundur
Firozpur ★

TIBET

Lhasa ○

Meerut ★
Badle-ke-Serai ✕   ○ Rampur   Sitapur
Delhi   Bareli
Bolandshar   NEPAL
             Lucknow   Raptee ○ Kathmandu   BHUTAN
Agra ★   Busherut-Gunge
Mainpura ★ Kanpur ★   Azamgarh   ○ Darjeeling
○ Ajmer   Cawnpore ★ Arrah ★
Jodhpur ○   ★ Patna
Gwalia ★   Kalpi ★   Benares
Erinpura ★ Jhansi ★   Dum-Dum   Dacca ○
Neemuch ★   Chandernagore ○   Goomtee
        Jabalpur ★   Allahabad   Calcutta ○
Indore ★   Fatehpur
Mhow ★
Baroda   Chittagong
○
Diu ○   ○ Surat   ○ Nagpur   Cuttack ○
Daman ○
        INDIA
○ Bombay
○ Poona
ARABIAN
SEA   Hyderabad ○   Yanam ○   Bay of
        Bijapur ○   Bengal
Goa ○

Madras ○

CEYLON

✕	Battle site
★	Major centre of uprising
⬭	Area affected by Indian Mutiny 1857

400 miles
600 kilometres

INDIAN OCEAN

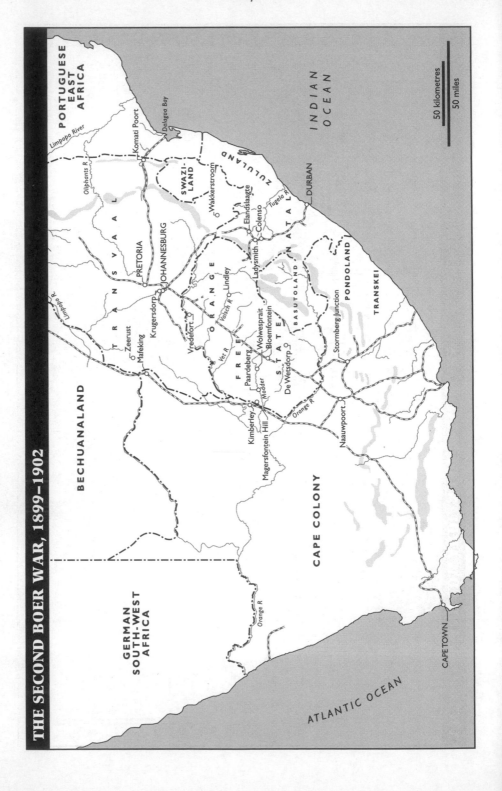

THE SECOND BOER WAR, 1899–1902

PORTUGUESE EAST AFRICA

Limpopo River

Oliphants R.

Komati Poort

Delagoa Bay

SWAZI-LAND

Wakkerstroom

ZULULAND

T R A N S V A A L

Limpopo R.

PRETORIA

JOHANNESBURG

Krugersdorp

Zeerust

Mafeking

Vredefort

Lindley

Vet R.

Valsch R.

Elandslaagte

Colenso

Ladysmith

Tugela R.

DURBAN

N A T A L

O R A N G E

F R E E   S T A T E

Paardeberg

Wolwespruit

Modder

Bloemfontein

De Wetsdorp

Kimberley

Magersfontein Hill

Orange R.

Naauwpoort

Stormberg Junction

BASUTOLAND

PONDOLAND

TRANSKEI

BECHUANALAND

GERMAN SOUTH-WEST AFRICA

Orange R.

CAPE COLONY

CAPETOWN

ATLANTIC OCEAN

INDIAN OCEAN

50 kilometres

50 miles

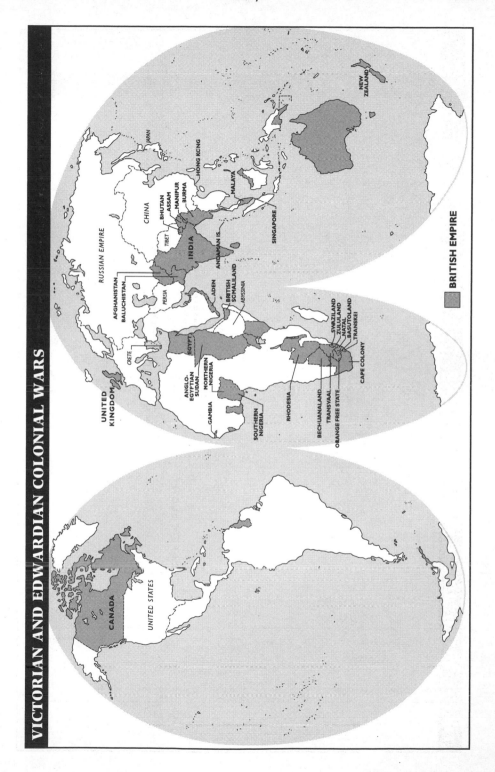

VICTORIAN AND EDWARDIAN COLONIAL WARS

BRITISH EMPIRE

THE WESTERN FRONT

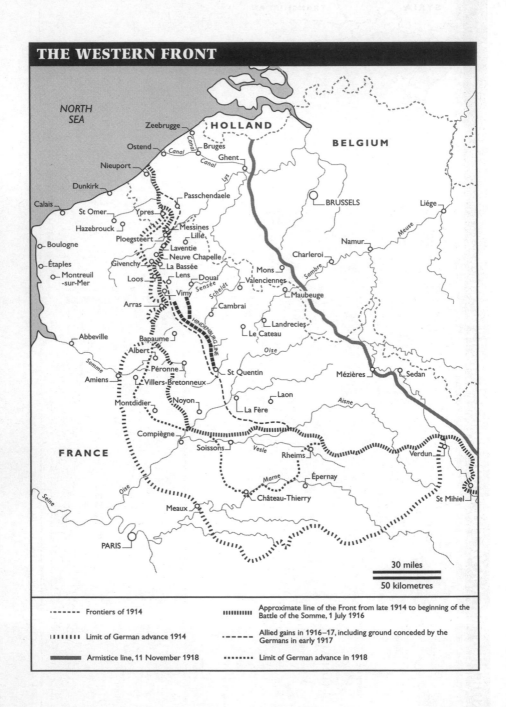

30 miles

50 kilometres

- - - - - - - Frontiers of 1914	⑴⑴⑴⑴⑴ Approximate line of the Front from late 1914 to beginning of the Battle of the Somme, 1 July 1916
⑴⑴⑴⑴⑴ Limit of German advance 1914	- - - - - Allied gains in 1916–17, including ground conceded by the Germans in early 1917
▬▬▬ Armistice line, 11 November 1918	• • • • • • • Limit of German advance in 1918

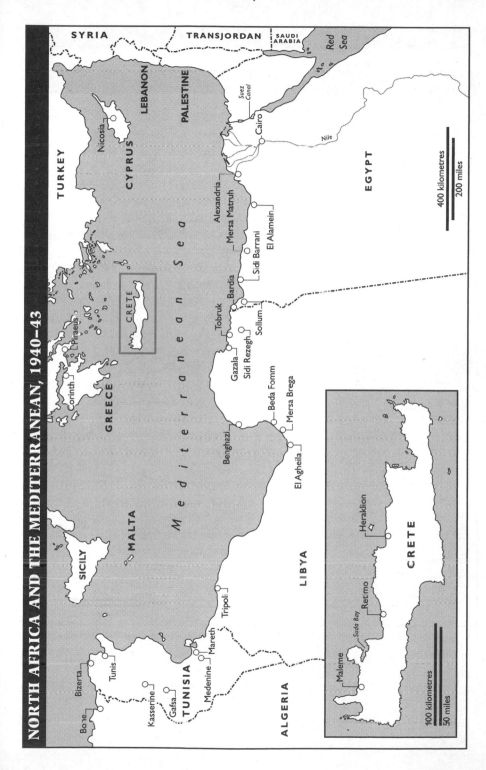

NORTH AFRICA AND THE MEDITERRANEAN, 1940–43

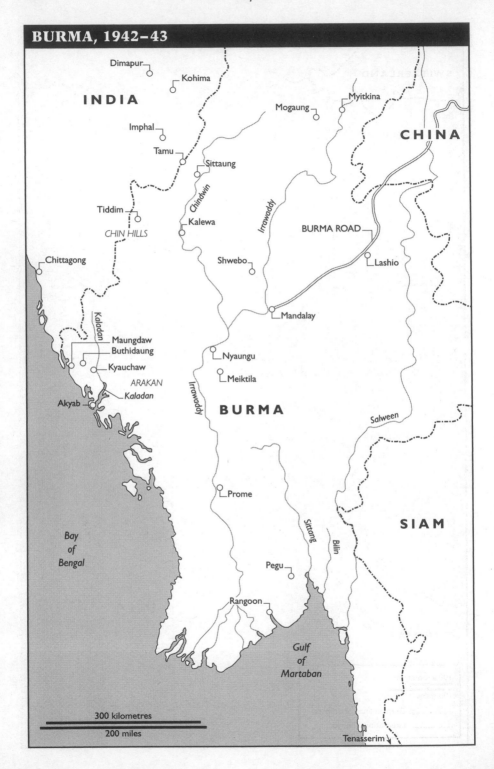

BURMA, 1942–43

INDIA

Dimapur

Kohima

Mogaung

Myitkina

CHINA

Imphal

Tamu

Sittaung

Chindwin

Irrawaddy

BURMA ROAD

Tiddim

Kalewa

CHIN HILLS

Shwebo

Lashio

Chittagong

Kaladan

Mandalay

Maungdaw
Buthidaung
Kyauchaw

Nyaungu

Meiktila

ARAKAN

Kaladan

Irrawaddy

BURMA

Salween

Akyab

Prome

Bay
of
Bengal

Sittang

Bilin

SIAM

Pegu

Rangoon

Gulf
of
Martaban

300 kilometres

200 miles

Tenasserim

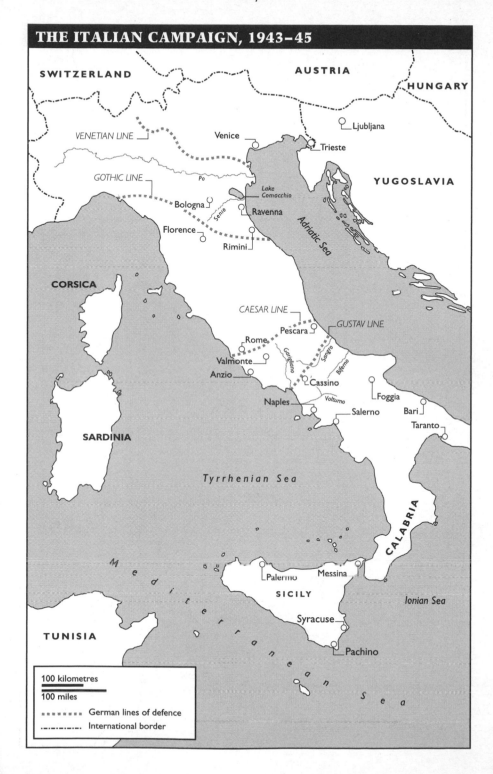

THE ITALIAN CAMPAIGN, 1943–45

SWITZERLAND

AUSTRIA

HUNGARY

VENETIAN LINE

Venice

Ljubljana

Trieste

GOTHIC LINE

Po

YUGOSLAVIA

Lake Comacchio

Bologna

Senio

Ravenna

Florence

Rimini

Adriatic Sea

CORSICA

CAESAR LINE

Pescara

GUSTAV LINE

Rome

Garigliano

Sangro

Valmonte

Liri

Anzio

Cassino

Foggia

Volturno

Naples

Salerno

Bari

SARDINIA

Taranto

Tyrrhenian Sea

CALABRIA

M
e
d
i
t

Palermo

Messina

SICILY

Ionian Sea

Syracuse

TUNISIA

Pachino

e
r
r
a
n
e
a
n

S
e
a

100 kilometres

100 miles

••••••••• German lines of defence

-·-·-·-·- International border

THE CRIMEAN WAR

1854–56

THE CAUSES OF WAR

During Queen Victoria's sixty-four-year reign, Britain only once fought a war against an established European power. In March 1854, standing alongside her traditional enemy France, she declared war on Russia.

Although the war arose ostensibly out of a dispute between the Catholic Church and the Russian Orthodox Church over precedence at the Holy Places of Jerusalem and Nazareth, the real causes lay deeper. The Tsar, Nicholas I, wanted to increase Russia's power and his most obvious area of expansion was south towards the Turkish-owned Dardanelles, which would give the Russian fleet access to the Mediterranean and a port that was not frozen up in winter. Britain was intent on maintaining her own domination of the Mediterranean and feared the Russians taking control of Constantinople. France was equally wary of Russia and keen on making her own territorial gains. Turkey, the 'sick man of Europe', merely wanted to keep hold of existing territory.

At the time, the Ottoman Empire controlled Palestine, Egypt and a large portion of the Middle East. The Porte, Sultan Abdul Medjid I, the Muslim ruler of Turkey, could grant privileges to the rival Christian Churches, allowing them to protect the Holy Places under his jurisdiction, and he now came under pressure from France and Russia to allocate them. The French threatened military action against him if he did not offer them rights over the Church of the Holy Sepulchre in Jerusalem, whilst the Russians threatened to occupy Moldavia and Wallachia if he did. With nowhere to turn, the Porte gave his word to both the French and the Russians. When his deception was discovered, the French sent a warship to Constantinople and ships to the Bay of Tripoli, causing the Porte to accede to their demands in December 1852. The Tsar reacted angrily, mobilizing two army corps and sending his ambassador, Prince Menshikov, to Constantinople to demand concessions from the Porte including recognizing the Tsar's right to the protectorate of all Orthodox laymen under Turkish rule. The Porte rejected the Russian demands in May; on 22 June Russia invaded Moldavia and Wallachia. Weighing up the situation, Britain (who viewed Turkey as an insurance against Russian expansion) felt it necessary to send the Mediterranean Fleet to the Dardanelles in June 1853, followed by the French, to support her solution, a promise by the Porte to protect the Christian religion; this was rejected by Turkey, not least because it did nothing about the occupied territories. The drift towards war had become an irresistible flow. On 4 October the Ottoman Empire demanded Russia withdraw her troops by the 18th then made a formal alliance with Britain and France. Tsar Nicholas had been convinced that Britain wanted to avoid war, but after the Russian fleet had defeated the Turkish fleet off the coast of Sinope on 30 November, he was proved wrong. On 3 January 1854 Britain and France moved their fleets into the Black Sea, and on 27 March declared war on Russia. At first, the Allies planned to fight the war in two distinct theatres. A British Expeditionary Force of twenty-seven thousand men (four, eventually five, infantry divisions and one cavalry) was sent to the Balkans under Commander-in-Chief Lord Raglan, an experienced administrator who had lost his right arm at Waterloo, the French sent the *Armée de l'Orient* under Marshal de Saint-Arnaud, and at the same time, an Allied fleet set sail for the Baltic under the command of Sir Charles Napier, a prickly Scot notorious for his refusal to wear naval uniform.

THE WAR IN THE BALTIC

As Napier's fleet sailed towards the Baltic, its most obvious targets were Sveaborg, the fort protecting Helsingfors (now Helsinki), Bomarsund, a fortress on an island in the middle of the Baltic, and Kronstadt, an island protecting the approaches to St Petersburg. It reached Kronstadt in June, but the Russian navy stayed in port and refused to confront the Allies. There was little that the Allies could do. They could not effect a landing, and whilst their guns could do no damage at long range, they could not risk approaching any closer and coming under fire themselves. After three days, Napier was forced to report to London that an assault was impossible. All his fleet could do was implement a blockade to prevent the Russian fleet from sailing to the Balkans.

On 21 June, Bomarsund was bombarded by the steam frigate *Hecla*, under the command of Captain Hall. His action angered Napier, who complained: 'If every Captain when detached chose to throw away all his shot against stone walls, the fleet would soon be inefficient'. The action was notable, however, for the conduct of a midshipman, Charles Lucas, who picked up a live shell and heaved it overboard. He was immediately promoted to lieutenant and his was the first action for which the Victoria Cross was awarded.

In August, under considerable pressure to achieve some kind of result and reinforced by the arrival of ten thousand French soldiers and marines, Napier decided to launch a full-scale attack on Bomarsund. The plan was to surround the island to prevent the Russian navy from intervening, while

Allied troops besieged the fortress, which consisted of three round towers and a 'Great Fort' built in a semi-circle. The first landings took place on 8 August, and on the following day two Victoria Crosses were earned by men involved in daring intelligence work on nearby Waldo Island. Within eight days, the Russian garrison of two thousand men had surrendered and the fortress had been reduced, in Napier's words, to 'a heap of ruins'. This first victory excited the British public into believing that the war might be over by Christmas. Napier set his sights on attacking the fortress of Sveaborg and a plan was formulated for a landing by five thousand men, but almost at once he began to have doubts about its feasibility and the French, by now suffering badly from cholera, refused to commit so many men to another landing. The plan dissolved into confusion and although the Baltic blockade continued until October, the offensive campaign had come to an effective end.

Even though he had conducted a prudent and reasonably successful campaign, Napier paid the price for not delivering the quick and glorious knockout blow expected by the British public. On his return to Portsmouth at the end of the year, he was asked to resign his commission.

LUCAS, Charles Davis *Mate, Royal Navy*
21 June 1854 – A live shell from an enemy battery landed on the upper deck of HMS *Hecla* in the Baltic Sea. All hands were ordered to fling themselves flat on deck. Without a moment's hesitation, he coolly picked it up and threw it overboard. He was immediately promoted to lieutenant.

BYTHESEA, John *Lieutenant, Royal Navy*
9 August 1854 – Having obtained information that despatches from the Tsar were being landed at Waldo Island and forwarded to Bomarsund, Lieutenant Bythesea and Stoker JOHNSTONE proceeded on shore with a view to intercepting them. They attacked the five men in charge of the mail bags, took three of them prisoner and made the prisoners row themselves to HMS *Arrogant*.

JOHNSTONE, William (enlisted and served as John) *Stoker, Royal Navy*
9 August 1854 – Having obtained information that despatches from the Tsar were being landed at Waldo Island and forwarded to Bomarsund, Stoker Johnstone and Lieutenant BYTHESEA proceeded on shore with a view to intercepting them. They attacked the five men in charge of the mail bags, took three of them prisoners and made the prisoners row themselves to HMS *Arrogant*.

On 20 August 1857, he died from self-inflicted wounds whilst serving on board HMS Brunswick *in the West Indies. He cut his own throat after attacking another man with a knife.*

THE WAR IN THE BALKANS

As the British Expeditionary Force settled in Constantinople and Scutari in the spring of 1854, the Russians began to suffer defeats against the Turks and were soon in retreat to the north. By June they had abandoned Moldavia and Wallachia and were retreating towards Bucharest, and on the 27th the British cabinet authorized Lord Raglan to launch an assault on the Russian naval base of Sebastopol. The troops moved to Varna, where they were struck by an epidemic of cholera. Nevertheless, on 7 September, they sailed for the ominously named landing point of Calamita Bay, thirty miles north of Sebastopol. Although they were exhausted by the cholera, the landing, from the 14th to the 18th, was unopposed and together with the French army they began to march south. The French were on the right of the line, protected by the sea on one flank and the British on the other. At the River Alma, they encountered the Russian army led by Prince Menshikov, who had massed his army with ninety-six guns on the high ground above the river. Menshikov, who had been castrated by Turkish gunfire during a previous encounter, was an understandably motivated opponent.

THE BATTLE OF THE ALMA

On the morning of 20 September 1854, the Allies advanced along the Causeway, a track which led up a slope towards the heights. The Russians had built a telegraph station (known as Telegraph Hill) on high ground to the west of the causeway, and to the east stood Kourgane Hill, a key strategic point on which Prince Menshikov had placed his headquarters. The Russians had built two earthworks on the slopes of Kourgane Hill, the Greater and the Lesser Redoubt. The Russian forces were massed across the Causeway. In all, thirty-six thousand Russian infantry, three thousand four hundred cavalry and two and a half thousand artillerymen stood against the Allies. Russian batteries covered the hills and the valley between them. Such was the strength of the Russian position that Menshikov informed the Tsar that he would be able to hold this position for three weeks.

The Allies decided to launch a pincer movement. The French were to advance along the sea shore on the right flank before scaling the cliffs and capturing the heights, the British were to advance on the centre and left flank. The French made good initial headway, General Bosquet's division scaling the cliffs and driving the Russian infantry back, but reinforcements failed to appear. The advance was soon halted and the troops were forced to shelter near the village of Bourliouk. In the meantime, the British were coming under heavy fire. Lord Raglan and his staff moved freely and fearlessly among the men in full view of the enemy. At 3.00 p.m., Raglan gave the order: 'The Infantry will advance'. The British troops deployed into a long line, two deep across a two-mile front. A Russian captain later wrote: 'We did not think it possible for men to be found with such firmness of morale to be able to attack in this apparently weak formation our massive columns'.

The British crossed the river under heavy fire. On the far side they encountered steep rocky ground, but pressed on. As they approached the Greater Redoubt, the Russian guns which had been pounding them were pulled clear to safety, allowing the Light Division to capture it. It remained vulnerable without reinforcements, so the Scots Fusiliers, the Grenadier Guards and the Coldstream Guards marched forward to relieve the position, whilst the Highland Brigade pushed forward on their left. The Guards were met by three thousand Russian troops, who they mistook for their French allies. The British ceased firing and then, hearing a rogue bugle call, began to retire. As they retreated down the slope, they collided with advancing comrades. Chaos reigned so Raglan called up two 9pdr guns, which opened fire on the Russian positions. The second shot hit an ammunition wagon, which blew up, and the Russian artillerymen retreated, believing themselves to be in more danger than was the case. In the meantime, the Highlanders began to regroup on Kourgane Hill, and by 4.00 p.m. the Hill had been comprehensively taken and the Russians were in retreat to Sebastopol. The Allied victory was complete. Six Victoria Crosses were won during the battle, including four by men of the Scots Fusiliers. For two whole days, the Allies tended their wounded and buried their dead. On 23 September, they pushed on towards Sebastopol.

BELL, Edward William Derrington *Captain, 23rd Regiment*

The son of Lieutenant-General Edward Wells Bell of the Royal Fusiliers, Bell was born into a family with a military tradition (interestingly, his mother was the great-aunt of T. E. Lawrence), and was educated at Sandhurst.

At the Battle of the Alma, 20 September, Bell went out alone under his own initiative to capture a Russian gun which was limbered up and being dragged from the redoubt. Taking the driver totally by surprise, he levelled his revolver at his head – the driver dismounted and fled. With the help of another man, Bell turned the gun team around and started to return to his company with the captured gun, and was surprised when his superior officer, Sir George Brown, ordered him back to his place, with a reprimand for having left it without leave. He left the gun ruefully but he learned some time later that the gun had remained within English lines. The horses drawing it were used in one of the British batteries and the gun itself was taken to Woolwich.

Despite his being given a dressing down for leaving his position, other higher authorities had noticed Bell's courageous foray and he was awarded the VC – but it was generally felt that if he had not earned it at Alma, it would have been awarded to him later at Inkerman, where he also conducted himself with exceptional bravery.

KNOX, John Simpson *Sergeant, Scots Fusilier Guards*
20 September 1854 – He was conspicuous for his exertions in re-forming the ranks of the Guards at the Battle of the Alma. *18 June 1855* – At Sebastopol, he volunteered for the ladder party in the attack on the Redan and behaved admirably, remaining on the field until twice wounded. He lost his arm during this action.

LOYD-LINDSAY, Robert James (later Lord WANTAGE) *Captain, Scots Fusilier Guards*
20 September 1854 – When the formation of the line of the regiment was disordered at the Alma, he stood firm with the colours and by his brave conduct and splendid example helped to restore confidence and order. *5 November 1854* – At Inkerman, he charged a party of Russians, driving them back and running one through the body.

McKECHNIE, James *Sergeant, Scots Fusilier Guards*
20 September 1854 – When the formation of the line of the regiment was disordered at the Alma, he stood firm alongside Captain LINDSAY and called out: 'By the centre, Scots, by the centre. Look to the colours and march by them.'

O'CONNOR, Luke *Sergeant, 23rd Regiment*
20 September 1854 – At the Battle of the Alma, he snatched the fallen colours from the hands of Lieutenant Anstruther, whose blood stained them as he fell. Although severely wounded himself, he held the Queen's Colour aloft, which by day's end had twenty-six holes through it. *8 September 1855* – At the assault on the Redan, he behaved with marked gallantry although shot through both thighs.

PARK, John *Sergeant, 77th Regiment*
20 September 1854 and 5 November 1854 – He showed conspicuous bravery at the Battles of the Alma and Inkerman. *19 April 1855* – He distinguished himself highly at the taking of the Russian rifle pits at Sebastopol.

REYNOLDS, William *Private, Scots Fusilier Guards*
20 September 1854 – When the formation of the line of the regiment was disordered at the Alma, he rallied the men round the colours.

THE SIEGE OF SEBASTOPOL

The Allies now had to decide how best to attack Sebastopol. Although Raglan was in favour of an immediate assault on the city (an assault that senior Russian officers greatly feared), the Allies finally settled on a plan submitted by Sir John Burgoyne, the Inspector General of Fortifications, for a formal siege from the south, using Balaklava and Kamiesch as supply bases, and wearing down the defences by prolonged heavy artillery. Sir George Cathcart, commander of the 4th Division and Raglan's proposed successor in the event of his death, felt that an ideal opportunity to take Sebastopol quickly was being wasted. 'I am sure I could walk into it with scarcely the loss of a man at night or an hour before day break, he wrote to Raglan. Nevertheless, the Allies spent three weeks hauling their guns into position and building breastworks, whilst on the Russian side, two men led the preparations for the defence of the city: Admiral Kornilov, the naval commander and governor of the city, and Colonel Totleben, an engineering officer. Kornilov oversaw the scuttling of seven Russian warships to form a barrier across the entrance to Sebastopol Harbour, while Totleben put together a series of earthwork defences, fortified by the guns from the scuttled ships. He began to construct two forts, the Redan and the Malakoff Tower, on separate eastern hills, connected by a system of trenches. Within only thirty-six hours, a hundred defensive guns were in position. In the meantime, the Russian army was being led into the heart of the Crimea, from where it could ensure that the supply lines to Sebastopol remained open. The Allied guns finally opened up on Sebastopol on 17 October. British troops believed that within a few days the city would be overrun. This proved to be hopelessly optimistic. Shelling continued apace, and although Admiral Kornilov was killed little permanent impact was made on the Russian defences.

DICKSON, Collingwood *Lieutenant Colonel, Royal Artillery*

17 October 1854 – Seeing that his men were running short of ammunition at Sebastopol, he carried barrels of powder from the magazine under a hurricane of shot and shell. He then stood for hours, exposed to a plethora of dangers, whilst he directed the unloading and storing of ammunition.

DANIEL, Edward St John *Midshipman, Royal Navy (Naval Brigade)*

The life of Edward St John Daniel is an extraordinary tale of youthful achievement, self-inflicted decline and enthralling mystery. There is no doubt that he won the Victoria Cross at the age of seventeen and that he became the first man to have his VC forfeited. Much of the rest of his life, however, is shrouded in intrigue. The offence for which he was due to be court-martialled when he deserted from the Royal Navy in June 1861 remains unknown. Whilst it is known that he subsequently sailed for Australia, it is not certain how he passed the next few years. He undoubtedly enrolled in 1864 to serve in the Maori Wars but no records state why he was court-martialled and sentenced to intensive labour in the same year. Without doubt the greatest mystery surrounding Daniel is whether he died aged thirty-one in New Zealand of 'delirium tremens' or whether he returned to England where he lived in poverty until at least 1902, when a man fitting his description was interviewed by the writer Jack London for a book on London's disenfranchised masses.

Daniel was born in Bristol on 17 January 1837, the son of a respected lawyer, who could supposedly trace his lineage directly back to Henry VII. At the age of thirteen, he joined HMS *Victory* as a naval cadet. A year later he experienced his first action whilst serving on HMS *Winchester* during the Second Burmese War. Then in 1854 he sailed to the Crimea on HMS *Albion* as aide-de-camp to Captain William Peel. Peel was, by all accounts, a man of impressive bearing. His other ADC, Midshipman Wood (later Sir Evelyn Wood VC) recalled that Peel advised his men to walk under fire '. . . with head up and shoulders back and without due haste.' Daniel quickly became devoted to him. On 18 October 1854, during the siege of Sebastopol, a pack of horses bringing supplies of ammunition to a battery had refused to move under heavy fire so Daniel took it on himself to empty the wagon and carry the ammunition into the battery. During the Battle of Inkerman, he remained alongside Captain Peel as Peel led seven charges against the Russian enemy. At one point, they escaped despite being completely sur- rounded by Russians. Daniel then saved Peel's life after Peel had been shot through the arm during the attack on the Redan at Sebastopol. Daniel placed a tourniquet around his captain's wound and carried him to safety under a hail of bullets which cut through Daniel's clothes and sliced open his pistol case. For these acts of valour, Daniel was awarded the Victoria Cross at the age of just seventeen.

In 1857 Peel put together a naval brigade, known as Shannon's Brigade, which sailed to Calcutta to take part in the suppression of the Indian Mutiny. Daniel served in the brigade throughout the campaign as an artillery officer and must have been disconsolate when Peel died of smallpox in Cawnpore on 27 April 1858, especially when he learned that Peel had been transported in a cart that had carried smallpox victims. Nevertheless, in September 1859 he was promoted to lieutenant and shortly afterwards was presented to Queen Victoria at St James' Palace.

The first sign of Daniel's imminent self-destruction appeared on 24 May 1860. He was severely reprimanded for being twice absent without leave whilst serving on HMS *Wasp*. Two weeks later, he was discovered drunk and incapable when he should have been standing middle watch. He was court- martialled, but due to his sterling service record, his punishment was light. He was dismissed from HMS *Victor Emanuel* and relegated to the bottom of the list of lieutenants.

In June of the following year, whilst serving on *Victor Emanuel* in the Mediterranean, he committed an offence for which he was placed under arrest. There is no solid evidence as to the nature of this offence. The Secretary of War, Sir George Lewis, referred to it as 'disgraceful', whilst the captain of the ship, Captain Clifford, wrote of Daniel 'taking indecent liberties with four of the subordinate officers'. *Victor Emanuel* sailed to Corfu where Daniel was to face another court martial. However, upon arrival, he went missing. He could not be found and was marked as a deserter. He was removed from the Navy List and in September he became the first man to forfeit the Victoria Cross under Clause 15 of the Royal Warrant. It has been suggested that his 'disappearance' may have been encouraged by the authorities in order to avoid a court martial that could have proved very embarrassing to the navy.

Having managed to return to England, Daniel made his way to Melbourne, Australia, where he is known to have arrived in December 1861. He probably spent the next few years working in the goldfields, as he later described himself as a 'miner'. In January 1864, he enlisted for three years with the Taranaki Military Settlers, who promptly sailed for Taranaki Province on the North Island of New Zealand to fight in the Maori Wars. In August of that year, he was in trouble once again. He was court-martialled and sentenced to intensive labour for another unknown offence. In 1867, he enlisted with the New Zealand Armed Constabulary, with whom he helped to subdue skirmishes between Catholics and Protestants in the South Island goldfields. In May 1868, aged thirty-one, he is recorded as having died of 'delirium tremens' at Hokitika Hospital. He received a full military funeral and was buried in the Hokitika Cemetery.

But was he? Victor Tambling, a Victoria Cross expert, has produced a photograph taken in London of a man aged about forty, which was sold to him as a picture of Daniel. When the photograph was compared to a known picture of Daniel, a forensic pathologist, Dr Tim Koelmeyer, surmised that the photos were of one and the same person. The later photo was most probably taken after 1875, considerably after Daniel's supposed death. Tambling believes that Daniel must have returned to England between 1866 and 1868.

This theory is made more likely by an intriguing interview recorded in London by Jack London in his 1903 book *The People of the Abyss*. This book contained London's conversations with slum-dwellers and people of the workhouses. One interview, with an old man who professed to have won the Victoria Cross and to have fought in Burma, the Crimea and the Indian Mutiny, contained a fascinating story. In it, the old man told how he had once become so angry with a lieutenant who had called him a bastard that he attacked the officer with an iron bar, knocking him into the sea. He then jumped into the water after him, in an attempt to drown him. As a result he had his VC forfeited and ended up in prison. Whilst it is certainly true that Daniel did not end up in prison, the story fits well enough, though the dates are somewhat awry, with the known version of events to unite with the evidence of the photograph to suggest that Daniel may indeed have returned to England and that someone else died and was buried in New Zealand in 1868.

GRADY, Thomas *Private, 4th Regiment*

18 October 1854 – At Sebastopol, he repaired the embrasures of the battery on the Left Attack in clear daylight under a heavy fire. *22 November 1854* – During the repulse of an attack on the most advanced trenches, he refused to quit his post, although severely wounded. He kept encouraging his comrades to 'hold on' and was thus the means of saving the position.

PEEL, William *Captain, Royal Navy*

18 October 1854 – At Sebastopol, he picked a live 42pdr Russian shell with a burning fuse from the midst of several powder-cases and, clasping it to his chest, carried it until he could throw it over the parapet. *5 November 1854* – He warned the Grenadier Guards at the Sandbag Battery that their retreat had been cut off by the enemy. As a result, the Guardsmen made an orderly retreat. *18 June 1855* – He led the first scaling party at the assault on the Redan until he was struck and severely wounded in the arm.

He was the third son of the statesman Sir Robert Peel, the founder of the London Metropolitan Police. He contracted smallpox and died at Cawnpore, India, after being carried in a dhoolie that had previously been used to carry a victim of the disease.

McWHEENEY, William *Sergeant, 44th Regiment*

20 October 1854 – At Sebastopol, he lifted Private John Keane, who had been dangerously wounded, onto his back and carried him for a long distance under heavy rifle-fire until he could place him in safety. *5 December 1854* – He brought Corporal Courtney, who had been severely wounded in the head, from under fire. He dug a cover with his bayonet where they sheltered until dark, when they made their escape.

THE BATTLE OF BALAKLAVA

As Sebastopol was being besieged, Menshikov saw an opportunity to attack Balaklava, the base supplying the besieging British army. Balaklava was defended by Royal Marines artillery on the heights outside the town, by six redoubts manned by four thousand four hundred Turkish troops on the Causeway Heights and by a force of Lord Lucan's cavalry and Sir Colin Campbell's 93rd Highlanders overlooking the South Valley. The Causeway Heights looked down onto the North Valley, which was to be the site of the infamous Charge of the Light Brigade.

At 5 a.m. on 25 October, a large force of Russian troops attacked the Turkish redoubts on the Causeway Heights, taking four by 7.30. The advance guard of Major General Rijov's 6th Hussar Brigade was closing on Balaklava; only the Highlanders stood in the way. Sir Colin Campbell (a carpenter's son from Glasgow who would doubtless have risen higher than brigadier general had he been of 'better stock') cautioned his men: 'Remember there is no retreat from here. You must die where you stand'. Heeding their commander's words, the Highlanders stood firm against three lusty attacks from the Russian cavalry. *The Times'* correspondent, William Russell, watching from the heights, described the conduct of the Highlanders:

> The Russians on their left drew breath for a moment, and then in one grand line dashed at the Highlanders. The ground flies beneath their horses' feet; gathering speed at every stride, they dash on towards that thin red streak tipped with a line of steel ... With breathless suspense everyone waits the bursting of the wave upon the line of Gaelic rock; but ere they come within 150 yards, another deadly volley flashed from the leveled rifle, and carries death and terror into the Russians. They wheel about, open files right and left, and fly back faster than they came.

The 'thin red streak tipped with a line of steel' (a phrase coined by Russell which Tennyson later popularized as the 'thin red line') paints a vivid picture of the Highlanders' exploits.

Meanwhile, to the west, the Heavy Brigade was neutralizing the remainder of Rijov's force in a brief and frantic engagement. Considerable casualties were inflicted by the Heavy Brigade's swords, blunted and weather-rusted though they were, but a great deal more damage was caused by the 24pdr howitzers brought to bear by the Royal Horse Artillery.

Throughout these actions, the Light Brigade had not been called on. Amongst the lancers themselves there was a feeling that they ought to have been sent in pursuit of the fleeing hussars. Little known to them, they were about to be sent on a mission of breathtaking futility.

THE CHARGE OF THE LIGHT BRIGADE

As he watched the battle unfold, Lord Raglan was vexed to discover that the Russians were removing abandoned British guns from the redoubts captured from the Turks. He sent Captain Nolan to deliver the following order to Lord Lucan, the commander of the cavalry: 'Lord Raglan wishes the cavalry to advance rapidly to the front, follow the enemy and try to prevent the enemy carrying away the guns. Troop Horse Attily may accompany. French cavalry is on y left. Immediate.'

Unfortunately, Lucan could not see the redoubts from his position. The only guns that he could see were the twelve guns of the mighty Don Battery, which had earlier been trained on the Turks. An attack on these guns was quite clearly suicidal.

'Attack, sir? Attack what? What guns, sir?' asked Lucan on receiving the order, to which Nolan flung out his arms in the general direction of the Don Battery and replied: 'There, my lord, is your enemy. There are your guns.'

When Lucan passed the order on to his brother-in-law, Lord Cardigan, the commander of the Light Brigade, Cardigan queried it. 'Allow me to point out that the Russians have a battery in the valley on our front and batteries and riflemen on both sides,' he said. 'I know it,' replied Lucan, 'but Lord Raglan will have it. We have no choice but to obey.'

Cardigan carried out what he believed were his orders. He led the 632 men of the Light Brigade against the mighty Russian guns. As they moved forward, Captain Nolan, who had received permission to charge with the 17th Lancers in the first line, suddenly rode ahead motioning wildly with his arms. It may be that the true nature of the order had occurred to him and he was attempting to call off the charge. If this was his intention, he had no chance to share it, as he was immediately struck in the chest by a shell splinter and killed. The Heavy Brigade, which had been following the Light Brigade into the charge, was suddenly halted on Lucan's orders, leaving the Light Brigade to continue alone towards the guns. The Russians were astonished at the sight hurtling towards them. A captured British lancer was later asked by a Russian general what he had been given to drink to encourage him to charge in so reckless a fashion. General Bosquet, watching on the heights, remarked: '*C'est magnifique, mais ce n'est pas la guerre.*' And yet in spite of the artillery fire, some of the cavalry did indeed reach the guns, sabring Russian gunners as they passed them, before confronting the Russian cavalry, positioned to the rear of the artillery. So astonished were these Russian horsemen to be confronted by the Light Brigade that many of them fled, as did a number of the gunners. Before long, however, the Russians returned to their guns, and the remains of the Light Brigade wheeled round and rode back up the valley, pounded by the artillery as they went. The entire event lasted twenty-five minutes, during which time 110 men were killed, 130 were wounded and 58 taken prisoner, with 475 horses lost. The fact that 375 men returned unharmed was considered remarkable, an extraordinary testament to the bravery of the men involved. Nine of the survivors were awarded the Victoria Cross.

The charge marked the end of the Battle of Balaklava. The town itself had not been captured, but the Russians viewed the battle as a significant victory. Winter was approaching and the Allied supply route had been cut with the loss of the Woronzoff Road. Yet an action described by William Russell in *The Times* as a 'hideous blunder' came to be remembered as a glorious, fearless act of obedience which represented the finest qualities of the British soldier. As Tennyson wrote:

> When can their glory fade?
> O the wild charge they made!
> All the world wonder'd.
> Honour the charge they made!
> Honour the Light Brigade,
> Noble six hundred.

BERRYMAN, John *Troop Sergeant Major, 17th Lancers*
  25 October 1854 – During the Charge of the Light Brigade at Balaklava, his horse was shot from under him and he stopped on the field with a wounded officer, Captain Webb. The officer told him to see to his own protection and leave him, but he refused to do so and carried Captain Webb to safety with the assistance of Sergeants FARRELL and MALONE. He then encountered the French General Morris, who said to him: 'If you were in the French service I would make you an officer on the spot.' Shortly afterwards Morris made his famous declaration: '*C'est magnifique, mais ce n'est pas la guerre.*'

DUNN, Alexander Roberts *Lieutenant, 11th Hussars*
  25 October 1854 – During the Charge of the Light Brigade at Balaklava, he saved the life of Sergeant Bentley: he rode at and cut down three Russian lancers who were attacking him from the rear, then dismounted and placed Bentley on his horse. A slap on its flanks sent it carrying Bentley to safety. He then rode to the assistance of Private Levett, cutting down a hussar who was assailing him.
  He sold his commission two weeks later and returned to his estates in Canada with Rosa, the wife of Colonel Douglas, his commanding officer. He returned to receive his VC, and was loaned a uniform by Douglas, an honourable act indeed! At one time, Dunn was the youngest colonel (at thirty-two years) in the British army.

FARRELL, John *Sergeant, 17th Lancers*
  25 October 1854 – During the Charge of the Light Brigade at Balaklava, he assisted Troop Sergeant Major BERRYMAN in carrying the wounded and dying Captain Webb out of immediate range of the cannon and, when a stretcher was obtained, assisted in carrying him from the field.

GRIEVE, John *Sergeant Major, 2nd Dragoons*
  25 October 1854 – During the Charge of the Heavy Brigade at Balaklava, he rescued an officer who was surrounded by the enemy. He killed one assailant by slicing off his head at a blow and drove off the others.
  Captain R. C. Grieve VC was his nephew.

MALONE, Joseph *Sergeant, 13th Dragoons*
  25 October 1854 – During the Charge of the Light Brigade at Balaklava, he stopped under very heavy fire and assisted Sergeant Major BERRYMAN and Sergeant FARRELL to carry the mortally wounded Captain Webb from the field.

PARKES, Samuel *Private, 4th Dragoons*
  25 October 1854 – During the Charge of the Light Brigade at Balaklava, he drove away two Cossacks who were attacking Trumpet-Major Crawford.

Then, whilst attempting to follow the retreat of the Light Brigade, he kept six Russians at bay until his sword was shattered by a shot.

He was captured and spent a year in captivity.

WOODEN, Charles *Sergeant Major, 17th Lancers*

Charles Wooden took part in the infamous Charge of the Light Brigade on 25 October 1854, and won his Victoria Cross on the following day when he went, with Dr MOUAT, to the assistance of Lieutenant Colonel Morris who was lying dangerously wounded. Wooden was either German-born or, more likely, was born in London to German parents. He was an eccentric man who died an eccentric death, but part of his eccentricity (at least so far as his comrades were concerned) must have stemmed from his strong German accent. On one evening, as Wooden stumbled drunkenly back to camp, he was challenged by the sentry on guard duty. Wooden could not remember the password but was equally unable to believe that the sentry did not know who he was. 'Tish me!' slurred Wooden. 'Who?' asked the sentry. 'Tish me! Tish me!' replied the infuriated Wooden. The sentry began to lower his lance at which point Wooden exploded: 'Tish me! The Devil!' The sentry must have recognized Wooden at this point (unless he had been teasing him all along) because he let him by with the words: 'Pass, tish me the Devil.' For the remainder of his life, Wooden was known by the nickname 'Tish me the Devil'.

Wooden's part in the Charge of the Light Brigade was undoubtedly courageous but he was somewhat fortunate to receive the Victoria Cross as he was not initially recommended for it. The Charge itself was a classic piece of military incompetence which came to be regarded as a testament to the disciplined obedience and fighting skills of the British soldier. A confused order sent by Lord Raglan and carried by Captain Nolan caused Lord Cardigan, the commander of the Light Brigade, to launch 632 men in a suicidal attack on the mighty Russian Don Battery.

During the Charge, Captain William Morris of the 17th Lancers came upon a squadron of Russian hussars. He rode directly towards the Russian leader, spearing him through the body with such force that he knocked the Russian off his horse and fell with him to the ground. The enemy, slashing wildly with their sabres, immediately set upon him. Morris lost consciousness and was taken prisoner. Some time later, in the confusion of the field, he escaped by jumping onto a horse and riding away. In agony from his wounds, he fell from the horse but managed to secure another which was promptly shot and fell on top of him. Freeing himself, he staggered towards the British lines, but suffering from a broken arm, broken ribs and three deep head wounds, he could not get far. He collapsed by the dead body of Captain Nolan, who, having brought the order from Lord Cardigan, had taken part in the Charge and been struck in the chest and killed by a shell splinter almost immediately. Morris and Nolan were great friends who had exchanged letters before the Charge to present to each other's families.

Seeing Morris lying badly wounded, Sergeant Wooden, accompanied by Surgeon Mouat of the 6th Dragoons, went out under heavy fire to bring him safely in. According to a contemporary report, 'it seemed like certain death to go to him'. Nevertheless, they managed to dress his wounds and bring him back to British lines. Morris survived and died four years later in action during the Indian Mutiny. Although Mouat and Wooden had acted together, originally only Mouat was recommended for the Victoria Cross. On hearing this, Wooden promptly wrote to Mouat saying that if Mouat was to receive the VC then so should he. Fortunately for him, Mouat agreed and wrote to the Horse Guards supporting Wooden's claim. The reply read: 'His Royal Highness feels very unwilling to bring any further claim for the Victoria Cross for an act performed at so distant a period but as the decoration has been conferred on Dr James Mouat for the part he took in the rescue of Lt. Col. Morris and Sergeant Major Wooden appears to have acted in a manner very honourable to him on the occasion and, by his gallantry, been equally instrumental in saving the life of this officer, His Royal Highness is induced to submit the case'. As a result, Wooden's VC was gazetted on 26 October 1858.

After the Crimean War, Wooden served with the 17th Lancers in India where the regiment was engaged in chasing down Tantia Topi, the last surviving leader of the Mutiny. In 1860 he received a commission as Quartermaster to the 6th (Inniskilling Dragoons) and five years later he transferred to the 5th Lancers. It seems that Wooden's accent and his eccentricity combined to make him unpopular amongst other officers. A feeling may well have existed that it was not quite 'the done thing' to put oneself forward for the Victoria Cross. Certainly, he was from a modest background and had no private income. His two sons joined the army as rankers and he was to receive no further promotion. Quite simply, he could not afford it. His financial situation must have compromised him greatly.

Wooden's life reached a bizarre conclusion on 14 April 1875. On that day, his wife summoned Dr Hooper. On arrival, he found Wooden lying in a pool of blood on the bed. Wooden was still conscious and pointing to the roof of his mouth, saying 'he had a tooth there that wanted pulling out'. The doctor found that the roof of Wooden's mouth was smashed. On the floor lay a pistol which contained an empty cartridge. The doctor found one bullet on the floor and another empty cartridge case showing that he had discharged the pistol twice. Wooden remained alive for twelve hours, during which time he was able to stand and talk, but eventually his wound took its toll and he died.

Various theories have arisen as to the circumstances of Wooden's death. It has been alleged that in a drunken state he had resolved to shoot a painful tooth out of his mouth, blinded by alcohol to the likely consequence. A coroner's inquest was held in the aftermath of the incident, which heard evidence that Wooden had been recently suffering from severe headaches, neuralgia and depression. It also heard that he had suffered from sunstroke during his twelve years in India and had been 'queer ever since'. This comment, however, may only reflect the attitude of fellow officers to a man cut from different cloth. The inquest finally decided that he had taken his own life 'while in a state of temporary insanity'. Whatever the reason for Wooden's action, the verdict ensured that he could receive a Christian burial. His funeral was led through Dover by three military bands and attended by his regiment. Wooden lay in a black upholstered coffin on a gun carriage. His hat and sword rested on the coffin. As he was lowered into his grave, the chaplain spoke of 'a brave soldier who had upheld the honour and fame of England in many battles'.

CONOLLY, John Augustus *Lieutenant, 49th Regiment*
26 October 1854 – When his company was under attack by the Russians outside Sebastopol, he mounted frequent short, sharp charges and engaged several Russians in hand-to-hand fighting. At length, he had to be carried off the field, wounded, having lost much blood.

HEWETT, William Nathan Wrighte *Lieutenant, Royal Navy (Naval Brigade)*
26 October 1854 – As the Russians swarmed towards his battery at Sebastopol, word was passed: 'Spike the guns and retire,' to which he replied: 'Retire? Retire be damned! Fire!' He swung the gun towards the advancing thousands and poured into them so steady a fire that the advance was checked.

MADDEN, Ambrose *Sergeant, 41st Regiment*
26 October 1854 – At Little Inkerman, he led a party of men of the 41st Regiment in capturing one Russian officer and fourteen privates, three of whom he took with his own hand.

MOUAT, James *Surgeon, 6th Dragoons*
26 October 1854 – At Balaklava, he went to the assistance of Lieutenant Colonel Morris who was lying dangerously wounded in a very exposed place. He dressed his injuries under severe fire and stopped a serious haemorrhage, saving his life.

RAMAGE, Henry *Sergeant, 2nd Dragoons*
26 October 1854 – At the Battle of Balaklava, he saved the life of Private McPherson who was severely wounded and surrounded by seven Russians. On the same day, he carried Private Gardiner to the rear, after the private's leg had been fractured by a round shot. Almost immediately, the spot where he had fallen was covered by Russian cavalry.

STANLAKE (called STANLOCK in the *Gazette*), **William** *Private, Coldstream Guards*

26 October 1854 – He crawled up to within six yards of a Russian sentry near Inkerman and brought back information that allowed his officer (Major GOODLAKE) to mount a surprise attack. He was warned in advance of the risk he would be running.

THE BATTLE OF INKERMAN

As the siege of Sebastopol continued, six battalions of Russian infantry, supported by four artillery pieces, launched an attack on 28 October which was halted by a unit of the Coldstream Guards led by Major Goodlake, who was subsequently awarded the Victoria Cross. This was merely a prelude to a much larger Russian attack on several fronts, intended to break the siege and rid the Crimea of the Allies before the winter descended. An assault was to be made on the three thousand three hundred men of the 2nd Division and the Guards at Home Ridge; General Soimonov was to lead nineteen thousand infantry from Sebastopol towards Shell Hill, where he would be joined by forty thousand infantry commanded by General Dannenberg; covering fire would be provided by two Russian warships and by the artillery inside Sebastopol.

The conditions on the morning of 5 November were abysmal. Heavy rain had subsided, leaving behind a thick layer of mud, and worse still – for both armies – a thick fog lay over the area. The soldiers involved in hand-to-hand fighting at Shell Hill were unaffected by any sense of the larger battle unfolding around them. There could be no sense of the larger battle – nobody could see more than two yards ahead. Plans and strategies meant less to the outcome of the Battle of Inkerman than fierce private struggles engaged in by corporals and colonels alike.

The focus of the battle soon became an unimportant earth wall to the right of the British on Home Ridge, named the Sandbag Battery. It was seized by the Russians, who mistakenly thought it to be an important British position. It soon gained a psychological importance and was taken and retaken several times by both sides. The Grenadier Guards captured it at one point (during this fighting 3 men, including Sir Charles Russell, earned the Victoria Cross), only to abandon it as worthless, yet as soon as the Okhotsk Regiment had walked back into it, the Scots Fusiliers launched an attack to take it back. Allied reinforcements arrived in the form of the formidable North African Zouaves, who succeeded in taking the right flank and putting an end to the fighting for the battery. They were assisted by two British 18pdr guns, which caused confusion in the Russian positions. The battle wore on for three more hours until eventually the 21st and 88th Foot made a successful attack on the Russian artillery positions, after which General Dannenberg ordered the Russians to retreat. During the battle, the Russians had suffered 10,729 casualties, the British 2,457 and the French 763. Certainly, the Russians lost the battle – they failed to take their objectives and suffered enormous casualties. Nevertheless, it was no great victory for the Allies. Raglan was criticized for a lack of effective leadership and it was clear that the Allies had moved no closer to taking Sebastopol.

Ten days after the Battle of Inkerman, hurricane-force winds struck the Crimea, sinking twenty-one British ships in Balaklava harbour. One of these ships, *The Prince*, was carrying a large supply of cold-weather clothing and medical supplies, which were desperately needed as the bitter Russian winter began to take hold. The weather was, in fact, to take a terrible toll on the British soldiers but this was regrettably in large part due to the British army's lack of facilities and organization.

GOODLAKE, Gerald Littlehales *Bt/Major, Coldstream Guards*
28 October 1854 – As the sole officer present, he commanded the sharpshooters of his battalion at Inkerman, holding the Windmill Ravine against a much larger force of the enemy, killing 38 and taking 3 prisoners.

OWENS, James *Corporal, 49th Regiment*
30 October 1854 – He greatly distinguished himself in personal encounters with the Russians at Sebastopol, and nobly assisted Lieutenant CONOLLY, who had been severely wounded and was surrounded by the enemy.

BEACH, Thomas *Private, 55th Regiment*
5 November 1854 – At the Battle of Inkerman, whilst on picket duty, he attacked several Russians who were plundering Lieutenant Colonel Carpenter as he lay wounded on the ground. He killed two of the Russians and protected the lieutenant colonel until some men of the 41st Regiment arrived.

BYRNE, John *Private, 68th Regiment*
5 November 1854 – At the Battle of Inkerman, when the regiment was ordered to retire, he advanced towards the enemy, and at risk of his own life brought in a wounded soldier under fire. *11 May 1855* – At Sebastopol, he engaged in a hand-to-hand contest with one of the enemy on the parapet of the work he was defending, killing his antagonist and capturing his arms.

On 10 July 1879, at Newport in Gwent, Byrne accused a man of insulting the Victoria Cross. He shot the man in the shoulder, and when the police arrived he fatally shot himself through the mouth.

CLIFFORD, the Hon. Henry Hugh *Lieutenant, Rifle Brigade*
5 November 1854 – At the Battle of Inkerman, he led a charge against the Russian lines, cutting off the head of one man and the arm of another,

and succeeded in driving the Russians back. He saved the life of a wounded soldier during the contest.

GORMAN, James *Seaman, Royal Navy (Naval Brigade)*

As was the case with Edward St John Daniel, some confusion exists as to the identity of James Gorman VC. Was he an Islington boy who died in Australia in 1882 or was he a native of Suffolk who died in Southwark in 1890?

The confusion appears to have arisen because, unlikely as it seems, two James Gormans served alongside each other in the Royal Navy during the Crimean War. The first Gorman was born in Islington in 1834. The second Gorman (also known as Devereux) was born in Suffolk in 1819. Gorman joined the navy in 1850 and was serving on HMS *Albion* when the Crimean War broke out. Gorman/Devereux was probably a rating on the *Beagle* at the same period. It seems Gorman/Devereux was one of the naval gunners serving alongside William Hewett during the latter's VC action at Sebastopol on the day after the Battle of Balaklava. Whilst Gorman/Devereux's bravery in repulsing a fierce Russian attack was undoubtedly marked, it was Hewett alone who was awarded the Victoria Cross as a result of the action.

By contrast, Gorman did receive the Victoria Cross. He was one of five sailors from the *Albion* who ignored orders to withdraw and leave the wounded at the Battle of Inkerman on 5 November 1854. As the Russians advanced up the Careenage Ravine, the 5 sailors were supposed to have said that they wouldn't 'trust any Ivan getting within bayonet range of the wounded.' The five then mounted the defence works banquette and began firing continuously at the approaching Russians. Men lying wounded in the trench below continuously reloaded their rifles, until the enemy were finally forced to retreat. During the encounter two of the sailors were killed. The surviving three, Gorman, Reeves and Scholefield, were awarded the Victoria Cross.

James Gorman VC was one of the first groups of boys to be accepted into the Royal Navy as apprentices. He entered HMS *Victory* (Nelson's former flagship, which was then in service as a training ship) on 2 March 1848 as Boy Second Class. He was thirteen and a half years old. Two years later, when he joined HMS *Albion*, his records show that he was just five feet two inches tall, with blue eyes and light brown hair. After the Crimean War, Gorman entered hospital at Gosport, suffering from rheumatism. At the age of only twenty-two, he was invalided out of the navy. Very soon afterwards, however, he re-enlisted on the twelve-gun sloop HMS *Elk*, which was one of the first ships to become part of the Royal Naval Australian section. He visited Australia three times between 1858 and 1860. After he was finally paid off at Sheerness in 1860, Gorman sailed to Sydney to make a new life for himself.

Once there, he became a foundation staff member on Australia's first Nautical School Ship, NSS *Vernon*. The purpose of these ships was to relieve the growing numbers of homeless, orphaned boys on the streets of Sydney. The boys would live on board the ship, and would receive training, a rudimentary education and plenty of discipline. They would ultimately be apprenticed as seamen. During his time on the ship, Gorman saw to it that the boys received ever more schooling, recreation and rewards for good behaviour. There were no appointed officers to look after those in the sick bay, but Gorman regularly carried out this duty in addition to his appointed duties. He retired from the *Vernon* in 1881 and died the following year at the age of forty-seven. He was described by another who served on the *Vernon* as 'always among the boys. He was a terror to the bad boys and the good boys regarded him with affection and would not do anything to displease him. In fact he had only to speak and all was peace and quietness.' During his time on the *Vernon*, a total of 1,130 boys passed through his care.

Gorman/Devereux died in 1889 and his obituary was published in the *South London Press* of 4 January 1890. The obituary related the true facts of Gorman/Devereux's service history but declared that he had received the VC for his role at Balaklava alongside Hewett. This was not true. The real James Gorman VC, born in Islington in 1834, was buried at Balmain Cemetery, Norton Street, Balmain, Sydney on 20 October 1882.

HENRY, Andrew *Sergeant Major, Royal Artillery*
5 November 1854 – At the Battle of Inkerman, he defended the guns of his battery against enemy troops who charged in with bayonets, 'howling like mad dogs'. He wrestled a bayonet from one of the Russians, threw the man down and fought against other assailants before he was stabbed in his chest, arms and back. He received twelve wounds yet survived.

McDERMOND, John *Private, 47th Regiment*
5 November 1854 – At Inkerman, he saved the life of Colonel Hely, who was lying wounded and surrounded by a number of Russians. He rushed to Hely's rescue and killed the soldier who had disabled him.

MILLER, Frederick *Lieutenant, Royal Artillery*
5 November 1854 – At the Battle of Inkerman, he attacked three Russians and led a charge on a battery which prevented the guns from coming to any harm.

PALMER, Anthony *Private, Grenadier Guards*
5 November 1854 – At the Battle of Inkerman, he was one of three men who charged with Major RUSSELL as he attempted to dislodge a party of Russians from the Sandbag Battery. He saved Russell's life by shooting down a Russian who was about to bayonet him. He was also one of a small band

which, by a desperate charge against overwhelming numbers, saved the colours of the battalion from capture. He was made a corporal on parade the next morning.

PERCY, the Hon. Henry Hugh Manvers (later Lord Henry) *Colonel, Grenadier Guards*

5 November 1854 – At Inkerman, he charged alone into the Sandbag Battery, where he engaged in single combat with and disabled a Russian soldier. Later in the battle, he mounted a parapet and became a mark for a hundred Russian muskets. He was knocked backwards by a stone and fell senseless to the ground, where he lay bleeding and half blinded, until, hearing the word 'Charge!', he rose to his feet and joined the advance. He soon found himself with soldiers of various regiments, almost surrounded by the Russians and without ammunition. He led them unperceived to safety down a path through some brushwood.

He was MP for North Northumberland 1865–68.

PRETTYJOHN, John *Corporal, Royal Marine Light Infantry*

5 November 1854 – At the Battle of Inkerman, his platoon used up nearly all its ammunition, clearing caves occupied by Russian snipers. Noticing parties of Russians creeping up the hillside towards his men, he ordered them to collect as many stones as they could find. He seized the first Russian and threw him down the hill. The other Russians were attacked by a shower of stones and retreated down the hill.

REEVES, Thomas *Seaman, Royal Navy (Naval Brigade)*

5 November 1854 – He was one of five sailors who, whilst under fierce attack from the Russians at Inkerman, mounted a defence work banquette and fired on the enemy. Wounded soldiers lying in the trench below reloaded and passed up their rifles. The sailors continued with this rapid fire until the attack was repulsed. Two of the sailors were killed during the action, the survivors being Reeves, GORMAN and SCHOLEFIELD.

ROWLANDS, Hugh *Captain, 41st Regiment*

5 November 1854 – At Inkerman, he saved the life of Colonel Hely of the 47th Regiment who was wounded and surrounded by Russian soldiers. He also acted with great gallantry at the commencement of the battle in holding the ground occupied by his advance picket.

He was Lieutenant of the Tower of London in 1893.

RUSSELL, Sir Charles *Bt/Major, Grenadier Guards*

5 November 1854 – At the Battle of Inkerman, he offered to dislodge a party of Russians from the Sandbag Battery if anyone would follow him. His call was quickly answered by Sergeant Norman, Private PALMER and Private Bailey. The attack was a success, although Russell, wearing no overcoat, was a prominent mark for the enemy. He was a man of slight build, yet he was able to tear a rifle from the hands of a Russian soldier.

SCHOLEFIELD, Mark *Seaman, Royal Navy (Naval Brigade)*
   5 November 1854 – He was one of 5 sailors who, whilst under fierce attack from the Russians at Inkerman, mounted a defence work banquette and fired on the enemy. Wounded soldiers lying in the trench below reloaded and passed up their rifles. The sailors continued with this rapid fire until the attack was repulsed. Two of the sailors were killed during the action, the survivors being Scholefield, REEVES and GORMAN.

WALKER, Mark *Lieutenant, 30th Regiment*
   5 November 1854 – At the Battle of Inkerman, he was in position with his battalion behind a low wall as two columns of Russian infantry approached. The battalion's arms had become wet and useless. He jumped up on the wall and, calling on his men to follow him with the bayonet, led them straight at the Russian ranks. This caused a panic amongst the enemy, who, in spite of their greater numbers, turned and bolted.

WALTERS, George *Sergeant, 49th Regiment*
   5 November 1854 – At Inkerman, he went to the rescue of Brigadier General Adams, who was in great peril, surrounded by Russians. He bayoneted one of the assailants and saved the brigadier general's life.

THE WINTER

The winter of 1854/55 was the coldest in Sebastopol for many years. The Tsar was well aware of its value to the Russians, noting that he had three generals – January, February and March – any of whom could overcome the British army. Nevertheless, the British soldiers were living in appalling conditions before the cold weather had even begun. The wind had forced many to abandon their tents, the rain kept their inadequate uniforms constantly wet and the deep mud infiltrated everything they possessed.
   When the freezing weather arrived life became unbearable. Food was scarce, forcing British troops to go begging to their French counterparts, offering their boots in exchange for something to eat. Lightweight tents and uniforms did not keep out the cold. Frostbite became a deadly enemy as any uncovered piece of the body turned into a sheet of ice. Whilst thousands of men were dying, supplies were failing to reach the troops. One reason was that the supply line from the harbour at Balaklava was barely functioning: twenty days' forage had been lost in the hurricane, the baggage animals had starved, and provisions arriving at the harbour were left to rot by the quayside. The well-built Woronzoff Road had been lost at the Battle of Balaklava and the alternative country roads were choked with mud, ice,

snow and dead animals, making them impassable. Matters were made worse by the stifling bureaucracy and lack of any organized system within the army, which prevented crucial decisions from being made. On 23 December 1854, *The Times* thundered that the army was governed by 'incompetence, lethargy, aristocratic hauteur, official indifference, favour, routine, perverseness and stupidity'. Lord Aberdeen resigned and was replaced as Prime Minister by Lord Palmerston.

Of more immediate concern to the troops were the improvements that were beginning to be made in terms of healthcare. Sidney Herbert, the Secretary at War, had decided to send female nurses into the military hospitals, and placed Florence Nightingale (the manager of 'The Establishment for Gentlewomen During Illness' in Harley Street) in charge of the operation. She and her charges set out for the Scutari Hospital, where on her arrival on 3 November she found poor hygiene, undisciplined staff and limited supplies. Bed linen went unwashed, soap was a rarity and the patients only received a bath every eighty days. She set about tackling these issues straightaway, instigating a new drainage system and paving the hospital floors, and kept up an insistent correspondence with Herbert, urging him to treat the bureaucratic paralysis that she found everywhere within the army medical system. In February 1855, the *Illustrated London News* christened her 'The Lady With The Lamp'.

Improvements were made in other areas. Alexis Soyer, the flamboyant ex-chef of the Reform Club in London, came out to the Crimea in February 1855 and immediately set about improving army catering. He improved the meat preparation, introduced salt and pepper, invented a new type of teapot that prevented tea from stewing, designed a portable cooking stove and stopped the cooks from throwing away the water in which meat was boiled, turning it instead into a nutritious soup.

Such improvements were welcomed but they came too late. Many more British soldiers were killed by the weather and the lack of military organization during the Crimean War than were killed by the enemy.

WHEATLEY, Francis *Private, 1st Bn., Rifle Brigade*

10 November 1854 – He tackled a live shell that fell in the midst of his party at Sebastopol, and after vainly endeavouring to knock out the burning fuse with the butt of his rifle, he picked it up and flung it over the parapet of the trench, where it immediately exploded.

BOURCHIER, Claude Thomas *Lieutenant, Rifle Brigade*

20 November 1854 – Lieutenant Bourchier and Lieutenant CUNNINGHAME were with a party detailed to drive the Russians from some rifle pits at Sebastopol. They launched a surprise attack and drove the Russian riflemen from their cover. Fighting continued throughout the night, but the two lieutenants held the position until relieved the following day.

CUNNINGHAME, William James Montgomery (later Sir William)
Lieutenant, Rifle Brigade

20 November 1854 – Lieutenant Cunninghame and Lieutenant BOUR-CHIER were with a party detailed to drive the Russians from some rifle pits at Sebastopol. They launched a surprise attack and drove the Russian riflemen from their cover. Fighting ensued throughout the night, but the two lieutenants held the position until relieved the following day.

He was MP for Ayr, 1874–80.

LENNOX, Wilbraham Oates   *Lieutenant, Royal Engineers*

20 November 1854 – At Sebastopol, he led a hundred men into the rifle pits taken by Lieutenant CUNNINGHAME and Lieutenant BOURCHIER. The men entrenched themselves under extreme exposure and repulsed the attempts of the enemy to dislodge them during the night.

NORMAN, William   *Private, 7th Regiment*

19 December 1854 – Whilst he was on single sentry duty in the White Horse Ravine at Sebastopol, three Russians crept up under cover of brushwood to reconnoitre the position. He saw them and fired his rifle to alarm the post. Without waiting for his comrades, he jumped almost on top of the three Russians, one of whom bolted off to his own lines. He seized the other two and made them prisoner.

THE SPRING

As the spring thaw began, news arrived of the death of Tsar Nicholas I. He was succeeded by his son Alexander II, who adopted a more liberal approach to home affairs by abolishing serfdom but refused to compromise his country's stance on the war. He declared that he would 'perish sooner than surrender' in the Crimea. A great deal of diplomatic chess had been played over the winter months but the result was stalemate. The siege of Sebastopol was to continue but conditions on the ground for the British troops had improved beyond recognition. Huts and medical supplies had started to arrive, as had horses, mules, buffalo and camels, the water supply had been purified, and most positively of all a railway leading from the harbour at Balaklava to the Allied camps that were besieging Sebastopol had been built – seven miles in seven weeks. A visitor to Balaklava in April was 'not prepared to find the harbour in so good a state. All dead animals were towed out to sea, and no pains seemed spared to keep it clean'.

Nevertheless, the problem remained for the Allies of agreeing on tactics to pursue. The Russians, under the capable leadership of Totleben, had never ceased fortifying Sebastopol. The batteries were strongly defended and capable of being swiftly repositioned whilst a complex network of tunnels had been dug underneath the city. The Russian positions were described as one entrenched camp stretching from Sebastopol Harbour towards Bala-klava. In response, the Allies dug trenches of their own. Fighting took on a new aspect, in which men crept out of one trench with fixed bayonets to attack enemy soldiers in an adjacent trench. A form of warfare had been born that would reach its climax sixty years later during the Great War.

The first significant action of the new year took place on 22 February on a hill known as the Mamelon Vert, several hundred yards from the Malakoff Tower (the large stone tower at the heart of the city's defences). Totleben ordered two new redoubts to be built overnight on the Mamelon Vert, merely for the purpose of luring the French into a trap. On the night of 24/25 February the French duly sent fourteen hundred men to attack the redoubts, only to find the Russians waiting for them. Two hundred French soldiers were killed. After the failure of a French sap towards the Mamelon that was bloodily repulsed on the night of 23/24 March, the Allies deter-mined that no further attacks would be made on Sebastopol until a heavy artillery bombardment had been launched. For ten days, beginning on 9 April, 138 British guns and 362 French guns bombarded Sebastopol. Every night, the Russians repaired the damage caused during the day. It was clear that Totleben's remarkable defences would not wither under an onslaught.

LENDRIM, William James (also known as LENDRUM) *Corporal, Royal Engineers*
14 February 1855 – He was superintending a party of French chasseurs during the building of a battery at Sebastopol when a tremendous fire made a series of small breaches in the parapet. He zealously went from gap to gap and ensured that all the capsized gabions were replaced. *11 April 1855* – He extinguished a fire which had broken out among some sandbags on the parapet of the battery, all the time under fire from the enemy. *20 April 1855* – He was one of four volunteers to destroy screens which the Russians had erected to conceal their advanced rifle pits.

GARDINER, George *Sergeant, 57th Regiment*
22 March 1855 – During a sudden Russian attack on the trenches at Sebastopol, he rallied the men, led them on and drove the enemy away. *18 June 1855* – During the assault on the Redan, he jumped into a shell crater, made a parapet from the dead bodies of his comrades and began a steady fire. He encouraged others to do the same, and the fire was kept up until all ammunition was exhausted.

WRIGHT, Alexander *Private, 77th Regiment*
22 March 1855 – He demonstrated particular bravery in repelling a Russian sortie from Sebastopol. *19 April 1855* – During the taking of some rifle pits, he showed tremendous courage and gave the other men great encouragement while they were being held.

COFFEY, William *Private, 34th Regiment*
29 March 1855 – At Sebastopol, he threw a lighted shell, which had fallen into the trench, over the parapet.

ELTON, Frederic Cockayne *Bt/Major, 55th Regiment*
29 March 1855 – He was with a working party in the trenches at Sebastopol, close up to the Quarries. A terrible fire was directed at the party, which made the work extremely dangerous, but he took a pick and shovel and worked fearlessly, encouraging the men by his fine example.

SULLIVAN, John *Boatswain's Mate, Royal Navy (Naval Brigade)*
10 April 1855 – A concealed Russian battery was doing a great deal of damage to No. 5 Greenhill Battery at Sebastopol. He volunteered to go forward to place a flag on a mound to act as an aiming point against the Russian battery. He did this with great coolness, taking care to ensure that the flag was in perfect line with the target, even though he was under heavy fire from snipers.

EVANS, Samuel *Private, 19th Regiment*
13 April 1855 – When most of the gunners attached to a battery had been killed by concentrated Russian fire at Sebastopol, he entered the embrasure and repaired the damage done. He was under heavy fire all the while and persevered until the breach was mended and replacement gunners had arrived.

DIXON, Matthew Charles *Captain, Royal Artillery*
17 April 1855 – At Sebastopol, he was in command of a battery which was hit by a shell that blew up the magazines, destroyed the parapet and killed or wounded ten men. Instead of retiring, he helped his men to keep the one remaining gun in action. He continued firing for seven hours until sunset, working as a gunner himself.

MacDONALD, Henry *Colour Sergeant, Royal Engineers*
19 April 1855 – His bravery was conspicuous whilst effecting a lodgement in the enemy's rifle pits, in front of the left advance of the right attack on Sebastopol. Later in the day, when the command devolved on him, he persisted in carrying on the sap, in spite of the repeated attacks of the enemy.

BRADSHAW, Joseph *Private, Rifle Brigade*
22 April 1855 – The Russians had constructed rifle pits amongst rocks overhanging the Woronzoff Road. A bandsman of the Rifle Brigade was killed by a shot from one of the pits. This enraged the men to such a degree that Bradshaw, accompanied by Private HUMPSTON, attacked and captured one of the pits in broad daylight, holding it until support arrived, when the rest of these 'wasps' nests', as they were called, were destroyed.

HUMPSTON, Robert *Private, 2nd Bn., Rifle Brigade*

22 April 1855 – The Russians had constructed rifle pits amongst rocks overhanging the Woronzoff Road at Sebastopol. A bandsman of the Rifle Brigade was killed by a shot from one of the pits. This enraged the men to such a degree that Humpston, accompanied by Private BRADSHAW, attacked and captured one of the pits in broad daylight, holding it until support arrived, when the rest of these 'wasps' nests', as they were called, were destroyed.

McGREGOR, Roderick *Private, 1st Bn., Rifle Brigade*

22 April 1855 – At the Quarries, Crimea, a bandsman was killed when he went to a well in front of the advanced trench by Russians in rifle pits. Private McGregor and two others drove the Russians out, killing some. *July 1855* – Two Russians occupying a rifle pit at Sebastopol were most annoying by their continuous fire. He crossed the open space under a hail of bullets, took shelter under a rock and dislodged them, occupying the position himself.

HAMILTON, Thomas de Courcy *Captain, 68th Regiment*

11 May 1855 – He boldly charged the enemy at Sebastopol with a small force from a battery, thereby saving the works from falling into the hands of the Russians. He was conspicuous for his gallantry and daring conduct.

THE SEA OF AZOV

Enthusiasm for the war was on the wane in England. The British guns had been of insufficient calibre to make a real impact on the Sebastopol defences and the large numbers of well-trained British soldiers lost over the winter had not been adequately replaced. As a maritime nation, Britain saw sea-power as the logical means of victory. The theory was that if the Allies could gain control of the Sea of Azov at Kertch, 120 miles away, the supply line into Sebastopol could be cut. The first Kertch expedition, consisting of British, French and Turkish troops, was aborted as it approached its objective because the ships were needed to bring the French Army of the Reserve from Constantinople. A second attempt was made on 22 May 1855. Two days later the Allied troops landed at Kertch and took the town with ease. Whilst this episode was soured by looting and pillaging, the victory promised much for the Allies. Control of the Sea of Azov meant that a great deal of the supplies intended for Sebastopol could be destroyed or rerouted.

BUCKLEY, Cecil William *Lieutenant, Royal Navy*

29 May 1855 – He landed on a beach near Genitchi, with Lieutenant BURGOYNE and Gunner ROBARTS, at a point where the Russian army were in strength. Despite encountering considerable enemy opposition, they set fire to corn stores and ammunition dumps and destroyed enemy equipment before embarking again. *3 June 1855* – He landed with Boatswain COOPER at the town of Taganrog and fired government buildings and stores and destroyed equipment and arms before embarking again.

He was the first winner of the VC to be gazetted.

BURGOYNE, Hugh Talbot *Lieutenant, Royal Navy*

29 May 1855 – He landed on a beach near Genitchi, with Lieutenant BUCKLEY and Gunner ROBARTS, at a point where the Russian army were in strength. Despite encountering considerable enemy opposition, they set fire to corn stores and ammunition dumps and destroyed enemy equipment before embarking again.

He was the son of Sir John Burgoyne, who served under Wellington through the Peninsular War and was Lord Raglan's adviser in the Crimean War, and grandson of John Burgoyne, playwright and general, who surrendered to the American general Gates at Saratoga.

ROBARTS, John *Gunner, Royal Navy*

29 May 1855 – He landed on a beach near Genitchi, with Lieutenant BURGOYNE and Lieutenant BUCKLEY, at a point where the Russian army were in strength. Despite encountering considerable enemy opposition, they set fire to corn stores and ammunition dumps and destroyed enemy equipment before embarking again.

COOPER, Henry *Boatswain, Royal Navy*

3 June 1855 – In a four-oared gig, he landed with Lieutenant BUCKLEY at the town of Taganrog and fired government buildings and stores and destroyed equipment and arms before embarking again.

TREWAVAS, Joseph *Seaman, Royal Navy*

3 July 1855 – He was a member of a party which set off in a four-oared gig to cut the pontoon bridge which the Russians had built across the Genitchi Strait. The single gun on the gig was out of action but the party was told by Lieutenant HEWETT to continue or risk court martial. The gig reached the bridge where Trewavas began to cut the hawsers. He was under fierce fire from enemy riflemen less than 80 yards away. Eventually, the strands of the bridge gave way and Trewavas was able to get back into the gig. As he did so, he was struck in the shoulder, but the gig escaped, riddled with bullet holes and filled with water and blood.

KELLAWAY, Joseph *Boatswain Third Class, Royal Navy*

31 August 1855 – He was one of a party of five from HMS *Wrangler* put ashore in daylight near Marionpol in the Sea of Azov. The party's intention was to burn boats, fishing stations and haystacks. They were ambushed by about 50 Russian riflemen who had cut off their retreat. In trying to escape, one of the party fell, and Kellaway, thinking he was injured, went to his assistance. They were surrounded by the enemy and taken prisoner after a gallant resistance.

THE QUARRIES, THE REDAN AND THE MALAKOFF TOWER

With control of the supply route secured, the Allies focused once more on the siege. On 6 June 1855, a third great bombardment of Sebastopol by British and French guns began, followed the next day by an attack. The attackers and defenders were both aware that the key to taking and holding the city was control of the Malakoff Tower. The plan was that the British would attack an area known as 'the Quarries', whilst the French launched another attack on the Mamelon Vert, control of which would place the Allies in prime position to move on the Malakoff Tower. The French captured the Mamelon quickly, and pushed on, believing that they could take the Malakoff Tower, but the Russians counter-attacked, forcing the French from the Mamelon. By the evening, they had retaken the Mamelon but had suffered 5,443 casualties in the process. In the meantime, the British took the Quarries, suffering 671 casualties.

Buoyed by this success, the Allies planned to capitalize immediately. Raglan and the French commander General Aimable Pélissier (who had replaced Canrobert on 16 May) agreed that the French should advance on the Malakoff Tower whilst the British attacked the Redan. Six hundred Allied guns, supported by naval guns lying offshore, opened fire on the Russian defences on 17 June. It was the fiercest bombardment so far. Yet, for some reason, Pélissier decided to bring the French attack forward from 8 a.m. to 3 a.m. Raglan was left with no option but to bring the British attack forward to fall in line with the French plans. The night was clear, and as the British troops moved into position they were plainly observed by the Russian defenders, who made appropriate preparations. As the French advanced in chaotic formation – one column had mistaken a signal and advanced at 2 a.m. – they were mowed down by the defenders of the Malakoff. As he watched this fiasco, Raglan felt that he had no option but to send the British forces forward. He explained in a subsequent dispatch that if the British troops 'had remained in our trenches, the French would have attributed their non-success to our refusal to participate in the operation.'

The British attack on the Redan took place under the heaviest fire imaginable. Splinters of shell and bullet rained down so heavily on the men that they ran forward over 400 yards of open ground with their heads down as if running into a storm. The attack on both positions was a disastrous failure: the French suffered three and a half thousand casualties, the British fifteen hundred. Twelve men won the Victoria Cross during the assault on the Redan, many of them for rescuing wounded comrades.

The defeat began to weigh heavily on Lord Raglan. His health declined rapidly and on 28 June he died, worn out by the pressures he was forced to endure. He was replaced by Lieutenant General Sir James Simpson, who is supposed to have remarked on receiving the promotion: 'They must indeed be hard up when they appointed an old man like me.'

SYMONS, George *Sergeant, Royal Artillery*
6 June 1855 – He opened the embrasures of a five-gun battery under terrific fire from the enemy at Sebastopol. He uncovered the last embrasure by mounting the parapet and throwing down sandbags. Whilst completing the task, he was badly wounded by a shell.

ARTHUR, Thomas (real name McARTHUR) *Gunner and Driver, Royal Artillery*
7 June 1855 – Having been taken suddenly ill whilst his battery was in action at Sebastopol, he left it without leave, returning to find that the guns were gone. Noticing that the 7th Fusiliers were running short of ammunition, he ran to a magazine and brought as many cartridges as he could to the front under heavy fire. He was marched away in custody for having been absent from his gun but the colonel of the infantry intervened and his dereliction was turned into an act of heroism. *18 June 1855* – He volunteered for and formed one of the party who spiked the guns in the assault on the Redan.

HUGHES, Matthew *Private, 7th Regiment*
Among the first recipients of the VC to be presented with their medals by Queen Victoria in Hyde Park on the 'proud and gratifying day', 26 June 1857, was an unlikely Yorkshireman. A perusal of the Royal Fusiliers' list of VC recipients provides a very mixed picture of Matthew Hughes. According to these scant but telling records, Hughes was born in 1822 and at the age of eighteen joined the 7th Royal Fusiliers. Four years later he was discharged by purchase in January, but then re-enlisted in June of the same year. During this period of service, the diminutive Hughes, who stood just five feet tall, spent a month 'in custody of the Civil Powers' during 1845, then achieved the rank of corporal in 1855, during which year in the Crimea he earned his VC. On 7 June 1855, during the attack on 'the Quarries' at Sebastopol, he twice went for ammunition across open ground. He also brought Private John Hampton, who was lying wounded, in from the front. On 18 June he volunteered to bring in Lieutenant Hobson of his regiment, who was lying wounded. He was severely wounded himself in the course of this act.

Following this feat of extraordinary bravery and, indeed, physical exertion for a man so short, he was promoted to sergeant in September 1855. This was the pinnacle of his military career. There then followed a court martial, a demotion to private, reinstatement, a further court martial – and his record lists twenty-one entries in the regimental defaulters' book.

Hughes finished his twenty-five-year service aged forty-three, still a private – but one with the rare accolade of being among the very first recipients of the Victoria Cross, presented by Queen Victoria herself.

JONES, Henry Mitchell *Captain, 7th Regiment*
7 June 1855 – During the attack on 'the Quarries' at Sebastopol, he encouraged the men around him to repel the continual assaults of the enemy throughout the night. Although he was suffering from severe wounds received earlier in the day, he unflinchingly remained at his post until daylight.

WILKINSON, Thomas *Bombardier, Royal Marine Artillery*
7 June 1855 – Russian fire having demolished much of the earthworks in the advanced batteries before Sebastopol, he went up to the parapet and called for sandbags to be handed up to him. He proceeded to repair the damage under heavy fire from the enemy, cheered on as he worked by the men in the nearby trenches.

LYONS, John *Private, 19th Regiment*
10 June 1855 – He picked up a live shell which had fallen among the guard in the trenches and threw it over the parapet.

PROSSER, Joseph *Private, 2nd Bn., 1st Regiment*
16 June 1855 – At Sebastopol, he chased and apprehended a deserter making his way towards the Russian camp, whilst crossfire from two points raked the ground. *11 August 1855* – He left the most advanced trench under heavy fire to carry in a soldier of the 95th Regiment who lay severely wounded and unable to move.

ALEXANDER, John *Private, 90th Regiment*
18 June 1855 – After the attack on the Redan at Sebastopol, Alexander went out of the trenches and brought in several wounded under heavy fire. *6 September 1855* – He went out and helped bring in Captain Buckley, who was lying dangerously wounded in an exposed position.

CURTIS, Henry *Boatswain's Mate, Royal Navy (Naval Brigade)*
18 June 1855 – Following the assault on the Redan at Sebastopol, he went to the assistance of a soldier of the 57th Regiment, who had been shot through both legs and was sitting up and calling for help. He (together with Lieutenant Henry D'Aeth, Captain of the Forecastle John TAYLOR and Lieutenant Henry RABY) proceeded 70 yards across an open space under heavy fire and brought the man back to a place of safety.

ELPHINSTONE, Howard Craufurd *Lieutenant, Royal Engineers*
18 June 1855 – On the night following the unsuccessful attack on the Redan at Sebastopol, he volunteered to command a party to search for the scaling ladders left behind after the attack. Whilst performing this task, he brought 20 wounded men back to the trenches.

ESMONDE, Thomas *Captain, 18th Regiment*
18 June 1855 – During the attack on the Redan at Sebastopol, he displayed great gallantry in rescuing the wounded, all the time under heavy fire from the enemy. *20 June 1855* – Whilst in command of a covering party, a fireball fell close by. He called out to his men to take shelter and dashed out to extinguish it himself. As he had anticipated, a hail of fire was directed upon him, but he put out the fireball and escaped unscathed.
Lieutenant Commander E. K. Esmonde VC was his great-nephew.

GRAHAM, Gerald *Lieutenant, Royal Engineers*
18 June 1855 – During the attack on the Redan at Sebastopol, he was conspicuous for his bravery at the head of the ladder party. He rescued a wounded man under terrific fire and later brought in some abandoned scaling ladders.

HOPE, William *Lieutenant, 1st Bn., 7th Regiment*
18 June 1855 – During the attack on the Redan at Sebastopol, he was informed that an officer, Lieutenant Hobson, was lying severely wounded outside the trenches. Hope went to search for him, found him and returned to him with four others. Seeing that he could not be moved without a stretcher, Hope went back to Egerton's Pit, found a stretcher and brought Hobson to shelter. All the time, he was under continuous fire.
He was the inventor of the shrapnel shell for rifled guns.

LEITCH, Peter *Colour Sergeant, Royal Engineers*
18 June 1855 – During the assault on the Redan at Sebastopol, he struggled to form a ramp across the ditch of the Redan by tearing down the gabions, filling them with earth and placing them in position in the ditch. He continued in this attempt, under very heavy fire, until he was disabled by wounds.

PERIE, John *Sapper, Royal Engineers*
18 June 1855 – He bravely assisted Lieutenant GRAHAM in leading the sailors with the ladders at the attack on the Redan at Sebastopol. He rescued a wounded soldier who was lying in the open, despite the fact that he had been hit in his right side by a rifle ball. He also risked his life to rescue scaling ladders left on the ground.

RABY, Henry James *Lieutenant, Royal Navy (Naval Brigade)*
18 June 1855 – Following the assault on the Redan at Sebastopol, he went to the assistance of a soldier of the 57th Regiment, who had been shot through both legs and was sitting up and calling for help. He (together with Lieutenant Henry D'Aeth, Captain of the Forecastle John TAYLOR and Boatswain's Mate Henry CURTIS) proceeded 70 yards across an open space under heavy fire and brought the man back to a place of safety.
On 26 June 1857, he was the first man to be invested with the VC by the

Queen. The story is told that he stood impressively to attention as Her Majesty accidentally pushed the pin straight into his chest and fastened it through his skin.

SIMS, John Joseph *Private, 34th Regiment*

18 June 1855 – After his regiment had retired from the attack on the Redan at Sebastopol, he went out to the open ground under heavy fire and brought in several wounded men who had fallen outside the trenches.

SMITH, Felix Philip *Corporal, 17th Regiment*

18 June 1855 – After the column had retired from the assault on the Redan at Sebastopol, he went out repeatedly in front of the advanced trenches to bring in wounded comrades under heavy fire.

TAYLOR, John *Captain of the Forecastle, Royal Navy (Naval Brigade)*

18 June 1855 – Following the assault on the Redan at Sebastopol, he went to the assistance of a soldier of the 57th Regiment, who had been shot through both legs and was sitting up and calling for help. He (together with Lieutenant Henry D'Aeth, Lieutenant Henry RABY and Boatswains Mate Henry CURTIS) proceeded 70 yards across an open space under heavy fire and brought the man back to a place of safety.

Taylor's widow wrote to the Admiralty in March 1857 asking whether she could be present at her late husband's investiture on 26 June. He had died on 25 February, in Woolwich. A letter was written back to her on 25 June stating: 'It would not be necessary for you to come to London as you suppose in connection with the ceremony to take place tomorrow, the 26th instant.'

McCORRIE, Charles (also known as McCURRY) *Private, 57th Regiment*

23 June 1855 – He threw a live shell, which had been thrown into the trenches at Sebastopol, over the parapet.

THE BATTLE OF TCHERNAYA

The war was placing a considerable strain on the economies of all the countries involved, but undoubtedly the greatest financial pressure was felt by Russia. The blockades and the loss of imports from Britain and France had taken their toll whilst huge loans supplied by European banks were looking increasingly insecure. Alexander II was having to compromise his pugnacious stance. Yet while he could no longer think in terms of victory at any price, he refused to sanction the possibility of retiring from Sebastopol. Rather, he ordered a decisive attack that, if successful, would put Russia in the strongest possible negotiating position. His plan was to march across the River Tchernaya and capture the Fediukhin Heights, a position held by French and Sardinian troops. The Russian commander, Prince Gorchakov, who had very little faith in the likely success of the attack, produced only an outline plan, giving very general directions to his generals. To make matters worse, Gorchakov's plan, such as it was, had become common knowledge in St Petersburg and was soon revealed to the Allies.

The attack began before dawn on 16 August and was defeated by 10 a.m. Although the Russian troops gained their initial objectives and forced a gap to open between French and Sardinian forces, this early momentum was quickly lost and the attack dissolved into confusion. Huge Russian casualties outnumbered those of the Allies. Indeed, the Sardinians (who had joined the Alliance in January in the hope of gaining support for a united Italy) lost only fourteen men.

THE SECOND BALTIC EXPEDITION

Once the winter ice had thawed, a second expedition set sail for the Baltic. Led by Rear Admiral Sir Richard Dundas, it was intended to enforce the naval blockade and to mount attacks on the fortresses that Sir Charles Napier had failed to secure. Captain Bartholomew Sulivan, the fleet hydrographer who was undertaking a detailed reconnaissance of the area, advised Dundas firmly that he should not attempt to attack Kronstadt, so he turned his attention to Sveaborg. The Russians had fortified Sveaborg's defences in the year since the last expedition, and they now laid nearly a thousand mines, a recently developed weapon in use for the first time, around the area. On the morning of 9 August the Allied fleet lined up in battle formation two miles off shore. The bombardment of the fortress began at 7 a.m. and continued until the next day. Sveaborg was effectively destroyed as a base for the Russian navy yet throughout this time not a single Allied vessel was hit by Russian guns nor was a single Allied casualty recorded. Once the bombardment subsided, the people of Helsingfors, convinced that an Allied invasion was to follow, hurried to evacuate the city. But no invasion came. The Allies were content that the bombardment should stand as a lesson to the Russians that they could never hope to defeat the Allied navies and that Kronstadt and St Petersburg would be next.

DOWELL, George Dare *Lieutenant, Royal Marine Artillery*
    13 July 1855 – He was on board HMS *Ruby* in the Gulf of Finland when an explosion took place on a cutter belonging to HMS *Arrogant*. Under great fire, he jumped into a boat, rescued three crew of the stricken cutter and took them aboard the *Ruby*. He went out again, picking up Captain of the Mast INGOUVILLE and the rest of the cutter's crew before towing the cutter out of range of the Russian guns.

INGOUVILLE, George *Captain of the Mast, Royal Navy*
    13 July 1855 – He was on board HMS *Arrogant*'s second cutter when a Russian shell blew up the cutter's magazine and it began to drift under a

battery. Despite a wound in his arm he jumped overboard, swam round to the bows, took hold of the painter and tried to tow her out to sea. Whilst doing this, he was picked up by Lieutenant DOWELL, who towed the cutter out of range of the Russian guns.

THE FALL OF SEBASTOPOL

Following the defeat of the Russian army at the Battle of Tchernaya, Pélissier gave orders to recommence the bombardment, and eight hundred Allied guns and three hundred mortars began to rain fire onto Sebastopol. By now, the damage caused was too extensive to repair effectively, but Alexander II insisted that there was to be no retreat and Gorchakov was not willing to disobey. However, on 26 August, a Russian pontoon bridge linking the south side of Sebastopol to the north side was completed, preparing the ground for an eventual evacuation. Pélissier's plan of attack, disclosed to the British on 7 September, once again concentrated its focus on the Malakoff Tower. Twenty-five thousand French troops were to attack it, whilst a general advance was to be made along the entire front. Once again, the British were to attack the Great Redan, led by the 2nd and the Light Divisions whilst the Guards and Highlanders were held in reserve. One lesson had been learnt from the disastrous assault of 18 June: the British were not to attack until they were sure that the French had taken the Malakoff Tower.

The attack began, unusually, at midday on 8 September. The French 1st Division stormed the Malakoff from their trenches only a few yards away. The Russians were taken completely by surprise, and within ten minutes, the tower, the key to overall control of Sebastopol, had fallen to the French. Seeing the British white ensign raised above the tower, the 90th and 97th Foot of the British army charged towards the Redan without even waiting for orders. Although a very few fought their way into the Redan (including Captain Lumley of the 97th and Sergeant Moynihan of the 90th, who were awarded the Victoria Cross for their efforts), the vast majority were quickly shot down by a murderous fire from the bastions. They were followed by the 23rd Foot who were similarly cut down. Before long, the British troops began to waver and troops in the salient even refused to advance. The indignity of the episode could have been prevented, many thought, had the Guards and Highlanders been used in the attack, rather than men who had spent so long in the trenches.

Another attack was quickly planned for the following morning, but it never took place. Despite the failure of the British troops, the French capture of the Malakoff Tower convinced Gorchakov that the day was lost. At 5.30 p.m., he ordered a retreat across the pontoon bridge. Riflemen and some of the gun crews remained behind to cover the retreat while for six or seven hours, a huge wave of carts, horses and people swarmed across the bridge.

As they retreated, the Russians spiked their guns, mined their bastions and detonated their powder stores. The Redan was blown up. Anything that could prove useful to the Allies was destroyed. Finally, when all but the most seriously wounded had retreated, the bridge itself was destroyed. As the dust settled, the British were able to walk into the ruins of the Redan, despite never having captured it. Henry Clifford VC, a captain in the Rifle Brigade, recalled:

> If a few days before I had been told 'on the morning of the 9th September at five o'clock Sebastopol will be in the hands of the Allies and you will stand in the Redan held by the English', I should have said 'Oh, that will be a proud and happy moment, that will repay us for all we have gone through, even the loss of so many lives, so much suffering and hardship will not have been thrown away in vain!' But no, I stood in the Redan more humble, more dejected and with a heavier heart than I have felt since I left home.

SHEPPARD, John *Boatswain's Mate, Royal Navy (Naval Brigade)*
15 July 1855 – Having designed a canoe with a freeboard of only three inches which carried explosives to attach to an enemy ship, he proposed that the canoe be used to destroy the Russian flagship. His proposal was rejected as unsporting by the British but the French heard of the idea and encouraged him to try it out. On his first attempt in Sebastopol harbour he slipped unobserved past Russian steamboats but was prevented from going further by a long string of boats carrying troops. A second attempt, made the next day, was also unsuccessful, but he brought back much valuable information.

ROSS, John *Corporal, Royal Engineers*
21 July 1855 – He displayed great bravery in connecting the 4th Parallel Right Attack with an old Russian rifle pit at Sebastopol. All the work was carried out at night, only 40 yards from the Russian lines. *23 August 1855* – Whilst in charge of the advance from the 5th Parallel Right Attack on the Redan, he placed and filled twenty-five gabions under severe fire from the Russians. *8 September 1855* – During the night, he crept on his own right up to the Redan and found that the enemy had evacuated it. He reported this information enabling the Redan to be taken.

COLEMAN, John *Sergeant, 97th Regiment*
30 August 1855 – The enemy attacked a new sap at Sebastopol and drove the working party in. He remained in the open, completely exposed to the enemy's rifle pits, until all around him had been killed or wounded. He finally carried one of his officers, who was mortally wounded, to the rear.

ABLETT, Alfred *Private, Grenadier Guards*
2 September 1855 – A shell from the Russian batteries at Sebastopol fell among a number of cases containing powder and ammunition. He instantly seized it and flung it over the trench.

MAUDE, Frederick Francis *Bt/Lieutenant Colonel, 3rd Regiment*
5 September 1855 – Whilst in command of the covering-party of the 2nd Division at Sebastopol, he dashed for a traverse, which he held, and only retired when all hope of support was lost. During this action, he was severely wounded and accompanied by only nine or ten of his men, the rest having fallen.
Captain F. C. Maude VC was his cousin.

CRAIG, James *Colour Sergeant, Scots Fusilier Guards*
6 September 1855 – At Sebastopol, he volunteered to go out under heavy fire to look for Captain Buckley, supposed at the time to be only wounded. With the help of a drummer, he brought in the dead body of that officer. He was badly wounded in the course of this action.

CAMBRIDGE, Daniel *Sergeant, Royal Artillery*
8 September 1855 – At Sebastopol, he volunteered to lead a spiking party on the Redan and remained with it despite being severely wounded. Later in the day he went out in front of the advanced trench and brought in a wounded man under very heavy fire, badly injuring himself a second time.

CONNORS, John *Private, 3rd Regiment*
8 September 1855 – During the assault on the Redan at Sebastopol, he rescued an officer of the 30th Regiment, who was surrounded by Russians. He shot one and bayoneted another and was observed inside the Redan in close combat with the Russians for some time.

DAVIS, Gronow *Captain, Royal Artillery*
8 September 1855 – During the attack on the Redan at Sebastopol, he was in command of the spiking party. Noticing Lieutenant Sanders lying wounded with a broken leg, he sprang over the parapet, braved a murderous fire, and succeeded in carrying the lieutenant to safety.

HALE, Thomas Egerton *Assistant Surgeon, 7th Regiment*
8 September 1855 – During the attack on the Redan at Sebastopol, he remained with the dangerously wounded Lieutenant HOPE, when all men in the immediate vicinity had retreated. He was conspicuous in his attempts to rally the men. On the same day, he carried several wounded men from the open to the shelter of a sap, under heavy fire the entire time.

LUMLEY, Charles *Captain, 97th Regiment*
8 September 1855 – During the attack on the Redan at Sebastopol, he was one of the first to gain access to the inside of the work. He attacked three Russian gunners who were reloading a gun, shooting two of them with his revolver. He was himself stunned by a large stone but recovered quickly to draw his sword and cheer on his men. He was severely wounded by a bullet which hit him in the mouth.

MOYNIHAN, Andrew *Sergeant, 90th Regiment*

8 September 1855 – During the attack on the Redan at Sebastopol, he encountered five Russians hand-to-hand and killed them all. He also rescued a wounded officer under heavy fire.

SHIELDS, Robert *Corporal, 23rd Regiment*

8 September 1855 – After the attack on the Redan at Sebastopol, he went out under terrific fire to bring in Lieutenant Dynely, who had fallen wounded, mortally as it transpired.

SYLVESTER, William Henry Thomas *Assistant Surgeon, 23rd Regiment*

8 September 1855 – After the attack on the Redan, he went out under terrific fire to where Lieutenant Dynely was lying mortally wounded and attended to him in that exposed and dangerous position.

STRONG, George *Private, Coldstream Guards*

September 1855 – Whilst he was on duty in the trenches at Sebastopol, he picked up and threw aside a live shell which had fallen among the men.

THE GARRISON AT KARS

On 18 June 1855, the Russian Caucasus Army began a siege of the Turkish garrisons at Kars and Erzerum in Asia Minor. These garrisons were attractive to the Russians as their capture would give Russia free access to the east. Omar Pasha had spent much of July and August trying to get the Allies' permission to release Turkish troops from the Crimea so that they could be redeployed across the Black Sea. The Turkish Minister of Foreign Affairs stressed that these garrisons were 'the key of the frontiers of Asia' and Britain, ever alert to the threat of Russian expansion in the east, was sympathetic to the Turkish dilemma.

On the morning of 23 September, the Russians launched a fierce assault on the defenders of Kars. A bloody contest followed during which the garrison, led by General Williams and inspired by British officers, managed to repel the Russians, who did not retreat far. They simply returned to their positions and continued the siege. They intensified the blockade and began sending deserters from the garrison straight back in. On the same day, a conference of Allied generals had agreed to allow Omar Pasha's force to travel across the Black Sea to relieve the city, but he took an agonizingly long time to arrive. In the meantime, disease, cold and lack of food took their toll. General Williams had no choice. On 25 November, General Muraviev accepted his surrender, but allowed him to lead his men out bearing their arms.

TEESDALE, Christopher Charles *Lieutenant, Royal Artillery*
29 September 1855 – At Kars, he took command of the force defending the most advanced part of the works, forcing the enemy out of the redoubt. He rallied the Turkish artillerymen and induced them to return to their posts under heavy Russian fire. He led the final charge which secured victory and afterwards, at great risk to himself, stepped in to prevent the Turks, in their fury, from killing Russians lying wounded outside the works.

THE SEA OF AZOV

DAY, George Fiott *Lieutenant, Royal Navy*
17 September 1855 – He landed behind Russian lines at Genitchi to reconnoitre the southern shore where the enemy had four gunboats. He approached to within 200 yards and concluded that the vessels were not strongly manned. *21 September 1855* – He returned to the same spot. On this occasion he observed that the boats were manned and ready for action. He wandered for nine hours, lay down to sleep in the weeds and was found next morning more dead than alive.
It was supposedly the sight of Day wearing three orders and nine medals ranged across his uniformed chest that prompted the Prince of Wales (later Edward VII) to suggest in about 1870 that medals should be collected together and worn neatly on one bar.

COMMERELL, John Edmund *Commander, Royal Navy*
11 October 1855 – He (together with Quartermaster William RICKARD and Seaman George Milestone) landed on the Spit of Arabat and set fire to 400 tons of corn and forage belonging to the Russians. They accidentally alerted Cossacks to their presence and were pursued by about 30 of them two and a half miles back to their boat. Milestone became exhausted and begged to be left behind. The others removed his boots and half-carried him back to the boat, arriving just ahead of the Russians. In spite of heavy fire, they made good their escape.
He was MP for Southampton, 1885–88.

RICKARD, William Thomas *Quartermaster, Royal Navy*
11 October 1855 – He (together with Commander John COMMERELL and Seaman George Milestone) landed on the Spit of Arabat and set fire to 400 tons of corn and forage belonging to the Russians. They accidentally alerted Cossacks to their presence and were pursued by about 30 of them two and a half miles back to the boat. Milestone became exhausted and begged to be left behind. The others removed his boots and half-carried him back to the boat, arriving just ahead of the Russians. In spite of heavy fire, they made good their escape.

PEACE

Despite the varied national motives for prolonging the war, it soon became clear that the Allies could not agree on how it should be pursued. At a meeting in Paris in January 1856, no firm strategy was agreed upon: the British argued for an attack on Russian territory on the east coast of the Black Sea whilst the French favoured an attack on Kronstadt. Both of these plans came to nothing and the Allied armies sat out another winter in the Crimea. Fortunately, it was a mild one and this time the British, who were now well supplied and living in healthy conditions, fared far better than the French, who lost between twenty-five and forty thousand men from typhus and cholera between January and March 1856.

Despite the loss of Sebastopol, Tsar Alexander II was feeling reasonably confident. He had won a victory at Kars, albeit a minor one, and had begun making plans for a fresh campaign in the spring. The Allies' inertia and the Tsar's confidence were soon undermined, however, by Austria's entry into the fray as a 'broker'. She offered an ultimatum to the Russians, that they should either agree to the Allies' demands or she would enter the war. Boxed into a corner, the Russians agreed to the demands.

On 30 March 1856, the peace treaty that brought an end to the Crimean War was signed in Paris. Crimea was returned to Russia and Kars was returned to Turkey. Moldavia and Wallachia were granted independent national administrations whilst remaining under Turkish sovereignty. The Black Sea was neutralized and no Russian naval bases were to be maintained on its shores. The Danube was opened up to free navigation and the Turkish Porte agreed to guarantee the rights of his Christian subjects. A war that had claimed the lives of half a million Russians, a hundred thousand Frenchmen, a hundred thousand Turks and twenty-two thousand British soldiers came to a formal end with the ratification of the treaty on 27 April.

In January 1856, Queen Victoria approved the design of the Victoria Cross. It was conceived as a medal that could be won by men of any rank within the army and navy who performed an act of conspicuous bravery in the presence of the enemy. The first investiture of the medal, a 'cross patté' made from the bronze of two Russian cannon captured at Sebastopol, took place in Hyde Park on 26 June 1857. On that day, 62 of the 111 men who earned their crosses in the Crimea received their medals in front of an assortment of dignitaries including the Earl of Cardigan (the man who had led the Charge of the Light Brigade) and Sir Colin Campbell (the man whom many thought should have succeeded Lord Raglan). The VC winners were drawn up in single file near a small table on which stood the medals. The boom of the Royal Salute fired from field batteries indicating that Queen Victoria was approaching. She rode forward on horseback, accompanied by Prince Albert, the Prince of Wales and (rather poignantly) the Crown Prince of Russia. One by one, led by Lieutenant Henry Raby RN, these brave men came forward to accept the Cross from Her Majesty. As the men filed past, she leant down from her charger and pinned a medal onto each proud breast.

THE INDIAN MUTINY

1857–59

Although it was ultimately unsuccessful, the Indian or Sepoy Mutiny against colonial rule in India tested Britain's military resources to the limits. The ferocious and sustained uprisings across the north of India which began in May 1857 and lasted until late 1858 afforded many situations in which British and native soldiers demonstrated extreme courage in the face of the enemy.

Since the establishment of British rule in India there had been a steady Westernization of Indian traditions – a breaking-down of both the Hindu and Muslim lore which struck at the very heart of Indian life – until every aspect of Indian culture and religion was threatened. Lord Dalhousie, Governor and High Commissioner from 1847 to 1856, wanted the way cleared to allow Hindu widows to remarry (the Hindu tradition was for widows to commit suttee on their husband's death), and the whole caste system was being systematically dismantled. Feelings were running very high in northern India long before the sepoys (native Indian soldiers) in the Bengal Army found cause to rebel. Throughout British-ruled India there was unrest and a sense of outrage at the British destruction of the national culture, but it was only in the military sector that Indians were organized enough to take action. It would only take one trigger to set off a full-scale rebellion, and that trigger appeared in the form of a religious taboo. In order to load the newly supplied Enfield rifles, the sepoys had to bite the ends off paper cartridges which they believed – rightly or not – were lubricated with pig and cow lard. To touch this with their mouths would be an affront to both Muslim and Hindu.

The first trouble arose on 27 February, when the 19th Bengal Infantry refused their new cartridges; the regiment was disbanded and British troops were sent for from Burma. But on 24 April, 85 troopers at Meerut garrison refused to use the cartridges. Their punishment was ten years' hard labour, and on Saturday 9 May they were stripped of their uniforms and clapped in irons. Their comrades were outraged, but waited to strike until the following evening, when the main body of British soldiers of the garrison were in their quarters some distance away and their officers were unarmed attending church parade. Seizing the moment, they massacred most of the British at the garrison, including the women and children. The mutineers were joined by the two native infantry regiments at Meerut, and gaining in numbers

47

some two thousand advanced on Delhi, leaving a trail of murder, arson, looting and rape in their wake. In an act of defiance against British rule, the ageing Moghul Emperor Bahadur Shah II, who lived in Delhi's Red Fort as a pensioner of the Honourable East India Company, was nominally restored to power.

As the mutineers neared Delhi on 11 May, their ranks were swelled by sepoys of the city's garrison and some of the civilian population, and there ensued a horrific massacre of British and European men, women and children, and widespread looting and burning of their property and any Christian places of worship. As the mutineers swept through the city, the nine British officers remaining in the arsenal which lay within the Red Fort realized that it would be a prime target for the rebels and made a courageous stand to prevent the arms and ammunition from falling into enemy hands.

The Delhi sepoys deserted as the mutineers assaulted the walls of the fort. Inside, Lieutenant Willoughby had all available guns set up to fire grapeshot at any breach of the courtyard walls, and in consultation with the other officers, decided to blow up the whole arsenal with themselves inside rather than let it be taken. Powder trails were laid, ready for firing should the enemy break through into the courtyard. Met first with devastating grapeshot and then with individual rifle fire, the mutineers swarmed over the arsenal walls, then, after five hours' fierce fighting, Willoughby ordered the powder trails to be fired. Despite there being no real hope of surviving, Conductor Scully volunteered to fire the gunpowder, and in a massive explosion heard forty miles away, the 40ft walls around the arsenal collapsed, burying hundreds in rubble. Scully was killed in the explosion, but miraculously, Willoughby, along with Lieutenants Raynor and Forrest and Deputy Assistant Commissary John Buckley survived and struggled out to the city gates. The latter three were all awarded the VC – however, the VC was not awarded posthumously at this time, and the bravery of Scully and Willoughby (who was killed shortly after their escape by insurgents in a nearby village) went unrecognized.

Although deprived of the contents of the arsenal, the mutineers now controlled Delhi, and it was around the city that the first major operations of the mutiny were centred. It was a backs-to-the-wall struggle with no help from reinforcements, and unprecedented numbers of the hard-pressed defenders behaved with extraordinary courage.

BUCKLEY, John *Deputy Assistant Commissary of Ordnance Commissariat Department (Bengal Establishment)*
    11 May 1857 – He was with seven others inside the Delhi Magazine when Lieutenant FORREST brought the news that mutineers were approaching. The men resolved to defend the magazine until overpowered, at which point they would blow the building into the air. The gates were barricaded and two 6pdr guns loaded with grapeshot were trained on the entrances. The rebels

began scaling the building with ladders, at which point the entire native-born garrison went over to the mutineers. The nine men fired their guns ceaselessly until, with ammunition running out and rebels forcing their way in on all sides, Willoughby gave the order for the building to be fired. Five of the men, including Buckley, survived the explosion and fled to safety.

FORREST, George *Lieutenant, Bengal Veteran Establishment*
11 May 1857 – He brought news to Lieutenant George Willoughby, Lieutenant William RAYNOR, Commissary John BUCKLEY and five others inside the Delhi Magazine that mutineers were approaching. The men resolved to defend the magazine until overpowered, at which point they would blow the building into the air. The gates were barricaded and two 6pdr guns loaded with grapeshot were trained on the entrances. The rebels began scaling the building with ladders, at which point the entire native-born garrison went over to the mutineers. The nine men fired their guns ceaselessly until, with ammunition running out and rebels forcing their way in on all sides, Willoughby gave the order for the building to be fired. Five of the men, including Forrest, survived the explosion and fled to safety.

RAYNOR, William *Lieutenant, Bengal Veteran Establishment*
11 May 1857 – He was with Commisary John BUCKLEY, Lieutenant George Willoughby and 5 others inside the Delhi Magazine when Lieutenant George FORREST brought the news that mutineers were approaching. The men resolved to defend the magazine until they were overpowered, at which point they would blow the building into the air. The gates were barricaded and two 6pdr guns loaded with grapeshot were trained on the entrances. The rebels began scaling the building with ladders, at which point the entire native-born garrison went over to the mutineers. The nine men fired their guns ceaselessly until, with ammunition running out and rebels forcing their way in on all sides, Willoughby gave the order for the building to be fired. Five of the men, including Raynor and Willoughby, survived the explosion and fled. Willoughby, however, was killed shortly afterwards by villagers near Koomhera.
At sixty-one years ten months, he remains the oldest winner of the VC.

THE SIEGE OF DELHI (1)

Control of Delhi was the key to putting down the rebellion, so all available troops were called in. The Delhi Field Force of four thousand British, Sikh and Pathan troops, including the remnants of the Meerut garrison, approached the city under command of General Sir Harry Barnard – and sent out to meet them was a force of thirty thousand mutineers with thirty guns. They met in a battle on 8 June against vastly superior numbers at Badle-ke-Serai. Good military tactics and leadership, solid discipline and great individual courage prevailed, and the Delhi Field Force was able to occupy the strategically important area of the ridge to the north-west of the city walls.

LISLE-PHILLIPPS, Everard Aloysius *Ensign, 11th Bengal Native Infantry*
30 May to 8 September 1857 – He performed many gallant acts during the siege of Delhi. He took the Water Bastion from the rebels with a small party of men and was wounded three times. He was killed during street fighting in the city.
He performed the first acts for which the VC was posthumously awarded.

COUGHLAN, Cornelius (also known as COGHLAN) *Colour Sergeant, 75th Regiment*
8 June 1857 – At Badle-ke-Serai he ventured into a building held by the rebels and rescued Private Corbett who lay severely wounded. *18 July 1857* – At Delhi, his party was hesitating before charging down a lane raked with crossfire. He encouraged and cheered them. They then entered an enclosure filled with armed mutineers and killed every one. He also returned under crossfire to collect litters and carry off the injured.

HARTIGAN, Henry *Pensioned Sergeant, 9th Lancers*
8 June 1857 – At Badle-ke-Serai, he went to the assistance of Sergeant Helstone who was wounded and surrounded by the enemy and at great risk to himself carried the sergeant to the rear. *10 October 1857* – At Agra, he ran unarmed to the assistance of Sergeant Crews who was being attacked by four rebels. He wrenched a tulwar from the first rebel with one hand, punched him in the mouth with the other, and turned and attacked the other three, killing one and wounding two.

JONES, Alfred Stowell *Lieutenant, 9th Lancers*
8 June 1857 – At Badle-ke-Serai, Delhi, he commanded a squadron which charged the rebels, riding straight through them, killing drivers and capturing one of their guns. He trained the gun on a village held by the mutineers and drove them out. *10 October 1857* – At Agra, he received twenty-two wounds, including part of his head being cut away and the loss of one eye.
He later recalled that on the day of his investiture he was sporting such a shocking bruise above his blind eye that the Queen became so nervous that she pricked him through his tunic as she pinned on his cross. In 1912 he published the book Will a Sewage Farm Pay?.

GOUGH, Charles John Stanley *Major, 5th Bengal European Cavalry*
15 August 1857 – He saved the life of his brother, Lieutenant H. H. GOUGH, killing two of his assailants. *18 August 1857* – He led a troop of the Guide Cavalry in a charge against the enemy, killing two sowars after hand-to-hand combat with one of them. *27 January 1858* – At Shunshabad, he tackled the leader of the rebel cavalry, running him through with his sword.

The sword lodged in his body, and Gough was reduced to his revolver, with which he shot two more. *23 February 1858* – At Meangunge, he ran to the aid of Bt/Major Anson and cut down his opponent, despatching another immediately afterwards.

Lieutenant H. H. Gough VC was his brother and Bt/Major J. E. Gough VC was his son.

THE SPREAD OF MUTINY

Once the news of the Meerut mutiny reached other garrison towns, insurrection spread across the north. In Benares, in the south-east of the Oudh region, Colonel Gordon believed that his Sikh soldiers would stay loyal, while having misgivings about the native infantry. A disarmament parade was hurriedly planned for the afternoon of 4 June and was under way when a shout came from among the sepoys that they were being disarmed so that the Europeans could shoot them down unopposed. Chaos broke out as the sepoys rearmed themselves, opened fire on the European troops and rampaged through the town looting, killing and setting fire to buildings – three VCs were awarded during this action. The mutiny was quashed in a day, but the backlash lasted much longer, and anyone even suspected of mutiny or inciting rebellion was publicly hanged.

GILL, Peter *Sergeant Major, Loodiana Regiment*
4 June 1857 – He was at Benares where the mutineers were setting light to bungalows and killing the inhabitants. Alongside Sergeant Major ROSAMUND and Private KIRK, he made his way to the residence of Captain Brown and his family, who were in great peril, and brought them all to safety. He also saved the life of a sergeant who had been bayoneted by slicing off the head of his assailant. On the same evening, he faced a guard of 27 mutineers, despite being armed with just a sword.

KIRK, John *Private, 10th Regiment*
4 June 1857 – He was at Benares where the mutineers were setting light to bungalows and killing the inhabitants. Alongside Sergeant Major GILL and Sergeant Major ROSAMUND, he made his way to the residence of Captain Brown and his family, who were in great peril, and brought them all to safety.

ROSAMUND, Matthew *Sergeant Major, 37th Bengal Native Infantry*
4 June 1857 – He was at Benares where the mutineers were setting light to bungalows and killing the inhabitants. Alongside Sergeant Major GILL and Private KIRK, he made his way to the residence of Captain Brown and his family, who were in great danger, and brought them all to safety. He also

volunteered with Lieutenant Colonel Spottiswoode to set fire to the sepoy lines to drive out the enemy.

THE SIEGE OF DELHI (2)

At the ridge, the Delhi Field Force, six hundred cavalry and two thousand three hundred infantry, with just twenty-two field guns, was now led by Colonel Archdale Wilson. The Field Force was constantly attacked by the mutineers in attempts to drive off the ridge, but they were held off, despite cholera and battle injuries seriously depleting their strength. Although reinforcements arrived, the Field Force still numbered only six thousand six hundred men by the end of July, and Wilson and Nicholson, seeing that disease and injuries would only deplete their numbers if they didn't strike fast, decided to storm the breaches around Delhi on 13 September. During the period while they held the ridge, an extraordinary sixteen VC awards were made, mostly for the rescue of comrades, with some being decided by ballot.

CADELL, Thomas *Lieutenant, 2nd Bengal European Fusiliers*
12 June 1857 – During an attack by the rebels at Delhi, he saw a bugler fall wounded and carried him from the enemy under severe fire. On the same evening, he went with three others towards the advancing mutineers to save the life of a wounded man who had been left behind.
Lieutenant S. H. Lawrence VC was his cousin.

HANCOCK, Thomas *Private, 9th Lancers*
19 June 1857 – When Sir Hope Grant's horse was shot under him at Delhi, he offered Sir Hope his own horse and (along with Private PURCELL and Roopur Khan) remained by him in the midst of the enemy cavalry. Sir Hope's life was undoubtedly saved by their actions.

PURCELL, John *Private, 9th Lancers*
19 June 1857 – At Delhi, he (along with Private HANCOCK and Roopur Khan), remained alongside Sir Hope Grant in the midst of the enemy cavalry, after Sir Hope's horse had been shot under him at Delhi. Sir Hope's life was undoubtedly saved by their actions.

TURNER, Samuel *Private, 1st Bn., 60th Rifles*
19 June 1857 – At Delhi, he carried the mortally wounded Lieutenant Humphreys from the midst of the enemy under heavy fire. Whilst perform-ing this act, he was severely wounded by a sabre.

GARVIN, Stephen *Colour Sergeant, 1st Bn., 60th Rifles*
23 June 1857 – At Delhi, he showed great courage in leading a small party in an assault on a well-defended post, the Sammy House. The post was

captured after a sharp contest, his party being under terrific fire all the while.

McGOVERN, John *Private, 1st Bengal Fusiliers*

23 June 1857 – At Delhi, he saved the life of a wounded comrade by carrying him into camp under heavy fire from the enemy.

HEATHCOTE, Alfred Spencer *Lieutenant, 60th Rifles*

June–September 1857 – He volunteered for services of extreme danger throughout the siege of Delhi, especially during the six days of the assault against the rebels.

He was elected by the officers of his regiment under Rule 13 of the Royal Warrant.

HILLS, James (later HILLS-JOHNES) *Second Lieutenant, Bengal Horse Artillery*

9 July 1857 – During the siege of Delhi, whilst on picket duty with two guns on a hill near the camp, his force was suddenly attacked by rebel cavalry. Without hesitation, he rode straight at the enemy, single-handed, in order to cause a commotion and give the guns time to load. He cut down two rebels before being thrown from his horse by two sowars charging together. Now on foot, he managed to fight off two more assailants and was about to be killed by a third when Major TOMBS came to his assistance.

Lieutenant W. G. Cubitt VC was his brother-in-law.

TOMBS, Henry *Major, Bengal Horse Artillery*

In Lord Roberts' introduction to the memoir of Sir Henry Tombs, he writes: 'Tombs was gifted with a bright and cheerful nature, great charm of manner, good looks and a fine soldierly bearing, which all contributed to make "Harry" Tombs the attractive and remarkable figure we knew and loved'. However, in *Forty-One Years in India*, Roberts describes Tombs as 'a strict disciplinarian and more feared than liked by his men until they realized what a grand leader he was.' Clearly, Sir Henry Tombs was a man to be reckoned with.

Tombs's father, John, left Gloucestershire for India in 1797 to join the 1st Bengal Cavalry. Tombs, the youngest of 8 children, was born on 10 November 1824 in Calcutta. His eldest brother took holy orders, the next one became a lawyer and all the others joined the army. Tombs was sent to Sandhurst, after which he joined the Bengal Artillery. He fought bravely in many campaigns over the next few years, beginning with the Gwalior Campaign of 1843–44, during which he was promoted to first lieutenant. In 1854 he became a captain, and two years later he assumed command of the 2nd Troop, 1st Brigade, Bengal Horse Artillery, which was to become renowned during the Mutiny under his leadership. His appointment gave rise to a joke: 'Why are men of the 2–1 Horse Artillery like men buried in the Crimea?' 'They are under Tombs.'

Tombs' troop was the first to respond to the massacre at Meerut on 10 May 1857. On seeing the troop approaching, the rebels moved off to Delhi. Tombs himself was mentioned in despatches following a two-hour confrontation with rebels by the Hindun River, during which the troop lost 13 of its 50 men. Shortly afterwards, an incident occurred which gives a flavour of the army of the period. One of Tombs' limber gunners had appeared drunk and insubordinate at Meerut. He was tried by court martial and awarded twenty-four lashes after which he was taken to hospital. Two days later, rebels attacked the camp and the limber gunner rose from his hospital bed to serve on No. 4 gun. No sooner had he taken his place than a shrapnel bullet pierced his lung and he was carried back to hospital, gravely wounded. When Tombs was brought to see him, the gunner told him that he was dying but was far more upset about his flogging. He begged Tombs not to record it on his defaulter sheet. Tombs agreed. The gunner was invalided home to England and lived for another two years.

Tombs recalled a strange event that occurred on 30 May. One of the officers of the troop, a lieutenant named Perkins, normally a quiet man, was particularly lively on that day. He was singing, humming and quoting bits of Thackeray. When Tombs asked him why, he said it was because he *knew* that he was going to die on 30 or 31 May but he did not know in which year. And as the enemy had just been driven off with the loss of their guns, he must now be safe for another year. Later that day, Perkins went off, under Tombs' instruction, to find a ford in a nearby river. Whilst gone, he was shot in the head and killed instantly.

Tombs was once again mentioned in despatches at Badli-ke-Serai on 7 June, after two horses were shot from under him whilst leading the troop over a series of ditches. The troop then became fully engaged in the siege of Delhi. Tombs was wounded and had two more horses shot from under him on the 17th. On that day, the Indian Civil Commissioner said of him: 'We are all very proud of him but nothing can make him vain.'

On 9 July, Tombs' subaltern, Lieutenant Hills, was on picquet duty on a mound to the side of the camp, when he heard a rumour that the rebel cavalry was approaching. As he moved to a better vantage point, the rebels appeared out of nowhere. Hills charged alone at the enemy column. He cut down one man and struck a second but was thrown off his horse. Three men came at him – he wounded one with his pistol, caught the lance of the second in his hand and slashed at him with his sword. The third man pulled the sword from Hills' hand and was about to kill him, when Tombs arrived, saw what was happening, and shot the rebel with his pistol at 30 paces. Tombs and Hills then went together to attend to wounded men. Before they had got far, they were confronted by a rebel carrying Hills' pistol and flourishing a sword. He ran at Hills, slashing him in the head. Tombs rushed in and put his sword through the rebel, although not before he too had been slashed in the head (he was only saved from a severe head wound by the wadded headdress he wore). Both Tombs and Hills were awarded the Victoria Cross. Immediately afterwards, Tombs had to deal with a more mundane sort of difficulty. A limber gunner complained that the lead driver of his gun had called him a coward, adding that he would have thrashed him had they not been on active service. Tombs told the driver to withdraw his remark and ordered the men to shake hands 'for there is no man in this troop who is a coward.' The driver looked at Tombs and said, 'But he bobbed his head when a shot passed over it!' 'Nonsense!' said Tombs. 'Shake hands and say you're sorry.' The driver shook hands, said he was sorry, but added: 'He bobbed his head, he *did.*'

During the final assault on Delhi in September, Tombs was in command of No. 4 battery (four batteries were placed to the north of Delhi for the purpose of breaching the walls and allowing the infantry to enter the city). No. 4 battery was positioned near the Kudsia Bagh and was armed with four 10in and six 8in mortars. On 14 September, the day of the infantry assault, Tombs' troop lost half of its men and seventeen horses. A false report reached the commanding officer that Tombs himself had been killed. Once Delhi was finally taken, the troop was ordered to Meerut to refit. Tombs was subsequently mentioned in the House of Lords by the Secretary of State for War. On 29 April 1861, he relinquished command of the troop and was promoted to lieutenant colonel and again a year later to brigadier general. In 1865, he commanded the right column of the Bhutan Field Force during a campaign intended to punish the Bhutanese for outrages committed on British territory. By the time peace terms were agreed in the autumn, Tombs had been appointed ADC to Queen Victoria and shortly afterwards, he was promoted to major general.

During the Christmas of 1873 Tombs fell ill, and though his condition did not seem serious, he journeyed from Lucknow to England to seek further medical advice. Whilst en route, he grew worse and underwent an operation in Paris. He was told by French doctors that he was now completely cured, but on reaching London he discovered that his condition was in fact terminal. He went to live out his days on the Isle of Wight, where he died on 2 August 1874, aged forty-nine.

WADESON, Richard *Lieutenant, 75th Regiment*
18 July 1857 – At Delhi, men collapsing from the effects of the sun were being attacked by prowling horsemen as they fell. Wadeson saved the life of Private Michael Farrell by bayoneting a sowar who was attacking him in this manner. Towards sunset, he saved the life of Private John Barry by cutting down a sowar attacking him.
He was Lieutenant Governor of the Royal Hospital, Chelsea, 1881–85.

DIVANE, John (also known as DEVINE) *Private, 60th Rifles*
10 September 1857 – He headed a charge made by the Beloochee and Sikh troops on the enemy's trenches at Delhi. Followed closely by the troops,

he made straight for the enemy's breastworks but was shot down within a few yards of his goal.

He was elected by the privates of the regiment under Rule 13 of the Royal Warrant.

GREEN, Patrick *Private, 75th Regiment*

11 September 1857 – At Koodsia Bagh, Delhi, whilst in the midst of large numbers of the enemy, he rescued a comrade who had fallen wounded.

REBELLIONS IN THE SOUTH

Mutiny flared up in Indore on 1 July, when the maharaja's troops attacked the Residency. Here Colonel James Travers led a five-man charge to drive the rebels from a gun battery, earning the VC. In the far north, in the largely peaceful Punjab region at Jhelum, mutiny broke out on 7 July, in Kolapore in the far south on the 10th and at Oonao on the 29th. These rebellions were quickly suppressed, but the fighting was vicious and VCs were earned at all three uprisings.

TRAVERS, James *Colonel, 2nd Bengal Native Infantry*

1 July 1857 – When the Indore Residency was suddenly attacked by Holkar's troops, he led a charge against the guns with only five men. He drove the rebels from the battery and created a diversion which allowed many lives to be saved and enabled the Bhopal artillery to man their guns. During the charge, his horse was shot in three places and his clothes were riddled with bullets.

CONNOLLY, William *Gunner, Bengal Horse Artillery*

7 July 1857 – At Jhelum, he replaced a wounded sponge man attached to one of the guns. After two rounds had been fired he received a bullet through the left thigh. Nevertheless he mounted his horse and stayed with the gun as the battery retired to another position. He continued sponging out his gun until he was struck again, in the hip. When urged by his officer to retire he replied, 'I'll not go whilst I can work here.' Late in the afternoon, a third bullet tore through his right leg. Still he carried on sponging, until he collapsed unconscious into the arms of Lieutenant Cookes, at which point he was carried from the fight.

KERR, William Alexander *Lieutenant, 24th Bombay Infantry*

10 July 1857 – On learning that rebels had risen at Kolapore and had murdered some officers and besieged others in the residency, he collected 50 troopers and led them 75 miles to Kolapore. On reaching the rebels' fortifications, his men charged the doors, broke them down and he was first into the building. The rebels were forced out into another building which was in turn stormed. Finally, the rebels took refuge in a temple, which was razed to the ground. At a stroke, the mutiny on the Malabar coast was practically stamped out.

BOGLE, Andrew Cathcart *Lieutenant, 78th Regiment*

29 July 1857 – At Oonao, he got together a few men and stormed a contested passage, opening a way for the force to advance. Under heavy fire, he and his men attacked a loopholed house held by sepoys, captured it and cleared it of the enemy. He was badly wounded during this attack.

LAMBERT, George *Sergeant Major, 84th Regiment*

29 July 1857 – At Oonao. *16 August 1857* – At Bithoor. *25 September 1857* – At Lucknow. On all these occasions he demonstrated great courage.

ARRAH

On 25 July, at Dinapore in the north-east, the garrison commander attempted to disarm the sepoys, but over two thousand escaped to nearby Arrah, and besieged the garrison there. Three men of a small force sent to relieve this siege were awarded the VC when their party of just four hundred was ambushed outside the town and forced into retreat – only half of the force survived the encounter.

DEMPSEY, Denis *Private, 10th Regiment*

30 July 1857 – During the retreat from Arrah, he carried the mortally wounded Ensign Erskine for two miles. *12 August 1857* – He was the first man to enter the village of Jugdispore under heavy fire. *14 March 1858* – He carried a powder bag through a burning village in order to mine a passage to the rear of the enemy's position, all the while exposed to heavy fire.

McDONELL, William Fraser *Mr, Bengal Civil Service*

30 July 1857 – During the retreat from Arrah, he was in a boat with 35 men attempting to escape. It was discovered that the enemy had bound the boat to the bank and fixed the rudder to the right. Exposed to heavy enemy fire, he cut away the rope holding the rudder. He then took the rudder himself whilst a fortunate breeze carried the boat halfway across the stream, from where he and all but two of the men were able to swim to safety.

He was one of the first two civilians to win the VC – Mr R. L. Mangles won his VC on the same day.

MANGLES, Ross Lowis *Mr, Bengal Civil Service*

30 July 1857 – During the retreat from Arrah, a wounded soldier of the 37th, Richard Taylor, begged not to be left at the mercy of the mutineers. Mangles bound up Taylor's wounds, lifted him on his back and carried him across swampy ground for six miles. The sun was fierce and he had neither eaten for twenty-four hours nor slept for forty-eight. At last, he reached the river and swam to the safety of a boat with his comrade in his arms.

He was one of the first two civilians to win the VC – Mr W. F. McDonell won his VC on the same day.

OUDH

In late July, Brigadier General Sir Henry Havelock marched his men into Oudh. He had just seventeen hundred men and twelve field guns and rebel resistance was spirited, so that, despite initial victories, by the 31st a sixth of his original force had been lost through battle casualties and disease, ammunition was running low and there was insufficient transport to deal with the wounded. On that day he received the unwelcome news that the much needed reinforcements he had been expecting would be held up dealing with the rebellion at Bihar. The planned advance to retake Lucknow now seemed unlikely, despite successful actions at Busherut-Gunge on 5 and 12 August (the latter against an enemy force of some four thousand), and Havelock moved back to Cawnpore.

CROWE, Joseph Petrus Hendrick *Lieutenant, 78th Regiment*
12 August 1857 – At Busherut-Gunge, a redoubt was strongly defended by the enemy. A decision was made to take the redoubt by storm as no guns were at hand and night was falling. He was the first of the Highlanders to reach the redoubt and within one minute the place was captured and the enemy scattered or slain.

On 14 August, Havelock learned that some two thousand Indians, mutineers from Sagar and some of the Nana's forces, had assembled at Bithoor. His troops found the rebels well dug in in front of the Nana's palace, but they held out despite concentrated pounding with heavy guns, and victory was achieved only after several bayonet charges – during which sixty British soldiers were killed or wounded and twelve died from sunstroke.

NEEMUCH

In mid-August, at Neemuch (the most southerly point to which the mutiny extended), the garrison of European officers remained under siege by a local rebel force which had moved in after the native Bengal troops had abandoned the fort for Delhi.

BLAIR, James *Captain, 2nd Bombay Light Cavalry*
12 August 1857 – At Neemuch, sword in hand, he burst in on 8 mutineers who had shut themselves in a house. A struggle ensued during

which he was badly injured and the rebels escaped through the roof. In spite of his wounds he pursued them, finally losing sight of them in the darkness. *23 October 1857* – At Jeerum he was surrounded by a party of rebels. He broke his sword on the head of one of them who then wounded him in the arm. He escaped to rejoin his men and led them in pursuit of the rebels, who were eventually routed.

Lieutenant R. Blair VC was his cousin.

CHOTA BEHAR

During September and early October, widespread fighting continued to relieve the besieged British strongholds, including Chota Behar, where two VC awards were made.

DAUNT, John Charles Campbell *Lieutenant, 11th Bengal Native Infantry*
2 October 1857 – At Chota Behar, he, together with Sergeant DYNON, charged the guns of the Ramgurh Battalion. They captured two of the guns and pistolled the gunners who had mowed down a third of their detachment. *2 November 1857* – He chased a body of mutineers across a plain.

DYNON, Denis *Sergeant, 53rd Regiment*
2 October 1857 – At Chota Behar, he, together with Lieutenant DAUNT, charged the guns of the Ramgurh Battalion. They captured two of the guns and pistolled the gunners who had mowed down a third of their detachment.

ASSAULT ON DELHI

From the relative calm of the Punjab, Chief Commissioner Sir John Lawrence despatched a mainly Sikh force under command of Brigadier General John Nicholson. A dour but ruthlessly effective soldier, he led from the front and, despite owning personally to hating the Indians as a nation, earned the respect and loyalty of all his men through his own example. He had not been averse to blowing mutineers from the mouths of his cannon in the past, and his Movable Column had been responsible for quashing any potential uprising in the Punjab region. Deemed the ideal man for the job, he set out with three cavalry regiments, seven infantry battalions and a heavy siege engine to strengthen the Delhi Field Force and retake the city.

For Nicholson, contemplating an assault with just five thousand men on a stronghold of more than thirty thousand, failure was not an option. The attack was to be launched in five columns, his own being directed to storm the main breach at the Kashmir Bastion. The operation would leave just a handful of troops and the sick to man the guns and defend the ridge.

On 7 September, the chief engineer, Lieutenant Colonel Richard Baird-

Smith, began building four powerful batteries to the north of the city. The rebels, who had been expecting a British attack from the west, were taken by surprise, but very soon began raining fire on the unarmed Indian workmen constructing the siege batteries. On 12 September, fifty guns and mortars were in place and they opened fire on the walls, causing the rebels to retire from the ruined bastions and take up positions in the open. The five columns approached the city walls under cover of darkness on the morning of 14 September. As light dawned it became apparent that the mutineers had sandbagged the breaches, so time was lost as the siege guns shot these down. Now in daylight, the parties tasked with storming the walls found that the ladders were too short, and casualties mounted as mounds of anything available, including bodies, were stacked up to support the ladders. A 'forlorn hope' party sent to blow the Kashmir Gate came under heavy fire as the men led by Lieutenant Home moved in to position the gunpowder sacks at the gates, and a second party, led by Lieutenant Salkeld, then followed to tamp down the charges. Several men from these parties were killed, but Sergeant John Smith managed to light the fuses and the right-hand gate was blown off its hinges. With most of the sepoys inside killed or stunned in the blast, the column stormed the entrance and continued, according to plan, to clear the narrow streets of the city.

Fierce hand-to-hand fighting ensued, but the column led by Colonel George Campbell made good progress – so good, in fact, that he feared he had advanced so far as to be in danger of being cut off. He decided to make a tactical withdrawal, which was seen by the mutineers as an opportunity to give chase, and casualties mounted as the retiring troops came under attack. Any wounded men left to be taken by the enemy would be killed with terrible savagery, so every attempt was made to carry out fallen comrades – the heroic rescue by Lance Corporal Smith of a wounded man while under heavy fire earned him the VC. Later in the day, Surgeon Reade also received the VC for saving the wounded at a dressing station from certain slaughter as the mutineers stormed the area, and two more awards were made, to Sergeant McGuire and Drummer Ryan, who picked up and disposed of two burning cases of ammunition, so averting a massive explosion.

In an error of judgement, the Kashmiri contingent made a premature and unsupported assault, and as they turned and fled, followed by a horde of mutineers, No. 4 column, which was to have entered the city via the Kabul Gate, came under attack from the pursuing enemy. Chaos ensued as the column was driven back towards the ridge, and only the cool thinking and decisive action of Lieutenant Robert Shebbeare (later awarded the VC) in rallying a rearguard to cover the withdrawal prevented disaster. Even then, the mutineers surged on, and were held off only by the fire of one troop of guns and a thin line of cavalry. British casualties were heavy, as holding their position in defence of the guns but unable to charge due to tangled under-growth in front of them, the cavalry was trapped under musket and gunfire.

By the afternoon Nicholson was mortally wounded, shot by a sepoy sniper, and about a quarter of the Delhi Field Force who had taken part in the assault were dead or injured, but a quarter of Delhi was back under British control. Wilson assumed command from a position holed up in St James' Church and, after much deliberation, decided to continue the attack. But his troops had found the city's wine warehouses and soon anaesthetized themselves against the horror of that day and the preceding months by drinking themselves into a stupor. This delayed progress by some thirty-six hours, but the mutineers too seemed to have run out of steam and they made no attempt at a counter-attack.

On 16 September the Delhi Field Force resumed the fight, this time with more sustained success. Siege guns supported the assault on the arsenal walls (repaired since the May explosion), and as a group led by Surgeon Herbert Reade spiked the enemy guns, the Field Force stormed and took control of the arsenal.

The mutineers had now lost 171 guns and a huge supply of ammunition, but launched a last-ditch counter-attack, setting fire to a thatched building full of explosives. The actions of two men, Second Lieutenant Thackeray and Lieutenant Renny, in extinguishing the fire, then throwing grenades from the arsenal into the midst of the enemy turned the tide, and quashed the attack. Delhi was effectively back in British control.

SUTTON, William *Bugler, 60th Rifles*
13 September 1857 – At Delhi, on the day before the assault, he volunteered to reconnoitre the breach. Throughout the siege, his behaviour was noticeable, particularly on one occasion when he killed an enemy bugler about to sound an order.

HAWTHORNE, Robert *Bugler, 52nd Regiment*
14 September 1857 – In advance of the assault on Delhi, he (together with Lieutenant HOME, Sergeant SMITH, Sergeant Burgess and Lieutenant SALKELD) was a member of the party which blew up the Kashmir Gate under heavy fire from the enemy. His role was to sound the advance once the gate was blown. He had to sound it three times before it was heard by the waiting column.
He was elected by the privates of the regiment under Rule 13 of the Royal Warrant.

HOME, Duncan Charles *Lieutenant, Bengal Engineers*
Home, like so many of the Indian Army, was born in India, the son of a major general in the Bengal Army. He was sent to boarding school in England and then attended the East India Company's cadet school at Addiscombe near Croydon (the Indian Army's equivalent of the Royal Military Academy) before completing his training at the Royal Engineer Establishment at Chatham (which he attended alongside his engineer con-

temporaries in the British army). He arrived back in India in 1848 and joined the Bengal Engineers, fighting at the Battle of Mujarat in the Second Sikh War. After the war he worked on a number of engineering projects. He built roads and canals near the Afghan border, supervised the construction of a portion of the Ganges Canal and spent five years in Malikpore working on the Bari Doab Canal. He built himself a reputation as a pillar of the military community, often leading church services at his own home in the absence of a minister. When he was summoned to join the siege force at Delhi in August, he brought with him five loyal companies of Sikh sappers from the Punjab. On 13 September, he was instrumental in making the final decision to launch the assault on Delhi – Baird-Smith sent him with Lieutenants Lang, Medley and Greathed to reconnoitre the damage that had been done to the walls. He reported back that the breaches were 'practicable' and the assault was launched the following morning.

After dawn on the morning of 14 September, Home formed his party of sappers into two groups. He led the first group, an emplacement party carrying 25lb bags of gunpowder, across the single remaining beam of the bridge that led to the Kashmir Gate. His men had to brave heavy gunfire coming from the top of the gate and through its open wicket. As they nailed the bags of gunpowder to the gate, one of their number, Sergeant Carmichael, fell dead. Having attached his own bag, Sergeant Smith nailed Carmichael's, prepared the fuse and called, 'All ready.' The second party came across the bridge, led by Lieutenant Salkeld who was holding the slow match ready to set light to the charge and ignite the gunpowder. In stooping down to light the charge, he was shot through the thigh. He held out the match to Corporal Burgess before toppling into the ditch beneath the bridge. Burgess took the match and, thinking it had gone out, reached for a box of lucifers. Just as he leant down, he was shot. Sergeant Smith grabbed the match before the corporal fell back on top of Salkeld. Realizing that the match was still alight, Smith quickly lit the fuse, picked up his gun and jumped into the ditch. Before he even reached the ground, the gunpowder exploded. When the dust cleared, he looked about him in the ditch and saw Burgess lying dead, Salkeld with two broken arms as well as a wounded leg and Home crouching uninjured. Enough of a gap had been blown in the gateway to allow men of the Third Column to enter. These men were able to throw the gate wide open and the infantry poured into the city of Delhi.

Home, Salkeld, Smith and Bugler Hawthorne were awarded the Victoria Cross. Carmichael and Burgess did not receive the honour because there was no provision at this time to make an award posthumously. Although both Home and Salkeld were dead weeks later (Salkeld died from his wounds in hospital on 10 October), their commanding officer had conferred the award on both men on the spot. Home, Salkeld and Smith were the first members of the East India Company to receive the award. Until this date, only officers and men of the British army were eligible for the Victoria Cross.

Indeed, it was not until 1911 that native Indian officers and men became eligible.

Five days after the blowing of the Kashmir Gate, Home was instrumental in the demolition of the Lahore Gate of the Red Fort (the palace of the King of Delhi), an event which consolidated the British recapture of the city. While he was supervising the destruction of an abandoned fort at Malagarh on 2 October, he was killed by the accidental detonation of the final mine. Lieutenant Lang (with whom he had earlier reconnoitred the Delhi walls) recalled him laughing and joking as he made final preparations to the mine. A split second later, his body was lying mangled, 20 yards from where he had been standing.

McGUIRE, James *Sergeant, 1st Bengal Fusiliers*
14 September 1857 – During the assault on Delhi, ammunition was being distributed at the Kabul Gate, when five boxes caught fire. Three of the boxes exploded. McGuire (together with Drummer RYAN) dashed for the two remaining boxes and hurled them over the parapet. Confused, many soldiers had begun running towards the explosions, so by their action the 2 men saved many lives.

His name was erased from the VC Roll and his medal confiscated in 1862 after he was convicted of the theft of a cow. His name was restored to the register after his death.

READE, Herbert Taylor *Surgeon, 61st Regiment*
14 September 1857 – During the siege of Delhi, he was ministering to the wounded when a party of rebels began firing on him from the roofs of nearby houses. Drawing his sword, he gathered together nine fit soldiers and after heavy fire succeeded in dislodging the enemy from their position. Two of his party were killed and six wounded. *16 September 1857* – At the assault on Delhi, he was one of the first up at the breach of the magazine and he successfully spiked one of the enemy's guns.

RYAN, Miles *Drummer, European Bengal Fusiliers*
14 September 1857 – During the assault on Delhi, ammunition was being distributed at the Kabul Gate, when five boxes caught fire. Three of the boxes exploded. Ryan (together with Sergeant McGUIRE) dashed for the two remaining boxes and hurled them over the parapet. Confused, many soldiers had begun running towards the explosions, so by their action the two men saved many lives.

SALKELD, Philip *Lieutenant, Bengal Engineers*
14 September 1857 – In advance of the assault on Delhi, he (together with Lieutenant HOME, Sergeant SMITH, Sergeant Burgess and Bugler HAWTHORNE) blew up the Kashmir Gate under heavy fire from the enemy. In stooping down to light the quick match he was shot in the thigh, but in falling he held out the slow match, telling Sergeant Smith to fire the charge

and stay calm. Once the gate was blown, he was carried away by stretcher but died of his wounds almost a month later.

This was the first time that the VC was gazetted and presented (to Lieutenant Salkeld's father) after the recipient's death. A poem commemorating his deeds was written by William Barnes (a fellow Dorset man) in 1860.

SHEBBEARE, Robert Haydon *Lieutenant, 60th Bengal Native Infantry*
    14 September 1857 – At the assault on Delhi, he led the Guides and twice charged a loopholed serai but failed to achieve a breach. He was under terrible fire and received one bullet through the cheek and another in the back of the head.

SMITH, Henry *Lance Corporal, 52nd Regiment*
    14 September 1857 – During the retreat from the Chaudney Chouk in the assault on Delhi, he carried a wounded comrade to safety through murderous fire.

SMITH, John *Sergeant, Bengal Sappers and Miners*
    14 September 1857 – In advance of the assault on Delhi, he (together with Lieutenant HOME, Lieutenant SALKELD, Sergeant Burgess and Bugler HAWTHORNE) was a member of the party which blew up the Kashmir Gate under heavy fire from the enemy. He placed his bag of explosives, arranged the fuse and reported all ready to Lieutenant Salkeld. About to light the fuse, the lieutenant was shot. Sergeant Burgess took over but was instantly killed. Left on his own, Smith realized the fuse had somehow been lit and jumped into the ditch just in time to save himself from the explosion. He then went to fetch stretchers for his comrades.

WALLER, George *Colour Sergeant, 60th Rifles*
    14 September 1857 – At Delhi, he charged and captured the enemy's guns near the Kabul Gate. *18 September 1857* – He showed conspicuous bravery in repulsing an enemy attack on a gun near the Chaudney Chouk.
    He was elected by the non-commissioned officers of the regiment under Rule 13 of the Royal Warrant.

RENNY, George Alexander *Lieutenant, Bengal Horse Artillery*
    16 September 1857 – After the capture of the Delhi Magazine, the rebels kept up a concerted attack on the post. Shells with lighted fuses were thrown onto the thatched roof. Renny leapt onto the wall above the magazine and flung several shells back down into the enemy's midst. Almost at once the attack became less severe and ceased entirely shortly afterwards.

THACKERAY, Edward Talbot *Second Lieutenant, Bengal Engineers*
    16 September 1857 – He extinguished a fire in a shed at the Delhi Magazine. The shed contained large quantities of ammunition and he was under heavy fire from the enemy all the while.

The reinstated king had fled the Red Fort with his family as the British approached, and had taken refuge in a mausoleum outside the city. Wilson sent a party led by Major William Hodson to bring them back. This group found themselves surrounded by armed rebels, but Hodson faced them down and persuaded the king and queen to accompany him back to Delhi. He returned for the rest of the royal party and started to escort two of the king's sons and one grandson, all of whom had joined in the massacre of women and children in the initial assault, and the same armed mob threatened to attempt a rescue. Hodson summarily shot all three, so removing the mutineers' only remaining figureheads.

The siege of Delhi and the operations to retake it had cost the Delhi Field Force 992 killed and 2,795 wounded, for the loss of a great many more enemy lives.

THE DELHI FIELD FORCE

Columns of troops from the Delhi Field Force were sent out to hound down the scattering groups of mutineers and resistance eventually petered out, despite a few more spirited attempts at defiance, as at Bolandshahr on 28 September, when seven VCs were awarded for what Home later described as 'tolerably sharp action'.

ANSON, the Hon. Augustus Henry Archibald *Captain, 84th Regiment*
28 September 1857 – After the 9th Light Dragoons had charged through Bolandshahr, the enemy drew carts across the gateway, blocking the dragoons' path. Anson dashed out of the gateway and knocked the rebel drivers off their carts. Suffering from an injured left hand and unable to control his horse, he plunged into the midst of the enemy. He was fired upon but though a bullet passed through his coat, he escaped unharmed.

BLAIR, Robert *Lieutenant, 2nd Dragoon Guards, attached 9th Lancers*
28 September 1857 – At Bolandshahr, his party of twelve men and a sergeant was ambushed by sixty enemy horsemen. He fought his way through the rebels, killing four of them himself. He brought all of his men safely back to camp, despite having been seriously wounded by a rebel officer, whom he ran through with his sword.

DIAMOND, Bernard *Sergeant, Bengal Horse Artillery*
28 September 1857 – At Bolandshahr, together with Gunner FITZGERALD, he continued working a gun after every other man had been killed or wounded. By this action, the road was completely cleared of the enemy.

DONOHOE, Patrick *Private, 9th Lancers*
28 September 1857 – At Bolandshahr, he went to the assistance of a wounded officer and brought him back to camp through the rebel cavalry.

FITZGERALD, Richard *Gunner, Bengal Horse Artillery*
28 September 1857 – At Bolandshahr, together with Sergeant DIAMOND, he continued working a gun after every other man had been killed or wounded. By this action, the road was completely cleared of the enemy.

KELLS, Robert *Lance Corporal, 9th Lancers*
28 September 1857 – At Bolandshahr, he dashed to the rescue of Captain Drysdale, whose horse had been shot from under him. He kept the enemy at bay and saved the captain from certain death.

ROBERTS, James Reynolds *Private, 9th Lancers*
28 September 1857 – At Bolandshahr, he carried a mortally wounded comrade through the streets under heavy fire. He was seriously wounded himself whilst carrying out this action.

BROWN, Francis David Millett *Lieutenant, 1st European Bengal Fusiliers*
16 November 1857 – At Narnoul, near Delhi, he rushed to the assistance of a wounded soldier whom he carried to safety under heavy fire. The enemy cavalry was within 50 yards of him at the time.

THE SIEGE OF LUCKNOW

To the east of Delhi lay the Oudh region, where the mutiny found some of its strongest support. Oudh, at one time an independent kingdom, had been so badly misruled that the Honourable East India Company, effectively wielding administrative power in India on behalf of the British government, annexed it. Many of the inhabitants were high-caste Hindus, fiercely protective of their traditions and way of life, who served in the Bengal Army. Always resentful of this British intervention, these Hindus sided with the mutineers and formed the strong core of the mutiny. The centre of activity in Oudh was the capital, Lucknow, which lay between the River Goomtee to the east and a canal to the south. The British Residency, like the other important buildings in the city, was situated by the river and was contained by high defensive walls.

The Chief Commissioner for Oudh, Brigadier General Sir Henry Lawrence (brother of Sir John), had foreseen a local rebellion in the wake of events in Meerut and Delhi. He accordingly stockpiled food and ammunition in the grounds of the Residency against a siege, fortified the perimeter, setting up defensive gun positions, and laid plans for evacuating all non-Indians in the city into the Residency in the event of an uprising. Sure enough, on 30 May the garrison's Indian regiments joined the mutiny – but were driven out of the city. As all other British garrisons fell to the mutineers during June 1857, only Lawrence's fortified Residency offered resistance – and refuge for the European inhabitants.

On 29 June, Lawrence received news of an enemy force approaching and sent out troops to drive them back. The encounter was a disaster for the garrison. Enemy numbers had been massively underestimated and, hugely outnumbered, the British were driven into retreat, leaving some two hundred dead and losing five guns. The mutineers now closed in around the Residency and kept it under constant attack. Lawrence was killed by a shell on 4 July and was succeeded by Colonel J. E. W. Inglis, whose robust policy of frequent aggressive forays kept the enemy's forward positions under pressure. Throughout July, August and September, forays continued, during which more individual acts of bravery were recognized with VC awards.

CUBITT, William George *Lieutenant, 13th Bengal Native Infantry*
30 June 1857 – He was sent from the Lucknow Residency as part of a force to fight the advancing rebels. He showed great courage in this ill-fated contest and when the retreat to Lucknow began, saved the lives of three men as the rebels were surging around him.
Second Lieutenant J. Hills VC was his brother-in-law and Lieutenant Colonel Evans VC his nephew.

OXENHAM, William *Corporal, 32nd Regiment*
30 June 1857 – At Lucknow, he saved the life of Mr Capper, a civil service official, by digging him out from the ruins of a veranda that had collapsed underneath him. This courageous act lasted ten minutes throughout which he was under tremendous fire from the enemy.

DOWLING, William *Private, 32nd Regiment*
4 July 1857 – At Lucknow, he went out with two others and spiked two of the enemy's guns, killing a subadar of the enemy. *9 July 1857* – He went out again with three men to spike an enemy gun but on this occasion the spike was too small to be serviceable. *27 September 1857* – He successfully spiked an 18pdr gun. On all these occasions he was under heavy fire.

LAWRENCE, Samuel Hill *Lieutenant, 32nd Regiment*
7 July 1857 – At Lucknow, he led the attack up a scaling ladder placed against the window of a house where it was believed a mine was being laid. A rebel knocked his pistol from his hand, but the house was captured and all the occupants killed or taken prisoner. *26 September 1857* – He charged well ahead of his party and recaptured a 9pdr gun.
Lieutenant T. Cadell VC was his cousin.

THOMPSON, James *Private, 60th Rifles*
9 July 1857 – At Lucknow, he saved the life of Captain Wilmot who was surrounded by a party of Ghazis. Before any assistance arrived, he killed two of the enemy.
He was elected for the award under Rule 13 of the Royal Warrant.

BOULGER, Abraham *Lance Corporal, 84th Regiment*
    12 July to 25 September 1857 – He was engaged almost daily with the enemy at Lucknow, either in pitched battles or as a scout and skirmisher. He helped to storm a bridge over the canal during the relief of the residency and shot a rebel gunner who was in the act of firing a 68pdr.

MYLOTT, Patrick *Private, 84th Regiment*
    12 July to 25 September 1857 – He was conspicuous for his bravery at every engagement at which he was present at Lucknow, including on one occasion rushing across a road under fierce fire to seize an enclosure.
    He was elected for the award under Rule 13 of the Royal Warrant.

AITKEN, Robert Hope Moncrieff *Lieutenant, 13th Bengal Native Infantry*
    20 August 1857 – At Lucknow, he extinguished a fire at the Baillie Guard Gate by rushing out and removing the combustibles. *25 September 1857* – He, with his soldiers, attacked and seized two guns and prevented them being used on General Havelock's column. *26 September 1857* – During an assault on a gateway at the Furreed Buksh Palace, he threw himself against the gate, preventing it from being closed. As a result, his men were able to force the door, gain entry and capture the position. *29 September 1857* – He led a sortie to capture a gun that had been harassing his troops. Under great fire he worked his way through lanes and houses, reached the gun, and held his ground until reinforcements arrived.

GORE-BROWNE, Henry George *Captain, 32nd Regiment*
    21 August 1857 – During the siege of Lucknow, he led a sortie to spike two heavy guns which were doing great damage to the defences. He was the first to enter the battery, which was protected by high palisades. He removed the shutters blocking the embrasures and attacked the gunners. About a hundred of the enemy were killed and the guns were spiked.

CAWNPORE

In Britain the news of the atrocities against women and children in Meerut, Delhi and the other fallen garrisons had hit hard – the relief of the Lucknow Residency was now paramount.
    A movable column was formed, commanded by Brigadier General Sir Henry Havelock, of about a thousand men and six guns. It set out from Allahabad on 7 July, intending to relieve the besieged garrison at Cawnpore then march on Lucknow. On 25 June, as the garrison at Cawnpore had run out of food and ammunition, the defenders finally sought terms for a surrender. It was agreed that the British would march out on 27 June, under arms with sixty rounds of ammunition; carriages would be provided to carry the women, children and infirm to the landing place on the Ganges about a mile

from the city, where boats would be ready; and they would then be given safe conduct to Allahabad. A jittery peace prevailed as the embarkation went ahead, but suddenly there was a shot. The British, on a knife edge after the three-week siege, opened fire and the Nana's troops replied, so that the boats were set on fire. The 60 men who survived this attack were summarily killed, and the women and children were disembarked and imprisoned. There they remained until the Nana received news on 15 July that the British were nearing the city – and the Nana gave the order for them all to be killed. A combined effort by his sepoys and butchers with knives left a few still alive by the following morning. These were thrown down a well and left to die. This atrocity, above all, was the spur for Havelock's men to exact fierce and bloody revenge when they arrived outside Cawnpore to begin the assault on 17 July. They hoped to free the women and children left in the city, but instead found a scene of carnage. Every captured rebel was made to go to the scene of the slaughter to assist in cleaning up – especially humiliating to high-caste Indians, as it was abhorrent to them to touch blood – and all were then hanged, whether guilty or not.

During the advance to Cawnpore, Havelock's small force was facing an enemy with around thirteen thousand Indian troops, but managed to proceed until confronted by a 24pdr gun. Havelock sent his aide (who happened to be his son), Lieutenant Henry Havelock, to command the storming of this gun. Seeing no other officer, young Havelock led the 64th Regiment into the attack himself and successfully captured it. However, he had failed to notice Major Stirling of the 64th, whose horse had been shot from under him. Stirling should properly have led this attack and was galled at being upstaged by a younger officer – and his rancour was increased when Havelock senior recommended his son for the VC. It was duly awarded, but was hotly opposed by the officers of the 64th and, on hearing their complaints, by the Commander-in-Chief, Lieutenant General Sir Colin Campbell. Lieutenant Havelock was evidently embarrassed, both by his father's nominating him and by the upset the award had caused, but he demonstrated extraordinary courage during the advance on Lucknow, following which he was recommended for the VC. He would have been the first man to receive a bar to his VC, but Campbell opposed it, arguing that he shouldn't even have received the first award.

HAVELOCK, Henry Marsham (later HAVELOCK-ALLAN) *Lieutenant, 10th Regiment*

16 July 1857 – At Cawnpore, the rebels were rallying their last 24pdr. He was sent to the 64th Staffordshire Regiment to order them forward to take the gun. On seeing that the regiment had no mounted officers remaining, he volunteered to lead them. He rode ahead under a shower of shot and grape and moved at a foot pace opposite the muzzle of the gun. The gun was taken and the rebels retreated.

He was MP for Sunderland, 1874–81, 1884–92 and 1895–97, first as a Liberal but later as a Unionist due to his belief that Home Rule for Ireland threatened the integrity of the Empire.

MAHONEY, Patrick *Sergeant, 1st Madras Fusiliers*
    21 September 1857 – Whilst on cavalry duty at Mungulwar, near Cawnpore, he was prominent in capturing the colours of the 1st Regiment of Native Infantry, who had mutinied.

RENNIE, William *Lieutenant, 90th Regiment*
    21 September 1857 – During the advance on Lucknow, he charged the enemy's guns in advance of the skirmishers of his regiment and prevented the rebels from carrying one of the guns away. The gun was captured when support arrived. *25 September 1857* – Whilst advancing on a battery under heavy grapeshot fire, he charged ahead of his men and forced the enemy to abandon its guns.

GRANT, Robert *Sergeant, 5th Regiment*
    24 September 1857 – At the Alum Bagh, he went to the assistance of Private Deveny, whose leg had been shot away. Under heavy fire he, Lieutenant Brown and others carried Deveny to safety.

FIRST RELIEF OF LUCKNOW, SEPTEMBER

On 25 September, Havelock's column arrived at Lucknow. By now it was about three thousand strong and comprised a portion of the 1st Madras Fusiliers, the 64th and 78th Regiments, with some Sikhs, together with the 5th, from Mauritius, and the 90th, which had been en route to China, and with Major General Sir James Outram, military commander of the Cawnpore and Dinapoor regions, acting in his capacity as Chief Commissioner of Oudh, but the troops had fought their way through considerable opposition and searing heat, and they were exhausted, with many sick or wounded – all they could do was get to the Residency and take refuge, without any hope of breaking out without major reinforcements. To add to the woes of the garrison, disease was now rife in the Residency, with many dying of cholera, dysentery, smallpox and heatstroke. They could only sit tight and wait for much-needed support.

HOLMES, Joel *Private, 84th Regiment*
    25 September 1857 – At Lucknow, he was the first to volunteer to replace the fallen gunners in Captain MAUDE's battery, where he worked the guns through terrific fire. His conduct was also noted while in General Havelock's Field Force.

JEE, Joseph *Surgeon, 78th Regiment*

25 September 1857 – At Lucknow, he displayed great courage in tending to the wounded. He escorted them towards the Residency on cots and on the backs of his men as many dhoolie bearers had fled. Whilst approaching the Residency, he was besieged by the enemy in the Mote Mahal. He continued to tend the wounded in an open position. On the following day, he managed to bring many of them into the Residency under heavy crossfire.

McMASTER, Valentine Munbee *Assistant Surgeon, 78th Regiment*

25 September 1857 – At Lucknow, he exposed himself to the heavy fire of the enemy throughout the night, whilst bringing in and attending to the many injured.

MACPHERSON, Herbert Taylor *Lieutenant, 78th Regiment*

25 September 1857 – At Lucknow, he led a charge on two 9pdr guns which the rebels had trained on the 78th Regiment along the Cawnpore Road. His attack was successful and the guns were captured, and dumped into a canal. It is said that in spite of the dangers he faced, he treated the thing as a matter of little importance.

MAUDE, Francis Cornwallis *Captain, Royal Artillery*

25 September 1857 – While in command of a battery at Lucknow, one third of his men were shot down at their guns, but he replaced them with volunteers from the infantry, and with his small force he bore down on the opposition. Sir James Outram reported that 'but for Captain Maude's nerve and coolness on this trying occasion, the army could not have advanced'.

OLPHERTS, William *Captain, Bengal Artillery*

25 September 1857 – When the British force penetrated into Lucknow, he charged on horseback with the 90th Regiment and assisted in capturing two cannon. He then galloped back to his battery for horses and limbers to carry the guns away. All this was achieved under heavy fire.

He was nicknamed 'Hell Fire Olpherts'.

WARD, Henry *Private, 78th Regiment*

25 September 1857 – At Lucknow, he was escorting the dhoolie containing Lieutenant HAVELOCK. Another wounded man, Private Pilkington, threw himself into the dhoolie. The bearers were about to drop this double load, but Ward compelled them to remain by his example, exertions and cheerfulness. Under heavy fire, the dhoolie was brought to the 'Baillie Guard' in safety.

Ward later became Lieutenant Havelock's servant.

BRADSHAW, William *Assistant Surgeon, 90th Regiment*

26 September 1857 – At Lucknow, as the British column was forcing its way into the Residency, many wounded were left behind in the streets.

Under heavy fire from the enemy, he persuaded many litter bearers to retrieve the wounded and without the aid of any troops led them to the safety of the Residency.

DUFFY, Thomas *Private, 1st Madras Fusiliers*
26 September 1857 – At Lucknow, the enemy kept up such a fire on a 24pdr gun that it could not be reached. Duffy managed to fasten a rope to the gun and retrieve it, keeping it out of the hands of the enemy.

HOLLOWELL, James (also known as HOLLIWELL) *Private, 78th Regiment*
26 September 1857 – As the British column was forcing its way into the Residency at Lucknow, he was one of those (along with Surgeon HOME) in charge of the wounded men left behind in the streets. Under fierce fire, he and others were forced to take refuge in a house, which was soon set ablaze by rebels. The occupants retreated into a shed from which they fired at the rebels who climbed onto the roof. Soon after dawn, when the small party had lost all hope of survival, they were rescued.

HOME, Anthony Dickson *Surgeon, 90th Regiment*
26 September 1857 – At Lucknow, as the British column was forcing its way into the Residency, he was in charge of the wounded men left behind in the streets. Under fierce fire, he and others were forced to take refuge in a house. He continued tending to the wounded and firing on the enemy until the house was set ablaze. The occupants retreated to a shed, firing at rebels who had climbed onto the roof. Soon after dawn, when the small party had lost all hope of survival, they were rescued.

McMANUS, Peter *Private, 1st Bn., 5th Regiment*
26 September 1857 – At Lucknow, as the column was forcing its way into the Residency, he was one of those (along with Surgeon HOME and Private RYAN) in charge of the wounded men left behind in the streets. Under fierce fire, he and others were forced to take refuge in a house. He kept up a steady and unerring fire, shooting rebel after rebel, whilst his comrades shouted in chorus to make the enemy think they were more numerous. After half an hour, the house was set ablaze and the occupants retreated to a shed, firing at rebels who climbed onto the roof. Soon after dawn, when the small party had lost all hope of survival, they were rescued.

McPHERSON, Stewart *Colour Sergeant, 78th Regiment*
26 September 1857 – Under fierce fire he rescued a private of his company who was lying bleeding to death in an exposed position at Lucknow.

RYAN, John *Private, 1st Madras Fusiliers*
26 September 1857 – As the British column was forcing its way into the Residency at Lucknow, many of the wounded were abandoned by the litter bearers. The rebels were firing into the litters and cutting the throats of the

wounded. Ryan and McMANUS were conspicuous for their rescue of many of these wounded.

THOMAS, Jacob *Bombardier, Bengal Artillery*

27 September 1857 – He was returning from a sortie when one of his comrades fell severely wounded at Lucknow. He picked up the injured man and carried him a great distance to safety under heavy fire.

McHALE, Patrick *Private, 5th Regiment*

2 October 1857 – At the capture of the Cawnpore Battery, Lucknow, he was the first man to leap into the embrasure and bayonet the rebel gunners. *22 December 1857* – At Alum Bagh, the enemy fled a village, leaving behind a loaded gun which their bullocks could not carry away. He arrived at the gun, turned the bullocks round with a stroke from the butt of his rifle, set the gun and began firing it into the retreating rebels.

SINNOTT, John *Lance Corporal, 4th Regiment*

6 October 1857 – At Lucknow, he went several times with Lieutenant Gibaut to extinguish a fire in a breastwork. When the lieutenant fell mortally wounded, he (together with two sergeants and a private) carried him into a shelter under heavy fire.

MILLER, James William *Conductor, Bengal Ordnance Depot*

28 October 1857 – At Futtehpore, he went to the assistance of Lieutenant Glubb, who was severely wounded, and at great personal risk, he carried him to safety. He was subsequently wounded himself and sent to Agra.

FLINN, Thomas *Drummer, 64th Regiment*

28 November 1857 – At Cawnpore, despite being himself wounded, he engaged in a hand-to-hand encounter with two rebel artillerymen during a charge on the enemy's guns.

At fifteen years three months, he was one of the two youngest winners of the VC, the other being Hospital Apprentice Andrew Fitzgibbon.

SECOND RELIEF OF LUCKNOW: THE ALUM BAGH

A united force under Brigadier General Hope Grant and Sir Colin Campbell, well equipped and with a greater strength of numbers, set out at the end of October and arrived on 12 November at the royal summer resort of Alum Bagh a few miles from Lucknow, where Outram had left a small garrison before moving on to the city. From outside at Alum Bagh and within the city at the Residency, plans were laid to effect a breakout. Outram, in the Residency, was anxious that the incoming forces should have a knowledge-able local guide to get them through the labyrinth of narrow streets, cul-de-sacs and enclosed courts. One local Indian spy, Kanauji Lal, was prepared to leave the Residency and join Campbell's men – but Outram rightly feared that the relief commander would not trust him. So it was that a civilian volunteer, a thirty-six-year-old clerk called Thomas Kavanagh, who was fluent in Hindustani, stained his skin, donned native Indian clothes and undertook the almost suicidally risky challenge of breaking out through enemy lines with Lal, then guiding the relief column back through the city to the Residency.

KAVANAGH, Thomas Henry *Mr, Bengal Civil Service*

Kavanagh had been a civilian clerk to Sir Henry Lawrence. He was nearly relieved of his position as a result of his profligate approach to his work and he was seeking to make amends. When news arrived at the Residency that Campbell's relief force was approaching, he had an idea:

> I had some days previously witnessed the preparation of plans which were being made by direction of Sir James Outram to assist the Commander in Chief in his march into Lucknow for the relief of the besieged and it occurred to me that someone with the requisite local knowledge ought to attempt to reach His Excellency's camp beyond or at Alumbagh. The news of Sir Colin's advance revived the idea and I made up my mind to go myself.

He discovered that Kanauji Lal was to be travelling to Alum Bagh that night and he persuaded the spy to allow him to keep him company. It was a harder task to persuade Sir James Outram, who argued that it would be impossible for a European to get through to Alum Bagh. Such an atmosphere of suspicion prevailed amongst the mutineers that they barely trusted each other. Any stranger would find himself minutely questioned and under suspicion. A badly disguised European would be quickly detected and brutally slaughtered. Eventually, Outram agreed that if Kavanagh was able to satisfy him with his disguise, then he would allow him to go. Kavanagh covered his face and hands in lamp black, dipping the cork in oil to help it adhere. He wore a yellow silk coat over a white muslin shirt, tight trousers, a white waist band, tight native shoes turned up at the toe, a yellow chintz sheet thrown round his shoulders, a cream-coloured turban, a sword and a shield. In this camouflage, he walked into Outram's quarters and sat down uninvited. The officers present took exception to an Indian behaving in such a disrespectful manner and berated him in Hindi. Outram came into the room to discover what the fuss was about and he too failed to recognize Kavanagh. Clearly the disguise was a success and Kavanagh was given consent to carry out his mission. Outram, cigar in mouth, added a few finishing touches to Kavanagh's make up and Captain Sitwell gave him a double-barrelled pistol to use on himself should he be taken. He took the plans to pass on to Campbell and at 8.30 p.m., he and Kanauji Lal set off.

At first, they made their way across the Goomtee River. Halfway across, Kavanagh's courage deserted him and he almost turned back. Kanauji Lal, however, had surged ahead and Kavanagh resolved to follow him. On the other bank, they confronted a rebel sepoy with a matchlock. Kavanagh, whose confidence had returned, spoke to the man about the weather. Six hundred yards further on, they reached an iron bridge where they were stopped and called over by a native officer. This time Kanauji Lal spoke, explaining that they had come from Mundeon (a town held by the rebels) and were going back to their homes. They were allowed to pass. They moved into the busy main street of Lucknow, where Kavanagh jostled against several armed men without being spoken to and passed a guard of seven sepoys engaged in conversation with prostitutes.

Before long, they had reached the countryside and they walked on several miles, before realizing that they had taken the wrong road and were now in Dilkusha Park, an area swarming with rebels. It was now midnight and they had lost a great deal of time by walking in the wrong direction. If they did not reach Alum Bagh by daybreak, they would be discovered. They had to move quickly. Kavanagh asked for directions from a man who looked at him and ran off to a nearby village to raise the alarm. The two men hurried away. Kavanagh's shoes had begun cutting into his feet and progress became more difficult. Over paddy fields and along irrigation cuts they went until they came across a small village, where they entered a hut. Groping around in the dark, Kavanagh's hand encountered a sleeping woman, who received a tremendous fright but did not panic or scream and gave them the necessary directions.

Eventually they arrived near Alum Bagh, which they could not approach directly as the area was crowded with pickets and rebel rifle pits. Instead they went round to Bunnee. At about 3 a.m., they were spotted by a sepoy on guard duty, who shouted for assistance. At once they were surrounded by 25 sepoys, all of them asking questions. Kanauji Lal panicked and threw away the dispatch that he was carrying. Kavanagh cleverly played on Kanauji Lal's fear, begging the sepoys not to terrify poor travellers. He told them that they were two poor men walking to the village of Umzoula to inform a friend that his brother had been killed by the British. The sepoys believed the story and allowed them to pass. Some time later, they arrived at a marshy swamp. For two hours they waded, sometimes waist deep, sometimes up to their necks in water. When they finally scrambled out of the marsh, the lamp black had washed off Kavanagh's hands and he had to rest for quarter of an hour, exhausted. As they continued, they heard a shout in English: 'Who goes there?' They had reached a British cavalry outpost. Kavanagh was so relieved, his eyes filled with tears and he shook the Sikh officer in charge warmly by the hand. Kavanagh was taken to a tent where he was given a glass of brandy and then taken to Sir Colin Campbell. Kavanagh handed over his map and was received with astonishment.

Two days later, Campbell began his advance on Lucknow, with Kavanagh at his side. Within days, the Residency was relieved and its occupants freed. Kavanagh received the Victoria Cross for his daring mission. At a time when native Indians were not eligible for the award, Kanauji Lal did not. Kavanagh lived on for another twenty-five years, dying in Gibraltar on 13 November 1880 at the age of sixty-one.

GOUGH, Hugh Henry *Lieutenant, 1st Bengal European Light Cavalry*
12 November 1857 – At Alum Bagh, he charged his party of Hodson's Horse across a swamp and captured two guns. His turban was cut through and he was twice wounded in the process. *25 February 1858* – When charging enemy guns near Jellalabad, he engaged in numerous single combats. Two horses were shot under him and he received bullets through his helmet and scabbard before being disabled by a shot to the leg as he was charging two sepoys with fixed bayonets. The guns were taken.
Major C. J. S. Gough VC was his brother and Bt/Major J. E. Gough VC his nephew. He was Keeper of the Crown Jewels at the Tower of London, 1898–1909.

HARINGTON, Hastings Edward *Lieutenant, Bengal Artillery*
14–22 November 1857 – He acted with conspicuous bravery throughout the Relief of Lucknow.
He was elected for the award under Rule 13 of the Royal Warrant.

JENNINGS, Edward *Rough Rider, Bengal Artillery*
14–22 November 1857 – Throughout the relief of Lucknow, his bravery in working the guns was noticed by all.
He was elected for the award under Rule 13 of the Royal Warrant.

LAUGHNAN, Thomas *Gunner, Bengal Artillery*
14–22 November 1857 – He acted with conspicuous bravery throughout the Relief of Lucknow.
He was elected for the award under Rule 13 of the Royal Warrant.

McINNES, Hugh *Gunner, Bengal Artillery*
14–22 November 1857 – He acted with conspicuous bravery throughout the Relief of Lucknow.
He was elected for the award under Rule 13 of the Royal Warrant.

PARK, James *Gunner, Bengal Artillery*
14–22 November 1857 – He acted with conspicuous gallantry through-out the Relief of Lucknow.
He was elected for the award under Rule 13 of the Royal Warrant.

WATSON, John *Lieutenant, 1st Punjab Cavalry*
14 November 1857 – Coming across a troop of enemy cavalry at Lucknow, he was attacked by the rebel leader who fired at him from a yard away. His death seemed inevitable but he was not hit. He ran his opponent through with his sword, but was instantly set upon by a number of the

enemy, who slashed at him with tulwars. His head, arms and legs were cut and a bullet passed through his coat. However, some cavalry arrived and the rebels were routed.

SECOND RELIEF OF LUCKNOW: THE SECUNDRA BAGH

Kavanagh's bravado and daring were rewarded as he led Campbell's men into Lucknow in an assault on 16 November, a period of ferocious close-quarters fighting. The plan was to take control of the strategically important fortified palaces along the troops' riverside line of advance, and the first fortress to fall was the Secundra Bagh.

Here Campbell's 93rd Highlanders expressed their fury at the earlier sepoy atrocities with a savage attack. Four VCs were won for the initial attack to open the gates, and a further seven as the 53rd Regiment's grenadier company surged through. As house-to-house fighting developed, Lieutenant Colonel Ewart personally killed eight of the enemy; when he was wounded, he was rescued by Private Grant (later awarded the VC), who killed five of the enemy using a captured sword.

DUNLAY, John *Lance Corporal, 93rd Regiment*
16 November 1857 – At the attack on the Secundra Bagh, he was the first man of his regiment to enter one of the breaches, gallantly supporting a captain against heavy odds. During the action he was shot through the knee.
The musket ball that pierced his knee is displayed, attached to his VC, in the Sheesh Mahal Museum, India.

FFRENCH, Alfred Kirke *Lieutenant, 53rd Regiment*
16 November 1857 – He was in command of the grenadier company at the taking of the Secundra Bagh. He was one of the first to enter the building and behaved with conspicuous gallantry.
He was elected for the award under Rule 13 of the Royal Warrant.

GRANT, Peter *Private, 93rd Regiment*
16 November 1857 – At the Secundra Bagh, he killed five rebels with a sword whilst defending a colonel who had captured the enemy's colours.
He was elected for the award under Rule 13 of the Royal Warrant.

GUISE, John Christopher (later Sir John) *Major, 90th Regiment*
16–17 November 1857 – He was one of the leaders of the attack on the Secundra Bagh. He (together with Sergeant HILL) saved the life of Captain Irby before going out under heavy fire to help two other wounded men. He acted most gallantly throughout the Relief of Lucknow.
He was elected for the award by the officers of his regiment under Rule 13 of the Royal Warrant.

HILL, Samuel *Sergeant, 90th Regiment*

16–17 November 1857 – At the attack on the Secundra Bagh, he (together with Major GUISE) saved the life of Captain Irby by warding off a tulwar blow aimed at his head by a rebel. He also went out under heavy fire to help two wounded men. He acted most gallantly throughout the Relief of Lucknow.

IRWIN, Charles *Private, 53rd Regiment*

16 November 1857 – Although severely wounded in his shoulder, he was one of the first of his regiment to enter the Secundra Bagh.

He was elected for the award by the privates of his regiment under Rule 13 of the Royal Warrant.

KENNY, James *Private, 53rd Regiment*

16 November 1857 – At the assault on the Secundra Bagh he volunteered to bring fresh ammunition up to his company in spite of a heavy crossfire.

He was elected for the award under Rule 13 of the Royal Warrant.

MACKAY, David *Private, 93rd Regiment*

16 November 1857 – At the attack on the Secundra Bagh, he captured one of the standards of the enemy despite their resistance. He was severely wounded afterwards during the attack on the Shah Nujeff mosque.

He was elected for the award under Rule 13 of the Royal Warrant.

MUNRO, James *Colour Sergeant, 93rd Regiment*

16 November 1857 – At the attack on the Secundra Bagh, he rushed to the rescue of Captain Walsh, who was in danger of being cut down. He carried him away and saved his life.

SMITH, John *Private, 1st Madras Fusiliers*

16 November 1857 – He was one of the first to enter the north gateway when the Secundra Bagh was stormed. He was instantly surrounded by the enemy but despite receiving a sword cut to the head and a bayonet wound to the side he fought his way out and continued fighting all day.

He was elected for the award under Rule 13 of the Royal Warrant.

STEWART, William George Drummond *Captain, 93rd Regiment*

16 November 1857 – At the Secundra Bagh, he led a brilliant charge on two enemy guns which were commanding the Mess House and inflicting severe damage. The guns were taken.

He was elected for the award under Rule 13 of the Royal Warrant.

HACKETT, Thomas Bernard *Lieutenant, 23rd Regiment*

17 November 1857 – At the Secundra Bagh, he and Private MONGER rushed out and rescued a corporal of the 23rd Regiment under heavy fire. On the same date, he prevented a fire spreading from a burning bungalow by jumping onto the roof and cutting the thatch away whilst under fire from hundreds of rebels.

MONGER, George *Private, 23rd Regiment*

17 November 1857 – At the Secundra Bagh, he and Lieutenant HACKETT rushed out and rescued a corporal of the 23rd Regiment under heavy fire.

THE SHAH NUJEFF MOSQUE

The Secundra Bagh being cleared of mutineers, Campbell ordered his men to the Shah Nujeff Mosque. This domed building lay in a walled enclosure, the entrance blocked with masonry, and on the roof a parapet allowed the defenders a panoramic vantage point from which to fire. In addition, to one side, a barracks or mess house offered a further post from which to pour in crossfire. Campbell's battle plan was to bring heavy field guns into close range for maximum effect, but this brought the gun crews within range of snipers and grenade throwers, causing heavy casualties. Seeing the imminent annihilation of the troops manning the guns, Lieutenant Salmon RN, Leading Seaman Harrison and an able seaman from the naval brigade climbed a tree whose branches abutted the mosque walls, and picked off the snipers and grenade throwers, in doing so saving the gun crews and earning themselves VC awards. (The third man, because he died in the attack, remained unrecognized.)

As dusk fell, after three hours of fighting, the mosque walls were still intact, so Captain William Peel RN (awarded the VC in the Crimea) brought his guns into action with great effect – especially in destroying enemy morale. Under the feint of a bugle sounding an advance, the defenders left through a breach in a rear wall. Sergeant Paton discovered this and, despite coming under heavy fire, led his regiment in to occupy the now deserted mosque – for which he earned a VC.

HALL, William *Able Seaman, Royal Navy (Naval Brigade)*

William Hall was the first black man to win the Victoria Cross. In 1852, when slavery was still accepted in the United States, Hall (who had been born a British subject in Canada) was able to join the Royal Navy. Attitudes towards him can perhaps be glimpsed in the words of one of these shipmates who served with him on HMS *Hero*: 'We had one Victoria Cross man amongst us; curious to say, he was a Negro, by name William Hall.' He may have been a curiosity, an oddity, but he was at least a free man and a heroic one at that.

William Hall was born in Horton Bluff, Nova Scotia, in 1829. There are two conflicting stories as to how he came to be born in Canada. The first story states that his parents were part of a slave cargo bound for America during the War of 1812. The ship on which they were being transported was captured by the British who then set the intended slaves free in Halifax,

Nova Scotia. The second story alleges that William's father escaped from his master in Virginia during the same war and joined up with the British in return for a guarantee of freedom in Canada. Whichever story is true, it is clear that Canada was a land of relative opportunity for black people at the beginning of the nineteenth century.

In 1851, at the age of twenty-two, Hall joined the Royal Navy. He was to be appointed to HMS *Rodney*, a ship detailed to patrol the English Channel, but in the meantime, he was billeted to and received training on HMS *Victory*, Nelson's flagship. He subsequently took part in the Crimean War as a member of the naval brigade, with which he fought on land, often serving as a member of the crew on guns brought ashore to provide artillery fire. In this capacity, he took part in the Siege of Sebastopol. He was then transferred to HMS *Shannon*, a frigate on active service in the Far East.

At the outbreak of the Indian Mutiny in 1857, he became part of Shannon's Brigade, a land-based force (of which Edward St John Daniel was also a member), set up by Captain Peel. The brigade, which consisted of 250 sailors accompanied by their naval cannons, sailed up the River Ganges from Calcutta to Cawnpore. The journey lasted over two months. From Cawnpore, the soldiers marched to Lucknow, where rebels were besieging British troops, East India Company officials and their families in the Residency. Just outside Lucknow stood the Shah Nujeff Mosque. Each time the infantry had tried to storm it, they had been driven back. It became clear that the brigade's guns would have to be used to blow apart its walls. The guns were moved up to within 350 yards of the walls but failed to make an impression. In desperation, Captain Peel ordered two of the guns to a position so close to the mosque that after firing each round the gun crews were in danger of being hit by bricks and stones torn from the walls. One of the crews was a man short, so Hall volunteered to fill the position. He was warned that the defenders of the mosque were directing all their fire at these two crews and that he faced almost certain death but he insisted. Before long the entire crew of one gun was dead and only Hall and his badly wounded officer remained alive at the other. Single-handedly, Hall dragged the cannon backwards and forwards, reloading and firing until the walls of the mosque were breached, allowing soldiers to rush in and take the building. It took nine days of hard fighting, but eventually Lucknow was successfully relieved. Hall's action was described by Sir Colin Campbell as 'an action almost unexampled in war'.

Hall was presented with his Victoria Cross on board HMS *Donegal* in Queenstown, Ireland, by Rear Admiral Charles Talbot in October 1859. He remained in the navy until 1876, retiring with the rank of first class petty officer. On retirement, he was offered a well-paid desk job in Whitehall (at a time when there could not have been many black civil servants in London) but he declined it, preferring to return to Nova Scotia. He settled down on a farm in Avonport, where he lived a quiet life with his two sisters. In October

1901, the Duke and Duchess of York (later to become George V and Queen Mary) visited Halifax, Nova Scotia, where they were introduced to Hall, who rode in a carriage in their procession and was given a place of honour at the subsequent ceremonies. He died on 25 August 1904 at his farm, aged seventy-five. He was described after his death by a minister who knew him well: 'He was a peaceable God-fearing citizen. He was honoured and respected by all who knew him. He was ever humble.'

HARRISON, John *Leading Seaman, Royal Navy (Naval Brigade)*
16 November 1857 – The naval brigade accompanied Sir Colin Campbell's relieving force on its march to Lucknow. During the assault on the Shah Nujeff Mosque, Captain PEEL asked for volunteers to climb a tree and dislodge rebels who were tossing grenades at the gun crews to deadly effect. At first Harrison handed loaded rifles up to Lieutenant SALMON, but after the lieutenant was wounded, he climbed the tree and continued firing. They succeeded in significantly weakening the mutineers' defences and the mosque was taken.

PATON, John *Sergeant, 93rd Regiment*
16 November 1857 – The Shah Nujeff mosque had been fired upon at close range by the naval brigade for three hours but little damage seemed to have been done. Paton reconnoitred for a means of entry and found a small gap in the rear defences. He fearlessly guided his regiment in and found that the mutineers had retreated. Within a few minutes, the mosque was taken.

SALMON, Nowell (later Sir Nowell) *Lieutenant, Royal Navy (Naval Brigade)*
16 November 1857 – The naval brigade accompanied Sir Colin Campbell's relieving force on its march to Lucknow. During the assault on the Shah Nujeff Mosque, Captain Peel asked for volunteers to climb a tree and dislodge rebels who were tossing grenades at the gun crews to deadly effect. The first volunteer was killed but he was replaced by Salmon who picked off rebel after rebel until he was hit by a musket ball in the thigh and replaced by Leading Seaman HARRISON. They succeeded in significantly weakening the mutineers' defences and the mosque was taken.

YOUNG, Thomas James *Lieutenant, Royal Navy (Naval Brigade)*
16 November 1857 – The naval brigade accompanied Sir Colin Campbell's relieving force on its march to Lucknow. During the assault on the Shah Nujeff mosque, Young was in command of the gun crews who brought their guns up so close to the mosque walls that their muzzles almost touched the brickwork. He moved from one gun to another giving encouragement, and when he saw that Seaman HALL was the sole survivor of his crew, he stood beside him helping him to load and fire the gun. After this pounding, the mosque was taken within minutes.
Midshipman D. G. Boyes VC was his brother-in-law.

RELIEF OF LUCKNOW: THE FINAL ASSAULT

Further fierce fighting ensued the next day, as Campbell's men stormed the Mess House and Moti Mahal buildings, while the Residency garrison sent out men to attack the now demoralized mutineers. The way was at last clear to evacuate the Residency.

GRAHAM, Patrick *Private, 90th Regiment*
    17 November 1857 – At Lucknow, he brought in a wounded comrade under very heavy fire.
    He was elected for the award under Rule 13 of the Royal Warrant.

PYE, Charles Colquhoun *Sergeant Major, 53rd Regiment*
    17 November 1857 – At Lucknow, he demonstrated great courage when he carried ammunition up to the mess house under terrific fire.
    He was elected for the award by the non-commissioned officers of his regiment under Rule 13 of the Royal Warrant.

The mutineers moved in and occupied the ruins of the Residency and resumed control in Lucknow, but the main British objective had been achieved and the garrison had been rescued. Campbell engineered a masterly evacuation, leaving the mutineers still firing for hours over his deserted trenches.

UPRISINGS IN THE NORTH, SEPTEMBER 1857 TO FEBRUARY 1858

From September 1857 to February 1858 troops were called to put down uprisings throughout the north – Bolandshahr, Agra, Mundisore, Dacca, Khodagunge, Rowa, Shunsabad, Choorpoorah, Sultanpore, Azamgarh – at all of which fierce fighting was seen and VC awards were made.

PROBYN, Dighton MacNaughten *Captain, 2nd Punjab Cavalry*
    1857–58 – He performed many acts of gallantry during this period. At Agra, he defended himself against five or six rebels, killing two of them before support arrived. On another occasion, he cut down a rebel who had bayoneted him in the wrist and later in the same day he killed an enemy standard bearer and captured the colours.
    He was Comptroller to Queen Alexandra, 1910–24.

FREEMAN, John *Private, 9th Lancers*
    10 October 1857 – At Agra, he went to the assistance of a lieutenant who had been severely wounded. He killed the leader of the enemy cavalry and kept the rebels at bay.

PRENDERGAST, Harry North Dalrymple *Lieutenant, Madras Engineers*

21 November 1857 – At Mundisore, he noticed a mutineer training his musket on Lieutenant Dew, so he charged at the mutineer who turned and fired a bullet through his left side. The rebel was then killed by Major Orr. He also distinguished himself at Ratgurh and Betwa, where he was severely wounded.

MAYO, Arthur *Midshipman, Indian Navy (Naval Brigade)*

22 November 1857 – At Dacca, he collected a few men and charged two 6pdr guns manned by mutineers. He was 20 yards ahead of his party and under heavy fire throughout the charge.

ROBERTS, Frederick Sleigh (later Earl Roberts of Kandahar) *Lieutenant, Bengal Artillery*

2 January 1858 – Seeing two rebels escaping with a standard at Khoda-gunge, he dashed at them, cut one of them down and snatched the standard. The surviving rebel fired point-blank at him but the musket misfired. Earlier on the same day he had ridden to the aid of a sowar who was being attacked by a rebel. Although the rebel had the advantage of a bayonet, Roberts killed him on the spot with one slash of his sword.

In 1880, he set out with ten thousand men on his celebrated march through Afghanistan to relieve Kandahar. He was created Commander-in-Chief in 1901 and superintended the arrangements for the funeral of Queen Victoria. Lieutenant the Hon. F. H. S. Roberts VC, fatally wounded at the Battle of Colenso, South Africa, was his son.

McQUIRT, Bernard *Private, 95th Regiment*

6 January 1858 – At the capture of Rowa, he engaged in a hand-to-hand fight with three men, killing one and wounding the others. During this action, he received a bullet wound and five sabre cuts.

SPENCE, David *Troop Sergeant Major, 9th Lancers*

17 January 1858 – He went to the defence of Private Kidd at Shunsabad, cutting his way through several rebels to reach him.

TYTLER, John Adam *Lieutenant, 66th Bengal Native Infantry*

10 February 1858 – Whilst approaching the enemy's position at Choor-poorah his men began to waver under heavy grapeshot fire so he dashed forward alone on horseback to attack the rebel gunners. Whilst engaging the enemy in hand-to-hand fighting, he was shot through the left arm, took a spear wound in his chest and had a ball through the right sleeve of his coat. When his men caught up, the position was taken.

INNES, James John McLeod *Lieutenant, Bengal Engineers*

23 February 1858 – During the attack on Sultanpore, he dashed ahead alone and shot a rebel gunner who was about to fire a heavy piece into the advancing columns. He then remained at the gun, under fire from hundreds of riflemen in huts close by, until support arrived. The guns were taken and the rebels routed.

LUCKNOW RETAKEN

Campbell eventually returned his attention to Lucknow at the start of March 1858. Since occupying the city in November the rebels had strengthened the surrounding defences and increased their numbers to over a hundred thousand. The operation to retake the city began on 2 March and lasted until the 21st – the rebels contested every stronghold fiercely and a further thirteen VCs were awarded during the fighting.

AIKMAN, Frederick Robertson *Lieutenant, 4th Bengal Native Infantry*
   1 March 1858 – He led a hundred men against a large body of rebels (five hundred infantry, two hundred horse and two guns). His force killed a hundred of them, captured the guns and drove the survivors into and over the Goomtee River. During the mêlée, he was slashed across the face by a sabre. This wound ultimately compelled him to retire on half-pay.

GOATE, William *Lance Corporal, 9th Lancers*
   6 March 1858 – At Lucknow, he pulled up his charger and sprang down to help the wounded Major Smith to safety. On foot, reins in hand, he carried the officer several hundred yards until he was engulfed by the enemy. He vaulted back into the saddle and desperately fought off the rebels swarming around him until relieved by his comrades. He then went back to search for the major, who was not to be found. His headless corpse was brought in the following morning.

BUTLER, Thomas Adair *Lieutenant, Bengal European Fusiliers*
   9 March 1858 – As the heavy guns were being placed in position during the capture of Lucknow, a message had to be sent to the infantry on the other side of the fast-flowing Goomtee River. The message could not be shouted across so he swam to the other side under heavy fire. Once there, he contacted the infantry before swimming back. As a result of his information, the infantry took and secured an abandoned enemy battery.

FARQUHARSON, Francis Edward Henry *Lieutenant, 42nd Regiment*
   9 March 1858 – Whilst leading a party of men at Lucknow, he stormed a bastion and spiked two guns. This ensured that advanced positions taken and held during the night were made secure from artillery fire.

HAWKES, David *Private, 2nd Bn., Rifle Brigade*
   11 March 1858 – At Lucknow, he found himself at the end of a street with Captain WILMOT and three others facing a large body of the enemy.

One of the men was shot through both legs and, despite being himself wounded, he (together with Corporal NASH) lifted the man up and carried him a considerable distance under heavy fire.

McBEAN, William *Lieutenant, 93rd Regiment*
11 March 1858 – At the assault on the Begum Bagh, Lucknow, he killed 11 rebels, one after the other. Confronted by a twelfth, a havildar, several men came to his assistance. He called to them not to interfere and he and the havildar set to with their swords. He made a feint cut but instead gave the point and pierced the heart of his opponent. When presented with his medal and congratulated on a good day's work, he replied, 'Tutts, it didna tak' me twenty minutes.'
Shortly after he enlisted as a private, a drill corporal made adverse comments about his rolling gait. A fellow recruit suggested that they should give the drill corporal a good hiding. 'That would never do,' replied McBean. 'I am going to command this regiment before I leave it and it would be an ill beginning to be brought before the colonel for thrashing the drill corporal.' He went on to hold every rank from private to major general.

NASH, William *Corporal, 2nd Bn., Rifle Brigade*
11 March 1858 – At Lucknow, he found himself at the end of a street with Captain WILMOT and three others facing a large body of the enemy. One of the men was shot through both legs and he (together with Private HAWKES) lifted the man up and carried him a considerable distance under heavy fire.

WILMOT, Henry *Captain, 2nd Bn., Rifle Brigade*
11 March 1858 – At Lucknow, he found himself at the end of a street with only four of his men facing a large body of the enemy. One of his men was shot through both legs and was taken up by Corporal NASH and Private HAWKES. As his party retreated he covered the men by firing their rifles at the enemy.

ROBINSON, Edward *Able Seaman, Royal Navy (Naval Brigade)*
13 March 1858 – At Lucknow, some sandbags on top of the battery operated by the naval brigade caught fire. He jumped up and extinguished the fires in some of the bags and threw others clear. Whilst performing this deed, he was hit by musket fire in the shoulder and knocked back into the trenches, unconscious.

BANKES, William George Hawtry *Cornet, 7th Hussars*
19 March 1858 – He led a charge against 50 rebels who had rushed the guns near Lucknow. He shot three of the rebels before he was felled by a young mutineer who hamstrung his horse with a tulwar. He was instantly set upon and hacked almost out of recognition, losing an arm and a leg with

his other limbs remaining barely attached. He died of his wounds eighteen days afterwards.

He was the first VC to have been educated at Westminster School.

NEWELL, Robert *Private, 9th Lancers*
   19 March 1858 – At Lucknow, he rescued a comrade whose horse had fallen, and brought him to safety under very heavy fire.

RUSHE, David *Troop Sergeant Major, 9th Lancers*
   19 March 1858 – At Lucknow, he attacked eight rebels posted in a ravine, killing three of them.

FIELD FORCES, SPRING AND SUMMER 1858

On 29 March the army was reorganized into three all-arms forces, the Azamgarh Field Force under General Lugard, the Lucknow Field Force under General Sir Hope Grant, and the Rohilcund Field Force under Brigadier General Walpole. All three saw action in mopping-up operations against fierce and often skilled resistance.

CARLIN, Patrick *Private, 13th Regiment*
   6 April 1858 – At Azamgarh, he was carrying an injured man off the field of battle when they were fired upon by a rebel. He took the wounded man's sword and killed the mutineer before bringing his comrade to safety.

NAPIER, William *Sergeant, 13th Regiment*
   6 April 1858 – Whilst on baggage guard at Azamgarh, he coolly bandaged the wounds of an injured private and carried him to safety despite being surrounded by rebels firing steadily.

CAFE, William Martin *Captain, 56th Bengal Native Infantry*
   15 April 1858 – During the attack on Fort Ruhya, he (together with Lance Corporal THOMPSON) went to the assistance of a wounded lieutenant. Seeing that the officer was dead, they removed the body under severe fire, to prevent its mutilation by the enemy.

The lieutenant whom he attempted to save was the brother of Captain Willoughby, one of the nine who blew up the Delhi Magazine.

DAVIS, James *Private, 42nd Regiment*
   15 April 1858 – Under a brutal fire beneath the walls of Fort Ruhya, he volunteered to bring the mortally wounded Lieutenant Bramley to safety. He began to lift the lieutenant with the aid of a private who was instantly shot and then carried the officer back to the regiment before returning to fetch the private's body.

MORLEY, Samuel *Private, 2nd Bn., Military Train*
15 April 1858 – At Azamgharh, he (together with Farrier MURPHY) went to the assistance of Lieutenant Hamilton, who had been struck from his horse and set upon by the rebels. The two men dashed in on foot and fought the rebels hand-to-hand until assistance arrived.

MURPHY, Michael *Farrier, 2nd Bn., Military Train*
15 April 1858 – At Azamgharh, he (together with Private MORLEY) went to the assistance of Lieutenant Hamilton, who had been struck from his horse and set upon by rebels. The two men dashed in on foot and fought the rebels hand-to-hand, although severely wounded, until assistance arrived.
His name was erased from the VC Roll and his medal confiscated in 1872 following his conviction for the theft of ten bushels of oats. His name was restored to the register after his death.

SIMPSON, John *Quartermaster Sergeant, 42nd Regiment*
15 April 1858 – During the assault on the fort at Ruhya, he rescued Lieutenant Douglas and a private soldier from an exposed point 40 yards from the fort under terrific fire.

SPENCE, Edward *Private, 42nd Regiment*
15 April 1858 – During the attack on Fort Ruhya, he and others went to the assistance of a wounded lieutenant. Seeing that the officer was dead, they removed the body under severe fire, to prevent its mutilation by the enemy.

THOMPSON, Alexander *Lance Corporal, 42nd Regiment*
15 April 1858 – During the attack on Fort Ruhya, he (together with Captain CAFE) went to the assistance of a wounded lieutenant. Seeing that the officer was dead, they removed the body under severe fire to prevent its mutilation by the enemy.

GARDNER, William *Colour Sergeant, 42nd Regiment*
5 May 1858 – At Bareilly, he went to the assistance of the commanding officer, who had been knocked off his horse and set upon by three Ghazis. He bayoneted two of the Ghazis and was in the midst of attacking the third when his opponent was shot down by another soldier.

BAMBRICK, Valentine *Private, 60th Rifles*
Born in Cawnpore, India, in 1837 into a family with a long military tradition, it was expected that Bambrick would join the army – and as soon as he turned sixteen he enlisted in the 60th Rifles, stationed in India. Three years later the Indian Mutiny spread like wildfire across the north of India and Bambrick's regiment was engaged in raising the siege of Delhi and the subsequent drive to capture the mutineers. In the narrow streets of Bareilly, 140 miles east of Delhi, three fanatical Muslim rebels cornered Bambrick and his company commander, Lieutenant Ashburnham, and despite being wounded twice, Bambrick fought furiously to save both their lives. For this

action, on 6 May, Ashburnham recommended him for the VC, which was awarded to him in 1859.

Having lived all his life in India, Bambrick chose to transfer to the 87th Regiment when his battalion was ordered back to England in 1860. With no mutiny to suppress, it seemed that what is called 'fighting spirit' and earns VC honours in the face of the enemy can make an 'unruly soldier' in more peaceful times – and perhaps that is why Bambrick never rose above rifleman.

In 1863, the 87th too left India for England and Bambrick took his discharge from the army at Aldershot on 16 November. There then began to unfold a tragic sequence of events which would only be finally put to rights in 2002.

Bambrick repaired to an Aldershot hostelry to celebrate his discharge from the army – and on hearing screams coming from the floor above, ran up to discover a woman being beaten by a commissariat sergeant called Russell. Bambrick hauled him off and gave him a sound beating, but the next day Russell had mustered the support of some cronies and brought a charge of assault against Bambrick, accusing him too of stealing his medals. The woman Bambrick had rescued was his only witness, so he paid for her to stay in a local hotel until the hearing – but on the day of the trial she had disappeared. Russell's witnesses seemed to convince the judge – perhaps assisted in their cause by Bambrick's outburst of verbal abuse – and he found Bambrick guilty on both counts and sentenced him to three years in Pentonville. The fact of his being imprisoned had no bearing on his right to keep his VC – however, under a Royal Warrant dated 4 September 1861, anyone found guilty of stealing another man's medals would forfeit his own. This last injustice was more than Bambrick could stand, and after just three months in prison he penned a note expressing his despair at the loss of his hard-earned award and was found on 1 April 1864 hanged in his cell.

He was buried in a plot in St Pancras and Islington with no sign that he had been awarded the nation's highest award for bravery. It was over half a century later in 1920, that George V decreed that, 'Even were a VC to be sentenced to be hanged for murder, he should be allowed to wear the VC on the scaffold.' Bambrick was one of eight VC recipients who had their awards restored under this new ruling. In 2002, in their campaign to locate unmarked VC holders' graves and honour their memory, the King's Royal Rifle Corps Association dedicated a plaque with proper honours to remember a man of courage whose honour was impugned and his good name sadly wronged.

SHAW, James (also known as John) *Private, 3rd Bn., Rifle Brigade*
    13 June 1858 – At Lucknow, he came upon a Ghazi flourishing his tulwar. Shaw tackled him, armed only with a short sapper's sword. The Ghazi struck him a heavy blow on the face. Infuriated, he flung himself on the rebel and sawed him to death with the serrated edge of his sword.

BROWNE, Samuel James *Captain, 46th Bengal Native Infantry*
31 August 1858 – During an engagement with rebels at Seerporah, he charged a 9pdr gun to prevent it firing on infantry who were advancing to the attack. He cut down several of the gunners but received one slash across the left knee and another which severed his left arm at the shoulder.
He was the inventor of the Sam Browne belt.

CHAMPION, James *Troop Sergeant Major, 8th Hussars*
8 September 1858 – When both of his troop officers had been wounded early in the day at Beejapore, he took command of the troop. He was shot through the body soon afterwards but remained in the saddle all day, disabling several of the enemy with his revolver.

MAJOR GENERAL SIR HUGH ROSE'S CAMPAIGN, 1858 TO 1859

Most of the fighting in 1857–58 had been in the north, and although there had been two rebellions in central India, at Gwalia and Jhansi, they were not put down until 1858, when Sir Hugh Rose, in command of the Central India Field Force (two brigades), advanced from Bombay in a campaign of unsurpassed speed and effectiveness. He set out on 6 January, and on 3 February relieved Saugor, which had been besieged for eight months, then marched for Jhansi.

KEATINGE, Richard Harte *Major, Bombay Artillery*
17 March 1858 – On the night before the assault on Chundairee, he had discovered a small path leading across the ditch. During the assault, he used this knowledge to lead his men through the breach. As he led the men forward, he received a severe wound but struggled to his feet only to be struck down by another bullet as he entered the fort. His discovery and leadership undoubtedly saved the column from dreadful loss.

CAMERON, Aylmer Spicer *Lieutenant, 72nd Regiment*
30 March 1858 – At Kotah, he led an attack on a strongly defended loopholed building, killing three of the defenders single-handed. The attack was successful but he was severely wounded during the action, losing half of one hand to a stroke from a tulwar.

Mutiny had broken out at the Jhansi garrison to the south-west of Lucknow in June 1857. As at Cawnpore, when the beleaguered occupants of the besieged fort offered to turn it over to the rebels in exchange for their lives, the mutineers went back on their word and massacred them as they left. The fort remained in rebel control, but now it had become imperative for the British to remove the threat posed by this major rebel stronghold, which had a garrison of eleven thousand men.
At the start of the rebellion it was questionable as to whether the Rani of Jhansi had condoned the massacre – her letter guaranteeing the safety of

the evacuees had either been a sham, or perhaps had been ignored by the rebel troops. However, in February 1858, her stance was unequivocal – her troops insisted that she fight the approaching British force. When the column under the command of Sir Hugh Rose arrived and surrounded the town on the 21st the Rani had made preparations for a long siege, but, despite an attempt to relieve it by twenty thousand men led by Tantia Topi that was defeated at the Betwah River by a thousand native troops and five hundred British, by 3 April the town was in British hands. Savage close-quarters fighting, spurred no doubt by vengeance for the earlier massacre, saw the award of seven VCs.

COCHRANE, Hugh Stewart *Lieutenant and Adjutant, 86th Regiment*
1 April 1858 – During the siege of Jhansi, his company was ordered to take a gun. He dashed forward alone, hundreds of yards in advance of his men, and took the gun, holding it until support arrived. He then had three horses shot from under him as he mounted an attack on the enemy's rearguard.

LEITH, James Edgar *Lieutenant, 14th Light Dragoons*
1 April 1858 – At Betwah, he charged a party of rebel infantry single-handed, rescuing Captain Need, who was on the point of being bayoneted.

BRENNAN, Joseph Charles *Bombardier, Royal Artillery*
3 April 1858 – During the assault on the fort at Jhansi, he brought up two guns, placing each under very heavy fire from the walls, and directed them so well that the rebels were forced to abandon their battery.

BYRNE, James *Private, 86th Regiment*
3 April 1858 – Whilst under heavy fire during the assault on the fort at Jhansi, he (together with Captain JEROME) rescued Lieutenant Sewell, who was severely wounded at an exposed part of the fort.

JEROME, Henry Edward *Captain, 86th Regiment*
3 April 1858 – Whilst under heavy fire during the assault on the fort at Jhansi, he (together with Private BYRNE) rescued Lieutenant Sewell, who was severely wounded at an exposed part of the fort. *28 May 1858* – His bravery was most conspicuous in action against a rebel force at Jumna, where he was gravely wounded, part of his head being torn away.

PEARSON, James *Private, 86th Regiment*
3 April 1858 – At Jhansi, he attacked a number of armed rebels, killing one and bayoneting two others. He was himself severely wounded in this action. At Calsee, he carried the mortally wounded Private Burns out of the line of fire.

SLEAVON, Michael *Corporal, Royal Engineers*
3 April 1858 – During the assault on the fort at Jhansi, he worked under fire at the head of a sap, and maintained his position for hours in the broiling sun.

WHIRLPOOL, Frederick *Private, 3rd Bombay European Regiment*

3 April 1858 – At Jhansi, he twice went out to bring wounded men to safety under very heavy fire from the wall of the fort. *2 May 1858* – He went to the rescue of Lieutenant Doune under such heavy fire that he received seventeen desperate wounds, one of which almost severed his head from his body.

Frederick Conker changed his name to Whirlpool. He later changed it again, to James.

Tantia Topi had occupied the town of Koonch, which was held by a strong fort, but on 7 May it was taken, though the temperature was 110°F in the shade and many on both sides died from the heat.

LYSTER, Harry Hammon *Lieutenant, 72nd Bengal Native Infantry*

23 May 1858 – After the defeat of the rebels at the Battle of Koonch, he was sent with an order to the cavalry to charge the remnants of the mutineers. Seeing that some of the rebels had rallied into a square, he charged alone into the midst of the square, broke it and killed two or three of the sepoys. He escaped without a wound.

Captain H. L. Reed VC was his nephew.

The next objective was Kalpi, which controlled the road from Lucknow across the Yamuna River, and which fell on 22 May, though the rebel force was ten times the British and Rose had his fifth sunstroke during the action. Once Kalpi was secure Rose was able to go on medical leave, but Tantia Topi and the Rani of Jhansi joined forces, and Gwalior went over to their side. Rose resumed his command, routed the rebels at the cantonments at the River Morar, and took Gwalior.

On 17 June the Rani assumed the red uniform of a sowar and led her troops against the British. Five VCs were awarded for a fierce charge against the enemy, during which the Rani was wounded. Although out of the action with her injury, she took aim at a British soldier who, mistaking her for a rebel sepoy, shot her before she could fire. With her death the rebels lost a major figurehead, and when Rose led his men to occupy the town on 19 June there was only scant resistance.

RODGERS, George *Private, 71st Regiment*

16 June 1858 – At Marar, he single-handedly attacked seven well-armed rebels who had taken up a strong position. One of the rebels was killed.

HENEAGE-WALKER, Clement (later known as WALKER-HENEAGE)
Captain, 8th Hussars

17 June 1858 – He was part of a squadron which charged at Gwalior. During the charge, the Rani of Jhansi (the twenty-two-year-old ruler of Jhansi who led her followers into battle) was killed and the rebels routed. The squadron charged through the enemy camp and into two batteries, which they took, bringing back two of the rebels' guns.

He was one of the six hundred who rode in the Charge of the Light Brigade at Balaklava. He was elected for the award under Rule 13 of the Royal Warrant.

HOLLIS, George *Farrier, 8th Hussars*
17 June 1858 – He was part of a squadron which charged at Gwalior. During the charge, the Rani of Jhansi was killed and the rebels routed. The squadron charged through the enemy camp and into two batteries, which they took, bringing back two of the rebels' guns.

PEARSON, John *Private, 8th Hussars*
17 June 1858 – He was part of a squadron which charged at Gwalior. During the charge, the Rani of Jhansi was killed and the rebels routed. The squadron charged through the enemy camp and into two batteries, which they took, bringing back two of the rebels' guns.
He was one of the six hundred who rode in the Charge of the Light Brigade at Balaklava.

WARD, Joseph *Sergeant, 8th Hussars*
17 June 1858 – He was part of a squadron which charged at Gwalior. During the charge, the Rani of Jhansi was killed and the rebels routed. The squadron charged through the enemy camp and into two batteries, which they took, bringing back two of the rebels' guns.

WALLER, William Francis Frederick *Lieutenant, 25th Bombay Light Infantry*
20 June 1858 – He attacked and successfully took the Gwalior fort with only a handful of men. They climbed onto the roof of a house, shot the gunners opposing them and entered the fort killing every rebel inside it.

The mutiny was effectively over, though there were more VCs to be won in defeating small uprisings and dealing with bands of rebels who had turned to open lawlessness. It was in one of these last that Sir Evelyn Wood won his VC.

BAKER, Charles George *Lieutenant, Bengal Police Battalion*
27 September 1858 – He led a mixed party of 108 cavalry and mounted police in a charge against seven hundred mutineers encamped at Suhejnee. The rebels were utterly routed.
He later took command of the Egyptian police.

CHICKEN, George Bell *Mr, Volunteer with Indian Naval Brigade*
27 September 1858 – Having openly declared his intention to win a VC, he was one of those who charged against the mutineers encamped at Suhejnee. When they fled, he rode recklessly in pursuit, catching up with 20 armed rebels whom he charged. He killed five with his sword, but was knocked off his horse and about to be butchered when four native troopers rode to his rescue.

RODDY, Patrick *Ensign, Bengal Army*

27 September 1858 – When engaged with the enemy at Kuthirga, he charged a rebel armed with a percussion musket. The rebel shot down his horse and came at him with his sword. He seized the mutineer until he could get at his own sword and ran him through the body.

He was offered a bar to his VC but chose promotion instead. He would have been the first VC and bar.

ANDERSON, Charles *Private, 2nd Dragoon Guards*

8 October 1858 – At Sundeela, he was in a party attacked suddenly by 20–30 mutineers. He (together with Trumpeter MONAGHAN) came to the rescue of Colonel Seymour, who had been cut down by two blows from a sword. He drove at the enemy with his sword, keeping them at bay until the colonel recovered himself and together the men routed the entire rebel force.

MONAGHAN, Thomas *Trumpeter, 2nd Dragoon Guards*

8 October 1858 – At Sundeela, he was in a party attacked suddenly by 20–30 mutineers. He (together with Private ANDERSON) came to the rescue of Colonel Seymour, who had been cut down by two blows from a sword. He killed the rebel swordsman and kept the remainder at bay until the colonel recovered himself and together the men routed the entire rebel force.

JARRETT, Hanson Chambers Taylor *Lieutenant, 26th Bengal Native Infantry*

14 October 1858 – At Baroun, 70 rebels had fortified themselves in a brick building, the only entrance to which was from a narrow alley under fierce constant fire. He called for volunteers to storm the house but only four responded. Undeterred he led these four men through the alley to the house and forced his way in, fending off enemy bayonets with his sword. Being so feebly supported, he was forced to abandon the attack and return under fire to his men.

FRASER, Charles Crauford (later Sir Charles) *Major, 7th Hussars*

31 December 1858 – Captain Sisted and some men of his regiment were drowning in the River Raptee, having plunged in whilst pursuing the enemy. Asked if he could swim, Fraser replied, 'Like a duck,' and hastily stripped and dived into the river. Despite heavy rebel fire and a severe wound in his own thigh, he succeeded in rescuing the officer and his men.

He was MP for North Lambeth, 1884–92.

ADDISON, Henry *Private, 43rd Regiment*

2 January 1859 – At Kurrereah, he rushed to the aid of Lieutenant Osborn who was being attacked by a number of rebels. He succeeded in keeping the rebels at bay until support arrived. He was terribly wounded, losing his leg during the action.

CLOGSTOUN, Herbert Mackworth *Major, 19th Madras Native Infantry*

15 January 1859 – At Chichumbah he charged the rebels, with only eight men of his regiment, forcing them into the town and causing them to relinquish their plunder. During this action, he lost seven out of the eight men.

COOK, Walter *Private, 42nd Regiment*

15 January 1859 – At Mayla Ghat, when the fighting was at its fiercest, the only officer was wounded and the colour sergeant had been killed, he (together with Private MILLAR) took command and led the men on with courage, coolness and discipline.

MILLAR, Duncan *Private, 42nd Regiment*

15 January 1859 – At Mayla Ghat, when the fighting was at its fiercest, the only officer was wounded and the colour sergeant had been killed, he (together with Private COOK) took command and led the men on with courage, coolness and discipline.

RICHARDSON, George *Sergeant, 34th Regiment*

27 April 1859 – Despite being wounded so severely that one of his arms was disabled, he closed with and secured a rebel armed with a loaded revolver at Kewanie.

GOODFELLOW, Charles Augustus *Lieutenant, Bombay Engineers*

6 October 1859 – During an attack on the Fort of Beyt, he carried off a mortally wounded soldier of the 28th Regiment under heavy fire and conveyed him to a place of shelter.

WOOD, Henry Evelyn *Lieutenant, 17th Lancers*

29 December 1859 – At Sindhora, a band of 80 rebels had captured an informant, Chemmum Singh, and were intending to hang him. Wood gathered together a small party and went in pursuit of the rebels. Perceiving a campfire through the thick jungle, he crept towards it, coming close to the sleeping rebels. He ran at a sentry, slashing him in the thigh, before running into the midst of the rebels. He was ably supported by a duffadar and a sowar and several rebels were killed. The remainder fled into the jungle, leaving the informant behind unharmed.

He served with the naval brigade in the Crimea and was badly injured in an assault on the Redan. His autobiography, 'From Midshipman to Field Marshal', was published in 1906. Constable of the Tower of London, 1911–19.

VICTORIAN COLONIAL WARS

THE PERSIAN WAR (1856–57)

In the days of British rule in India, a major influence on Britain's foreign policy was the threat of incursions into this part of the Empire by Russia or her minion states. Since the Russia's victory over Persia in 1828, her influence over Persian policy had become evident, and was posing a latent threat to British India.

It was with the Russian threat in mind that Britain had helped to create the buffer state of Afghanistan between India and Persia, and although the Afghan city of Herat had long been part of Persia, the British supported its incorporation into Afghanistan. So began a sporadic battle to hold the city. The Persian army invested Herat on 23 November 1838, but lifted the siege when Britain threatened to intervene. In 1851, the Shah in Herat allowed Persian troops to enter the city – and again British diplomatic pressure ousted them. When Persia annexed Herat in October 1856 and diplomatic measures failed, Britain declared war on 1 November.

Within five days, a British division from Bombay under Major General Foster Stalker launched an amphibious attack in the Persian Gulf, landing south of Bushire. Under heavy naval bombardment and following the capture of the city's defensive forts, during which Captain John Wood of the 20th Bombay Native Infantry was awarded a VC, Bushire's governor surrendered, and soon after, four thousand five hundred British troops under overall command of Lieutenant General Sir James Outram arrived as reinforcements. These men – from the 64th and 68th Regiments – came under attack at Khoosh-ab by a Persian force of six thousand nine hundred on 8 February and, at the loss of just 10 killed and 62 wounded, routed the enemy, leaving some seven hundred Persians dead. This action saw the award of two VCs, to Lieutenant John Malcolmson and Lieutenant Arthur Moore of the 3rd Bombay Light Infantry. Outram crossed the Persian Gulf to Mohamrah on the Euphrates delta, where his men took the city easily after fierce naval bombardment, sending the Persians into retreat. A small force under Commander Rennie pursued them up the Karoon River to Akwaz and captured the town on 1 April, but a peace treaty had already been signed on 4 March, resulting in the Persian withdrawal from Herat and the opening up of Persia for British trade.

WOOD, John Augustus *Captain, 20th Bombay Native Infantry*
   9 August 1856 – At Bushire, he led his company in an assault on the fort. He was the first man on the parapet and was instantly fired upon by the enemy from three feet away. Despite being hit by seven bullets, he threw himself at the enemy, killing their leader. His company followed him closely, the enemy was routed and the position taken.

MALCOLMSON, John Grant *Lieutenant, 3rd Bombay Light Cavalry*
   8 February 1857 – At the Battle of Khoosh-ab, he saved the life of Lieutenant MOORE who was surrounded by a crowd of the enemy and attempting to fight his way through them with a broken sword. He rode his way through the Persians to his brother officer, offered him a stirrup and carried him away to safety.

MOORE, Arthur Thomas *Lieutenant, 3rd Bombay Light Cavalry*
   8 February 1857 – At the Battle of Khoosh-ab, he took part in a mounted charge on an infantry square of five hundred Persians. He was the first to arrive at the square and he took the first line of bayonets like a fence. As he landed in the midst of the enemy, his charger fell dead. He attempted to fight off the Persians with only a broken sword. He would undoubtedly have lost his life had not Lieutenant MALCOLMSON come to his assistance.

THE TARANAKI MAORI WAR, NEW ZEALAND (1860–61)

As more immigrants from the northern hemisphere flooded into New Zealand's North Island in the 1850s, there was an increasing demand for land to accommodate them – and this had to be bought from the native Maoris by the British government. As a lever, the Governor announced a policy that the government would buy land from any individual, and that anyone obstructing this would be committing treason against the crown. This was put to the test when a local Te Atiawa chief offered to sell an area of land in North Taranaki, known as the Pekapeka Block, to the British government. Not surprisingly, the two thousand or so Te Atiawa Maoris living there were fiercely opposed to the sale, and their paramount chief, Wiremu Kingi, spoke for them – while they wanted no war, he could not let the sale go through. The local people obstructed attempts to survey the area, refused to move out, and instead built up a fortified village or *pah* at Te Kohia, just inside the Block.
   On 17 March 1860, the British army attacked the *pah* to begin the First Taranaki War. There followed more attacks, where the army, including the 40th Regiment and servicemen from HMS *Niger*, besieged pahs at Puketekauere, Mahoetahi, Orongomai, Omata (at which action Leading Seaman William Odgers of HMS *Niger* was awarded the VC). With the exception of the June attack on Puketekauere, where the Te Atiawa people put up spirited

resistance to defeat the British forces, these sieges were successful. In a skirmishing foray near Huirangi Bush on 18 March 1861, Colour Sergeant John Lucas of the 40th Regiment earned a VC for bravery under heavy fire, but weight of numbers and military muscle prevailed, and after the final attack on Te Arei pah in March 1861, a truce was signed, although the disputed block of land became British-owned territory and the Maori people remained in possession of the area.

ODGERS, William *Leading Seaman, Royal Navy*
28 March 1860 – He was one of a party of 48 from HMS *Niger* who went to relieve the 65th Regiment at Omata, New Zealand. At the storming of a Maori *pah* (fort), he was the first to enter under fearsome fire, capturing the enemy's largest flag.

LUCAS, John *Colour Sergeant, 40th Regiment*
18 March 1861 – Near the Huirangi Bush in New Zealand, he was one of a party of skirmishers ambushed by Maoris. Under heavy fire, he ran to assist a wounded lieutenant and sent him to the rear. He collected the arms of the killed and injured and, taking post behind a tree, returned enemy fire for fifteen minutes until support arrived.

THE THIRD CHINA WAR (1860)

Chinese resentment of European traders and diplomats had already resulted in the First China War (or Opium War) of 1840–42, following which Hong Kong was ceded to Britain and five ports were opened up to European trade. An uneasy peace came to an end when the Chinese executed a French missionary and five Chinese sailors were taken off a British schooner and tried for piracy. The resulting conflict – the Second China War (1846–47) – was concluded with lengthy negotiations leading to the Treaty of Tientsin in June 1858, which opened eleven more ports to European trade, allowed European missions into Peking and guaranteed the safety of missionaries and travellers in China. The British and French commissioners set sail up the Pei-ho River to ratify the treaty, but their vessels were fired on from the three Taku forts at the swampy mouth of the river. A combined Anglo-French expedition under Lieutenant General Sir James Hope Grant (who had served with distinction in the Indian Mutiny) and General de Montauban landed at Peh-Tang on 1 August 1860 to teach the Chinese a lesson – so initiating the Third China War. The force, some ten thousand British (one cavalry regiment and six infantry battalions) and seven thousand French, advanced almost unopposed, but were halted before the Taku Forts while engineers set about making roads to cross the surrounding swamps. The assault to take the forts was launched on 21 August, during which action seven men earned VCs. After fierce fighting, the combined force took the forts and carried on towards Peking with the objective of ratifying the Tientsin Treaty, arriving in early October. The Chinese finally signed the Treaty of Peking on the 24th, ratifying the former treaty, adding Tientsin to the tally of open ports and ceding Kowloon to Britain on a ninety-nine-year lease.

BURSLEM, Nathaniel Godolphin *Lieutenant, 67th Regiment*
21 August 1860 – During the storming of the Taku Forts, China, he swam across the ditch in front of a fort, and together with Private LANE, endeavoured to enlarge an opening in the wall and gain entry. Both men eventually forced their way in and were severely wounded.

CHAPLIN, John Worthy *Ensign, 67th Regiment*
21 August 1860 – During the storming of the North Taku Forts, China, he planted the regimental colours on the breach made by the storming party and subsequently on the bastion of the fort, which he was the first to mount. During the action, he was severely wounded.

FITZGIBBON, Andrew *Hospital Apprentice, attached 67th Regiment*
21 August 1860 – During the storming of the Taku Forts, China, he went out under severe fire to bind up the wounds of a litter bearer. He then ran to the aid of another man in an exposed position and was himself severely wounded.
At fifteen years three months, he was one of the two youngest winners of the VC, the other being Drummer T. Flinn.

LANE, Thomas *Private, 67th Regiment*
21 August 1860 – During the storming of the Taku Forts, China, he swam across the ditch in front of a fort, and together with Lieutenant BURSLEM, endeavoured to enlarge an opening in the wall and gain entry. Both men eventually forced their way in. He received a slight wound to the face.
His name was erased from the VC Roll and his medal confiscated in 1882 after he was convicted of desertion on active service and theft of a horse, arms and accoutrements. His name was restored to the register after his death.

LENON, Edmund Henry *Lieutenant, 67th Regiment*
21 August 1860 – During the storming of the Taku Forts, China, together with Lieutenant ROGERS and Private McDOUGALL, he sprang into a ditch filled with stagnant water in front of a fort, swam to the walls and forced his way in through an embrasure. He was the third man to gain a footing on the walls.

McDOUGALL, John *Private, 44th Regiment*
21 August 1860 – During the storming of the Taku Forts, China, together with Lieutenant ROGERS and Lieutenant LENON, he sprang into a ditch filled with stagnant water in front of a fort, swam to the walls and forced his

way in through an embrasure. He was the second man to gain a footing on the walls.

ROGERS, Robert Montresor *Lieutenant, 44th Regiment*

21 August 1860 – During the storming of the Taku Forts, China, together with Lieutenant LENON and Private McDOUGALL, he sprang into the ditch filled with stagnant water in front of the fort, swam to the walls and forced his way in through an embrasure. He was the first man to gain a footing on the walls.

THE T'AI P'ING REBELLION (1851–64)

In 1850, eight years after the Manchu Ch'ing Empire's defeat by the British in the Opium War, the popular leader Hung Hsiu-ch'an raised an army of T'ai P'ing rebels in Guangxi Province. His aim was to overthrow the weak Manchu Ch'ing emperor and declare a Utopian Christian 'Heavenly Kingdom of Great Peace'. Hung was a charismatic character and his philosophy – a mix of Chinese thinking and Protestant ethics – offered an end to the oppressive traditions of foot-binding, slavery, arranged marriages, concubinage, idol-worship and the destructive culture of opium-smoking. The rebels declared their new republic in 1851, and in March 1853 seized Nanking, establishing a new regime in which peasants owned the land in common.

An American adventurer named Frederick T. Ward became an unlikely ally for the Ch'ing Empire – he raised a small force of foreigners and led them against the T'ai P'ings. This motley group had the mercenary goal of plunder in mind, but they responded to discipline to achieve their own purposes, and were very successful against the rebels. Ward led this 'Ever Victorious Army' to take back Shanghai, but he was killed in battle. When his successor, an American called Burgevine, proved ineffectual, his place was taken, with the approval of the British authorities, by Major Charles Gordon (who was killed at Khartoum). Britain saw how the T'ai P'ing regime had paralysed trade and wanted positive action to restore commerce. Under Gordon's leadership the T'ai P'ings' strongholds were reduced until only Nanking remained to be retaken. During this campaign, at an engagement at Fung Wha, a VC was earned by Able Seaman George Hinckley from HMS *Sphinx*. Imperial troops finally retook Nanking in July 1864, and the rebellion was over after eleven years. With the loss of an estimated thirty million lives, it was the bloodiest civil war in history, and the second bloodiest war of any kind. Only the Second World War was worse.

HINCKLEY, George *Able Seaman, Royal Navy (Naval Brigade)*

9 October 1862 – At Fung Wha, China, he was part of a force which attacked the fortified town. The force found the main gate blocked and had to retreat under an intense fire of musket balls, stink pots, slugs, nails and jagged lumps of iron fired from loopholes in the walls. Noticing the assistant master of his ship, HMS *Sphinx*, lying wounded in the open, he ran to him and carried him to the safety of a temple. He ran back to rescue another man and then returned to the fight.

He lost his medal at a funeral in 1863 and had to pay twenty-four shillings for a replacement.

THE WAIKATO-HAUHAU MAORI WAR (1863–66)

The truce which concluded the Maori War in 1861 had dealt only with the immediate territorial problem. By 1863, the increasing flow of settlers to New Zealand's North Island and the consequent demand for land was once more the cause of fighting.

The 18th, 43rd, 57th, 65th and 68th Regiments and the 107th Bengal Infantry, the Royal Regiment of Artillery and detachments from HMS *Foretop* and the Auckland Militia launched a massive invasion of the Maori king Tawhiau's home area – the Waikato – in July 1863. They set about expelling the Maori people from their holdings and they swept south, claiming land as they went, their route taking them through battles at Cameron Town, Pontoko, Rangiriri, Mangapiko River, Ohanpu, Tauranga and Nukumaru. The Waikato people and their allies were defeated at Orakau in 1864, following which Tawhiau fled west to the dense bushland where the Ngati people lived. The British pursued the king with an aim to 'repress the Maori' – which they did ruthlessly. Major battles were fought at Gate Pa and Te Ranga, and the Maoris put up spirited resistance defending their strongholds, taking full advantage of their local knowledge, but the British forces' superior organization and firepower finally forced the Maori to capitulate.

McKENNA, Edward *Colour Sergeant, 65th Regiment*
7 September 1863 – At Cameron Town, New Zealand, he took command of thirty-five men, a bugler and two sergeants of his regiment and charged a much larger Maori force, causing the enemy to disperse into the bush. His force then held its ground under fire and moved on as darkness fell, spending the night in perfect silence. Support arrived at daybreak.

RYAN, John *Lance Corporal, 65th Regiment*
7 September 1863 – At Cameron Town, New Zealand, he removed the mortally wounded Captain Swift from the field of battle, holding the Captain's hand as he died. He stayed with the body, covering it with leaves to hide it from the surrounding Maoris, until support arrived the following morning.

DOWN, John Thornton *Ensign, 57th Regiment*

2 October 1863 – At Pontoko, New Zealand, a soldier fell wounded 50 yards from the bush which was swarming with Maoris. He, together with Drummer STAGPOOLE, volunteered to bring the man in under intense fire.

STAGPOOLE, Dudley *Drummer, 57th Regiment*

2 October 1863 – At Pontoko, New Zealand, a soldier fell wounded 50 yards from the bush which was swarming with Maoris. He, together with Ensign DOWN, volunteered to bring the man in under intense fire.

PICKARD, Arthur Frederick *Lieutenant, Royal Artillery*

20 November 1863 – During the assault on the *pah* (fort) at Rangiriri, New Zealand, he (together with Assistant Surgeon TEMPLE) went to the assistance of Captain Mercer of the Royal Artillery, who had received a bullet in the jaw and was lying at the entrance of the keep. He went back and forth under heavy fire to bring water and showed great calmness in trying circumstances.

TEMPLE, William *Assistant Surgeon, Royal Artillery*

20 November 1863 – During the assault on the *pah* (fort) at Rangiriri, New Zealand, he (together with Lieutenant PICKARD) went to the assistance of Captain Mercer of the Royal Artillery, who had received a bullet in the jaw and was lying at the entrance of the keep. He dressed the wound and showed great calmness under the severest fire.

HEAPHY, Charles *Major, Auckland Militia, New Zealand Military Forces*

11 February 1864 – He went to the assistance of a soldier who had fallen into a hollow by the Mangapiko River, New Zealand, where the Maoris were concealed in great numbers. A volley was fired at him from a few feet away and he was hit in three places but he stayed with the wounded man, assisting him all day.

He had explored the Wellington area between 1839 and 1851 and the Heaphy River is named for him.

McNEILL, John Carstairs *Lieutenant Colonel, 107th Bengal Infantry Regiment*

30 March 1864 – Near Ohaupu, New Zealand, he was riding with his orderly, Private Vosper, when they suddenly came upon 50 of the enemy. They turned to gallop back but Vosper's horse went down under a hail of shot. McNeill rode after the horse, caught it, helped Vosper to mount and the pair rode to safety under heavy fire.

MANLEY, William George Nicholas *Assistant Surgeon, Royal Artillery*

29 April 1864 – At the attack on the *pah* (fort) near Tauranga, New Zealand, he accompanied the storming party into the stronghold and attended to the injuries of the mortally wounded Commander Hay. He then returned to see if any others required assistance. He was one of the last to leave the *pah*.

MITCHELL, Samuel *Captain of the Foretop, Royal Navy*
29 April 1864 – During the attack on the *pah* (fort) near Tauranga, New Zealand, Commander Hay was mortally wounded inside the *pah*. The commander ordered Mitchell to leave him and look to his own safety, but he refused and carried him out of the *pah* on his back. The commander died of his wounds the next day.

MURRAY, John *Sergeant, 68th Regiment*
21 June 1864 – At Tauranga, New Zealand, at the storming of the Maori position, he leapt into an enemy rifle pit containing ten men and killed or wounded every one of them. He then carried on up the works, attacking with his bayonet.

SMITH, Frederick Augustus *Captain, 43rd Regiment*
21 June 1864 – At Tauranga, New Zealand, he was wounded whilst leading his company in an assault on a Maori position. Ignoring his wounds, he sprang into the enemy rifle pit and engaged the enemy in a hand-to-hand fight.

SHAW, Hugh *Captain, 18th Regiment*
24 January 1865 – At Nukumaru, New Zealand, he commanded a force ordered to clear the bush. Having advanced to within 30 yards of the enemy, his men began to fall. Retiring the force behind a palisade, he rushed forward with four privates to bring in a wounded man close to the enemy.

THE UMBEYLA EXPEDITION (1863–64)

During the late 1850s, the Peshawar district of British-held India came under frequent attack by Hindustani Pathans based in the nearby Mahabun Mountains. The very warlike Pathans were vehemently opposed to British colonial rule. An expedition in 1858 under Sir Sydney Cotton drove the raiders from their base, but by 1863 they had regrouped around the mountain outpost of Malka. Without consulting the Commander-in-Chief, the Lieutenant-Governor of the Punjab authorized an expedition to destroy Malka – some six thousand men under Brigadier General Sir Neville Chamberlain were taken out of the frontier defence for this mission. Chamberlain chose the Chamla Valley as his operational base, and of the three points of access to it, he opted for the Umbeyla Pass, under the impression that the local Bunerwal people were friendly. The first of his 'Peshawar Column' reached the pass on 20 October, but it was a tough route and the rest of the column finally arrived two days later.

Unknown to Chamberlain, the Hindustanis had convinced the Bunerwals that the British would annexe their land if they failed to stand up to them, and on 22 October a reconnaissance party was attacked by Bunerwal tribesmen. Chamberlain fortified his position in the pass on two rocky outcrops – Eagle's Nest on Guru Mountain and Crag Piquet on the hills opposite – but these could only hold small numbers of men. In contrast, the Hindustanis had by now mustered the local tribesmen and moved in with a force of around fifteen thousand to trap Chamberlain and his men.

The two hilltop pickets were the focus of fierce action, as small companies of men defended them against massed swordsmen supported by accurate matchlock fire. On 30 October Crag Piquet was the centre of fierce hand-to-hand fighting, during which Lieutenant George Fosbery and Lieutenant Henry Pitcher earned VCs. Crag Piquet fell into Hindustani hands three times and was three times retaken in the next four weeks. On 20 November, Chamberlain was seriously wounded, but gradually reinforcements were drafted in on the orders of the C.-in-C., Sir Hugh Rose, and on 6 December Major General Garvock replaced Chamberlain. Nine days later he broke out of the pass with a two-column attack by four thousand eight hundred men, supported by the 11th Bengal Cavalry led by Colonel Dighton Probyn VC. On 17 December a Bunerwal deputation surrendered to Garvock and a small party was sent out to burn Malka as originally planned. Peace was restored, but at the cost of around a thousand British casualties.

FOSBERY, George Vincent *Lieutenant, 4th Bengal European Regiment*
30 October 1863 – During the Umbeyla Campaign in north-west India, he led a party of his regiment up one of two paths to recapture the Crag Piquet after its garrison had been attacked by the enemy. He led his men to the top of the cliff two abreast and was the first man atop the crag. He afterwards led his men in pursuit of the fleeing enemy and inflicted great losses on them.
He later brought the machine-gun to the attention of the British government.   *Maxim*

PITCHER, Henry William *Lieutenant, 4th Punjab Infantry*
30 October 1863 – During the Umbeyla Campaign in north-west India, he led a party of his regiment up one of two paths to recapture the Crag Picket after its garrison had been attacked by the enemy. He led his men up until he was knocked down and stunned by a large stone thrown from above. *13 November 1863* – He led the first charge during the recapture of the same post, it having fallen back into the enemy's hands.

THE SHIMONOSEKI EXPEDITION (1864)

The expansion of foreign trade into the Far East caused mounting resentment in Japan, and in 1863, the Daimyo (feudal landowner) of the Choshu clan began action to expel all foreigners from their land around the Straits of Shimonoseki. His forces launched attacks on European and American vessels, and naturally they fired back. Hostilities continued, so the European powers formed an international squadron, which quickly wiped out the Choshu clan's ships and forts. During these battles, fought mainly in the Shimonoseki Strait, Midshipman Duncan Boyes, Ordinary Seaman William Seeley and Captain of the After Guard Thomas Pride were awarded the VC, and a British force including the 20th and 67th Regiments, the Royal Artillery, Royal Engineers and Royal Marines supported the united offensive. A treaty was signed with the Japanese government barring the fortification of the Straits of Shimonoseki and providing a large indemnity to the injured Europeans.

BOYES, Duncan Gordon *Midshipman, Royal Navy*
   6 September 1864 – During the attack on the batteries and defences of Shimonoseki, Japan, he carried the colour ahead of the storming party under a shower of fire. The colour was pierced six times by musket balls. He (together with Captain of the After Guard PRIDE) was only prevented from advancing still further by an order from his flag captain. The stockades and batteries were captured and destroyed.
   Lieutenant T. J. Young VC was his brother-in-law.

PRIDE, Thomas *Captain of the After Guard, Royal Navy*
   6 September 1864 – During the attack on the batteries and defences of Shimonoseki, Japan, he ran ahead, turning and cheering his comrades on, despite being shot in the chest. He (together with Midshipman BOYES) was only prevented from advancing further by an order from his flag captain. The stockades and batteries were captured and destroyed.

SEELEY, William Henry Harrison *Ordinary Seaman, Royal Navy*
   6 September 1864 – Before the attack on the batteries and defences of Shimonoseki, Japan, he was sent ashore alone to ascertain the enemy's positions and strength. He carried out this duty with great daring and intelligence and afterwards took part in the final assault despite being shot through the arm. The stockades and batteries were captured and destroyed.
   He was the first American citizen to win the VC, at a time when American nationals were forbidden from enlisting in the British services.

THE BHUTAN WAR (OR DUAR WAR) (1864–65)

The Indian state of Bhutan lies just to the east of Nepal, and in 1864, following a civil war in the region, Britain, protecting her interests in her Indian Empire, sent a peace mission to restore order.
   The leader of the victorious Punakha people had broken with the central administration and set up a rival government. The legitimate governor was

deposed, so the British mission mediated, dealing alternately with the supporters of the deposed and the new government. The latter, however, rejected all British attempts to broker peace, so in November 1864, Britain declared war on the new Bhutan regime. It was an ill-matched contest, as Bhutan had no regular army, and such forces as it had were armed with matchlocks, bows and arrows, swords, knives and catapults. Wearing chain armour and carrying shields, these guards engaged the well-equipped British forces.

On 30 April 1865, a sharp engagement at Dewan Giri in the south-east of Bhutan drove the Bhutanese out of their positions, but the resistance of a stubborn pocket of about two hundred men prompted a courageous assault on their blockhouse by men of the Royal (later Bengal) Engineers – Lieutenant James Dundas and Major William Trevor were awarded VCs for their actions at this engagement.

Although the Bhutanese gained some battlefield victories, they were defeated in just five months. In the ensuing treaty, Bhutan lost part of her sovereign territory and was forced to relinquish formerly occupied territories in the Assam and Bengal Duars – and the much-contested Dewan Giri area.

DUNDAS, James *Lieutenant, Bengal Engineers*
30 April 1865 – At Dewan Giri, he (together with Major TREVOR) led an attack on a blockhouse containing two hundred of the enemy. To gain entry, the two men had to climb up a 14-foot-high wall and then enter the blockhouse head-first through a small gap between the wall and roof. At once Sikh soldiers followed the officers in. He was wounded during the action, but the blockhouse was taken, 60 of the enemy surrendering, the others killed, fighting to the last.

TREVOR, William Spottiswoode *Major, Bengal Engineers*
30 April 1865 – At Dewan Giri, he (together with Lieutenant DUNDAS) led an attack on a blockhouse containing two hundred of the enemy. To gain entry, the two men had to climb up a 14-foot-high wall and then enter the blockhouse head first through a small gap between the wall and roof. At once Sikh soldiers followed the officers in. He was severely wounded by a spear thrust, but the blockhouse was taken, and the enemy routed. Sixty of the enemy were taken prisoner.

CANADA – THE FENIAN RAIDS (1866)

Determined to liberate Ireland from British rule, the fiery Irish-American Fenian Brotherhood planned to spark a war between Britain and the US – and to do so they decided to carry out attacks on the British dominion of Canada. Two raids were carried out across the US–Canadian border in early June 1866, and were repulsed by Canadian volunteers.

On 9 June Private Timothy O'Hea of the Rifle Brigade was awarded the VC for his actions in dealing with a fire in an ammunition van on a train – this action was responsible for the appending of a new Royal Warrant to the existing criteria of eligibility for receiving the VC. Previously awards were only made in recognition of deeds performed in action against the enemy – but henceforth, awards would be made for acts of bravery carried out 'in circumstances of extreme danger'.

Although US authorities took action to subdue the Fenians, they still went ahead with further raids into Canada in late May 1870, from Vermont and New Hampshire – again unsuccessfully. Public pressure and a firm crackdown on Fenian activities in the US finally eliminated the threat.

O'HEA, Timothy *Private, 1st Bn., Rifle Brigade*
9 June 1866 – At Danville, Quebec, a railway van laden with 2,000lb of powder and ammunition caught fire. Whilst others took cover, waiting for the inevitable explosion, he set to wrenching open the door of the van, collecting water and suppressing the fire. By his actions, the lives of everyone within reach and a good part of the town were saved.

THE GAMBIA (1866)

In 1866 British forces were involved in trouble with a West African tribe in the Gambia. A punitive expedition having been organized by Colonel D'Arcy, the Governor of Gambia, the kingdom of Barra, in which the tribe resided, was invaded. One of the first actions in this campaign was the assault on the stockaded town of Tubabecolong. When the small force reached the town, D'Arcy called for volunteers to break down the stockade with axes. Private Hodge and another pioneer plied their axes in the face of intense fire until a breach had been made. The regiment struggled through, but the tribesmen had been reinforced, and so strongly that they were able to beat the British off for a time.

D'Arcy recalled later that he found himself left alone in the breach with only Hodge by him. He continued firing at the enemy while the big West Indian standing coolly by his side, conspicuous in his scarlet uniform with white facings, supplied him with loaded muskets. After a while, the rest of the men re-formed and came once more into the attack. Hodge then went ahead again, breaking a way for them through the bush-work defences.

To give his men a better chance of storming the place, Hodge ran round to the main entrance, drove off the enemy and forced open the two great gates which had been barricaded from within. Through these the West Indian Regiment charged with their bayonets, and when they emerged at the other side of the smoke-enveloped village they left some hundreds of the enemy dead and dying in their wake.

HODGE, Samuel *Private, 4th West India Regiment*

30 June 1866 – At the storming of Tubabecelong, he sprang forward and began to hew down the blockade. He then followed his colonel into the town, smashing open two barricaded gates with his axe, thus allowing support to enter the town. The enemy was routed and he was proclaimed the bravest man of his corps.

THE ANDAMAN ISLANDS EXPEDITION (1867)

Britain needed a new penal settlement to deal with prisoners from the Indian Mutiny (1857–59) and returned in 1858 to the former penal colony of the Andaman Islands in the Bay of Bengal to establish Fort Blair – despite concern over native cannibals' attacks on shipwrecked crews washed up on the islands.

The ship *Assam Valley* put in at the island of Little Andaman in 1867 and a small party of men went ashore, never to be seen again. Suspecting that they had been attacked by cannibal natives, part of the 24th Regiment – later the South Wales Borderers – were sent by steamer from Rangoon and arrived to investigate on 7 May. They were attacked by natives shortly after landing, but on retreating to the beach were prevented from leaving by a sudden fierce storm. A party of five men from the steamer volunteered to rescue them – all five were awarded the VC under the new clause added at the time of the Fenian raids into Canada in 1866, for extraordinary courage in the face of great danger.

BELL, David *Private, 2nd Bn., 24th Regiment*

7 May 1867 – Seventeen men of the 24th Regiment had been sent ashore at Little Andaman Island, Bay of Bengal, to track down a party of missing British sailors. On landing, they were attacked by natives and their boat swamped by the sea. Bell was amongst those sent to rescue the soldiers. A storm was raging and the rescuers' gig began to fill up, forcing them to retire. Another two attempts were made until all 17 soldiers were safely brought back off the island.

COOPER, James *Private, 2nd Bn., 24th Regiment*

7 May 1867 – Seventeen men of the 24th Regiment had been sent ashore at Little Andaman Island, Bay of Bengal, to track down a party of missing British sailors. On landing, they were attacked by natives and their boat swamped by the sea. Cooper was amongst those sent to rescue the soldiers. A storm was raging and the rescuers' gig began to fill up, forcing them to retire. Another two attempts were made until all seventeen soldiers were safely brought back off the island.

DOUGLAS, Campbell Mellis *Assistant Surgeon, 2nd Bn., 24th Regiment*

7 May 1867 – Seventeen men of the 24th Regiment had been sent ashore at Little Andaman Island, Bay of Bengal, to track down a party of missing British sailors. On landing, they were attacked by natives and their boat swamped by the sea. Douglas led the party sent to rescue the soldiers. A storm was raging and the rescuers' gig began to fill up, forcing them to retire. Another two attempts were made until all 17 soldiers were safely brought back off the island.

GRIFFITHS, William *Private, 2nd Bn., 24th Regiment*

7 May 1867 – Seventeen men of the 24th Regiment had been sent ashore at Little Andaman Island, Bay of Bengal, to track down a party of missing British sailors. On landing, they were attacked by natives and their boat swamped by the sea. Griffiths was amongst those sent to rescue the soldiers. A storm was raging and the rescuers' gig began to fill up, forcing them to retire. Another two attempts were made until all 17 soldiers were safely brought back off the island.

MURPHY, Thomas *Private, 2nd Bn., 24th Regiment*

7 May 1867 – Seventeen men of the 24th Regiment had been sent ashore at Little Andaman Island, Bay of Bengal, to track down a party of missing British sailors. On landing, they were attacked by natives and their boat swamped by the sea. Murphy was amongst those sent to rescue the soldiers. A storm was raging and the rescuers' gig began to fill up, forcing them to retire. Another two attempts were made until all 17 soldiers were safely brought back off the island.

THE ABYSSINIAN EXPEDITION (1867–68)

The Christian Emperor of Abyssinia, Theodor III (Tewodros), had consolidated his control in the mid-1850s, and pursued an anti-Muslim crusade to reform the country, the present-day Ethiopia. In February 1862, a new British consul, Captain Charles Cameron, arrived, bearing a pair of pistols as a gift from Queen Victoria. He suggested that Theodor approach the Queen to negotiate a treaty of friendship, and a letter was sent, proposing an alliance with Britain to wipe out Islam. It seems that this letter went astray, and on getting no response the volatile Theodor imprisoned Cameron (who had angered him by visiting the Muslim Sudan) and some British missionaries. Diplomatic means failed to resolve the problem, so Britain sent an ultimatum to Theodor – which he ignored. Plans were made for an attack on Theodor at his mountain capital of Magdala, to be led by Lieutenant General Sir Robert Napier, Commander-in-Chief of the Bombay Presidency Army in India since 1865.

Napier arrived at Zula in Annesley Bay with a force of thirteen thousand fighting men and thirty-six thousand pack animals (including forty-four elephants) to negotiate the mountainous route to Magdala – a journey of over forty days. Arriving at the plateau below the citadel, the British force repelled a charge by six thousand five hundred tribesmen, shooting down seven hundred and wounding twelve hundred for the loss of only two dead and eighteen wounded. Theodor panicked, attempted suicide and then escape, but had to return to Magdala with just a few hundred followers. On the same day, 13 April 1868, Napier's troops assaulted the citadel gates – an action in which only fifteen were wounded and two VCs were awarded. Theodor shot himself with one of Queen Victoria's pistols, Magdala was blown up and peace was restored.

BERGIN, James *Private, 33rd Regiment*
13 April 1868 – During the storming of Magdala, the head of the main column of attack, moving in fours, was obstructed by obstacles at the gate. He was one of a small party of officers and men who climbed a cliff and forced their way in through a strong fence of thorns and fought the enemy hand-to-hand. He and Drummer MAGNER were the first men to enter.

MAGNER, Michael *Drummer, 33rd Regiment*
13 April 1868 – During the storming of Magdala, the head of the main column of attack, moving in fours, was obstructed by obstacles at the gate. He was one of a small party of officers and men who climbed a cliff and forced their way in through a strong fence of thorns and fought the enemy hand-to-hand. He and Private BERGIN were the first men to enter.

THE LUSHAI EXPEDITION (1872)

Since 1850, Lushai tribesmen (later called the Mizo) had gradually migrated from the Chin Hills into Assam, subjugating the local people and imposing their own rule. They remained untouched by foreign political influence until Britain annexed Assam in north-eastern India in 1862. The Lushai were furious at this foreign intrusion and responded with raids into British territory – to which Britain replied with punitive expeditions. On one occasion in 1872, the Lushai kidnapped a girl, Mary Winchester, and a field force under General Brownlow set out to save her and punish her kidnappers. It was in the storming of the stockaded village of Lalgnoora that a VC was awarded to Major Donald MacIntyre.

MACINTYRE, Donald *Major, Bengal Staff Corps and 2nd Gurkha Rifles*
4 January 1872 – Leading a small party of Gurkhas in an assault on the stockaded village of Lalgnoora, he was the first to reach the nine-foot-high stockade. Climbing over it, he ran into the flames and smoke of the burning village. He was followed by his men, who stormed the village.

THE FIRST ASHANTI EXPEDITION (1873–74)

In 1872, the coastal fort of Elmina in Ashanti (present-day Ghana) came into British possession. This had been the last trade outlet to the sea for the native Ashanti people and their king, Kofi Karikari, was ready to fight to protect it. Early in 1873, he mustered a twelve-thousand-strong army, crossed the Pra River and invaded the coastal area. British forces defeated them at Elmina and, to emphasize their domination in the area, the British government appointed Major General Sir Garnet Wolseley as governor and commander-in-chief, tasked with driving the Ashanti from the coastal region. In December, several British units arrived to reinforce Wolseley's African levies, and in January, Wolseley issued a warning to Karikari that he was ready to attack. He also offered an armistice if the Ashanti would retreat from the coast, but as negotiations failed, war became inevitable.

The battle at Amoaful on 31 January typified the imbalance of strength – the Ashanti fought bravely, using the camouflage of tall undergrowth, but superior British numbers and firepower prevailed. In this instance the Ashanti lost 150 men to just 4 on the British side. Wolseley's men captured the settlements of Abogu, Amoaful, Becquah and Ordashu – for which attacks four VCs were awarded. Wolseley went on to take and burn the capital, Kumasi, where stacks of human skulls pointed to a tradition of human sacrifice. On 17 March 1874 the Treaty of Fomena brought the war to a close and hammered home British victory. The Ashanti had to pay an indemnity of 50,000 ounces of gold, renounce all claims to Elmina and to any payment from Britain for use of the forts for trade. They also had to break off their alliances with nearby states and, thus weakened, they withdrew from the coast, leaving trade routes open, with an agreement to abandon their custom of human sacrifice.

GIFFORD, Lord Edric Frederick *Lieutenant, 2nd Bn., 24th Regiment*
1873–74 – Throughout the campaign, his conduct was exceptional. He was placed in command of the native scouts, and hung upon the rear of the enemy, dogging their movements, noting their positions and capturing many enemies single-handed. Before the taking of Becquah (1 February 1874) he entered the city and took note of the enemy positions, enabling it to be swiftly carried.
Captain J. F. P. Butler VC was his nephew.

SARTORIUS, Reginald William *Major, 6th Bengal Cavalry*
17 January 1874 – During an attack on Abogu, he went to the assistance of a mortally wounded Houssa non-commissioned officer and brought him to safety under heavy fire.
Captain E. H. Sartorius VC was his brother.

McGAW, Samuel *Lance Corporal, 42nd Regiment*

21 January 1874 – At the Battle of Amoaful, he led his section through heavy fighting in the bush all day, despite having received a serious wound early that morning.

BELL, Mark Sever *Lieutenant, Royal Engineers*

4 February 1874 – At the Battle of Ordashu, he was at the head of a working party of Fanti labourers, who were exposed not only to the enemy's fire in front but also to the wild fire of native troops to the rear. He urged them to work on without a covering party, contributing materially to the success of the day.

MALAYA (1875–76)

Britain had occupied Singapore since 1819, and exercised a policy of not getting involved in local upheavals in the Malay states to the north. However, in 1871, civil war broke out in nearby Selangor, and Britain intervened, annexing the region. The next year, trouble flared in Perak and threatened to spread to Singapore, so it too was annexed. These areas proved difficult to administer, with the British Resident James Birch's measures to keep law and order and stamp out slavery bringing him into direct conflict with the local Malay leaders.

In July 1875, seeing their power and revenue seriously threatened, the Malay tribal chiefs had Birch murdered. All Britain could muster was a scratch force of sixty men of the 1st and 10th Regiments, fifty Sikhs, twenty Penang police, fifteen Malay volunteers and four sailors – and these men were repulsed near Birch's former base on 4 November. Reinforcements arrived from Hong Kong and India and the tide was turned. The 1st Gurkhas captured the assassins' base of Kintra and nearby Kotah Lama, taking on the Malays in guerrilla-style fighting. The British force went on to take Perak on 20 December, in which action Captain George Channer of the Bengal Staff Corps earned the VC. After a major breakthrough at the Bukit Putus Pass, the dissident chiefs were arrested and the Sultan of Perak was deposed.

CHANNER, George Nicholas *Captain, Bengal Staff Corps and 1st Gurkha Rifles*

20 December 1875 – In advance of an attack on the enemy stockade at Perak, he crept up so close to it that he could hear men talking. Seeing there was no watch, he signalled his troops to attack. He himself shot the first man dead and the stockade was taken. His action undoubtedly saved a great many lives.

BALUCHISTAN (1877)

During the Anglo-Indian War of 1838–42, Britain had briefly occupied Baluchistan in the north-west of India to protect her lines of communication, but had been forced to leave in 1841. However, relations improved when treaties were signed in 1859 and 1876, strengthening Baluchistan's ties with the British Indian Empire, and in 1876 British forces set up a strongly garrisoned army station at Quetta in the west of Baluchistan, commanding the vital Bolan and Khojak passes through the mountains. It was on 26 July 1877 that officers at this station were attacked by a group of coolies and Captain Andrew Scott of the Bengal Staff Corps serving with the 4th Sikh Infantry earned a VC for his courage during the attack.

Five districts of Baluchistan were divided off later that year to become the British Province of Baluchistan.

SCOTT, Andrew *Captain, Bengal Staff Corps attached 4th Sikh Infantry*
26 July 1877 – Hearing that two engineer officers were being attacked at Quetta, he rushed to their assistance. Finding one officer cut down and the other wounded, he bayoneted two of the enemy and closed with a third. His actions saved the life of one of the officers.

THE NINTH CAPE FRONTIER WAR (1877–78)

The Cape Frontier Wars spanned a century – a hundred years of intermittent warfare between the Cape colonists and the pastoral Xhosa tribes of South Africa's Eastern Cape – during which the African people struggled against the intrusion of the British and European settlers. In the so-called Ninth War, the Ngika and Gaika sections of the Xhosa tribe took arms against the Fingoes, whom they felt to be favoured by the British colonists. What started as a beer brawl between Gaikas and Fingoes near the old mission station at Butterworth suddenly blew up into a full-blown tribal conflict.

The ensuing war drew in British forces in support of colonial police to support the Fingoes against the Gaikas. It was an intermittent war of raids, ambushes, skirmishes and some small pitched battles around the Cape region, notable for the British troops using the machine-gun for the first time in action. The first VC in South Africa was awarded to Major Hans Garrett Moore for an action at Draaibosch near Komgha on 29 December, when men of the 88th Regiment supported the police against a Gaika attack. This ninth war concluded with Xhosa lands being incorporated into Cape Colony.

MOORE, Hans Garrett *Major, 88th Regiment*
29 December 1877 – Near Komgha, he was part of a small party forced to retreat before a large body of Gaikas. Seeing a private unable to mount

his horse with the enemy surrounding him, he turned back to save him. He killed two Gaikas and received an assegai in the arm but could not prevent the death of the private.

THE SECOND AND THIRD AFGHAN WARS (1878–80)

Britain had been keeping a watchful eye on this important buffer area to the north-west of British-ruled India as part of a policy of 'masterly inactivity'. In 1866 the Emir, Sher Ali, came to power. He was well disposed towards Britain and feared Russian encroachment in the region as much as Britain, but although prepared to support the Emir with arms and funds, Britain would promise no other help. In 1872, Britain and Russia had signed an agreement that the latter would respect Afghanistan's northern borders – there would be no need, the British government thought, to give any promises of support to Afghanistan.

However, alarm bells sounded in the British corridors of power when, in 1876, Sher Ali reluctantly allowed a Russian mission to Kabul – and then, significantly, refused to admit Lord Lytton, sent out as Viceroy, to the country. This Russian encroachment into Central Asia was too close to British-ruled India to go unopposed. Lytton decided that Sher Ali must be removed – and when his ultimatum demanding that a British envoy be admitted to Kabul was ignored, three columns of British troops moved into Afghanistan in November 1878.

One column, under Major General Sir Donald Stewart, advanced from Quetta over the Bolan Pass to Kandahar, a second, under Lieutenant General Sir Samuel Browne, marched through the Khyber Pass, taking the fortress of Ali Masjid. The third, including the 5th Gurkha Rifles, under Major General Frederick Roberts, set out along the Kurram Valley towards Kabul, but he was met on 2 December at Peiwar Kotal by an Afghan force of about eighteen thousand men and eleven guns. After a careful reconnaissance, Roberts made a dummy attack, under cover of darkness, leading his troops in a flanking movement to dislodge the Afghans, inflicting heavy injuries and capturing their guns.

Fighting in the harsh mountainous terrain continued into 1879 – engagements on 31 January at the Bazar Valley, on 17 March and 21 April at the Khyber Pass and on 2 April at Futtehabad saw extraordinary acts of courage by men of the Royal Engineers and the Bengal Staff Corps rewarded by VC citations.

As the British advanced on Kabul, Sher Ali fled, leaving his son Yakub Khan to deal with the situation. He signed the treaty of Gandamak on 26 May 1879, under which he relinquished control of foreign affairs to Britain in return for an annual subsidy and promises of support in the event of foreign aggression. He also had to accept a British envoy in Kabul, and as well as extending British control as far as the Michni and Khyber passes, he was made to cede various frontier areas to Britain.

In 1879, the Afghan army mutinied, killing the British envoy and his escort. Roberts responded by occupying Kabul and deposing Yakub Khan on 6 October, after a sharp action, in which a VC was won by Major George White of the 92nd Regiment, to dislodge the Afghanis from their hillside base at Charasiah, outside the city. Further punitive action on 24 October involved the 59th Regiment in an assault on an enemy stronghold on a hill at Shahjui, but a popular uprising in December forced Roberts and his occupying troops to fall back to their base at Sherpur, just north of Kabul, where they were besieged for three weeks by a huge Afghan army, during which time men of the Gordon Highlanders, Seaforth Highlanders, the 5th Punjab Cavalry and the Bengal Staff Corps distinguished themselves by acts of extraordinary bravery. Roberts' men beat back a major attack on the night of 22/23 December, after which they returned to occupy Kabul again.

Abdur Rahman, Sher Ali's nephew, was instated as Emir in July 1880, but on 27 July, Ayub Khan (Yakub Khan's brother) led a rebel force to defeat the British at Maiwand, then laid siege to the occupying troops at Kandahar. Under severe pressure, the besieged force held out until, in a celebrated feat of endurance, Roberts marched from Kabul to Kandahar in three weeks and defeated the rebels on 1 September.

In March 1887, British troops were finally withdrawn. Abdur Rahman remained in power until his death in 1907, and British troops had no occasion to re-enter Afghanistan until 1919.

COOK, John *Captain, Bengal Staff Corps and 5th Gurkha Rifles*

2 December 1878 – At Peiwar Kotal, he went to the assistance of Major Galbraith who was about to be slain by a powerful Afghan. He parried the Afghan's bayonet and the men wrestled for some time until the Afghan bit into his sword arm, hurled him over and shortened his bayonet to give the final stroke. At this point a Gurkha shot the Afghan in the head.

HART, Reginald Clare *Lieutenant, Royal Engineers*

31 January 1879 – In the Bazar Valley, he ran to the assistance of a wounded sowar, 1,200 yards away, exposed to enemy fire. He reached the man as the enemy were about to cut him up, drove them off and brought him to safety with the help of others.

LEACH, Edward Pemberton *Captain, Royal Engineers*

17 March 1879 – In the Khyber Pass, he was covering the retirement of a survey escort. As the enemy began to press on all sides, he led a charge of the 45th Sikhs. Killing three Afghans single-handed and suffering a severe knife wound in his arm, he prevented the annihilation of the party.

HAMILTON, Walter Richard Pollock *Lieutenant, Bengal Staff Corps and Corps of Guides*
    2 April 1879 – At Futtehabad, he led a charge and scattered the enemy. During the charge, he rescued Dowlut Ram, a sowar whose horse had fallen and was under attack by three of the foe. He cut down the three Afghans and rescued Dowlut Ram from the mêlée.

CREAGH, O'Moore *Captain, Bombay Staff Corps*
    21 April 1879 – At Kam Dakka in the Khyber Pass, he retired his detachment of 150 men into a cemetery and repelled an Afghan force of fifteen hundred with the bayonet until a charge by the 10th Bengal Lancers routed the enemy.
    He was the author of The Victoria Crosss 1856–1920.

WHITE, George Stuart *Major, 92nd Regiment*
    6 October 1879 – At Charasiah, artillery and rifle fire had failed to dislodge the enemy from a hill. He led his men up the rocks, from ledge to ledge, until they were faced with the Afghan force, which outnumbered them by eight to one. He ran straight at the enemy, by himself, shooting the Afghan leader. Taken by surprise, the enemy fled in disarray.
    He commanded the garrison at the siege of Ladysmith.

SARTORIUS, Euston Henry *Captain, 59th Regiment*
    24 October 1879 – At Shahjui, he led a party of four or five in a surprise attack on an enemy stronghold on top of an almost inaccessible hill. Creeping up on the picket unawares, the position was taken with the loss of only one man. He was wounded by sword cuts in both hands.
    Major R. W. Sartorius VC was his brother.

ADAMS, James William *The Reverend, Bengal Ecclesiastical Department*
    11 December 1879 – At Killa Kazi, he spotted two lancers drowning, trapped underneath their horses in a deep ravine. Aware from the shouting and firing that the enemy were nearly upon them, he jumped into the water, pulled the men clear of their frantic horses and escaped on foot.
    He was known as the 'Fighting Parson'.

DICK-CUNYNGHAM, William Henry *Lieutenant, 92nd Regiment*
    13 December 1879 – During the attack on the Sherpur Pass, the 92nd Regiment were on the point of wavering under heavy fire. Aware of this, he rode out, exposing himself to the fire, raised his claymore aloft and called on his men to follow him. With a cheer they charged, and the pass was taken.

HAMMOND, Sir Arthur George *Captain, Bengal Staff Corps and Corps of Guides*
    14 December 1879 – On the Asmai Heights, he fought off the advancing enemy with rifle and fixed bayonet whilst his men were retreating. He then

stopped to carry a wounded sepoy to safety although the Afghans were only 60 yards away and firing heavily.

SELLAR, George *Lance Corporal, 72nd Regiment*

14 December 1879 – During the attack on the Asmai Heights, he dashed up the slope in front of his party and engaged in hand-to-hand fighting with an Afghan whom he defeated despite receiving a knife wound in his arm.

VOUSDEN, William John *Captain, 5th Punjab Cavalry and Bengal Staff Corps*

14 December 1879 – On the Asmai Heights, he charged 12 men at an enemy force numbering three or four hundred. He led his men through the Afghan ranks, backwards and forwards, cutting down 30, five of whom he killed himself. Six of his men were wounded, three later died.

COLLIS, James *Gunner, Royal Horse Artillery*

27 July 1880 – During the retreat to Kandahar after the defeat at Maiwand, he behaved splendidly, fetching water, tending to the wounded and maintaining his humour whilst many died of fatigue on the road. Whilst riding with No. 2 gun, he saw 12 of the enemy cavalry approaching. He broke off, lay down in a ravine, and opened fire. Thinking that he was several men, the enemy halted and returned bullet for bullet. He killed two of their number before he was relieved. His action undoubtedly saved the gun and the lives of his comrades.

He was convicted of bigamy in 1895, imprisoned and his name erased from the VC Roll. His medal was redeemed from a pawnshop and returned to the War Office, which sold it at auction in 1910. After he died, his widow wrote to King George V, asking that his name should be restored to the register. Shortly afterwards, the King declared that the VC should never be forfeited. 'Even were a VC to be sentenced to be hanged for murder,' wrote the King, 'he should be allowed to wear the VC on the scaffold.'

MULLANE, Patrick *Sergeant, Royal Horse Artillery*

27 July 1880 – During the retreat to Kandahar after the defeat at Maiwand, he saw his driver lying bleeding on the ground. Although the Afghans were only 10 yards away, he sprang from his horse, lifted the mortally wounded man onto the limber of his gun and got him away. During the retreat he entered several villages under heavy fire to procure water for the wounded.

His medal was sold at auction by his family, whilst he was abroad, believed dead, in 1904. On his return, the medal was restored to him.

ASHFORD, Thomas Elsdon *Private, 7th Regiment*

16 August 1880 – Near Kandahar, he (together with Lieutenant CHASE) carried the wounded Private Massey for over 200 yards. Bullets fired from both sides were raising dust all around them and they fell three times but eventually reached shelter.

CHASE, William St Lucien *Lieutenant, 28th Native Infantry, Indian Army*
   16 August 1880 – Near Kandahar, he (together with Private ASHFORD) carried the wounded Private Massey for over 200 yards. Bullets fired from both sides were raising dust all around them and they fell three times but eventually reached shelter.

THE ZULU WAR (1879)

Imperial fervour was growing in Britain in the 1870s, and in 1877, to secure the stability of lands in South Africa contested by both Britain and the Boers, Sir Bartle Frere was sent as British High Commissioner to create a federal dominion of British Colonies and Boer Republics. To do this, he needed Britain to control the land bordering Natal and the Transvaal which belonged to the Zulu tribesmen. Cetshwayo, the Zulu king, refused to give up his land, so it was on 11 January that Lieutenant General Lord Chelmsford invaded Zululand. Three columns of troops set out into Zulu territory, and it was the centre column under Chelmsford himself which went in search of Cetshwayo and his army, across the Buffalo River towards Rorke's Drift.
   Chelmsford had underestimated the Zulus' speed and military prowess and split his column in two. On 22 January, his unprepared and under-strength camp at Isandlwana, including men of the 24th Regiment under command of Lieutenant Colonel Henry Pulleine, was surprised by the main Zulu army, numbering some fourteen thousand. Sheer weight of Zulu numbers swamped the camp, and thirteen hundred of the seventeen hundred defenders were massacred – a massive blow to British military prestige and confidence. The Zulus moved straight on to Rorke's Drift, a small mission station consisting of two clay-brick thatched buildings, where B Company of the 2nd Battalion 24th Regiment of Foot was stationed with elements of the Army Medical Department, the Commissariat and Transport Department and the Natal Native Contingent. In a masterly defensive action, 139 men, mostly from the 24th Foot, held back the attack by about four thousand Zulus armed with assegais for over twelve hours, during which time 11 men earned VCs – the most ever in a single action. When Chelmsford finally arrived with reinforcements some four to five hundred Zulus lay dead for the loss of just 17 British lives.
   As the men at Rorke's Drift regrouped, the column to the east under Colonel Charles Pearson had driven east across the Tukela River to Eshowe, where they occupied the former Norwegian mission station. The defeat at Isandlwana had left the flanking columns dangerously exposed, so Pearson was faced with a choice – stay put and risk attack from the full Zulu army

or try to return south to the border with a view to returning with greater strength, thereby risking being caught defenceless in the open. They opted to stay, and as time passed, cut off and in cramped and unhygienic conditions, many lives were claimed by typhoid. At last, after three months under siege, Chelmsford broke through the Zulu cordon at Gingindlovu and arrived to relieve Pearson's men on 2 April.

To the north, in the wake of the defeat at Isandlwana, only the left-hand column under Colonel Evelyn Wood remained operational, and it was left for them to carry out diversionary attacks while Chelmsford went to Pearson's rescue. They fought a major action at the Ntombe River on 12 March, where one VC was earned, then met heavy opposition at Hlobane Mountain on the 28th, where that day five VCs were won. The army had fallen back on Khambula, where they inflicted a major defeat on the Zulus: the concentrated British fire was devastating, and defeat was turned to a rout as a cavalry party pursued and dispatched the fleeing Zulu warriors.

With his troops consolidated and regrouped, Chelmsford planned his attack. His first division, made up of relief troops and Pearson's men, would proceed under Pearson's command up the eastern coast, and the second, under his own command, would advance through the centre of Zulu territory, via Rorke's Drift – an opportunity to reclaim the military debris around Isandlwana and bury their dead.

By the end of June, Chelmsford's men had fought through to the heart of Zulu territory – the capital of Ulundi, taking the surrender en route of many individual Zulu chiefs, who sensed imminent defeat. On 3 July, Lieutenant Colonel Redvers Buller, who had earned a VC at Hlobane with a supply train of the 80th Regiment, which was all but wiped out, led his 'Irregular Cavalry' on an ambush party – and only narrowly escaped capture. The following day, however, there was no such uncertainty. Some twenty thousand Zulu came face to face with a massive imperial army, and in an action which took just forty-five minutes, the British routed the Zulu at their capital of Ulundi – which they put to the torch. This last battle left two British officers and ten men dead, compared with fifteen hundred Zulus lost. Cetshwayo escaped and remained on the run for two months, after which he was rounded up and sent into exile in Cape Town. The whole conflict had cost some two thousand British lives and £5m – and the matter of the confederation of British colonies and Boer republics remained unsettled.

ALLAN, William Wilson *Corporal, 2nd Bn., 24th Regiment*

A small, tough Geordie, William Allen, from Belford Moor, Northumberland, enlisted in the army at the age of fifteen at York and joined the 2nd Battalion, 24th Regiment of Foot. Although only five feet four inches tall, Allen was no retiring violet, and ended up confined in the cells on several occasions between 1860 and 1864. After serving in Mauritius and spending thirteeen years in the East, he returned to Brecon in 1864. He married two years later, and after acquiring a second class Certificate of Education was appointed Assistant School Master at the Brecon Barracks – where he was awarded a prize for Good Shooting and Judgement of Distance.

Posted to his battalion in January 1878. February saw him in South Africa and, after serving in the Cape Frontier War, he found himself among the defenders of Rorke's Drift on 22 January 1879.

When the Zulus attacked, Allen was posted as a sharpshooter on the southern rampart, where two wagons hade up part of the perimeter. Zulu attackers came within 50 paces of the barricade – and were mown down by British fire – but the Zulus still held the hills to the south, and could fire at will, causing serious casualties. Allen was determined to eliminate this threat and from the start, laid himself open to great danger as he positioned himself over the top of the barricade to fire on the enemy.

Inside the compound, Allen and Hitch between them kept communications open with the main building as the patients were rescued from the hospital. They helped the patients out through a high window together, and held a perilously exposed post in the middle of the compound in order to keep back the attackers who were climbing over the barricades. Most of the patients were withdrawn safely without further injury.

Like Hitch, Allen was shot in the shoulder – Surgeon Reynolds dressed his wound and he was quickly back in action. Although to badly injured to fight, he distributed ammunition as the night's fighting wore on.

As he recovered at Helpmakaar, he wrote to his wife, 'Everything is quiet and we don't expect any fighting till the arrival of troops from home. My dear wife, I trust you will feel too thankful to God for having preserved my life to fret over what might have been a great deal worse. I feel very thankful to God for leaving me in the land of the living.'

Allen's arm remained partly disabled, but back in Brecon in 1886, he became Sergeant, Instructor of Musketry to C Company 4th Volunteer Battalion, South Wales Borderers at Monmouth.

In February 1890 a flu epidemic struck the Welsh town, and after several weeks of serious illness Allen died of complications. His death left his family unprovided for, so the Mayor of Monmouth set up a benefit appeal to help them. Although his wife had to sell his medal, it was eventually returned to the South Wales Borderers Museum in Brecon, along with an inscribed pocket watch, given to the museum by his grandson.

BROMHEAD, Gonville *Lieutenant, 2nd Bn., 24th Regiment*

22–23 January 1879 – At Rorke's Drift, he and Lieutenant CHARD commanded a hundred men posted in a missionary station against an attacking Zulu force of four thousand warriors. The Zulus arrived only half an hour after the first warning was received and in that time they had supervised the erection of barricades. From 4 p.m. until daybreak next morning, they kept up a steady fire and directed the operation, which ensured the successful defence of the post and paved the way for the success of the campaign.

CHARD, John Rouse Merriott *Lieutenant, Royal Engineers*
22–23 January 1879 – At Rorke's Drift, he and Lieutenant BROMHEAD commanded a hundred men posted in a missionary station against an attacking Zulu force of four thousand warriors. The Zulus arrived only half an hour after the first warning was received and in that time they had supervised the erection of barricades. From 4 p.m. until daybreak next morning, they kept up a steady fire and directed the operation, which ensured the successful defence of the post and paved the way for the success of the campaign.

COGHILL, Nevill Josiah Aylmer *Lieutenant, 2nd Bn., 24th Regiment*
22 January 1879 – After the disaster at Isandlwana, he joined Lieutenant MELVILL, who was endeavouring to bring the Queen's Colour of the regiment to safety, and together they rode, pursued by Zulu warriors, to the Buffalo River. He crossed safely, but looked back to see Melville being carried away in the torrent. As he plunged back into the river to assist his brother officer, his horse was shot under him. Both men struggled to the Natal bank, where they were engulfed by Zulus, a people who took no prisoners. When their bodies were discovered, a ring of dead Zulus was found around them.

DALTON, James Langley *Acting Assistant Commissary, Commissariat and Transport Department*
22–23 January 1879 – Before the attack by the Undi Regiment at Rorke's Drift, he argued that the party should fortify the post and not retreat to Helpmakaar. When this was agreed, he set about superintending the erection of barricades. When the attack began, he was at the corner of the hospital. He later rushed forward and shot a Zulu as he was about to assegai one of the defenders, saving the man's life.

HITCH, Frederick *Private, 2nd Bn., 24th Regiment*
Born the tenth of 11 children to shoemaker John Hitch and his wife Sarah, Fred grew up in Southgate, North London. With no education or training, he had little choice when it came to a trade, and he found employment as a bricklayer's labourer. On these meagre wages he struggled to make ends meet, and for some unspecified crime he ended up before the magistrates of Westminster Police Court in March 1877. Police reports were destroyed during the Second World War, but it seems to have been a minor offence, as it was tried only in a police court, and his sentence offered him an option – go to prison, or join the army. Although neither offered much comfort for the future, the army at least promised food and clothing. The young, fresh-faced Fred, just five feet eight inches tall, enlisted by signing with an X – and was soon with the 2nd Battalion, 24th Regiment of Foot.

After seeing action in South Africa towards the end of the Cape Frontier War, Fred, stationed at Mount Kemp, sent the princely sum of £2 to his mother at home . . .

By June 1878 the threat of the growing Zulu nation had become impossible to ignore – and so it was that by mid-January 1879, Hitch was among five thousand troops under Lord Chelmsford garrisoned at the Swedish missionary base of Rorke's Drift. On 22 January Chelmsford moved out with his troops, leaving B Company of 2/24th to defend the base, which was a vital staging post for supplies. Fortunately for him, Major Spalding of the 2/24th rode out the same day to see what had become of the company which was to relieve them. In his absence, B Company carried on building an enclosure around the post and men were sent to build a pont across the Buffalo River.

Hitch provided two accounts of the events of 22–23 January. One, dictated to a reporter, appeared in the *Cambrian* newspaper; the other, written by hand and expressed in his own words, paints a very personal picture of the Zulu attack.

Back on that terrible night of 22 Jan 1897, it was about 3.30 o'clock that we heard of that fatal disaster at Isandhlwana. I was cooking the tea for the company. I tried to get it done before the Zulus attacked the little post, Rorke's Drift, which I managed – taken the tea and my rifle and ammunition and four kettles [of] tea. I just got into the fort when Bromhead asked me to try and get on to the top of the house. I at once mounted it. As soon as I got on top I could see that Zulus had got as near to us as they could without us seeing them. I told Bromhead that the were at the other side of the rise . . . Mr Bromhead asked me how many there were. I told him that I thought [they] numbered four to six thousand. A voice from below – "Is that all? We can manage that lot very well."'

. . . I told Mr Bromhead that they would be all around us in very short time. He at once told the company to take up their post. The enemy making a right wheel, they attacked us in the shape of a bullock's horns, and in a few minutes was all round us. I found as they got close to the laager, I was out of the fighting, so I slid down the thatch roof, dropping into the laager, fixing my bayonet as I ran across the laager, taking up my position on an open space which we had not time to complete. The deadly work now commenced.

The Zulus pushing right up to the pint, it was not until the bayonet was freely used that they flinched the least bit. Had the Zulus taken the bayonet as freely as they took the bullets, we could not have stood more than fifteen minutes. They pushed on right up to us, and not only got up to the laager, but got in with us – but they seemed to have a great dread of the bayonet, which stood to us from beginning to end. During that struggle there was a fine big Zulu, see me shoot his mate down. He sprang forward, dropping his rifle and assegais, seizing hold of the muzzle of my rifle with his left hand, and the right hand [had] hold of the bayonet. Thinking to disarm me, he pulled and tried hard to get the rifle from me, but I had a firm hold of the small of the butt of my rifle with my left hand, my cartridges on top of the mealie bag, which enabled me to load my rifle and shoot the poor wretch whilst holding on to his grasp...

Their next object was to get possession of the hospital, which they did, by setting fire to it. The greatest task was in getting the sick and wounded out of the hospital, [of] which the Zulus had bursted open the doors and killed them in their beds. Whilst doing this I noticed it was with great difficulty they were kept back. They [were] keeping up a heavy fire from front and rear, from which we suffered very much. It was then about when Mr Dalton was shot – and Mr Dunn. Mr Dalton was very active up 'til he was wounded. We had to fall back to the second line of defence.

When the Zulus took possession of the hospital, Bromhead and myself and five others took up the position on the right of the second line of defence, [by] which we were exposed to three cross-fires. Bromhead took the centre, and was the only one that did not get wounded. There were 4 killed and 2 wounded – myself was the last of the 6 – one shot. Bromhead and myself had it to ourselves an hour and a half – Bromhead using his rifle and revolver with deadly aim. Bromhead kept telling the men not to waste one round...

We were so busy that one had got inside and was in the act of assegai-ing Bromhead. Bromhead not knowing he was there, I put my rifle on him, knowing at the same time it was empty. Instead of him delivering the assagai, which no doubt would have been fatal, he dodged down and hopped out of the laager again. This was just before they tried to fire the other building. They seemed to me as if they made up their minds to take Rorke's drift with this rush. They rushed up madly, notwithstanding the heavy loss they had all suffered. It was in this struggle that I was shot. They pressed us very hard, several of them mounting the barricade. I knew this one had got his rifle presented at me, but at the same time I had got my hands full in front and I was at the present when he shot me through the right shoulder blade and passed through my shoulder– which splintered the shoulder bone very much, as I have had in all thirty-eight pieces of broken bone taken from my shoulder. I tried to keep my feet, but could not. He could have assegai-ed me, had not Bromhead shot him with his revolver. Bromhead seemed very sorry when he sees me down, bleeding so freely, saying, "Mate, I am very sorry to see you down." I was not down more than a few minutes, stripped in my shirtsleeves, with my waist belt on and fleece [?] straps. I put my wounded arm under my waist belt. I was able to make another stand. Getting Bromhead's revolver, and with his assistance in loading it, I managed very well with it. At this time we were fighting by the aid [?] from the burning hospital, which was very much to our advantage. Bromhead at this time was keeping a strict eye on the ammunition and telling the men not to waste one round as we were getting short. I was serving out ammunition myself when I became thirsty and faint. I got worse. A chum tore out the linen of Mr Dun's coat and tied it round my shoulder. I got so thirsty that I could not do much – in fact we were all exhausted and the ammunition was beginning to be counted. Deacon [?] a comrade said to me as I was leaning back against a biscuit box, "Fred, when it comes to the last, shall I shoot you?" I declined. "No, they have very near done for me and they can finish me right out when it come to the last." I don't remember much after that. When I came to myself again, Lord Chelmsford had relieved us of our task. Bromhead brought his lordship to me and his lordship spoke very kindly to me, and the doctor dressed my wound. Bromhead was my principal visitor and nurse while I was at the Drift.

Hitch had collapsed exhausted and badly wounded, and woke to learn that their defence had been successful. Chelmsford and his men were marching back to Rorke's Drift, and there would be no further attack.

Hitch and other surviving wounded were sent back to Helpmakaar to recover. He fared better than most in unhygienic conditions, and lived to be shipped back to England.

By July, he had recovered – but was ruled unfit for further duty and discharged from the army. The state of his injured arm precluded his return to building work, so he received £10 a year as a War Office pension for his VC (upped to £50 in 1898). However, he was eligible to join the Corps of Commissionaires, which recruited ex-servicemen to guard business premises – and his prospects seemed to be improving as he became a commissionaire and married in 1881. He had sporadic postings from the Corps – his wedding certificate has him down as a labourer. In the ensuing years he worked as a railway porter, caretaker and messenger, and in 1893 he acquired a publican's licence – but lost it the following year. It was around this time he got a hackney coach; although not qualified to drive it for a living, he could rent it to a licensed hackney cab driver.

In July 1901, Hitch fell from a ladder at work and was knocked unconscious. When he came to in hospital at Charing Cross, he asked after his VC medal – it had been on his tunic. Someone was sent back to the Royal United Services Institute in Whitehall where he had been working, but it was gone. He would have to pay to have it replaced – at which he was made to sign a declaration that he would return it should the original reappear. (The family eventually located the first medal and had to pay £85 to buy it back at auction.)

The Institute management accepted no responsibility, even suspecting that Hitch might have set up his fall to cover for the 'loss' of the medal, when he had possibly sold it. He and the Institute parted company, and he now lived with his wife and three children on just his income as a cab proprietor. By the time his eighth child was born, however, Hitch was driving his own cab, drawn by his own horses, and making a comfortable living – and he was able to upgrade to a motorized vehicle when horsepower became obsolete.

An enigma surrounds his last years. Newspaper reports of 1910 stated that the cabbie VC had turned down profitable work offers due to family commitments – but at his death in 1913, he was apparently alone. He collapsed while talking to a neighbour and his landlady found him dead the following morning. It's unclear what had happened to his wife and children. At his funeral, his cab was pulled manually by taxi drivers, and his coffin was borne on a gun carriage with outriders from the Army Service Corps. It was followed by a firing party from the South Wales Borderers, the Chiswick firefighters, a troop of Boy Scouts and trainees from the Duke of York's Headquarters – and some two hundred cab drivers. It was an amazing tribute to a man of the people who had earned the highest award for gallantry for his part in what is recognized as one of the greatest defence actions in history.

HOOK, Alfred Henry *Private, 2nd Bn., 24th Regiment*
22–23 January 1879 – At Rorke's Drift, he first shot several Zulus through a loophole in the hospital building. As the Zulus burst their way into the building and set its roof ablaze, he bayoneted countless attackers through the smoke as Private WILLIAMS pickaxed one partition wall after another until they had moved eight patients through four rooms and into the inner defence. At that moment, the roof collapsed, crushing and burning the pursuing Zulus.

JONES, Robert *Private, 2nd Bn., 24th Regiment*
22–23 January 1879 – During the attack at Rorke's Drift, he and Private William JONES had seven patients in their care at the back of the hospital. They kept attackers out by crossing bayonets at the door and hurried six of the patients out of the window and into the Inner Defence. The seventh patient, delirious with fever, refused to move and was stabbed by Zulus.

JONES, William *Private, 2nd Bn., 24th Regiment*
22–23 January 1879 – During the attack by the Undi Regiment at Rorke's Drift, he and Private Robert JONES had seven patients in their care at the back of the hospital. They kept attackers out by crossing bayonets at the door and hurried six of the patients out of the window and into the inner defence. The seventh patient refused to move, delirious with fever, and was stabbed by Zulus.

MELVILL, Teignmouth *Lieutenant, 2nd Bn., 24th Regiment*
22 January 1879 – After the disaster at Isandlwana he rode off, endeavouring to bring the Queen's Colour of the regiment to safety, and together

with Lieutenant COGHILL, he rode, pursued by Zulu warriors, to the Buffalo River. He was swept away by the torrent, but, with Coghill, struggled to the Natal bank, where they were engulfed by Zulus, a people who took no prisoners. When their bodies were discovered, a ring of dead Zulus was found around them.

REYNOLDS, James Henry *Surgeon-Major, Army Medical Department*
22–23 January 1879 – During the attack by the Undi Regiment at Rorke's Drift, he was constantly moving, attending to the wounded under heavy crossfire from the Zulus on the hills above the post and a constant shower of assegais from those attacking the barricades. He also carried ammunition to the men from the magazine.

SCHIESS, Ferdnand Christian *Corporal, Natal Native Contingent, South African Forces*
22–23 January 1879 – During the attack by the Undi Regiment at Rorke's Drift, he left his hospital bed – he was suffering from a severe foot injury – and took part in the defence. He jumped onto the barricade and bayoneted a Zulu, jumped back and shot another and leapt onto the wall again to bayonet a third.

WASSALL, Samuel *Private, 80th Regiment*
22 January 1879 – After the disaster at Isandlwana, he rode to the Buffalo River and was fording it when he saw Private Westwood being swept away by the current. He tied his horse up on the Zulu side of the river and dragged the private across the river to safety.

WILLIAMS, John *Private, 2nd Bn., 24th Regiment*
22–23 January 1879 – At Rorke's Drift, he was posted with two others (William Horrigan and Joseph Williams) in a distant ward of the hospital. They held out for an hour until cartridges ran short. The Zulus burst in and speared Joseph Williams and two of the patients to death. John Williams grabbed a pickaxe and broke a wall down through which he passed the two surviving patients to Private HOOK. He pickaxed one partition wall after another as Hook bayoneted countless attackers until they had moved eight patients through four rooms and into the inner defence. At that moment the roof collapsed, crushing and burning the pursuing Zulus.
He was born John Fielding but enlisted as Williams to prevent his parents from discovering that he had joined the army.

BOOTH, Anthony Clarke *Colour Sergeant, 80th Regiment*
12 March 1879 – After four thousand Zulus had attacked a convoy of twenty wagons at the Ntombe River, slaying the officers present, he took command of the few surviving men and led them to safety, despite being followed by the enemy for three miles.

BULLER, Redvers Henry *Bt/Lieutenant Colonel, 60th Rifles*
28 March 1879 – During the retreat from Hlobane, he saved the lives of two officers (Captain D'ARCY and Lieutenant Everitt) and a trooper of the Frontier Light Horse when their horses had been shot or assegaied under them. Rallying his men, he rode time and time again at the Zulus, under heavy attack from gun and spear.

FOWLER, Edmund John *Private, 2nd Bn., 26th Regiment*
28 March 1879 – At the Hlobane Mountain, he (together with Lieutenant LYSONS and Captain Campbell) advanced between rocks and over fallen boulders to a cave commanded by the Zulus. Advancing in single file to the mouth of the cave, they opened fire, driving the enemy away in disarray. The captain was shot dead during the action.
He was subsequently convicted of embezzlement but unlike Frederick Corbett his medal was not confiscated and his name was not erased from the VC Roll.

LEET, William Knox *Major, 1st Bn., 13th Regiment*
28 March 1879 – During the retreat from Hlobane, he rescued Lieutenant Smith, whose horse had been speared under him, by picking him up and riding him to safety under a shower of assegais and bullets.

LYSONS, Henry *Lieutenant, 2nd Bn., 26th Regiment*
28 March 1879 – At the Hlobane Mountain, he (together with Private FOWLER and Captain Campbell) advanced between rocks and over fallen boulders to a cave commanded by the Zulus. Advancing in single file to the mouth of the cave, they opened fire, driving the enemy away in disarray. The captain was shot dead during the action.

BROWNE, Edward Stevenson *Lieutenant, 1st Bn., 24th Regiment*
29 March 1879 – During the retreat from Hlobane, he twice rode back to assist men whose horses had fallen, only yards from the pursuing Zulus.
In fact he received the VC for saving the life of Colonel Russell at Kamlula, the following day – a clerical error.

BERESFORD, Lord William Leslie de la Poer *Captain, 9th Lancers*
3 July 1879 – At Ulundi, he went to the assistance of Sergeant Fitzmaurice, whose horse had been speared under him by the Zulus. The sergeant urged him to ride on and save himself. 'If you don't get up, I'll punch your head for you!' replied Beresford, helping him into his saddle. They were joined by Sergeant O'TOOLE, who rode alongside, shooting Zulu after Zulu, as well as propping the wounded sergeant up in the saddle.

D'ARCY, Henry Cecil Dudgeon *Captain, Cape Frontier Light Horse, South African Forces*
3 July 1879 – At Ulundi, seeing Trooper Raubenheim fall from his horse, he stopped to pick him up, but the horse kicked them both off. The trooper

was stunned and D'Arcy made several vain attempts to lift him into the saddle as the Zulus closed in. Eventually, he was forced to ride on alone to safety.

His own life had been saved three months previously by Lieutenant Colonel Buller VC.

O'TOOLE, Edmund *Sergeant, Cape Frontier Light Horse, South African Forces*
3 July 1879 – At Ulundi, he rode alongside Captain BERESFORD, keeping the pursuing Zulus in check with a steady fire and holding the wounded Sergeant Fitzmaurice steady in the saddle until they all reached safety.

He was awarded the VC after Beresford told Queen Victoria that he could not in honour receive the decoration unless it was shared by O'Toole.

THE BASUTO WAR (1879–82)

Basutoland, on the borders of Natal, had been a British Protectorate since 1868, but in 1871, British Cape Colony annexed the Basutos' land, interfering with the chiefs' authority and the tribes' traditional laws. Resentment grew and in 1879 troops from Cape Colony were sent to quell the unrest. Following a severe defeat, the Basutos retreated into the hills and made a determined stand on a mountain named after their chief, Morosi. This naturally almost impregnable stronghold was further defended by a series of stockade barriers on the one side which offered any access to attackers. In an action lasting from April to June, men of the Cape Mounted Rifles carried out attacks on the mountain, for which three VCs were awarded. In another significant attack, this time against the Bapedi stronghold of Sekukuni's Town, men of the 21st and 94th Regiments under Sir Garnet Wolseley reinforced the assault force on 27 November 1879. At first light the following morning, a three-pronged attack was launched against the hillside stronghold, during which two men of the 94th Regiment earned VC citations. The campaign was concluded with Sekukuni's surrender on 2 December 1879.

In 1880, the Cape Colony authorities prepared to enforce the Cape Peace Preservation Act of 1878, which disarmed the natives, in Basutoland – which gave rise to the Gun War. The Basutos rebelled and, taking up defensive positions in the rugged, mountainous terrain, they held the Cape Colony troops at bay with guerrilla-style attacks and sudden charges. On 14 January 1881, the Basutos charged a contingent of the 1st Cape Mounted Yeomanry, which action left 37 dead or wounded – it was here that the only doctor present earned a VC in recognition of his courage. Eventually the Cape government decided to seek a settlement. In the ensuing peace, the Cape Colony administration was unable to reassert control, and on the appeal of the Basutos the British government in London took over responsibility for Basutoland in 1884.

BROWN, Peter *Trooper, Cape Mounted Riflemen, South African Forces*
8 April 1879 – Hearing three wounded men crying piteously for water on Morosi's Mountain, South Africa, he said, 'I can't stand this any longer, has anyone any water?' Someone handed him a tin and he walked across open ground to the men and began pouring water into their mouths. As he did this, one bullet shattered his arm and another struck his leg but he did not stop until the tin was shot through and useless.

SCOTT, Robert George *Sergeant, Cape Mounted Riflemen, South African Forces*
8 April 1879 – During an assault on Morosi's Mountain, South Africa, he crept up to the enemy's defences and attempted to fling two time-fuse shells into their midst. He had retired his own men lest a grenade burst prematurely, and indeed the second exploded almost in his hand, blowing the hand away and shattering his leg.
He commanded the Kimberley Commando during the First World War.

HARTLEY, Edmund Barron *Surgeon-Major, Cape Mounted Riflemen, South African Forces*
5 June 1879 – During an attack on Morosi's Mountain, South Africa, he crossed open ground under severe enemy fire and carried Corporal Jones to safety. He continued to dress the wounds of other injured and bleeding men throughout the day.

FITZPATRICK, Francis *Private, 94th Regiment*
28 November 1879 – During an attack on Sekukuni's Town, South Africa, he, Private FLAWN and six men of the Native Contingent were carrying a wounded lieutenant. Suddenly, thirty of the enemy appeared in pursuit. The six men fled leaving Fitzpatrick and Flawn to alternate between carrying the lieutenant and firing into the pursuers. The wounded officer was brought to safety.

FLAWN, Thomas *Private, 94th Regiment*
28 November 1879 – During an attack on Sekukuni's Town, South Africa, he, Private FITZPATRICK and six men of the Native Contingent were carrying a wounded lieutenant. Suddenly, thirty of the enemy appeared in pursuit. The six men fled leaving Fitzpatrick and Flawn to alternate between carrying the lieutenant and firing into the pursuers. The wounded officer was brought to safety.

McCREA, John Frederick *Surgeon, 1st Cape Mounted Yeomanry, South African Forces*
14 January 1881 – During the action against the Basutos at Tweefontain, South Africa, an enemy charge resulted in 37 casualties. He was the only

doctor present, and despite incurring a serious chest wound, which he dressed himself, he attended to the wounded under a shower of bullets throughout the day.

THE SECOND NAGA HILLS EXPEDITION, INDIA (1879–80)

Although the control of the British Empire still held in most of India, the tribal people in the mountainous north were turbulent and resisted British rule. On 14 October 1879, the Naga people in the Eastern Bengal/Assam region of India had murdered a British commissioner and besieged the garrison at Kohima, so in December 1879 Brigadier General J. L. Nation led a punitive expedition to the Naga Hills to restore order. One column was sent to relieve the garrison and the second, including men of the Bengal Staff Corps and 44th Gurkha Rifles, under Nation's command, went to capture the Naga stronghold of Konoma, where Captain Richard Ridgeway earned the VC. The Nagas were eventually forced into submission in March 1880.

RIDGEWAY, Richard Kirby *Captain, Bengal Staff Corps and 44th Gurkha Rifles*
    22 November 1879 – During the attack on Konoma on the eastern frontier of India, he charged up to a barricade and attempted to tear down the planking surrounding it under very heavy fire. During this brave action, he was severely wounded in the shoulder.

THE FIRST BOER WAR (1880–81)

At the end of the Zulu War in 1879, Britain's High Commissioner had failed to deliver the desired federal dominion of British colonies and Boer republics. Tension between the British and the Boer farmers was mounting – Gladstone's government was not prepared to give back the Boer territory of the Transvaal which Britain had annexed, and Boer resentment was escalated further by the revenue-collecting activities of the Administrator of the Transvaal, Sir Owen Lanyon. This, with allegations of undisciplined behaviour by British troops in the Transvaal garrisons, drove the Boers to boiling point, and on 16 December 1880 they declared a republic. Four days later, a small column of 257 men of the 94th Regiment of Foot were ambushed at Bronkhorstspruit, en route to the garrison at Lydenburg – unprepared, the British lost 57 dead and over a hundred wounded and all the survivors were taken prisoner.
    There were just seven British garrisons in the Transvaal, and the Boers were quick to surround them. On 16 January the 94th Regiment and

Nourse's (Transvaal) Horse were engaged near the Boers' camp at Elands-fontein. The Boers' next strategic move was to cut off access to the Transvaal across the Drakensberg at Laing's Nek for the two thousand British troops based in Natal. On 28 January 1881, Major General Sir George Pomeroy Colley, who had succeeded Sir Garnet Wolseley as High Commissioner for South-East Africa on 24 April, ordered an assault on the Boer position at Laing's Nek which was repulsed, leaving 83 dead and 111 wounded. Reinforcements under Brigadier General Sir Evelyn Wood – a veteran of the Zulu War – were due, but Colley had to keep communications open with the base at Newcastle. He and his small column of three hundred men from the 60th Rifles was pinned down by just two hundred and fifty Boers at Ingogo, where the British suffered a hundred and fifty casualties.

These losses prompted Gladstone to try to open negotiations with the Boers. While waiting for a response to the proposed armistice, on 22 February forces at Wesselstroom including the 58th Regiment came under Boer attack and, there being no reply to Gladstone's overtures by the 26th, Colley went ahead with a move to outflank the Boers at Laing's Nek. His aim was to take the high ground of Majuba Hill, 2,500 feet above the Boer camp, and that night he sent 554 men to secure the summit. and it took them all night to scale the steep face of the extinct volcano. On reaching the top unopposed, Colley ignored recommendations to entrench; the following morning the Boers, taking advantage of their knowledge of the land and their mobility, scaled the hill under cover of fire from below. They easily overran the vulnerable British with a hail of rapid fire. Colley was killed at the start of the attack, the British lost 96 officers and men, with 132 wounded and 96 prisoners, and a VC was won as a few men put up a spirited resistance to cover the retreat from the summit.

Wood, now in command of the army in Natal, arrived with reinforce-ments on 4 March, and was immediately ordered to seek an armistice. He confirmed the right to self-government for Transvaal, and on 23 March, the Pretoria Convention was signed, granting the Boers independence under British Sovereignty. With 390 British dead and 502 wounded, the British could only retire licking their wounds with the shame of defeat.

DANAHER, John *Trooper, Nourse's (Transvaal) Horse, South African Forces*
16 January 1881 – At Elandsfontein, seeing two wounded men of the Royal Scots Fusiliers lying in the open, he and Lance Corporal MURRAY advanced towards them under brutal fire. On reaching them, Murray, by now wounded himself, ordered him to take his carbine and escape.

MURRAY, James *Lance Corporal, 2nd Bn., Connaught Rangers*
16 January 1881 – At Elandsfontein, seeing two wounded men lying in the open, he and Private DANAHER rode out to them under fire. Instantly, his horse was shot from under him but he continued on foot. On reaching the men, a bullet entered his right side, passing out near his spine. He

ordered Danaher to take his carbine and escape. He was taken prisoner but released the next day.

DOOGAN, John *Private, 1st Dragoon Guards*
28 January 1881 – At Laing's Nek, Major Brownlow was surrounded by the enemy during a charge. Seeing this, Doogan sprang from his horse and persuaded the major to take his mount. Doogan was twice wounded whilst performing this service.

HILL, Alan Richard (later HILL-WALKER) *Lieutenant, 2nd Bn., Northamptonshire Regiment*
28 January 1881 – At Laing's Nek, whilst hurrying to cover with a wounded comrade, Lieutenant Baillie, in his arms, a bullet struck and killed the lieutenant. Twice more he braved the open ground, each time rescuing a wounded man.

OSBORNE, James *Private, 2nd Bn., Northamptonshire Regiment*
22 February 1881 – At Wesselstroom, he galloped in the direction of a large force of Boers, picked up Private Mayes, who was lying wounded, and brought him back to camp under tremendous fire.

FARMER, Joseph John *Provisional Lance Corporal, Army Hospital Corps*
27 February 1881 – At Majuba Hill, he was helping a surgeon to dress the wounded when the Boers made their rush. He held up a white bandage, expecting the enemy to respect the fallen, but instead was shot through the wrist. The surgeon and the man being treated were also hit. He raised the bandage with his other arm and was instantly shot through that elbow. Lying in agony, he was injected with morphine by the mortally wounded surgeon.

SUDAN (1881–85)

In 1881 the political situation in Sudan was descending into chaos. The previous year, General Charles Gordon had resigned as Governor-General, and his successor, receiving no direction from the British-run government in Cairo, lost control. Soon the illegal slave trade returned, the army to whom the governor looked to keep order was woefully under-resourced, and the people were subjected to higher and higher taxes.

It was in this atmosphere of disorder and dissatisfaction that the self-styled Mahdi (or 'guide') gathered the support of Islamic fanatics and started a full-scale revolt in 1881. By the end of 1882, the Mahdi's forces controlled much of the country. In occupying Egypt, Britain had also taken on responsibility for Egyptian Sudan, and it became apparent that military action would have to be taken to suppress this revolt.

On 5 November 1883, at El Obeid, the Mahdists wiped out an Egyptian force of ten thousand men sent to restore order under Colonel William Hicks: only the uncommitted reserve of three hundred survived. Egyptian forces suffered another defeat when the Beja tribesmen (dubbed 'fuzzy-wuzzies' by the British for their extravagant hair) rose up in support of the Mahdi and, under the leadership of Osman Digna, captured most of the Red Sea garrisons. Then at El Teb on 4 February 1884 they annihilated the forces under General Valentine Baker sent to prevent the capture of the Red Sea port of Suakim. Admiral Sir William Hewett VC landed with a naval brigade of men from HMS *Decoy, Euryalus, Ranger* and *Sphinx* and defended it fiercely, preventing it from being overrun. Reinforcements then began to arrive from Aden and Egypt, and on 29 February, the Beja were defeated at El Teb by a force comprising three thousand men under Major General Gerald Graham VC and a naval brigade under Commander E. N. Rolfe.

In a form of battle unfamiliar to the Mahdists, the naval brigade formed up in a huge square and advanced steadily upon the enemy, who sent small parties out to attack – but found themselves shot down or bayoneted before they could strike. The attacks continued, however, the strongest being directed against the side of the square defended by Captain Wilson's men and their Gardner guns.

In a headlong rush, the Mahdists managed to force a gap in the square, and were followed by further troops, hoping to capitalize on this break to infiltrate the formation. Wilson took on the enemy single-handed, running the first man through with his sword, breaking it off at the hilt so it was useless. Unarmed and using just his fists, Wilson kept up a furious whirlwind and managed to hold the enemy off until reinforcements came to his aid and the square was re-formed. Amazingly, he was only very slightly wounded during this furious onslaught.

MARSHALL, William Thomas *Quartermaster Sergeant, 19th Hussars*
29 February 1884 – During the charge of the cavalry at El Teb, he stayed close by the wounded and the unhorsed Lieutenant Colonel Barrow, seizing his hand and dragging him through the midst of the enemy back to the regiment.

WILSON, Arthur Knyvet *Captain, Royal Navy (Naval Brigade)*
29 February 1884 – During the advance on El Teb, he attached himself to the naval brigade (ostensibly as a spectator – he later explained that he had nothing else to do that day) and marched on the enemy's Krupp battery. Whilst attacking an Arab spearman, his sword stuck in the man's ribs and snapped in two. He fought on with his fists and received a sword slash to the head before he was relieved by men of the York and Lancashire Regiment.
He was an early advocate of the torpedo but a committed opponent of the submarine, describing it as 'a damned un-English weapon'. Admiral of the Fleet (1907) and First Sea Lord (1909–12).

The Beja were further defeated at Tamai on 13 March (when VCs were earned by Lieutenant Sir Percival Marling and Private Thomas Edwards), but instead of pressing home their advantage, the British troops withdrew to Suakim on the orders of Sir Evelyn Baring, in command of the army, who had instructions from London to insist on evacuation. The force was pulled out in April and May and the rebels were allowed to regroup.

In the meantime, the former Governor-General of Sudan, General Gordon, arrived back in Khartoum on 18 February 1884 under orders to evacuate Egyptian garrisons and civilians from Sudan. He evacuated some two thousand women, children, sick and wounded, but after his candidate for the governor of the country was rejected by London on the grounds that he was a notorious slave trader, opted to stay and defend the city. The Mahdists' siege began on 13 March. In April, Gordon stated that he had five months' provisions, but it was not until October that Sir Garnet Wolseley's relief column left Cairo, in the belief that Gordon could hold out until 15 November. Part of this relief mission, under Sir William Butler, travelled by specially constructed whale boats up the Nile; the other half, a camel corps and naval brigade under Brigadier General Sir Herbert Stewart, set out across dangerous desert terrain directly towards Metemma, only 100 miles to Khartoum, intending to bypass the Fifth Cataract of the Nile. This Desert Column, of eighteen hundred men, came under attack by ten thousand of the Mahdi's troops at Abu Klea on 17 January 1885, and there ensued what Winston Churchill later described as 'the most savage and bloody action fought in the Sudan by British troops', during which Gunner Albert Smith earned the VC. British casualties were 168 killed and wounded.

The Desert Column, now under General Sir Charles Wilson (Stewart had been fatally wounded in action on the 19th), reached the Nile, where on 21 January steamers sent north by Gordon from Khartoum joined him. Wilson waited three days to take care of his wounded and establish his defence before setting off with two of the steamers. He arrived with 20 soldiers and 280 Sudanese on the 28th – but too late. On 26 January the city had fallen, and Gordon had been killed.

On 1 February, Wilson's two steamers were found wrecked on the river just outside the city and he and his men were holed up on an island in the river, in danger of imminent attack by several thousand Mahdist troops on the opposite bank. A day later, a naval brigade from the steamer *Safieh* under command of Admiral Beresford, set out to rescue Wilson, but were delayed by damage to the ship's boiler from enemy fire, and it did not reach them until the 4th. So it was that Major General Redvers Buller VC was sent to oversee the withdrawal of Wilson's men towards Korti.

Fighting continued through February, when on the 10th, the River Column under Major General W. Earle, which had followed the course of the Nile, drove the Sudanese from near Kirbekan. Although casualties were few,

Earle was killed. Back at Suakim, Lieutenant General Graham had landed with thirteen thousand men, to lay a railway to link the port with Berber, 280 miles away on the Nile, and then systematically retake control of Sudan. They moved out on 20 March in a defensive square formation against the threatened Beja attack, but it was Major General Sir John McNeill's force, leaving Suakim two days later, which came under attack at Tofrek. The Royal Marines, the Berkshire Regiment and the 15th Sikhs were successful in beating off this attack, and the railway advanced to Otao – but these four years of bitter fighting and the many lives lost would be in vain. A Russian incursion into Afghanistan, exaggerated in London into a full-scale invasion threat, required the troops from the Sudan, and withdrawal was ordered on 11 May. On 17 May, British troops were withdrawn from Sudan, the Mahdi died on 22 June, and the Mahdists were left to set up their new government.

EDWARDS, Thomas *Private, 1st Bn., Royal Highlanders*
    13 March 1884 – At Tamaii, he was with No. 4 gun in charge of two mules loaded with Gatling ammunition. When the gun was attacked by a large enemy force, he bayoneted two Arabs and shot another who had just cut through the arm of a lieutenant. Soon outnumbered, he was wounded in the hand and forced to retreat.

MARLING, Sir Percival Scrope *Lieutenant, King's Royal Rifle Corps, attached Mounted Infantry*
    13 March 1884 – At Tamaii, under terrific fire, he lifted the wounded Private Morley into the saddle in front of him. The private immediately fell off so he dismounted and carried him 80 yards to safety.

SMITH, Alfred *Gunner, Royal Artillery*
    17 January 1885 – When an assailant ran at Lieutenant Guthrie with a spear at Abu Klea, Smith warded off the blow with a handspike. In the ensuing struggle, the assailant managed to stab the lieutenant in the leg with a long knife. Smith forced the handspike into his foe and killed him. Lieutenant Guthrie died a few days later.

THE OCCUPATION OF EGYPT (1882)

By the late 1800s Egypt had suffered almost a century of misgovernment. Control had been returned to Turkey in 1801 after Napoleon had been driven out, so the country was part of the Ottoman Empire. The Sultan forbade the Khedive (the viceroy) to impose taxes or contract loans in Egypt – a policy which spelled financial disaster – but with the opening of the Suez Canal in 1869, influence in Egypt took on a new significance and Disraeli's government was quick to buy up the Khedive's shares in the canal in 1875. By 1878, Egypt was virtually bankrupt and, to protect their interests in the canal, England and France took joint control of Egypt's finances, effectively running the country.

Nationalist feeling in Egypt ran high against the Khedive for allowing this and in May 1882, the Egyptian Minister of War, Colonel Ahmed Arabi, led a revolt against this interference in the country's affairs. When the Khedive tried to dismiss Arabi in June, rioting broke out in Alexandria, and over 50 Europeans were killed. Despite British protests, Arabi continued to fortify the forts guarding the harbour at Alexandria, so Admiral Seymour, who led the British element of the joint Anglo-French squadron moored offshore, threatened to bombard the city and harbour. At this point, the French withdrew, relinquishing their interest in Egypt's affairs. On 11 July the British bombarded Alexandria for over ten hours (during which Gunner Israel Harding earned the VC), then withdrew. Overnight rioters set fire to the city and freed prisoners looted and murdered unchecked. By the following morning a white flag flew over Alexandria and a force of marines landed to accept the surrender. Arabi and his rebel army were still at large, however.

Skirmishes continued while the British waited for reinforcements – Arabi's forces attacked a reconnaissance group at Kafr Dowar on 5 August, when a VC was awarded to Private Frederick Corbett of the King's Royal Rifle Corps. On 15 August, Lieutenant General Sir Garnet Wolseley landed at Alexandria and immediately sent contingents to take control of Port Said and the canal itself. With access routes to Egypt secured, Wolseley sent troops to drive rebels from Mukfar, where sabotage activities threatened to cut the fresh-water supply between Ismailia and Cairo. These rebels were pursued to Kassassin, where they were defeated on 26 August by troops who then held the town despite continued heavy attacks.

During the night of 12/13 September, Wolseley's force of 17,400 attacked the fortifications at Tel-el-Kebir, held by forty thousand Egyptians with seventy guns – when a VC was earned by Lieutenant William Edwards – and two hours' fighting produced a resounding victory with only 469 British casualties. Wolseley went straight on to Cairo the next day to accept Arabi's surrender. The Khedive was restored to power, but a British presence remained to oversee Egypt's return to financial stability.

HARDING, Israel *Gunner, Royal Navy*

11 July 1882 – Eight Royal Navy ships were bombarding Alexandria, but were themselves under fire from the shore. A 10in shell penetrated the side of HMS *Alexandra* and rolled along the deck, near the magazine. Hearing screams, he dashed up from below, seized the hot shell and plunged it into a tub full of water. His actions undoubtedly saved many lives.

He served in minesweepers during the First World War, although aged over eighty.

CORBETT, Frederick *Private, 3rd Bn., King's Royal Rifle Corps*

5 August 1882 – During the reconnaissance of Kafr Dowar, his officer, Lieutenant Howard-Vyse, was struck and mortally wounded. He stayed by him attempting to stem the flow of blood until relieved. All the while, he was subject to fierce fire.

His name was erased from the VC Roll and his medal confiscated after his conviction for embezzlement and theft from an officer in 1884. His name was restored to the register after his death.

EDWARDS, William Mordaunt Marsh *Lieutenant, 2nd Bn., Highland Light Infantry*

13 September 1882 – At Tel-el-Kebir, whilst leading an attack on a redoubt, he charged ahead of his men and dashed alone into the enemy battery, killing the officer in charge. He was knocked down and about to be killed by an Egyptian gunner when three of his men arrived, saving his life.

THE CHIN FIELD FORCE (1889) AND THE KAREN-NI EXPEDITION (1888–89)

Following the British victory in the Third Anglo-Burmese war, many native Burmese refused to accept the authority of the British army of occupation, and resorted to guerrilla action. The guerrillas were led mainly by former officers of the disbanded Burmese royal army, village headmen and even royal princes. To the British they were not patriots but rebels and bandits, and their measures to suppress the rebel activity were severe and ruthless. Even those who aided the rebels were punished and British troops were responsible for many atrocities, including mass executions. The British adopted a punitive strategy: families of the village headmen were packed off to the secure territory of Lower Burma and their villages were burned, then new villages, led by strangers loyal to the British cause, were established. The guerrilla troops targeted these new villages, and by 1890 more than three thousand British troops were involved in the battle to maintain order and suppress the rebels' activities. On 1 January 1889, the Karene Field Force engaged the rebels at Lwekaw in the eastern Karenni region, where the bravery of Surgeon John Crimmin was recognized with the VC, and again on 4 May, at the village of Tartan, Surgeon Ferdinand Le Quesne of the Chin Field Force earned the VC. Action against the Chin rebels continued when 3,500 men were sent to avenge raids in the Chin and Lushai areas on 15 November 1889, and eventually only sheer weight of numbers brought the military struggle to a close.

CRIMMIN, John *Surgeon, Bombay Medical Service*

1 January 1889 – Whilst attending a wounded man at Lwekaw in the midst of a skirmish with bullets flying around him, he was attacked by several of the enemy. Jumping up, he ran his sword through one assailant and engaged boldly with another causing them to flee into the bush.

LE QUESNE, Ferdinand Simeon *Surgeon, Medical Staff*

4 May 1889 – During the attack on the village of Tartan, he dressed the wounds of a mortally wounded officer for ten minutes, five yards from the loopholes of the enemy's stockade from which a steady fire poured. He was later wounded whilst dressing the wounds of another officer.

THE MANIPUR EXPEDITION (1891)

Tucked between Assam and Burma on India's north-east frontier was the small hill state of Manipur, cut off from India by mountains, jungle and rivers. In September 1890, the Raja of Manipur was ousted in a palace coup and the British government in India saw this as a rebellion. In March 1891, they sent the Chief Commissioner in Assam, James Wallace Quinton, with a force of Gurkhas under the command of Lieutenant Colonel Charles Skene, to the capital Imphal to settle the uprising and banish the Commander-in-Chief of the Manipuri army, the Sennaputti, who had engineered the coup. On 24 March, after refusing to be arrested, the Sennaputti drove off Skene's men, inflicting considerable casualties, and bombarded the British Residency. Along with Britain's political agent in Manipur, Frank St Clair Grimmond, Skene and Quinton went to the palace to parley – and on leaving were seized and beheaded.

Of Skene's men, three hundred Gurkhas remained to fight on, fifty were taken prisoner and thirty-five broke out of Imphal. Some troops, and some wounded, were led out through the jungle into the mountains towards British territory in Assam by Grimmond's young widow, Ethel.

On 27 March, in the Burmese village station of Tammu, a young British officer, Lieutenant Charles Grant of the 12th Madras Infantry, heard of the rebellion in Manipur and set out with a group of 80 Punjabi and Gurkha troops across the mountains to come to Skene's aid (news of his death had not yet reached the nearby areas). Only after a short but fierce engagement with Manipuri troops at Palel did Grant learn from prisoners that the three men had been killed. Believing Skene's troops to be besieged, he continued towards Imphal and his men stormed and held Thobal near Manipur from 21 March to 9 April when he was finally relieved. Grant was later awarded the VC for the action at Thobal.

At the end of April, three columns under Major General Thomas Graham set out for Manipur – of which only the Tammu column saw action. On arriving at the palace, Graham found it deserted. A thorough search found the Sennaputti disguised as a coolie, and he was duly tried and publicly hanged. Ethel Grimmond, dubbed 'the Heroine of Manipur', was awarded the Royal Red Cross and given a pension for life – the men who escaped with her, however, were court-martialled.

GRANT, Charles James William *Lieutenant, Indian Staff Corps*
21 March to 9 April 1891 – After the massacre at Manipur, he marched day and night through northern Burma to relieve the survivors at Thobal. He held the place for ten days despite receiving a bullet through the root of his neck which carried part of his shirt and uniform collar through his neck and out the other side.

THE HUNZA-NAGA EXPEDITION (1891)

Late in 1891, following tribal unrest, an expedition was sent to the mountainous Hunza-Naga region in north-eastern India to storm the fort at Nilt and restore order. The thousand-strong expedition, consisting mainly of Kashmir Imperial Service troops with 16 British officers, arrived at the fort on 2 December, and found it protected on three sides by precipices. The only approach to the gate was blocked by a rampart of felled trees. Since it was impossible to drag mountain guns up the surrounding cliffs, the storming party had to rely on rifle fire to cover their advance towards the gate in order to set explosive charges. Captain Fenton Aylmer and Lieutenant Guy Boisragon, who led the assault, were awarded VCs for their actions, which ensured its capture. On 20 December, near the Nilt fort, Lieutenant John Smith was also awarded the VC for his bravery in storming an enemy position while under constant attack. Having achieved the capture of enemy strongholds, the expedition effectively ended the localized unrest.

AYLMER, Fenton John *Captain, Royal Engineers*
2 December 1891 – During the assault on Nilt fort, whilst forcing the Inner Gate open with gun cotton, he was shot in the leg and wounded in the hand by a rock dropped from above. Nevertheless, he dashed through and engaged the enemy hand-to-hand, killing several, until he collapsed from loss of blood.

BOISRAGON, Guy Hudleston *Lieutenant, Indian Staff Corps and*
5th Gurkha Rifles
2 December 1891 – After the Gurkhas had cut through the defensive scrub protecting the Nilt fort, he led the assault on the Outer Gate. Finding his force insufficient, he went back under a heavy cross-fire to collect more men to relieve the first party. His actions ensured that the fort was taken.

SMITH, John Manners *Lieutenant, Indian Staff Corps and 5th Gurkha Rifles*
20 December 1891 – At Nilt, he led his small party up a precipitous cliff in an attack on a strong enemy position which had barred any advance for

seventeen days. Avoiding rocks dropped from above, the summit was reached and he charged his men at the enemy, shooting the first tribesman himself. The position was successfully taken.

THE SECOND GAMBIA EXPEDITION (1892)

Early in 1891, a party from the Anglo-French Boundary Commission was attacked by tribesmen led by the local chief, Fodeh Cabbah, and several of the group were wounded. HMS *Alecto* was joined by a gunboat at Kansa on the Gambia River, and a landing party went ashore. This situation was defused when a local chief, hearing of the shore expedition, came to meet them and apologized. The men returned to their ships, but Fodeh Cabbah continued to cause trouble. Evading an expedition sent to capture him, he escaped on horseback into French territory. The naval brigade proceeded to burn down any towns and villages considered to be Fodeh Cabbah's strongholds and established a small entrenched post at Kaling, garrisoned by some 60 men of the West India Regiment.

The garrison remained into 1892, and during ensuing engagements against Fodeh Cabbah's men more villages were destroyed. Notably, on 13 March at Toniatabe, in an action to break down the town gates, Lance Corporal William Gordon of the West India Regiment earned the VC.

As a punitive campaign, this was not a success, as Foteh Cabbah's men retreated into French territory where the British were unable to follow them.

GORDON, William James *Lance Corporal, West India Regiment*
13 March 1892 – At Toniatabe, West Africa, he was one of a party of twelve men under Major Madden attempting to break down the south gate of the town with a battering ram. Several musket barrels were pushed through loopholes in the walls and aimed at the major whilst his back was turned. Gordon called, 'Look out!' and flung himself between the officer and the guns as they were fired. Gordon was shot through the lungs, Madden was unhurt.

THE KACHIN HILLS EXPEDITION, BURMA (1892–93)

During the later 1880s, British and Indian troops were deployed throughout the separate operational zones of Burma to control the rebellious border bandits, or 'dacoits', who rose up against the British presence in their territory. By 1891 the northern area of Burma held by Britain was largely under control, but the Kachin tribe continued to cause trouble, plundering caravans travelling through the region and preying on travellers. On 28 December 1885, a British force moved in to occupy the Bhamo region in the

Kachin Hills of Upper Burma. The Kachin people resisted British annexation fiercely and the military police were constantly called on to quell uprisings and restore peace. In December 1892, the Kachins attacked a military police column en route to establish a post at Fort Sima, and simultaneously launched a raid on the town of Myitkyna. An expedition of British and mixed forces was sent to put down the uprising, during which campaign, at Fort Sima on 6 January, Surgeon-Major Owen Lloyd earned the VC. The Kachins were finally defeated at Palap after a short campaign during which 3 officers were killed and 102 sepoys and followers were killed or wounded.

LLOYD, Owen Edward Pennefather *Surgeon-Major, Army Medical Service*
   6 January 1893 – At Fort Sima, he ran to the assistance of the mortally wounded Captain Morton and treated his wounds although the enemy were less than 15 paces away and firing heavily. He was himself wounded whilst returning to the fort.

THE NORTH-WEST FRONTIER (1895)

In 1889 the British entered the Chitral district of what is now northernmost Pakistan and established an agency, to which the local tribesmen remained very hostile. In January 1895, the Chitrali chief was overthrown and murdered, and this signalled the start of fighting amongst local tribes. When Umrah Khan, ruler of the Narai district, invaded Chitral, Britain's political agent in Gilgit, Surgeon-Major George Robertson, arrived with four hundred men to occupy the Chitral Fort. Umrah Khan joined forces with the Pathan chief Sher Afzal to remove the British from Chitral.

   The British garrison at the Chitral fort amounted to just 419 fighting men when, on 3 March, Afzal arrived with around four thousand men and took up positions around the fort. A recce party went out from the fort and suffered heavy casualties before making a difficult retreat: during the sortie Surgeon-Captain Harry Whitchurch earned the VC. They remained under siege until 19 April, when a small force under command of Lieutenant Colonel James Kelly drove the Chitralis back, and the main relief party, fifteen thousand men led by Major General Sir Robert Low, seized Afzal. A new British-backed chief, Shuja-ul-Mulk, was confirmed as ruler and a British garrison was established at Chitral to keep the peace.

WHITCHURCH, Harry Frederick *Surgeon-Captain, Indian Medical Service*
   3 March 1895 – He carried the wounded Captain Baird three miles to Chitral fort under heavy fire from the enemy. Several times he was forced to lay the captain down to mount a charge on the enemy. Just as he reached the fort the captain was shot in the face, dying the next day.

THE MATABELELAND REBELLION (1896)

In 1895, all the territories subject to the British South Africa Company were drawn together under the new name of Rhodesia, after the company's leading spirit, Cecil Rhodes. By the end of March 1896, conditions for the Matabele people in the new Rhodesia drove them to rise up in rebellion. A VC was awarded to Trooper Herbert Henderson following an ambush by Matabele tribesmen at Campbell's Store. The uprising continued as, driven to desperation by the death of their cattle from disease, and enslaved by forced labour on the settlers' farms and in mines, their witch doctors incited them to take action, and they murdered all the men and women on the outlying farms. In a further Matabele attack on 22 April, during which a small group was surrounded near Bulawayo, a VC was awarded to Trooper Frank Baxter

The BSAC could not keep control, so a relief force – the Bulawayo Field Force – was raised, comprising one group under Major Herbert Plumer, which entered the chief town of Bulawayo in May, and additional imperial troops under Sir Frederick Carrington, who joined Plumer's men in June. Notably, in this latter force, Baden-Powell – who later founded the Boy Scout movement – was the chief of staff, and it was his prowess in scouting out and spying on the enemy that was responsible for much of its success. The Matabele tribesmen worked in small groups, using their knowledge of the terrain to set up mountain strongholds from which to carry out raids and ambushes, and the campaign was one of small encounters, which were finally brought to an end when Baden-Powell's chief native scout, Jan Grootboom, managed to get the Matabele chiefs to attend a parley with Cecil Rhodes. It took months to bring the whole region under control, and it was not until early 1897 that Baden-Powell was able to leave Africa to return home.

HENDERSON, Herbert Stephen *Trooper, Bulawayo Field Force, attached Rhodesian Horse, South African Forces*

30 March 1896 – At Campbell's Store, having been caught in an ambush by the Matebele, he lifted the wounded Trooper Celliers onto his horse and led him 35 miles to Bulawayo, hiding by day and travelling at night. They arrived three days later having eaten only a few plums on the way. Celliers died two months later of his wounds.

BAXTER, Frank William *Trooper, Bulawayo Field Force, South African Forces*

22 April 1896 – Whilst surrounded by Matebele near Bulawayo, he selflessly gave his horse to the wounded Trooper Wise who galloped away to safety. As the enemy approached Baxter, three comrades rode past and tried to lift him to safety, but they all failed and he was killed moments later.

THE MASHONA REBELLION, RHODESIA (1896–97)

Anti-colonial feeling among the tribal peoples of the newly created state of Rhodesia had long run high, but in June 1896, the Mashona tribe were fired to revolt by their spirit mediums, who convinced them that they would be impervious to bullets.

The main action of the revolt centred around the Alice Mine in the Mazoe Valley, where a group of Mashona surrounded the miners and their families. On 17 June, the Chief Inspector of the Chartered Company's Telegraphs organized and led a party from Salisbury to rescue the miners, but it was on the 19th that a second party, led by Captain R. C. Nesbitt, joined the rescue mission to bring the miners and their families to safety, for which he was awarded the VC.

NESBITT, Randolph Cosby *Captain, Mashonaland Mounted Police, South African Forces*
19 June 1896 – He set out with thirteen men to relieve the Alice Mine, which was surrounded by hordes of rebels. They reached the miners and brought them out despite the enemy creeping through the long grass and firing from close range. Only three men were killed and five wounded during the action.

THE NORTH-WEST FRONTIER WAR (1897–98)

In 1894, Colonel Sir Mortimer Durand's commission finalized the demarcation of new frontiers between India and Afghanistan, thereby bringing many frontier tribes into the British sphere of influence. These tribesmen were extremely hostile to this annexation and there was widespread unrest. Anti-British feeling was already running high when, in 1897, the Amir of Afghanistan (only superficially pro-British) published a fiercely anti-Christian religious work in his assumed capacity of the King of Islam. This provoked a warlike spirit among the border Muslims, inciting uprisings against the British garrisons all along the frontier. Furthermore, since Britain had backed Greece in her recent war against Turkey, the Turkish sultan took revenge by sending agents to Afghanistan to spread word that Britain's empire was crumbling and that there would be no troops available to contain an uprising in the frontier region. This coincided with the retirement of Colonel Robert Warburton as political officer in the Khyber Pass. The son of an Afghan mother, he was fluent in Persian and Pushtu and was well respected by the tribesmen – and although he had set up the Khyber Rifles to man the forts along the pass, it was his personal influence which maintained the tenuous peace.

On 26 July 1897, the garrison at Malakand in the Swat Valley was alerted to an imminent attack across the border by Swati tribesmen led bythe so-called 'Mad Mullah'. The garrison commander ordered a force to leave the garrison and secure the Amandra Pass five miles to the north, but they were delayed and never left. Word soon came from the Chakandra Fort, near the pass, that the Mullah and his horde were approaching Malakand. Although there was a fort at Malakand, many men were camped outside, so when the alarm sounded, Lieutenant Colonel McRae and Major Taylor led out a party of Sikhs to a narrow defile where, despite Taylor being killed, they prevented the enemy from surrounding the camp and cutting it off from the fort. For his bravery on the first day of the Malakand attack, Lieutenant Edmond Costello was awarded the VC. The garrison held out against day and night attacks from 26 to 30 July, finally scattering the tribesmen with a bayonet charge on the night of the 30th. The Chakdara garrison also saw action – an estimated two thousand tribesmen were killed there for the loss of five dead and ten wounded in fighting which lasted until 2 August. A punitive expedition of three brigades led by Brigadier General Sir Bindon Blood arrived to reinforce the garrisons on 31 July and remained in the region, quelling tribal unrest until late October.

COSTELLO, Edmond William *Lieutenant, 22nd Punjab Infantry*
26 July 1897 – At Malakand, he saved the life of a wounded lance halvidar lying 60 yards away on a football field. The field was swarming with the enemy's swordsmen and raked with rifle fire.

On 8 August 1897, Mohmand tribesmen raided Shabkadar near Peshawar, but the means to quash this uprising was already in the region. Two divisions of Sir Bindon Blood's expedition had advanced from Malakand to meet up at Bajour with another division under Major General Edmund Elles from Peshawar.

Blood's men reached Nawagai on 14 September, having detached a brigade to cross the Rambat Pass. These men were attacked in their camp the same night, but advanced the next day to deal with the rebel tribes in the Mohmand Valley. A further three columns under Brigadier General Jeffreys moved up the valley on 16 September, and met with fierce opposition. It was here that Lieutenant James Colvin, Corporal James Smith and Lieutenant Thomas Watson earned their VCs in an action to hold a small group of buildings at Bilot as Jeffreys retired.

At Nawagai, Blood's troops came under heavy attack from four thousand men led by Hadda Mullah, but although sustaining losses, he was able to link up with Elles, dispatching him to deal with the Upper Mohmands. Elles' well-conducted operation brought the Mohmand uprising to a close – one of a number of short campaigns to be fought in the frontier area.

COLVIN, James Morris Colquhoun *Lieutenant, Royal Engineers*
16 September 1897 – In the Mohmand Valley, he took part in a bayonet rush on the burning village of Bilot. After Lieutenant WATSON was injured, he continued to lead the men in two more attempts to clear the enemy from the village. His conduct was brave and his devotion to his men most noticeable.

SMITH, James *Corporal, East Kent Regiment*
16 September 1897 – In the Mohmand Valley, he took part in a bayonet rush on the burning village of Bilot. Although himself injured, he assisted in removing the wounded to shelter. When placed in charge of the men, he behaved with exemplary courage, standing fully exposed in order to watch the enemy.
His VC was not granted until seventeen months after the action and only after the matter had been raised in Parliament.

WATSON, Thomas Colclough *Lieutenant, Royal Engineers*
16 September 1897 – In the Mohmand Valley, he led a party of volunteers in a bayonet rush on the burning village of Bilot. Although his hand had been smashed by a bullet, he made two gallant attempts to dislodge the enemy from the village. He did not desist in his efforts until so severely wounded that he had to be carried back to the entrenchment.

In the spate of individual tribal uprisings by Afghanis against the British, fighting broke out at Nawah Kili in the Swat Valley on 17 August – where, in rescuing a war correspondent, VCs were earned by Brevet Lieutenant Colonel Robert Adams, Lieutenant Alexander Fincastle and Lieutenant Hector MacLean. On 25 August 1897, Pathan Afridi tribesmen succeeded in taking control of the Khyber Pass. By the end of 1897, three field forces were needed to control the north-west frontier, and the authorities in Simla issued an order at the end of September that the Khyber Pass must be retaken.

The Afridis were the largest and most aggressive of the frontier tribes – fine fighters who were well armed with long-range breech-loading rifles. Their neighbours in the Kohat and Khyber passes and the Tirah area, to the south-west of the Peshawar Valley, were the Orakzais, and although less warlike, they were willing to join them to regain their homeland. The Tirah was an oval-shaped plain of some 900 square miles – jealously guarded by the Afridis, and never ventured into before by Europeans because of the almost impassable mountains which bordered it.

As Lieutenant General Sir William Lockhart's thirty-five-thousand-strong Tirah Expeditionary Force set out, it was notionally the best-equipped yet in the frontier conflict. His plan was to enter the Tirah before the first snows, cross the Samana Range which bordered it to the south and subdue the Afridis and their allies by the end of December.

On 18 October, Lockhart's men stormed the cliffs leading to the strategically important Dargai Heights – but having insufficient supplies, they withdrew. The Afridis reclaimed the position and it was not until 20 October, when supplies arrived, that another attack was made to regain the Heights. The well-armed Afridis fired at will on the exposed attackers, causing devastating casualties, but the heights were retaken – and VCs were earned by Private Edward Lawson, Lieutenant Henry Pennell, Private Samuel Vickery and Piper George Findlater.

On eventually reaching the Tirah plain, the Expeditionary Force found the villages deserted, so Lockhart summoned the chiefs of the tribes to meet with him to discuss the terms of their surrender. No one appeared, and instead, the Afridi warriors embarked on a guerrilla campaign of sniping and ambushing. In retaliation, Lockhart's men were ordered to raze the Tirah villages to the ground – only mosques remained untouched. As the harsh winter approached, the Orakzais were driven to surrender – but the Afridis remained defiant, their hatred of the British more intense than ever.

The Khyber was still not reclaimed, and on 9 December, to avoid being trapped in the Tirah for the winter, Lockhart started a withdrawal in bitter weather. Freezing and without winter shelter, the columns had to bivouac by night around guttering camp fires and were subjected to constant night attacks over the five-day journey. However, despite heavy casualties, the columns reached familiar territory and, carrying out a scorched-earth campaign, began to gain the upper hand. By the early spring of 1898, the Khyber Pass was retaken; the Afridis had had enough and gave up the fight for their homeland.

Although the Tirah campaign proper started with Lockhart's punitive expedition, an action at Nawah Kili on 17 August 1897 in which three VCs were earned is considered to be part of this overall campaign.

ADAMS, Robert Bellew *Bt/Lieutenant Colonel, Staff Corps and Corps of Guides*

17 August 1897 – At Nawah Kili during the Tirah Campaign, Lieutenant Greaves (correspondent for the *Times of India*) fell from his pony and was set on by the enemy with tulwars and knives. Lieutenant Colonel Adams (together with Lieutenant FINCASTLE, Lieutenant MACLEAN and five guides) dashed to his aid. The enemy was driven away and Adams held them off whilst Fincastle and MacLean attempted to move Greaves. In the ensuing chaos, Greaves was killed by a second bullet and MacLean also received a mortal wound.

FINCASTLE, Alexander Edward Murray, Viscount *Lieutenant, 16th Lancers*

17 August 1897 – At Nawah Kili during the Tirah Campaign, Lieutenant Greaves (correspondent for the *Times of India*) fell from his pony and was set on by the enemy with tulwars and knives. Lieutenant Fincastle (together with Lieutenant Colonel ADAMS, Lieutenant MACLEAN and five guides) dashed to his aid. The enemy was driven away and Adams held them off whilst Fincastle and MacLean attempted to move Greaves. In the ensuing chaos, Greaves was killed by a second bullet and MacLean also received a mortal wound.

Fincastle was acting as a war correspondent himself.

MACLEAN, Hector Lachlan Stewart *Lieutenant, Staff Corps and Corps of Guides*

17 August 1897 – At Nawah Kili during the Tirah Campaign, Lieutenant Greaves (correspondent for the *Times of India*) fell from his pony and was set on by the enemy with tulwars and knives. Lieutenant MacLean (together with Colonel ADAMS, Lieutenant FINCASTLE and five guides) dashed to his aid. The enemy was driven away and Adams held them off whilst Fincastle and MacLean attempted to move Greaves. In the ensuing chaos, Greaves was killed by a second bullet and MacLean also received a mortal wound.

LAWSON, Edward *Private, 1st Bn., Gordon Highlanders*

20 October 1897 – At the attack on the Dargai Heights, during the Tirah Campaign, he carried Lieutenant Dingwall out of danger and then ran back to pick up Private MacMillan. He was under severe fire all the while and was himself twice wounded.

PENNELL, Henry Singleton *Lieutenant, 2nd Bn., Derbyshire Regiment*

20 October 1897 – At the attack on the Dargai Heights, during the Tirah Campaign, he ran to the wounded Captain Smith and twice attempted to carry him into shelter under a terrific hail of bullets. He only ceased in his efforts on finding that the officer was dead.

FINDLATER, George *Piper, 2nd Bn., Gordon Highlanders*

As a piper in the Gordon Highlanders, George Findlater's duty was to lead the men of his regiment into an attack, playing stirring and emotive songs on the bagpipes. During the assault on the Heights of Dargai in the Tirah campaign, he carried out this role so courageously that on his return to Britain he was contracted by the music halls to reenact his actions nightly on the stage. In doing so, he fell foul of the stuffy military establishment but he nevertheless came to be regarded as the epitome of the fearless piper.

Findlater was born on 16 February 1872 at Forgue near Huntly in Aberdeenshire. At the age of sixteen (and against the wishes of his parents) he enlisted in 2nd Battalion Gordon Highlanders. Almost at once, he began learning to play the bagpipes. In 1896, he was promoted to the rank of piper in the regimental band. In 1897, a force of thirty thousand men was sent to the Tirah province of India (nowadays part of Pakistan) to deal with a revolt by Afridi tribesmen. The British commander's intention had been to advance on the tribesmen through the Chagru valley, but army working parties were spotted preparing a mountain road and the tribesmen moved quickly to occupy the village of Dargai and block the intended advance. The British launched a series of attacks on Dargai, but the tribesmen's position on well-defended high ground was so strong that each attack failed. The Gurkhas, the Dorsetshire Regiment and the Derbyshire Regiment all suffered heavy casualties in the attacks. The tribesmen were seen waving standards and beating drums, believing victory to have been achieved. At this point, the Gordon Highlanders advanced. The Gordon Highlander's Pipe Major was busy bringing up reserve ammunition, so Lance Corporal Piper Milne and Pipers Findlater, Fraser, Wills, Walker and Kidd led the men into action.

Findlater recalled the event: 'I remember the Colonel addressing the regiment, telling them what they were expected to do. I remember the order for the regiment to attack, and the order "Pipers to the front". I am told that the "Cock of the North" was the tune ordered to be played, but I didn't hear the order, and using my own judgement I thought that the charge would be better led by a quick strathspey, so I struck up "The Haughs o' Cromdale". The "Cock o' the North" is more of a march tune and the effort we had to make was a rush and a charge. The battle fever had taken hold of us and we thought not of what the other was feeling. Our whole interest being centred in self. Social positions were not thought of, and officers and men went forward with eagerness shoulder to shoulder.' Men including Milne began falling all around Findlater. Soon, he too was hit: 'I got about half across when I was struck on the left foot, but as the bullet only grazed my toes that did not matter. Then a stray shot broke my chanter ... (it did not stop my playing) because the break did not make it impossible to play. I had not gone much further when a third bullet went through my right ankle. I could not stand. My leg went under me, and as a result my pipes slid off my shoulder. But I managed to keep on playing to cheer on the other fellows. I got my back against a stone, and that helped me wonderfully.' As Findlater played on, the men poured forward, reaching the top and overcoming the tribesmen, who began retreating. By mid-afternoon the position was won. Findlater was subsequently recommended for the Victoria Cross by Major General Yeatman-Biggs.

Findlater returned invalided home to Scotland to find that news of his exploits had turned him into something of a celebrity. Indeed, he soon found that he could earn good money by appearing in music halls, but his unusual act was soon brought to a halt by the military authorities, who declared sniffily that it was 'repugnant to military feeling that an exhibition should be made at a music hall of a soldier who had so recently been decorated by the Queen'. This attitude not only smacked of snobbery, it failed to consider the fact that Findlater might now possess a Victoria Cross but he had no income and no obvious means of obtaining one. The outraged public reaction caused by Findlater's treatment forced the government to substantially increase the pensions given to soldiers decorated for bravery.

Findlater settled in Mountlairy, Banffshire. In 1899, he married his cousin Nellie Findlater, the daughter of his father's brother. In the following year, he took a holding in Forglen and began life as a farmer. When the

Great War broke out in 1914, he volunteered to join the Gordon Highlanders once again. He went to France with his battalion in 1915 but was wounded at Loos and was again invalided out of the army. He continued farming until his death in March 1942, aged seventy.

VICKERY, Samuel *Private, 1st Bn., Dorsetshire Regiment*
20 October 1897 – At the attack on the Dargai Heights during the Tirah Campaign, he ran down the slope under severe fire and carried a wounded comrade to shelter. *16 November 1897* – In the Waran Valley, he killed three men who had attacked him after he had become separated from his company.

THE SUDAN CAMPAIGN (1896–1900)

The defeat of General Gordon at Khartoum in 1885 was seen as a major British humiliation, and there were calls for revenge. No action was taken, however, until a new Conservative government under Lord Salisbury came to power in 1895. By then the government was also concerned about the Khalifa's regime in Sudan, which bordered British-held Egypt, and needed to restore the perception of European strength in the region following Italy's thwarted attempt to expand her territories in Eritrea in March 1896.

In March 1896, the Egyptian army under Kitchener was ordered to retake the Dongola Province in Sudan. On 7 June, Kitchener led five Egyptian and five Sudanese battalions, one British engineer company and the machine-gun sections of the 1st North Staffords and the Connaught Rangers to defeat the dervish force at Firket. He then advanced, with reinforcements, to Hafir, where his men encountered the last organized resistance before reaching Dongola, which they occupied on 23 September.

In 1897, Kitchener planned a rail link between Wadi Halfa (at what is now the southern end of Lake Nasser) and Abu Hamed on the Nile to the south and east, so as not to have to rely on the looping course of the river for transport. Work began on 1 January 1897, with the route for the track being cleared of opposition by a force under Major General Sir Archibald Hunter, who reached Abu Hamed on 7 August and went on to occupy Berber, further south down the river, on 5 September. The Khalifa's army now threatened action, so Kitchener called in more British troops, who joined him in January 1898.

Kitchener attacked Emir Mahmoud's camp at Atbara, on the Nile to the south-east of Berber, routing the dervish defenders and capturing the Emir. Now with some twenty-six thousand men, Kitchener advanced along the Nile towards the Khalifa's base at Omdurman, and by 1 September he arrived within artillery range. In a grave tactical error, the Khalifa, instead of waiting for an attack in the hills around Omdurman, lined up his forty thousand men on the plain before the town. Early on the morning of 2 September, the Khalifa's troops attacked, but the superior artillery and massive fire power repelled two attacks, inflicting massive losses – eleven thousand killed, sixteen thousand wounded and four thousand taken prisoner. Kitchener then marched out from his defended positions and in the following engagement, Colonel Hector Macdonald's Sudanese Brigade and the 21st Lancers came under heavy attack, the latter carrying out one of the last major cavalry charges in history, during which VCs were earned by Private Thomas Byrne, Lieutenant the Honourable Raymond de Montmorency, Captain Paul Kenna and Captain Nevill Smyth. For the loss of just 48 dead, Kitchener advanced victorious into Omdurman. On 4 September, British and Egyptian flags were raised over Omdurman and, to exact due revenge for Gordon's death, Gordon's nephew blew up the tomb of the Mahdi who had defeated him.

Dervish resistance persisted, and on 7 September a small force under Colonel Parsons marched on Gedarif, south-east of Khartoum, and occupied the town on 22 September, during which action Captain the Honourable Alexander Hore-Ruthven earned the VC. It was not until November 1899 that British control was finally established in Sudan.

BYRNE, Thomas *Private, 21st Lancers*

2 September 1898 – At the Battle of Khartoum, Sudan, despite having received a bullet in his right arm, he went to the assistance of the wounded Lieutenant Molyneux who was unhorsed and surrounded by dervishes. Byrne's arm had lost its power so his sword dangled uselessly from his hand as he charged the enemy time and time again, giving the lieutenant a chance to escape. Byrne received a spear wound in his chest but rode away to safety.

His identity as Molyneux's saviour was discovered by Winston Churchill (the Morning Post*'s correspondent in the Sudan) some days later. Skin taken from Churchill's chest was grafted onto Molyneux's wounds, helping to save his life.*

DE MONTMORENCY, the Hon. Raymond Harvey Lodge Joseph
Lieutenant, 21st Lancers

2 September 1898 – At the Battle of Khartoum, Sudan, he rode to the assistance of Lieutenant Grenfell, who had been slashed through the head and was lying surrounded by dervishes. After dismounting and finding Grenfell dead, De Montmorency's horse bolted, leaving him in the midst of the enemy. Captain KENNA and Corporal Swarbrick rode to his aid.

KENNA, Paul Aloysius *Captain, 21st Lancers*

2 September 1898 – At the Battle of Khartoum, Sudan, seeing that Major Crole Wyndham's horse had been killed, he rode up to the major, took him up onto his own horse and rode him to safety. He then (together with

Corporal Swarbrick) rode to the assistance of Lieutenant DE MONTMO-
RENCY who was dismounted in the midst of the enemy. He kept the enemy
off with his revolver whilst the corporal caught the lieutenant's horse and
retrieved it.

SMYTH, Nevill Maskelyne *Captain, 2nd Dragoon Guards*
   2 September 1898 – At the Battle of Khartoum, Sudan, he killed an Arab
who had run amok among some war correspondents. He received a spear
wound in the arm whilst performing the deed. His action saved at least one
of the correspondents.

HORE-RUTHVEN, the Hon. Alexander Gore (later Earl of Gowrie) *Captain,
3rd Bn., Highland Light Infantry*
   22 September 1898 – At Gedarif, Sudan, he went to the aid of a wounded
Egyptian officer 50 yards from the advancing dervishes. Several times he lay
down the officer to return fire, keeping the enemy in check, until he reached
shelter.

CRETE (1898)

For two hundred years, the Turkish Muslim regime had oppressed the
Christian population of the Mediterranean island of Crete, but in 1897, with
the support of the Greek government and the Greek military, the Christians
rose up in revolt. Britain, France, Russia, Italy, Germany and Austria sent
warships to restore peace, but no lasting political solution was reached – the
Christians controlled the countryside while the Turks held the towns.
Austria and Germany withdrew, leaving Britain, France, Russia and Italy
overseeing one district of the island each.
   By 1898 the garrison in Candia, the British quarter, was down to a single
regiment of the Highland Light Infantry. On 6 September, the colonel of this
regiment attempted to install a new collector of taxes to gather revenue
from the export customs duties, at which a Muslim mob rose up in protest,
killing nearly a hundred British soldiers and a thousand Christian inhabitants in the town of Candia. They went on to burn the British vice-consul in
his home, set the town on fire and besiege the customs house. The beleaguered customs house garrison called on the British fleet under Admiral Noel,
which bombarded the town. Two parties of 50 men from the torpedo boat
HMS *Hazard* came ashore, and it was during the landing under fire that
Surgeon William Maillard earned the VC – an unusual citation in that he
was the first naval medical officer to receive the award, which was made in
what was technically peacetime and therefore not against a declared 'enemy
of the Crown'. The situation was brought under control and the seven
Muslim ringleaders were tried for the murder of two privates of the Highland
Light Infantry, and hanged.

MAILLARD, William Job *Surgeon, Royal Navy*

6 September 1898 – At Candia, Crete, his party was attacked whilst being brought ashore from HMS *Hazard*. Although he had already reached shelter, he ran back to the boat to help a wounded seaman. He tried to carry him to shelter but found it impossible to steady himself on the boat. After this action, his clothes were found to be riddled with bullet holes.

He remains the only naval medical officer to win the VC.

THE THIRD ASHANTI EXPEDITION (1900–1901)

First suppressed in the cause of protecting trade routes and British nationals on the western coast of Africa in 1874, the Ashanti people of Gambia had risen again against British dominance in 1895. This had been quashed and a peace, albeit a resentful one, had continued until 1900, when the British decided to capture the symbolic 'Golden Stool', regarded by the Ashanti as a sign of authority.

In April 1900, on hearing of this, the Ashanti rebelled and besieged the fort of Kumassi, where the visiting governor, Sir Frederick Hodge, took refuge with his wife and some thousand others, and it was around this siege that the main action centred. Imperial troops were tied up in the Boer War in southern Africa and in the Boxer Rebellion in China, so few men were available to relieve the siege. An initial group of 50 men broke through on 15 April, and a further group on the 17th – but by the time 230 reinforcements arrived on 15 May, the situation in the fort was getting desperate without food or medical supplies. Not until 23 June was it possible to evacuate the six hundred troops and around a thousand civilians from Kumassi, leaving a garrison of about a hundred men.

In the meantime, a relief party under Brigadier General James Willcocks was making its way to the fort – in an engagement at Dompoassi on 6 June, Sergeant John Mackenzie of the Seaforth Highlanders earned a VC. The column eventually relieved Kumassi on 23 July, but further fighting ensued as flying columns pursued the Ashanti, destroying their villages. Significantly, at Obassa, Willcocks' men inflicted a decisive defeat on 30 September, after which Captain Sir Charles Melliss was awarded the VC, and by November, Ashanti opposition had been suppressed. In 1902, Ashanti was formally annexed as a Crown Colony.

MACKENZIE, John *Sergeant, 2nd Bn., Seaforth Highlanders attached West African Frontier Force*

6 June 1900 – At Dompoassi, during the Ashanti Expedition, he worked two Maxim guns, receiving a severe wound. He nevertheless volunteered to clear an enemy force from strongly held stockades with the bayonet. His own company was ordered up from the rear of the column and he led his men into the charge. The enemy fled in confusion.

MELLISS, Sir Charles John *Captain, Indian Staff Corps attached West African Frontier Force*

30 September 1900 – At Obassa, during the Ashanti Expedition, he collected as many men as he could find and led a charge through the bush. A hand-to-hand fight ensued during which he grappled with one of the foe before running him through. As the enemy fled in panic, they were pursued and routed by the Sikhs.

He was attacked by a lion whilst hunting in Somaliland in 1903 and was severely wounded, almost losing his arm.

THE BOXER REBELLION (1900)

In the late nineteenth century, a society was formed in China called the I-ho chuan, or 'Society of Righteous and Harmonious Fists', known in the West as the 'Boxers'. Its objective was to rid China of foreigners and Christians – and with the appointment of one of its founder members, Yu Hsien, as Governor of Shantung Province in March 1899, the way was clear for the Boxers to start their campaign. On 30 December, a clergyman, Reverend Brooks, was murdered in Shantung, and the Chinese Manchu regime's response on 11 January 1900, that the Boxers should not be regarded as a criminal organization, encouraged other fiercely xenophobic secret societies. By May the situation in Peking was so dangerous that the British Ambassador telegraphed the British Naval Commander-in-Chief, Vice Admiral Sir Edward Seymour, to send guards to protect the legations. The Great Powers demanded that the Chinese Empress and her court take action to suppress these groups, but the request was ignored. On 2 June, two missionaries were killed, and seven days later a royal edict was issued, openly encouraging the murder of foreigners.

Britain, America, Russia, France, Japan, Italy, Austria and Germany all had warships in Chinese ports to protect their nationals and their trade interests, and contributed to an allied force of two thousand marines and sailors which formed to relieve Peking. Seymour's column advanced by railway as far as Langfang, about 70 miles inland, but there the line was too damaged for it to advance further. Isolated and with 230 casualties, it was compelled to fall back towards Tientsin, about 35 miles inland; it took the arsenal near Hsiku, a few miles outside the city, on the 22nd, and waited for reinforcements. The Taku Forts at the entrance to the Pei-Ho River had been captured on 17 June, an essential preliminary to a relief of Peking, but on 21 June, war was declared on all foreigners, and now able to act freely, the Boxers attacked the foreign settlements in Tientsin. Seymour's column was rescued by an international force of two thousand men and Tientsin was captured on 14 July after fierce fighting, in which Midshipman Basil Guy was awarded the VC.

Meanwhile in Peking, in compliance with an imperial order of 18 June, the Boxers had begun massacring Christians and foreigners and burning their buildings. The compound that held the foreign legations became a refuge for about three and a half thousand foreigners and Chinese Christians: besieged by about three hundred thousand Chinese, it was defended by 407 men. Fifty men of the Royal Marine Light Infantry from HMS *Orlando*, under the command of Captain Sir Lewis Halliday (who was awarded the VC for his actions here), fought a fierce battle to protect the besieged British Legation.

Atrocities continued as a Roman Catholic bishop was burned alive in Mukden, and 54 missionaries were murdered in Shansi Province. With the arrival of British and allied troops in Shanghai in early August, fighting between the Chinese and Europeans began in earnest. An allied force of some eighteen thousand British and Americans advanced on Peking, reaching the outer city on the 14th, where men of the 14th Infantry scaled the Tartar Wall, raised the first ever foreign flag to fly there and opened up the way for British units to raise the fifty-five-day siege of the compound.

The Manchu court fled the capital, but eventually had to accept the terms of the Boxer Protocol, which allowed the permanent stationing of fortified foreign legations in Peking, foreign garrisons along the Tientsin–Peking railway and the payment of a large indemnity.

HALLIDAY, Lewis Stratford Tollemache *Captain, Royal Marine Light Infantry*
24 June 1900 – When Boxers attacked the British Legation at Peking, setting light to the stable quarters and occupying adjoining buildings, he led 20 marines in a charge at the enemy through a hole in the Legation wall. During the hand-to-hand fighting that ensued, he killed three Boxers despite being shot through the left shoulder and having part of his lung torn away. When incapable of fighting on, he ordered his men to continue without him.

GUY, Basil John Douglas *Midshipman, Royal Navy*
13 July 1900 – During the attack on Tientsin, he went to the assistance of the wounded Able Seaman McCarthy, 50 yards from cover. Whilst he bound McCarthy's wounds the entire enemy fire from the city walls was concentrated on the pair. He ran to fetch stretcher bearers but McCarthy was hit again and killed before he could be brought to safety.

THE SECOND BOER WAR

1899–1902

THE CAUSES OF WAR

Having subjugated the local southern African tribes to create the colonies of Natal and Cape Colony by the end of the nineteenth century, Britain wanted to bring together her colonies and the Boer republics – the Orange Free State and the Transvaal (the South African Republic) – in one British-dominated South African Federation.

The Boers, Dutch-speaking Calvinist farmers, had already suffered incursions from 'Uitlanders' (outsiders, chiefly Britons, who now formed a majority in the population) after gold had been discovered in the Transvaal in 1886, and had no wish to lose their independence. The war that resulted from this clash of wills lasted almost three years and cost Britain around £210 million, and 52,156 casualties, including 20,721 dead. It was also a war in which, for the first time, technical innovations such as the electric telegraph, the field telephone and eventually steam traction engines were used, the latter to spare pack animals which, ill-suited to the harsh conditions and long distances covered, died in their thousands.

The High Commissioner in South Africa, Sir Alfred Milner, decided to use the representation of the Uitlanders in the Transvaal's government as the lever with which to remove Paul Kruger, President of the Transvaal. In August 1899, Kruger made the last of a series of concessions, offering to extend the franchise to the Uitlanders in return for Britain's agreeing not to interfere in Boer affairs and to relinquish claims to the Transvaal. Although conflict seemed inevitable, Britain did little to prepare for war. Only on 8 September were troops ordered from India to reinforce Natal, and mobilization from Britain was not ordered until 7 October. Kruger mobilized on 27 September and on 9 October, with President Steyn of the Orange Free State, presented an ultimatum, demanding that within forty-eight hours Britain should submit to arbitration on all points of difference, withdraw her troops from the Transvaal's borders and return all reinforcements that had arrived since 1 June. The Boers, foreseeing no peaceful resolution, seized the initiative, struck first and invaded Cape Colony and Natal on 11 and 12 October 1899.

MAFEKING AND LADYSMITH

The Boers immediately cut off Mafeking, the northernmost town in Cape Colony, and surrounded Kimberley on 15 October. The Natal Field Force, under Lieutenant General Sir George White VC, set out towards Ladysmith and recorded initial successes on 20 and 21 October at Talana and Elandslaagte (at the latter of which four VCs were earned), but soon found itself driven into the town and under siege, with thirteen thousand five hundred troops and seven thousand five hundred civilians surrounded by seventeen thousand Boers. Well equipped with modern rapid-fire arms and heavy artillery, and tactically very cunning, they posed a very different sort of opposition from the South African tribesmen who had been relatively easily suppressed.

FITZCLARENCE, Charles *Captain, Royal Fusiliers*

14 October 1899 – In the winter of 1899 Colonel Robert Baden-Powell and his men were besieged by the Boers in the small railway town of Mafeking on the north-west border of Cape Colony. This force, the Bechuanaland Protectorate Regiment, had been gathered from local Rhodesians, and to help him in his recruitment and training, Baden-Powell called on Captain Charles Fitzclarence of the Royal Fusiliers. His friends called him Fitz – Baden-Powell referred to him as 'the Demon'.

Charles Fitzclarence and his twin brother Edward were born on 8 May 1865 to Captain George Fitzclarence RN and Lady Maria Henrietta Scott in County Kildare – and in the tradition of aristocratic families, Charles attended Eton and Wellington, where he had the values of empire and 'muscular Christianity' instilled into him. Unlike their father, both Charles and Edward opted for the army.

Fitzclarence was commissioned as a lieutenant in the Royal Fusiliers, and quickly applied for special service in Egypt, where he joined the Mounted Infantry in Kitchener's army fighting against the Mahdi and his dervish followers. His twin, in the Dorset Regiment, had also applied to serve in Egypt, but he was killed in the attack on the dervish garrison at Abu Hamed on 7 August 1897. Charles had no chance to avenge his twin as the Mounted Infantry were left behind in Egypt when Kitchener led his forces to the Sudan. Already engaged to Lady Violet Spencer Churchill, before leaving Egypt he arranged for the wedding to be performed in Cairo in April 1898.

Now a captain, he was once again engaged on special service – this time with Baden-Powell in South Africa – in command of B Squadron of the Bechuanaland Protectorate Regiment, known disparagingly as 'the Loafers'. This motley bunch consisted of frontier adventurers and not a few villains, but this formula had proved remarkably effective in the Zulu War, provided they were well trained and strongly led. As Baden-Powell assessed, Fitzclarence was the man for the job.

B Squadron were drawn straight into the action two days after the Boer War began. On 14 October the Boers attacked an armoured train outside Mafeking at Five Mile Bank and B Squadron arrived to find themselves heavily outnumbered. Even though Fitzclarence had not had all the time he wanted to train his men, he led from the front, inspired his men, and they drove the Boers back – leaving 50 dead and many wounded. However, the following day the Boers regrouped and encircled the town – Mafeking was under siege with Baden-Powell, Fitzclarence and their men inside and was to remain so for the next eight months.

Baden-Powell was charged with keeping the Boers on their toes and tying up as many of them as possible in the siege. Outgunned by the Boer artillery, he opted for covert strikes and planned an attack on the night of 27 October. 'The Demon' led 60 of his own squadron and a few Cape Police in a charge against the Boer positions under cover of dark. Fitzclarence went in first, sword drawn, and accounted for four killed in hand-to-hand fighting. The enemy retreated and in their panic fired on their own men. At the end of the attack, 150 Boers lay dead or wounded for just 6 dead and 9 wounded among Fitzclarence's men. Baden-Powell recorded that without Fitz-clarence's 'extraordinary spirit and fearlessness, the attacks would have been failures and we should have suffered heavy losses in both men and prestige.'

To keep the Boers alert, Baden-Powell planned another raid on Boxing Day, this time on Game Tree Fort, 3,000 yards outside the town. The armoured train sent out to support the attack couldn't get through as the Boers had destroyed the rails and any attack launched against the Boer stronghold was cut down in a hail of bullets. The Protectorate Regiment was called to storm the fort. Despite suffering casualties, they reached their objective – but were thwarted by heavy sandbagging and impenetrable iron roofing. It was left for Fitzclarence and B Squadron to break through in the second wave of the attack. The Boers fired constantly through loopholes, but according to one reporter, 'Fitzclarence alone got inside and stabbed two or three. They shot him once, but he proceeded to bayonet another when they shot him a second time and he dropped down ... though not dead.' He had been shot in both legs, but was recovered enough to play cricket within the beleaguered town.

For his bravery at Game Tree Fort and previously on 27 October, Baden-Powell recommended him for the VC – the first of the Boer War.

Back in England he was appointed Brigade Major of the 5th Brigade, Irish Guards, then given command of the 1st Battalion. By 1913 he was colonel of the regiment and, when war broke out in 1914, at the age of forty-nine he took command of the 1st Guards Brigade in France. At Polygon Wood during the First Battle of Ypres, fierce fighting drove the British back and the Germans overran some of the foremost British trenches on 11 November. The order came to retake those trenches and, as the reserve regiments were not familiar with the territory, Fitzclarence led them into the assault. The night, previously overclouded, was suddenly lit up by bright moonlight. Now exposed, the advance was subjected to intense machine-gun fire and Fitzclarence fell dead. Further shelling devastated the ground and his body was never found. His name is inscribed on the Menin Gate along with 6 other VCs who have no known grave. He is one of very few VC recipients who have earned their award in one conflict only to die in a later one.

JOHNSTON, Robert *Captain, Imperial Light Horse (Natal), South African Forces*
21 October 1899 – At the charge on the ridge at Elandslaagte, when the advance was met with such a terrific fire that the men wavered for an instant, he and Captain MULLINS rushed forward, ignoring the hail of bullets and rallied the men. The operation was a success from that moment onward.
He was Commandant of Prisoners of War in Meath, Ireland, 1914–15.

MEIKLEJOHN, Matthew Fontaine Maury *Captain, 2nd Bn., Gordon Highlanders*
21 October 1899 – At the Battle of Elandslaagte, the Gordon Highlanders started to waver under heavy fire when about to charge a kopje. Sensing the danger, he sprang forward, calling on the men to follow him. The kopje was captured, although he was severely wounded, losing an arm.

MULLINS, Charles Herbert *Captain, Imperial Light Horse (Natal), South African Forces*
21 October 1899 – At the charge on the ridge at Elandslaagte, when the advance was met with such a terrific fire that the men wavered for an instant, he and Captain JOHNSTON rushed forward to rally the men, showing no regard to danger. The operation was a success from that moment onward.

ROBERTSON, William *Sergeant Major, 2nd Bn., Gordon Highlanders*
21 October 1899 – At the Battle of Elandslaagte, during the final advance he led each successive rush of his battalion. Once the main position was captured, he led a party to seize the Boer camp. He held this position under deadly fire even after he was dangerously wounded.

NORWOOD, John *Second Lieutenant, 5th Dragoon Guards*
30 October 1899 – At Ladysmith, whilst retiring his small patrol from the enemy under heavy fire, he noticed a trooper fall from his saddle. He rode back 300 yards to the fallen man, dismounted and carried him on his back out of range. He then remounted and rejoined his troop.

MARTINEAU, Horace Robert *Sergeant, Protectorate Regiment (North-West Cape Colony), South African Forces*
26 December 1899 – At Game Tree, he remained behind after the retire had been sounded to assist Corporal Le Camp who was lying wounded ten

yards in front of the Boer trenches. Whilst half dragging, half carrying the corporal to the cover of a bush 150 yards away, he was himself hit three times, losing his left arm as a result.

RAMSDEN, Horace Edward *Trooper Protectorate Regiment (North-West Cape Colony), South African Forces*
26 December 1899 – At Game Tree, he remained behind after the retire had been sounded to assist his brother who had been shot through both legs and was lying wounded 10 yards from the main Boer trench. He carried him 800 yards under heavy fire until he met some men who were able to carry him on to safety.

MAJOR GENERAL SIR REDVERS BULLER VC

Maintaining three major sieges (Mafeking, Ladysmith and Kimberley) seriously diluted the Boer strength – but the British relief troops were similarly weakened. The newly arrived Commander-in-Chief Sir Redvers Buller split his force of some forty-seven thousand men, directing his own efforts into relieving Ladysmith, while Lieutenant General Lord Methuen was to reclaim Kimberley and Lieutenant General Sir William Gatacre was ordered to keep potential Boer reinforcements occupied. Disaster ensued. In what became known as 'Black Week', 10 to 17 December, Gatacre's force was defeated at Stormberg on the 10th, and two days later, Methuen's men, weakened by an earlier battering in an ambush at Modder River just south of Kimberley, suffered a defeat at Magersfontein. Here, once again, the British walked into a well-laid trap as the Boers waited unseen in camouflaged trenches – three VCs were awarded for actions during the costly retreat. On Friday 15th Buller attempted to cross the River Tugela at Colenso to the east, just ten miles south of Ladysmith, and despite commanding the largest British force amassed since the Battle of the Alma in the Crimea, was no match for the Boers and their well-directed mobility, and was badly defeated. During the rout seven VCs were earned.

DOUGLAS, Henry Edward Manning *Lieutenant, Royal Army Medical Corps*
11 December 1899 – At Magersfontein, he attended to the wounds of Captain Gordon, Major Robinson and many other stricken men under a hail of bullets.

SHAUL, John David Francis *Corporal, 1st Bn., Highland Light Infantry*
11 December 1899 – At Magersfontein, where the Highlanders were being mown down by Boer rifle fire, he was in charge of the stretcher bearers. He went from one man to another, dressing wounds under terrific fire. At one point, he was seen encouraging men to advance across open ground.

TOWSE, Ernest Beachcroft Beckwith (later Sir Ernest) *Captain, 1st Bn., Gordon Highlanders*

11 December 1899 – At Magersfontein, he carried the mortally wounded Colonel Dowman out of action and supported him until help arrived. *30 April 1900* – At Mount Theba, a force of a hundred and fifty Boers dashed to within 40 yards of his party of twelve men and called on him to surrender. Refusing, he charged his few men at the enemy, driving them off. He was shot through both eyes during the charge and blinded for life.

BABTIE, William *Major, Royal Army Medical Corps*

15 December 1899 – At the Battle of Colenso, he rode across open ground and attended to wounded exposed to heavy rifle fire. He later went out and assisted Captain CONGREVE to bring in Lieutenant ROBERTS.

CONGREVE, Walter Norris *Captain, Rifle Brigade*

15 December 1899 – At the Battle of Colenso, he answered General Buller's call for volunteers to save the guns of the 14th and 66th Batteries. Under terrific fire, he managed to hook a gun to a limber and bring it in. With the aid of Major BABTIE, he brought in the mortally wounded Lieutenant ROBERTS.

He was the father of Major W. La T. Congreve VC.

NURSE, George Edward *Corporal, 66th Bty, Royal Field Artillery*

15 December 1899 – At the Battle of Colenso, he answered General Buller's call for volunteers to save the guns of the 14th and 66th Batteries. Under terrific fire, he helped to hook a gun to a limber and bring it in.

RAVENHILL, George *Private, 2nd Bn., Royal Scots Fusiliers*

15 December 1899 – At the Battle of Colenso, he answered General Buller's call for volunteers to save the guns of the 14th and 66th Batteries. Under heavy fire, he helped to limber up one of the guns which was saved.

His name was removed from the VC Roll in 1908 after he was convicted of the theft of less than six shillings' worth of iron. He was sentenced to a month in prison. Shortly before Ravenhill's death, King George V declared that the VC should never be forfeited. 'Even were a VC to be sentenced to be hanged for murder,' wrote the King, 'he should be allowed to wear the VC on the scaffold.' His name was returned to the register.

REED, Hamilton Lyster *Captain, 7th Bty, Royal Field Artillery*

15 December 1899 – At the Battle of Colenso, he galloped down with three teams from his battery to help to save the guns of the 14th and 66th Batteries. Five of his thirteen men were hit, one being killed, and thirteen of his twenty-one horses were killed, forcing him to abandon the attempt. He himself was wounded.

He was nephew of Lieutenant H. H. Lyster VC.

ROBERTS, the Hon. Frederick Hugh Sherston *Lieutenant, King's Royal Rifle Corps*

15 December 1899 – At the Battle of Colenso, he answered General Buller's call for volunteers to save the guns of the 14th and 66th Batteries. He dashed out with Lieutenant CONGREVE and Lieutenant SCHOFIELD to help to limber up one of the guns. During this action he was mortally wounded.

Field Marshal Earl Roberts VC was his father.

SCHOFIELD, Harry Norton *Captain, Royal Field Artillery*

15 December 1899 – At the Battle of Colenso, he answered General Buller's call for volunteers to save the guns of the 14th and 66th Batteries. He dashed out and got together a team which brought in one gun. He was unharmed although six bullets passed through his uniform.

FIELD MARSHAL LORD ROBERTS VC

The British military leadership was unequal to the challenge, and in response to the defeats of Black Week, Field Marshal Lord Roberts was despatched to take supreme command, with Major General Kitchener as his Chief of Staff. He appreciated better than Buller the importance of public morale and the power of well-planned publicity for gains – and a light hand in reporting reverses. More materially, he addressed the problems of bad management and poor leadership, logistical shortcomings and lack of mobility.

The Boers surrounding Ladysmith now drove to storm the town, but were thwarted at unsuccessful attacks on Caesar's Camp and Waggon Hill on 6 January – five VCs were earned, two awarded posthumously.

MILBANKE, John Peniston (later Sir John) *Lieutenant, 10th Hussars*

5 January 1900 – Whilst on a reconnaissance near Colesberg, the horse of one of his men was unable to keep up with the others. He rode back under heavy fire from a party of Boers close by, took the man up on his own horse and brought him into the camp.

ALBRECHT, Herman *Trooper, Imperial Light Horse (Natal), South African Forces*

6 January 1900 – During the attack on Ladysmith, he (together with Lieutenant DIGBY-JONES) led a party of men to the crest of Waggon Hill. They scrambled to the gun pits before the enemy could reach them. He killed at least two Boers before he was shot dead.

DIGBY-JONES, Robert James Thomas *Lieutenant, Royal Engineers*

6 January 1900 – During the attack on Ladysmith, he (together with Trooper ALBRECHT) led a party of men to the crest of Waggon Hill. They scrambled to the gun pits before the enemy could reach them. Once there, he shot the Boer leader De Villiers, killed three others with successive rounds and brained another with the butt of his revolver before he was killed by a bullet through the throat.

The South African Review *of 24 February 1900 declared that he 'saved Ladysmith and the British arms from defeat'.*

MASTERSON, James Edward Ignatius *Lieutenant, 1st Bn., Devonshire Regiment*

6 January 1900 – At Waggon Hill, near Ladysmith, having led his company in a successful attack on a ridge, he crossed an open plain under fierce enemy fire to request support from the Imperial Light Horse. Before crossing this ground, he was shot through both thighs yet he crawled on and delivered his message before collapsing exhausted.

PITTS, James *Private, 1st Bn., Manchester Regiment*

6 January 1900 – He and Private SCOTT were the last surviving defenders of a sangar at Caesar's Camp. They held their post for fifteen hours without any food or water whilst the enemy poured continuous fire on them from close by. They were eventually relieved.

SCOTT, Robert *Private, 1st Bn., Manchester Regiment*

6 January 1900 – He and Private PITTS were the last surviving defenders of a sangar at Caesar's Camp. They held their post for fifteen hours without any food or water whilst the enemy poured continuous fire on them from close by. They were eventually relieved.

THE RELIEF OF LADYSMITH

Buller still drove on to lift the Ladysmith siege, but through naive military strategy and lack of foresight, suffered a costly defeat at Spion Kop on 23/24 January 1900 where nearly twelve hundred were killed or wounded in a bloody massacre. This disaster had dented Buller's confidence and even when the strategically vital Val Krantz to the south-east of Ladysmith had been secured he hesitated, failed to press home the attack to take the equally important Green Hill nearby and forty-eight hours later his men had withdrawn back across the Tugela – no ground had been gained, but 34 men had been killed and 335 wounded.

A week later, when his troops had had a much-needed respite, Buller led a successful attack which drove the Boers from south of the river. The same could not be said of the north side, however. Here the Boers were well dug in, and it took two days of fierce and costly fighting to dislodge them. There was a further setback at Hart's Hill on the Tugela on 23 February, as Major General Fitzroy Hart launched an ill-advised attack against unassailably strong Boer positions with further loss of life, but Buller finally moved in to relieve Ladysmith on 28 February – not a moment too soon for the inhabitants, who had been reduced to practically nil rations.

INKSON, Edgar Thomas *Lieutenant, Royal Army Medical Corps, attached Royal Inniskilling Fusiliers*
24 *February 1900* – At Hart's Hill, he carried the wounded Lieutenant Devenish 400 yards through intense fire, bringing him to safety.

PAARDEBERG

To the west, Roberts planned his advance on Kimberley, finally relieving the four-month siege on 15 February. Then as Buller was finally lifting the siege at Ladysmith, the tide of the war also turned in the west, as the Boers surrendered to Roberts at Paardeberg on 27 February.

ATKINSON, Alfred *Sergeant, 1st Bn., Yorkshire Regiment*
18 *February 1900* – During the Battle of Paardeberg, he carried water backwards and forwards to the wounded seven times before he was shot through the head. He died three days later.

PARSONS, Francis Newton *Lieutenant, 1st Bn., Essex Regiment*
18 *February 1900* – During the Battle of Paardeberg, he went to the assistance of the wounded Private Ferguson. He dressed his wounds and twice fetched him water before carrying him to safety. He was under terrific fire all the while.

KORN SPRUIT

Roberts' progress was now held up for seven weeks by a serious outbreak of typhoid. During this period there was a setback at the Korn Spruit tributary of the Modder River on 31 March, where again there was needless loss of life in an ill-advised attack.

GLASOCK, Horace Henry *Driver, Q Bty., Royal Horse Artillery*
31 *March 1900* – His battery was ambushed by the Boers at Korn Spruit. The fire he faced was so fierce that the sand around him looked like the surface of a lake in a downpour. When Major PHIPPS-HORNBY gave the order to retire, he helped to bring two guns to safety. He tried three times to hook horses on to a third gun, but each time the horses were killed. He was himself shot in the leg and the hand.
He was elected for the award under Rule 13 of the Royal Warrant by the drivers of the battery.

LODGE, Isaac *Gunner, Royal Horse Artillery*
31 March 1900 – His battery was ambushed by the Boers at Korn Spruit.
When Major PHIPPS-HORNBY gave the order to retire, he helped bring the
guns to safety by hand, the fire being too heavy for horses to face.
*He was elected for the award under Rule 13 of the Royal Warrant by the
gunners of the battery.*

MAXWELL, Francis Alymer *Lieutenant, Indian Staff Corps, attached
Roberts's Light Horse*
31 March 1900 – When Q Battery was ambushed by the Boers at Korn
Spruit, he helped the men of that battery to save the guns. Five times he
went out under a hail of bullets, bringing in two guns and three limbers,
one of which was dragged in by hand. He was one of those trying to bring
in the last gun until the attempt had to be abandoned.

PARKER, Charles Edward Haydon *Sergeant, Q Bty., Royal Horse Artillery*
31 March 1900 – His battery was ambushed by the Boers at Korn Spruit.
When Major PHIPPS-HORNBY gave the order to retire, he helped bring the
guns to safety by hand, the fire being too heavy for horses to face.
*He was elected for the award under Rule 13 of the Royal Warrant by the
non-commissioned officers of the battery.*

PHIPPS-HORNBY, Edmund John *Major, Royal Horse Artillery*
31 March 1900 – He was in command of one of the batteries ambushed
by the enemy at Korn Spruit. He retired his battery 800 yards, unlimbered
and began firing. The Boers returned such a fire that bullets were rattling on
his guns like hail. As the fire was too fierce for his horses to face, he gave
the order for the guns to be retired by hand. All but one of the guns were
saved.

THE RELIEF OF MAFEKING TO THE PEACE OF VEREENIGING

However, Roberts resumed the drive eastward with a force of around a
hundred thousand men, mustered from Kimberley, Pretoria and the north
of Natal – and the Boers, with no more than thirty thousand men, were
unable to sustain the 217-day siege at Mafeking, and were driven away on
17 May.

The drive continued as Lieutenant General Sir Archibald Hunter crossed
into the Transvaal at the start of May and Roberts pressed on to take
Johannesburg, Pretoria and, to the far east, Koomati Poort. By June Britain
had overrun the Orange Free State and annexed the gold-rich Transvaal.

However, despite jubilation in Britain, this was not the end of the war.
The President of the Orange Free State, Marthinus Steyn, fled as Roberts'
troops overran his capital, and remained at large, inciting determined and

skilled resistance, as did Kruger's deputy, Burgher. Boer commandos under the inspired command of Christiaan Rudolf de Wet and Jacobus Hercules de la Rey continued to harass the British troops for a further eighteen months after the so-called end of the war. Kitchener's response was to deprive the Boers of reinforcements, food, supplies and information by burning down their homesteads and gathering their families into concentration camps – a policy deplored at home, and which backfired as fatal diseases spread through the camps and which, having removed the distraction of dependents, left the Boer guerrillas free to fight single-mindedly. (Some eighteen to twenty thousand Boers – mainly women and children – died in the camps, along with around fourteen thousand black Africans in separate refugee camps.) Most effectively, however, Kitchener dealt with the Boers' mobility by building a network of blockhouses, linked by barbed wire, which also guarded the railway tracks, and by sending out frequent columns of mounted infantry, one to two thousand strong, to sweep the veld to seek out the enemy – if necessary in quick response to a telegraphed warning,

On 31 May 1902, the Boers had finally had enough and, in signing the Treaty of Vereeniging, they surrendered their territories to British colonial rule, with a promise of self-government later.

During the course of the war, seventy-eight VC awards were made. Much of the action was directed at lifting the sieges at Ladysmith, Kimberley and Mafeking and VCs were earned in strategic battles to achieve these ends. However, the Boers' guerrilla ambush tactics also occasioned acts of great bravery and following the notional end of the war proper, VCs were also awarded for actions during the policing of the region prior to the treaty being signed.

CURTIS, Albert Edward *Private, 2nd Bn., East Surrey Regiment*
23 February 1900 – At Onderbank Spruit, Colonel Harris lay wounded in the open. The Boers were firing at any sign of life and he was shot eight or nine times. After several failed efforts, Curtis succeeded in reaching the colonel, attending to his wounds, giving him a drink and carrying him to safety with the assistance of Private Morton.

FIRTH, James *Sergeant, 1st Bn., Duke of Wellington's Regiment*
24 February 1900 – At Plewman's Farm, he carried Lance Corporal Blackman and Lieutenant Wilson over the crest of a ridge to safety. On both occasions he was under severe fire from the Boers who had advanced to within 500 yards. Whilst rescuing the officer, he received a bullet through the eye and nose.

MANSEL-JONES, Conwyn *Captain, West Yorkshire Regiment*
27 February 1900 – During the attack on Terrace Hill, the advance of the West Yorkshire Regiment was momentarily checked. He rallied his men, and although he fell severely wounded, the ridge was swiftly taken.

ENGLEHEART, Henry William *Sergeant, 10th Hussars*

13 March 1900 – Returning from blowing up the Bloemfontein railway, his party found a Boer picquet and four deep spruits in their path. He led the way into the first spruit causing the Boers to flee. At the last spruit, he went back to pull Sapper Webb and his horse to safety under fierce enemy fire.

NICKERSON, William Henry Snyder *Lieutenant, Royal Army Medical Corps, attached Mounted Infantry*

20 April 1900 – At Wakkerstroom, he went out under shell and rifle fire and stitched up the stomach of a man whose entrails were protruding. He stayed with the man until the fire slackened and stretcher bearers arrived.

He served in an Atlantic convoy during the Second World War.

BEET, Harry Churchill *Corporal, 1st Bn., Derbyshire Regiment*

22 April 1900 – During a retreat near Wakkerstroom, he dragged the wounded Corporal Burnett to cover, bound up his wounds and kept up such a hot fire that the enemy were prevented from approaching until darkness fell. He was himself subjected to fierce fire throughout the afternoon.

MACKAY, John Frederick *Lance Corporal, 1st Bn., Gordon Highlanders*

20 May 1900 – At Crow's Nest Hill, he was conspicuous for his bravery in attending to the wounded close to the enemy, far from any cover. He carried one man from open ground to shelter under very heavy fire.

KIRBY, Frank Howard *Corporal, Royal Engineers*

2 June 1900 – He was one of a party sent to cut the Delagoa Railway. Whilst retiring, the party was attacked by the Boers. One man had his horse shot from under him. Kirby turned and rode back towards the enemy under heavy fire, picked up the man and rode with him to rejoin the troop.

WARD, Charles Burley *Private, 2nd Bn., King's Own Yorkshire Light Infantry*

26 June 1900 – At Lindley, a picket of his regiment was attacked by five hundred of the enemy on three sides. Reinforcements were necessary and he volunteered to deliver the message. His offer was at first refused – the mission was too dangerous – but he insisted. Crossing 150 yards of open ground, he delivered the message and returned to his comrades. Reinforcements arrived and the post was saved. He was severely wounded during the action.

He was the last VC winner to be decorated by Queen Victoria.

RICHARDSON, Arthur Herbert Lindsay *Sergeant, Lord Strathcona's Horse, Canadian Forces*

5 July 1900 – Whilst retreating from a large force of Boers at Wolwe-spruit, he spotted a badly wounded comrade who had been thrown from his horse. He rode back towards the enemy, picked the man up and carried him away to safety. He was under heavy fire all the while.

GORDON, William Eagleson *Captain, 1st Bn., Gordon Highlanders*
11 July 1900 – Near Krugersdorp, the fire from the Boers was too fierce for the artillery horses so he resolved to drag one of the guns to shelter by hand. He attached a drag rope to the gun under a hail of bullets and called for volunteers to pull it to safety. He gave a sign, the men dashed out and began pulling. Four men were wounded, Captain YOUNGER mortally so. Realizing that to continue would only lead to further casualties, he ordered the men to take cover.

YOUNGER, David Reginald *Captain, 1st Bn., Gordon Highlanders*
11 July 1900 – Near Krugersdorp, under fire too heavy for horses, he went out with a few men and dragged an artillery wagon into shelter by hand. He then helped Captain GORDON to drag in one of the guns. He was wounded whilst doing this and died shortly afterwards.

HOWSE, Neville Reginald *Captain, New South Wales Medical Staff Corps, Australian Forces*
24 July 1900 – At Vredefort, he carried a wounded trumpeter to shelter under severe crossfire.
He was the first Australian recipient of the VC.

HOUSE, William *Private, 2nd Bn., Royal Berkshire Regiment*
2 August 1900 – At Mosilikatse Nek, he went out into the open under heavy fire to assist a wounded sergeant, although he had been warned that to do so would mean almost certain death. On reaching the sergeant, he was himself severely wounded so that the two men now lay side by side. In spite of his agony, he called to his comrades not to risk their lives coming to his aid.

LAWRENCE, Brian Turner Tom *Sergeant, 17th Lancers*
7 August 1900 – Near Essenbosch Farm, he was on patrol duty with Private Hayman when they were attacked by 14 Boers. Seeing that Hayman's horse had thrown him, he dismounted, lifted Hayman onto his own horse and told him to ride towards the picket. He walked on for two miles, keeping the enemy at bay with two carbines until help arrived.
He was a member of the English riding team at the 1912 Olympics in Stockholm, which also included Paul Kenna VC.

HAMPTON, Harry *Sergeant, 2nd Bn., King's (Liverpool) Regiment*
21 August 1900 – At Van Wyk's Vlei, he was in command of a party of mounted infantry forced to retire. He saw all his men safely to cover, and although he was himself wounded in the head, supported a badly hurt lance corporal until the man was killed by another shot.

KNIGHT, Henry James *Corporal, 1st Bn., King's (Liverpool) Regiment*
21 August 1900 – At Van Wyk's Vlei, he and four others were covering the rear of his detachment, when they were attacked by about fifty Boers. He directed his small party to retire one by one to better cover whilst he maintained his position for nearly an hour. He lost two of his four men. When he retired, he carried a wounded man with him for nearly two miles.

HEATON, William Edward *Private, 1st Bn., King's (Liverpool) Regiment*
23 August 1900 – At Geluk, his company was surrounded by the enemy and suffering severely. He volunteered to take a message back asking for relief. Under heavy fire, he accomplished his mission. Had he not done so, his company would have suffered very heavily.

DURRANT, Alfred Edward *Private, 2nd Bn., Rifle Brigade*
27 August 1900 – At Bergendal, Acting Corporal Wellar became dazed and began running towards the enemy. Durrant started after him, caught him, pulled him down and carried him 200 yards back to a safe position under tremendous fire. He then returned to his place in the firing line.

BISDEE, John Hutton *Trooper, Tasmanian Imperial Bushmen*
1 September 1900 – He was one of the advanced scouts with a foraging party near Warm Baths when the enemy suddenly opened fire from behind nearby trees. Six out of eight men were hit, including an officer. Bisdee dismounted, placed the officer on his horse, mounted behind him and rode him out of range of the Boers.

WYLLY, Guy George Egerton *Lieutenant, Tasmanian Imperial Bushmen*
1 September 1900 – He was one of the advanced scouts with a foraging party near Warm Baths when the enemy suddenly opened fire from behind a copse. Six out of eight men, including Wylly, were hit. Nevertheless, he raised the badly wounded Corporal Brown onto his horse and opened fire on the Boers, covering the retreat of the others.

BROWN (later Brown-Synge-Hutchinson), **Edward Douglas** *Major, 14th Hussars (King's)*
13 October 1900 – At Geluk, he saved the lives of 3 men. First, he helped a dismounted sergeant into the saddle behind him and rode him to safety. Shortly afterwards, he held a lieutenant's horse steady so it could be mounted. Finally, he carried a wounded lance corporal out of action. All of these acts were carried out under heavy fire.

DOXAT, Alexis Charles *Lieutenant, 3rd Bn., Imperial Yeomanry*
20 October 1900 – Near Zeerust, whilst reconnoitring an enemy position, his men came under heavy fire. Seeing a man thrown by his wounded horse, he galloped back, took the man on his own horse and rode him out of range.

COCKBURN, Hampden Zane Churchill *Lieutenant, Royal Canadian Dragoons*

7 *November 1900* – At the Komati River, two hundred mounted Boers charged in an attempt to take two Canadian 12pdr guns. He and a few men held them off long enough to enable the guns to be got away to safety. All of his men were killed, wounded or captured. He himself was wounded.

HOLLAND, Edward James Gibson *Sergeant, Royal Canadian Dragoons*

7 *November 1900* – At the Komati River, after Lieutenant COCKBURN had carried out his act of valour, the Boers again threatened to capture the Canadian guns. Holland worked his Colt to deadly effect, until finding the enemy almost on top of him, and the horse attached to the carriage dead, he lifted the gun and rode it away under his arm.

TURNER, Richard Ernest William *Lieutenant, Royal Canadian Dragoons*

7 *November 1900* – At the Komati River, after Lieutenant COCKBURN had carried out his act of valour, the Boers again threatened to capture the Canadian guns. Turner, although twice wounded, dismounted, deployed his men at close quarters and drove off the enemy. The guns were again saved.

KENNEDY, Charles Thomas *Private, 2nd Bn., Highland Light Infantry*

22 *November 1900* – At Dewetsdorp, seeing one of his comrades bleeding to death, he carried the man nearly a mile under brutal fire to hospital. The following day, he volunteered to carry a message across an open space swept so heavily by rifle fire that it was almost certain death to anyone attempting it. He was shot and wounded after only 20 yards.

FARMER, Donald Dickson *Sergeant, 1st Bn., Queen's Own Cameron Highlanders*

13 *December 1900* – At Nooitgedacht he was part of a small force that went to the assistance of a picket which had lost most of its men. The Boers opened fire on the party from close range. Seeing his officer wounded, he carried him to safety under heavy fire and then returned to the fight. He was taken prisoner after a desperate resistance.

BARRY, John *Private, 1st Bn., Royal Irish Regiment*

7 *January 1901* – During the attack on Monument Hill, his party was surrounded by Boers. To prevent their Maxim gun from being used by the enemy, he smashed the breech, rendering it useless.

HARDHAM, William James *Farrier-Major, 4th New Zealand Contingent*

28 *January 1901* – Whilst retiring from an engagement with a band of 20 Boers near Naauuwpoort, he noticed Trooper McCrae wounded on the ground. He rode to him under a galling fire, dismounted, helped him onto his own horse and then ran alongside until he was out of danger.

He later served at Gallipoli, in 1915.

TRAYNOR, William Bernard *Sergeant, 2nd Bn., West Yorkshire Regiment*
    6 February 1901 – When Bothwell Camp was under night attack, he dashed out of his trench to help a wounded man but was himself shot. Unable to continue alone, he called for help. Corporal Lintott ran to him and they carried the man to safety. He remained in command of his section until the attack was repulsed.

CLEMENTS, John James *Corporal, Damant's Horse (Rimington's Guides)*
South African Forces
    24 February 1901 – He was lying wounded near Strijdenburg, shot through the lungs, when five Boers came towards him, calling on him to surrender. He jumped up, shot and wounded three of the Boers and forced them all to surrender to him.

DUGDALE, Frederic Brooks *Lieutenant, 5th Lancers (Royal Irish)*
    3 March 1901 – Whilst retiring from an outpost near Derby, his party came under brutal fire. He dismounted and placed an injured man on his horse. Catching a riderless steed, he jumped into the saddle and lifted another wounded man up behind him. He then rode away with both men to safety.

BELL, Frederick William *Lieutenant, West Australian Mounted Infantry*
    16 May 1901 – At Brakpan, whilst retreating under fierce fire he saw a trooper dismounted. He took him up behind him on his horse but the weight was too great for the animal and it fell. He ordered the trooper to save himself whilst he remained behind firing at the Boers until his comrade was out of danger.

COULSON, Gustavus Hamilton Blenkinsopp *Lieutenant, 1st Bn., King's Own Scottish Borderers*
    18 May 1901 – Whilst under heavy fire at Lambrechtontein, Corporal Cranmer's horse had fallen. Coulson was lifting Cranmer into the saddle behind him when his own horse was shot and both men were thrown. With the enemy approaching rapidly, he ordered Cranmer to ride the wounded horse away to safety as best he could. Another corporal came to Coulson's aid, taking him upon his horse but almost at once both men were shot and killed.

ROGERS, James *Sergeant, South African Constabulary*
    15 June 1901 – When his rearguard of eight was attacked by sixty Boers at Thaba 'Nchu, he saved the lives of five men. First, he lifted an officer into his saddle and rode him half a mile until cover was reached. He then brought two comrades to safety whose horses had been shot. Finally, he brought two riderless horses under control and helped two more comrades to mount them and escape.
    He was wounded at Gallipoli in 1915.

ENGLISH, William John *Lieutenant, 2nd Scottish Horse*

3 July 1901 – At Vlakfontein, he and his five men were holding a position under attack by the Boers. As ammunition ran short, he crossed 15 yards of open ground to fetch a fresh supply. All the while he was fired upon by the enemy only 30 yards away. The position was held.

He served in the First World War and with the Royal Ulster Rifles in the Second World War, and died on active service in 1941.

CRANDON, Harry George *Private, 18th Hussars (Queen Mary's Own)*

4 July 1901 – At Springbok Laagte, he dismounted and gave his horse to the wounded Private Berry, whose mount had fallen. He ran, leading his comrade's horse for over a thousand yards under fire, until shelter was reached.

YOUNG, Alexander *Sergeant Major, Cape Police, South African Forces*

13 August 1901 – At Ruiterskraal, his small party took a kopje held by Commandant Erasmus and 20 Boers. The enemy fled towards another hill. Dashing ahead on his own, he charged the Boers before they reached the hill, shot one of them and captured Erasmus.

PRICE-DAVIES, Llewellyn Alberic Emilius *Lieutenant, King's Royal Rifle Corps*

17 September 1901 – At Blood River Poort, four hundred Boers were charging the gun drivers, calling on them to surrender. He drew his revolver and dashed in firing amongst the enemy in an effort to rescue the guns. He was shot and knocked off his horse.

BRADLEY, Frederick Henry *Driver, 69th Bty., Royal Field Artillery*

26 September 1901 – At Itala, a driver who volunteered to carry ammunition 150 yards up a hill was struck by a bullet. Bradley rushed out and brought him to safety and then proceeded to carry the ammunition up the hill. All the while he was subject to constant fire.

BEES, William *Private, 1st Bn., Derbyshire Regiment*

30 September 1901 – At Moedwil, six of the nine men attached to a Maxim gun were wounded. Unable to bear their cries any longer, he dashed forward under a raking fire to a spruit 500 yards away, filled his camp kettle with water and returned to quench the men's thirsts. His kettle was struck by several bullets during the dash, but he was unharmed.

MAYGAR, Leslie Cecil *Lieutenant, 5th Victorian Mounted Rifles, Australian Forces*

23 November 1901 – At Geelhoutboom, seeing a man's mount shot from under him, he lifted the man up onto his own horse. The animal, not up to the double weight, bolted into a swamp. Maygar ordered the man to ride to safety whilst he made his own way to shelter on foot. He was under heavy fire all the while.

CREAN, Thomas Joseph *Surgeon-Captain, 1st Imperial Light Horse*

18 December 1901 – At Tygerkloof Spruit, he ministered to the injured under heavy fire only 150 yards from the enemy. He only ceased his efforts when struck by a second bullet. His wounds were so serious that he was not at first expected to live.

IND, Alfred Ernest *Shoeing Smith, Royal Horse Artillery*

20 December 1901 – Near Tafelkop, he stuck to his gun under heavy fire when the rest of his team had been shot down. He continued firing into the advancing Boers until the last possible moment.

MARTIN-LEAKE, Arthur *Surgeon-Captain, South African Constabulary*

8 February 1902 – Of the group of just three men who earned a bar to his VC, Martin-Leake was the only one to gain his in two different wars – the Boer War and the Great War. He was also the first of these elite, showing that the medical corps was no easy option in the army.

Arthur Martin-Leake was born in High Cross, Hertfordshire, and was educated at Westminster and University College Hospital in London. He served first with the South African Constabulary during the Boer War as surgeon-captain. At Vlakfontein in the Transvaal, he risked his life to tend a wounded man, going 100 yards into open ground under fire from forty Boer riflemen. Although wounded himself while dressing an officer's injuries, he gave up his efforts only when completely exhausted – and even then he refused water until all the other wounded had been served. For this he earned his VC.

When war again broke out in 1914, Martin-Leake was working as a doctor with the Indian railways. In this protected occupation, there would have been no need for him to join up, but he was driven by his sense of duty. At forty, he was concerned that he might not be accepted for military service, but all the same, he travelled to Paris and enlisted at the British Consulate – then attached himself to the first medical unit he could find. This was the 5th Field Ambulance, which was soon sent north for the First Battle of Ypres. The British situation here in October 1914 was desperate. Casualties were heavy and Martin-Leake worked tirelessly throughout the battle from 29 October to 8 November, personally rescuing many wounded men lying close to the enemy while constantly under heavy fire. This sustained period of selfless courage and unwavering care for others earned him the bar to his VC.

Demobilized after the war, he returned to the Indian railways and continued to work there until his retirement in 1932. Many who were treated by him must have been unaware that their doctor had that most prestigious honour of being the first man ever to win the VC twice.

EDWARDIAN COLONIAL WARS

SOMALILAND (1902–05)

Since the middle of the nineteenth century, Britain had been securing her territory in Somaliland and defining its boundaries with those of French, Italian and Abyssinian Somaliland. The majority of local tribal chiefs accepted Britain's protection, but the most belligerent of the hostile chiefs was Mahommed bin Abdullah, a mullah of the Habr Suleiman Ogaden tribe. Claiming supernatural powers in support of his cause against the infidel, he gathered followers, mustering an army of some fifteen thousand dervishes. In 1899 bin Abdullah, dubbed the Mad Mullah, declared himself Mahdi and launched attacks against pro-British tribes, These tribes requested British protection and Colonel E. J. Swayne raised a body of about two thousand mainly local troops – the Somali Levy – to take on the dervish rebels.

Starting in April 1901, Swayne carried out cat-and-mouse attacks, but these were indecisive – in June, after setbacks and suffering heavy casualties, the Mad Mullah retreated and regrouped, gathering more support in order to renew his campaign in October 1902. On 6 October Swayne's troops followed the dervishes into Italian territory (with permission) and were ambushed at Erego where, despite heavy casualties, they drove off the enemy in an action where the only VC of the campaign was earned by Captain Alexander Cobbe of the King's African Rifles. Unfortunately, the Somali troops did not press home this defeat and again, the Mad Mullah withdrew to regroup.

COBBE, Alexander Stanhope *Captain, Indian Army, attached King's African Rifles*
   6 October 1902 – At Erego, Somaliland, the retirement of some companies left him alone in front of the line with a Maxim gun. He brought it in single-handed and worked it gallantly. Then, seeing an orderly lying wounded 20 yards from the enemy, he dashed out and carried him to safety under heavy fire.

As the Mullah retreated to Mudug it became apparent that the levies were not seasoned enough troops to deal with the continuing threat he posed, so a third expedition was planned with an increased force. The existing two thousand four hundred rifles were reinforced by nine hundred men of the

King's African Rifles and three hundred Indian infantry. This strengthened column advanced from the port of Obbia in Italian Somaliland towards Mudug on 22 February 1903 while an Abyssinian force led by British officers cut off the Mullah's retreat to the west. On 17 April a British advance guard pursued the Mullah's dervishes into Abyssinia and were annihilated in a two-and-a-half-hour battle at Gumburu – not one officer survived to report on the battle. On 22 April the dervishes, their leaders wearing the uniforms of British officers killed at Gumburu, attacked again at Daratoleh, but this time suffered heavy losses during a battle in which three VCs were earned.

GOUGH, John Edmund *Bt/Major, Rifle Brigade*
22 April 1903 – During the retreat from the fight at Daratoleh, Somaliland, he received news from Captain ROLLAND that Captain Bruce was wounded and that the rearguard was under attack. He immediately rushed back to assist in the fight and helped to lift Bruce (who died soon afterwards) onto a camel.
Major C. J. S. Gough VC was his father and Lieutenant H. H. Gough VC was his uncle.

ROLLAND, George Murray *Captain, 1st Bombay Grenadiers*
22 April 1903 – Whilst retiring from Daratoleh, Somaliland, he (together with Captain WALKER and 4 men) was in the rearguard under heavy fire from the pursuing enemy when Captain Bruce was shot through the body. He ran 500 yards to fetch help whilst the other men fired ceaselessly to keep the enemy in check. Returning with Major GOUGH, he helped to lift Captain Bruce onto a camel. The enemy remained in close pursuit for a further three hours, during which time Captain Bruce died.

WALKER, William George *Captain, 4th Gurkha Rifles*
22 April 1903 – Whilst retiring from Daratoleh, Somaliland, he (together with Captain ROLLAND and four men) was in the rearguard under heavy fire from the pursuing enemy when Captain Bruce was shot through the body. Whilst Rolland ran to fetch help, he kept up a desperate fire to keep the enemy at bay. When Rolland returned with Major GOUGH, he helped to lift Captain Bruce onto a camel. The captain died soon afterwards.

Despite a rout of the dervish troops by the Abyssinians on 31 May, the Mullah once again retreated unhindered and took refuge in the Nogal Valley.

The British government saw the Mullah's presence in Nogal as a continuing threat, and decided to destroy his power once and for all. Some eight thousand British troops led by Major General Sir Charles Egerton advanced on the Mullah's force of around seven thousand dervishes at Jidballi in British Somaliland in December 1903. During a reconnaissance foray, a small mounted party were pursued by a large force of dervishes – for returning to save one of the party, Lieutenant Herbert Carter was awarded the VC. The second VC of the expedition was awarded to Lieutenant Clement Smith in the conclusive engagement against the Mullah's forces at Jidballi on 10 January. The British square withstood repeated attempts to charge it down, and superior firepower and discipline eventually broke up the Mullah's forces, which fled, pursued by the cavalry.

CARTER, Herbert Augustine *Lieutenant, Mounted Infantry, Indian Army*
    19 December 1903 – During a reconnaissance at Jidballi, Somaliland, he rode 400 yards towards a huge force of dervishes to assist Private Jai Singh, who had lost his horse. He brought the private to safety, closely followed all the while by the enemy.

SMITH, Clement Leslie *Lieutenant, 2nd Bn., Duke of Cornwall's Light Infantry attached 5th Bn., Somaliland Light Infantry*
    10 January 1904 – At Jidballi, Somaliland, the enemy ambushed the 5th Somaliland Light Infantry. During the ensuing fight, he and Lieutenant Welland tried to rescue a wounded hospital assistant by placing him on a horse. The enemy surrounded them, killing the hospital assistant and wounding Welland with spears. Smith stayed with the lieutenant, endeavouring to keep the enemy at bay with his revolver.

Although the Mullah himself evaded capture, his troops were reduced to around eight hundred, and his wealth – mainly livestock – was impounded. The Royal Navy temporarily occupied the port of Illig, which had formerly been seized by the Mullah, and at last, with the fourth expedition, Somaliland was restored to peace as a British protectorate.

THE KANO–SOKOTO EXPEDITION (1903)

In January 1900, Sir Frederick Lugard, the creator of the West African Frontier Force, arrived in Northern Nigeria as High Commissioner, with the temporary rank of brigadier general. The British government had recently terminated the Niger Company's charter and declared a protectorate over Northern and Southern Nigeria, and Lugard was tasked with building a new state in the undeveloped region, where Muslim emirates drew their prosperity from trading in slaves taken from among their pagan neighbours. Lugard set about subjugating the emirs to bring them under the overall British protectorate – freeing the non-Muslim states from the threat of slavery and clearing the way for an infrastructure of transport routes and communications to support foreign trade.

    In 1902, he ordered a series of raids against the Fulani emirates of Sokoto, Kano, Gando and Katsina, which were resisting his rule. With a force quite disproportionate to the task, a column of seven hundred men was sent to invade the ancient city of Kano. In February 1903, field guns delivered a devastating barrage, ripping through the mud-brick walls and causing massive casualties. The Emir's troops put up what resistance they could, but, inadequately armed, they were no match for the invaders' superior power. One group of just 45 men under the command of Lieutenant Wallace Wright (later awarded the VC for this action) held off cavalry and infantry charges by some three thousand of the Emir's troops and eventually sent them into retreat in disarray.

Lugard then sent forces to the Fulani federation's capital of Sokoto, where the swords and spears of the Emir's men were useless against the heavy guns, and the city surrendered before it suffered the same damage as Kano. These two raids effectively quashed the Muslim emirates' opposition, the remaining cities surrendered, and Lugard was careful to appoint new emirs who were amenable to British control to avoid further opposition.

WRIGHT, Wallace Duffield *Lieutenant, Queen's Royal West Surrey Regiment attached Northern Nigeria Regiment*

26 February 1903 – In Nigeria, with only one other officer and forty-four men, he withstood the charges of one thousand cavalry and two thousand infantry for two hours. His little force inflicted such losses that the enemy fell back, breaking into a full retreat when pursued.

THE ARMED MISSION TO TIBET (1903–1904)

Although notionally under Chinese rule, Tibet had never subscribed to the trade regulations and border demarcations agreed by China with Britain in the late 1890s. This led to considerable unrest, but this alone was not the spur to military intervention. Word had reached the British government that China was engaged in secret negotiations to cede her interest in Tibet to Russia. This would provide a base from which Russia could threaten India's north-eastern frontiers, so in July 1903 a commercial mission with military escort under Colonel Francis Younghusband was sent to talk with the Chinese and Tibetans at Khamba Jong. The Tibetans refused to negotiate, so Britain sent him with a military mission to Lhasa to force the Tibetans to cooperate. Some eleven hundred and fifty troops entered Tibet on 12 December but their commander, Brigadier General J. R. L. Macdonald, was not prepared to overwinter in Tibet and the advance was held up until March 1904. Macdonald's forces dispersed the opposition as they swept through Red Idol Gorge to Gyantse on 12 April. Although the *jong* or fortress surrendered, it was not until 6 July, when the British stormed it, that the capture was consolidated. The sheer rock face of the approach offered no cover from fire, and after a day of artillery pounding, a breach was finally made to allow the attacking forces in. Lieutenant Grant led a company under heavy fire to make the first assault, for which action he was awarded the VC.

The advance reached Lhasa on 3 August, and it was left to Younghus-band to reach an agreement with the Tibetans, which was concluded on 7 September. The expedition returned safely to India at the end of October.

GRANT, John Duncan *Lieutenant, 8th Gurkha Rifles*

6 July 1904 – At the attack of the Gyantse Jong, Tibet, he led the storming company up a precipitous rock face in single file, on hands and knees, under heavy fire. Near the top, he was hurled back wounded but he refused to give up and was the first man to enter the fort. Once inside, the Gurkhas quickly routed the enemy with bayonet and kukri.

THE FIRST WORLD WAR

1914–18

1914

History has the beginning of the 'War to end all Wars' or the 'Great War' as 28 June 1914, when the Austro-Hungarian Archduke Franz Ferdinand was assassinated during a visit to Sarajevo. The Balkans and particularly Bosnia had been in ferment. The attack was blamed on the Serbs by Austria-Hungary and on 6 July the German government confirmed that it would support Austria-Hungary in reprisals against the Serbs. The First World War might have ended as a localized Balkan war except for two factors: Imperial Germany's ambition to overtake Great Britain as the world's superpower, and Britain's desire to retain her position; and a complex series of treaties that locked countries together with promises of mutual support in the event of war.

On 24 July Serbia appealed for help to Russia and two days later Austria-Hungary declared war on Serbia. At the end of July, Russia, linked by treaty to France, began to mobilize; and although this was more of a bluff, Germany presented ultimatums to Russia and France threatening war if they did not demobilize. On 1 August 1914 Germany declared war on Russia and a day later entered the tiny principality of Luxembourg. On 3 August Germany declared war on France and a day later German troops entered neutral Belgium in the first moves of the Schlieffen Plan. The violation of Belgian neutrality brought Britain into the war against Germany. There was a rush to recruiting offices as thousands of young men were drawn by a mixture of patriotism and a desire to join their mates in a challenging adventure that would prove their manhood. There was also a conviction that the war would be quick and would be 'Over by Christmas'.

The Schlieffen Plan called for a knockout blow to be delivered to France before Britain became involved in a Continental land war. The German army would push through Belgium and in a sweeping manoeuvre cut off Paris from the north and west. It envisaged a war of manoeuvre similar in character to the Franco-Prussian War of 1870–71. With France out of the war and the British army locked in the British Isles, the German army could then deliver the final knockout blow to Russia.

On 5 August Austria-Hungary declared war on Russia. Five days later France declared war on Austria-Hungary. On 12 August Belgian cavalry halted German mounted attacks at a bridge at Haelen, one of many small but determined actions that were beginning to slow down the impetus of the Schlieffen Plan. By 23 August, German hopes of keeping Britain from the Continent had been dashed.

MONS

In support of the principle of Belgian neutrality, British forces crossed the Channel, and at Mons in Belgium the British Expeditionary Force (BEF), a small force of tough well-trained professional soldiers, was in action: seventy thousand British troops with three hundred guns faced a hundred and sixty thousand Germans with six hundred guns.

It was here that the first VCs of the war were won. Mons was a striking demonstration of quality versus quantity: the excellent training and marksmanship of the British forces imposed a further delay on the German advance.

DEASE, Maurice James *Lieutenant, 4th Bn., Royal Fusiliers*

Born into the affluent family of JP Edmund Fitzlawrence Dease, Maurice Dease went to school in Hampstead, London, and then to Stonyhurst, the Jesuit public school in Lancashire. Here, in the Officer Training Corps, he proved a rather poor shot (just 121 out of 200 in the Annual Course of Musketry). Notwithstanding, he went on to the Army College, Wimbledon, and then Sandhurst.

In May 1910, Dease was commissioned and joined the 4th Battalion, Royal Fusiliers (City of London) and in April 1912 was promoted to lieutenant, and machine-gun officer of the battalion.

Dease's battalion was mobilized on 7 August 1914, and a week later arrived at Le Havre. In command was Lieutenant Colonel McMahon, DSO, who had introduced the standard rate of fire – fifteen aimed rounds a minute – that was to be directed against the enemy.

On 22 August the battalion marched out around dawn and by evening arrived in Nimy, a village just north of Mons, where they were warmly welcomed by the local people. It was here that the lines were drawn for the forthcoming battle of Mons. The BEF's I Corps, under Sir Douglas Haig, and II Corps (including the Royal Fusiliers), under Sir Horace Smith-Dorrien, were deployed on a 25-mile front to the north, west and east of the Mons–Condé Canal, which curved around Mons towards Nimy and Obourg, passing through a cluster of mining villages. The salient formed as the canal looped around Mons was a natural weak point in the lines – and it was here that the 4th Battalion Royal Fusiliers and the 4th Battalion Middlesex Regiment were positioned. As this was a vulnerable site from which to face a major attack, they were ordered back to the canal later in the day. Here they spread out along the west of the canal bend. From there they were tasked with covering all crossings, including the Nimy road and rail bridges.

The 4th Middlesex defended the eastern side of the canal salient and Dease, with C Company, set up his two machine guns at the railway bridge. Despite their long march, the 4th Royal Fusiliers began to dig in and set up defences. Dease got flour sacks from the local mill and filled them with shingle to protect his guns on either side of the bridge, and they worked into the night, all the time hearing the sounds of the Germans moving in the woods to the north of the canal.

The following morning, around seven o'clock, Private Barnard, manning the left-hand gun, saw a German aircraft flying low over them, and soon a German cavalry patrol came down the Nimy road towards the bridge. Of the seven men, four were shot and the officer was wounded and taken prisoner. However, the main attack was launched at nine o'clock, when columns approaching the canal towards the bridges were mown down by Dease's guns. The rear of the columns then retreated as German artillery was called down on the British positions. Unable to respond in kind, the British now came under further infantry attack, concentrating on the bridges – and, on finding the road bridge swung back, they directed all their efforts into taking the railway bridge. Dease's guns, though as well positioned and defended as the location allowed, were the focus of fierce German fire.

As fighting continued, the officer commanding the first reinforcements from Nimy was shot in the head and killed. Two more officers were killed on arrival at the railway bridge and the machine-gunners, under constant fire, were killed and wounded in such numbers that bodies had to be moved aside so that replacement gunners could take their place. Dease had been directing fire from a trench 50 yards from the bridge, but quickly went forward when he saw any break in the fire. He was wounded for the first time when attending to the left-hand gun, which had been silenced shortly after the action began. His commanding officers tried to persuade him to go to get the wound in his leg dressed, but he refused and was again shot, this time in the side, as he crawled across to the other gun. Lieutenant Steele could not convince him that he should rest – in spite of his wounds, he returned to the guns, where he was hit again. Private Barnard on the left-hand gun reported later:

'The section continued to suffer casualties. I saw both Lieutenant Dease and Sergeant Haycock fall – they had been controlling the guns from the middle of the bridge. I was the only man left on my gun, and all the crew on the other had been knocked out, so Corporal Parminter, the section corporal, took it over.' Parminter too was shot in the head and was seen to roll down the embankment by the bridge.

Lieutenant Steele, seeing both guns silenced, asked for a volunteer to man one of them, and Private Godley went forward under heavy fire, eventually reaching the right-hand gun, which he used to good effect, buying valuable time for the rest of C Company to retreat. Godley himself was badly wounded and the gun rendered inoperable, but he disabled it anyway, throwing it into the canal before attempting to retire. The able-bodied rushed back across open ground under shell and rifle fire, but the wounded were left – including Godley, who was taken prisoner.

The straggling remains of C Company finally rested in a field near Mons hospital and Lieutenant Steele, one of the few officers unwounded in the battle, paused to write reports recommending Dease and Godley for the VC. The two sheets of paper he wrote on during the retreat are now in the Regimental Museum of the Royal Fusiliers in the Tower of London. He clearly felt that their acts of bravery should not go unregistered should he be killed – along with many others who had witnessed their actions.

Questions raised as to who, of the two, had the right to the first VC of the war were settled by reports of Dease being already dead or dying at the bridge, well before Godley volunteered to go out to the guns. There was no question, under the rules governing the awarding of the VC, that Dease would take precedence due to rank – but his action was undoubtedly the first of the two, and his was the first VC gazetted for the Great War.

GARFORTH, Charles Ernest *Corporal, 15th Hussars*
23 August 1914 – Whilst his troop was fighting a rearguard action near Harmignies, he cut through a wire fence which was under heavy machine-gun fire, enabling the troop to escape. *3 September 1914* – By opening fire on an enemy machine-gun position, he drew fire away from a sergeant whose horse had been shot. *6 September 1914* – Under heavy fire, he pulled Sergeant Scatterfield from under his wounded horse and brought him to safety.

GODLEY, Sidney Frank *Private, 4th Bn., Royal Fusiliers*
23 August 1914 – At Mons, he took over the machine-gun defending the Nimy Bridge after Lieutenant DEASE had been fatally wounded. He held the enemy from the bridge for two hours, covering the retreat of his comrades. Twice wounded, he succeeded in breaking up his gun and throwing the pieces into the canal before he was taken prisoner.

JARVIS, Charles Alfred *Lance Corporal, 57th Field Coy., Royal Engineers*
23 August 1914 – At Jemappes, he successfully demolished a bridge over the Mons canal. Working for an hour and a half under continuous fire from the enemy, he fixed twenty-two slabs of gun cotton onto the bridge's three girders. Finding himself without exploder and leads, he commandeered a bicycle from a Belgian to search for them. He returned, connected up the leads and destroyed the bridge.

WRIGHT, Theodore *Captain, 57th Field Coy., Royal Engineers*
23 August 1914 – At Mons, he attempted to connect up a lead to demolish a bridge under heavy fire. Despite being wounded in the head, he refused assistance and redoubled his efforts. *14 September 1914* – He helped the 5th Cavalry Brigade to cross a pontoon bridge over the Aisne by laying

straw across it and repairing shattered sections. The bridge was under fire and he received a fatal wound just after the last men had crossed.

AISNE

About 1 a.m. on 24 August the BEF was ordered to retreat towards the River Aisne, which flowed east–west about 50 miles north-east of Paris.

ALEXANDER, Ernest Wright *Major, 119th Bty., Royal Field Artillery*
24 August 1914 – At Audregnies, whilst under attack by a German corps, he successfully saved all the guns of his battery even though all his horses had been killed and almost every man in his detachment had been killed or wounded. With the help of Captain GRENFELL and officers and men of the 9th Lancers, the guns were all withdrawn by hand.

GRENFELL, Francis Octavus *Captain, 9th Lancers*
24 August 1914 – At Audregnies, he took part in a cavalry charge against the massed German infantry. Men and horses fell and he soon found himself senior officer. Despite being severely wounded in the hand and thigh, he then assisted in saving the guns and limbers of the 119th Battery, Royal Field Artillery (commanded by Major ALEXANDER). This was achieved by slowly turning the guns and lifting them over the dead gunners. A shell landed under a gun he was lifting but did not explode. The guns were eventually brought to safety.

WYATT, George Harry *Lance Corporal, 3rd Bn., Coldstream Guards*
25–26 August 1914 – At Landrecies, whilst a part of his battalion was engaged beside a farmyard, the enemy set light to some straw sacks. The fire began to spread and it seemed as though his battalion would have to abandon its position. He dashed out in full view of the enemy and single-handedly extinguished the burning straw. Later, he received a head wound from which blood poured until he could no longer see. Although ordered to the rear, he returned to the line and continued to fight.

LE CATEAU

The BEF's II Corps was caught at Le Cateau, 30 miles from Mons, on 26 August, and turned to fight. The battle lasted eleven hours and was the British army's biggest since Waterloo, but allowed the BEF to evade destruction by the German 1st Army.

DRAIN, Job Henry Charles *Driver, 37th Bty., Royal Field Artillery*
26 August 1914 – At Le Cateau, the Germans swept in dense formation towards the guns of the 37th. He helped Captain REYNOLDS to limber up

two guns and drove the horses, enabling one of the guns to be brought safely out of action. During this action the enemy were keeping up a constant fire from 100 yards away.

HOLMES, Frederick William *Lance Corporal, 2nd Bn., King's Own Yorkshire Light Infantry*
26 August 1914 – At Le Cateau, he carried a wounded comrade out of action and a little later helped to save a gun by taking a wounded driver's place.

LUKE, Frederick *Driver, 37th Bty., Royal Field Artillery*
26 August 1914 – At Le Cateau, the Germans swept in dense formation towards the guns of the 37th. He helped Captain REYNOLDS to limber up two guns and drove the horses, enabling one of the guns to be brought safely out of action. During this action the enemy were keeping up a constant fire from a hundred yards away.

REYNOLDS, Douglas *Captain, 37th Bty., Royal Field Artillery*
26 August 1914 – At Le Cateau, the Germans swept towards the guns of the 37th. He raised two teams of volunteers to save them. Two guns were limbered up but one gun was lost when its team was shot down. The other gun was brought safely out of action by Reynolds, Driver LUKE and Driver DRAIN. Reynolds was forced to ride alongside the unguided centre pair of horses after their driver fell dead. *9 September 1914* – At Pysloup, whilst reconnoitring, he discovered a battery and silenced it.

YATE, Charles Allix Lavington *Major, 2nd Bn., King's Own Yorkshire Light Infantry*
26 August 1914 – At Le Cateau his company was subject to a heavy artillery bombardment resulting in the loss of all but 19 of his men. Rather than surrender, he led the survivors in a charge against the surrounding Germans. When the charge was over only three of the company could be formed up. He was taken prisoner, dying of his wounds a month later.

NERY

The BEF fell back towards Paris, amidst rumours that the French government had left for Bordeaux and the BEF was to be evacuated from Nantes. About 12 miles from Le Cateau the River Oise runs from east to west; just south of it is a small village called Nery. There, on 1 September, the rearguard of III Corps, 1st Cavalry Brigade and L Battery RHA, encountered and held back the German 4th Cavalry Division.

BRADBURY, Edward Kinder *Captain, L Bty., Royal Horse Artillery*
1 September 1914 – Within two minutes of enemy shells starting to fall at Nery, most of the members of L Battery were dead or wounded. He

managed to bring one gun into action before a shell severed his leg. Mortally wounded, he directed the fire of the gun until he died. The gun did not cease firing until all ammunition was expended, by which time it had knocked out four German guns.

DORRELL, George Thomas *Battery Sergeant Major, L Bty., Royal Horse Artillery*
   1 September 1914 – Whilst in action with L Battery at Nery, he helped Captain BRADBURY to bring a gun into action under tremendous fire. After the captain had been killed, he took over command and with the assistance of Sergeant NELSON, continued to fire the gun until all ammunition was expended.

NELSON, David *Sergeant, L Bty., Royal Horse Artillery*
   1 September 1914 – Whilst in action with L Battery at Nery, he helped Captain BRADBURY to bring a gun into action under tremendous fire. He then assisted Sergeant Major DORRELL to fire the gun until all ammunition was expended, although he was by then severely wounded.

AISNE

France began to feel the pressure; the government left Paris on the 2nd and on the 6th the First Battle of the Marne began. The Rive Marne is south of the Aisne and to the east of Paris, and the battle was fought on a line from Compiègne to Verdun. The Germans began to retreat on the 9th. Paris was saved. The German line in northern France went firm on the Aisne by the 13th. The position was immediately assaulted by the French 5th and 6th Armies, with the BEF in their centre, and although the 6th crossed the river with the help of a pontoon bridge and secured the north bank, they were driven back by a counter-attack and no further progress was made.

FULLER, William Charles *Lance Corporal, 2nd Bn., Welch Regiment*
   14 September 1914 – At Chivy-sur-Aisne, he ran forward under machine-gun fire, lifted up the mortally wounded Captain Haggard and carried him 100 yards to the shelter of a ridge where he dressed his wounds. At Haggard's request, he ran back out to retrieve the captain's rifle to prevent it falling into enemy hands.

JOHNSTON, William Henry *Captain, 59th Field Coy., Royal Engineers*
   14 September 1914 – Whilst the Royal Engineers were constructing pontoon bridges across the River Aisne, he worked two rafts across the river all day, ferrying supplies of ammunition over to one side and returning wounded men to the other. This action, carried out under heavy fire, enabled an advanced brigade to maintain its position.

TOLLERTON, Ross *Private, 1st Bn., Queen's Own Cameron Highlanders*
    14 September 1914 – At the Battle of the Aisne, he carried the wounded Captain Matheson to the safety of a corn field and returned to the firing line. On receiving orders to retire, he returned to the captain and stayed with him for three days until the Germans retired from the area. During this ordeal, he received bullet wounds to the temple and the right hand.

WILSON, George *Private, 2nd Bn., Highland Light Infantry*
    14 September 1914 – At Verneuill, he detected the position of an enemy machine-gun and, alone, dashed towards it. Jumping into a hollow, he found a group of eight Germans holding two British prisoners. 'Come on, men, charge!' he shouted as though his regiment was at his heels. The Germans instantly surrendered. Once they were secured, he continued his attack on the machine-gun, shooting six of the enemy, bayoneting the officer in charge and capturing it.

HORLOCK, Ernest George *Bombardier, 113th Bty., Royal Field Artillery*
    15 September 1914 – At Vendresse, whilst his battery was under fire, a shell burst wounded him in the thigh. The doctor ordered him to hospital. Instead of complying, he returned to the battery. Five minutes later, he was wounded in the back. Again the doctor ordered him to hospital. Again, he returned to the battery. A few minutes later, he was hurt in the arm. Not wanting to explain himself to the doctor, he stayed where he was.
    As well as the VC, Horlock received a promotion to sergeant and a reprimand for disobeying orders.

RANKEN, Harry Sherwood *Captain, Royal Army Medical Corps, attached 1st Bn., King's Royal Rifle Corps*
    19–20 September 1914 – At Hautes-Avesnes, whilst he was attending to the wounded, a shell blew his leg to pieces. He arrested the bleeding, bound his leg up and immediately returned to dressing the wounds of his men. When he could no longer continue, he was carried to the rear. He died shortly afterwards.

DOBSON, Frederick William *Private, 2nd Bn., Coldstream Guards*
    28 September 1914 – At Chavanne, Aisne, a thick mist cleared near the German lines leaving three British soldiers clearly visible. Two of them were instantly shot. Dobson crawled out to assist them. Finding only one alive, he dressed the man's wounds before returning to find a stretcher. He then crawled out again with Corporal Brown, and together they dragged the man to safety.

THE RACE TO THE SEA

German and Allied forces raced northwards towards the Channel, attempting to find an open flank, and by October the Western Front had reached the sea. By the 18th it was continuous. Trenches with barbed-wire obstacle belts in front and linking communications trenches and dugouts or bunkers were constructed. These field fortifications dominated fighting on the Western Front and restricted the scope for manoeuvre by all sides, although the autumn of 1914 saw many attempts by both sides to penetrate the enemy line.

MAY, Henry *Private, 1st Bn., Cameronians*
 22 October 1914 – At La Boutillerie, he ran across the firing line under a hail of fire to assist a wounded comrade. As he brought him in, the man was shot dead in his arms. He then went to the aid of the wounded Lieutenant Graham and succeeded in dragging him to safety.

THE FIRST BATTLE OF YPRES

The battle for Flanders centred on Ypres ('Wipers' to the British soldiers). The BEF took and held it early in October, and on 15 October, when the first heavy German attack was launched on the town, Ypres entered British history.

KENNY, William *Drummer, 2nd Bn., Gordon Highlanders*
 23 October 1914 – At Ypres, he rescued wounded men on five occasions under heavy fire. Previously he had carried two machine-guns out of action and conveyed many messages under dangerous circumstances over fire swept ground.

BROOKE, James Anson Otho
 29 October 1914 – At Fayet, whilst carrying a message from his colonel, he noticed that the Germans were breaking through part of the line. He immediately gathered 100 men around him and led them in a charge against the advancing Germans, saving the situation and a huge number of British lives. He was shot dead during the action.

★ **MARTIN-LEAKE, Arthur** *Lieutenant, Royal Army Medical Corps, attached 5th Field Ambulance*
 29 October to 8 November 1914 – Near Zonnebeke, Belgium, Lieutenant Martin-Leake won a bar to his VC. See p. 176 for his entry.

KHUDADAD KHAN *Sepoy, 129th Duke of Connaught's Own Baluchis*
 31 October 1914 – At Hollebeke, Belgium, after all but one of the machine-guns of his detachment had been destroyed by a shell, he fired the

remaining gun until all the other men of his detachment had been killed. Badly wounded himself, he was left for dead by the enemy but managed to crawl back to his unit.

Khudadad Khan was the first soldier of the Indian Army to win the VC in the war. He was later commissioned, and died in Pakistan aged eighty-three.

BENT, Spencer John *Drummer, 1st Bn., East Lancashire Regiment*
1–2 November 1914 – Near Le Gheer, Belgium, he was sent to bring back the members of his platoon who had mistakenly begun to retire from their trench. The men reassembled but were then attacked by the Germans who believed the trench to be empty. On finding it occupied, the Germans attacked vigorously and the officers and the platoon sergeant were all struck down. Bent took command of the platoon, and with great valour and coolness succeeded in holding the position until relieved later in the day. *3 November 1914* – About to lift the wounded Private McNulty onto his back, he slipped and fell. Realizing that bullets were flying over his head he remained on the ground, hooked his feet under McNulty's armpits and worked his way backwards with his hands, dragging McNulty to the safety of his trench.

VALLENTIN, John Franks *Captain, 1st Bn., South Staffordshire Regiment*
7 November 1914 – At Zillebeke, Belgium, whilst leading an attack against the Germans, he was struck down, and on rising to continue the attack was killed. He had instilled in his men such confidence that the enemy trenches were taken.

BRODIE, Walter Lorrain *Captain, 2nd Bn., Highland Light Infantry*
11 November 1914 – At Becelaere, Belgium, he led a gallant bayonet charge and cleared the British trenches of enemy troops who had slipped in under a thick mist. His actions led to the deaths of 80 Germans and the capture of 51.

DIMMER, John Henry Stephen *Lieutenant, 2nd Bn., King's Royal Rifle Corps*
12 November 1914 – At Klein Zillebeke, Belgium, he fired his machine-gun at the Prussian Guard, mowing them down as they advanced. Owing to the belt getting wet, his gun jammed. Whilst mending it, he was shot in the jaw. He got the gun going again but was struck by a bullet in the shoulder. Then a shrapnel shell burst above him and he was hit for the third time. With blood streaming from his wounds, he continued firing until his gun was hit and destroyed by a rain of shrapnel.

The First Battle of Ypres lasted until 22 November; it almost destroyed the original BEF but halted German progress. The Ypres salient was the site of three major actions fought at huge cost in 1914, 1915 and 1917.

AFRICA

Allied strategy in the war was concentrated on taking German colonies, particularly Togoland, Cameroon, South-West Africa and German East Africa. Fighting in 1914 was in West Africa, where an Anglo-French invasion of Cameroon made swift progress, and in German East Africa, where twelve thousand troops of the Indian Army's Expeditionary Force C were thrown back after an ill-prepared attack on the main port, Tanga.

BUTLER, John Fitzhardinge Paul *Lieutenant, King's Royal Rifle Corps, attached Pioneer Coy., Gold Coast Regiment*
17 November 1914 – In the Cameroons with a party of 13 men he went into thick bush and attacked and defeated a much greater force of the enemy. A machine-gun and many loads of ammunition were captured. *27 December 1914* – Whilst on patrol duty with a few men, he swam the Ekam River under heavy fire, carried out his reconnaissance on the far bank and swam back to safety.
Lord Gifford VC was his uncle.

RITCHIE, Henry Peel *Commander, Royal Navy*
28 November 1914 – He took a small steam boat into the harbour at Dar-es-Salaam to lay demolition charges on any German ships he found. The harbour was almost deserted and he scented a trap so he lashed two steel lighters to his boat, one on either side, as protection. Suddenly an immense fire opened up from all sides. Taking over at the wheel, he guided his boat towards the mouth of the harbour. He was hit eight times in the next twenty minutes, fainting from loss of blood just before the boat reached safety.

TURKEY

In the Black Sea, the Ottoman Empire made a pre-emptive attack on Russian naval bases on 29 October and on the 31st declared an Islamic holy war – against the British Empire. The Allies blockaded the Dardanelles.

HOLBROOK, Norman Douglas *Lieutenant, Royal Navy*
13 December 1914 – He was in command of *B.11*, a submarine built in 1905, which was keeping watch on the western end of the Dardanelles. Not only did *B.11* have to maintain a depth of 80 feet for much of the time to avoid mines but she also had to battle against the current running through the narrows. Sighting a Turkish warship through his periscope, Holbrook fired his starboard torpedo and sank the 10,000-ton battleship *Messudiyeh*. Diving immediately to avoid Turkish shells, *B.11* retreated to the Mediterranean and eventually surfaced nine hours later.
B.11 was the first submarine to sink a battleship.

TRENCH WARFARE

By November the Western Front had become locked into trench warfare as both sides dug deep and complex field fortifications. Barbed wire provided an effective obstacle against infantry attacks and machine-guns cut down the soldiers trapped by the wire in 'no-man's-land'. Heavy rain had turned the low-lying ground of Flanders into a brown mush. Churned up by shell fire, in places the mud was so deep and glutinous that men drowned in it.

HOGAN, John *Sergeant, 2nd Bn., Manchester Regiment*
  29 October 1914 – After his trench had been taken by the Germans, near Festubert, France, he, Second Lieutenant LEACH and ten volunteers launched a counter-attack on the trench. As the Germans were pushed into the next traverse, he and the lieutenant advanced farther into the trench shooting round corners with their revolvers until they had cornered the fourteen remaining Germans, who surrendered on their knees with cries of 'Mercy!' They had killed eight of the enemy and wounded two others.

LEACH, James Edgar *Second Lieutenant, 2nd Bn., Manchester Regiment*
  29 October 1914 – After his trench had been taken by the Germans, he, Sergeant HOGAN and ten volunteers launched a counter-attack on the trench. As the Germans were pushed into the next traverse, he and the sergeant advanced farther into the trench, shooting round corners with their revolvers until they had cornered the fourteen remaining Germans, who surrendered on their knees with cries of 'Mercy!' They had killed eight of the enemy and wounded two others.

RENDLE, Thomas Edward *Bandsman, 1st Bn., Duke of Cornwall's Light Infantry*
  20 November 1914 – Having seen sights in the trenches that were 'enough to move the heart of a stone', he determined to carry as many wounded comrades as possible from the shattered trenches near Wulverghem. At one point he took the injured Lieutenant Colebrook on his back and wormed his way across an open gap. Two or three bullets narrowly missed his head as he brought the officer to safety.

DARWAN SING NEGI *Naik, 1st Bn., 39th Garhwal Rifles*
  23/24 November 1914 – At Festubert, he was one of a party which successfully cleared the enemy from a British trench. During the action, he was always either first or among the first to push round each traverse that was taken. He did not even report the fact that he was wounded until the fighting had entirely ceased, by which time 32 Germans were dead and 105 prisoners had been taken.

1. Edward Bell, with Private Styles, captured a Russian gun at the Battle of the Alma, Crimea, 1854 (p. 7).

2. Charles Lucas, the very first VC, who at great personal risk, picked up and threw overboard a live shell, Crimea, 21 June 1854 (p. 5).

3. Joseph Trewavas, a Cornish sailor who cut loose a pontoon bridge at Genitchi, Crimea, 1855, thereby considerably hindering the enemy (p. 30).

4. Thomas Flinn, who as a fifteen-year-old drummer boy was one of the youngest VCs. Wounded, he fought off the enemy at Cawnpore during the Indian Mutiny (p. 73).

5. Robert Kells, who saved an officer from certain death by fighting off the enemy at Bolandshahr, during the Indian Mutiny, September 1857 (p. 66).

6. Thomas Kavanagh, a civilian with local knowledge, infiltrated enemy lines in disguise to carry out an important mission at Lucknow, Indian Mutiny, 9 November 1857 (p. 74).

7. David Spence ventured out under fire to retrieve a fallen soldier who was surrounded by the enemy at Shunsabad, Indian Mutiny, 17 January 1858 (p. 83).

8. Francis Farquharson, who although wounded led a party of men to spike two guns, depriving the enemy of firepower, Lucknow, Indian Mutiny, 9 March 1858 (p. 84).

9. Samuel Hodge (on the right, kneeling), axed down two gates of a stockade to enable his comrades to gain an entry, Gambia, 30 June 1866 (p. 109). He was the first black soldier to be awarded the VC.

10. *Below, left*. Timothy O'Hea, while others stood undecided, took action to prevent ammunition from exploding on a train, Canada, 9 June 1866 (p. 108). One of only six VCs to be awarded 'under circumstances of extreme danger' rather than in the 'presence of the enemy'.

11. *Below, right*. Lord Leslie Beresford, with a sergeant, rescued an NCO from attacking Zulu warriors, at Ulundi, Zululand, 3 July 1879 (p. 128).

12. Henry D'Arcy, a commanding officer, did not hesitate to ride out to save one of his men from Zulu attack in Ulundi, Zululand, 3 July 1879 (p. 128).

13. *Left.* Frederick Corbett volunteered to go out under heavy fire to rescue a fallen officer, Egypt, 5 August 1882 (p. 138). One of only eight cases of forfeiture, resulting from his conviction for embezzlement and theft from an officer.

14. *Below.* George Findlater (sitting with bagpipes), a piper who, although severely wounded and under heavy fire, inspired his comrades by playing his pipes throughout the attack on the Dargai Heights, India, 20 October 1897 (p. 148).

15. *Above, left.* Hamilton Reed helped his men to try to retrieve horses and guns from capture, while under intense fire at Colenso, Boer War, 15 December 1899 (p. 164).

16. *Above, right.* James Firth, under heavy fire, rescued a comrade who was wounded, and later an officer, although shot through the nose and eye himself at Plewman's Farm, Boer War, 24 February 1900 (p. 169).

17. *Right.* Sir Walter Congreve, with several other ranks, went out in order to save the guns and later, with another man, rescued one of the original party who was wounded at Colenso, Boer War, 15 December 1899 (p. 164).

18. *Above*. Basil Guy (second from right), a sailor with the naval brigade, tended the wounds of an injured comrade; he ran to get help and returned but the man had died, at Tientsin, Boxer Rebellion, 13 July 1900 (p. 155). Seen here at his investiture, Buckingham Palace.

19 *Left*. Herbert Carter, when severely outnumbered, rode 400 yards towards the enemy to rescue a severely wounded man at Jidballi, Somaliland, 19 December 1903 (p. 181).

DE PASS, Frank Alexander *Lieutenant, 34th Prince Albert Victor's Own Poona Horse*

24 November 1914 – Near Festubert, he entered an enemy sap and crawled along it until he reached a traverse from which the Germans had been lobbing bombs into a British trench. He placed a charge in the loophole and fired it, demolishing the traverse. Later in the day, he carried a wounded sepoy to safety under heavy fire.

He was the first Jewish VC of the war.

ROBSON, Henry Howey *Private, 2nd Bn., Royal Scots*

14 December 1914 – During an attack on a German position near Kemmel, France, he left his trench under heavy fire and rescued a wounded non-commissioned officer. During a subsequent attack, he tried to bring another wounded man to safety. He had already been wounded once during the attack and he was forced to abandon his attempt when he was shot again.

BRUCE, William Arthur McCrae *Lieutenant, 59th Scinde Rifles*

19 December 1914 – During a night attack near Givenchy, France, his party captured an enemy trench. In spite of the pain from a severe neck wound, he paced back and forth for several hours urging his men to hold the trench against repeated German attack. It was due to his example and encouragement that the trench was held until dusk, when it was finally taken by the Germans and he was killed.

MACKENZIE, James *Private, 2nd Bn., Scots Guards*

19 December 1914 – After a stretcher-bearer party had failed to rescue a wounded man in front of the German trenches at Rouges-Bancs, he went out under very heavy fire and accomplished the task.

NEAME, Philip *Lieutenant, 15th Field Coy., Royal Engineers*

19 December 1914 – He arrived at a captured trench at Neuve Chapelle just as the Germans were counter-attacking with bombs. Almost alone in the trench, he trimmed the damp fuses on the home-made British 'jam tin' bombs. He then lit them with matches and began hurling them over the traverse of the trench. Huge explosions were followed by yells and groans from the Germans, who responded from two directions. A machine-gun opened up on him every time he stood up on the fire step but failed to hit him. Single-handedly, he halted the German advance for an hour. He was later told that from a distance it had looked as though he and the Germans were throwing coconuts at each other.

ACTON, Abraham *Private, 2nd Bn., Border Regiment*

21 December 1914 – At Rouges Bancs, France, he and Private SMITH left their trench and went to the aid of a wounded soldier who had lain exposed near German lines for seventy-five hours. Together, they dragged him to safety. Later they went out again and brought another wounded man to safety. They spent an hour risking their lives in this manner under heavy fire.

SMITH, James Alexander *Private, 3rd Bn., Border Regiment, attached 2nd Bn.*

21 December 1914 – At Rouges Bancs, France, he and Private ACTON left their trench and went to the aid of a wounded soldier who had lain exposed near German lines for seventy-five hours. Together, they dragged him to safety. Later they went out again and brought another wounded man to safety. They spent an hour risking their lives in this manner under heavy fire.

On the Western Front fighting stopped on Christmas Day and tentative contact was made between the two sides in no-man's-land. The front-line soldiers had a great deal in common and the informal truce lasted for most of the day, but in the earliest carrier-launched air attack of naval history, the same Christmas Day, British aircraft attacked the naval base at Cuxhaven in Germany.

1915

As the first full year of the Great War began, France had lost ten per cent of her territory to the German invaders – and, significantly, a third of her industrial capacity. Nevertheless, there was a massive increase in munitions production, both in France and in Britain, to supply the 110 Allied divisions on the Western Front.

Stretched out along the Eastern Front, 83 Russian divisions defended against the irresistible impetus of 80 highly professional German and Austro-Hungarian divisions, with the result that the advancing Germans drove the Russians out of Poland and went on to overrun Serbia. This was a massive territorial conquest – but of little avail as Russia remained in the war.

This year Ypres saw the Germans make the first use of chlorine gas to make a break-through – but as would be the case after numerous sub-sequent Allied successes, no follow-up troops were available to capitalize on the gap breached, and the impetus of the attack was lost. Although the Ypres gas attack was condemned as an atrocity, the Allies also began to produce chemical weapons.

Since Turkey had joined the German side in October 1914, the Allies launched a diversionary attack against the Ottoman Empire, starting on 19 March with a naval assault at the Dardanelles. This was beaten off, so the next move was a landing by ground forces at Gallipoli on 25 April. Allied forces including Australians and Indians won a limited beachhead – but spent the rest of the year in static trench warfare in which no ground was permanently gained but thousands of lives were lost.

THE WESTERN FRONT: TRENCH WARFARE

More British troops poured into the trenches – but the tiny pre-war army was ill-equipped to train these new volunteers. Although veteran officers and NCOs were recalled from retirement, the early loss of so many regular troops made the British Expeditionary Force an essentially amateur army by 1915.

Certainly it was proven by the small success at Neuve Chapelle that, with good artillery preparation, the German trenches could be stormed – but such operations were on a small scale with modest objectives. Increas-ingly ambitious Allied assaults came to grief as the year wore on, and the casualty lists grew alarmingly. June marked the start of production in Britain of the Mills bomb, a well-designed and effective hand grenade. With two safety features, a pin and a handle that could be held down until the last moment, it was the ideal weapon for trench warfare, and the design remained in service until the 1970s.

The first VC won on the Western Front in 1915 was won in February, when the Irish Guards repelled an attack at Cuinchy, in the Loos battlefield at the junction of the French and British lines.

O'LEARY, Michael John *Lance Corporal, 1st Bn., Irish Guards*

1 February 1915 – At Cuinchy, France, he took part in an attack to recapture trenches lost the previous day. Remembering the position of a German machine gun (which he knew was about to start firing), he ran towards it. Finding his path blocked by a barricade, he killed the five men who held it and hurried on, arriving to find five Germans working feverishly to remount the gun. He shot three of them, including the officer in charge, at which point the other two surrendered. The enemy trenches were taken and O'Leary was immediately promoted sergeant.

WOODROFFE, Sidney Clayton *Second Lieutenant, 8th (S) Bn., Rifle Brigade*

30 July 1915 – At Hooge, Belgium, he defended his position and skilfully withdrew his men when heavily attacked with bombs from the flank and the rear. He then led his party forward in a counter-attack under tremendous fire but was killed whilst cutting through some barbed wire holding up the attack.

BOYD-ROCHFORT, George Arthur *Second Lieutenant, Scots Guards (Special Reserve), attached 1st Bn.*

3 August 1915 – He was standing with a working party of his battalion in a communication trench between Cambrin and La Bassée, France, when a German mortar bomb landed on the side of the parapet. Instead of stepping round the corner to perfect safety, he shouted to his men to look out, rushed at the bomb, seized it and hurled it over the parapet, where it instantly exploded. His action undoubtedly saved many lives.

HALLOWES, Rupert Price *T/Second Lieutenant, 4th Bn., Middlesex Regiment*

25–30 September 1915 – During four heavy and prolonged bombardments at Hooge, he climbed onto the parapet to put fresh heart into his men, made daring reconnaissances of the German positions and, when ammunition was running short, went back under heavy fire to bring up fresh supplies. Even when mortally wounded, he carried on inspiring those around him.

KULBIR THAPA *Rifleman, 2nd Bn., 3rd Gurkha Rifles*

25 September 1915 – At Fauquissart, France, whilst himself wounded, he found a badly wounded man of the Leicestershire Regiment behind the first-line German trench and, though urged by the soldier to save himself, he remained with him all day and night. The next morning he brought him through the German wire and placed him in a shell hole. He then returned to the German wire to bring in two wounded Gurkhas before returning to the shell hole to bring the first man in.

MALING, George Allen *T/Lieutenant, 12th (S) Bn., Rifle Brigade*
25–26 September 1915 – Near Fauquissart, he worked for nearly twenty-six hours, collecting and treating three hundred men in the open under heavy shell fire. At one point he was stunned by a high-explosive shell which killed several of his patients. A second shell covered him with debris but he never wavered from his work.

KENNY, Thomas *Private, 13th (S) Bn., Durham Light Infantry*
4 November 1915 – Near La Houssoie, whilst on patrol in thick fog, his lieutenant was shot through both thighs. He placed the officer on his back and crawled for more than an hour, under fire, hoping to find the British lines. The officer urged him to go on alone but he refused. At last he came to a familiar ditch, where he placed the lieutenant and went to find help. Finding an officer and a few men, he guided them to the ditch and together they carried the lieutenant to safety.

CAFFREY, John Joseph *Private, 2nd Bn., York and Lancaster Regiment*
16 November 1915 – Near La Brique, together with an RAMC corporal, he set out to rescue a man lying wounded in the open, 300 yards from the enemy trenches. As they reached the man, under heavy shrapnel, sniper and machine-gun fire, the corporal was shot in the head. Caffrey bandaged the corporal and brought him to safety, before returning to and bringing in the other wounded man.

MEEKOSHA, Samuel (in 1941 changed to INGHAM by deed poll) *Corporal, 1/6th (T) Bn., West Yorkshire Regiment*
19 November 1915 – Near the Yser, France, his trench was hit by a heavy bombardment, killing or wounding the senior NCOs. He took command, sent a runner for assistance, and dug out buried and wounded men in full view of the enemy. Even though ten large shells fell within 20 yards of him as he dug, he worked on. His actions saved at least four lives.

DRAKE, Alfred George *Corporal, 8th (S) Bn., Rifle Brigade*
23 November 1915 – Near La Brique, whilst on patrol with an officer, they came under rifle and machine-gun fire. The officer was hit, so Drake knelt beside him and bandaged his wounds. Some time later, a rescue party found the officer lying unconscious but alive and beside him the bullet-riddled corpse of Drake.

YOUNG, William *Private, 8th (S) Bn., East Lancashire Regiment*
22 December 1915 – Whilst attending to his wounded sergeant under heavy fire near Fouqevillers, his jaw was shattered by a bullet. In spite of the

pain, he managed to bring the sergeant to safety. He then went unaided to the dressing station, where it was discovered that he had also been wounded by a bullet in the chest.

NEUVE CHAPELLE

The spring offensive on the British sector of the Western Front began with a demonstration of British attacking capability. Four divisions of 1st Army would attempt to break the German lines at Neuve Chapelle, capture the Aubers Ridge, then threaten Lille, well inside German-occupied France. The attack, by IV Corps on the left and Indian Corps on the right, made swift progress through the German lines, held by a single division, and by nightfall the village was captured, but the relatively narrow front made exploitation by reserves difficult and the Germans soon had reinforcements to check further progress. Many of the VCs were won by soldiers using 'bombs', crude hand-thrown charges that had a short length of safety fuse that was normally lit with a cigarette. Empty jam tins were popular for 'bomb-making'.

BUCKINGHAM, William *Private, 2nd Bn., Leicestershire Regiment*
10 and 12 March 1915 – At Neuve Chapelle, he carried several wounded men to safety under heavy fire. Those he rescued included a corporal and a German soldier whose leg had been blown off.
He became known as the 'Leicester VC' and said of his action, 'Of course I did what I could, but really, it's not worth talking about.'

GOBAR SING NEGI *Rifleman, 2nd Bn., 39th Garhwal Rifles*
10 March 1915 – He was a member of a bayonet party accompanying bombers into the German trenches west of Neuve Chapelle. Despite encountering determined resistance, he was the first man to go round each traverse. He killed several Germans and forced the remainder back until they surrendered. He was killed during this action.

ANDERSON, William *Corporal, 2nd Bn., Yorkshire Regiment*
12 March 1915 – At Neuve Chapelle, he led three men with bombs against a large party of Germans who had entered the British trenches. He threw his own bombs and then those of his comrades, who had fallen wounded. Standing alone against the enemy, he then opened rifle fire on them.

BARBER, Edward *Private, 1st Bn., Grenadier Guards*
12 March 1915 – At Neuve Chapelle, he ran ahead of his grenade company and began hurling bombs at the enemy, many of whom instantly surrendered. When his company caught up with him, they found him alone, surrounded by surrendered Germans.

DANIELS, Harry *Company Sergeant Major, 2nd Bn., Rifle Brigade*
12 March 1915 – At the start of the Battle of Neuve Chapelle, more shells were fired by the British than in the whole of the Boer War. Nevertheless, as Daniels' battalion approached the section of German trenches which they had been ordered to take, they found the wire entanglements practically intact. Whilst others threw themselves to the ground to take cover from the brutal fire, Daniels and Corporal NOBLE ran directly to the entanglements and began to cut through them. Numerous rifles and several machine-guns fired at them but they succeeded in cutting through the wire, allowing the riflemen to rush through the breach and take the trenches. Daniels was seriously wounded during the action.

FOSS, Charles Calveley *Captain, 2nd Bn., Bedfordshire Regiment*
12 March 1915 – After the enemy had captured a part of one of the British trenches and a counter-attack on the trench had failed, he dashed forward with eight men under heavy fire and attacked the enemy with bombs. The trench was captured, as were the 52 Germans occupying it.

FULLER, Wilfred Dolby *Lance Corporal, 1st Bn., Grenadier Guards*
12 March 1915 – At Neuve Chapelle, he noticed about 50 Germans trying to escape along a communication trench. Despite being on his own, he ran towards them and killed the leading man with a bomb. The rest instantly surrendered.

NOBLE, Cecil Reginald *A/Corporal, 2nd Bn., Rifle Brigade*
12 March 1915 – As Noble's battalion approached the section of German trenches which they had been ordered to take, they found the wire entanglements practically intact. Whilst others threw themselves to the ground to take cover from the fire, Noble and Sergeant Major DANIELS ran directly to the entanglements and began to cut through them. Numerous rifles and several machine-guns fired at them but they succeeded in cutting through the wire, allowing the riflemen to rush through the breach and take the trenches. Noble died soon afterwards from wounds sustained.

RIVERS, Jacob *Private, 1st Bn., Sherwood Foresters*
12 March 1915 – At Neuve Chapelle, he observed a large number of Germans massed on the flank of an advanced company of his battalion. He crept up to them and hurled bomb after bomb among them, throwing them into confusion and forcing them to retire. He repeated this action later in the day and was killed by a bullet through the heart.

YPRES SALIENT AND HILL 60

The Ypres salient also saw a VC won by the commander of a bombing party, and one by a private who rescued wounded men. Hill 60 was the site of a

British tunnelling attack in April. It took its name from its height, 60 metres: it was formed out of spoil from a railway cutting, and at about 9 p.m. on 17 April it exploded. The British assaulted at once, and held it until 5 May.

MARTIN, Cyril Gordon *Lieutenant, 56th Field Coy., Royal Engineers*
12 March 1915 – At Spanbroek Molen, Belgium, in spite of his wounds, he led a party of six bombers against a section of the enemy's trenches. The Germans were driven out in confusion, and he proceeded to strengthen his new position with sandbags. The Germans counter-attacked, but his men held them off for two and a half hours until orders arrived to abandon the post.

MORROW, Robert *Private, 1st Bn., Royal Irish Fusiliers*
12 April 1915 – Near Messines, he rescued and carried to places of comparative safety several men who had been buried in the debris of trenches wrecked by shellfire.

DWYER, Edward *Private, 1st Bn., East Surrey Regiment*
20 April 1915 – At Hill 60, near Ypres, he found himself alone in his trench, from which his comrades had been driven by a party of German bomb throwers. He collected all the grenades he could find, climbed onto the parapet and began throwing them at the Germans. He came under immediate fire but managed to keep the enemy at bay until reinforcements arrived and the trench was saved. Earlier in the day, he had gone out into the open under heavy shellfire to bandage the wounded.

GEARY, Benjamin Handley *Second Lieutenant, 4th Bn., East Surrey Regiment attached 1st Bn.*
20–21 April 1915 – From 5 p.m. until nearly dawn on Hill 60, near Ypres, he held the left crater with his platoon, some men of the Bedfordshire Regiment and a few reinforcements. His men were first subjected to heavy artillery fire and then to repeated bomb attacks throughout the night. He used his rifle to great effect, threw grenades and exposed himself to view the enemy's position by the light of flares. He also arranged for ammunition and reinforcements.

ROUPELL, George Rowland Patrick *Lieutenant, 1st Bn., East Surrey Regiment*
20 April 1915 – He was in command of a company of his battalion at Hill 60 near Ypres, during the massive bombardment by German artillery. Despite being wounded in several places, he refused to quit his post when the attack came. Later that evening, faint from loss of blood, he made his way across the shell-swept open ground to the reserve trench to fetch reinforcements. The position was held until 2 a.m. when the Devons arrived to relieve his company.

WOOLLEY, Geoffrey Harold *Second Lieutenant, 1/9th Bn., London Regiment*
20–21 April 1915 – The British had taken control of Hill 60, near Ypres, but the Germans were doing their utmost to take it back. At daybreak, when only 30 men were holding the position, Woolley made his way up the hill under fearful fire to take charge of the men. His arrival put fresh heart into the survivors and several attacks were repelled before relief arrived several hours later.

He was the first Territorial Army officer to win the VC. He was later ordained and served as a chaplain in North Africa during the Second World War.

SECOND BATTLE OF YPRES

The first Zeppelin raid on Britain was launched on 19 January, and with it arose a sense of outrage at a technique of waging war that targeted civilians. Accusations of 'Hun atrocities' increased when the Germans employed poison gas at Ypres in April. They had experimented with irritant gas inside shrapnel canisters at Neuve Chapelle, but with no effect (the gas was not even noticed by the French), and on 31 January, at Bolimov in northern Galicia on the Eastern Front, they employed gas for the first time on a wide scale. Though it was not a success – the tear gas froze in the cold – it marked a grim change in land warfare: by the close of the war all sides had developed a range of chemical weapons. Their effect was either to cause choking and a condition called 'dry land drowning' in which the lungs filled with liquid and mucus, or to bring up blisters on exposed skin. The blister agents, universally known as 'mustard gas' or simply 'mustard', caused temporary or permanent blindness.

The Ypres battle began on 22 April to the north-east of the town with a limited German gas offensive, this time using chlorine. The point of the attack was held by two French divisions, the 45th (Algerian) and the (87th) Territorial, and faced by this novel and terrifying weapon they fled or died, but the Canadian 1st Division stayed at their posts and fought, then counter-attacked the cautiously advancing Germans.

FISHER, Frederick *Lance Corporal, 13th Bn. (Royal Highlanders of Canada)*
23 April 1915 – On the previous day, the Germans had used poison gas for the first time in the war, releasing 168 tons of chlorine over a four-mile front, before making an attack on the Canadian Division. Setting up his machine-gun in an exposed position, Fisher opened fire in defence of a battery of Canadian 18pdrs. The pressure of his finger never relaxed on the trigger until the guns were dragged back to safety. Even though all the men assisting him had been put out of action, he took up a new position and continued firing until he was killed.

He was the first Canadian-born man to win the VC while serving with the Canadian army.

BELLEW, Edward Donald *Lieutenant, 7th Bn. (1st British Columbia Regiment)*
24 April 1915 – During the German attack on the Canadian Division at the Ypres salient, he sited his machine-gun on high ground and fired at the enemy until his gun was smashed. Although there was no assistance in sight, he continued to fire relays of loaded rifles until he was wounded and taken prisoner. His action saved the Gravenstafel Ridge and therefore the entire Canadian position.
His captors sentenced him to death for continuing to fire after part of his unit had surrendered and he was brought before a firing squad. He protested vehemently and at the last moment his sentence was commuted.

HALL, Frederick William *Company Sergeant Major, 8th Bn. (90th Rifles)*
24 April 1915 – During the German attack on the Canadian division at the Ypres salient, a wounded man lay crying for help 15 yards from the trench. As bullets whined and hummed around him, Hall squirmed out of the trench and crawled to the soldier. He slid himself underneath the man to lift him but as he raised his head slightly to assess his position he was shot and killed.

SCRIMGER, Francis Alexander Carron *Captain, Canadian Army Medical Corps, attached 14th Bn. (Royal Montreal Regiment)*
25 April 1915 – At St-Julien, he was in charge of an advanced dressing station being heavily shelled by the enemy. He directed the removal of the wounded and himself carried a severely wounded officer (who had been abandoned as a hopeless case when the remainder of the staff left the building) as far as he could, staying with him until the fire slackened. For three days and nights he continuously displayed the greatest devotion to duty amongst the wounded.

MIR DAST *Jemadar, 55th Coke's Rifles (Frontier Force), attached 57th Wilde's Rifles (Frontier Force)*
26 April 1915 – At Wieltje, Belgium, he led his platoon with great gallantry during an attack. Afterwards, when no British officers were present, he collected various parties of the regiment together and kept them under his command until the order was given to retire. He subsequently helped to carry 8 officers to safety whilst exposed to intense fire.

SMITH, Issy (born Ishroulch SMEILOWITZ) *Acting Corporal, 1st Bn., Manchester Regiment*
26 April 1915 – At St-Julien, Belgium, he went out on his own initiative under heavy machine-gun and rifle fire to carry a wounded soldier 250 yards to safety. He then brought in many other wounded men throughout

the day, attending to them with the greatest devotion to duty, regardless of personal risk.

WARNER, Edward *Private, 1st Bn., Bedfordshire Regiment*
    1 May 1915 – After a gas attack had forced the evacuation of a trench near Hill 60, Ypres, he entered the trench alone to defend it against the enemy. The gas had prevented reinforcements from reaching him so he went himself to fetch more men. In the end the trench was held thanks to his efforts. He died the following day from the effects of gas poisoning.

LYNN, John *Private, 2nd Bn., Lancashire Fusiliers*
    2 May 1915 – During a German attack at Ypres ('Suicide Corner' as it was known) a cloud of gas was seen rolling forward from the enemy trenches. Lynn rushed to his machine gun without fixing his gas mask, and began firing at the Germans advancing behind the greenish-yellow cloud. Even as the gas was killing him, he hoisted the gun onto a parapet to get a better field of fire. Once he had single-handedly seen the enemy off, he collapsed, gasping for breath. His face had turned black. 'This is the last carry, Flash,' were his last words uttered to a friend just before he died.

BELCHER, Douglas Walter *Lance Sergeant, 1/5th Bn., London Regiment*
    13 May 1915 – South of the Wieltje–St-Julien road, and whilst in charge of an advanced breastwork during a fierce German bombardment, he decided to stay and defend the position with a handful of men even though the troops near him had been withdrawn. Throughout the day, he fired at the enemy, who were 150–200 yards away, whenever he saw them collecting for an attack. His bold stand prevented the Germans from breaking through.
    He was the first Territorial to be awarded the VC.

THE BATTLE OF AUBERS RIDGE

Aubers Ridge lay to the east of Neuve Chapelle, about a mile from the British line. The country in this sector was flat and low-lying, and occupation of the ridge gave the Germans a considerable advantage in observing the British positions. The attack, six divisions in three corps, was preceded by four days of defensive patrols by 1 Wing RFC, then by a forty-minute artillery bombardment.
    In the southern sector, the first wave suffered from machine-gun fire in the attempt to penetrate barbed wire, and by 8 a.m. were trapped in no-man's-land. VCs were won by the Black Watch, which went over the top at 3.57 p.m. after a second bombardment. Some reached the enemy line, but almost all were then killed or captured. In the northern sector, success was quickly achieved, but the forward troops in the German lines were cut off and had to withdraw the following morning.

FINLAY, David *Lance Corporal, 2nd Bn., Black Watch*
    9 May 1915 – Near Rue de Bois, he led a bombing party in an attack on enemy trenches that were heavily protected by machine-guns. After 80 yards, a shell burst just behind him, knocking him unconscious. When he recovered consciousness, he saw one of his comrades lying badly wounded beside him. He bandaged him up and half carried, half dragged him back to the British trenches.

RIPLEY, John *Corporal, 1st Bn., Black Watch*
    9 May 1915 – Leading his men in an assault at Rue de Bois, he was the first man of his battalion to reach the enemy's parapet. He directed the men to gaps in the barbed wire and led them through a breach in the parapet to a second line of trenches. He, together with seven or eight others, held this position until all his men had fallen and he himself was badly wounded in the head.

SHARPE, Charles Richard *A/Corporal, 2nd Bn., Lincolnshire Regiment*
    9 May 1915 – Whilst in charge of a blocking party sent forward at Rouges Bancs to take a portion of the German trench, he was the first man to reach the enemy's position. He began using his bombs to great effect, but by the time he had cleared the Germans from a trench 50 yards long, every member of his party had fallen. He was then joined by four other men with whom he successfully captured a trench 250 yards long.

UPTON, James *Corporal, 1st Bn., Sherwood Foresters*
    9 May 1915 – At Rouges Bancs, he crawled out to a sergeant lying in the open with a broken leg. He bandaged the limb with an old flag and carried him back to the trench. He returned to help a wounded man, but he was too heavy to carry so he placed him on his waterproof sheet and dragged him in. Even though a high-explosive shell burst behind him while he was carrying another soldier, he continued his work, bringing another ten men back to the trench.

THE BATTLE OF FESTUBERT

More than eleven thousand casualties were taken at Aubers. The attack on Festubert was an attempt to renew the offensive about two miles south. Preparations included a long preliminary bombardment and aerial bombing of communication points. The initial advance was very rapid, but the Germans withdrew to prepared lines and the attack had to be halted because of a lack of ammunition.

BARTER, Frederick *Company Sergeant Major, 1st Bn., Royal Welch Fusiliers*
    16 May 1915 – As his battalion reached the first line of German trenches at Festubert, he called for volunteers to engage in close-quarter fighting.

Eight men came forward and together they attacked the German position with bombs to such effect that in a very short time they had cleared 500 yards of hostile trenches and captured 3 officers and 102 men.

SMYTH, John George (later the Rt Hon. Sir John) *Lieutenant, 15th Ludhiana Sikhs*

18 May 1915 – Two companies attempting to hold a captured German trench 300 yards in front of the British front line near Richebourg l'Aouve, France, were coming under severe attack. Three attempts had been made to supply them with bombs and ammunition, but each attempt had failed with the deaths of all those involved. Smyth was asked to make another attempt. Together with ten volunteers, he wriggled his way through the mud and over and around dead bodies, pulling and pushing two boxes of bombs. Rifle and machine-gun fire ripped up the ground all around them and churned up the water as they forded a stream. Only Smyth and two of his companions reached the trench safely.

He was life-President of the VC and George Cross Association and author of The Story of the Victoria Cross.

MARINER, William (enlisted as William Wignall) *Private, 2nd Bn., King's Royal Rifle Corps*

Born in Chorley, Lancashire, to a Mrs Alice Wignall, it was not under his own name that this enigmatic hero was gazetted for his VC. William Wignall joined the 2nd Battalion, King's Royal Rifle Corps in 1902. His military record says he served for seven years in India with the colours and a further five years in the reserve – then was discharged around 1913/14. At the outbreak of war he re-enlisted with his old battalion and was in action in France by November 1914. By August 1915, he was invalided back to the UK, but was back in France by mid-October and stayed there at the front until his death.

In this history, however, are buried two seemingly incongruous details. Firstly, at some point between his periods of service abroad, Wignall acquired a criminal record – apparently for breaking and entering – and became closely acquainted with the constabulary. According to a newspaper report following his death, he enlisted at the outbreak of war under an assumed name for this reason. Secondly, having shown extraordinary and almost suicidal bravery in the trench battles of May 1915, he was awarded the VC. His citation reads:

> He crept up to a German gun emplacement near Cambrin, climbed onto the parapet and threw a bomb in under the roof. He heard the enemy running away and when, fifteen minutes later, he heard them return, he climbed onto the other side of the emplacement and threw another bomb in. He then lay still while the Germans opened fire. Fifteen minutes after that, he returned to his trench.

Because of his alias, the newspaper which reported the death and disappearance in action of a VC hero (the *Daily Sketch*) was unable to find any relatives for him back home – instead they feted him as having a hero's grave on a famous battlefield, and cited the police as his only 'friends'. This was pure melodrama for the public, who loved nothing better than a tale of a sinner redeemed – even if dead – but the truth was that the police were keeping an eye on this unlikely hero. He had become well known to Scotland Yard for his less commendable activities and the police had, indeed, been his friends since 1914. A detective whose job was to keep an eye on the ex-con was quoted in the *Sketch* as saying, 'We're proud to have known such a man.' Although Wignall may have shown considerable disregard for the letter of the law, 'the law' in person was apparently conscientious in keeping its protégé supplied with cigarettes, tobacco and creature comforts while he was at the front.

Even following his VC investiture by the King at Buckingham Palace, Mariner (for such was the name under which he was recommended and awarded his medal) had a further run-in with the law by overstaying his leave by two days. At his court appearance he wore his VC – and the judge ticked him off and warned him 'not to bring that Cross into court again in such circumstances'.

Back at the front in 1916, Mariner VC was killed on 1 July, the first day of the Battle of the Somme. His body was not found, so he has no grave, but he is remembered at the Thiepval Memorial – and the nation was told of an apparent ne'er-do-well who redeemed himself by making the ultimate sacrifice. The Commissioner of the Metropolitan Police issued a Roll of Honour in 1921 to recognize the heroism of 283 convicted criminals and their contribution to the war effort. Among them were two DCMs, three MMs and one Russian Order of St George, 4th Class: Mariner was the only VC.

THE ARTOIS OFFENSIVE

KEYWORTH, Leonard James *Lance Corporal, 1/24th Bn., London Regiment*
  25–26 May 1915 – He took part in a bomb attack on German positions near Givenchy. Standing on the parapet of a German trench for two hours, he hurled 150 bombs down until the trench was choked with bodies. When he ran out of bombs he took more from the bag of a dead comrade before returning to the parapet.

ANGUS, William *Lance Corporal, 8th (T) Bn., Highland Light Infantry*
  12 June 1915 – At Givenchy he volunteered to bring in Lieutenant Martin, who lay wounded a few yards from the German lines. When warned that he was going to certain death, he replied, 'It does not matter much, sir, whether sooner or later.' He crawled to the lieutenant, gave him brandy and

brought him back under bomb and rifle fire. During the action, he received forty separate wounds.

CAMPBELL, Frederick William *Lieutenant, 1st Bn. (Western Ontario)*

15 June 1915 – At Givenchy, he commanded two machine-gun crews in an attack on a German trench. After all the members of one crew had been killed, he kept the other gun in action until only he and Private Vincent were left standing. Failing to find a firm base on which to set the gun, he mounted the tripod on Private Vincent's back and continued firing, keeping the enemy at bay until a bullet shattered his hip bone.

TOMBS, Joseph Harcourt *Lance Corporal, 1st Bn., King's (Liverpool) Regiment*

16 June 1915 – Near Rue de Bois, he crawled out repeatedly under heavy shell and machine-gun fire to bring in four wounded men lying 100 yards away. He brought one man back by putting a rifle sling round his neck and looping it round the man's body and dragging him slowly to safety.

THE BATTLE OF LOOS

The attack on Loos was the British contribution to the northern element of the autumn offensive of 1915; the French attacked Vimy Ridge, near Arras. The British deployed six divisions (seventy-five thousand men) on a wide front, with six more in reserve seven miles from the front. There was a four-day barrage, with a final four hours that exceeded in intensity any yet seen. Smoke barrages hid the advancing troops, and chlorine gas was used by the British for the first time. The RFC provided artillery reconnaissance and bombed communications targets. Loos was a coal-mining area before the war, and much of the fighting was for occupation of spoil heaps, such as Fosse 8, or the fortifications built into them, such as the Hohenzollern Redoubt.

The attack began at 7.05 a.m. In the south, the village of Loos was taken by 8.00, and troops advanced to Hill 70, where they saw retreating Germans; but in following them were caught by fire from the prepared second line, and were stopped by 10.30. In the north the Hulloch Quarries were taken by 9.30; casualties approached 70 per cent. The German observation posts were at the Hohenzollern Redoubt and Fosse 8, on the British left; the Camerons reached Little Willie Trench, directly in front of the redoubt, quickly, and after failing to make much further progress were supported by artillery in the afternoon. By midnight, Loos, Fosse 8 and the quarries were all in British hands.

The Germans counter-attacked at about 1.00 a.m., taking the Quarries but failing at Fosse 8; the British attack was renewed at 9.00, with an assault on Hill 70, which failed. These positions were attacked and counter-attacked many times, with gas attacks by both sides, until 13 October, when the failure of the French 10th Army to draw off German reserves, severe casualties and bad weather brought the offensive to an end with Loos village in British hands.

DOUGLAS-HAMILTON, Angus Falconer *T/Lieutenant Colonel, 6th (S) Bn., Queen's Own Cameron Highlanders*
  25–26 September 1915 – At Hill 70, France, when the battalions on his right and left had retired, he rallied his own battalion again and again and led his men forward four times. Whilst leading the 50 remaining men, he was killed at their head. It was mainly due to his bravery, untiring energy and splendid leadership that the enemy's advance was checked.

JOHNSON, Frederick Henry *T/Second Lieutenant, 73rd Field Coy., Royal Engineers*
  25 September 1915 – During the attack on Hill 70, France, although wounded in the leg, he led several charges against one of the German redoubts. He repeatedly rallied his men under very heavy fire and was instrumental in saving the situation.

KILBY, Arthur Forbes Gordon *Captain, 2nd Bn., South Staffordshire Regiment*
  25 September 1915 – Near Cuinchy, he was selected at his own request to attack a strong enemy redoubt with his company. Despite being wounded at the outset, he led the charge along a narrow path up to the enemy wire, where his foot was blown off. The last anyone saw of him alive, he was firing his rifle and cheering his men on.
  A few weeks after these events, the Germans erected a cross with an inscription bearing his name on the towpath outside their redoubt.

KENNY, Henry Edward *Private, 1st Bn., Loyal North Lancashire Regiment*
  25 September 1915 – Near Loos, he went out six times in one day under heavy shell, rifle and machine-gun fire and each time he carried a wounded man from open ground to safety. He was himself wounded in the neck as he brought the last man over the parapet.

LAIDLAW, Daniel Logan *Piper, 7th (S) Bn., King's Own Scottish Borderers*
  25 September 1915 – As the bugles sounded an advance near Hill 70, France, he mounted the parapet and played his company out of the trench. He ran forward with his comrades, playing 'Blue Bonnets over the Border', until he was struck by shrapnel in the left leg as he approached the German lines. He then changed tune to 'The Standard on the Braes o' Mar' until, seeing that the German position had been taken, he struggled back to his trench.

PEACHMENT, George Stanley *Private, 2nd Bn., King's Royal Rifle Corps*
  25 September 1915 – During heavy fighting near Hulluch, France, he saw his company commander lying wounded. The enemy's fire was intense but a shell hole, in which a few men had already taken cover, was close by.

However, he had no intention of saving himself. Instead, he crawled over to the officer, but as he reached him was wounded by a bomb. A minute later, he was killed by a rifle bullet.

READ, Anketell Moutray *Captain, 1st Bn., Northamptonshire Regiment*
25 September 1915 – Although partially gassed, he went out several times near Hulloch to prevent disorganized parties of men from retiring. He led them back into the firing line and moved freely amongst them under ferocious fire. He was killed in the course of this action. He had previously shown great courage when he carried a mortally wounded officer out of action under intense rifle fire and grenade attacks.

VICKERS, Arthur *Private, 2nd Bn., Royal Warwickshire Regiment*
25 September 1915 – During an attack by his battalion on the first-line German trenches at Hulloch, he went out in front of his company under very heavy shell, rifle and machine-gun fire and, standing in broad daylight, cut the wires which were holding up the progress of a large part of the battalion. This action contributed greatly to the success of the attack.

WELLS, Harry *Sergeant, 2nd Bn., Royal Sussex Regiment*
25 September 1915 – He took command of his platoon after its commander had been killed near Le Rutoire, Loos, and led the men forward to within 15 yards of the German wire. Nearly half the platoon had been killed or wounded but he rallied them and led them forward. Urging the few survivors forward once more, he was killed.

DUNSIRE, Robert *Private, 13th (S) Bn., Royal Scots*
26 September 1915 – At Hill 70, France, he went out under very heavy fire and rescued a wounded man from between the firing lines. Hearing another man shouting for help, he then crawled close to the German lines to bring that man to safety. Shortly after these actions, the Germans attacked over the very same ground.

SAUNDERS, Arthur Frederick *Sergeant, 9th (S) Bn., Suffolk Regiment*
26 September 1915 – Near Loos, despite a severe thigh wound, he took charge of two machine-guns and a few men and followed closely the last four charges of another battalion, rendering every support. Later, when that battalion retired, he remained with one of his guns, gave clear orders and did his best to cover the retirement.

BURT, Alfred Alexander *Corporal, 1st Bn., Hertfordshire Regiment*
27 September 1915 – At Cuinchy, his company had lined the front trench in preparation for an attack when a large bomb fell amongst the men. Instead of seeking cover behind a traverse, he stepped forward, put his foot on the fuse, wrenched it out of the bomb and threw it over the parapet, rendering the bomb harmless. His presence of mind and great pluck saved a great many lives.

POLLOCK, James Dalgleish *Corporal, 5th (S) Bn., Queen's Own Cameron Highlanders*

27 September 1915 – Near the Hohenzollern Redoubt, France, when the enemy's bombers were advancing up the 'Little Willie' trench towards his position, he got out of the trench alone, walked along the top under machine-gun fire and began bombing the Germans from above, forcing them to retire. At length he was wounded, but not before holding up the Germans' advance for an hour.

Corporal J. L. Dawson VC was his cousin.

TURNER, Alexander Buller *Second Lieutenant, 3rd Bn., Royal Berkshire Regiment, attached 1st Bn.*

28 September 1915 – At Fosse 8, near Vermelles, France, the regimental bombers were unable to make any headway so he headed down the communication trench alone, throwing bombs with such dash and determination that he drove the Germans back 150 yards. As a result the reserves were able to advance with very little loss. Died shortly afterwards from his wounds.

Colonel V. B. Turner VC was his brother.

FLEMING-SANDES, Arthur James Terence *T/Second Lieutenant, 2nd Bn., East Surrey Regiment*

29 September 1915 – At the Hohenzollern Redoubt, France, men of his company were beginning to retire, so he collected together a few bombs, jumped on the parapet in full view of the Germans, and threw them. He was severely wounded almost at once, but he struggled to his feet and continued to advance and throw bombs until he was wounded again. His action put new heart into the men and saved the situation.

HARVEY, Samuel *Private, 1st Bn., York and Lancaster Regiment*

29 September 1915 – He volunteered to bring urgently needed ammunition to the 'Big Willie' trench near the Hohenzollern Redoubt. Ignoring intense enemy fire, he carried thirty boxes of bombs across open ground before he was wounded in the head. It was mainly thanks to his action that the enemy was driven back.

BROOKS, Oliver *Lance Sergeant, 3rd Bn., Coldstream Guards*

8 October 1915 – Near Loos, he gathered together a party of bombers and led them forward in an attempt to recapture 200 yards of trenches that had been lost to the enemy. His bravery in the midst of a hail of bullets ensured the complete success of the operation.

RAYNES, John Crawshaw *A/Sergeant, A Bty., 71 Brigade, Royal Field Artillery*

11 October 1915 – At Fosse 7 de Bethune, he dashed out under shellfire to assist a sergeant who was lying wounded. He bandaged him and went back to his gun but when 'Cease fire' was ordered, he returned to the sergeant and carried him into a dugout, in which a gas shell burst. He ran to fetch his gas helmet, which he placed on the sergeant before staggering back to his gun, badly gassed. The next day he was buried under a house which had been shelled, and although he was the first man rescued, insisted on remaining to assist with the rescue of all the other men. Then, having had his wounds dressed, he reported for duty.

DAWSON, James Lennox *Corporal, 187th Field Coy., Royal Engineers*
13 October 1915 – During a gas attack at the Hohenzollern Redoubt, he walked up and down under heavy fire, clearing infantry out of sections of the trench that were full of gas. Finding three leaking gas cylinders, he rolled them away from the trench and fired rifle bullets into them allowing the gas to escape. His coolness saved many men from being gassed.
He was cousin of Corporal J. D. Pollock VC.

VICKERS, Charles Geoffrey (later Sir Geoffrey) *T/Captain, 1/7th (T) Bn., Sherwood Foresters*
14 October 1914 – When nearly all his men had been killed or wounded at the Hohenzollern Redoubt, and with only two men to hand him bombs, he held a barrier for some hours against heavy German attacks. He then ordered a second barrier to be built behind him to ensure the safety of the trench in the full knowledge that his own retreat would be cut off. By the time he was finally severely wounded, the barrier was complete and the situation was saved.

CHRISTIAN, Harry *Private, 2nd Bn., King's Own (Royal Lancaster Regiment)*
18 October 1915 – At Cuinchy, a heavy bombardment forced him to withdraw from a crater that he was holding with several others. When he found that three men were missing, he returned alone to the crater, where he found, dug out and carried all three men to safety, undoubtedly saving their lives. He later placed himself where he could see the bombs coming and directed his comrades when and where to seek cover.

INDIA

Tribesmen in the northern Indian states continued to rebel against British influence and in January, Captain Jotham of the 51st Sikhs was awarded the VC for his courage in a small-scale mounted action. In the autumn, Charles Hull of the 21st Lancers won his when he saved his officer's life when they were attacked by tribesmen.

JOTHAM, Eustace *Captain, 51st Sikhs (Frontier Force)*
7 January 1915 – At Spina Khaisora, whilst in command of a party of 40 who were attacked by fifteen hundred tribesmen, he gave the order to retire, but in the knowledge that he was almost certainly sacrificing his life, he

turned back to save one of his sowars who had been knocked off his horse. He killed seven of the enemy before his death.

HULL, Charles *Private – Shoeing Smith, 21st Lancers*
   5 September 1915 – At Hafiz Kor, he rescued Captain Learoyd, whose horse had been shot, by taking him up behind him and galloping to safety. All the while he was under fire from the enemy, who were only a few yards away.
   He was one of the honour guard at the interment of the Unknown Soldier at Westminster Abbey on 11 November 1920.

THE DARDANELLES

On 19 February Anglo-French naval forces began attacks on Turkish forts protecting the narrows of the Dardanelles. This was part of a bold plan proposed by Winston Churchill, First Lord of the Admiralty, to drive Turkey out of the war and open up a supply route to Russia via the Black Sea.

ROBINSON, Eric Gascoigne *Lieutenant Commander, Royal Navy*
   26 February 1915 – He led a demolition party ashore in the Dardanelles to destroy the guns at Achilles' tomb, Kum Kale and Orkanie. His sailors' white uniforms made them conspicuous so he went alone to Achilles' tomb where he demolished two guns with gun cotton. The entire party then proceeded to Orkanie to destroy the remaining gun mountings.

GALLIPOLI

The landings at Gallipoli were part of the larger campaign to drive Turkey out of the war, and more immediately to divert her troops from the Caucasian Front. The specific aim was to secure the peninsula, clear it of Turkish defences and thus allow a British fleet to enter the Sea of Marmara. General Sir Ian Hamilton was given command of the British Mediterranean Force, of seventy-five thousand men, but the well-prepared Turkish Fifth Army, under the command of the German Liman von Sanders, had eighty-four thousand men distributed in six divisions across the peninsula. The principal assault was by the British 29th Division at Cape Helles, followed up by the French, and the secondary assault was by the Anzac Corps, twelve miles north, near Gaba Tepe.
   Following the bombardment of Turkish positions and two diversionary landings, the Allies landed at Gallipoli between 4.45 and 8 a.m. The main point of attack, at Helles (X, W and V Beaches), was defended by only a thousand Turks, and X Beach was secured by 6.20, but the V and W Beaches had mined underwater barbed wire and machine-guns, which were not

affected by the naval bombardment. Of the leading battalion at W Beach, 1st Lancashire Fusiliers, only two of the twenty-four boats in the first wave reached the shore, and although they had driven the Turks off by 8 a.m. they had lost eleven officers and three hundred and fifty men killed or wounded. Their sanguinary landing was remembered as the day they won 'Six VCs Before Breakfast'. At V Beach the tramp steamer *River Clyde*, modified as an assault ship to land men, took two thousand men into shore, supported by a thousand men in ships' boats, but her steam hopper, planned to form a gangway to the shore, swung sideways, and the lighters drifted out of position. Five VCs were won in the struggle to resecure them. By 9.00 a.m. only three hundred of the seven hundred men of the Royal Dublin Fusiliers had landed, and had only reached a bank ten yards inland.

The Allies held W and V Beaches that night, but were driven from Y Beach, and by morning the Turks had pulled back to a new line across the peninsula.

BROMLEY, Cuthbert *T/Major, 1st Bn., Lancashire Fusiliers*
25 April 1915 – At Gallipoli, he was one of those rowed ashore at the seemingly deserted W Beach. As the boats neared land, it became clear that the British naval bombardment had failed to clear the barbed-wire entanglements. As they reached the shore, a hail of bullets swept across them from hidden Turkish machine guns. Sailors were shot dead at their oars. The relentless fire continued as the Fusiliers hurled themselves ashore and cut their way through the entanglements. Although most of the men were killed or wounded, the beach was taken.

DREWRY, George Leslie *Midshipman, Royal Naval Reserve*
25 April 1915 – At Gallipoli, he was on board the *River Clyde*, a tramp steamer attempting to land two thousand troops onto V Beach, when lighters forming the bridge between the steamer and the shore began to drift apart. Under fierce machine-gun fire, he waded ashore and attempted to rescue a wounded soldier who was shot dead in his arms. He then returned to the steamer and collected a rope, which he delivered to Commander UNWIN, enabling the latter to secure the lighters. When they again came adrift, he swam across with another rope clamped in his teeth, despite a head wound caused by a fragment of shell.

GRIMSHAW, John Elisha *Corporal, 1st Bn., Lancashire Fusiliers*
25 April 1915 – At Gallipoli, he was one of those rowed ashore to the seemingly deserted W Beach. As the boats neared land, it became clear that the British naval bombardment had failed to clear the barbed-wire entanglements. As they reached the shore, a hail of bullets swept across them from hidden Turkish machine-guns. The relentless fire continued as the Fusiliers hurled themselves ashore and cut their way through the entanglements. Although most of the men were killed or wounded, the beach was taken.

KENEALLY, William *Private, 1st Bn., Lancashire Fusiliers*

25 April 1915 – At Gallipoli, he was one of those rowed ashore at the seemingly deserted W Beach. As the boats neared land, it became clear that the British naval bombardment had failed to clear the barbed-wire entanglements. As they reached the shore, a hail of bullets swept across them from hidden Turkish machine-guns. Sailors were shot dead at their oars. The relentless fire continued as the Fusiliers hurled themselves ashore and cut their way through the entanglements. Although most of the men were killed or wounded, the beach was taken.

MALLESON, Wilfred St Aubyn *Midshipman, Royal Navy*

25 April 1915 – At Gallipoli, he was on board the *River Clyde*, a tramp steamer attempting to land two thousand troops onto V Beach, when lighters forming the bridge between the steamer and the shore began to drift apart. The lighters were repositioned by Commander UNWIN but they came adrift again after a shot severed a rope. Another rope brought by Midshipman DREWRY proved too short, so Malleson threw himself over the side with a fresh line and managed to reconnect the lighters. They subsequently came adrift again, and although he made two courageous efforts, he was unable to reposition them.

RICHARDS, Alfred Joseph *Sergeant, 1st Bn., Lancashire Fusiliers*

25 April 1915 – At Gallipoli, he was one of those rowed ashore at the seemingly deserted W Beach. As the boats neared land, it became clear that the British naval bombardment had failed to clear the barbed-wire entanglements. As they reached the shore, a hail of bullets swept across them from hidden Turkish machine guns. Sailors were shot dead at their oars. The relentless fire continued as the Fusiliers hurled themselves ashore and cut their way through the entanglements. Although most of the men were killed or wounded, the beach was taken.

SAMSON, George McKenzie *Seaman, Royal Naval Reserve*

25 April 1915 – At Gallipoli, he was on board the *River Clyde*, a tramp steamer attempting to land two thousand troops onto V Beach, when lighters forming the bridge between the steamer and the shore began to drift apart. Under fierce machine gun fire, he busied himself among the wounded and offered assistance to those repairing the bridge. He was hit over and over again, and when he returned to England his body still contained a dozen pieces of shrapnel.

Whilst walking in civilian dress to a public reception in honour of his VC, he was presented with a white feather – a symbol of cowardice – by a stranger.

STUBBS, Frank Edward *Sergeant, 1st Bn., Lancashire Fusiliers*

25 April 1915 – At Gallipoli, he was one of those rowed ashore at the seemingly deserted W Beach. As the boats neared land, it became clear that the British naval bombardment had failed to clear the barbed-wire entanglements. As they reached the shore, a hail of bullets swept across them from hidden Turkish machine guns. Sailors were shot dead at their oars. The relentless fire continued as the Fusiliers hurled themselves ashore and cut their way through the entanglements. Although most of the men were killed or wounded, the beach was taken.

TISDALL, Arthur Walderne St Clair *Sub-Lieutenant, Royal Naval Volunteer Reserve (Anson Bn.)*
25 April 1915 – At Gallipoli, he was one of those on board the tramp steamer *River Clyde*, waiting his turn to land on V Beach as the Turkish machine guns mowed down those who came ashore. Unable to bear the cries of wounded men, he jumped into the water and called for assistance. First one man and later three others answered his call, and the rescuers made five boat journeys, each time bringing as many men as they could back to the *River Clyde*. Only darkness prevented them from continuing.

UNWIN, Edward *Commander, Royal Navy*
25 April 1915 – At Gallipoli, he was in command of the *River Clyde*, a tramp steamer attempting to land two thousand troops onto V Beach, when lighters forming the bridge between the steamer and the shore began to drift apart. Under fierce machine-gun fire, he waded into the water and (together with Seaman WILLIAMS) secured a line to one of the lighters and towed it into position. The line was not long enough, but when Midshipman DREWRY returned with a longer one, he secured the lighter, allowing the attack to continue. On his return to the steamer, he was ordered to rest by the doctor but instead made several journeys to pick up wounded men as they lay helpless in the shallow water. He was eventually overcome by sheer physical exhaustion.

WILLIAMS, William Charles *Able Seaman, Royal Navy*
25 April 1915 – At Gallipoli, he was on board the *River Clyde*, a tramp steamer attempting to land two thousand troops onto V Beach, when lighters forming the bridge between the steamer and the shore began to drift apart. Under fierce machine-gun fire, he (together with Commander UNWIN) secured a line to one of the lighters and towed it into position. The line was not long enough, and after waiting for over an hour, neck-deep in water whilst Midshipman DREWRY fetched another, he was shot. He died in the arms of Unwin.

WILLIS, Richard Raymond *Captain, 1st Bn., Lancashire Fusiliers*
25 April 1915 – At Gallipoli, he was one of those rowed ashore at the seemingly deserted W Beach. As the boats neared land, it became clear that the British naval bombardment had failed to clear the barbed-wire entanglements. As they reached the shore, a hail of bullets swept across them from hidden Turkish machine guns. Sailors were shot dead at their oars. The relentless fire continued as the Fusiliers hurled themselves ashore and cut

their way through the entanglements. Although most of the men were killed or wounded, the beach was taken.

COSGROVE, William *Corporal, 1st Bn., Royal Munster Fusiliers*
   26 April 1915 – During an attack from the beach to the east of Cape Helles at Gallipoli, he set about clearing a way though the Turkish wire single-handedly. Using great strength, he managed to wrench one of the stanchions clean out of the ground under terrific fire from the front and flanks. He contributed greatly to the success of the operation.

DOUGHTY WYLIE, Charles Hotham Montagu *Lieutenant Colonel, Royal Welch Fusiliers, attached HQ Mediterranean Expeditionary Force*
   26 April 1915 – He was one of those who landed on V Beach at Gallipoli with the Mediterranean Expeditionary Force. Together with Captain WAL-FORD, he led an attack on a strongly held enemy position in the Old Castle. It was mainly due to the skill and initiative of the two officers that the attack was a complete success. He was shot through the head whilst leading the last assault.

WALFORD, Garth Neville *Captain, Royal Artillery*
   26 April 1915 – He was one of those who landed on V Beach at Gallipoli with the Mediterranean Expeditionary Force. Together with Lieutenant Colonel DOUGHTY WYLIE, he led an attack on a strongly held enemy position in the Old Castle. It was mainly due to the skill and initiative of the two officers that the attack was a complete success. He was killed at the moment of victory.

PARKER, Walter Richard *Lance Corporal, Royal Marine Light Infantry*
   30 April/1 May 1915 – Whilst a stretcher bearer, he volunteered to go to the assistance of a party of marines in an isolated trench at Gaba Tepe even though several men had already been killed attempting to reach them. Ignoring an Australian officer who threatened to shoot him if he went any further, he dashed across an open space swept by machine-gun fire. He was shot in two places, but inspired by cheers from his comrades, ran on until he reached the marines. He gave first aid to the wounded. When the trench was evacuated, he was again shot several times.

ANZAC COVE

The line constructed on 25 April held against repeated attacks that by 4 May cost the Turks around fourteen thousand casualties; there had been very limited successes in counter-attacks but a breakout looked impossible, and the sector was quiet for the next two weeks. Then at 3 a.m. on 19 May about forty thousand Turks headed by the 2nd Division began a frontal infantry assault. Anzac lines were well sited and the enemy took nearly ten thousand casualties in the first two hours. The attack failed by midday, but at one position the Turks briefly broke through. They were killed by Albert Jacka, who won the first Australian VC of the war.

JACKA, Albert *Lance Corporal, 14th Bn. (Victoria), Australian Imperial Force*
Albert Jacka came from a farming family in Victoria, South-Eastern Australia. He grew up in the great outdoors, helping with his father's dairy herd and timber business, and was working for the Victorian State Forests Department when war broke out in 1914. The Australian government quickly offered Britain twenty thousand men to fight, and on 10 August recruiting offices opened. There was no need, then or at any other time in the Great War, for conscription to fill the ranks with Australian men. Jacka was among those keen to see action and adventure – he joined up on 18 September and was soon training with the 14th Battalion. By Christmas Jacka was in Egypt and the Australians were joined by a large contingent from New Zealand.

By 19 May, Jacka's 14th Battalion had lost 75 per cent of its strength and was grimly defending the line from a point known as Quinn's post to that of Courteney, Jacka's commanding officer. At Courtney's Post, he rushed alone into a communications trench occupied by seven Turks. He kept them at bay until three Anzacs came to his aid. 'Keep them here and I will take them at the other end of the trench,' he told his comrades, as he ran round and fell on the astonished Turks from the rear, shooting five and killing two with his bayonet. 'I think I lost my nut,' he explained afterwards.

Two lieutenants of the 14th were killed by Turkish fire and Lieutenant Crabbe from battalion headquarters rushed down the communications trench towards where Jacka was holding back the enemy. He pulled up as Jacka warned him what was going on ahead, then asked Jacka if he thought, given enough support, he could make a charge. Without hesitation, Jacka asked for a few volunteers and prepared to attack. Under heavy fire, he leapt across the gap into the trench with Crabbe and, bayonets fixed, he and his two volunteers charged into heavy Turkish fire. Jacka's comrades were wounded and fell back into the side trench. As the dust settled, Crabbe and Jacka planned a diversion.

Under a hail of crossfire, Jacka climbed out of the trench and crawled over open ground to the south. When they reckoned he had time to reach his position, the men in the trench threw two hand-made bombs towards the Turks. Both bombs malfunctioned, but they had the desired effect in creating a diversion. In the ensuing noise and smoke, Jacka seized his opportunity. Jumping into the trench from behind the Turks, he shot five of them with his rifle and bayoneted two more before the others could turn to defend themselves. Thrown into disarray, the remaining Turks scattered, scrambling out of the trench. Jacka shot two as they tried to escape and the rest were accounted for by others from the battalion. Crabbe entered the now secured trench to find Jacka caked in dust and sweat – surrounded by Turkish dead. Flushed from the exertions of an hour's fierce fighting, he had an unlit cigarette in the corner of his mouth. Grinning, he welcomed Crabbe, 'I managed to get the beggars, sir!'

The trenches were the scene of further acts of courage by Jacka as the Anzac troops were withdrawn from Gallipoli and sent to the Western Front in July 1916 after a spell recuperating in Egypt. With so many killed in the Gallipoli battle, promotion was rapid for experienced soldiers, and Jacka got his commission in March 1916.

On 7 August 1916, the Germans had overrun part of the line at Poziers where the 14th Battalion had joined the British in the Somme. Jacka had returned to his dugout following a reconnaissance foray when the enemy charged down the trench, killing two men in the dugout with a grenade. Jacka rushed forwards, firing as he went up the steps – to find a large number of Germans rounding up Australian prisoners. He charged with two men in support and, firing at point-blank range or clubbing down the Germans with his gun, he was wounded three times, once through the neck, but the 'prisoners' needed no second bidding and attacked their captors with any weapons they could lay their hands on. The situation was reversed – now the Germans were the prisoners and the security of the line was restored. Jacka was awarded the Military Cross for this action – but there were many who felt he should have received a bar to his VC. Official War Historian C. E. W. Bean described Jacka's action at Poziers as 'the most dramatic and effective act of individual audacity in the history of the Australian Imperial Force'. However, the Australian command seemed loath to heap further supreme honours on Jacka in case he became even more of an icon among the men – following his VC award, his face had appeared on recruitment posters in his homeland. Jacka does not seem to have been the sort of man to have cared that much about medals, but after recovering from his wounds in England, the newly promoted Lieutenant Jacka was invested with his VC by the King at Buckingham Palace on 29 September 1916.

Back in France at the front, Jacka was evidently unchastened by his narrow escape at Poziers, as on 18 April 1917 he earned a bar to his MC with another audacious action. By then a captain, and the intelligence officer for the 14th Battalion, he went out alone under cover of darkness to recce the wires blocking the way to the objective of the imminent attack. He managed to penetrate the wire in two places, then returned to his trench – only to crawl back out over the churned-up ground to mark the breaches for the assault. It was then that he was confronted by two Germans. He challenged them, but as they continued to approach him, he drew his revolver and fired – but the gun was jammed with mud and nothing happened. He rushed the two Germans – one an officer – and knocked them to the ground, then pushed his captives ahead of him to the Australian lines just minutes before the attack began. As the troops went into action, his markers enabled them to assemble in silence – so preserving the element of surprise.

It seems there was no end to Jacka's appetite for battle – on a later occasion he led a company to take half a mile of ground and capture a field gun, and later, although not fully recovered from an injury, took charge of the battalion during fierce fighting. Jacka was eventually evacuated to England suffering from the effects of poison gas, and took a long recovery before returning to Australia, the nation's most decorated hero.

Back at home, Jacka became Mayor of the City of St Kilda in Melbourne, but his business was destroyed by the post-war economic depression and his health suffered under the stress and the aftermath of his wounds. He died in hospital aged only thirty-nine. His father was at his bedside as he whispered, 'I'm still fighting, Dad,' before he passed away. Tributes poured in. His former brigade commander summed up the mettle of the man. 'Jacka was more than a fighter – he was a genius. He had that superb quality of knowing when to act and how to act, and the sublime courage that made that which seemed impossible, possible.'

TRENCH WARFARE

June saw an attempt to break out in the south, at Krithia, where initial advances fell back after Turkish counter-attacks. After these repeated failures, Britain sent three more divisions, which effected a landing at Suvla Bay to the north of Anzac cove on 6 August. A number of VCs were won here, most notably in the attack on Chunuk Bair, in the Sari Bair Ridge, control of which would prevent Turkish reinforcement, and in two diversionary attacks, on Lone Pine, to the south-east, and the Nek, south-west of Chunuk Bair. The Chunuk Bair and Nek attacks failed, but Lone Pine, which saw some of the bitterest fighting of the campaign (ninety per cent of the casualties were killed), was secured by the Australian 1st Division on 8 August and held against repeated counter-attacks. The attack continued until the 10th, when, after twelve thousand Allied and twenty thousand Turkish casualties had been taken, both sides were exhausted. The final Allied offensive at Gallipoli was a second attempt to link Suvla Bay with Anzac Cove: the principal objectives were W Hills and Scimitar Hill (Hill 70), and the secondary was Hill 60. As so often before, a frontal assault against well-defended lines found limited success but was thrown back, and General Hamilton asked for ninety-five thousand men. He was offered twenty-five thousand, and in September had to send one division to the defence of Serbia and another to Egypt, to recuperate. He was replaced on 15 October by General Sir Charles Monro, who on 28 October recommended withdrawal, which was ordered on 7 December. Suvla Bay and Anzac Cove were completed on 19/20 December. The last VC of the campaign was won at Helles, from which withdrawal was completed on 8/9 January 1916.

MOOR, George Raymond Dallas *Second Lieutenant, 3rd (R) Bn., Hampshire Regiment*
    5 June 1915 – Near Krithia, Gallipoli, noticing a detachment of a battalion falling back under Turkish attack, he shot the leading four men of the battalion. His action stopped the retreat and he was able to lead the battalion forward. As a result, the lost trench was recaptured.

JAMES, Walter Herbert *Second Lieutenant, 4th Bn., Worcestershire Regiment*
    28 June 1915 – At Gallipoli, when a portion of his regiment had been checked and its officers put out of action, he gathered a party of men and advanced them under heavy fire. He then returned and advanced with a second party, putting fresh life into the attack. *3 July 1915* – He headed a party of bomb throwers up a Turkish communications trench, and after nearly all his men had been killed or wounded kept the enemy back single-handed until the trench was secured.

O'SULLIVAN, Gerald Robert *Captain, 1st Bn., Royal Inniskilling Fusiliers*
    1–2 July 1915 – At Gallipoli, when it was essential that a portion of trench should be regained, he took charge of a party of bomb throwers and advanced them onto the enemy parapet in order to throw his bombs with greater effect. He was eventually wounded, but his example inspired his party to make further efforts which resulted in the recapture of the trench.

SOMERS, James *Sergeant, 1st Bn., Royal Inniskilling Fusiliers*
    1–2 July 1915 – At Gallipoli, whilst alone in a sap after his comrades had retired, he climbed into a Turkish trench and began bombing with great effect. He then advanced into the open under heavy fire and held the enemy back by throwing bombs into their flank until a barricade was established. All the while, he was running to and from the trenches receiving fresh supplies of bombs.

BASSETT, Cyril Royston Guyton *Corporal, New Zealand Divisional Signal Coy., New Zealand Expeditionary Force*
    7 August 1915 – At Chunuk Bair Ridge, Gallipoli, in full daylight and under continuous fire, he succeeded in laying a telephone line from the New Zealand Brigade's old position to its new one. He did further gallant work repairing telephone lines by day and night.

FORSHAW, William Thomas *Lieutenant, 1/9th (T) Bn., Manchester Regiment*
    7–9 August 1915 – At Gallipoli, he held the north-west corner of the 'Vineyard' against a sustained attack by the Turks. Whilst directing operations, he threw bombs continuously for forty-one hours, even after his

detachment had been relieved. At one point the Turks got over the barricade, but he shot three of them, led his men forward and recaptured the trench. When he finally rejoined his battalion, he was choked by bomb fumes, wounded by shrapnel and could barely lift his throwing arm.

KEYSOR, Leonard Maurice *Private, 1st Bn. (New South Wales), Australian Imperial Force*

7–8 August 1915 – At Lone Pine, Gallipoli, during bomb fighting between Anzac and Turkish trenches, he threw bombs, smothered them with his coat and even caught bombs in the air as though they were cricket balls before throwing them back. Twice wounded but refusing to retire, he remained in action almost continuously for fifty hours.

SYMONS, William John (later PENN-SYMONS) *Second Lieutenant, 7th Bn. (Victoria), Australian Imperial Force*

8–9 August 1915 – At Lone Pine, Gallipoli, whilst defending a section of newly captured trenches, he made an attack on an isolated sap which the Turks had retaken. He shot two Turks with his revolver and built up a sandbag barricade. When the Turks set fire to the barricade, he extinguished the flames and rebuilt it. His coolness and determination compelled the enemy to abandon their attack.

BURTON, Alexander Stewart *Corporal, 7th Bn. (Victoria), Australian Imperial Force*

9 August 1915 – At Lone Pine, Gallipoli, he (together with Lieutenant TUBB, Corporal DUNSTAN and a few men) repulsed a Turkish attack on a newly captured trench. Three times the Turks advanced up the sap and blew in a sandbag barricade, leaving only a small part standing, but each time they were pushed back and the barricade rebuilt. Burton was killed whilst building the parapet under a hail of bullets.

DUNSTAN, William *Corporal, 7th Bn. (Victoria), Australian Imperial Force*

9 August 1915 – At Lone Pine, Gallipoli, he (together with Lieutenant TUBB, Corporal BURTON and a few men) repulsed a Turkish attack on a newly captured trench. Three times the Turks advanced up the sap and blew in a sandbag barricade, leaving only a small part standing, but each time they were pushed back and the barricade rebuilt.

HAMILTON, John Patrick *Private, 3rd Bn. (New South Wales), Australian Imperial Force*

9 August 1915 – At Lone Pine, Gallipoli, as the Turks attempted to retake a position, he climbed on top of a parapet, arranged a makeshift shelter from sandbags and kept a sharp lookout for hours. Despite being exposed to Turkish guns, rifles and bombs, he shot many Turks and observed all their movements so that each enemy advance ended in failure.

HANSEN, Percy Howard *Captain, 6th (S) Bn., Lincolnshire Regiment*

9 August 1915 – At Yilghin, Burnu, Gallipoli, his battalion was forced to retire in the face of intense heat from scrub set on fire by shell bursts. Calling for volunteers, he dashed into the blazing scrub to rescue the wounded. Choked by thick black smoke and under a hail of Turkish bullets, he saved six men from being burnt alive.

SHOUT, Alfred John *Captain, 1st Bn. (New South Wales), Australian Imperial Force*

9 August 1915 – At Lone Pine, Gallipoli, with a small party, he charged enemy trenches hurling bombs into them. He killed eight men and routed the rest. Whilst capturing a further length of trench, laughing and joking all the time, a bomb blew up in his right hand, shattering it and destroying his left eye. Carried out of action, he remained conscious, talking cheerfully and drinking tea, until he succumbed to his wounds.

TUBB, Frederick Harold *Lieutenant, 7th Bn. (Victoria), Australian Imperial Force*

9 August 1915 – At Lone Pine, Gallipoli, he (together with Corporal BURTON, Corporal DUNSTAN and a few men) repulsed a Turkish attack on a newly captured trench. Three times the Turks advanced up the sap and blew in a sandbag barricade, leaving only a small part standing, but each time they were pushed back and the barricade rebuilt. During the action, Tubb was wounded in the head and arm, but he held his ground nonetheless.

LAUDER, David Ross *Private, 1/4th (T) Bn., Royal Scots Fusiliers*

13 August 1915 – At Cape Helles, Gallipoli, he threw a bomb which failed to clear the parapet and landed back amongst his own comrades. Realizing there was no time to smother the bomb, he put his foot on top of it to limit the explosion. His foot was blown off but the rest of his party escaped unhurt.

POTTS, Frederick William Owen *Private, 1/1st Berkshire Yeomanry*

21 August 1915 – During the attack on Hill 70, Gallipoli, he spent over forty-eight hours in the open with a severely wounded comrade, despite an injury to his own thigh. Eventually, under heavy Turkish fire and tormented by thirst, he laid his comrade on a shovel and dragged him over 600 yards to safety.

THROSSELL, Hugo Vivian Hope *Second Lieutenant, 10th Light Horse Regiment, Australian Imperial Force*

Hugo Throssell, better known to his friends as Jim, joined the 10th Light Horse in December 1914. In May 1915, when it became clear that reinforcements were needed in the Dardanelles, the 10th Light Horse volunteered for dismounted service. Throssell, by then a lieutenant, arrived at Gallipoli in

August, in time for an attack on Turkish positions at the Nek. His troop was to take part in the fourth wave of the attack. The first and second waves were cut down instantly by Turkish machine guns. At this point, a major of the 10th Light Horse pleaded to Command HQ that the attack be halted. The plea was ignored because somebody had reported seeing a flag of the 8th Horse within yards of the Turkish lines. The third wave charged and was cut down. The commanding officer of the 10th echoed the major's plea. He was ignored. The fourth wave went forward and was shot to pieces. Throssell and his troops on the left flank were lucky enough to find a hollow in which they could lie underneath the hail of Turkish machine-gun bullets. No part of the Turkish trench was taken in the attack but Throssell and his men survived. A dramatic (and to some degree dramatically licensed) reconstruction of this attack can be seen in the 1981 Australian film *Gallipoli*, directed by Peter Weir.

Almost immediately, Throssell and his men were sent to Hill 60, an important tactical feature which faced 150 yards of Turkish-held trench which the Allies desperately wanted to capture. During the subsequent attack, Throssell's heroism earned him the Victoria Cross. He led the second wave of the attack, which took a part of the Turkish trench. Throssell and his few remaining men despite being outnumbered held the trench in the face of a fierce counter-attack. Throssell himself was shot through the right shoulder; the bullet exited through the back of his neck and a piece of bomb laid his left shoulder open to the bone, but so intent was he on resisting the attack that he barely felt the wounds. He recalled: 'When the first of the Turks got within 10 yards we cheered and shouted and started firing as fast as we could. There was no thought of cover. We just blazed away until the rifles grew red-hot and the chocks jammed and then picked up the rifles the killed men had left. When we were wondering how long we could stand against such numbers the Turks turned and fled.' The Turks mounted two further counter-attacks (the final one from all sides as day was breaking) but he and his men stood firm and repulsed them all. Throssell's wounds were so severe that he was twice ordered from the firing line, but he refused to retire. On several occasions he picked up bombs thrown by the Turks into the trench and returned them before they could explode, all the time keeping up the morale of his men, for more than six hours.

Throssell was sent to London where he recuperated from his ordeal. He was temporarily deaf from the concussion of the bombs, and had contracted meningitis from the wounds for which he had refused treatment in the trench. He immediately became a hero in the popular imagination. In a Victoria Cross issue of Will's cigarette cards he was described as 'Seven Feet of Gallant Manhood' and in an article in the *Daily Mail* as 'The Man I Want to Follow'. When speaking privately, he called the attack at the Nek 'that fool charge', but on his return to Australia, he was publicly paraded by the army recruiting office. He was feted wherever he went before returning to the regiment in March 1917 in Palestine, where his brother had been killed in the Second Battle of Gaza. On 11 December 1917, he led the guard of honour of men of the 10th Light Horse through which General Allenby made his entry into Jerusalem for the city's formal surrender ceremony. Shortly afterwards, he fell ill again, contracting malaria. He spent the next few months in and out of hospitals, malaria clinics and convalescent centres.

When he was recovering in London, Throssell met and took a shine to a young Australian writer named Katherine Pritchard. On his return to Australia they renewed their friendship, and once the armistice was signed, they married. Katherine was a politically aware young woman who felt that the success of the Russian Revolution demonstrated that an organization of working people in Australia could similarly succeed. She soon began to educate Throssell in the political theories of the day. As a man who had been brought up to believe in God, King and Country but who had become disillusioned by his own war experiences and the death of his brother, he did not need a great deal of persuasion. He made his new politics public in July 1919, when he was asked to lead the Victory Parade in Northam. He rode at the head of the cavalcade in full Light Horse uniform. A huge crowd cheered him as he rode by and climbed onto the podium to speak. The cheers turned to silence, however, when he declared: 'I have seen enough of the horrors of war and I want peace. War has made me a socialist.' From that moment on, friends and family disowned him. People felt that he was trading on his reputation to promote 'the tiger of socialism'. He claimed that for the rest of his life, only four old friends stuck by him. It was not long before he was under surveillance by Australian military intelligence.

Over the next few years, Throssell worked at the Australian Agriculture Department, but money started becoming a problem. He suffered from a number of bad investments and 1931, leaving Katherine behind, he travelled to the gold fields of South Australia but came back empty handed a few weeks later. Undeterred, he soon set out again, this time taking Katherine with him to cook and wash in the camp. Once again, they returned goldless, but by then he had debts of more than $4,000. To make matters worse his old job at the Agriculture Department had been filled. In 1933, he decided to set up a dude ranch and pony trail on his land. He put all the money that he could borrow into this venture, expecting a roaring success. On its opening day, he organized a rodeo and car and motorcycle races as well as horse riding. A large crowd turned up but Throssell had miscalculated and organized the opening for a Sunday. By law, he could not charge admittance. He suffered a monumental loss.

Throssell's debts mounted up. His wife had no idea of the scale of them. He tried to pawn his Victoria Cross but the pawnbroker only offered him ten shillings for it. On 19 November 1933, having lost his self-respect and seeing no other solution, Hugh Throssell shot himself in the head on the veranda of his home. He had been determined that Katherine would not be deprived of his war pension, so he had changed his will to state that his suicide was a result of terrible suffering caused by his war wounds. He left a note behind, which read: 'I can't sleep. I feel my old war head. It's going phut and that's no use for anyone concerned.'

He was buried with full military honours. As he was laid to rest, his coffin was draped in the Union Flag.

SMITH, Alfred Victor *Second Lieutenant, 1/5th (T) Bn., East Lancashire Regiment*

22 December 1915 – At Helles, Gallipoli, whilst he was throwing a grenade, it slipped from his hand and fell to the bottom of his crowded trench. He shouted a warning and jumped clear, but aware that others were not taking cover, ran back to the grenade and threw himself onto it. The explosion killed him instantly but his action saved many lives.

SUBMARINE WARFARE

BOYLE, Edward Courtney *Lieutenant Commander, Royal Navy*

27 April to 18 May 1915 – Whilst in command of Submarine *E.14*, he made the first successful submarine patrol of the Sea of Marmara. Whilst still in the Dardanelles, sank a 700-ton Turkish gunboat and then, avoiding the minefields, sunken ships and hostile patrols, she entered the Sea of Marmara, where she sank a transport, a 200-ton gunboat and a 5,000-ton liner carrying six thousand troops. For three weeks, *E.14* disrupted Turkish troop movements and avoided detection in an area only 75 miles long and 50 miles wide.

DUNBAR-NASMITH, Martin Eric *Lieutenant Commander, Royal Navy*

20 May to 8 June 1915 – Whilst in command of Submarine *E.11*, he mounted a patrol in the Sea of Marmara, during which he sank eleven Turkish ships. His first victim was a gunboat which shot a hole in his periscope as it sank. He then surfaced near a large Turkish steamer. An American journalist on board the steamer asked if there was time to get off. 'Yes, but be damned quick about it,' replied Nasmith before sinking the ship. Soon afterwards, he entered the port of Constantinople itself, where he sank a barge, forced a transport to run ashore and damaged the quayside. The civilian population flew into a panic, believing that the Allies' fleet had arrived. On his return through the Dardanelles, he noticed that a mine had become entangled in his forward hydroplanes. Keeping the discovery to himself, he towed the mine for 11 miles until he reached an area free of patrol boats, where he surfaced delicately, allowing the mine to float free.

PARSLOW, Frederick Daniel *Lieutenant and Master, Royal Naval Reserve*

4 July 1915 – He was in command of the unarmed horse transport *Anglo-Californian* in the Atlantic south-west of Queenstown, Ireland, when

it came under steady fire from a submarine. For ninety minutes, he constantly altered course, keeping the submarine astern, and was on the point
of abandoning ship when he received a wireless message urging him to hold
on as long as possible. He did so, and remained on the bridge without
protection until the bridge was wrecked and he was killed.

MESOPOTAMIA

The campaign in Mesopotamia began in 1914 with the Indian Expeditionary
Force D's investment of Basra and the oilfields of Abadan, and the defeat on
8 December 1914 of the Turkish 38th Division sent to oppose it. The Battle
of Shaiba, on 12–14 April, saw the destruction of the planned Turkish
counter-offensive. The summer saw a succession of victories as the Anglo-
Indian force proceeded towards Baghdad, and in August the force was
authorized to advance on Kut, 120 miles up the Tigris from the current
position at Amara and 380 miles from the sea. The town fell on the 28th
after a deception that involved two brigades crossing the river on a pontoon
bridge built under cover of darkness.

WHEELER, George Godfrey Massy *Major, 7th Hariana Lancers*
   12 April 1915 – Together with a Gurkha officer and eight men, he
rushed an enemy trench at Shaiba, Mesopotamia, under heavy bombing,
rifle, machine-gun and artillery fire. He was then counter-attacked by a
strong enemy party with bombers. He at once led a charge with one officer
and three men that dispersed the enemy although he received a severe
bayonet wound to the head.

COOKSON, Edgar Christopher *Lieutenant Commander, Royal Navy*
   28 September 1915 – At Kut-el-Amara, Turkish machine-guns and rifles
opened up on the river gunboat HMS *Comet* as it approached a large
obstruction placed across the river. Cookson, who was commanding the
Comet, ordered her to be brought alongside the central dhow of the obstruction. He then leapt on to the dhow and began to hack at the hawsers. He
was shot in seven places and dragged back on board the *Comet*, where he
died. His last words were, 'I am done. It's a failure. Get back at full speed.'

THE AIR WAR

British military aviation in the First World War was carried out by the Royal
Naval Air Service and the Royal Flying Corps, merged on 1 April 1918 as the
Royal Air Force. The RNAS was used for fleet reconnaissance, anti-ship and
anti-submarine patrols on the enemy's coasts, army reconnaissance in
coastal areas, the destruction of airships in their bases (as at Cuxhaven in

December 1914) and defending British airspace; the *Ark Royal* was deployed in support of the Gallipoli landings, and in 1916 a wing was sent to support the RFC at the Somme. The smaller RFC was initially used for reconnaissance and bombing missions, but in August 1915, when General Hugh Trenchard became its field commander in France, the focus changed to constant aggressive patrols over enemy lines and the support of ground attacks.

RHODES-MOORHOUSE, William Bernard *Second Lieutenant, 2 Squadron, Royal Flying Corps*

26 April 1915 – Flying at a height of 300 feet, he dropped a 1,000lb bomb on the railway junction at Courtrai. The bomb hit its target. Thousands of rifles and a machine-gun mounted in a church tower immediately opened fire on him. A bullet struck him in the thigh, but instead of landing amongst the enemy he descended to 100 feet, increased his speed and made for the British lines. He was struck by another bullet that ripped open his abdomen but flew back to his own aerodrome, where he executed a perfect landing. He died of his wounds the following day.

His promotion to lieutenant with effect from 24 April was notified posthumously.

WARNEFORD, Reginald Alexander John *Flight Sub-Lieutenant, 1 Squadron, Royal Naval Air Service*

7 June 1915 – Whilst flying a Morane monoplane over Ghent, he spotted a Zeppelin airship which opened fire on him, dropped her ballast, and rose to a height of 6,000 feet. He pursued her until she began to descend, at which point he was able to get above her. He dropped six bombs onto her, the last of which blew her up, killing all 28 of her crew, but also overturned Warneford's aircraft and stopped its engine. He regained control, planed to earth, refilled his tanks and was airborne again within fifteen minutes.

HAWKER, Lanoe George *Captain, Royal Engineers and 6 Squadron, Royal Flying Corps*

25 July 1915 – Whilst on patrol over France, he engaged three enemy aircraft in combat. The first aircraft went spinning down, the second was driven to ground damaged and the third, which he attacked at a height of 10,000 feet, crashed in flames.

LIDDELL, John Aiden *Captain, 3rd Bn., Argyll and Sutherland Highlanders and Royal Flying Corps*

31 July 1915 – Whilst flying an RE5 over the Ostend–Bruges–Ghent area, he was attacked from above and badly wounded in the right thigh. Despite becoming temporarily unconscious, he recovered partial control of his machine and brought it in to land safely behind Allied lines. He was taken to hospital at La Panne, where septic poisoning set into his leg. He died a month later with his mother at his side.

INSALL, Gilbert Stuart Martin *Second Lieutenant, 11 Squadron, Royal Flying Corps*

7 November 1915 – Whilst on patrol in a Vickers fighter near Achiet, he forced a German plane down into a field. Seeing the Germans scramble out and prepare to fire at him, he dived to 100 feet and opened fire. Under renewed attack, he dropped an incendiary bomb before firing into German trenches at a height of only 2,000 feet. Although his fuel tank was hit, he succeeded in landing near a wood, where he and his gunner repaired the damage, returning to base at dawn.

He was shot down and taken prisoner by the enemy a week later. In August 1917, he escaped from his prison camp at Strohen near Hanover and walked 150 miles, travelling by night, until he reached the safety of the Dutch border.

BELL-DAVIES, Richard *Squadron Commander, 3 Squadron, Royal Naval Air Service*

19 November 1915 – As he prepared to land to rescue a stranded airman, during an attack on Ferrijik Junction, Bulgaria, the airman set fire to his aircraft to prevent it from being captured. Davies landed, collected the airman in full view of advancing Bulgarian troops and returned to his aerodrome.

AFRICA

German forces in East Africa were led by General Paul von Lettow-Vorbeck. After his success at Tanga, in 1914, he retreated into the country and with his three thousand troops began a highly successful guerrilla warfare campaign that at its height occupied the attention of three hundred and fifty thousand Allied troops and auxiliaries. A VC was won by Lieutenant Dartnell when the Germans attacked a force of Royal Fusiliers and 130th Baluchis that was protecting a railway line under construction.

DARTNELL, Wilbur Taylor *T/Lieutenant, 25th (S) Bn., Royal Fusiliers*

3 September 1915 – Near Maktau, Kenya. Whilst he was being carried to safety with a leg wound, the enemy came so close that it became impossible to rescue any more injured men. Seeing this and knowing full well that he would be murdered by the enemy, he insisted on being left behind to help the remaining wounded.

1916

January 1916 brought the stark realization to the British War Cabinet that volunteers alone could not adequately make up for the losses on the Western Front, and on 27 January conscription was introduced in the form of the Military Service Act. With massively increased firepower and still more men brought in to the trenches, the scale of operations was increased, and with it the level of violence and devastation – and the number of casualties in the battle at Verdun in June and later in July, at the Somme.

The German strategy in 1916 was to force the Allies to defend at points of the Germans' choosing. The objective was not to win ground but to cause unsustainable casualties; Verdun, which was fought from February to December, was expressed as an attempt 'to bleed the French army white'.

The next major battles of the year began on 1 July at the River Somme, where the Allies had agreed on a joint offensive. The battles on the Somme continued into November as the British commanders pursued their objectives of inflicting as great as possible losses on the enemy while relieving the pressure on the French at Verdun.

At sea, the Battle of Jutland, fought between 31 May and 2 June, saw the Royal Navy sustain worse losses than those of the German fleet – but it ultimately proved a strategic victory for Britain as German surface ships ventured out sea only twice more, and never challenged the Royal Navy. This task was delegated to the U-boats, which continued to harry British shipping.

On the home front, civilians had a first-hand taste of war as Zeppelin raids affected the south and east coasts. One was shot down in flames over Cuffley in Hertfordshire – but they had no conception of the carnage and devastation in the trenches and battlefields across the Channel.

Although withdrawn from Gallipoli at the end of 1915, British troops – apart from the massive concentration of manpower on the Western Front – were also still in action in Mesopotamia and East Africa.

MESOPOTAMIA: THE RELIEF OF KUT

Major General Charles Townshend's march on Baghdad reached its limit at Ctesiphon, about 10 miles from the city, in a closely fought battle on 22–25

November 1915, after which the force retreated to Kut. There they made a stand, just as he had done at Chitral in 1895 (see p. 142), and was besieged with the ten thousand men of 6th Division. Tigris Force, the relief force of fourteen thousand men under Lieutenant General Sir Fenton Aylmer VC, who had played an important part in the relief of Chitral, reached the first Turkish positions, about 25 miles from Kut, in January. There they were soundly beaten in a succession of attacks in which the Turks withdrew to prepared positions and the Anglo-Indian troops made little progress in the thin strip of land between marsh and river, now churned to mud by weeks of rain.

Aylmer wanted to wait for the 13th Division, on its way from Gallipoli, but was ordered to renew the attempt. After two attacks failed, the 1st Manchesters and 59th Royal Scinde Rifles were sent in a last-ditch attempt across two miles of open ground; they got into the Turkish trenches, but were beaten back, and the force lost 3,500 men. Aylmer was replaced by Major General Sir Frederick Gorringe, but the next major attacks, frontal assaults by the 13th Division against prepared positions on the north bank, saw 2,800 casualties taken (with five VCs won) and no progress; there was more success at Beit Ayeesa, on the south bank, but the Turks drove the 3rd Division back with 1,150 casualties; and a further attempt in terrible weather at Sanna-i-Yat by 7th Division failed on the 20th. With little water, food or fodder for the relieving force, this was the final attempt to break through to the garrison except for a gallant effort to bring in 270 tons of supplies in an armour-plated hospital ship, an action that won two VCs. On 30 April, after 143 days of defending Kut, Townshend surrendered to the Turks – the largest British force ever to yield to an enemy.

CHATTA SINGH *Sepoy, 9th Bhopal Infantry*
13 January 1916 – At the Battle of the River Wadi, Mesopotamia, he went out into the open to assist his commanding officer, who was lying wounded under heavy fire. He dug a parapet around the officer with his entrenching tool and remained beside him until dark, shielding his exposed side with his own body. After nightfall, he brought the officer to safety.

LALA *Lance Naik, 41st Dogra Regiment*
21 January 1916 – At El Orah, Mesopotamia, he dragged a wounded officer to a temporary shelter which he had constructed. Hearing the cries of his adjutant, who was lying wounded only 100 yards from the enemy, he then crawled to the adjutant, staying with him until dark, taking off his own clothes to keep him warm. After night fell, he carried both the wounded officer and the adjutant to safety.

SINTON, John Alexander *Captain, Indian Medical Service*
21 January 1916 – At Orah Ruins, Mesopotamia, he remained on duty and tended to the wounded all day under very heavy fire. Even after he was

shot through both arms and through the side, he refused to go to hospital. In three previous actions, he had displayed the utmost bravery.

STRINGER, George *Private, 1st Bn., Manchester Regiment*
8 March 1916 – After the capture of an enemy position at Es Sinn, Mesopotamia, he was posted on the extreme right of his battalion. When an enemy counter-attack forced the battalion back, he held his ground single-handed and kept the enemy at a distance until all his grenades were expended. His gallant stand made a steady withdrawal possible.

BUCHANAN, Angus *T/Captain, 4th (S) Bn., South Wales Borderers*
5 April 1916 – At Falauyah Lines, Mesopotamia, he went out under heavy machine-gun fire to bring in a wounded officer who was lying 150 yards from cover. He then went out again to bring in a man who had been wounded whilst helping him to save the officer.

WARE, Sidney William *Corporal, 1st Bn., Seaforth Highlanders*
6 April 1916 – When the order was given to withdraw at Sanna-i-Yat, Mesopotamia, he picked up a wounded man, carried him 200 yards to cover and then spent two hours bringing in all the wounded under very heavy fire.

ADDISON, William Robert Fountains *The Revd T/Chaplain, Army Chaplains Department*
9 April 1916 – At Sanna-i-Yat, Mesopotamia, he carried a wounded man to the cover of a trench and assisted several others to the same cover after binding up their wounds under heavy rifle and machine-gun fire. By his splendid example, he encouraged the stretcher bearers to go forward under heavy fire and collect the wounded.

FYNN, James Henry *Private, 4th (S) Bn., South Wales Borderers*
9 April 1916 – Whilst dug in forward of the advance line, 300 yards from the enemy's trenches at Sanna-i-Yat, Mesopotamia, he went out and bandaged several men lying wounded in the open. Unable to get a stretcher, he carried one of the men to safety on his back. He then returned to carry in another man. He was constantly under severe fire.

MYLES, Edgar Kinghorn *Second Lieutenant, 8th (S) Bn., Welch Regiment attached 9th (S) Bn., Worcestershire Regiment*
9 April 1916 – At Sanna-i-Yat, Mesopotamia, he went out alone on several occasions in front of the advanced trenches and assisted wounded men lying in the open. On one occasion, he carried a wounded officer to safety. Throughout this action, he was under heavy rifle fire.
He ended his life in a British Legion home after he was found living destitute in a railway carriage.

SHAHAMAD KHAN *Naik, 89th Punjab Regiment*

12–13 April 1916 – Near Beit Ayeesa, Mesopotamia, he was in charge of a machine-gun section 150 yards from the enemy. He beat off three enemy attacks and worked his gun single-handed after all his men except two belt-fitters had become casualties. He held the position for three hours and when his gun was knocked out continued to hold it with a rifle until ordered to retire. He then brought the gun, ammunition and a wounded comrade to safety.

COWLEY, Charles Henry *Lieutenant Commander, Royal Naval Volunteer Reserve*

24–25 April 1916 – He (together with Lieutenant FIRMAN and 12 ratings) volunteered to take supplies to the garrison at Kut, Mesopotamia, in the steamer *Julnar*. The task was so dangerous that no married man was allowed to volunteer. The steamer encountered heavy fire from both banks and passed safely through one steel cable that had been placed across the river by the Turks. She was then fired on by Turkish field guns brought down to the water's edge. One shell hit the bridge, killing Lieutenant Firman. She then fouled another steel cable and the remaining crew had no option but to surrender.

FIRMAN, Humphrey Osbaldston Brooke *Lieutenant, Royal Navy*

24–25 April 1916 – He (together with Lieutenant Commander COWLEY and 12 ratings) volunteered to bring supplies to the garrison at Kut, Meso-potamia, in the steamer *Julnar*. The task was so dangerous that no married man was allowed to volunteer. The steamer encountered heavy fire from both banks and passed safely through one steel cable that had been placed across the river by the Turks. She was then fired on by Turkish field guns brought down to the water's edge. One shell hit the bridge, killing Firman. The remaining crew had no option but to surrender when the steamer fouled another steel cable.

TRENCH WARFARE

The first year and a quarter of war had seen the Allied armies of France and Britain sustain horrific losses. Although new recruits were brought in, they were no replacement for the seasoned, career-trained men who had been lost – and in 1916 Germany set out to capitalize on both the impact of earlier losses and the inexperience of the fresh troops.

No British or Dominion units were involved in Verdun, which cost the French about five hundred and fifty thousand casualties and the Germans four hundred and thirty thousand, but VCs were won in defeating and turning diversionary attacks that spring, and in continued trench warfare along the line. Major General Sir Douglas Haig became C.-in-C. France on 16 December 1915, and these minor actions between 19 December 1915 and

30 June 1916 cost him more than one hundred and twenty-five thousand casualties.

McNAIR, Eric Archibald *T/Lieutenant, 9th (S) Bn., Royal Sussex Regiment*
14 February 1916 – When the enemy exploded a mine at Hooge, Belgium, many men were buried. Although shaken by the blast, he immediately organized a machine-gun party to repel the advancing Germans. He then ran to fetch reinforcements, but finding the communication trench blocked, went across open ground under heavy fire and led the reinforcements up the same way. His prompt action saved the situation.

COTTER, William Reginald *Acting Corporal, 6th (S) Bn., East Kent Regiment*
6 March 1916 – Near the Hohenzollern Redoubt, France, his leg was blown off at the knee and he was wounded in both arms. Unaided, he struggled to a crater 50 yards away, and for the next two hours steadied the men who were holding it and encouraged them to face a fresh counter-attack. Only when the attack had abated did he allow his wounds to be dressed. He then had to wait fourteen hours to be moved back for treatment, but throughout this time he had a cheery word for all.

MELLISH, Edward Noel *Captain, The Revd T/Chaplain, Army Chaplains Department*
27–29 March 1916 – During three days of fighting at St Eloi, Belgium, he went repeatedly under heavy and continuous shell and machine-gun fire to tend and rescue wounded men. He brought in ten badly wounded men on the first day, twelve on the second and on the night of the third, took charge of a party of volunteers who went out to rescue the remainder. He is said to have carried a prayer book under his arm.
The story goes that one of the men he rescued, who was known for his anti-religious views, asked, 'What religion is 'e?' When told, he declared, 'Well, I'm the same as 'im now, and the bloke as sez a word against our Church will 'ave 'is bloody head bashed in.'

BAXTER, Edward *Second Lieutenant, 1/8th Bn., King's (Liverpool) Regiment*
17–18 April 1916 – On the two nights before an attack on the enemy near Blairville, France, he was cutting wire close to the enemy trenches. At one point he dropped a bomb with the pin withdrawn. Instantly, he picked it up, unscrewed the base plug and smothered the detonator in the ground. His action saved lives and prevented the alarm from being given. When the attack later commenced, he was the first man into the enemy trench. He was never seen alive again.

JONES, Richard Basil Brandram *T/Lieutenant, 8th (S) Bn., Loyal North Lancashire Regiment*
21 May 1916 – As the enemy advanced on a crater near Vimy which his platoon had recently taken, he kept his men in the crater and raised

himself over the parapet to fire, counting off his victims as they fell. He shot 15 Germans before he ran out of ammunition. He then attempted to throw a bomb but was shot through the head before he could release it.

CHAFER, George William *Private, 1st Bn., East Yorkshire Regiment*
3–4 June 1916 – In a trench near Meaulte, France, despite being choked and half-blinded by gas, bruised and dazed from concussion and with a hand shot through and a leg torn by shell wounds, he took a written message from a fallen orderly and dragged himself along the trench parapet under brutal fire to deliver it to a corporal.

PROCTER, Arthur Herbert *Private, 1/5th Bn., King's (Liverpool) Regiment*
4 June 1916 – Near Ficheux, France, he noticed two men lying wounded in the open in full view of the enemy. He jumped out of his trench under heavy fire and crawled to the men. He dragged them to the cover of a small bank, dressed their wounds, left some of his clothes with them for warmth and promised them rescue after dusk. He then returned to his trench under fire. The men were rescued that night.
He was later ordained, and served as a chaplain with the RAF during the Second World War.

ERSKINE, John *A/Sergeant, 5/6th Bn., Cameronians*
22 June 1916 – At Givenchy, France, he rushed out under continuous fire to rescue a wounded sergeant and a private. Later, seeing his officer (who was thought dead) showing signs of movement, he ran over, bandaged him and stayed with him for an hour under steady fire before bringing him in, shielding him with his own body.

HACKETT, William *Sapper, 254th Tunnelling Coy., Royal Engineers*
22–23 June 1916 – Whilst tunnelling in Shaftesbury Avenue mine near Givenchy, an explosion trapped him and four others in a gallery. After twenty hours of digging, a hole was made and he was able to pass three of the men through to a rescue party. He could easily have followed but chose to remain with the fourth man, who was seriously injured. 'I am a tunneller and must look after the others first,' he said. Not long afterwards, the gallery collapsed and both he and the wounded man were killed.

BATTEN-POOLL, Arthur Hugh Henry *Lieutenant, 3rd Bn., Royal Munster Fusiliers*
25 June 1916 – Whilst in command of a raiding party near Colonne, France, he was severely wounded by a bomb which mutilated all the fingers of his right hand. In spite of this, he refused to retire and continued to direct operations. He was twice further wounded whilst assisting in the rescue of others and collapsed on returning to his own lines.

JACKSON, William *Private, 17th Bn. (New South Wales), Australian Imperial Force*

25–26 June 1916 – After returning from a raiding party near Armentières with a prisoner, he went straight out again into no-man's-land and brought in a wounded man. Then, as he was carrying in another man with the help of a sergeant, a shell exploded nearby tearing off his arm and knocking the sergeant unconscious. He returned to his trench, obtained assistance, and went out again to look for the sergeant and the man they had been carrying.

HUTCHINSON, James *Private, 2/5th Bn., Lancashire Fusiliers*

28 June 1916 – During a raid on a German position near Ficheux, he was the first bayonet man. On entering the trench, he shot a machine-gunner through the head, bayoneted another and shot a third. In the second traverse he shot and bayoneted two more, and in the third traverse another three, before his ammunition ran out. He then covered the retirement under fierce machine-gun fire. His brother was killed during the same raid.

CARTER, Nelson Victor *Company Sergeant Major, 12th (S) Bn., Royal Sussex Regiment*

30 June 1916 – He was in command of the fourth wave of an assault on enemy lines at 'Boar's Head', Richebourg l'Avoue, France. Under intense shell and machine-gun fire, he penetrated into the German second line, where he captured a machine-gun, shot the gunner and inflicted heavy casualties with bombs. As he retired, carrying wounded men to safety on his back, he was shot through the chest and died instantly.

THE BATTLE OF JUTLAND

In 1914, the popular and professional expectation was that the Royal Navy's Grand Fleet would 'Trafalgar' the smaller German High Seas Fleet, but to universal disappointment the Germans refused battle, and instead spent sixteen months trying to weaken the Royal Navy with mines and torpedoes until eventual victory could be assured. On 24 January 1916, however, Admiral Reinhard Scheer took command of the fleet, determined to refute charges of inactivity.

Scheer planned a trap for Vice Admiral Sir David Beatty's Battlecruiser Fleet: in its final form, his battlecruisers under Admiral Hipper would steam up the Jutland coast of Denmark, and when Beatty attacked they would turn and draw him onto the battleships of the High Seas Fleet. U-boats at the exits of the Grand Fleet anchorages would disrupt or prevent rescue by Admiral Sir John Jellicoe's battleships. Unfortunately for this German strategy, the British had been reading German naval wireless traffic since 1914.

The Grand Fleet left harbour by 11 p.m. on 30 May, four and a half hours before the High Seas Fleet, and avoided the U-boat threat.

Four VCs were won in the action: in the *Lion*, Beatty's flagship; in the cruiser *Chester*; and in the destroyers *Shark* and *Nestor*.

Beatty sighted the German battlecruisers at about 1530 on 31 May; Hipper turned south-east towards the High Seas Fleet and opened fire at 18,500 yards. Beatty ordered a course south-south-east, but his 5th Battle Squadron did not see it, and continued north; they only opened fire, at extreme range, at 1605. The *Lion* was hit almost at once; the fire was prevented from spreading to the magazine by Major Harvey, but two other battlecruisers were not so lucky, and *Indefatigable* and *Queen Mary* had blown up by about 1615. The destroyers went into action, but about 1633 light cruisers scouting ahead saw the High Seas Fleet, and at 1640 Beatty ordered a turn to the north, towards Jellicoe, and at 1814 signalled the High Seas Fleet's position. Jellicoe thus deployed his twenty-four battleships in line, and opened fire. Jellicoe had crossed Scheer's 'T'; Scheer, outnumbered, outgunned and outmanoeuvred, ordered a 'battle turn away'. This took his ships safely into the mist, and Jellicoe turned south to intercept the likeliest German course. At 1855 Scheer turned east, either to renew the attack or to steam past the Grand Fleet's rear; at 19.10 the British opened fire again, and at 1918 Scheer turned west, covering his retreat with an attack by his battlecruisers and destroyers. At 2019 Beatty met the German battlecruisers again and opened fire, sinking one and damaging two. Although there were continued destroyer and cruiser actions through the night, Scheer returned home to claim a victory. The Royal Navy had lost three battlecruisers, three armoured cruisers, eight destroyers and 6,094 men and boys dead, as against one German battlecruiser, one predreadnought, four light cruisers, five destroyers and 2,551 deaths, but the High Seas Fleet was never used in a major action again: after Jutland it only left port twice before it surrendered in 1918.

BINGHAM, the Hon. Edward Barry Stewart *Commander, Royal Navy*

31 May 1916 – At the Battle of Jutland, whilst in command of HMS *Nestor*, he led his division of destroyers towards the enemy battlecruisers. On his way, he engaged a flotilla of enemy destroyers, sinking two of them. He then sighted the enemy fleet and closed to within 3,000 yards to obtain a good position to fire his torpedoes. His division was under concentrated attack throughout this attack and *Nestor* was subsequently sunk. He was picked up by a German destroyer and taken prisoner.

CORNWELL, John Travers *Boy First Class, Royal Navy*

31 May 1916 – Despite being mortally wounded within the first few minutes of the Battle of Jutland, he remained standing alone by his gun on HMS *Chester* in an exposed position until the end of the action. As the gun crew lay dead and wounded around him, he stood waiting quietly for orders. He died after being brought ashore at Grimsby.

He was buried in a pauper's grave, but after the story of his death had caught the public imagination, his body was exhumed and he was given an impressive funeral. Several months later, his father, Eli Cornwell, who had joined the army, was buried in the same grave.

HARVEY, Francis John William *Major, Royal Marine Light Infantry*

31 May 1916 – At the Battle of Jutland, despite being mortally wounded by a shell which exploded in the gunhouse of HMS *Lion*, he displayed sufficient presence of mind to order the magazine to be flooded. His action saved the ship, but he died shortly afterwards.

JONES, Loftus William *Commander, Royal Navy*

31 May 1916 – At the Battle of Jutland, whilst in command of HMS *Shark*, he led a division of destroyers in an attack on the enemy battlecruiser squadron. When *Shark* was disabled by enemy fire, Jones helped in attempts first to connect and man the after wheel and then to keep the midship gun in action. Eventually he was hit by a shell which took off his leg above the knee, but he carried on giving orders, including one to properly hoist the ensign. Soon afterwards, *Shark* was hit by a torpedo and sank. His body was washed ashore some time later in south-west Sweden.

THE BATTLE OF THE SOMME

German defences at the Somme had been set up with professional thoroughness. The line ran along a low chalk ridge, and they used the contours of the land to their best advantage, digging successive lines of trenches connected by communications trenches and leaving impenetrable thickets of barbed wire as deadly obstacles to any infantry advance at points of perceived weakness. Concrete gun emplacements were strategically place to overlap zones of fire and, as protection, they dug deep tunnels to shelter the front-line defenders. Camouflaged artillery posts were indiscernible from the air, and with well-buried telephone lines, fire could be called down from distant observation posts with ruthless efficiency.

The objectives of the Somme offensive were strategic, not tactical: according to Sir William Robertson, Chief of the Imperial General Staff, 'The necessity of relieving pressure on the French Army at Verdun remains, and is more urgent than ever. This is, therefore, the first objective to be obtained by the combined British and French offensive. The second objective is to inflict as heavy losses as possible upon the German armies.' The Somme was in part chosen because it was where the British and French lines joined, and the French could make a smaller attack to the south. The part of the line chosen for the French attack ran from just north of Lihons to Curlu on the river (about nine miles), and then to Maricourt (3,000 yards). The British sector ran from there north-west to Fricourt, then to the River Ancre, then north in front of Beaumont-Hamel and Serre. The total British frontage was more than 25 miles; the French, 11. A subsidiary attack was to be made at the German salient at Gommecourt, further north.

The German lines in the British sector were defended by the 2nd Army (sixteen divisions), and against it was ranged Sir Henry Rawlinson's 4th Army (eleven divisions), with nine in reserve, and two divisions from 3rd Army to attack Gommecourt. Haig's plan was for an eight-day artillery bombardment of one million six hundred thousand rounds, with artillery spotting provided by the Royal Flying Corps, together with gas attacks and infantry raids and deceptions, before a daylight assault on a 15-mile front between Serre and Curlu; the infantry would consolidate there (each man went over the top carrying 66lb of equipment) and be followed up by General Sir Hubert Gough with three cavalry and two infantry divisions which would circle north behind the enemy lines, cutting them off as far as Arras, 14 miles away.

THE BATTLE OF THE SOMME: 1 JULY 1916

At 7.20 a.m. on 1 July, Hawthorn Mine was detonated under a strongpoint protecting the village of Beaumont-Hamel. It left a crater 40 feet deep and 300 feet wide, but only alerted the Germans. Beaumont-Hamel was not finally taken until 13 November. The barrage lifted at 7.30 a.m. on 1 July, and sixteen more mines were detonated. The Allies went over the top, to find that along most of the line the dugouts had not been destroyed and the wire was intact. The British army took 57,470 casualties, 19,240 of them fatal. It remains the army's greatest loss on a single day.

Haig's despatch on the situation at the end of the first day painted a rosier picture of progress than was apparent to those in the action, and, by omission, denied the terrible losses and the desperate situation in which nine men acquitted themselves with such courage as to be awarded the VC.

BELL, Eric Norman Frankland *T/Captain, 9th Bn., Royal Inniskilling Fusiliers, attached 109th Light Trench Mortar Battery*
1 July 1916 – When an attack at Thiepval, France, was halted by a machine-gun, he crept forward and shot the gunner. When subsequent bombing parties were unable to progress, he went forward alone three times and cleared enemy trenches with trench mortar bombs. He then stood on his parapet firing at the counter-attacking enemy. He was killed whilst rallying and reorganizing groups of infantry that had lost their officers.

CATHER, Geoffrey St George Shillington *T/Lieutenant, 9th (S) Bn., Royal Irish Fusiliers*
1/2 July 1916 – Between 7 p.m. and midnight, and again the following morning, he searched no-man's-land near Hamel, France, for wounded

men. He brought four men to safety and gave water to others under direct machine-gun fire and in full view of the enemy, before he was himself killed.

GREEN, John Leslie *Captain, Royal Army Medical Corps, attached 1/5th Bn., Sherwood Foresters*
   1 July 1916 – At Foncquevillers, France, whilst himself wounded, he dragged an officer who was lying on the enemy's barbed wire into a shell hole. He dressed the officer's wounds under bomb attack and rifle fire and tried to carry him to safety but was killed in the attempt.

LOUDOUN-SHAND, Stewart Walker *T/Major, 10th (S) Bn., Yorkshire Regiment*
   1 July 1916 – As his company climbed over the parapet to attack the enemy at Fricourt, France, they were met by fierce machine-gun fire which stopped them in their tracks. He immediately leapt onto the parapet and began helping the men over it and encouraging them until he was mortally wounded. Even then, he insisted on being propped up in the trench and went on encouraging the men until he died.

McFADZEAN, William Frederick *Private, 14th (S) Bn., Royal Irish Rifles*
   1 July 1916 – As preparations were being made for an attack on Thiepval Wood, grenades were handed to the bombers. McFadzean picked up a box containing twelve Mills grenades, but unknown to him the ropes securing the boxes had been cut and all twelve bombs spilled into the trench. Without a moment's hesitation, he threw himself flat on the bombs. The safety pins had dropped out of two of them and they exploded killing him and wounding the man on his left. His action saved the lives of many of his comrades. It was recalled that just before he died he had been singing his favourite song, 'My Little Grey Home in the West'.

QUIGG, Robert *Rifleman, 12th (S) Bn., Royal Irish Rifles*
   1 July 1916 – Having advanced with his platoon three times near Hamel, Somme, he heard that his officer was lying wounded in no-man's-land so he went out seven times to look for him under heavy shell and machine-gun fire. Each time he brought back a wounded man. He dragged the last man in on a waterproof sheet from within a few yards of the enemy's wire, before having to give up through exhaustion.

RITCHIE, Walter Potter *Drummer, 2nd Bn., Seaforth Highlanders*
   1 July 1916 – He stood on the parapet of an enemy trench at Y Ravine, near Beaumont-Hamel, Somme, under heavy machine-gun fire and repeatedly sounded the 'Charge'. He rallied many men of various units, who, having lost their leaders, were wavering and beginning to retire. Throughout the remainder of the day, he carried messages over fire-swept ground.

SANDERS, George *Corporal, 1/7th Bn., West Yorkshire Regiment*

1 July 1916 – Following an advance near Thiepval, Somme, he became isolated in enemy trenches with a party of 30 men. He organized a defence, detailed a bombing party and impressed upon the men that their duty was to hold the position. His party was eventually relieved thirty-six hours later, having seen off three advances and bombing attacks. Throughout the period, they had been without food and water.

He was later commissioned, and won the MC. He was taken prisoner in April 1918.

TURNBULL, James Youll *Sergeant, 17th (S) Bn., Highland Light Infantry*

1 July 1916 – Having, with his party, captured a post of great importance at Authuille, Somme, the post was subjected to severe counter-attacks throughout the day. Although his party was wiped out and replaced several times over, he never wavered and almost single-handedly maintained the position. He was killed later in the day whilst repelling a counter-attack.

THE BATTLE OF THE SOMME: 2–17 JULY

Haig halted the attack north of the Ancre, and gave the sector La Boiselle to Serre to Gough, telling him to 'make steady pressure' and 'act as a pivot' to the eventual success to the south. By midday on the 2nd, Fricourt had been taken, Fricourt Wood that night, on the 4th the railway at Mametz and La Boiselle, and on the 6th the front-line trenches were consolidated. On 7 July, Ovillers, Contalmaison and Mametz Wood, and to the right Trones Wood, were attacked and although Trones Wood changed hands several times they were secure by the 13th. Haig was then in a position to attack the second line, which he did at 3.25 a.m. on 14 July. By the 17th, the British line was established from Maltz Horn Farm to the north of Ovillers. High Wood (marked on contemporary French maps as Bois des Foureaux), a crucial position at the top of the ridge, was not held; despite the cavalry finally coming into action and clearing it on the 14th, it was counter-attacked, the flanks could not advance to support it, and the troops were pulled back on the 15th. This left Delville Wood and Longueval, which had been taken at great cost by the South African Brigade, as a vulnerable salient, and the next stage of the battle was to secure it and to take Pozières.

CARTON de WIART, Adrian *T/Lieutenant Colonel, 4th Dragoon Guards, attached 8th (S) Bn., Gloucestershire Regiment*

2–3 July 1916 – After three other battalion commanders had become casualties at La Boiselle, Somme, he took over their commands and ensured that the ground won was maintained at all costs. He organized positions and supplies under intense fire and it was due to his courage and example that a serious reverse was averted.

He had by this time already lost an eye (in Somaliland) and his left hand (at Zonnebeke).

In October 1943 he went to China as Winston Churchill's personal representative to Chiang Kai-Shek.

TURRALL, Thomas George *Private, 10th (S) Bn., Worcestershire Regiment*
3 July 1916 – When the officer commanding a bomb attack at La Boiselle, Somme, was wounded, and his party forced to retire, Turrall remained with the officer for three hours under continual bomb and machine-gun attack, holding his ground with determination. He was finally able to carry the officer to safety behind his own lines.

BELL, Donald Simpson *T/Second Lieutenant, 9th (S) Bn., Yorkshire Regiment*
Donald Bell is the only professional footballer to have won the Victoria Cross. Born in Harrogate on 3 December 1890, he attended St Peter's School, Harrogate, and then trained to be a teacher at Westminster College in London. He was appointed assistant master at Starbeck Council School near Harrogate but decided to supplement his income of £2 10s per week by becoming a professional footballer with Bradford Park Avenue. He had already played for Crystal Palace and Newcastle United as an amateur and he made his debut for Park Avenue against Wolverhampton Wanderers at full back on 13 April 1913. He made five appearances for the club before the war broke out in August of the following year. The club's secretary, T. E. Maley, recalled his ability: 'He was about 6 feet tall and when fit about 13 stone 8 lbs. With it all he was most gentle. He played many fine games for our team. At Nottingham against Notts County he played grandly but the best of games was that against the Wolves, when he completely eclipsed Brooks and co.'

Having been released from his professional contract, he signed up as a volunteer with the West Yorkshire Regiment in November 1914 at the age of twenty-four. He was the first professional footballer to enlist. He soon became an NCO and was promoted to sergeant in 1915. He was then recommended for a commission and by June was a second lieutenant in the Yorkshire Regiment (in 1921 renamed the Green Howards). In November, he travelled to France with the regiment. Whilst on leave in June 1916, he married Rhoda Margaret Bonson in the Wesleyan Chapel in Kirkby. He returned at once to fight in the Battle of the Somme.

He won his Victoria Cross during the attack on the Horseshoe Trench near La Boiselle on 5 July 1916. The 8th and 9th Battalions launched the assault on the trench, sixteen hundred yards long, which was taken together with 146 prisoners. During the attack, a German machine-gun began to enfilade the 9th Battalion. Bell, together with Corporal Colwill and Private Batey, decided to put the gun out of action. In a letter to his mother, Bell modestly described his action:

When the battalion went over, I with my team crawled up the communication trench and attacked the machine gun and the trench and I hit the gun first shot from about 20 yards and knocked it over. We then bombed the dugout and did in about 50 Bosches. The GOC has been over to congratulate the battalion and he personally thanked me. I must confess that it was the biggest fluke alive and I did nothing. I only chucked the bomb and it did the trick . . . I believe God is watching over me and it rests with him whether I pull through or not.

Bell did not pull through. Five days later, he was sent with a bombing party to the 8th Battalion, which had been ordered to attack a position at Contalmaison. The attack was successful but the Germans began mounting counter-attacks and erected a machine-gun nearby. Once again, Bell led his bombing party in a charge at the gun in an attempt to put it out of action. He was killed during the charge. In a letter to Bell's wife of just five weeks, his batman, Private John Bayers, wrote:

I would to God that my late master and friend had still been with us, or, better still, been at home with you. The men worshipped him in their simple, wholehearted way and so they ought, he saved the lot of us from being completely wiped out by his heroic act.

WILKINSON, Thomas Orde Lauder *T/Lieutenant, 7th (S) Bn., Loyal North Lancashire Regiment*

5 July 1916 – Whilst a party was retiring from an attack at La Boiselle without their machine-gun, he rushed forward and with two others got the gun into action and held up the enemy until the party was relieved. Later, when he spotted men of different units trapped behind a block of earth over which the enemy was throwing bombs, he mounted a machine-gun on the parapet and dispersed the Germans.

Later in the fight, he attempted to bring in a wounded man but was killed.

CONGREVE, William La Touche *Bt/Major, Rifle Brigade*

6–20 July 1916 – For two weeks at Longueval, France, he inspired all those around him with acts of gallantry. He carried out personal reconnaissances of the enemy lines, established himself in an exposed forward position to observe the enemy and removed the wounded from brigade headquarters while suffering from the effects of gas. On returning to the front line to ascertain the position after an unsuccessful attack, he was shot killed.

He was the son of Captain W. N. Congreve VC and the first officer to receive the VC, DSO and MC.

BOULTER, William Ewart *Sergeant, 6th (S) Bn., Northamptonshire Regiment*

14 July 1916 – When his company was held up during an attack on Trones Wood, Somme, by a machine-gun causing heavy casualties, he advanced alone towards the gun and bombed it. This act saved many casualties and was instrumental in clearing the enemy from the wood.

THE BATTLE OF THE SOMME: 18 JULY TO 9 SEPTEMBER

By 17 July, the British had secured a foothold on the ridge of about six thousand yards, with its highest point at Delville Wood, north-east of Longueval village, but to the left Pozières and Thiepval and to the right Guillemont remained in German hands. The forward troops were therefore in a sharp salient onto which heavy and concentric fire could be concentrated, and the immediate objective was to prevent the salient being driven in. The difficulties were immense: the attack would be uphill against very strongly held and newly reinforced positions, onto which artillery would be less than usually effective, since direct observation was rarely possible and weeks of low cloud and rain prevented RFC spotting. Haig paused to relieve his front-line troops, move guns forward and improve his communications, but on 18 July the Germans made their expected counter-attack on Delville Wood.

This phase of the battle saw a succession of small advances and fierce counter-attacks, with the key positions changing hands many times. Delville Wood was finally taken on the 27th; High Wood to the west and Pozières were finally taken by 1st Australian Division on the 25th. An advance on a wide front to the village of Guillemont, the immediate objective on Haig's right, on the 23rd had been checked, but with these intermediate positions secure, new assaults were launched on 30 July and 8 and 16 August, and on the 23rd the railway station on the outskirts was held against a counter-attack. Simultaneously, what were deemed to be 'minor' attacks – but nonetheless involving savage fighting – continued: 'Our lines were pushed forward wherever possible by means of local attacks and by bombing and sapping, and the enemy was driven out of various forward positions from which he might hamper our progress.'*

By the end of August, there were five times as many German divisions on the British front as on 1 July, but they were believed to be exhausted and short of ammunition, particularly in artillery. Accordingly, at noon on 3 September a general assault was made from the Ancre in the north to the extreme right of the line, supported by the French in their sector. By the 9th, Beaumont-Hamel and Thiepval remained in German hands, as did the ground initially captured between High Wood and Delville Wood, but Guillemont and Ginchy had fallen, the second line penetrated, and about five miles of the nearer crest of the ridge held.

---

* Haig's despatch dated 23 December 1916 was published as a supplement to the *London Gazette* of 29 December 1916.

FAULDS, William Frederick *Private, 1st Bn., South African Infantry*

18 July 1916 – Spotting a wounded lieutenant lying in the open midway between two lines of trench at Delville Wood, Somme, he climbed over the parapet with two others, ran to the officer and carried him back to his trench. Two days later he went out alone under fierce artillery fire and brought in another wounded man.

He was the first man born in South Africa to win the VC whilst serving with South African forces.

DAVIES, Joseph John *Corporal, 10th (S) Bn., Royal Welch Fusiliers*

20 July 1916 – Prior to an attack on the enemy at Delville Wood, Somme, he became separated with 8 men from the rest of his company. The enemy surrounded his small party, but he got his men into a shell hole, threw bombs, opened fire and succeeded in routing the Germans. He then followed the enemy's retreat and bayoneted several of them.

HILL, Albert *Private, 10th (S) Bn., Royal Welch Fusiliers*

20 July 1916 – During an attack at Delville Wood, he dashed forward and bayoneted two Germans. Finding himself suddenly surrounded by twenty of the enemy he attacked them with bombs, killing and wounding many and scattering the rest. He then fought his way back to his lines, accompanied by a sergeant, before going straight out again to bring in a wounded officer. His final act on this astonishing day was to capture two Germans and bring them in as prisoners.

On his return home to Manchester, he was greeted by a crowd of thousands who sang 'See, the Conquering Hero Comes'.

VEALE, Theodore William Henry *Private, 8th (S) Bn., Devonshire Regiment*

20 July 1916 – At High Wood, Somme, he heard cries and left his trench to investigate. He was immediately fired upon but ran on until he reached Lieutenant Savill, who was lying wounded only 10 yards from the German lines. He pulled him back and brought him water before returning with a waterproof sheet, on which he dragged him into a shell hole. That evening, he led a party of volunteers to the shell hole. When the party was approached by an enemy patrol, he ran to fetch a Lewis gun with which he covered the party whilst they brought the lieutenant to safety.

Three Devonians were awarded the VC in the First World War, rejoicing in the names of Veale, Sage and Onions!

BLACKBURN, Arthur Seaforth *Second Lieutenant, 10th Bn. (South Australia), Australian Imperial Force*

23 July 1916 – At Pozières, Somme, he captured 120 yards of a German trench after leading four separate bombing parties against it. He then crawled forward with a sergeant to reconnoitre, returned and led another attack which seized a further 120 yards of trench, enabling communication to be established with another battalion.

LEAK, John *Private, 9th Bn. (Queensland), Australian Imperial Force*
    23 July 1916 – During an assault on an enemy strongpoint at Pozières, Somme, he ran forward into heavy machine-gun fire and threw bombs into the enemy's bombing post, before jumping into the post and bayoneting three Germans. Later, as his party was driven back, he was the last to withdraw at each stage and continued throwing bombs. His courage had such an effect on the enemy that when reinforcements arrived, the whole trench was recaptured.

COOKE, Thomas *Private, 8th Bn. (Victoria), Australian Imperial Force*
    24–25 July 1916 – After a Lewis gun had been disabled at Pozières, he took his gun and gun team to a dangerous part of the line. He did fine work but came under very heavy fire until he was the only man left. He stuck to his post and continued firing. When assistance came, he was found dead at his gun.
    He played first cornet in a leading band.

GILL, Albert *Sergeant, 1st Bn., King's Royal Rifle Corps*
    27 July 1916 – At Delville Wood, France, after the enemy had rushed a bombing post and killed all the bombers, he rallied the remnants of his platoon, none of whom were skilled bombers, and reorganized the defences. As the enemy surrounded the position, creeping through thick undergrowth and sniping from 20 yards away, he stood up to direct his men's fire, enabling the German advance to be held up. Whilst doing this, he was shot in the head and killed.

CASTLETON, Claude Charles *Sergeant, 5th Coy., Machine-Gun Corps, Australian Imperial Force*
    28–29 July 1916 – When the infantry was driven back at Pozières by enemy machine-gun fire, many wounded men were left lying in shell holes. Castleton went out twice into the teeth of this fire to carry in wounded men on his back. When he went out a third time, he was shot and died instantly.

MILLER, James *Private, 7th (S) Bn., King's Own (Royal Lancaster Regiment)*
    30–31 July 1916 – At Bazentin-le-Petit, France, he was ordered to take an important message through heavy shell and rifle fire and to bring back a reply at all costs. He was shot almost immediately in the back, the bullet coming out of his abdomen. In spite of this, he compressed the gaping wound with his hand, delivered the message and staggered back with the answer. He died at the feet of the officer to whom he delivered it.
    Whilst on leave for the last time, he told his sister that he had a premonition that the end was near, but that he would like to die a hero.

EVANS, George *Company Sergeant Major, 18th (S) Bn., Manchester Regiment*
    30 July 1916 – After five runners had been shot and killed whilst attempting to deliver an important message at Guillemont, Somme, he

volunteered to try. He covered 700 yards under constant fire, dodging from shell hole to shell hole, and succeeded in delivering the message. Whilst returning to his company over the same ground, he was wounded. He was taken prisoner several hours later and remained in captivity until 1918.

Following the deaths of both his parents, he had looked after himself from the age of thirteen. From 1902 he was an inspector for the National Society for the Prevention of Cruelty to Children.

SHORT, William Henry *Private, 8th (S) Bn., Yorkshire Regiment*
6 August 1916 – He was foremost in the attack at 'Munster Alley', Pozières, Somme, bombing the enemy fearlessly, but was severely wounded in the foot. He refused to be treated until his leg was shattered by a shell and he was unable to stand. He then lay in his trench, adjusting detonators and straightening bomb pins for his comrades, until he died of his wounds.

COURY, Gabriel George *Second Lieutenant, 3rd Bn., South Lancashire Regiment attached 1/4th Bn.*
8 August 1916 – Whilst in command of two platoons ordered to dig a communication trench from the old firing line to a position won at Guillemont, Somme, he kept up the spirits of his men under intense fire. He then ran forward to rescue his commanding officer who was lying wounded on ground swept by machine-gun fire.

O'MEARA, Martin *Private, 16th Bn. (South Australia and Western Australia), Australian Imperial Force*
9–12 August 1916 – At Pozières, Somme, he went out repeatedly to bring in wounded officers and men from no-man's-land under intense machine-gun and artillery fire. He also carried bombs and ammunition to a portion of the trench that was being heavily shelled. Throughout this action, he showed an utter contempt for danger.

CHAVASSE, Noel Godfrey *Captain, Royal Army Medical Corps, attached 1/10th Bn., King's (Liverpool) Regiment*
One of seven children born in Oxford to the Reverend Francis and Edith Chavasse, Noel was the second of twins – both he and his brother Christopher in their respective fields of medicine and the Church would be a credit to the family name.

In 1900, the family moved to Liverpool, where Francis was ordained, and despite both twins returning to Oxford to study, it was Liverpool which Noel regarded as his home, and where, once he qualified as a doctor, he returned to work in 1912. Notably, both twins excelled at sports while at university, and represented Great Britain in the 400 metres at the 1908 Olympics.

Chavasse applied to join the Royal Army Medical Corps and was accepted into the 10th Battalion, the Liverpool Scottish, of the King's (Liverpool) Regiment as surgeon-lieutenant. It was a territorial battalion, but at the start of November 1914 it was in France, where Christopher Chavasse was already at the front as chaplain to No. 10 General Hospital at St-Nazaire. Tetanus was a major concern for Noel Chavasse in looking after the men's health, as there was no vaccine developed – but he obtained and was one of the first to use an anti-tetanus serum. (Over eleven million doses of the serum were administered during the war and very few patients developed tetanus.) Moved up to the front line, Chavasse often had cause to be thankful for his sprinting speed as he dodged sniper fire to run across open ground to treat the injured. Filthy trench conditions and the standing water and mud caused trench foot in epidemic proportions, and he found that in cutting away the clothes of injured men, his hands ended up as filthy as they were.

By the Second Battle of Ypres in March 1915, the battalion had moved to the Ypres Salient near Hill 60. Here the Germans used chlorine gas for the first time and, although the Scottish were not directly affected, alarm spread among the men. Concerned for all aspects of the men's well-being, Noel had his father send out a gramophone to lift morale. Trench life continued until 10 June 1915, when the battalion went into action at the Battle of Hooge, in which Chavasse lost most of his friends. Only 140 men and 2 officers remained fit for action – and for his bravery in treating the wounded his commanding officer recommended him for the Military Cross. The recommendation was lost at division level, but he was finally awarded the honour in January 1916.

Committed and caring, Chavasse openly criticized some areas of the RAMC and had great sympathy for those suffering from shell shock, their nerves in tatters after months of constant bombardment – these reasons probably account for his never being promoted above captain.

At the end of July 1916, the battalion moved to the Somme near Mametz, and on 7 August it was ordered to take part in an assault on Guillemont at dawn the next day as part of the 166th Brigade. Initially in reserve, it was called to action when the 164th Brigade got cut off. Unfortunately the guides did not turn up to lead them and while waiting the men were caught in shellfire and suffered early casualties. Then, when guides finally arrived, they were uncertain of their route and the battalion struggled into the jumping-off trenches with only minutes to spare. The attack was intended to capture the German front-line trench and press on to Guillemont – but from the off, the men came under sweeping machine-gun and artillery fire in no-man's-land. Four times the men tried to go forward, and were driven back while suffering many losses. Of the 23 officers of the Liverpool Scottish who began the attack, 5 were killed, 5 were missing and 7 wounded – and of the 600 men, 69 were killed, 27 missing and 167 wounded.

Chavasse received two shell splinters in his back, but went on treating the injured, and in a sustained effort which earned him his first VC, he led a party of volunteers to bring in the wounded from no-man's-land. At one point he came to within 25 yards of the German line to rescue three men –

and the rescue effort lasted throughout the night as they worked under a constant hail of bullets and artillery bombardment. After a short sick leave, Chavasse was returned in September to the thick of the fighting near Delville Wood. Here he learned from his father (who had been tipped off by Lord Derby) that he was to be awarded the VC – he commented, ''Til I see it in print I will not believe it.'

The honours for the Guillemont action were finally announced – two of Chavasse's stretcher bearers were awarded the DSM, two more the Military Medal, and Chavasse's VC was confirmed.

Late in 1916, Chavasse spent a short posting with a small hospital away from his battalion – probably a reaction to his persistent criticism of RAMC methods and policies – but was back with his men by Christmas. Then in 1917 the Liverpool Scottish were in action in the Third Battle of Ypres. At dawn on 31 July, they launched an attack across open ground, but were held up by uncut wire, at which point they came under heavy machine-gun fire. A tank finally broke through the wire, allowing the men to go forward to take their first objectives. Chavasse moved his aid post from the Weiltje dugout (which was away from the immediate action) to a captured German dugout at Setques Farm, where he remained under heavy fire to help the wounded. After getting a shell splinter in the head (and possibly a fractured skull), the wound was dressed and he was back at the aid post, where he worked until sundown. When light failed, he took a torch and went in search of survivors in the wrecked landscape.

The next day, along with a German prisoner who was a medic, Chavasse worked in rain-sodden and mud-drenched conditions to treat the wounded. When a shell flew past him at the doorway and killed the man waiting to be carried out, it seems that Chavasse was wounded again in the head – but a stretcher bearer sent from the Weiltje dugout to bring him back reported, 'The doc refused to go and told us to take another man instead.' Around three o'clock next morning another shell entered the aid post, killing or wounding everyone inside. Chavasse, resting in a chair, received a wound to the stomach but, although bleeding heavily, he managed to drag himself out to the muddy road, and crawled to a dugout where a Lieutenant Wray of the Loyal North Lancashire Regiment sent for help – and later sent his account of events to his local paper.

Chavasse was operated on at the casualty clearing station at Brandhoek, which specialized in abdominal surgery, and he came round from the operation. He was reported as being very weak, but speaking cheerfully – but he died at 1.00 p.m. on 4 August.

Chavasse's father, the bishop, received a letter in September from Lord Derby.

> I signed something last night which gave me the most mixed feelings
> of deep regret and great pleasure, and that was the submission to his

majesty that a Bar should be granted to the Victoria Cross gained by your son ... It is a great pleasure to think that your son, in laying down his life, laid it down on behalf of his fellow countrymen, and that it is recognised, not only by those who knew him, but by the King and Country as a whole.

The medals of Noel Godfrey Chavasse are on permanent loan to the Imperial War Museum, where they can be seen in the Victoria Cross and George Cross Gallery. Chavasse himself – a devoted Liverpudlian – is remembered and honoured in the city to this day.

It is interesting that there is a link between the only three men to have earned a bar to their VC awards. Lieutenant Colonel Arthur Martin-Leake was with the 46th Field Ambulance which brought Chavasse back to Brandhoek, and Captain Charles Upham was distantly related to Chavasse by marriage.

ALLEN, William Barnsley *Captain, Royal Army Medical Corps, attached 246th Brigade Royal Field Artillery*
3 September 1916 – Whilst high-explosive ammunition was being unloaded near Mesnil, Somme, it was struck by an enemy shell. The resulting explosion caused many casualties. He immediately ran across the open and began to dress the wounded, saving many from bleeding to death. Over the next hour, he was hit by four shell fragments, one of which fractured his ribs, but he continued helping others and did not even mention his own injuries until the last man had been treated.

HOLLAND, John Vincent *Lieutenant, 3rd (R) Bn., Prince of Wales Leinster Regiment, attached 7th (S) Bn.*
3 September 1916 – At Guillemont, Somme, he led his bombers fearlessly through an artillery barrage and cleared a large part of the village, taking 50 prisoners despite losing 19 of his own men. This action undoubtedly broke the enemy's spirit and saved many subsequent lives.

HUGHES, Thomas *Private, 6th (S) Bn., Connaught Rangers*
3 September 1916 – After going over the top at Guillemont, Somme, and being hit four times, he spotted a machine-gun firing from the German lines. He rushed towards it, shot both gunners, captured the gun and brought 4 German prisoners back to his own lines. He then lost consciousness.

JONES, David *Sergeant, 12th (S) Bn., King's (Liverpool) Regiment*
3 September 1916 – As his platoon advanced on a forward position at Guillemont, Somme, enemy machine-guns opened up, killing the officer in charge. Jones sprang forward, took command and led the advance on, taking the position under intense shell fire. Despite having no food or water, he and his men drove off two fierce German attempts to regain the position and held it for two days until relief arrived. A fellow NCO described Jones as 'the right man in the right place at the right moment'.

CLARKE, Leo *Acting Corporal, 2nd Bn. (Eastern Ontario Regiment),*
Canadian Expeditionary Force

    9 September 1916 – He was covering construction work in a newly
captured trench near Pozières, Somme, when 20 of the enemy counter-
attacked. He emptied his revolver into the attackers before firing two enemy
rifles which he found in the trench. A German officer lunged at him with a
bayonet and caught him just below the knee but Clarke shot him dead. The
enemy then ran away but he was able to shoot four of them as they ran. A
fifth begged so hard for his life that he was spared. In total, Clarke killed 2
officers and 16 men.

THE BATTLE OF THE SOMME: 10 SEPTEMBER TO 3 OCTOBER

Haig paused a further week to allow replacement forces to be brought to
the line, including New Zealanders, and Canadians to replace the Australians. He also brought forward tanks, which were used for the first time –
he had been promised a hundred and fifty, but received only forty-nine. Key
objectives were the village of Courcelette, just west of the Albert–Bapaume
road; and east of the road High Wood, Flers, Lesboeufs and Morval. On the
left Courcelette was captured by the Canadians and the ridge in the centre
was held, but on the right the Guards and 6th Divisions failed to reach
Lesboeufs and Morval respectively after tanks broke down.
    The attack on Morval was renewed on the 25th and taken that day, and
the next day the village of Guedecourt fell. Thiepval was finally taken, with
a thousand prisoners, on the morning of the 27th, and after a struggle for
Eaucourt l'Abbaye and Sers, in Haig's words, 'with the exception of his
positions in the neighbourhood of Sailly–Saillisel, and his scanty foothold
on the northern crest of the high ground above Thiepval, the enemy had
now been driven from the whole of the ridge lying between the Tortille and
the Ancre'.

BROWN, Donald Forrester *Sergeant, 2nd Bn., Otago Infantry Regiment,*
New Zealand Expeditionary Force

    15 September 1916 – At High Wood, France, when his company's
advance was held up by a machine-gun, he and a comrade rushed the gun,
killed four of its crew and captured the weapon. He and his comrade then
rushed a second gun and killed its crew. On a third occasion, he attacked a
gun single-handed, killing its crew and capturing it.

CAMPBELL, John Vaughan *T/Lieutenant Colonel, 3rd Bn., Coldstream*
Guards

    15 September 1916 – During an attack at Ginchy, Somme, the first two
waves of his battalion had been decimated by machine-gun and rifle fire so
he took personal command of the third line, rallied his men and led them

against the machine-guns, capturing them and killing the gun teams. Later in the day, he led the survivors of the battalion through a heavy barrage. His gallantry and initiative turned the fortunes of the day and enabled tactically vital objectives to be taken.

He was ADC to the King, 1919–33.

McNESS, Frederick *Lance Sergeant, 1st Bn., Scots Guards*
15 September 1916 – As he led an attack near Ginchy, Somme, the enemy began bombing his left flank, so he gathered together a party to clear the Germans from their trench. When his men ran short of grenades, he discovered a supply of German bombs, which he had just begun to use when a bomb burst near him, blowing away the left side of his neck, his lower jaw and upper teeth, leaving his jugular vein and windpipe fully exposed. Refusing to retire, he led five bomb-carrying parties to his men until another shell burst near him, destroying more of his jaw, blinding him with blood and preventing him from walking. At this point, he was taken from the field.

In 1958 he took his own life whilst 'the balance of his mind was disturbed'.

KERR, John Chipman *Private, 49th Bn. (Edmonton Regiment), Canadian Expeditionary Force*
16 September 1916 – Shortly after a bomb had blown away his right forefinger, he took part in an attack on enemy trenches at Courcelette, Somme. He ran along the top of the trench and opened fire at point-blank range on the Germans who, thinking they were surrounded, surrendered. Sixty-two prisoners and 250 yards of trench were taken. Having delivered his prisoners, he returned to action without having his finger dressed.

JONES, Thomas Alfred *Private, 1st Bn., Cheshire Regiment*
25 September 1916 – Whilst entrenching a position near Morval, Somme, his company came under sniper fire. Declaring, 'If I am to be killed, I'll be killed fighting, not digging,' he set out in search of the sniper. Five bullets pierced his tunic and helmet before he spotted the sniper and shot him dead. He then shot two of the enemy who were firing whilst waving white flags, before rushing into an enemy trench and single-handedly taking 102 Germans prisoner.

His nickname was Dodger. He said later in an interview, 'Up went their hands and I laughed like blazes. It fairly tickled me to death, that did, and I couldn't stop laughing.'

EDWARDS, Frederick Jeremiah *Private, 12th (S) Bn., Middlesex Regiment*
26 September 1916 – When the infantry's advance was held up by a machine-gun and all the officers had been hit at Thiepval, Somme, he dashed alone towards the gun and knocked it out with bombs. His act resolved a dangerous situation and made a further advance possible.

RYDER, Robert Edward *Private, 12th (S) Bn., Middlesex Regiment*
26 September 1916 – When his company was held up by heavy rifle fire and all the officers had been hit at Thiepval, Somme, he dashed forward and by skilful use of his Lewis gun cleared the trench single-handedly. This turned possible failure into success and inspired the advance.

ADLAM, Tom Edwin *T/Second Lieutenant, 7th (S) Bn., Bedfordshire Regiment*
27 September 1916 – When an attack at Thiepval, Somme, came under heavy machine-gun and rifle fire, he ran from shell hole to shell hole under fire, collecting grenades and gathering men for a rush on an enemy-held village. Despite receiving a leg wound, he led the rush, captured the village and killed its occupiers.

WHITE, Archie Cecil Thomas *T/Captain, 6th (S) Bn., Yorkshire Regiment*
27 September to 1 October 1916 – Whilst in command of troops manning the southern and western faces of Stuff Redoubt, Thiepval, Somme, he held his position under heavy fire and constant attack for four days and nights. When the enemy attacked in vastly greater numbers and almost ejected his men from the redoubt, he led a counter-attack which repulsed the enemy.

BRADFORD, Roland Boys *T/Lieutenant Colonel, 1/9th (T) Bn., Durham Light Infantry*
1 October 1916 – At Eaucourt l'Abbaye, France, when a lead battalion had suffered severe casualties, including its commander, and its flank had become dangerously exposed, he took command of the battalion in addition to his own. By fearless energy and skilful leadership he rallied the attack, secured the flank and captured the objective.
At the time of his death, he was the youngest brigadier general in the army. He was the brother of Lieutenant Commander G. N. Bradford VC.

THE BATTLE OF THE SOMME: 4 OCTOBER TO 18 NOVEMBER

By 4 October, Haig was in a position to push forward the centre, turn the positions on the Ancre, and secure the ridge, while on the right smashing the Le Transloy line and, by advancing north and north-east, outflank the Beaumont-Hamel position then take the German position from the Ancre to Arras. This has been the original objective for the first day. Unfortunately, the weather changed and October and early November were very wet. In Haig's words: 'The country roads, broken by countless shell craters, that crossed the deep stretch of ground we had lately won, rapidly became almost impassable, making the supply of food, stores and ammunition a serious problem. These conditions multiplied the difficulties of attack to such an extent that it was found impossible to exploit the situation with the rapidity necessary to enable us to reap the full benefits of the advantages we had gained.' In the words of the *Official History*, the battlefield was now 'a wilderness of mud', where 'holding water-logged trenches or shell-hole posts, accessible only by night, the infantry abode in conditions which might be likened to those of earth-worms, rather than of human-kind'.

By 13 November, the weather had cleared, and Haig attacked on both sides of the Ancre. The 63rd (RN) Division took and held Beaucourt, and the 51st (Highland) Division finally captured Beaumont-Hamel. The last attack before foul weather precluded further offensives was on the high ground between Grandcourt and Pys. In four and a half months the Allied lines had advanced an average of five miles on the fourteen-mile front, two-thirds in the British sector. Haig wrote in the conclusion to his despatch:

> The enemy's power has not yet been broken, nor is it yet possible to form an estimate of the time the war may last before the objects for which the Allies are fighting have been attained. But the Somme battle has placed beyond doubt the ability of the Allies to gain those objects.

KELLY, Henry *T/Second Lieutenant, 10th (S) Bn., Duke of Wellington's (West Riding) Regiment*
4 October 1916 - During an attack at Le Sars, Somme, he twice rallied his company under heavy fire and led the only three available men into the enemy's trench, remaining there until two of his men became casualties and enemy reinforcements arrived. He then carried his wounded sergeant major 70 yards back before bringing in three other wounded men.
He won the Grand Laurelled Cross of San Fernando during the Spanish Civil War.

RICHARDSON, James Cleland *Piper, 16th Bn. (The Canadian Scottish), Canadian Expeditionary Force*
8–9 October 1916 – He piped his company over the top near Morval, Somme, but as the company approached its objective, it was held up by barbed wire and intense fire. He strode up and down in front of the wire, coolly playing his pipes. Inspired by his music and bravery, the company rushed the wire with such ferocity that the position was captured.
His favourite tune was 'Standard on the Braes o' Mar'.

DOWNIE, Robert *Sergeant, 2nd Bn., Royal Dublin Fusiliers*
23 October 1916 – When an attack by the Dublin Fusiliers at Lesboeufs, Somme, was checked after most of their officers had been killed or wounded, he rushed forward alone crying, 'Come on, the Dubs!' The line rushed forward and the attack resumed. Despite being himself wounded, he personally accounted for several of the enemy and captured a machine-gun, killing the gun team.
When his wife, back home in Glasgow, received the telegram informing

her of her husband's VC, she was afraid to open it, thinking it must contain news of her husband's death. 'Telegrams,' she explained, 'never bring very good news.'

BENNETT, Eugene Paul *T/Lieutenant, 2nd Bn., Worcestershire Regiment*
5 November 1916 – Whilst in command of the second wave of an attack at Le Transloy, Somme, he realized that the first wave was wavering due to heavy casualties and the death of its commander. He inspired his wave to continue and achieved his objective with only 60 men. Despite being wounded, he consolidated the position under heavy fire. Without his example, the attack would have been checked at the outset.

CUNNINGHAM, John *Private, 12th (S) Bn., East Yorkshire Regiment*
13 November 1916 – After the capture of the German front line near Hebuterne, Somme, he went with a bombing party to clear the German communication trench. The rest of his party was quickly killed or wounded, but he went on alone. After returning briefly to collect a fresh supply of bombs, he killed 10 Germans and cleared the trench up to the next enemy line.

FREYBERG, Bernard Cyril *T/Lieutenant Colonel, Queen's Royal West Surrey Regiment, commanding Hood Bn.*
13 November 1916 – After leading an attack through the enemy's front-line trenches at Beaucourt, Somme, his battalion became disordered, so he rallied and reorganized the men, leading them in a successful assault on the second objective, during which he was twice wounded. Throughout the following day and night, the battalion held the gained ground unsupported. When reinforced on the following day, he led an attack in which a village was taken and five hundred German prisoners captured. Despite two further wounds, he refused to leave the line until he had issued his final instructions. On arrival at the casualty station, he was put into a tent with those who were expected to die and so received no treatment except for pain-killing drugs. Fortunately he was later moved.
He gained the second bar to his DSO for an act carried out two minutes before the start of the armistice. He was C.-in-C. Allied Forces Crete (1941), Governor-General of New Zealand (1946–52) and Deputy Constable and Lieutenant-Governor of Windsor Castle (1953–63).

THE AIR WAR

Under the command of the former head of the Central Flying School, Major L. W. B. Rees, 32 Squadron, based in France from May 1916, had inspired leadership and training – a great advantage when the life expectancy of pilots over the Western Front was short. As the first battle at the Somme began on 1 July, the squadron flew from its base at Treizennes with orders to deny the enemy reconnaissance over the lines. Later in the afternoon six of the squadron's DH2 aircraft were sent as a bomber escort to attack the railway station at Don. It was around 5.30 p.m. that Rees himself set his squadron an example of flying skills which earned him the seventh Royal Flying Corps VC of the war.

REES, Lionel Wilmot Brabazon *T/Major, Royal Artillery and 32 Squadron Royal Flying Corps*
    1 July 1916 – Sighting a party of ten British aircraft flying over Double Crassieurs, France, he went up to escort them. On nearing them, however, he realized that they were actually enemy aircraft. One of them attacked him but he damaged it and it disappeared. Five others then came at him but he dispersed them and chased two before receiving a thigh wound and losing control of his machine. He regained control, closed with the enemy, used up all his ammunition and returned home safely.

EAST AFRICA

The British campaign in East Africa was invigorated in February, when General Smuts assumed command and began an advance to Kilimanjaro and then to Dar es Salaam, completed by the end of September.

BLOOMFIELD, William Anderson *Captain, Scout Corps*
    24 August 1916 – Whilst under attack at Miali, East Africa, he evacuated his wounded and withdrew his command to a new position. On arrival at the new position, he found that a wounded corporal had been left behind, so he went back over 400 yards of open ground swept by machine-gun fire to find him, before carrying him over the same ground to safety.

HOME DEFENCE

In September 1916 Germany began an all-out bombing offensive on England, always bombing at night. On 2/3 September twelve navy Zeppelins and four wooden-framed army airships, with thirty-two tons of bombs, appeared over England. Army airship SL-11, commanded by Wilhelm Schramm, dropped her bombs then turned north, when she was spotted by searchlights in Finsbury Park.

ROBINSON, William Leefe *Lieutenant, Worcestershire Regiment and 39 Squadron, Royal Flying Corps*
    3 September 1916 – During an attack on eastern England by sixteen German airships, he spotted one of them whilst flying over Cuffley, Hertford

shire. He attacked and destroyed it at a height of 11,500 feet, firing a new form of incendiary bullet. Its destruction was witnessed by thousands of people who had gathered in the streets to watch.

His was the only VC to be awarded for an act which took place on (or in this case above) British soil. Robinson was taken prisoner in 1917 and made several unsuccessful attempts to escape. His captors disliked him for these attempts and for his VC exploit. A fellow prisoner recalled: 'The Boche harried and badgered and bullied him every way possible.'

SALONIKA

The British 10th Division, taken from Gallipoli to protect Serbia from Bulgaria, arrived too late to prevent her defeat. King Constantine was determined to preserve Greek neutrality, and the troops remained in Salonika as part of an international force. A Bulgarian invasion of Greece was defeated at Lake Doiran, and a British VC was won during a limited counter-offensive against Bulgaria on the River Struma.

LEWIS, Hubert William *Private, 11th (S) Bn., Welch Regiment*
22–23 October 1916 – During a raid at Macakovo, Salonika, he was wounded twice and then again whilst searching enemy dugouts, but he refused medical attention. Observing three Germans approaching, he attacked them single-handedly and captured them all. He then carried a wounded man to safety under shell and rifle fire, before finally collapsing, weakened by his wounds.

1917

On the Western Front the start of 1917 saw the strength of the British Expeditionary Force increased to fifty-six divisions – with twice as many heavy guns as for the Somme offensive. Haig launched a series of minor attacks on the Somme in January to suggest that he planned to resume major operations there come the spring. Meanwhile, German strategy was to stay on the defensive, launching Operation Alberich – a tactical withdrawal with scorched-earth tactics, lasting to the end of March, which straightened out the front line and set them up in new, well-sited defensive positions on the pre-prepared Hindenburg Line – this despite having to yield previously hard-defended sites. The Allies pursued the withdrawing enemy, who left behind them poisoned water, booby traps and fields of mines.

The Hindenburg Line ran from Arras via Saint Quentin to Laffaux, six miles north-east of Soissons, and was a masterpiece of defensive strategy. The British launched attacks against these defences on 9 April at Arras, managing, with the support of four Canadian divisions, to send tanks over three miles into the defences. As the Canadians captured Vimy Ridge, ten thousand Germans were taken prisoner and despite a major German counter-offensive in early May, the Allies continued to gain ground.

The new French Commander-in-Chief, General Robert Nivelle, launched a tank attack at Chemin-des-Dames – which failed disastrously, with most of the eighty-two French Schneider tanks destroyed. French losses soared during April and mutiny began to break out in the French ranks. During May and early June, sixty-eight of France's hundred and twelve divisions reported 'acts of collective indiscipline' – strikes among the fighting men. Despite the best efforts of General Philippe Pétain, the Chief of the General Staff, to restore order, Britain's army was effectively now without support from France or Russia (now torn by revolution) – and America had not yet brought anywhere near enough troops in to change the course of the war.

On 6 April the United States declared war on Germany. This was a significant moment, there being in America a large population of emigrant Germans. By the end of June the first men of the American Expeditionary Force arrived in France to support the Allies.

Fighting continued on all fronts – in Mesopotamia the battle continued around Kut, and at the end of February, in modern Saudi Arabia, Wehj was captured in the course of the Arab Revolt. British troops of the Egyptian

Expeditionary Force pressed north into Palestine, with fierce fighting at Gaza during March. Fighting continued until Allenby's entry into Jerusalem on 11 December. The end of hostilities here released large numbers of veteran troops for the European offensive.

On 8 March (24 February in the Russian calendar), revolution erupted in Russia for a turbulent week – Tsar Nicholas abdicated on 15 March, and a provisional government was formed, but this still did not take Russia out of the war, and her troops continued fighting on the Eastern Front until autumn. On 8 October the Bolsheviks rose up to bring Lenin to power. On 2 December, a Russian peace delegation arrived at Brest-Litovsk, bringing Russia's part in the war to an end by the 16th.

TRENCH WARFARE

The year on the Western Front was dominated by the battles for Arras and Messines and the third battle for Ypres, and Cambrai – but fighting was not confined to these major offensives. Trench warfare continued throughout the year as forays ventured into no-man's-land to harry the enemy in their trenches, and 30 men distinguished themselves between January and December to earn the VC.

MURRAY, Henry William *Captain, 13th Bn. (New South Wales), Australian Imperial Force*
4/5 January 1917 – He successfully led his company in an assault on Stormy Trench, near Guedecourt, France, and then inspired his men to resist three fierce counter-attacks. Throughout the following night, his company suffered heavy casualties from shell fire and on one occasion briefly conceded ground, but he rallied the men, headed bombing parties, led bayonet charges, carried wounded men to safety and saved the situation.
Known as 'Mad Harry', he was the most decorated Australia soldier of the war.

MOTT, Edward John *Sergeant, 1st Bn., Border Regiment*
27 January 1917 – When an attack by his company near Transloy, France, was held up by machine-gun fire, he rushed forward, engaged in a fierce struggle with the gunner, took him prisoner and captured the gun. As a result, the attack succeeded. Throughout this action, he was suffering from a serious eye wound.

PALMER, Frederick William *Lance Sergeant, 22nd (S) Bn., Royal Fusiliers*
16–17 February 1917 – After all his officers had been cut down near Courcelette, France, he took command of the company, cut through wire entanglements under machine-gun fire and rushed the enemy's trench with 6 of his men. He then dislodged a machine-gun and established a block,

which he held for three hours against seven determined counter-attacks. Whilst he was collecting more bombs, an eighth counter-attack was mounted which threatened the flank. Despite exhaustion, he rallied the men, drove back the enemy and maintained the position.

CATES, George Edward *Second Lieutenant, 2nd Bn., Rifle Brigade*
8 March 1917 – Whilst he was deepening a captured trench with his men near Bouchavesnes, France, he struck a buried bomb with his spade. As the fuse started to burn, he placed his foot over the bomb to minimize the inevitable explosion. It killed him but all the others in the trench were saved.

COX, Christopher *Private, 7th (S) Bn., Bedfordshire Regiment*
13 March 1917 – During an attack by his battalion at Achiet-le-Grand, France, the first wave was checked by artillery and machine-gun fire, forcing the whole line to take cover in shell holes. He went out alone in this mayhem and single-handedly rescued four men and then brought in the wounded of another battalion. He repeated this exploit over the following two days.

CHERRY, Percy Herbert *Captain, 26th Bn. (Queensland and Tasmania), Australian Imperial Force*
26 March 1917 – When his company was storming a village at Langnicourt, France, and all the other officers had been killed, he organized machine-gun and bomb parties and captured the position. He then held it against continual counter-attacks. Despite receiving a serious wound, he remained at his post until killed by a shell.

HARVEY, Frederick Maurice Watson *Lieutenant, Lord Strathcona's Horse, Canadian Expeditionary Force*
27 March 1917 – During a mounted attack at Guyencourt, France, an enemy party ran forward to a wired trench and opened rapid rifle and machine-gun fire at very close range. He galloped ahead of his men, leapt into the trench, shot the machine-gunner and captured the gun.

JENSEN, Joergen Christian *Private, 50th Bn. (South Australia), Australian Imperial Force*
2 April 1917 – At Noreuil, France, with five comrades, he attacked a barricade defended by 45 of the enemy and a machine-gun. One of his party shot the gunner whilst he threw in a bomb. He then entered the position with a bomb in each hand and, drawing a pin with his teeth, told the enemy they were surrounded. Believing him, they surrendered. He then sent one of the prisoners to order a nearby enemy party to surrender, which they did, whereupon he stood on the barricade and sent the prisoners back to his own lines.
He was one of three Danish-born VCs. (The others were Anders Lassens

(1945) and Thomas Dinesen (1918), the brother of Karen Blixen of Out of Africa *fame.)*

LUMSDEN, Frederick William *Major, Royal Marine Artillery*
3/4 April 1917 – At Francilly, France, he undertook to bring in six enemy field guns which had been left 300 yards in front of the British lines. He led four artillery teams and a party of infantry through a hostile barrage. Although he had to make three journeys to the guns during which the party sustained casualties, all the guns were successfully brought in.
He was killed on 4 June 1918. He was one of the most decorated British soldiers.

GOSLING, William *Sergeant, 3rd Wessex Brigade, Royal Field Artillery*
5 April 1917 – After he had fired a trench mortar near Arras, France, he watched as the bomb fell just 10 yards from the mortar, due to a faulty cartridge. He instantly sprang out, lifted the nose of the bomb, which had sunk into the ground, unscrewed the fuse and threw it on the ground, where it immediately exploded. His prompt action undoubtedly saved the lives of the whole detachment.

CUNNINGHAM, John *Corporal, 2nd Bn., Prince of Wales' Leinster Regiment*
12 April 1917 – Whilst in command of a Lewis gun section at Bois-en-Hache, near Barlin, France, he came under heavy enfilade fire, but he got his gun into action despite being badly wounded. When attacked by 20 Germans, he exhausted his ammunition and started throwing bombs. He was wounded again but picked himself up and continued the fight before retiring with many injuries from which he died four days later.

FOSTER, Edward *Corporal, 13th (S) Bn., East Surrey Regiment*
24 April 1917 – At Villers Plouich, Cambrai, France, he was in charge of two Lewis guns during an advance held up by two entrenched enemy machine-guns. When a Lewis gun was lost, he rushed forward, recovered it and opened fire on one of the German gun teams, killing them and capturing the machine-gun, allowing the advance to continue.

BROOKS, Edward *Company Sergeant Major, 2/4th Bn., Oxfordshire and Buckinghamshire Light Infantry*
28 April 1917 – Whilst taking part in a raid on the enemy's trenches at St Quentin, France, he rushed forward from the second wave with the aim of capturing a gun that was checking the advance of the first wave. After he killed one of the gunners with his revolver and bayoneted another, the rest of the gun's crew ran off, so he turned the gun on the retreating Germans before carrying it back to his own lines.

DUNVILLE, John Spencer *Second Lieutenant, 1st Dragoons*
24–25 June 1917 – During a raid on the German lines near St Quentin, he was directing sappers laying a torpedo (an explosive tube pushed under

barbed wire and detonated to make a passage). The torpedo had become bent, and while a sapper corporal repaired it, Dunville lay between the corporal and the enemy's fire, protecting him and reassuring him that he was in no danger. He was later mortally wounded but continued to direct his men and walked unaided back to his lines. He died the following day.

WEARNE, Frank Bernard *Second Lieutenant, 3rd Bn., Essex Regiment, attached 11th (S) Bn.*
28 June 1917 – Whilst in command of a small party during a raid on enemy trenches east of Loos, France, he gained his objective and maintained it in the face of repeated counter-attacks. Aware of the danger to his left flank, he leapt onto the parapet and ran along the top of the trench firing and throwing bombs. He was severely wounded but remained in the trench directing the operation until he was wounded again, this time mortally.

YOUENS, Frederick *T/Second Lieutenant, 13th (S) Bn., Durham Light Infantry*
7 July 1917 – Having been wounded whilst on patrol near Hill 60, Belgium, he was taken to a dugout where his wounds were dressed. As he stood with tunic and shirt off, word came that his company was being attacked. He rushed out as he was to rally a Lewis gun team, and when a bomb was thrown into the midst of the team, he picked it up and threw it over the parapet. Another bomb landed in the same place but as he picked it up, it exploded in his hand. He died of his wounds two days later.

BARRATT, Thomas *Private, 7th (S) Bn., South Staffordshire Regiment*
27 July 1917 – Whilst acting as scout on a patrol near Ypres, Belgium, he twice stalked and killed enemy snipers firing at him. When a party of the enemy was spotted trying to outflank the patrol during its retirement, he covered the withdrawal and caused many casualties but was killed by a shell on returning to his lines.

ANDREW, Leslie Wilton *Corporal, 2nd Bn., Wellington Infantry Regiment, New Zealand Expeditionary Force*
31 July 1917 – Whilst leading his men against a machine-gun post located in an isolated building at La Bassée Ville, France, he encountered another machine-gun which he attacked and captured, killing several of the crew. He then continued the attack on the original machine-gun post, which he attacked from the rear. He threw bombs and rushed at the crew, killing four and capturing the gun. He then advanced further on a reconnoitring expedition and brought back valuable information.

BUTLER, William Boynton *Private, 17th (S) Bn., West Yorkshire Regiment attached 106th T.M. Bty.*
6 August 1917 – Whilst he was in charge of a Stokes gun near Lempire, France, there was a malfunction and a live shell fell into the emplacement. At that moment a party of infantry was passing so he placed himself between

them and the shell and shouted to them to hurry past. When they had gone, he picked up the shell and threw it out of the position. It exploded almost on leaving his hand and greatly damaged the emplacement, but he suffered only bruising.

On the day before his investiture, he went to visit his parents in Leeds but as a result of a misunderstanding they had already travelled up to London. He found himself locked out of the house and had to sit on the doorstep until someone recognized him.

HOBSON, Frederick *Sergeant, 20th Bn. (Central Ontario), Canadian Expeditionary Force*

15 August 1917 – During an enemy counter-attack near Lens, France, a Lewis gun was buried by a shell blast and all but one of the crew killed. He jumped out of his trench, dug out the gun and got it into action against the enemy who were advancing across the open. Almost at once the gun jammed, so he ran straight at the advancing enemy and with bayonet and clubbed rifle held them off until he was killed by a rifle shot. At the same moment, the surviving gunner cleared the gun and opened fire on the Germans, who were driven back. Hobson was found surrounded by dead.

O'ROURKE, Michael James *Private, 7th Bn. (1st British Columbia Regiment), Canadian Expeditionary Force*

15–17 August 1917 – Whilst he was a stretcher bearer at Hill 60, Lens, France, he worked unceasingly for three days and nights bringing the wounded to safety, dressing their wounds and giving them food and water. He was continually subjected to shelling, machine-gun and rifle fire and was knocked down and partially buried several times. On one occasion, he went out into no-man's-land and brought back a blinded man who was stumbling around in full view of the Germans.

BROWN, Harry W. *Private, 10th Bn. (Canadians), Canadian Expeditionary Force*

16 August 1917 – At Hill 70, near Loos, France, the enemy were seen massing for an attack. An artillery barrage was desperately needed but all the signal wires had been cut. He and another man were chosen to carry the message. His comrade was killed almost immediately and he went on alone. The ground around him was torn up savagely and his arm shattered as he ran, but he reached the support lines and delivered the message before collapsing unconscious. He died hours later.

LEARMONTH, Okill Massey *A/Major, 2nd Bn. (Eastern Ontario), Canadian Expeditionary Force*

18 August 1917 – During an enemy counter-attack near Loos, France, he charged and personally disposed of the enemy. Later, when under intense barrage fire, he stood on the parapet of his trench, directed its defence and bombed the enemy continuously. Several times he actually caught bombs that had been thrown at him by the enemy and threw them back. He was wounded three times but refused to be carried out of the line until the counter-attack was repulsed. He died of his wounds the following day.

PARSONS, Hardy Falconer *T/Second Lieutenant, 14th (S) Bn., Gloucestershire Regiment*

20–21 August 1917 – During a night attack by an enemy party on a post near Epehy, France, he single-handedly held them up with bombs despite being horribly scorched by liquid fire. His act of self-sacrifice delayed the Germans long enough to allow a bombing party to be organized which forced the enemy back before they could enter the trenches. He later died of his wounds.

HANNA, Robert Hill *Company Sergeant Major, 29th Bn. (Vancouver), Canadian Expeditionary Force*

21 August 1917 – Three attacks by his company on an enemy strong-point at Lens, France, had failed due to wire and heavy machine-gun fire. He collected a party of men, rushed through the wire and personally bayoneted three of the enemy, brained a fourth, silenced the machine-gun and captured the position. He then built a block and held the position under counter-attack until he was relieved later that day.

KONOWAL, Filip *A/Corporal 47Bn. (British Columbia), Canadian Expeditionary Force*

No one who ever won the Victoria Cross could be said to have lived an unexceptional life, but even by these standards, Filip Konowal's story is extraordinary. Before the First World War, he had left his native Ukraine for Canada in the hope of finding a better life. He left behind a wife who starved to death during Stalin's forced famine of 1932–33 and a daughter who lived on in the Ukraine until 1986. He was awarded the Victoria Cross for his bravery during mopping-up operations in France, but his wartime experiences left him damaged – physically and mentally. He was charged with manslaughter in Canada after a fight left a man dead from stab wounds but was found not guilty by reason of insanity and spent years in a mental institution. He lived out his life working as a janitor at the Canadian House of Commons. 'I mopped up overseas with a rifle and here I must mop up with a mop,' he laughed.

It seems that Konowal did not intend to abandon his family when he left the Ukraine in 1913. Contact with his wife Anna would have become impossible almost immediately. Between 1914 and 1918, the war would have prevented any communication. In 1918, a communist government took power in the Ukraine, and in 1922 the country became part of the Soviet Union. It is plain that Konowal had made genuine efforts to support his family in 1913. In that year, he sent two American $20 bills to Anna. Although she still had these bills during the famine, they were worthless to her. Even if she had tried to spend them, she would have been arrested for the possession of foreign currency. These bills still survive. They belong today to Konowal's granddaughter, who lives in the same house in the village of Kutkiv in which Anna starved to death during the 1930s.

Konowal spent a few months working as a lumberjack in western Canada after his arrival, before moving to Ottawa and working as a forester. In 1915, he joined the 77th Infantry Battalion, with which he sailed to Liverpool, arriving in June 1916. He was soon on his way to France, where he fought in the Battle of the Somme. He took part in the spring offensive at Vimy Ridge and was appointed an acting corporal in April 1917. In the summer of that year the Canadian army was redeployed further north, toward the German-held town of Lens, France. It was there, at the battle for Hill 70, that he won the Victoria Cross.

He led his section as it mopped up cellars of abandoned buildings, craters and machine-gun emplacements after the main attack had swept on. In one cellar he bayoneted three of the enemy, whilst in a crater he killed seven Germans single-handedly. On the following day, he rushed alone into a machine-gun emplacement, killing the crew and capturing the gun, and on the day after that he killed at least 16 of the enemy before being wounded. His behaviour was so courageous that on one occasion as he burst forward alone towards the German gun positions his own captain shot at him, thinking that he was trying to desert. It was simply inconceivable to the officer that a soldier could be acting as indifferently to his own safety as Konowal was doing. Years later, he explained his actions: 'I was so fed up standing in the trench with water up to my waist that I said the hell with it and started after the German army.' As well as being awarded the Victoria Cross, he was promoted to sergeant.

Shortly after receiving his citation and promotion, Konowal suffered a gunshot wound to the head which left him with a hairline fracture. This injury contributed to the event which led to years in a mental institution. Following his honourable discharge from the army and his return to Canada, he led Ottawa's Peace Day Parade in 1919. On the following day, he became involved in a fight outside a bootlegging operation between a friend of his and one William Artich, who was armed with a knife. During the fight, in which Konowal received a further blow to his already injured head, Artich was stabbed with his own knife and died. Konowal was arrested and charged with manslaughter. During his trial, medical evidence was presented that his head fracture had created intense pressure on his brain and that the further blow had exacerbated his condition. The court accepted this explanation and found him not guilty by reason of insanity, but he was sent to a mental institution in Montreal, where he remained for seven years.

On his release, he attempted to rebuild his life. He enlisted in the Governor General's Foot Guards in Ottawa in 1928. Six years later (and presumably aware that Anna had died during the famine) he remarried. He then found work as a junior caretaker in the Canadian House of Commons, thanks to the intervention of Major Milton Fowler Gregg (a fellow Victoria Cross holder who was also a member of the Governor General's Foot Guards). One day he was spotted washing the floors by the Prime Minister, William Lyon Mackenzie King, who was surprised to see a Victoria Cross holder engaged in such menial work. King immediately appointed him the custodian of his office, a post which Konowal retained until his death.

During his later years, Konowal received a good deal of recognition but money remained a constant problem. He was introduced to King George VI during the 1939 Royal Tour of Canada but he was forced to sell his Victoria Cross to pay for his mortgage. He attempted to re-enlist to fight for Canada during the Second World War but was rejected due to his age. In 1953, he was voted to become the patron of the Toronto branch of the Royal Canadian Legion and was invited to participate in the ceremony to mark the hundredth anniversary of the Victoria Cross in London. Although he did not have sufficient funds to travel to London, the Ukrainian Canadian branches of the Royal Canadian Legion paid for him to attend. On 26 June 1956, he participated in a march-past of Victoria Cross winners, which was reviewed by the Queen and Prince Philip. Konowal marched in the centre of the front rank of Canadian winners. He died three years later at the age of seventy-two and was buried at the St John the Baptist Ukrainian Catholic Church in Ottawa with full military honours.

DAY, Sidney James *Corporal, 11th (S) Bn., Suffolk Regiment*
26 August 1917 – Near Hargicort, France, he led a bombing section which cleared a maze of trenches held by the enemy, killed two machine-gunners and captured four prisoners. On his return to his section, a stick bomb fell into a trench occupied by five men. He picked it up and threw it over the trench where it immediately exploded. He then cleared the trench and established himself in an advanced position where he remained for sixty-six hours under severe shell and rifle-grenade attack.

GOURLEY, Cyril Edward *Sergeant, 276th (West Lancashire) Brigade, Royal Field Artillery*
30 November 1917 – Whilst he was in charge of a section of howitzers east of Epehy, France, the enemy advanced to within 400 yards in front, 300 yards on one flank and sent snipers around to the rear. He pulled his gun out of its pit and engaged a machine-gun at 500 yards, knocking it out with a direct hit. All day he held the enemy in check, firing over open sights on bodies of German troops. He saved his guns, which were withdrawn at nightfall.

NICHOLAS, Henry James *Private, 1st Bn., Canterbury Regiment, New Zealand Expeditionary Force*
3 December 1917 – When an advance was checked at Polderhoek, Belgium, by heavy fire from an enemy position, he charged the position

alone, with the rest of his Lewis-gun section 25 yards behind him. He shot the commander and overcame 16 other men using bayonet and bombs. He captured four men and a machine-gun.

MILLS, Walter *Private, 1/10th Bn., Manchester Regiment*

10–11 December 1917 – A strong enemy patrol attacked a British post at Givenchy, France, after a gas attack had overcome the garrison. Despite being badly gassed, he met the advance single-handed, threw bombs until reinforcements arrived and remained at his post until the attack had been driven off. He died from gas poisoning as he was being carried away. He had known that his only chance of survival had been to lie motionless but his sacrifice ensured that the enemy was defeated and the line remained intact.

THE BATTLE OF ARRAS

The Allies' major plan on the Western Front for 1917 was for a French breakthrough in Flanders, supported by limited British and French attacks between, respectively, Arras and Bapaume, and the Somme and the Oise. For this offensive, British forces in France were under French command. Just after this was agreed in London, the Germans redrew the map of the Somme–Oise salient by withdrawing to the Hindenburg Line, leaving a wasteland behind. The French view was that the planned attacks would outflank the new defensive line.

The Arras battlefield was dominated by Vimy Ridge, north-east of the town, which had been taken by the Germans in 1914. Haig assigned it to 1st Army (thirteen divisions) and the high ground beyond Arras to 3rd Army (eighteen divisions), with a diversionary attack at Bullecourt made by 5th Army (six divisions). He had five thousand guns and sixty tanks, and the Cavalry Corps (six divisions) to exploit success. The Germans had eight divisions with nine in reserve. Technical advances since the Somme included detailed maps provided by aerial reconnaissance, artillery fuses that burst on impact to cut wire, gas projectors with ranges of 1,200 yards and creeping barrages to precede infantry advances. Most importantly the infantry could move up to the start line through tunnels and caves, rather than under enemy fire.

After a five-day barrage, the attack began in a snowstorm at 5.30 a.m. on 9 April. Success that day was considerable, with two German lines occupied, and the all-important ridge taken by the Canadians at the cost of fourteen thousand casualties; on the right, the village strongpoint of Monchy-le-Preux was taken on the 11th after a cavalry charge. An advance against Bullecourt that day from the new positions against the Hindenburg Line was a bloody failure, and the advance was halted on the 14th, until the outcome of the Aisne offensive could be known.

By the 18th it was apparent that the Battle of Arras was a disastrous failure. Haig made a new assault at Arras on 3 May; fighting continued until the end of the month without further success.

NEWLAND, James Ernest *Captain, 12th Bn. (South Australia, Western Australia and Tasmania), Australian Imperial Force*
8/9 April 1917 – He organized an attack by his company on an important objective at Bapaume, France, and personally led the bombing attack under heavy fire. When the company suffered heavy casualties, he rallied the men and was one of the first to reach the objective, which was taken. On the following night, the enemy counter-attacked but he succeeded in dispersing them through personal exertion and the judicious use of reserves. On 15 April, near Langnicourt, when the company on his left was overwhelmed and his company attacked from the rear, his tenacity encouraged his men to hold out and repel the enemy.

BRYAN, Thomas *Lance Corporal, 25th (S) Bn., Northumberland Fusiliers*
9 April 1917 – Despite being wounded, he went forward alone during an attack near Arras, France, with a view to silencing an enemy machine gun which was inflicting a great deal of damage. He made his way along a communication trench, approached the gun from the rear, disabled it and killed two of its team as they tried to escape.

CATOR, Harry *Sergeant, 7th (S) Bn., East Surrey Regiment*
9 April 1917 – During an attack near Arras, France, his platoon was suffering severe casualties from machine-gun fire, so he advanced across open ground with another man to attack the gun. His comrade was soon shot but he continued, picked up a Lewis gun and reached the northern end of the hostile trench. Once there, he set up his gun and killed the entire German machine-gun team. He then held that end of the trench, with the result that an advancing British party was able to capture five machine-guns and a hundred prisoners. He was wounded three days later when his jaw was shattered by high-explosive shrapnel.

KENNY, Thomas James Bede *Private, 2nd Bn. (New South Wales), Australian Imperial Force*
9 April 1917 – When his platoon was held up by an enemy strongpoint at Hermies, France, and severe casualties prevented progress, he dashed alone under heavy fire towards the enemy's position. He killed a German who tried to bar his way, bombed the position, captured a machine-gun crew, killed an officer who fought back and captured the gun. His act enabled his platoon to occupy the position.

MacDOWELL, Thain Wendell *Captain, 38th Bn. (Ottawa), Canadian Expeditionary Force*
9 April 1917 – At Vimy Ridge, he advanced towards the enemy position in the company of two runners. As he went along, he bombed a machine-

gun out of action and attacked and killed the crew of another. Reaching a large dugout, he walked down a flight of stairs into a room containing 77 Prussian Guards. Thinking quickly, he shouted orders to an imaginary force behind him and instantly the Germans surrendered. He sent the Germans up the stairs in batches of twelve, marshalled by the runners. When the Germans emerged into daylight and saw that they had been captured by only three men, they opened fire, but the outbreak was quickly checked. MacDowell held the dugout (which was found to contain ammunition, rations and excellent cigars) for five days until he was relieved by his battalion.

MILNE, William Johnstone *Private, 16th Bn. (The Canadian Scottish), Canadian Expeditionary Force*

9 April 1917 – Near Thélus, France, he observed an enemy machine-gun firing on his comrades so he crawled to it, killed the crew with bombs and captured the gun. He then located a second machine-gun, made his way to it, put the crew out of action and captured that gun as well. He was killed shortly afterwards.

SIFTON, Ellis Welwood *Lance Sergeant, 18th Bn. (Western Ontario), Canadian Expeditionary Force*

9 April 1917 – During an attack on enemy trenches at Neuville-St-Vaast, France, his company was held up by machine-gun fire. Spotting the position of the gun, he leapt into the enemy trench and bayoneted every gunner. When another party of Germans appeared, he attacked them with his bayonet and clubbed rifle, managing to hold them off until his comrades arrived and joined the fight. When it seemed as though the danger had passed, one of the Germans who lay dying picked up a rifle and shot him dead.

WHITTLE, John Woods *Sergeant, 12th Bn. (South Australia, Western Australia and Tasmania), Australian Imperial Force*

9 April 1917 – Whilst he was in command of a platoon near Boursies, France, the enemy, under cover of an intense artillery barrage, attacked and took a small trench. He collected all available men and charged the enemy, regaining the trench. When the enemy later broke through the line and attempted to bring a machine-gun up to enfilade the position, he ran alone across the fire-swept ground and attacked and killed the entire gun crew before they could bring the gun into action.

PATTISON, John George *Private, 50th Bn. (Calgary), Canadian Expeditionary Force*

10 April 1917 – When an advance was held up by a machine-gun at Vimy Ridge, he sprang forward and jumped from shell hole to shell hole, until he was within 30 yards of the gun. He then hurled bombs at the gun, killing some of the crew, and rushed at them with his bayonet, killing the remainder. The advance was then able to continue.

WALLER, Horace *Private, 10th (S) Bn., King's Own Yorkshire Light Infantry*
10 April 1917 – As the Germans attacked near Heninel, France, he threw bombs for an hour and a half until they retreated. Five of his comrades were killed and one of his officers described the scene as 'the most violent hand-to-hand fighting I ever witnessed'. That evening, the Germans attacked again. This time he received a wound, but continued throwing bombs until he was eventually killed.

MACKINTOSH, Donald *Lieutenant, 3rd Bn., Seaforth Highlanders*
11 April 1917 – Despite being shot in the leg near Fampoux, France, he led his men on and captured a trench. Assuming command of another company which had lost its officer, he held the trench against a counter-attack, during which he received another leg wound. With only 15 men left, he ordered his party to advance on the final objective, but as he hauled himself out of the trench he was shot and killed.

MUGFORD, Harold Sandford *Lance Corporal, 8th Squadron, Machine-Gun Corps*
11 April 1917 – Under intense fire at Monchy-le-Preux, Arras, France, he got his machine-gun into a position from which he could fire on the enemy who were massing for a counter-attack. His No. 2 was instantly killed and he was severely wounded, but he refused to go to a dressing station and continued firing, inflicting severe loss on the enemy until a shell broke both of his legs. He remained with his gun for a while but was wounded again whilst being carried to safety.

ORMSBY, John William *Sergeant, 2nd Bn., King's Own Yorkshire Light Infantry*
14 April 1917 – Whilst his company cleared a village at Favet, France, under heavy machine-gun and rifle fire, he was acting as company sergeant major. When the only surviving officer was wounded, he took command and led the company 400 yards forward to a new position, which he skilfully organized until relieved of his command.
After he left the army, he was presented with a horse and cart and £500 to enable him to set up as a greengrocer.

POPE, Charles *Lieutenant, 11th Bn. (Western Australia), Australian Imperial Force*
15 April 1917 – He received orders to hold an important picket post at all costs at Louverval, France, so when hugely greater numbers of the enemy surrounded the post, he sent back for further supplies of ammunition. Before it could arrive, he charged the enemy, inflicting great losses. His body and those of most of his men were found beside 80 dead Germans.

SYKES, Ernest *Private, 27th (S) Bn., Northumberland Fusiliers*
19 April 1917 – When his battalion was held up by intense fire from front and flank near Arras, France, he went forward and brought back four wounded. He went out a fifth time under conditions which appeared to invite certain death and remained out until he had bandaged all those who were too badly wounded to be moved.

HIRSCH, David Philip *A/Captain, 1/4th Bn., Yorkshire Regiment*
23 April 1917 – Despite being wounded during an attack near Wancourt, France, he went back over fire-swept ground to ensure that the flank of the position was established. Machine-gun fire was so intense that he had to travel up and down the line encouraging his men to hold the position. He stood on the parapet to cheer them on until he was killed.

HENDERSON, Arthur *A/Captain, 4th (ER) Bn., Argyll and Sutherland Highlanders, attached 2nd Bn.*
23 April 1917 – During an attack on enemy trenches at Fontaine-les-Croisilles, France, he led his company through the enemy front line despite being wounded in the arm. He then consolidated the position under heavy artillery and machine-gun fire and bomb attack. By his cheerful courage and coolness, he maintained the spirit of his men. He was killed whilst holding the position.

HAINE, Reginald Leonard *Second Lieutenant, 1st Bn., Honourable Artillery Company*
28–29 April 1917 – He led six bombing attacks near Gavrelle, France, on an enemy position which was threatening communications. He captured the position, together with 50 prisoners and two machine-guns. When the enemy counter-attacked and regained the position, he formed a block in his trench and held firm throughout the night against repeated attacks. The following morning, he attacked and regained the position, pressing the enemy back several hundred yards. Throughout thirty hours of continuous fighting, his personal example inspired his men to continue.

POLLARD, Alfred Oliver *Second Lieutenant, 1st Bn., Honourable Artillery Company*
29 April 1917 – When troops of various units were disorganized after an enemy attack at Gavrelle, France, he dashed forward to prevent them from retiring. He started a counter-attack with only four men and pressed it home until he had regained all the lost ground and the enemy was forced to retire with many casualties. He infused courage into every man who came into contact with him.

WELCH, James *Lance Corporal, 1st Bn., Royal Berkshire Regiment*
29 April 1917 – After entering an enemy trench near Oppy, France, he killed a man after a severe hand-to-hand struggle. He then chased four

Germans across the open and captured them single-handed. He handled his machine-gun fearlessly and several times went into the open under heavy fire to collect ammunition and spare parts to keep his gun in action, which he did for over five hours until wounded.

COMBE, Robert Grierson *Lieutenant, 27th Bn. (City of Winnipeg), Canadian Expeditionary Force*

3 May 1917 – South of Acheville, France, he led his company through an artillery barrage, reaching the German line with only five men. Before reinforcements could arrive, he led his men, together with a few men from another company, into the trench. They bombed the Germans, took 250 yards of trench and captured 80 prisoners. He was killed by a rifle bullet as he led the band in yet another charge.

HARRISON, John *T/Second Lieutenant, 11th (S) Bn., East Yorkshire Regiment*

3 May 1917 – During an attack in darkness and smoke in a dense wood at Oppy, France, he led his company through heavy machine-gun fire towards a German trench. They were initially repulsed but he reorganized the men in no-man's-land and attacked again. When this attack also failed, he made a single-handed dash towards the machine-gun hoping to knock it out. He was never seen again.

He played professional Rugby league for Hull, and his record of fifty-two tries scored in a season still stands.

JARRATT, George *Corporal, 8th (S) Bn., Royal Fusiliers*

3 May 1917 – After being taken prisoner, he was placed with some wounded men in a dugout near Pelves, France. The enemy were soon driven back and the dugout attacked by British troops, who tossed in a grenade. Without hesitation, he placed his feet on the grenade, which exploded and blew off both his legs. The wounded were removed to safety but he died before he could be helped.

HEAVISIDE, Michael Wilson *Private, 15th (S) Bn., Durham Light Infantry*

6 May 1917 – At Fontaine-les-Croisilles, he observed a wounded man in distress and holding up a water bottle in a shell hole near the enemy. Under intense machine-gun and rifle fire, he ran to the man with food and water and discovered that he had been lying there for four days. That evening, he returned with a stretcher party and rescued the man.

HOWELL, George Julian *Corporal, 1st Bn. (New South Wales), Australian Imperial Force*

6 May 1917 – Seeing a party of the enemy heading to outflank his battalion near Bullecourt, France, he climbed alone to the top of his parapet and threw grenades down onto the Germans, pressing them back along the trench. When he had used up his bombs, he continued the attack with his bayonet until he was severely wounded.

DRESSER, Tom *Private, 7th (S) Bn., Yorkshire Regiment*

12 May 1917 – Near Roeux, France, he carried a crucial message from battalion headquarters to the front line of trenches despite being twice wounded on the way and arriving exhausted and in great pain.

MOON, Rupert Vance *Lieutenant, 58th Bn. (Victoria), Australian Imperial Force*

12 May 1917 – Near Bullecourt, France, he led an attack on three objectives: first a position in front of an enemy trench, second the trench itself and third a position behind the trench. He was wounded whilst achieving the first objective and wounded again whilst taking the trench, yet he continued to lead his men with great bravery. Only after he had been twice more wounded did he agree to retire from the fight.

WHITE, Albert *Sergeant, 2nd Bn., South Wales Borderers*

19 May 1917 – Realizing that an enemy machine-gun would hold up the advance of his company at Monchy-le-Preux, he dashed ahead of his company to capture the gun. He fell, riddled with bullets, within a few yards of the gun.

MAUFE, Thomas Harold Broadbent *Second Lieutenant, 124th Siege Bty., Royal Garrison Artillery*

4 June 1917 – Under intense artillery fire at Feuchy, France, unaided and on his own initiative, he repaired a telephone line between the forward and rear positions, enabling his battery to open fire on the enemy. He then extinguished a fire in an advanced ammunition dump, knowing the risk he ran from gas shells in the dump.

THE BATTLE OF MESSINES

The Battle of Messines was an essential first step for a British offensive in Flanders, necessary now the French army was exhausted and mutinous, and unfit for offensive action. The Messines Ridge was a German salient south-east of Ypres held since 1914; at 3.10 a.m. on 7 June, hundred of tons of explosive packed into nineteen mines went off simultaneously, killing ten thousand men in half a minute. Nine British and Anzac divisions attacked, with seventy-two tanks and following a creeping barrage, and took the ridge in thirty-five minutes. The positions held against counter-attacks, and in throwing them back more ground was gained. By 14 June the whole salient had been taken.

CARROLL, John *Private, 33rd Bn. (New South Wales), Australian Imperial Force*

7–12 June 1917 – During an attack at St Yves, France, he rushed an enemy trench and bayoneted four men. He then killed another of the enemy whilst assisting a comrade in difficulties before single-handedly attacking a machine-gun crew, killing three of them and capturing the gun. He later rescued two comrades buried by a shell. During the ninety-six hours his battalion was in the line, he displayed wonderful courage.

FRICKLETON, Samuel *Lance Corporal, 3rd Bn., 3rd New Zealand (Rifle) Brigade, New Zealand Expeditionary Force*
    7 June 1917 – During an attack at Messines, Belgium, he dashed forward into the barrage despite being wounded and personally destroyed an enemy machine-gun and crew which was causing heavy casualties. He then attacked a second gun, killing the whole of its crew of 12. His act ensured the capture of the objective. He was wounded again whilst consolidating the position.

GRIEVE, Robert Cuthbert *Captain, 37th Bn. (Victoria), Australian Imperial Force*
    7 June 1917 – At Messines, Belgium, two enemy machine-guns were holding up an advance. His company was sustaining heavy losses and all his officers had been killed so he single-handedly ran at the guns, bombed them and killed their crews. When he finally fell wounded, the few remaining enemy were in full flight.

RATCLIFFE, William *Private, 2nd Bn., South Lancashire Regiment*
    14 June 1917 – After an enemy trench had been captured at Messines, Belgium, he spotted a hostile machine-gun which was firing on his comrades from the rear, attacked it and bayoneted its crew. He then brought the gun back into action on the front line.
    At a dinner given in his honour in October 1917 by the National Union of Dock Labourers, Lord Derby made a speech in which he announced that a proposed monetary presentation would not take place whilst Ratcliffe was still serving as it breached army regulations but that it would be made when he returned to civilian life.

THE THIRD BATTLE OF YPRES (PASSCHENDAELE)

Encouraged by the success of the assault on Messines, Haig planned a conventional attack to gain the remainder of the ridge, as far north as Passchendaele. However, the next stage of his plan was subject to more than just enemy action – the constant, unremitting drizzle reduced shell craters in this lowland area to sludge and slime, the drainage system had been destroyed by savage bombardment, and with no sun or warmth to dry the ground the men of both sides fought and died in a man-made swamp. After a ten-day preliminary bombardment, the attack began at 3.50 a.m. on 31 July. A record for the war of eleven VCs were won that day. Ten British divisions went over the top, with 1st French Army (six divisions) to their left. They were supported by 136 tanks, but after four days of rain many bogged down in the deep mud before they could reach the line. The British made initial progress, especially at Pilckem Ridge, the French some, but both were thrown back by counter-attacks. The attacking forces had particular difficulties with pillboxes, also called at the time blockhouses or forts, which were equipped with machine-guns and were strong enough to survive direct hits with field artillery, and continued rain prevented major assaults. However, some ground was slowly retaken over the next few days, and on 16 August a new attack began: Wijdendrift and Langemarck were captured after several days of struggle and the French advanced from the Yser Canal on the left.

Nothing could be done except to hold positions until 20 September, when a limited attack on the Menin road advanced the front a mile. A series of limited advances, often checked or reversed by counter-attacks but never permanently halted, made slow and expensive progress, until the Canadians finally captured Passchendaele on 6 November and Haig called the offensive to a halt.

• **PILCKEM RIDGE** • The first battle, Pilckem Ridge, began on 31 July, but an artillery bombardment had been under way since 18 July – effectively giving the enemy good warning of the impending offensive. Battle raged overhead too, as Allied air forces fought to take out the observation balloons and shoot down German reconnaissance aircraft which were directing their artillery fire.

The rain, which along with the battle began on 31 July, was the worst for forty years – a major factor in the ensuing battle. The objective at Pilckem Ridge was an arc of small hills, which formed a saucer shape around the British positions in the valley around Ypres. The Germans held this ridge and had therefore the advantage of height, so the main thrust of the attack was aimed at wearing the enemy down at the crescent of high ground known as Passchendaele Ridge. As increasing use of aircraft had rendered major trenchworks inappropriate, the Germans instead used the craters made by artillery fire to conceal their gunners and snipers, and built concrete pillboxes as defences – but the main obstacle to the Allied advance was the terrain. Over the course of the battle from 30 July to 6 August there was only one day without rain. Troops arriving at the front carried up to 100lb of equipment. If they slipped from the duckboards or paths it was all too easy to slide into a crater and drown before anyone could help them.

ACKROYD, Harold *T/Captain, Royal Army Medical Corps, attached 6th (S) Bn., Royal Berkshire Regiment*
31 July to 1 August 1917 – He worked continuously for many hours in front of the line at Ypres, Belgium, tending the wounded and saving the

lives of officers and men. He carried a wounded officer to safety and brought in a wounded man under continuous sniping and machine-gun fire.

BEST-DUNKLEY, Bertram *T/Lieutenant Colonel, 2/5th Bn., Lancashire Fusiliers*
31 July 1917 – At Wieltje, Belgium, he was in command of a battalion which became disorganized under close-range machine-gun fire. He led a successful counter-attack and continued to lead the battalion until all its objectives had been gained. Later in the day, he led his battalion head-quarters to the attack and beat off the advancing enemy. He died later of his wounds.

BYE, Robert James *Sergeant, 1st Bn., Welsh Guards*
31 July 1917 – During an attack at the Yser Canal, Belgium, he saw the leading waves coming under fire from two enemy blockhouses so he rushed one of them and put it out of action. He then volunteered to take charge of a party which cleared another line of blockhouses and took many prisoners. He displayed remarkable initiative throughout the action.
He was the first Welsh Guards VC.

★ **CHAVASSE, Noel Godfrey** *Captain, Royal Army Medical Corps, attached 1/10th Bn., King's (Liverpool) Regiment*
31 July to 2 August 1917 – At Wieltje, Belgium, Captain Chavasse won a bar to his VC. See p. 252.

COFFIN, Clifford *T/Brigadier General, Royal Engineers, commanding 25th Infantry Brigade*
31 July 1917 – When his command was held up at Westhoek, Belgium, by heavy machine-gun and rifle fire, he walked quietly from shell hole to shell hole giving advice and cheering the men. Due to his courage and cheerfulness, the line was held.

COLYER-FERGUSSON, Thomas Riversdale *A/Captain, 2nd Bn., Northamptonshire Regiment*
31 July 1917 – Leading an attack at Bellewaarde, Belgium, with only a sergeant and five men he captured a trench and dealt with its garrison. He then resisted a fierce counter-attack by capturing an enemy machine-gun and turning it on the assailants. Later, assisted only by his sergeant, he captured a second machine-gun which enabled him to consolidate his position. He was killed shortly afterwards by a sniper.

DAVIES, James Llewellyn *Corporal, 13th (S) Bn., Royal Welch Fusiliers*
31 July 1917 – During an attack at Polygon Wood, Belgium, he single-handedly attacked a machine-gun emplacement after several men had been killed attempting to take it. He bayoneted one member of the crew, captured another and brought in the gun. Despite being wounded, he insisted on leading another attack on a defended house during which he shot a sniper.

EDWARDS, Alexander *Acting Company Sergeant Major, 1/6th Bn., Seaforth Highlanders*
31 July 1917 – At Pilckem Ridge, Belgium, he led an attack which killed a machine-gun team and captured the gun. Later, he crawled out to stalk a sniper, and although wounded in the arm, went on and killed him. He then led a successful attack on an objective and consolidated the position despite receiving two further wounds.

HEWITT, Denis George Wyldbore *Second Lieutenant, 14th (S) Bn., Hampshire Regiment*
31 July 1917 – Whilst organizing his company in advance of an attack near Ypres, Belgium, he was hit by a piece of shell which ignited the signal lights in his haversack and set fire to his clothes and equipment. He put out the flames and ignored the intense pain as he led his company forward. He captured and consolidated his objective but was killed by a sniper whilst inspecting the consolidation.

McINTOSH, George Imlach *Private, 1/6th Bn., Gordon Highlanders*
31 July 1917 – During the consolidation of a position at Ypres, Belgium, his company came under machine-gun fire at close range. He ran at the emplacement and threw a Mills grenade into it, killing two Germans and injuring a third. On entering the dugout he found two light machine-guns which he carried back to his own lines.

MAYSON, Tom Fletcher *Lance Sergeant, 1/4th Bn., King's Own (Royal Lancaster Regiment)*
31 July 1917 – When the leading wave of his platoon was held up by a machine-gun at Wieltje, Belgium, he ran to the gun and destroyed it with bombs, wounding four of the team. He chased the other three men into a dugout and killed them with his bayonet. He later tackled another gun single-handed, killing six of the team. Finally, during an enemy counter-attack, he took charge of an isolated post and held it until ordered to withdraw.
He wrote to his mother, 'I have been recommended for a great honour, but I leave you to guess what it is.'

REES, Ivor *Company Sergeant Major, 11th (S) Bn., South Wales Borderers*
31 July 1917 – When a hostile machine-gun opened fire at close range at Pilckem, Belgium, he led his platoon forward in short rushes, working his way round to the rear of the gun. When he was about 20 yards away, he charged the team, shooting one man and bayoneting another. He then bombed the concrete emplacement, killing five men and capturing thirty prisoners as well as the undamaged gun.

WHITHAM, Thomas *Private, 1st Bn., Coldstream Guards*
31 July 1917 – When an enemy machine-gun was enfilading his battalion during an attack at Pilckem, Belgium, he worked his way from shell

hole to shell hole towards the gun. When close enough, he rushed the gun and captured it together with an officer and 2 other ranks.

• **LANGEMARCK** • Following the modest advance gained during the Pilckem Ridge battle, the French kept up a constant bombardment to prevent any return by the German troops to the area lost. Bombardment kept the Germans held up in a forest area as the British troops advanced through waterlogged craters and oozing mud towards Langemarck next to the railway line leading to Staden and Bruges. The roads were a mass of shell holes and the village itself had been reduced to blackened ruins surrounded by entanglements of rusty wire.

On the morning of the attack, 16 August, the village was shrouded in mist and smoke from the battle and the advance was reduced to a crawl, so that the Germans were able to call in heavy fire before the infantry had a chance to move in following the preliminary barrage. Fierce resistance came from the strongly fortified concrete defences at Au Bon Gîte, but it was eventually taken in the afternoon. Despite bitter fighting in the swamp, the advancing British gained about a thousand yards, but had to draw back to better defensive positions under heavy counter-attack. Visibility was so bad that no aerial reconnaissance was possible to warn of German gun positions and often the men had to advance without artillery support and were consequently forced to cede positions they had earlier gained.

LOOSEMORE, Arnold *Private, 8th (S) Bn., Duke of Wellington's (West Riding) Regiment*
11 August 1917 – When his platoon was checked by machine-gun fire near Langemarck, Belgium, he crawled through partially cut wire with his Lewis gun and opened fire, killing about 20 of the enemy. His Lewis gun was then destroyed by a bomb so he pulled out his revolver and shot three Germans rushing him. He later shot several snipers and brought a wounded comrade to safety.

COOPER, Edward *Sergeant, 12th (S) Bn., King's Royal Rifle Corps*
16 August 1917 – At Langemarck, Belgium, he charged with 4 men towards a concrete blockhouse, 250 yards away, from which machine-guns were holding up the advance of a battalion. One hundred yards from the guns, he ordered his men to lie down and open fire. He then ran forward with a lance corporal and fired his revolver through an opening into the blockhouse. The machine-guns ceased firing and the garrison surrendered. Forty-five prisoners and seven machine-guns were taken.

EDWARDS, Wilfred *Private, 7th (S) Bn., King's Own Yorkshire Light Infantry*
16 August 1917 – Whilst under heavy machine-gun and rifle fire from a concrete fort at Langemarck, Belgium, he dashed forward, threw bombs through the loopholes of the fort, jumped on top of it and waved to his

company to advance. He took 3 officers and 30 other ranks prisoner in the fort and later did valuable work as a runner, guiding most of his battalion across difficult ground.

GRIMBALDESTON, William Henry *A/Company Quartermaster Sergeant, 1st Bn., King's Own Scottish Borderers*
16 August 1917 – Despite being wounded, he collected together a small party to fire rifle grenades at a blockhouse at Wijdendrift, Belgium. He then crawled alone towards the blockhouse until he reached its entrance, where he threatened the machine-gun teams inside with a grenade. The teams surrendered one after the other and he captured 36 prisoners, six machine-guns and a trench mortar.

ROOM, Frederick George *A/Lance Corporal, 2nd Bn., Royal Irish Regiment*
16 August 1917 – Whilst in charge of his company of stretcher bearers at Fezenberg, Belgium, he worked continuously under intense fire, dressing wounds and helping to evacuate the wounded. By his actions he saved many of his comrades' lives.

SKINNER, John Kendrick *A/Company Sergeant Major, 1st Bn., King's Own Scottish Borderers*
18 August 1917 – When his company's attack was held up by machine-gun fire at Wijdendrift, Belgium, he collected six men and worked round the left flank of three blockhouses from which the machine-gun fire was coming. He bombed and captured the first blockhouse on his own and cleared the other two with the help of his comrades. Sixty prisoners, three machine-guns and two trench mortars were captured.
He was killed in a later action, in March 1918, trying to bring in a wounded man. He had the rare distinction of six VC holders as his pallbearers.

MOORE, Montague Shadworth Seymour *Second Lieutenant, 15th (S) Bn., Hampshire Regiment*
20 August 1917 – He led 70 men in an assault near Ypres, Belgium, but resistance was so fierce that by the time the objective was reached, only 5 men remained. Undaunted, he bombed a large dugout and captured 28 prisoners, two machine-guns and a light field gun. Sixty reinforcements arrived and he held the position under continual shell fire for thirty-six hours until his party was reduced to 10 men and he was forced to withdraw under cover of a thick mist.

CARMICHAEL, John *Sergeant, 9th (S) Bn. (Pioneers), North Staffordshire Regiment*
8 September 1917 – Whilst he was excavating a trench at Hill 60, Zwarteleen, Belgium, he spotted an unearthed grenade which had started to burn. He realized that were he to throw it out of the trench it might kill men working on top, so he shouted to his men to get clear, placed his steel

helmet over the grenade and stood on the helmet. The grenade exploded and blew him out of the trench, seriously injuring him.

MOYNEY, John *Lance Sergeant, 2nd Bn., Irish Guards*

12–13 September 1917 – At Ney Copse, Broembeek, Belgium, he was in command of 15 men forming two advanced posts surrounded by the enemy. Despite having no water and little food, he held his post for ninety-six hours. On the fifth day, as a large enemy force advanced, his men attacked the enemy with bombs whilst he opened up with a Lewis gun from a flank. He then led a charge through the enemy and reached a stream which he instructed his party to cross while he and Private WOODCOCK covered their retirement. He was thus able to bring his entire force safely out of action.

WOODCOCK, Thomas *Private, 2nd Bn., Irish Guards*

12–13 September 1917 – At Ney Copse, Broembeek, Belgium, he was in one of the advanced posts commanded by Lance Sergeant MOYNEY. Wood-cock covered the retirement of the party across a stream with a Lewis gun but only retired himself when the enemy were yards away. After crossing the stream he heard cries for help so he waded back into the water and rescued a stranded comrade, whom he carried to safety under heavy machine-gun fire.

• **MENIN ROAD** • By the second week of September a concentration of heavy artillery was in place behind the British lines to support the forthcoming drive for the Menin Road ridge. Cables were buried deep below the ground; sappers built new gun positions and laid railways and tracks across the rain-sodden ground. 1,295 guns were brought in – approximately one gun for every five yards of the attacking front. On 14 September a five-day barrage opened up – giving the German commander, General von Armin, prior warning of an intended attack. In the early hours of 20 September he sent down a heavy barrage on the north of the British line, but in the blackness and drizzle this localized barrage did not touch the troops assembled for the dawn attack. British guns countered the German guns successfully, taking out dozens while flooding the gun positions with poison gas. As the troops finally advanced at zero hour, 5.40 a.m., they met with unprecedented success, taking all the high ground crossed by the Menin Road. Determined counter-attacks were quashed as, in the clearing air, planes flew overhead to direct artillery fire, and over the five-day battle, even ground which had to be ceded was recaptured. Overall the Allies gained about fifteen hundred yards for twenty-one thousand casualties.

INWOOD, Reginald Roy *Private, 10th Bn. (South Australia), Australian Imperial Force*

19–22 September 1917 – During an attack on Polygon Wood, Belgium, he moved forward alone through the barrage to an enemy strongpoint which he captured together with nine prisoners. That night, he went out on an all-night patrol and brought back valuable details of the enemy's movements. The next morning, he went out alone and bombed a machine-gun and team, killing all but one man whom he brought in as a prisoner with the gun.

BIRKS, Frederick *Second Lieutenant, 6th Bn. (Victoria), Australian Imperial Force*

20 September 1917 – At Glencorse Wood, east of Ypres, Belgium, accompanied only by a corporal, he rushed a strongpoint which was holding up the advance. He went on alone, killed the rest of the enemy holding the position and captured a machine-gun. He then attacked another enemy strongpoint with a small party and captured an officer and 15 men.

BURMAN, William Francis *Sergeant, 16th (S) Bn., Rifle Brigade*

20 September 1917 – When his company's advance was held up at Bulgar Wood, Ypres, Belgium, by a machine-gun firing at point-blank range, he shouted to the man next to him to wait a few minutes and went forward alone. He killed the enemy gunner and carried the gun to the company's objective where he used it to great effect. He then ran behind the enemy on his right with two others, killing 6 and capturing 2 officers and 29 men.

COLVIN, Hugh *Second Lieutenant, 9th (S) Bn., Cheshire Regiment*

20 September 1917 – When all the officers of his company and all but 1 officer of the leading company had become casualties at Hessian Wood, Ypres, Belgium, he led both companies forward under heavy machine-gun fire. He entered a dugout alone and brought out 14 prisoners. He stormed another dugout and captured the machine-gun. When attacked by 15 of the enemy, he shot 5 and, using another as a shield, forced the remainder to surrender. He took about 50 prisoners in all.

EGERTON, Ernest Albert *Corporal, 16th (S) Bn., Sherwood Foresters*

20 September 1917 – At Bulgar Wood, Ypres, Belgium, thick fog and smoke caused an attack to miss some hostile dugouts. Realizing this, he single-handedly attacked the dugouts. He shot in succession a rifleman, a bomber and a gunner, by which time he was supported, and 29 of the enemy surrendered. He relieved the entire situation in less than thirty seconds.

The motive for what his company commander called 'the most reckless piece of gallantry I ever saw' undoubtedly came from the news he received a few days before the attack in a letter informing him that his elder brother had been killed on 17 August. He said later: 'I was longing to get into action and pay back a debt.'

HEWITT, William Henry *Lance Corporal, 2nd South African Light Infantry*

20 September 1917 – During an attack on a pillbox with his section near Ypres, Belgium, he received a severe wound when he rushed the doorway.

He was then wounded in the arm as he tried to push a bomb through the loophole. He finally managed to get a bomb inside, which dislodged the occupants who were then dealt with by the remainder of his section.

KNIGHT, Alfred Joseph *Sergeant, 2/8th Bn., London Regiment*
20 September 1917 – During an attack at Hubner Farm, Ypres, Belgium, he rushed through the barrage, bayoneted a gunner and captured a position single-handed. He then ran at 12 of the enemy in a shell hole, bayoneted two of them, shot a third and scattered the remainder. He carried out further acts of bravery under heavy machine-gun and rifle fire before taking command of his platoon and other platoons without officers.

PEELER, Walter *Lance Corporal, 3rd Pioneer Bn., Australian Imperial Force*
20 September 1917 – Whilst accompanying the first wave of an assault near Ypres, Belgium, he rushed an enemy party which was sniping from a shell hole. He accounted for nine men with his Lewis gun and cleared the way for the advance. He twice repeated this action. He then shot another gunner and dislodged the remainder of his team from a dugout with bombs before disposing of them in the open.

REYNOLDS, Henry *T/Captain, 12th (S) Bn., Royal Scots*
20 September 1917 – During an attack near Frezenberg, Belgium, an enemy pillbox was causing heavy casualties. He tried to throw a grenade into it but found the entrance blocked, so he crawled up to it and forced a phosphorous grenade inside, which killed three of the enemy. He captured the remainder. He then led his company in a successful assault against another objective in which 70 prisoners and two machine-guns were captured.

HAMILTON, John Brown *A/Lance Corporal, 1/9th Bn., Highland Light Infantry*
25–26 September 1917 – During an enemy attack north of the Ypres–Menin Road, Belgium, difficulty was encountered in keeping the front and support lines supplied with small-arms ammunition. Several times he carried bandoliers of ammunition in full view of enemy snipers and machine-gunners. He inspired all who saw him.

• **POLYGON WOOD** • The objective of this battle was to take conclusively the ground dominating the Menin Road and the areas around it. Both sides were aware of the value of these positions, so Haig planned to force Armin to deploy a large proportion of his reserve troops against diversionary attack to the north provided by South African troops. The attack was launched a 5.50 a.m. on 26 September, with the infantry advancing behind a heavy artillery barrage across ground pitted with craters from previous bombardment. With the objective of making small, steady gains, General Sir Hubert Plumer directed his troops using 'bite-and-hold' tactics over the eight days of the battle to secure British possession of the strategically important ridge to the east of Ypres – a further two thousand yards had been gained, but at the cost of thirty thousand casualties.

BUGDEN, Patrick Joseph *Private, 31st Bn. (Queensland and Victoria), Australian Imperial Force*

26–28 September 1917 – When enemy pillboxes were holding up the advance at Polygon Wood, Belgium, he silenced the machine-guns with bombs and captured the garrisons at bayonet point. Then, spotting a captured corporal being taken to the rear by the enemy, he shot one of his captors and bayoneted the other two, allowing the corporal to escape. On five occasions, he rescued wounded men. He was killed on the last of these occasions.

DWYER, John James (later the Hon.) *Sergeant, 4th Coy., Machine-Gun Corps, Australian Imperial Force*

26 September 1917 – Whilst advancing with the first wave of the brigade at Zonnebeke, Belgium, he rushed his Vickers machine-gun to within 30 yards of an enemy gun and opened fire, killing the crew, before bringing the enemy gun back to his front line. When his Vickers was later hit by shell fire, he brought a reserve gun up through the enemy barrage in the shortest possible time.

He was Speaker of the Tasmanian House of Assembly (1941–48) and Deputy Premier (1958–61).

BENT, Philip Eric *T/Lieutenant Colonel, commanding 9th (S) Bn., Leicestershire Regiment*

1 October 1917 – During an enemy attack at Polygon Wood, he issued orders as to the defence of the line before collecting a reserve platoon and leading them forward in a counter-attack. The attack was successful and the enemy was checked. He was killed as he led a charge which he had inspired with the cry: 'Come on, the Tigers!'

• **BROODSEINDE** • In the early hours of 4 October, twelve divisions of British and Australian troops moved silently into position for the third stage of Plumer's drive to secure the ridges to the east of Ypres. The objectives were about fifteen hundred yards away, and the advance would be covered by a creeping barrage, which would protect them while they consolidated their positions. Before the attack began, the Australian troops were heavily shelled on their start line, losing about a seventh of their number as casualties. The Germans had chosen the same day – just fifteen minutes later – to launch their own attack, and as the Allied troops advanced, they were confronted by advancing Germans. The Australians fought through the German advance and took their objectives, but suffered six and a half thousand casualties as they fought to take the well-defended German pillboxes.

COVERDALE, Charles Harry *Sergeant, 11th (S) Bn., Manchester Regiment*
4 October 1917 – During an attack near Poelcapelle, Belgium, he killed an officer and captured two men sniping at the flank. He then rushed two machine-guns, killing or wounding the teams. He led his platoon in an attempt to capture another position but was twice forced to retire; first due to a barrage and then an enemy advance.

EVANS, Lewis Pugh *A/Lieutenant Colonel, Black Watch, commanding 1st Bn., Lincolnshire Regiment*
4 October 1917 – Whilst leading his battalion through a terrific enemy barrage near Zonnebeke, Belgium, he rushed single-handedly a machine-gun emplacement which was causing casualties and caused its garrison to surrender by firing his revolver through the loophole. He was twice badly wounded but refused treatment until a further two objectives had been captured. He then collapsed from loss of blood.
Lieutenant W. G. Cubitt VC was his uncle.

GREAVES, Fred *A/Corporal, 9th (S) Bn., Sherwood Foresters*
4 October 1917 – When his platoon was caught in heavy fire at Poelcapelle, Belgium, he rushed an enemy blockhouse, hurled bombs inside and brought out four machine-guns. He later took command of his company after all the officers had become casualties during a massive enemy counter-attack. He spurred the men on with his cheerfulness and courage and the enemy was repulsed in disorder.

HUTT, Arthur *Private, 1/7th Bn., Royal Warwickshire Regiment*
4 October 1917 – At Poelcapelle, Belgium, he assumed command when all the officers and NCOs of his platoon had become casualties. He ran ahead alone to a strong enemy post, where he shot an officer and three men and captured another 40 or 50. Having pushed too far, he covered his men's withdrawal by sniping at the enemy before carrying four wounded men in under heavy fire.

McGEE, Lewis *Sergeant, 40th Bn. (Tasmania), Australian Imperial Force*
4 October 1917 – When the advance of his company was held up by machine-gun fire from a pillbox near Ypres, Belgium, he rushed the pillbox single-handedly, armed only with a revolver. He shot some of its garrison and captured the rest, before reorganizing the remnants of his platoon. His coolness and bravery contributed largely to the success of his company's operations.

OCKENDON, James *Sergeant, 1st Bn., Royal Dublin Fusiliers*
4 October 1917 – When acting as company sergeant major he saw the platoon on his right was held up by machine-gun fire near Langemarck, Belgium, he rushed the gun and killed two of its crew. The third gunner ran across no-man's land but Ockenden followed him and shot him down. He

then led an attack on a farm, during which he ran ahead of his company and killed four of the enemy and accepted the surrender of another 16.

ROBERTSON, Clement *A/Captain, Queen's Royal West Surrey Regiment, Special Reserve (T/Lieutenant, A/Captain, Tank Corps)*

4 October 1917 – In the build-up to a tank attack at Zonnebeke, Belgium, he and his batman spent three days reconnoitring ground cut up by shellfire, trying to find routes for his tanks to follow. In the subsequent assault, he led the tanks on foot, guiding them to their objective. He was killed after the objective had been reached.

His was the first VC to be awarded to the Tank Corps.

SAGE, Thomas Henry *Private, 8th (S) Bn., Somerset Light Infantry*

4 October 1917 – At Tower Hamlets Spur, Ypres, Belgium, a live bomb fell into the shell hole that he was sharing with eight other men. He immediately threw himself on it, saving the lives of his comrades. He himself sustained very serious wounds.

• **POELCAPPELLE** • Following the advances at Broodseinde, the British line was now overlooked by the Germans on Passchendaele Ridge, and it became imperative to deprive the enemy of this vantage point. On 9 October, Allied troops from one Australian and two British divisions, already exhausted from fighting and worn down by the foul weather conditions, were tasked with taking the ridge. The pattern of attack was for a heavy artillery barrage to cover their advance, but torrential rain had waterlogged the already badly drained ground it was impossible to bring in adequate heavy guns to provide the necessary support. The men wallowed in the mud and, although able to secure some of their objectives, were unable to hold them without proper artillery support. The day had gained nothing for many casualties.

CLAMP, William *Corporal, 6th (S) Bn., Yorkshire Regiment*

9 October 1917 – When an advance was checked at Poelcapelle, Belgium, by machine-gun fire from concrete blockhouses, he dashed forward with two men and tried to rush the largest blockhouse. The two men were knocked out but he made another attempt with two others. He threw his bombs in, entered the blockhouse and brought out a gun and 20 prisoners. He then rushed several snipers' posts. He was killed by a sniper whilst encouraging and cheering the men.

DANCOX, Frederick George *Private, 4th Bn., Worcestershire Regiment*

9 October 1917 – At Boesinghe, Belgium, an objective had been taken but machine-gun fire from a concrete emplacement on the edge of the protective barrage was still causing problems. He was detailed to mop up, so he made his way through the barrage, entered the emplacement from the rear and threatened the gun team with a Mills bomb. He captured the gun and 40 of the enemy and kept the gun in action throughout the day.

LISTER, Joseph *Sergeant, 1st Bn., Lancashire Fusiliers*
9 October 1917 – When his company's advance was checked by machine-gun fire from near two pillboxes at Olga House, Ypres, Belgium, he dashed ahead of his men and shot two of the gunners. He ran on to the pillbox and shouted at the occupants to surrender, which they all did except for one man whom he shot dead. At that moment about one hundred of the enemy emerged from shell holes to the rear and surrendered.

MOLYNEUX, John *Sergeant, 2nd Bn., Royal Fusiliers*
9 October 1917 – When an attack was held up by machine-gun fire from a trench near Langemarck, Belgium, he organized a bombing party which captured the gun and killed the crew. He then jumped out of the trench, called for his comrades to follow him and ran to a nearby house occupied by the enemy. Before help could arrive, he became engaged in hand-to-hand fighting. The enemy quickly surrendered and 20–30 prisoners were taken.

RHODES, John Harold *Lance Sergeant, 3rd Bn., Grenadier Guards*
9 October 1917 – Whilst in charge of a Lewis-gun section covering the consolidation of the right front company at Houthulst Forest, Belgium, he accounted for several of the enemy with his rifle and Lewis gun. Seeing three Germans leave a pillbox, he went forward alone through the barrage and entered the pillbox. He captured nine of the enemy, including a forward observation officer.

HALTON, Albert *Private, 1st Bn., King's Own (Royal Lancaster Regiment)*
12 October 1917 – After an objective had been reached near Poelcapelle, Belgium, he rushed forward 300 yards under heavy rifle and shell fire and captured a machine-gun and its crew which was causing severe losses. He then went out again and brought in 12 prisoners.

• **THE FIRST BATTLE OF PASSCHENDAELE** • After the failure of the Poelcappelle attack on 9 October, the next drive to take the ridge was set for three days later. Again, mud and waterlogged ground prevented the Allies from bringing in enough artillery to support the attack and again, men exhausted and demoralized advanced against a well-prepared enemy and suffered thirteen thousand casualties with no real gains.

JEFFRIES, Clarence Smith *Captain, 34th Bn. (New South Wales), Australian Imperial Force*
12 October 1917 – When his company was held up by machine-gun fire at Passchendaele, Belgium, he organized a party and rushed a gun emplacement, capturing four guns and 35 prisoners. He then organized another attack which captured two guns and 30 prisoners. He was killed during this attack.

• **THE SECOND BATTLE OF PASSCHENDAELE** • The Allies had lost a hundred thousand men since the start of the battle at the end of July, and the Anzac forces were decimated. The Canadian Corps was brought in to replace them. Following their successes at Vimy Ridge and Hill 70 it gained a reputation as an elite force, and was brought into the thick of the battle for Haig's drive to take Passchendaele. On 26 October twenty thousand men of the 3rd and 4th Canadian Divisions advanced up the hills of the salient – the Allies suffered twelve thousand casualties during the day for just a few hundred yards gained. Undeterred by the losses and unwilling to call off the assault, a second offensive was launched on 30 October in driving rain. On this attempt the Allies took the ruined village of Passchendaele and there followed five days of grim defence against constant enemy shelling. When reinforcements arrived on 6 November four-fifths of the Canadian Corps had been lost. Finally, on 10 November the Allies succeeded in driving the enemy off the slopes to the east of the town to consolidate their hold on the hard-won high ground.

HOLMES, Thomas William *Private, 4th Bn., Canadian Mounted Rifles, Canadian Expeditionary Force*

26 October 1917 – When the right flank of an attack was held up by machine-gun fire from a pillbox at Passchendaele, he ran forward on his own and hurled two bombs into the pillbox which knocked out the guns and killed or wounded their crews. He then ran back, collected a bomb from a comrade, ran forward again and threw it into the entrance of the pillbox, causing the 19 occupants to surrender.

O'KELLY, Christopher Patrick John *Major, 52nd Bn. (New Ontario), Canadian Expeditionary Force*

26 October 1917 – At Passchendaele, Belgium, he organized and personally led a series of attacks which captured six pillboxes, one hundred prisoners and ten machine-guns. He later led his company as it repelled a strong counter-attack, taking more prisoners, and that night captured a hostile raiding party of one officer, ten men and a machine-gun.

SHANKLAND, Robert *Lieutenant, 43rd Bn. (Cameron Highlanders of Canada), Canadian Expeditionary Force*

26 October 1917 – At Passchendaele, he led his company to a position on the crest of a hill. He then held this line for four hours in the face of relentless enemy shelling that churned up so much mud that weapons became clogged. In spite of this he dispersed a counter-attack, which enabled supporting troops to come up unmolested. He then personally communicated to his headquarters an accurate report of the critical situation.

KINROSS, Cecil John *Private, 49th Bn. (Edmonton Regiment), Canadian Expeditionary Force*

30 October 1917 – Shortly after the attack was launched on Furst Farm, Passchendaele, Belgium, his company was held up by a hurricane of fire.

Throwing off all his equipment except his rifle and bandolier, he advanced alone over the open ground, charged an enemy machine-gun, killed the crew of six and destroyed the gun. His courage allowed a further advance of 300 yards to be made.

McKENZIE, Hugh McDonald *Lieutenant, 7th Coy., Canadian Machine-Gun Corps, Canadian Expeditionary Force*

30 October 1917 – Whilst in charge of a section of four machine-guns accompanying the infantry in an attack at Meescheele Spur, Belgium, and aware that the attack was faltering due to fire coming from a pillbox on the crest of a hill, he rallied the infantry and led an assault on the pillbox. He was shot through the head as the pillbox was captured.

MULLIN, George Harry *Sergeant, Princess Patricia's Canadian Light Infantry, Canadian Expeditionary Force*

30 October 1917 – An enemy pillbox at Passchendaele, Belgium, was causing heavy casualties and holding up an attack, so he rushed it, bombed the garrison, crawled on top of the pillbox and shot the two machine-gunners with his revolver. The garrison of ten surrendered. By the end of this action, his clothes were riddled with bullets.

PEARKES, George Randolph *A/Major, 5th Bn., Canadian Mounted Rifles, Canadian Expeditionary Force*

30–31 October 1917 – Just before the advance at Passchendaele, Belgium, he was wounded in the left thigh but insisted on leading his men into the attack. His advance was threatened by a strongpoint which another battalion had failed to capture so he led an attack which carried the place by storm. Although his force was reduced to 20 men, he held this point against repeated counter-attack until, eventually, support arrived.

He was Minister of National Defence (1957–60) and Lieutenant-Governor of British Columbia (1960–68).

BARRON, Colin Fraser *Corporal, 3rd Bn. (Toronto Regiment), Canadian Expeditionary Force*

6 November 1917 – When his unit was held up by three machine-gun posts at Vine Cottage, Passchendaele, Belgium, he charged them single-handedly, killing four of the enemy and capturing the remainder. He then turned one of the guns on the retiring enemy, causing them severe casualties.

ROBERTSON, James Peter *Private, 27th Bn. (City of Winnipeg), Canadian Expeditionary Force*

6 November 1917 – When his platoon was held up at Passchendaele, Belgium, by uncut wire and a machine-gun which was causing many casualties, he rushed the gun and after a desperate struggle with the crew, killed four and then turned the gun on the remainder who were running towards their own lines. Then, carrying the captured gun, he led his platoon to the objective and got the gun into action, firing on the retreating enemy. Later he went out under severe fire to bring two wounded men to safety. He was killed as he returned with the second man.

THE BATTLE OF CAMBRAI

Cambrai was conceived as a tank action, a raid that would destroy enemy guns and cause confusion, and withdraw the same day. By the time it was launched it had become intended as a major breakthrough, with 375 tanks and eleven divisions (six infantry and five cavalry). The objective was Cambrai, by autumn 1917 an important railhead. Only two German divisions were in defence in the Hindenburg Line, and there was no preliminary bombardment. The attack began at dawn on 20 November with an intense barrage, and the first two lines were taken by noon. By nightfall, 179 tanks were out of action but the forward troops had advanced 5 miles on a 6 mile front. The next week was spent deepening the salient, particularly the heights of Bourlon Wood, which controlled the Bapaume–Cambrai road, but by the end of the month it had become clear that Cambrai could not be encircled from the south, reserves could not be brought up quickly enough and the cavalry could not break out. On the 30th the Germans counter-attacked with twenty divisions. By 3 December they had pinched out the salient; the British held most of the ground captured on the first day, and had taken about fifty thousand casualties to the Germans' forty-five thousand.

McBEATH, Robert Gordon *Lance Corporal, 1/5th (T) Bn., Seaforth Highlanders*
   20 November 1917 – When the advance of his company was checked by a nest of machine-guns west of Cambrai, France, he went ahead with a Lewis gun and a revolver. He attacked the guns with the assistance of a tank and drove the gunners into a dugout. He rushed in after them, shot a man who opposed him on the steps and captured 3 officers and 30 men. He put five machine-guns out of action and cleared the way for the advance.

SHEPHERD, Albert Edward *Rifleman, 12th (S) Bn., King's Royal Rifle Corps*
   20 November 1917 – At Villers Plouich, France, he volunteered to rush a machine-gun holding up his company. He was ordered not to, but ran forward and threw a Mills bomb which killed two of the gunners. He then captured the remainder of the team. The company continued its advance but came under such heavy fire that the last officer and NCO became casualties. Taking command, he ordered the men to lie down while he went back 70 yards to obtain the help of a tank. He then led them to their final objective.

SHERWOOD-KELLY, John *A/Lieutenant Colonel, Norfolk Regiment, commanding 1st Bn., Royal Inniskilling Fusiliers*

20 November 1917 – When fierce fire prevented men of another unit from crossing a canal at Marcoing, France, he personally led the leading company of his battalion across, before reconnoitring high ground held by the enemy. The left flank of his battalion became held up by a thick belt of wire, so he crossed to that flank and with a Lewis gun team covered the advance. He later led a successful charge against some pits, during which he captured five machine-guns and 46 prisoners.

He was later court-martialled for publicly criticizing the handling of the BEF in Russia in 1919.

SPACKMAN, Charles Edward *Sergeant, 1st Bn., Border Regiment*

20 November 1917 – At Marcoing, France, the leading company was checked by heavy fire from a machine-gun commanding ground devoid of any cover. He went alone through the fire to attack the gun, killing all the crew but one and capturing the gun. The advance was able to continue.

STRACHAN, Harcus *Lieutenant, Fort Garry Horse, Canadian Expeditionary Force*

20 November 1917 – After his squadron leader had been killed at Masnières, France, whilst galloping towards the enemy, he took the squadron through a line of machine-gun posts, and then led a charge on an enemy battery, killing seven gunners with his sword. With the battery silenced, he rallied his men and fought his way back at night through the enemy's line, bringing 15 prisoners with him.

WAIN, Richard William Leslie *A/Captain, A Bn., Tank Corps*

20 November 1917 – After his tank was disabled by a direct hit from a trench mortar battery at Marcoing, France, he refused the attention of stretcher bearers, though bleeding profusely from his wounds. Instead, he rushed from behind the tank with a Lewis gun and attacked the battery and three nearby machine-guns. He put them all out of action and captured a number of men. He then picked up a rifle and continued firing at the fleeing enemy until he received a fatal wound in the head.

McAULAY, John *Sergeant, 1st Bn., Scots Guards*

27 November 1917 – When all his officers had become casualties at Fontaine Notre Dame, France, he assumed command of the company and successfully held and consolidated the objectives gained. When the enemy counter-attacked his left flank, he repelled them skilfully with his machine-guns, causing heavy casualties. He then carried his company commander, who was mortally wounded, to a place of safety. He was twice knocked down by shell bursts but refused to give up and killed two Germans who tried to intercept him.

CLARE, George William Burdett *Private, 5th Lancers*

28–29 November 1917 – Whilst acting as a stretcher bearer at Bourlon Wood, France, he dressed wounds under intense fire and carried the wounded to a dressing station. At one point, he crossed an area swept by fire to reach a detached post where all the men had been killed or wounded. He tended the men and manned the post single-handedly until relief was sent. He then carried a wounded man to a dressing station where he was informed that the enemy was using gas shells in the valley below, so he ran to every company post, warning them of the danger. At the end of this action, he was killed by a shell.

ELLIOTT-COOPER, Neville Bowes *T/Lieutenant Colonel, commanding 8th (S) Bn., Royal Fusiliers*

30 November 1917 – Seeing the Germans advancing across open ground near Cambrai, France, he mounted the parapet, called on the reserve company to follow him and dashed forward. Absolutely unarmed, he made straight for the enemy, and under his direction, the men forced them back 600 yards. Whilst out in front alone he was severely wounded, and aware his men were outnumbered he signalled to them to withdraw, knowing he would be taken prisoner. His wounds were eventually to kill him.

GEE, Robert *T/Captain, 2nd Bn., Royal Fusiliers*

30 November 1917 – Taken prisoner during an enemy attack near Masnières, France, he managed to escape after killing one of his captors with a pointed stick. He then organized a party of the brigade staff with which he attacked the enemy, closely followed by two companies of infantry. Whilst clearing the locality, he found that an enemy machine-gun was still in action so, with a revolver in each hand, he rushed and captured the gun, killing 8 of the crew. He was wounded but refused treatment until he was satisfied that the defence was secure.

McREADY-DIARMID, Allastair Malcolm Cluny *A/Captain, 17th (S) Bn., Middlesex Regiment*

30 November to 1 December 1917 – During an enemy attack on the Moeuvres sector, France, he led his company forward with such success that the enemy were pushed back 300 yards. The following day, he led another counter-attack. He was eventually killed by a bomb when the Germans had been driven back to their original starting point. It was entirely due to his throwing of bombs that the ground was regained.

STONE, Walter Napleton *A/Captain, 3rd Bn., Royal Fusiliers, attached 17th (S) Battalion*

30 November 1917 – Whilst in command of an isolated company, 1,000 yards in front of the main line, in the Cambrai sector, France, he observed the enemy massing for an attack and sent this information to battalion headquarters. He was ordered to withdraw but the attack developed quickly, so he sent three platoons back and remained with the rearguard. He stood on the parapet passing information by telephone under tremendous bombardment until the wire was cut. The rearguard was eventually surrounded and cut to pieces. He was seen fighting until he was shot through the head. The accuracy of his information enabled the line to be saved.

THOMAS, John *Lance Corporal, 2/5th Bn., North Staffordshire Regiment*
30 November 1917 – When he saw the enemy making preparations for a counter-attack at Fontaine, France, he crawled out in full view of the enemy, bluffing snipers by lying still and pretending to be hit. He shot 3 snipers and crawled on to a building from which he could see where the enemy was congregating. He worked his way from house to house, before returning to his lines. As a result of his information, the counter-attack was swiftly broken up.

WALLACE, Samuel Thomas Dickson
30 November 1917 – When enemy infantry surrounded his battery at Gonnelieu, France, and his men were reduced to five by fire from artillery, machine-guns, infantry and aeroplanes, he maintained fire by swinging the gun trails close together and keeping the men running from gun to gun. He was in action for eight hours firing the whole time. He withdrew when infantry support arrived but he took with him the essential gun parts and all wounded men.

GOBIND SINGH *Lance Duffadar, 28th Light Cavalry, attached 2nd Lancers*
1 December 1917 – East of Peizières, France, he volunteered on three separate occasions to carry messages between the regiment and brigade headquarters, a distance of one and a half miles over open ground under constant observation and heavy enemy fire. He delivered the messages successfully, although on each occasion his horse was shot and he had to finish his journey on foot.

PATON, George Henry Tatham *A/Captain, 4th Bn., Grenadier Guards*
1 December 1917 – When a unit on his left was driven back at Gonnelieu, France, leaving his company practically surrounded, he walked up and down under a ferocious fire readjusting the line. He personally removed several wounded men. When the enemy broke through on his left, he (with the help of a few men) forced them to withdraw. Whilst on the parapet, he received a fatal wound.

LASCELLES, Arthur Moore *A/Captain, 3rd Bn., Durham Light Infantry, attached 14th Bn.*
3 December 1917 – After he had been wounded during a heavy bombardment at Masnières, France, he refused treatment whilst he organized his men and repulsed an enemy attack. A second German attack captured the trench so he jumped on the parapet and, followed by 12 men, rushed

forward and drove 60 Germans back. He was captured during another enemy attack and became unconscious. He later escaped during a counter-attack.

EMERSON, James Samuel *T/Second Lieutenant, 9th (S) Bn., Royal Inniskilling Fusiliers*
6 December 1917 – He led an assault near La Vacquerie, France, which cleared 400 yards of trench. In the subsequent enemy counter-attack, one bullet hit his hand and another tore through his steel helmet, but he sprang out of his trench with 8 men and met the Germans in the open. For three hours he remained with his men and repelled repeated bombing attacks. He was mortally wounded whilst leading another attack.

THE AIR WAR

Increasing use was made on the Western Front of the Royal Flying Corps to provide reconnaissance, deliver localized bombardment, take out specific enemy targets and fly routine patrols to shoot down the German observation balloons and aircraft over the battlefield. During the major battles, the RFC's main task was to deprive the enemy of aerial reconnaissance – but some exceptional pilots excelled, not just in the routine tasks of aerial combat and routine duties, but also, with the licence enjoyed by the fledgeling air service, in 'freelance' missions to find their own targets and fly sorties as they chose.

MOTTERSHEAD, Thomas *Sergeant, 20 Squadron, Royal Flying Corps*
7 January 1917 – Whilst on flying patrol at 9,000 feet over Ploegsteert, Belgium, he came under attack. Bullets pierced his petrol tank, setting the aircraft on fire. Although his observer Lieutenant Gower was unable to subdue the growing flames, Mottershead flew back to his own lines and made a successful landing, but the aircraft collapsed on touching the ground and Mottershead was pinned underneath the burning wreckage. He died four days later. His remarkable endurance undoubtedly saved his observer's life.

McNAMARA, Frank Hubert *Lieutenant, 1 Squadron, Australian Flying Corps*
20 March 1917 – When a pilot was forced to land behind enemy lines near Tel-el-Hesi, Egypt, McNamara, seeing enemy cavalry approaching, flew down under heavy fire to rescue him. He landed and picked up the airman but was hit in the thigh and his machine turned over as he took off again. The two officers struggled over to the other aircraft and McNamara flew it 70 miles back to his aerodrome, although very weak from loss of blood.

BALL, Albert *T/Captain, 7th Bn., Sherwood Foresters and Royal Flying Corps*

At the outbreak of the Great War, Ball, being a Nottingham lad, joined the Sherwood Foresters before transferring to the RFC in 1915. His was an incongruous blend of deep religious belief combined with a killer instinct. In just three months of operations over the Somme, Ball notched up an amazing thirty victories, and this unassuming man became the first ace to be idolized by the British public – and to inspire the likes of Edward Mannock (later VC), to join the RFC.

The catalogue of his medals gives some idea of his skill and bravery. His Military Cross was awarded for consistent courage, including encounters where he brought down a German kite balloon in flames and took on six enemy aircraft in one fight, forcing two down and scattering the rest, all above enemy territory.

His DSO was awarded for a close-quarters air attack on a formation of seven enemy aircraft – he shot one down at 15 yards' range, closed to 10 yards to take out the next, then turned to confront an attacking aircraft and brought that down. Re-arming at a nearby aerodrome, he was quickly into action and destroyed three more of the enemy before returning with his own aircraft badly shot about.

The bar to his DSO followed, for several separate actions. On a bombing raid he dived on a formation of four enemy planes, and shot one of them down. On another occasion he picked off one of a twelve-plane formation and sent another spinning down out of control, after which he limped home at low altitude, his own plane badly damaged. The second bar came just months after the first, for an attack on three aircraft and for bringing down eight more over a short period of operations.

The crowning award, however, was made posthumously, for his acts of valour between 25 April and 6 May 1917. Always happy with his favourite Nieuport 17 aircraft, he bemoaned the arrival of the SE5. 'The SE5 has turned out a dud – it's a great shame, for everybody expects such a lot of them. It's a rotten machine.' These were prescient words indeed.

Cecil Lewis, who flew with him in 56 Squadron, recalled, 'Ball never flew for pleasure and never indulged in acrobatics, his tactics were point blank, going right in, sometimes within a few yards of the enemy, without the slightest hesitation. He never boasted or criticized, but his example was tremendous.'

On 6 May, he took off in an SE5. The VC citation details his actions throughout his last forays, but the final events of the day were not all made public. Ball encountered Lothar von Richthofen, the brother of the 'Red Baron', and in the course of the fight, both were seen entering a large dark thundercloud.

In the garden of her home in the village of Annoeulin in northern France, Mlle Cecile Deloffre suddenly became aware of a plane flying upside-down as it emerged from low cloud. It was alone and doomed to crash.

Gathering her skirts she ran to where it had fallen and with tremendous courage, for she knew the aircraft could burst into flames, she clambered onto the SE5. In the wreckage was a young pilot. She cradled him gently and lifted his head and spoke to him. He opened his eyes and as she held him he died. The fighter hero with forty-three victories to his credit had slipped away.

Germany was keen to claim the death of Britain's ace as a hit for von Richthofen, but years later, a German officer on the ground admitted that he saw Ball moments before he crashed. There was no evidence of damage to his aircraft, which emerged from the cloud some 200 feet above the ground – its propeller apparently not rotating.

Maurice Baring, who also served with the RFC and was foreign correspondent of *The Times*, wrote of his death in May 1917: 'Brief-fated among mortals, glorious was thy end, when peerless among the swift and most daring among those athirst for danger, after slaying so many of thy foes, thou at last didst fall, veiled in a cloud, in mortal combat with one second only to thyself.'

BISHOP, William Avery *Captain, Canadian Cavalry and 60 Squadron, Royal Flying Corps*
2 June 1917 – Flying over an enemy aerodrome near Cambrai he saw seven aircraft on the ground, some with their engines running. One took off but he fired fifteen rounds into it at close range and it crashed. Another got off the ground but he fired thirty rounds into it and it crashed into a tree. He sent a third side-slipping into a clump of trees before emptying the rest of his ammunition into a fourth which went down out of control. He then flew home.

He said in 1917, 'Give me the aeroplane I want and I'll go over to Berlin any night – or day – and come back too, with any luck.' He was Director of Recruiting, Royal Canadian Air Force, 1940–44.

McCUDDEN, James Thomas Byrford *T/Captain, General List and 56 Squadron, Royal Flying Corps*
23 December 1917 to 5 March 1918 – By March 1918, he had accounted for fifty-four enemy aeroplanes, forty-two of which had been definitely destroyed. On two occasions, he destroyed four two-seater enemy aeroplanes in a day, once in the space of an hour and a half. On 30 January 1918, during a single-handed attack on five enemy scouts, he shot down two and returned with his Lewis gun ammunition used up and the belt of his Vickers gun broken. As a patrol leader, he showed utmost gallantry and skill in the way he protected newer members of his flight, keeping casualties to a minimum.

AFRICA

In an extraordinary one-man campaign in German East Africa, the colony's military commander, General Paul Erich von Lettow-Vorbeck, harried the three-hundred-thousand-strong forces of the British Empire with his three thousand Europeans and eleven thousand native levies. His efforts tied up massive British resources during the course of the war, and cost some sixty thousand casualties. Lettow-Vorbeck was eventually forced to retreat into Mozambique, but only surrendered a few weeks after the end of the war.

BOOTH, Frederick Charles *Sergeant, British South African Police attached Rhodesia Native Infantry*
    12 January 1917 – During an attack mounted in thick bush near Songea, East Africa, he went forward alone under heavy rifle fire and brought in a dangerously wounded man. He later rallied disorganized native troops and brought them to the firing line. On many previous occasions, he had displayed bravery, coolness and resource in action.

MESOPOTAMIA

In November 1916, Anglo-Indian forces in Mesopotamia moved up the Tigris with the intention of forcing the Turks out of Kut. There were two corps: 1st Indian Army (the former Tigris Corps, under Lieutenant General Sir Alexander Cobbe, who had won a VC in Somaliland), which was given responsibility for Sanna-i-Yat; and 3rd Indian Army, which would attack Kut from the west. Attacks on Sanna-i-Yat and on the Shatt-al-Hai, south-west of Kut, began on 13/14 December, and by 15 February the Turks had lost all their defences south of the river. Sanna-i-Yat was attacked in force on 17 February, and although Sergeant Steele won a VC for rallying the line the counter-attack was ultimately successful and a new attack was made at first light on the 23rd at Shumran, a loop in the Tigris where the river was 400 yards wide. Thanks in part to Major Wheeler of the 2/9th Gurkhas, the far bank was held and by the afternoon a pontoon bridge was completed, but the Turks there and at Sanna-i-Yat fell back into Kut.

Nevertheless, Major General Stanely Maude, in command of the Mesopotamian Expeditionary Force, was allowed to proceed to Baghdad. He found little opposition until the Dialah (Diyala) River, a tributary of the Tigris abut 5 miles from the city; once it was successfully crossed the Turks again withdrew to the north. Maude then fought a series of actions to secure his position in Baghdad and prevent the Turkish forces against him combining, which, though costly in casualties, was largely complete when the heat drove the Turks into the mountains in July.

HENDERSON, Edward Elers Delaval *T/Lieutenant Colonel, North Staffordshire Regiment, attached 9th (S) Bn., Royal Warwickshire Regiment*

25 January 1917 – Whilst he was leading his battalion in an assault near Kut, Mesopotamia, the enemy counter-attacked and penetrated his line in several places. Although shot through the arm, he leapt onto a parapet, ran ahead of his men and cheered them on over 500 yards of open ground as they advanced. Despite receiving three more serious wounds, he led the bayonet charge which captured the position. He died from his wounds after he was brought in by Lieutenant PHILLIPS.

PHILLIPS, Robert Edwin *T/Lieutenant, 13th (R) Bn., Royal Warwickshire Regiment, attached 9th (S) Bn.*

25 January 1917 – Whilst attempting to lay a telephone wire after a successful assault near Kut, Mesopotamia, he noticed Lieutenant Colonel HENDERSON lying wounded in the open. Assisted by a corporal, he went out to rescue him under such heavy fire that it was thought they had little chance of getting back alive. The lieutenant colonel was brought in but died shortly afterwards.

STEELE, Thomas *Sergeant, 1st Bn., Seaforth Highlanders*

22 February 1917 – During a Turkish counter-attack at Sanna-i-Yat, Mesopotamia, he rushed forward, brought a machine-gun into position and kept it in action until he was relieved, thus keeping the British line intact. Several hours later during another Turkish counter-attack, he rallied wavering troops and led a number forward, again helping to re-establish the British line. On this occasion, he was badly wounded.

WHEELER, George Campbell *Major, 2nd Bn., 9th Gurkha Rifles*

23 February 1917 – At Shumran, Mesopotamia, he (together with a Gurkha officer and eight men) crossed the River Tigris and rushed a Turkish trench under heavy bombing, rifle, machine-gun and artillery fire. When his party was met by Turkish bombers, he led a charge against them during which he received a severe bayonet wound in the head. In spite of this, he dispersed the enemy and consolidated the position.

READITT, John *Private, 6th (S) Bn., South Lancashire Regiment*

25 February 1917 – At Alqayat-al-Gaharbigah Bend, Mesopotamia, he advanced five times along a water course in the face of heavy machine-gun fire and each time was the only survivor. These advances drove back the machine-guns and 300 yards were gained in an hour. He then made further advances until he reached the Turkish barricade. When support reached him, he held the forward bend by bombing until the position was consolidated.

WHITE, Jack *Private, 6th (S) Bn., King's Own (Royal Lancaster Regiment)*

7–8 March 1917 – During an attempt to cross the Dialah River, Mesopotamia, he watched the two pontoons ahead of his raked by machine-gun fire. When his own pontoon was hit and every man besides himself had been killed or wounded, he tied a telephone wire to the pontoon, dived overboard and towed it to shore. In this way, he saved the life of a wounded officer and salvaged the rifles and equipment of the dead and dying.

REID, Oswald Austin *Captain, 1st Bn., King's (Liverpool) Regiment, attached 6th (S) Bn., Loyal North Lancashire Regiment*
8–10 March 1917 – He consolidated a small post on the opposite side of the Dialah River, Mesopotamia, to the main body after his line of communication had been cut by the sinking of pontoons. He maintained this position for thirty hours against continuous attacks by bombs, machine-guns and shells. On the following night, the river was crossed, mainly due to his tenacity. He was wounded during the crossing.

MELVIN, Charles *Private, 2nd Bn., Black Watch*
21 April 1917 – At Istabulat, Mesopotamia, he rushed alone across fire-swept ground to an enemy trench. Once there, he shot several Turks, jumped in and attacked others with his bayonet (which he used as a dagger as his rifle was broken). The enemy fled to their second line but not before he had taken nine prisoners, whom he brought back to his own lines.

GRAHAM, John Reginald Noble (later Sir Reginald) *Lieutenant, 9th Bn., Argyll and Sutherland Highlanders, attached 136th Coy., Machine-Gun Corps*
22 April 1917 – Whilst in command of a machine-gun section at Istabulat, Mesopotamia, he carried ammunition and opened fire on the enemy who were massing for an attack, despite being twice wounded. After his gun had been damaged and he was again wounded, he brought a Lewis gun into action until he was severely wounded a final time and had to retire from loss of blood.

THE WAR AT SEA

At sea, although the full force of the German surface fleet was no longer operative after the Battle of Jutland in 1916, predations on Allied shipping by German U-boats resumed with renewed vigour, prompting the Royal Navy to resort to new measures – the Q Ships, or Mystery Ships, which were modified merchantmen with concealed guns – to lure the enemy submarines into surfacing and leaving themselves open to shelling. The first Q-ship VC was awarded for action in an encounter in the Irish Sea in mid-February, and men of the Q ships continued to distinguish themselves throughout the year, in the Irish Sea, the Atlantic and the Bay of Biscay.

CAMPBELL, Gordon *Commander, Royal Navy*
17 February 1917 – He was in command of HMS Q.5, a 'mystery ship', in the Irish Sea, when he spotted a German torpedo track. He altered course,

allowing the torpedo to hit *Q.5*. Mystery ships were apparently unarmed but had been fitted with carefully disguised guns to attack U-boats. He called the gun crews to their fighting stations and waited until the submarine surfaced about 300 yards away, at which point he gave the order to fire. The U-boat was quickly destroyed. He then signalled for friendly ships to come to the assistance of the stricken *Q.5*, before he eventually beached her to prevent her from sinking.

He was MP for Burnley, 1931–35.

BISSETT-SMITH, Archibald *T/Lieutenant, Royal Naval Reserve*
10 March 1917 – Whilst in command of SS *Otaki* in the Atlantic, which was armed with one 4.7in gun, he was called on to stop by the German raider *Moewe*, armed with four 5.9in guns, one 4.1in gun, two 22pdr guns and two torpedo tubes. He refused and a duel ensued at a range of 2,000 yards. The *Otaki* scored several hits on the *Moewe*, starting a fire which lasted for three days. The *Otaki* was seriously damaged herself and Smith gave orders for the boats to be lowered but he remained on board himself and went down with her when she sank with the British colours still flying. An enemy account described 'a duel as gallant as naval history can relate'.

SANDERS, William Edward *A/Lieutenant, Royal Naval Reserve*
30 April 1917 – Whilst in command of HMS *Prize*, a topsail schooner 'mystery ship', he spotted a German submarine south of Ireland. Mystery ships were fitted with carefully disguised guns and were designed to attack U-boats. When the submarine opened fire, a 'panic party' abandoned ship whilst the gun crews hid by lying face down on the deck. The submarine continued firing for twenty minutes, but only as she drew close did the schooner return fire. The submarine was sunk within four minutes.

WATT, Joseph *Skipper, Royal Naval Reserve*
15 May 1917 – Whilst in command of HM Drifter *Gowan Lea*, in the Straits of Otranto, Adriatic, an Austrian cruiser ordered him to surrender. Instead, he ordered full speed ahead and called on his crew to give three cheers and fight to the finish. The cruiser opened fire, disabling *Gowan Lea*'s only gun and causing many casualties. After the cruiser had passed on, he helped to remove the dead and wounded onto another drifter.

STUART, Ronald Niel *Lieutenant, Royal Naval Reserve*
7 June 1917 – Whilst he was serving on HMS *Pargust*, a 'mystery ship', in the Atlantic Ocean, an enemy submarine fired a torpedo at close range and damaged *Pargust*'s engine room. Mystery ships were fitted with carefully disguised guns and were designed to attack U-boats. A 'panic party' rowed away from *Pargust* but then its gunners opened fire, sinking the submarine.

He was elected for the award by officers of HMS Pargust *under Rule 13 of the Royal Warrant.*

WILLIAMS, William *Seaman, Royal Naval Reserve*

7 June 1917 – Whilst he was serving on HMS *Pargust*, a 'mystery ship', in the Atlantic Ocean, an enemy submarine fired a torpedo at close range and damaged *Pargust*'s engine room. Mystery ships were fitted with carefully disguised guns and were designed to attack U-boats. He noticed that the explosion had loosened the gun covers so he physically held them up to prevent the U-boat from spotting the guns. The submarine was successfully sunk.

He was elected for the award by officers of HMS Pargust *under Rule 13 of the Royal Warrant.*

BONNER, Charles George *Lieutenant, Royal Naval Reserve*

8 August 1917 – He served on HMS *Dunraven*, a 'mystery ship', shelled by an enemy submarine in the Bay of Biscay. Mystery ships were fitted with carefully disguised guns and were designed to attack U-boats. He was in the thick of the fighting, was twice blown up and showed a pluck and determination that influenced the crew.

PITCHER, Ernest Herbert *Petty Officer, Royal Navy*

8 August 1917 – He was the 4in gun-layer on HMS *Dunraven*, a 'mystery ship', shelled by an enemy submarine in the Bay of Biscay. Mystery ships were fitted with carefully disguised guns and were designed to attack U-boats. As the battle went on overhead, he and the rest of the crew stored the cartridges on their knees to prevent the heat from igniting them. When the magazine exploded they were all blown into the air.

He was elected for the award by the crew of a gun of HMS Dunraven *under Rule 13 of the Royal Warrant.*

CRISP, Thomas *Skipper, Royal Naval Reserve*

15 August 1917 – Whilst skipper of HM Armed Smack *Nelson* in the North Sea, he was below packing fish when an enemy submarine opened fire. The U-boat fired shell after shell but there was no panic on board even when the seventh shell struck him, passed through his side and continued through the deck. He remained in command but the ship began to sink so he ordered it to be abandoned. Both his legs were hanging off but he was smiling as he told his son (the second hand) not to lift him into a boat. He went down with his ship.

CARLESS, John Henry *Ordinary Seaman, Royal Navy*

17 November 1917 – During the Battle of Heligoland, North Sea, a light cruiser action, he received a severe wound to the abdomen but carried on serving his gun as rammer and helping to clear away casualties. He collapsed once but got up again and cheered on the new gun crew before he finally fell dead.

EGYPT

Anglo-Indian forces in Egypt in early 1917 were deployed in the defence of the Suez Canal and of the railway being built from El Kantara (on the Canal) along the coast, and in garrisoning towns, oases and key points. In the summer, they were ordered to prepare for a planned offensive into Palestine that autumn, for which the two key objectives were Gaza, on the coast, and Beersheba, 25 miles south-east. The first attack on Gaza, 16–27 March, failed, partly because of a Turkish advance from Beersheba; the second, on 17–18 April, a frontal infantry assault with the assistance of eight tanks, naval bombardment and gas, found strengthened defences, and was ordered to dig in on the position it reached on the second day.

CRAIG, John Manson *Second Lieutenant, 1/4th Bn., Royal Scots Fusiliers, attached 1/5th Bn.*

5 June 1917 – When an advanced post was rushed by a large number of Turks in Egypt, he organized a rescue party which tracked the enemy and removed the dead and wounded under heavy fire. He rescued an NCO and a medical officer and was himself wounded whilst bringing the latter to shelter.

PALESTINE

In the summer of 1917, the Egyptian Expeditionary Force went on to the offensive, under a new commander, General Sir Edmund Allenby. A mixed Turkish–German force was preparing to recapture Baghdad, and it was proposed to counter this threat by an attack on Palestine, which would remove its supplies and preclude any action. The starting point was Beersheba, taken on 31 October after a highly successful deception focused on Gaza. The first step, on 1 November, was to attack the positions at Tel-el-Khuweilfeh, which protected the road to Jerusalem, and at Tel-es-Sheria, the eastern end of the Turkish defences. The former held, but the latter was taken, and the Turks began a general withdrawal on the 7th. Unfortunately, poor logistics, reduced visibility from the hot south wind and determined resistance (and the award of two VCs) meant that the Turks were able to remove about fifteen thousand troops to a new line south-west of Jerusalem. They were disorganized, however, and by 15 November Allenby had reached Jaffa, where, encouraged by his success thus far, he set out for Jerusalem on the 18th. The Turks made repeated counter-attacks, but by the 21st he was within five miles of the city. Both sides had taken about 50 per cent casualties in two days; he paused to bring up relief troops, then launched the final assault on the night of 7/8 December. Jerusalem surrendered on the afternoon of the 9th. Allenby secured his position by clearing the Turks from the immediate area of Jaffa, which allowed its use as a port, and from Jerusalem, then on 26/27 December he turned a strong counter-attack just north of the city into a British advance that pushed the Turks as far east as Jericho.

LAFONE, Alexander Malins *Major, 1/1st County of London Yeomanry*
    27 October 1917 – Ordered to hold his post at Beersheba, Palestine, at all costs, he stood firm against repeated cavalry charges for over seven hours. After one charge, during which he personally bayoneted a man who entered his trench, 15 Turkish casualties lay nearby. Eventually, only three of his men remained unwounded but he continued to mount a heroic resistance. When finally surrounded, he stepped into the open and continued fighting until he was mortally wounded and fell unconscious.

COLLINS, John *A/Corporal, 25th Bn., Royal Welch Fusiliers*
    31 October 1917 – Prior to an attack at Wadi Saba, Beersheba, Palestine, his battalion was forced to lie out in the open under heavy shell and machine-gun fire. He went out repeatedly and brought many wounded back to cover. Whilst leading the subsequent assault, he bayoneted 15 of the enemy and with a Lewis gun section pressed on beyond the objective.

RUSSELL, John Fox *Captain, Royal Army Medical Corps, attached 1/6th Bn., Royal Welch Fusiliers*
    6 November 1917 – At Tel-el-Khuweilfeh, Palestine, he repeatedly went out to attend the wounded under murderous fire from snipers and machine-guns. He carried many of these men to safety until he was himself fatally wounded.

BORTON, Arthur Drummond *Lieutenant Colonel, 2/22nd Bn., London Regiment*
    7 November 1917 – In a dawn attack at Sheria, Palestine, he led his companies against a Turkish position. When the leading waves were checked by machine-gun fire, he moved up and down his lines under heavy fire. He then led his men forward and captured the position. He later led a party of volunteers against a battery of field guns, capturing the guns and their crews.

BOUGHEY, Stanley Henry Parry *Second Lieutenant, 1/4th Bn., Royal Scots Fusiliers*
    1 December 1917 – When large numbers of the enemy had crawled to within 30 yards of his lines at El Burf, Palestine, he rushed them with bombs and caused devastation. Just before they surrendered, as he turned to get more bombs, he was mortally wounded.

TRAIN, Charles William *Corporal, 2/14th Bn., London Regiment*
    8 December 1917 – When his company's assault was halted at Air Karim, near Jerusalem, Palestine, by Turkish machine-guns, he darted forward 20

yards, crept to the end of the enemy barricade and began firing and throwing bombs. He shot the officer in charge, at which point the remaining Turks ran to the other end of the barricade, where they were attacked by Train's comrades. He then shot a Turk who was escaping with one of the machine-guns. His action allowed his battalion to advance to their objective at a time when the situation seemed critical.

He was twice offered a commission but preferred to stay in the ranks.

CHRISTIE, John Alexander *Lance Corporal, 1/11th Bn., London Regiment*

21–22 December 1918 – After capturing a position at Fejja, Palestine, the enemy began making bombing attacks up communication trenches. In the darkness and confusion he filled his pockets with bombs and rained them down on the attackers until a block was established. Returning to his lines, he heard voices behind him so turned back and bombed another party moving up to mount an attack. Twenty-six dead Austrians were later found in the first trench.

DUFFY, James *Private, 6th (S) Bn., Royal Inniskilling Fusiliers*

27 December 1917 – He and another stretcher bearer went out to bring in a seriously wounded comrade at Kereina Peak, Palestine. When the other stretcher bearer was wounded, he returned to get another man, who was himself killed. Duffy then went forward alone and under heavy fire suc-ceeded in getting both wounded men under cover where he attended to their injuries. His gallantry undoubtedly saved both lives.

1918

At the end of 1917, the onus of the Allied war effort had devolved on the British Expeditionary Force with its Dominion troops and the French army. Russia had withdrawn from the war in the wake of the Revolution and Lenin's accession to power, Italy's efforts had collapsed and Rumania had sued for peace.

Following the Passchendaele offensive, the British Prime Minister, Lloyd George, considered Haig had squandered too many British lives and effectively left him hamstrung for any future offensives by depriving him of manpower.

Consequently, January to March was quiet on the Western Front – although the British command, especially Gough with the Fifth Army to the south, were aware that a German offensive was imminent. Interrogating German prisoners elicited the date of 21 March as its start. As the attack developed, Gough's thinly spread troops were forced to stand and fight till they could withdraw in good order. Attacked with gas, rifles and machine-gun fire, Gough's men had orders to delay the enemy while still keeping the option open to retire. Following this action, Gough was replaced by Sir Henry Rawlinson in April, but by now, although the Allied line had taken some dents, the German advance had outrun its lines of supply. During April, the focus of the German attack switched to advancing on the Channel ports – but at the end of the month this campaign was abandoned with no real gains. The knockout blow had not been delivered.

As Haig urged his forces to fight to the last with their 'backs to the wall' and making no retreat, the Germans prepared to launch an offensive against the French – a campaign which lasted from 27 May to 6 June. But then the British and Dominion troops, older and wiser with the lessons of four years of fighting, and with the increasing support of American forces, were preparing for a counterblow to end the war. The German army was short on reinforcements and equipment, morale was low and then was the time to strike decisively.

The new Allied assault began on 8 August, with a well-coordinated all-round operation using artillery, tanks, aircraft, armoured cars and motorized machine-guns, supported by vastly improved field communications. Within days of this attack beginning, German representatives were putting out feelers for peace through President Woodrow Wilson of the United States.

The Allied push continued, and by 26 September the Allied troops were up against the Hindenburg Line. The last period of the war took the form of a sequence of assaults to take a series of river lines. As each one fell to the Allies, the Germans fell back to the next, and despite heavy Allied losses, the writing was on the wall for Germany. After the fall of the Hindenburg Line, the British suffered a hundred and twenty thousand casualties, but German losses were comparable – and around a quarter of the German army surrendered. Pressing on and fighting to the last as Haig had demanded, the Canadian Corps finally took Mons on the morning of 11 November, and on the eleventh hour of the eleventh day the Armistice was signed and the guns were silenced.

TRENCH WARFARE

As in 1917, day-to-day fighting continued that was not part of any drive or attack. The war did not stand still, and operations were carried out to dislodge the enemy from their trench positions and capture their guns – and similarly a fierce defence had to be maintained to drive back German attacks on the Allied lines. A total of twenty-five VCs were awarded between March and October as the daily attrition continued.

ROBERTSON, Charles Graham *Lance Corporal, 10th (S) Bn., Royal Fusiliers*
    8–9 March 1918 – During an enemy attack at Polderhoek Chateau, Belgium, he sent two men to fetch reinforcements while he maintained a steady fire with his Lewis gun. No reinforcements arrived and he was twice forced to concede ground, but he continued firing. When he reached a defended post, he mounted his gun in a shell hole and started firing again. By now the enemy were pouring forward and he was severely wounded, but he managed to crawl to safety, bringing his gun with him.

SADLIER, Clifford William King *51st Bn. (Victoria), Australian Imperial Force*
    24–25 April 1918 – When his platoon was held up by a German machine-gun position at Villers-Bretonneux, France, he led his bombing section against the post. Two of the guns were captured but his men were all killed or wounded in the attack so he rushed the third gun on his own, armed only with a revolver. He killed the crew of four and took the gun, although he himself received a serious wound.

McKEAN, George Burdon *Lieutenant, 14th Bn. (Royal Montreal Regiment), Canadian Expeditionary Force*
    27–28 April 1918 – During a raid on enemy trenches in the Gavrelle sector, France, his party was held up at a block which was too close to the British trenches to have been destroyed by the preliminary bombardment. The block was protected by a machine-gun and heavy wire but McKean

leapt over and landed on top of a German soldier. Instantly another man rushed at him with a fixed bayonet but McKean shot both men in the course of the struggle. He then rushed a second block, killing two Germans, capturing four others and driving the remaining garrison into a dugout, which he then destroyed.

BEESLEY, William *Private, 13th (S) Bn., Rifle Brigade*
8 May 1918 – Armed only with a revolver, he rushed a machine-gun post at Bucquoy, France, where he killed two machine-gunners and an officer who tried to take their place. He then shot another officer who was trying to dispose of a map. By now a Lewis gun had been brought up, which he fired until nightfall, when he returned to his lines with the gun and a wounded comrade.

GREGG, William *Sergeant, 13th (S) Bn., Rifle Brigade*
8 May 1918 – When all the officers of his company had been put out of action during an attack at Bucquoy, France, he took command and rushed an enemy post where he personally killed an entire machine-gun team. He then rushed another post and killed two more men. He led his company to their objective which he consolidated. When his party was later driven back, he led a charge which put a machine-gun out of action.

RUTHVEN, William *Sergeant, 22nd Bn. (Victoria), Australian Imperial Force*
19 May 1918 – Whilst leading an advance at Ville-sur-Ancre, France, after his company commander had been wounded, he rushed an enemy machine-gun post, bayoneted one of the crew and captured the gun. He then wounded two Germans and captured six others as they came out of a shelter. He subsequently rushed an enemy position on a sunken road, shooting two men before single-handedly mopping up the post and taking 32 prisoners.

HALLIWELL, Joel *Lance Corporal, 11th (S) Bn., Lancashire Fusiliers*
27 May 1918 – During the withdrawal of the remnants of his battalion at Muscourt, near Reims, France, he captured a stray enemy horse, rode out under rifle and machine-gun fire and rescued a man from no-man's-land. He repeated this performance time and again until he had rescued nine men and an officer. His final effort to reach a wounded man was driven back by the advance of the enemy.

KAEBLE, Joseph *Corporal, 22nd Bn. (French Canadian), Canadian Expeditionary Force*
8–9 June 1918 – As the enemy barrage lifted at Neuville-Vitasse, near Arras, France, he observed 50 Germans advancing towards his post. All but one of his comrades had been killed or wounded so he jumped alone onto the parapet, held the Lewis gun at his hip and fired into the Germans. He was hit several times by shell and bomb fragments but continued firing

until he fell mortally wounded. As he lay dying, he shouted out, 'Keep it up, boys! Do not let them get through! We must stop them!'

DAVEY, Philip *Corporal, 10th Bn. (South Australia), Australian Imperial Force*

28 June 1918 – At Merris, France, under point-blank fire he attacked an enemy machine-gun with hand grenades. He put half the crew out of action before he ran out of grenades. He collected more, rushed back and killed the rest. He then mounted the gun in a new post and used it to repel a counter-attack.

AXFORD, Thomas Leslie *Lance Corporal, 16th Bn. (South Australia and Western Australia), Australian Imperial Force*

4 July 1918 – Observing an adjoining platoon taking casualties from a machine-gun during the advance at Vaire and Hamel Woods, France, he threw bombs at the gun position before charging alone into the trench. He killed ten Germans and took six prisoners before throwing the machine-guns over the parapet, allowing the platoon to advance. He then returned to his own platoon.

The first ever airborne supply drop to troops took place during this attack, when British aeroplanes dropped ammunition to Australian gunners.

DALZIEL, Henry *Driver, 15th Bn. (Queensland and Tasmania), Australian Imperial Force*

4 July 1918 – Whilst in action with a Lewis gun section at Hamel Wood, France, his company was held up by heavy machine-gun fire. Armed only with a revolver, he ran alone at the gun. His hand was almost shot away as he ran but he killed four of the crew and captured the others. 'Come on, lads! We've got 'em guessing!' he called to his comrades. Later, whilst dashing across no-man's-land to fetch ammunition, he was wounded in the head but he still continued to serve his gun.

At a dinner in his honour given by the Sailors' and Soldiers' Imperial League of Australia in May 1919, he was toasted with the words: 'Our guest, our hero, our cobber.'

BROWN, Walter Ernest *Corporal, 20th Bn. (New South Wales), Australian Imperial Force*

6 July 1918 – Fed up with persistent sniping from an enemy dugout at Villers-Bretonneux, France, he crept out alone and dashed towards it. With a Mills grenade in his hand, he called on the occupants to surrender. One of the Germans rushed out, a scuffle ensued and Brown knocked him down with his fist. An officer and 11 men then appeared from the dugout and surrendered to him. He led the entire party back to his own lines under heavy machine-gun fire.

At the outbreak of the Second World War he gave his age as thirty-nine (rather than fifty-four) and joined up. When the truth was discovered he was promoted to lance sergeant but insisted on being returned to the rank of gunner.

BORELLA, Albert Chalmers (changed his surname to CHALMERS-BORELLA in 1939) *Captain, 26th Bn. (Queensland and Tasmania), Australian Imperial Force*

17–18 July 1918 – At Villers-Bretonneux, France, he ran ahead of his men, shot 2 German machine-gunners with his revolver and captured their gun. He then led his party of ten against a strongly held trench, causing many casualties. Two large dugouts were also bombed and 30 prisoners taken. Subsequently when the enemy counter-attacked and his platoon was outnumbered by ten to one, his cool determination inspired his men to repulse the enemy.

TRAVIS, Richard Charles (born SAVAGE, Dickson Cornelius) *Sergeant, 2nd Bn., Otago Infantry Regiment, New Zealand Expeditionary Force*

24 July 1918 – At Rossignol Wood he crawled out alone and bombed an impassable wire block, enabling attacking parties to pass through. Minutes later he charged alone at two enemy machine-guns, killing the crews and capturing the guns. He then killed a German officer and three men who rushed at him in an attempt to retake the position.

KNIGHT, Arthur George *A/Sergeant, 10th Bn. (Canadians), Canadian Expeditionary Force*

2 September 1918 – Whilst leading a bombing section after an unsuccessful attack near Cagnicort, he dashed forward alone, bayoneting several enemy machine-gunners and trench-mortar crews, and forcing the remainder to retire in confusion. He then brought a Lewis gun forward and directed fire on the retreating enemy. Seeing about 30 Germans go into a deep tunnel which led off the trench, he ran forward alone, killed an officer and 2 NCOs and took 20 prisoners. He then single-handedly routed another enemy party opposing his platoon. He was subsequently fatally wounded.

McGUFFIE, Louis *A/Sergeant, 1/5th Bn., King's Own Scottish Borderers*

28 September 1918 – During the advance to Piccadilly Farm near Wytschaete, Belgium, he entered several enemy dugouts alone and took many prisoners. During subsequent operations he dealt similarly with dugout after dugout, forcing an officer and 25 other ranks to surrender. Whilst consolidating the position, he pursued and brought back several Germans who were slipping away. He also rescued some British soldiers being led away as prisoners. Later in the day, whilst in command of a platoon, he continued taking prisoners.

SEAMAN, Ernest *Lance Corporal, 2nd Bn., Royal Inniskilling Fusiliers*

29 September 1918 – When the right flank of his company was held up by a nest of enemy machine-guns at Terhand, Belgium, he rushed forward ❧

under heavy fire with his Lewis gun and engaged the nest single-handed, capturing two guns and 12 prisoners and killing an officer and 2 men. Later that day, he captured another machine-gun post under heavy fire, after which he was killed.

GORLE, Robert Vaughan *T/Lieutenant, A Bty., 50th Brigade, Royal Field Artillery*
   1 October 1918 – In command of an 18pdr gun during the attack on Ledeghem, Belgium, he sited his gun in the most exposed positions on four separate occasions and disposed of enemy machine-guns by firing over open sights at ranges of 500–600 yards. Later, when the infantry were driven back, he twice galloped his gun out and knocked out German machine-guns disrupting the attack. As a result, the northern end of the village was retaken.

JOHNSON, James *Second Lieutenant, 2nd Bn., Northumberland Fusiliers, attached 36th (T) Bn.*
   14 October 1918 – He repelled enemy counter-attacks for six hours under heavy fire near Wez Macquart, France. When he was eventually ordered to retire, he was the last to leave the advanced position, carrying a wounded man. He then returned three times to carry in other wounded men under intense machine-gun fire.
   According to the corporal who brought him the telegram informing him that he was to receive the VC, 'When I gave it to the officer, he read it, waltzed me round his billet and then threw every piece of his shaving kit through the window.'

MOFFAT, Martin Joseph *Private, 2nd Bn., Prince of Wales' Leinster Regiment*
   14 October 1918 – Whilst advancing with five comrades across open ground near Ledeghem, Belgium, the party came under heavy fire from an enemy-held house. Dashing towards the house through a hail of bullets, he threw bombs and then worked round to the back of the house, rushed the door single-handedly, killed 2 Germans and captured 30.
   He was buried in Sligo Town Cemetery. Seven holers of the VC were his pallbearers.

O'NEILL, John *Lieutenant, 2nd Bn., Prince of Wales' Leinster Regiment*
   14 October and 20 October 1918 – On 14 October, when the advance of his company was checked by two machine-guns and an enemy field battery firing over open sights near Moorseele, Belgium, he charged the battery at the head of a party of 11 men, capturing four field guns, two machine-guns and 16 prisoners. On 20 October, with one man, he rushed an enemy machine-gun position, routing about a hundred Germans and causing many casualties.

RICKETTS, Thomas *Private, 1st Bn., Royal Newfoundland Regiment, Canadian Expeditionary Force*
   14 October 1918 – At Ledeghem, Belgium, he volunteered to go with his section commander and a Lewis gun in an attempt to outflank an

enemy battery. Their ammunition was used up when still 300 yards from the battery so he doubled back 100 yards under heavy machine-gun fire, secured the ammunition, returned to the Lewis gun and drove the enemy gun teams into a farm. His platoon then advanced and captured the battery.

His investiture took place at York Cottage, Sandringham in early 1919 during the period of mourning for Prince John, the youngest son of George V. 'This is the youngest VC in my army,' the King said as he made the award.

McGREGOR, David Stuart *Lieutenant, 5/6th Bn., Royal Scots and 29th Bn., Machine-Gun Corps*

22 October 1918 – Whilst in command of a section of machine-guns during an advance near Hoogemolen, Belgium, he concealed his guns on a limber in the shelter of the bank of a sunken road. Knowing that the ground ahead was bare and swept by bullets, he ordered the gun teams forward by a safer route whilst he lay flat on the limber and told the driver to gallop straight ahead. The driver and the horses were hit but he managed to get the guns into action 600 yards further on, from where he effectively engaged the enemy. He continued to ignore enemy fire until he was killed an hour later.

HARVEY, Norman *Private, 1st Bn., Royal Inniskilling Fusiliers*

25 October 1918 – With his battalion held up and suffering severe casualties from machine-guns at Ingoyghem, Belgium, he ran forward and engaged the enemy single-handed, killing two, wounding one and capturing twelve men and two guns. He later rushed a machine-gun hidden in a farmhouse and put the enemy to flight. After night fell, he went out alone to gather important information. Throughout these actions he was limping with a sprained ankle. According to his sergeant, 'He seemed to bear a charmed life.'

He enlisted in November 1914 when he was only fifteen years old.

CALDWELL, Thomas *Sergeant, 12th (T) Bn., Royal Scots Fusiliers*

31 October 1918 – Whilst in command of a Lewis gun section engaged in clearing a farmhouse near Audenarde, Belgium, his men came under intense fire from another farm. He rushed the enemy position, which he captured single-handedly together with 18 prisoners. Having eliminated this obstacle, his section was able to capture eight machine-guns, one trench mortar and 70 more prisoners.

THE BATTLE OF THE SOMME

Shortly before 5 a.m. on 21 March, German artillery opened a gas and high-explosive bombardment along the front from the Scarpe River (Arras) to the Oise (La Fère) 100 miles to the south-east, with artillery targeting both the front lines and key points up to 12 miles behind, including headquarters, magazines and dumps, and road and rail junctions. By 9.45, sixty-four divisions had attacked on a 54-mile front between the Oise River and the Sensée (10 miles north-west of Cambrai): the British had eight divisions in the area Arras–Cambrai, with seven in reserve, and eleven in the area Cambrai–Barisis, with six divisions (three of them cavalry) in reserve. Haig's despatch stated that he had expected an attack in two prongs, between the Sensée River and the Bapaume–Cambrai road, and between the southern flank of the Flesquières salient and St-Quentin; the exceptionally dry spring in fact allowed six divisions to take his right flank, in the marshes beyond Moy-de-l'Aisne (seven miles north of La Fère). He believed the objective was to split the British and French armies and capture Amiens: in fact it was to break through the front, hold the French on the left, and roll up the British to the north, where an attack in Flanders would cut them off from the sea.

The attack was assisted by thick fog that reduced visibility to 50 yards and hid the distress signals from the front line, and by new infiltration tactics, in which strongpoints were bypassed and left for successive waves. Many fierce actions were fought as these redoubts held out – Haig's despatch reported, 'Wireless messages from their gallant defenders [18th Division, north of Quessy] were received as late as 8.30 p.m., and rifle fire was heard in their vicinity until midnight' – and many VCs were won, but whole companies and battalions were killed or captured, and brigades and even divisions destroyed.

From 22 March the British and French were driven back in disorder and confusion, despite determined resistance and well-planned and locally successful counter-attacks, including by horsed cavalry. On 5 April the forward troops were within 10 miles of Amiens, but the Germans had taken more than a quarter of a million casualties, resupply and communications across the ruins of the Somme battlefield, devastated in the retreat of 1917, were proving difficult, Arras had not been taken and the French and British armies had not been separated, and the advance finally halted. In the south, attacks against French positions continued until the 9th, when the Germans secured the Oise–Aisne Canal.

BEAL, Ernest Frederick *T/Second Lieutenant, 13th (S) Bn., Yorkshire Regiment*

21–22 March 1918 – When in command of a company occupying a section of trench at St-Leger, France, he was ordered to work his way along a communication trench to clear a 400-yard gap held by the enemy. Leading a small party, he captured four machine-guns and inflicted heavy casualties. Later that evening he brought in on his back a wounded man who was lying near enemy lines but was killed shortly afterwards.

BUCHAN, John Crawford *Second Lieutenant, 2/7th (T) Bn., Argyll and Sutherland Highlanders, attached 2/8th (T) Bn.*

21 March 1918 – Despite being wounded earlier in the day near Marteville, France, he remained in action under severe shell fire, continually visiting all his posts and encouraging the men as the enemy crept ever closer. Eventually the enemy rushed forward shouting 'Surrender!' 'To hell with surrender!' he replied. He repelled the attack and fought his way back to the support line where he held out until dusk. Totally cut off, he was last seen fighting against overwhelming odds.

DE WIND, Edmund *Second Lieutenant, 15th (S) Bn., Royal Irish Rifles*

21 March 1918 – He held the Racecourse Redoubt near St-Quentin, France, almost single-handedly for seven hours despite being twice wounded. On two occasions he climbed up under machine-gun and rifle fire and cleared the Germans out of a trench. He continued to repel attack after attack until he collapsed, fatally wounded.

ELSTOB, Wilfrith *T/Lieutenant Colonel, commanding 16th (S) Bn., Manchester Regiment*

21 March 1918 – During a bombardment of Manchester Redoubt near St-Quentin, France, he encouraged his men and when repeated attacks developed directed the defence. He repulsed a bombing assault single-handed and later made several journeys under severe fire to replenish ammunition. He sent his brigade commander the cable: 'The Manchester Regiment will defend Manchester Hill to the last.' After a long brave defence, the post was overcome and he was killed.

HAYWARD, Reginald Frederick Johnson *A/Captain, 1st Bn., Wiltshire Regiment*

21–22 March 1918 – Whilst in command of a company near Frenicourt, France, he displayed almost superhuman powers of endurance. He was buried by the explosion of a shell, wounded in the head and rendered deaf; two days later his arm was shattered and he was again wounded in the head: yet at no time would he leave his men. As the enemy attacked incessantly, he moved between trenches organizing the defence and encouraging his men until he eventually collapsed.

He was Commandant, Prisoner of War Camps, 1945–47.

JAMES, Manley Angell *T/Captain, 8th (S) Bn., Gloucestershire Regiment*

21 March 1918 – He led his company forward at Velu Wood, France, in an assault which captured two machine-guns and 27 prisoners. He then repulsed three enemy attacks, despite being wounded. Two days later, he stood firm as the Germans broke through and was wounded again whilst leading a counter-attack. He was eventually captured and held as a prisoner until the end of the war.

KER, Allan Ebenezer *Lieutenant, 3rd (R) Bn., Gordon Highlanders, attached 61st Bn., Machine-Gun Corps*

21 March 1918 – When the Germans penetrated the line near St-Quentin, France, he held up their advance with a machine-gun. He then found himself stranded with his sergeant and several badly wounded men for ten hours during which the small party was subjected to continuous bayonet and bomb attacks. He survived many hand-to-hand fights and refused to surrender until all his ammunition was spent and his position was rushed by five hundred of the enemy.

SAYER, John William *Lance Corporal, 8th (S) Bn., Queen's Royal West Surrey Regiment*

21 March 1918 – At La Verguier, France, he beat off a succession of enemy attacks on his isolated post. The mist was so thick that the Germans had been able to surround him undetected yet, for two hours, he inflicted heavy casualties on them. Under heavy fire he held out until nearly the whole party had been killed. He was himself wounded and captured.

STONE, Charles Edwin *Gunner, C Bty., 83rd Brigade, Royal Field Artillery*

21 March 1918 – After working his gun for six hours under heavy gas and shell fire at Caponne Farm, France, he was sent to the rear. He returned voluntarily with a rifle and lay in the open under heavy fire, shooting at the enemy. He later captured four Germans who had worked their way to the rear of the gun position armed with a machine-gun.

COLLINGS-WELLS, John Stanhope *A/Lieutenant Colonel, commanding 4th (ER) Bn., Bedfordshire Regiment*

22–27 March 1918 – During fighting between Marcoing and Albert, France, he led a small volunteer party which held the Germans for an hour and a half and allowed the rearguard to withdraw. His battalion was subsequently ordered to counter-attack. His men were exhausted after six days' fighting, but he led them forward and refused to leave them, even when twice wounded. He was killed as the objective was gained.

COLUMBINE, Herbert George *Private, 9th Squadron, Machine-Gun Corps*

22 March 1918 – At Hervilly Wood, France, he kept his machine-gun firing at the enemy from 9 a.m. until 1 p.m. in an isolated position with no wire in front. Wave after wave of advancing Germans failed to take the position and only succeeded when he came under attack from a low-flying aeroplane. He was then bombed from both flanks, but still kept his gun firing. He was finally killed by a bomb.

JACKSON, Harold *Sergeant, 7th (S) Bn., East Yorkshire Regiment*

22 March 1918 – At Hermies, France, he went out alone and brought back valuable information regarding enemy movements, before bombing the enemy into the open. He then stalked a German machine-gun single-

handedly and put the gun out of action with Mills bombs. When all his officers had become casualties, he led his company in an attack, before going out repeatedly under fire to carry in the wounded.

He was a well-known amateur boxer before the war.

KNOX, Cecil Leonard　*T/Second Lieutenant, 150th Field Coy., Royal Engineers*
22 March 1918 – Whilst supervising the demolition of a bridge at Tugny, France, he realized that the time fuse had failed. Without hesitation, he ran to the bridge under heavy fire, climbed underneath it and lit the instantaneous fuse. The bridge blew up as the enemy were crossing it.

ROBERTS, Frank Crowther　*A/Lieutenant Colonel, commanding 1st Bn., Worcestershire Regiment*
22 March to 2 April 1918 – During a major German offensive over twelve days around Pargny, France, he showed great bravery, military skill and an ability to motivate those around him. On one occasion, the enemy attacked a village and were about to clear it. He got together an improvised party, counter-attacked and drove the enemy back, preventing many men from being cut off.

BUSHELL, Christopher　*T/Lieutenant Colonel, commanding 7th (S) Bn., Queen's Royal West Surrey Regiment*
23 March 1918 – Whilst leading C Company of his battalion into heavy machine-gun fire near Tergnier, France, he was severely wounded in the head. Refusing assistance, he continued in front of both English and other allied troops, encouraging and reorganizing them. He eventually fainted and was carried to a dressing station.

GRIBBLE, Julian Royds　*T/Captain, 10th (S) Bn., Royal Warwickshire Regiment*
23 March 1918 – Whilst in command of the right company of his battalion at Beaumetz, Hermies Ridge, France, he was ordered to hold on at all costs during an enemy attack. His company became isolated but rather than withdraw he fought on and prevented the enemy from obtaining mastery of the crest of the ridge for some hours. When his company was eventually surrounded, he was seen fighting to the last.

HERRING, Alfred Cecil　*T/Second Lieutenant, Royal Army Service Corps, attached 6th (S) Bn., Northamptonshire Regiment*
23–24 March 1918 – After severe fighting at Montagne Bridge, France, the enemy gained a position on the south bank of the canal. Herring, whose post was cut off, immediately counter-attacked. He recaptured the position together with 20 prisoners and six machine-guns. During the night the Germans attacked repeatedly, but Herring's men responded to his bravery and initiative and held firm.

He was educated at Tottenham County School, where he was captain of the school at cricket and football.

DAVIES, John Thomas *Corporal, 11th (S) Bn., South Lancashire Regiment*
24 March 1918 – When his company was outflanked on both sides near Eppeville, France, he knew that the only line of withdrawal lay through a deep stream lined with a belt of barbed wire. To hold up the enemy as long as possible, he mounted the parapet, fully exposed, and fired his Lewis gun into the Germans and checked their advance sufficiently to allow part of his company to get across the obstacle. He was eventually captured and taken prisoner.
As he was not seen being captured the official Gazette *incorrectly related that he 'was in all probability killed at his gun'.*

ANDERSON, William Herbert *A/Lieutenant Colonel, commanding 12th (S) Bn., Highland Light Infantry*
25 March 1918 – As the Germans were about to overrun his flank at Bois Favières, near Maricourt, France, he hurried across the open under heavy fire, gathered his remaining companies together and led a counter-attack which drove the Germans back and captured twelve machine-guns and 70 prisoners. Later the same day, he was killed whilst leading another counter-attack which drove the enemy from their new position.

CROSS, Arthur Henry *A/Lance Corporal, 40th Bn., Machine-Gun Corps*
25 March 1918 – At Ervillers, France, he volunteered to reconnoitre a position recently captured by the enemy. He advanced alone to the position where he discovered two British machine-guns in enemy hands. Armed only with his revolver, he forced seven Germans to carry the guns with their tripods and ammunition back to the British lines. He handed over the prisoners, collected teams for the guns and immediately brought them into action against an attacking German force which was annihilated.
He lent his VC to David Niven to wear in the film Carrington VC.

TOYE, Alfred Maurice *A/Captain, 2nd Bn., Middlesex Regiment*
25 March 1918 – At Eterpigny Ridge, France, he recaptured a single post three times, before fighting his way through the enemy together with an officer and 6 men of his company. He then gathered together 70 men of his battalion and mounted an attack which held the line until reinforcements arrived. He later covered his battalion's retirement on two occasions and re-established a line that had been abandoned before his arrival.

YOUNG, Thomas (real name MORRELL) *Private, 1/9th (T) Bn., Durham Light Infantry*
25–31 March 1918 – Whilst working as a stretcher bearer at Bucquoy, France, he went out on nine separate occasions over five days to bring wounded men in from seemingly impossible places. He was under constant

rifle, machine-gun and shell fire and on several occasions dressed wounds in the open before carrying men in.

He enlisted as Young, his mother's maiden name.

MOUNTAIN, Albert *Sergeant, 15th/17th Bn., West Yorkshire Regiment*

26 March 1918 – As his company fell back at Hamelincourt, France, the enemy advanced in strength, preceded by an advanced guard of 200 men. He immediately offered to lead a counter-attack and with ten others went forward with a Lewis gun and killed about half of the German advanced guard. When the enemy main body appeared, Mountain steadied his small party and inspired them to hold 600 of the enemy for half an hour whilst the rest of his company retired. He then took command of the flank post of his battalion and held on there for twenty-seven hours before finally withdrawing.

HORSFALL, Basil Arthur *Second Lieutenant, 3rd (R) Bn., East Lancashire Regiment, attached 11th (S) Bn.*

27 March 1918 – During an enemy attack near Ablainzeville, France, his platoon was driven back and he was wounded in the head. He immediately reorganized his men, counter-attacked and regained his earlier position. He refused medical assistance and made a second successful counter-attack. When the order to withdraw was finally given, he was the last to leave his position. He was killed whilst retiring.

CASSIDY, Bernard Matthew *Second Lieutenant, 2nd Bn., Lancashire Fusiliers*

28 March 1918 – He was in command of the left company of his battalion at Arras, France, during the German offensive. He had been given orders that he must hold on to his position to the last and these orders he carried out to the letter. The enemy came on in overwhelming numbers but he rallied his men time and again. His company was eventually surrounded but he fought on until he was killed.

McDOUGALL, Stanley Robert *Sergeant, 47th Bn. (Queensland), Australian Imperial Force*

28 March 1918 – During an enemy attack at Dernancourt, France, the first wave broke through the Allied line. Acting on his own, he charged the second wave with rifle and bayonet, killing seven men and capturing a machine-gun. He turned the gun on the Germans, firing it from the hip, routing the entire wave. He then turned his attention to the enemy who had broken through the line, firing on them at close range until his ammunition ran out. After this he seized a bayonet and continued his attack, killing three men and an officer. His actions saved the line and stopped the enemy advance in its tracks.

WATSON, Oliver Cyril Spencer *A/Lieutenant Colonel, 1st City of London Yeomanry, commanding 5th Bn., King's Own Yorkshire Light Infantry*

28 March 1918 – At Rossignol Wood, north of Hebuterne, France, his command was continually subject to enemy attempts to pierce the line.

Leading a bombing party in an attempt to dislodge the enemy from two tactically important positions, his small party was outnumbered, and he ordered his men to withdraw. He stayed behind in a communication trench to cover their retirement, where he was killed.

FLOWERDEW, Gordon Muriel *Lieutenant, Lord Strathcona's Horse, Canadian Expeditionary Force*

30 March 1918 – As the men of his mounted squadron galloped through Bois de Moreuil, France, they came across two lines of Germans, each 60 strong, with machine-guns in the centre and on the flanks. He ordered his men to charge the lines. As they did so, the German machine-guns opened fire. The cavalrymen passed through both lines full tilt, cutting down Germans as they passed, before wheeling and riding through again. The Germans broke and fled in terror. By the end of the charge, 70 per cent of his squadron had been killed or wounded and Flowerdew himself had been shot through both thighs. He died the following day.

Haig's despatch noted: 'During the night, the enemy established a footing in Moreuil Wood, and on the following morning attacked on both sides of the River Luce. Our line in Moreuil Wood was restored by a brilliant counter-attack carried out by the Canadian Cavalry Brigade supported by the 3rd Cavalry Brigade'.

HARDY, Theodore Bailey *The Revd, T/Chaplain to the Forces, 4th Class, attached 8th (S) Bn., Lincolnshire Regiment*

5, 25 and 27 April 1918 – At Bucqouy, France, he tended a wounded officer 400 yards beyond the front line cut off by an enemy patrol. When a shell later exploded in a British post, he dug out the men who had been buried by the blast in spite of the danger posed by an unstable wall which threatened to fall on him as he worked. On a third occasion, he rescued a man who lay wounded 10 yards from a German pillbox.

STORKEY, Percy Valentine *Lieutenant, 19th Bn. (New South Wales), Australian Imperial Force*

7 April 1918 – At Bois de Hangard, France, he, together with another officer and 10 men, charged a German position containing 80–100 men. His small party drove the enemy out, killed or wounded 30 Germans and captured 50 men and a machine-gun.

He was later a judge on the District Court Northern Circuit, New South Wales.

THE BATTLE OF THE LYS

Haig wrote that 'the possibility of an early attack' in the Lys sector, between Béthune and Ypres, now 'became a matter for immediate consideration'. It was held by one Portuguese and three British divisions, and he arranged for the Portuguese to be replaced and the British reinforced by divisions resting after the Somme, but this was not complete when the Germans attacked with seventeen divisions at about 4 a.m. on 9 April. Originally planned as a diversion to the attack on the Somme, it was now launched as an attempt to force a decision by breaking through the front towards Hazebrouck then to continue towards Béthune and to the south. The attack was again preceded by a gas and high-explosive bombardment, and began in thick fog.

By the end of the first day a large breach had been effected between Givenchy and Bois Greniers, about 10 miles to the north. On the 10th the attack was renewed and extended north to the Messines Ridge; Messines was lost but retaken by the South African Brigade that afternoon. On the 11th Germans advanced to a line between Merville and Hollebeke, another two to three miles: their progress in the south had not been matched in the north, where Allied reinforcements had provided a check, but the British had pulled back from Messines. Haig issued his famous special order of the day.

> Three weeks ago today the enemy began his terrific attacks against us on a fifty-mile front. His objectives are to separate us from the French, to take the Channel ports and destroy the British army.
>
> In spite of already throwing 106 divisions into the battle and enduring the most reckless sacrifice of human life, he has as yet made little progress towards his goals.
>
> We owe this to the determined fighting and self-sacrifice of our troops. Words fail me to express the admiration which I feel for the splendid resistance offered by all ranks of our army under the most trying circumstances.
>
> Many amongst us are now tired. To those I would say that Victory will belong to the side which holds out the longest. The French army is moving rapidly and in great force to our support.
>
> There is no other course open to us but to fight it out. Every position must be held to the last man: there must be no retirement. With our backs to the wall and believing in the justice of our cause each one of us must fight on to the end. The safety of our homes and the Freedom of mankind alike depend upon the conduct of each one of us at this critical moment.

By the 13th reinforcements in the south had prevented the capture of Hazebrouck – the advance was held up all day by desperate fighting, in which the Allies' advanced posts fought with great tenacity, holding their ground even though entirely surrounded, as men stood back to back in the trenches, shooting to front and rear. A renewed attack on the 18th was defeated.

The sector was relatively quiet for a week, then after a diversionary attack at Villers-Brétonneux notable both for the first engagement between German and British tanks and for the skill of the Australian Brigade in its counter-attack, on 25 April nine divisions attacked the French and British positions in the Lys sector from Bailleul to the Ypres–Commines Canal. Its objective, Mt Kemmel, was taken by about 10 a.m., and on 26/27 April the Allies withdrew another mile, to a position that with some small improvements was held when the German attack ended. Givenchy, Festubert and Hazebrouck had not been captured, and the Germans had taken a hundred thousand casualties.

COLLIN, Joseph Henry *Second Lieutenant, 1/4th Bn., King's Own (Royal Lancaster Regiment)*
9 April 1918 – After his platoon of sixteen men had been reduced to five at Orchard Keep, Givenchy, he withdrew slowly, contesting every inch of ground. He put one German machine-gun out of action with a Mills bomb, before climbing onto the parapet and firing at another with a Lewis gun until he fell mortally wounded.

MASTERS, Richard George *Private, Royal Army Service Corps, attached 141st Field Ambulance*
9 April 1918 – After an enemy attack at Béthune, France, communications had been cut off, the road had been reported impassable and the wounded were not being evacuated. Masters volunteered to drive the wounded to safety. He cleared debris from the road as he passed along and made many trips under machine-gun and shell fire. He succeeded in evacuating most of the wounded single-handed.
He also won the Croix de Guerre for rescuing wounded men trapped in a quarry on the Somme.

SCHOFIELD, John *T/Second Lieutenant, 2/5th Bn., Lancashire Fusiliers*
9 April 1918 – Whilst leading a party of nine men against a German strongpoint at Givenchy, France, they were attacked by about a hundred of the enemy. His party returned fire with a Lewis gun and 20 of the Germans were captured. He then led his men on towards the front line where they met another large German force in a communication trench. His party opened rapid fire once again and the enemy surrendered. As a result 123 Germans were taken prisoner. Schofield was killed a few minutes later.

DOUGALL, Eric Stuart *A/Captain, Special Reserve, attached A Bty., 88th Bde, Royal Field Artillery*
10 April 1918 – During the withdrawal from Messines, he moved his guns to the top of a ridge. The infantry were being pressed back so he rallied them, supplied them with Lewis guns and formed a line in front of his guns, telling them, 'So long as you stick to your trenches, I will keep my guns here.' As a result, the German advance was checked for twelve

hours. In the evening, the battery received orders to withdraw. The guns were manhandled over 800 yards of shell-cratered ground under intense machine-gun fire.

POULTER, Arthur *Private, 1/4th Bn., Duke of Wellington's (West Riding) Regiment*
    10 April 1918 – At Lys, France, he carried 10 badly wounded men, one after the other, through heavy machine-gun and artillery fire. Two of the men were again shot whilst on his back. During the withdrawal over the River Lys, he ran back in full view of the enemy and carried away another man who had been left behind. He then bandaged 40 men under fire and was seriously wounded while attempting another rescue.
    After the war, Poulter's young son took the VC out of his father's drawer and swapped it with another boy for a bag of marbles. When the transaction was discovered, the medal was returned (as presumably were the marbles).

FORBES-ROBERTSON, James *A/Lieutenant Colonel, commanding 1st Bn., Border Regiment*
    11–12 April 1918 – Near Vieux Berquin, France, he conducted a mounted reconnaissance under heavy fire, before leading a counter-attack which re-established the line. His horse was shot under him but he continued on foot. The following day he covered the retreat. He organized, encouraged and cajoled his men until he had established a line to which they could withdraw.

PRYCE, Thomas Tannatt *A/Captain, 4th Bn., Grenadier Guards*
    11 April 1918 – At Vieux Berquin, France, he killed 7 Germans whilst leading an attack on a village. The following morning his men beat off four attacks on their position but by evening the enemy had approached to within 60 yards. He led a bayonet charge which drove them back 100 yards, but the enemy approached again in greater numbers. By now he had only 17 men left but he mounted another charge. He was last seen engaged in fierce hand-to-hand fighting.
    Haig wrote of the 4th Guards Brigade at Vieux Berquin on 11–13 April: 'No more brilliant exploit has taken place since the opening of the enemy's offensive, though gallant actions have been without number.'

CROWE, John James *Second Lieutenant, 2nd Bn., Worcestershire Regiment*
    14 April 1918 – He twice went forward at Neuve Église, Belgium, with two NCOs and seven men, to engage the enemy. On both occasions, he forced the Germans to withdraw from a position they were taking on high ground. Then, accompanied by just two men, he attacked two enemy machine-guns which were sweeping his post. He killed both gun crews and captured the guns.
    Recognizing the need for vegetables at the front during the early part of the

war, he turned the area around his quarters into a vegetable garden. The French government rewarded his efforts with the Diploma d'Honneur de l'Encouragement.

COUNTER, Jack Thomas *Private, 1st Bn., King's (Liverpool) Regiment*
   16 April 1918 – At Boisieux St-Marc, France, information had to be obtained from the front line but the only way to get there was along a sunken road swept by German machine-gun fire. Six men had tried to run this road, one after the other, but each man had been shot and killed in full view of his comrades. Counter volunteered to make the journey. He reached the front line and obtained the required information, and then turned round and delivered the information back to company headquarters. As a result, a successful counter-attack was launched.
   Arriving back in Blandford Forum he received a huge civic welcome, during which he was paraded in a landau through the crowded streets.

WOODALL, Joseph Edward *Lance Sergeant, 1st Bn., Rifle Brigade*
   22 April 1918 – When his platoon was held up by a machine-gun at La Pannerie, France, he rushed forward alone and captured the gun and eight prisoners. He then led an attack on an enemy-held farmhouse which secured 30 more prisoners. Shortly afterwards, when the officer in charge was killed, he took command and reorganized two platoons which he deployed skilfully throughout the day.

HEWITSON, James *Lance Corporal, 1/4th Bn., King's Own (Royal Lancaster Regiment)*
   26 April 1918 – He led an attack on a series of German crater posts at Givenchy, France. In one dugout, he killed six men who would not surrender. He then observed a hostile machine-gun coming into action in a crater so worked his way round it before attacking and killing the gunners. Shortly afterwards, he routed a German bombing party as it attacked a Lewis gun post, killing six of the party.
   He was a true victim of the war. He suffered mental problems and spent more than sixteen years in mental institutions.

THE THIRD BATTLE OF THE AISNE

In late May, Germany executed a highly successful attack on French and British positions on the Chemin des Dames Ridge. The British had four divisions in the front lines, which were destroyed by a surprise bombardment on 27 May: by nightfall the Germans had crossed the River Vesle and by the 30th the Marne. Allied counter-attacks and German difficulties with supplies and reserves prevented further progress.

GROGAN, George William St George *T/Brigadier General, Worcestershire Regiment, commanding 23rd Infantry Brigade*

27 May 1918 – Whilst in command of remnants of infantry at the River Aisne, France, he rode up and down encouraging his troops, reorganizing them and leading back into the line those who were about to retire. He was under artillery, trench-mortar, rifle and machine-gun fire throughout and was forced to walk the line for a while when his horse was shot from beneath him. As a result of his example the line held.

THE BATTLE OF THE MARNE

On 15 July, the Germans began a renewed offensive from the Marne towards Reims with twenty-five divisions, against two French armies (including two American divisions). Although the Marne was crossed on the first day, the advance stalled, and was thrown back by a counter-attack on the 18th by French, British and American forces. According to Haig, its 'complete success ... marked the turning-point in this year's campaign, and commenced the second phase of the Allied operations.' By 3 August the Germans were back east of the Aisne and Vesle.

MEIKLE, John *Sergeant, 1/4th (T) Bn., Seaforth Highlanders*

20 July 1918 – When his company was held up by machine-gun fire near Marfaux he rushed the position single-handed. He emptied his revolver into the crews of the two guns and put the remainder out of action with a heavy stick. When another machine-gun checked progress shortly afterwards, he again rushed forward but was killed almost at the gun position.

THE BATTLE OF AMIENS

On 8 August 1918 the British III Corps, and the Australian and Canadian Corps (of three, five and four divisions respectively), with 342 Mark V heavy and 732 light Whippet tanks, and supported by around 800 aircraft, attacked east of Amiens with the Somme as their left flank: the front was more than 11 miles from 'just south of the Amiens–Roye road to Morlancourt exclusive'. The French made a supporting attack immediately to the south. By midday Allied forces had reached their objectives, and by nightfall had advanced between six and seven miles. Haig particularly praised the 'brilliant and predominating part taken by the Canadian and Australian Corps'. The Germans, victims of a deception campaign, were taken by surprise: they suffered thirty thousand casualties and lost 300–400 guns. As Ludendorff famously recorded, it was 'the black day of the German army'.

By the evening of the 12th Allied infantry had reached the old German

Somme defences of 1916. North of the Somme they were approaching the outskirts of Bray-sur-Somme. The troops now faced a derelict battle area, rutted with old trench lines and pitted with shell holes, crossed in all directions with tangles of barbed wire, and eerily overgrown by the wild vegetation of two years. This grim terrain, however, offered good opportunities for setting up machine-gun posts.

BRILLANT, Jean *Lieutenant, 2nd Bn. (Eastern Ontario), Canadian Expeditionary Force*

8–9 August 1918 – During the advance of his company near Meharicourt, France, he rushed and captured an enemy machine-gun, personally killing two of the crew. Despite receiving a wound, he then led two platoons in an attack on a machine-gun nest which captured a hundred and fifty Germans and fifteen machine-guns. He personally killed five Germans and was wounded again but refused to retire. He then detected an enemy field gun, and was leading a party towards it when he received two more wounds and fell unconscious. Over the two days he advanced 12 miles.

He died the following day.

CROAK, John Bernard *Private, 13th Bn. (Royal Highlanders of Canada), Canadian Expeditionary Force*

8 August 1918 – While separated from his section during an attack at Amiens he bombed a machine-gun nest, capturing the gun and crew. Despite being severely wounded, he rejoined his platoon. Almost at once, he charged another machine-gun nest, followed closely by the remainder of his platoon. Three machine-guns were captured and the entire enemy garrison was bayoneted or captured. He was wounded again and died as a result.

GABY, Alfred Edward *Lieutenant, 28th Bn. (Western Australia), Australian Imperial Force*

8 August 1918 – Whilst leading his company from the front at Villers-Bretonneux, France, his advance was checked by four enemy machine-guns and numerous riflemen located in a strongpoint. Creeping forward alone, he slipped through a gap in the wire and emptied his revolver into the German garrison, who quickly surrendered. He captured 50 Germans as well as four machine-guns. He then reorganized his men and led them on to their final objective.

GOOD, Herman James *Corporal, 13th Bn. (Royal Highlanders of Canada), Canadian Expeditionary Force*

8 August 1918 – When his company was held up during an attack at Hangard Wood, France, by heavy fire from three machine-guns he dashed forward alone, killed several of the enemy and captured the remainder. He later collected three men of his section and charged a battery of 5.9in guns, capturing the guns and their crews.

His mother later recalled her reaction on hearing that her son had been gassed on the day after his VC action: 'I can't say that Victoria Crosses meant a great deal just then.'

MINER, Herbert Garnet Bedford *Corporal, 58th Bn. (Central Ontario), Canadian Expeditionary Force*

8 August 1918 – Despite being badly wounded, he single-handedly rushed an enemy machine-gun post at Demuin, killing the entire crew before turning the gun on the Germans. He then attacked a second machine-gun post with two others, putting the gun out of action. His final action was to charge alone at an enemy bombing post. He bayoneted two of the garrison and put the remainder to flight but was mortally wounded as he did so.

TAIT, James Edward *Lieutenant, 78th Bn. (Winnipeg Grenadiers), Canadian Expeditionary Force*

8–11 August 1918 – When his company's advance at Amiens was checked, he rallied the men and led them forward with great skill and dash under a hail of bullets. Taking a rifle and bayonet, he charged forward alone and killed an enemy machine-gunner who was causing many casualties. Inspired by his example, his men rushed the position and captured twelve machine-guns. During a later enemy counter-attack he continued to direct and aid his men though he was himself mortally wounded.

BEATHAM, Robert Matthew *Private, 8th Bn. (Victoria), Australian Imperial Force*

9 August 1918 – When the advance at Rosières was held up by heavy machine-gun fire, he dashed forward and, assisted by one man, attacked the crews of four enemy machine-guns, killing ten of them and capturing ten others. As the final objective was reached, he dashed forward again, although wounded, and bombed a machine-gun. As he did so he was riddled with bullets and killed.

BRERETON, Alexander Picton *A/Corporal, 8th Bn. (90th Rifles), Canadian Expeditionary Force*

9 August 1918 – When machine-guns opened fire on his platoon at Aubrecourt, France, and no cover was available, he ran forward alone, reached one of the machine-gun posts, shot the man operating the gun and bayoneted the man who tried to replace him. Nine Germans then surrendered to him. His action inspired his platoon to charge and capture the five remaining posts.

COPPINS, Frederick George *Corporal, 8th Bn. (90th Rifles), Canadian Expeditionary Force*

9 August 1918 – When his platoon came under unexpected machine-gun fire at Hackett Woods, near Amiens, France, he called on four men to follow him and ran forward. He was wounded and the four men with him killed but he reached the guns, killed the operator of the first gun and three of the crew and made prisoners of four others. Despite his wound, he continued with his platoon to the final objective and only left the line when ordered to do so.

HARRIS, Thomas James *Sergeant, 6th (S) Bn., Queen's Own Royal West Kent Regiment*

9 August 1918 – When the advance at Morlancourt, France, was impeded by hostile machine-guns concealed in crops and shell holes, he led his section against a gun, capturing it and killing seven Germans. He then single-handedly attacked another gun, capturing it and killing the crew, but was himself killed as he attacked a third gun. Throughout he showed total disregard for his own safety.

ZENGEL, Raphael Louis *Sergeant, 5th Bn. (Western Cavalry), Canadian Expeditionary Force*

9 August 1918 – Whilst leading his platoon in an attack near Warvillers, France, he rushed 200 yards ahead and tackled a machine-gun emplacement on his own, killing an officer and dispersing the crew. Later, when his battalion was held up by heavy machine-gun fire, he directed return fire with destructive results until he was knocked unconscious. The instant he regained consciousness, several minutes later, he resumed firing at the enemy.

DINESEN, Thomas *Private, 42nd Bn. (Royal Highlanders of Canada), Canadian Expeditionary Force*

12 August 1918 – He displayed continuous bravery during ten hours of hand-to-hand fighting at Parvillers, France, which resulted in the capture of over a mile of strongly garrisoned and stubbornly defended enemy trenches. On five separate occasions he rushed forward alone and put enemy guns out of action. He accounted for 12 Germans with bombs and bayonet.

Before he joined the Canadians, he had been turned down by the British, French and US forces. He was the brother of Karen Blixen, the author of Out of Africa, *and between 1921 and 1923 lived in a cottage on her farm in Kenya. He was himself the author of* No Man's Land *and* Twilight on the Betz.

SPALL, Robert *Sergeant, Princess Patricia's Canadian Light Infantry, Canadian Expeditionary Force*

12/13 August 1918 – When his platoon was isolated during an enemy counter-attack at Parvillers, France, he mounted the parapet with a Lewis gun and fired at the advancing enemy. He then directed his men into a sap 75 yards from the enemy, before climbing again onto the parapet and firing at the Germans. While holding up the enemy in this way, he was killed.

STATTON, Percy Clyde *Sergeant, 40th Bn. (Tasmania), Australian Imperial Force*

12 August 1918 – He engaged two machine-gun posts with Lewis-gun fire at Proyart, France, enabling his battalion to advance. Then, armed only with a revolver, he rushed four enemy machine-gun posts in succession, putting two out of action and killing five Germans. The remaining two posts were evacuated. Later, he went out under heavy fire and brought in two badly wounded men.

THE BATTLES OF THE SOMME AND ARRAS

Haig now decided to attack to the north, between Albert and Arras, where his tanks could be put to good use and where the Germans seemed ill-prepared, hoping thereby to 'turn the line of the Somme south of Peronne', with the strategic objective of St-Quentin and Cambrai. At 4.55 a.m. on 21 August, five divisions attacked in thick fog and reached the first day's objective, the Arras–Albert railway, having taken more than two thousand prisoners. The despatch noted particularly the hard fighting around Logeast Wood and Achiet-le-Petit. Albert was taken the next day. On the 29th the New Zealanders took Bapaume, and by nightfall Allied infantry had reached the left bank of the Somme on the whole front from the neighbourhood of Nesle north to Peronne. It now became clear that the Germans had reached a point at which they were prepared to stand, and the fight for Mont-St-Quentin and Peronne was met with determined opposition, but was success-ful. On 2 September the Drocourt–Quéant line was taken, and that night the Germans fell back to the Canal du Nord.

BEAK, Daniel Marcus William *T/Commander, Royal Naval Volunteer Reserve (Drake Bn.)*
21 August, 25 August and 4 September 1918 – Due to his skilful and fearless leadership at Logeast Wood, France, four enemy positions were captured under heavy fire. Four days later, though dazed by a shell frag-ment, he reorganized the whole brigade under heavy fire and led his men to their objective. When an attack was held up, he rushed forward accom-panied by only a runner and broke up a nest of machine-guns, personally bringing back nine or ten prisoners. On another occasion, his courage and leadership inspired the advance of his own and a neighbouring unit.
He was General Officer Commanding Malta, 1942. His VC, DSO and MC and bar group was sold at Spink in November 2003 for a world-record price of £155,000.

SMITH, Edward Benn *Lance Sergeant, 1/5th (T) Bn., Lancashire Fusiliers*
21–23 August 1918 – Whilst in command of his platoon near Serre, France, he charged alone at a machine-gun post, armed only with a rifle and bayonet. The enemy instantly scattered to throw hand grenades at him, but he shot and killed at least six of them. Later, observing another platoon in need of assistance, he led his men to them, took command of the situation and captured the objective.

A local newspaper described him in the following terms: 'Sergeant Smith is not only a VC but looks it. He is a British soldier every inch of him. He is an A1 man from the crown of his head to the soles of his feet. There is not a C3 part of him. He has not only won the VC but he has a chest on which to display it.' At the time, aged nineteen years nine months, he was the youngest VC holder in the army. At the outbreak of the Second World War, he was commissioned and killed in action in January 1940.

WEST, Richard Annesley *A/Lieutenant Colonel, North Irish Horse (SR), seconded 6th Bn., Tank Corps*

21 August, 2 September 1918 – On 21 August, when the infantry lost their bearings during an attack in dense fog at Courcelles, France, he collected and reorganized any men he could find and led them to their objective under heavy machine-gun fire. On 2 September 1918 he arrived at the front line at Vaulx Vraucourt as the enemy were counter-attacking. Aware the infantry might give way, he rode up and down in front of the men under brutal machine-gun and rifle fire encouraging them and calling, 'Stick it, men. Show them fight and for God's sake put up a good fight!' He fell riddled by machine-gun bullets.

ONIONS, George *Lance Corporal, 1st Bn., Devonshire Regiment*

22 August 1918 – Having been sent out with another man to make contact with the battalion on the right flank of his unit at Achiet-le-Petit, France, he observed the enemy advancing in great numbers. He and his comrade placed themselves on the flank of the advancing enemy and opened rapid fire. The Germans began to waver and some hands went up. He then rushed forward and with his comrade's assistance took two hundred of the enemy prisoner and marched them back to his company commander.

He had served in Ireland in 1916.

JOYNT, William Donovan *Lieutenant, 8th Bn. (Victoria), Australian Imperial Force*

23 August 1918 – During the attack on Herleville Wood, France, he took charge of his company after its commander had been killed. When the troops of the leading battalion began to waver, he rushed forward under heavy machine-gun and artillery fire and reorganized the men. Realizing that fire from the wood was checking the whole advance, he led a magnificent frontal bayonet attack. Later, after severe hand-to-hand fighting at Plateau Wood, he overcame a stubborn defence. He continued until he was badly wounded by a shell.

McCARTHY, Lawrence Dominic *Lieutenant, 16th Bn. (South Australia and Western Australia), Australian Imperial Force*

23 August 1918 – During an attack near Madame Wood, east of Vermandovillers, France, he dashed with two men towards an enemy machine-gun post. He outpaced his comrades and on his own captured the gun and continued down the trench, inflicting heavy casualties and capturing three more machine-guns. By this time he had been caught up by one of his comrades and together they continued to bomb the trench until contact was established with an adjoining unit. During this action, he killed 20 of the enemy and captured five machine-guns and 50 prisoners.

McIVER, Hugh *Private, 2nd Bn., Royal Scots*
    23 August 1918 – Whilst employed as a company runner near Courcelle-le-Compte, France, he pursued an enemy scout alone into a machine-gun post where he killed 6 of the garrison and captured 20 prisoners and two machine-guns. Later, at great personal risk and at close range, he stopped the fire of a British tank directed in error at British troops.
    He was killed on 2 September, south of Montdidier.

FORSYTH, Samuel *Sergeant, New Zealand Engineers, attached 2nd Bn., Auckland Infantry Regiment, New Zealand Expeditionary Force*
    24 August 1918 – When his company came under heavy machine-gun fire at Grevillers he led attacks on three machine-gun positions and captured their crews. He then got support from a tank in an attack on several other guns. When the tank was put out of action, he led the tank crew and several of his men in a charge which put the guns out of action. At the moment of victory, he was killed by a sniper.

MacINTYRE, David Lowe *T/Lieutenant, Argyll and Sutherland Highlanders, attached 1/6th (T) Bn., Highland Light Infantry*
    24–27 August 1918 – Whilst acting as adjutant of his battalion near Henin and Fontaine, Croisilles, France, his gallantry and leadership inspired those around him. During an attack, he supervised the cutting of gaps in a strong barbed-wire entanglement. He then rallied a small party which hunted down an enemy machine-gun detachment, killing three and capturing one officer, ten men and five guns. On another occasion, he rushed an enemy machine-gun single-handed, putting its crew to flight and capturing the gun.

COLLEY, Harold John *A/Sergeant, 10th (S) Bn., Lancashire Fusiliers*
    25 August 1918 – During an enemy counter-attack at Martinpuich, France, he ran forward without orders to assist two platoons in advance of his own which had been instructed to hold on at all costs. He rallied the platoons and threatened to shoot any man who retreated. The enemy were by now advancing quickly, so he formed a defensive flank and held it. The enemy were prevented from breaking through but out of the two platoons only three men remained unwounded. Colley himself received a fatal stomach wound.

GORDON, Bernard Sidney *Lance Corporal, 41st Bn. (Queensland), Australian Imperial Force*
    26–27 August 1918 – During an assault at Fargny Wood near Bray, France, he attacked an enemy machine-gun single-handed, killing the gun

ner and capturing the post which contained one officer and ten men. He then cleared more trenches and captured 51 prisoners and five machine-guns practically unaided.

JUDSON, Reginald Stanley *Sergeant, 1st Bn., Auckland Infantry Regiment, New Zealand Expeditionary Force*

26 August 1918 – During an attack on enemy positions near Bapaume, France, he led a small bombing party through heavy fire and captured a machine-gun. Proceeding up the sap alone, he bombed three more machine-gun crews. He ordered a fleeing group of two officers and ten men to surrender but they fired at him, so he threw a bomb and jumped amongst them, killing two and capturing two machine-guns.

RUTHERFORD, Charles Smith *Lieutenant, 5th Bn. (Western Cavalry), Canadian Expeditionary Force*

26 August 1918 – Finding himself a long way ahead of his men at Monchy, France, he observed an armed enemy party outside a pillbox ahead of him. He beckoned to the Germans to come to him; in return they waved to him to come to them. This he did and informed them that he was taking them prisoner. They disputed this at first but he persuaded them by bluff that they were surrounded. As a result, 45 Germans (including 2 officers and with three machine-guns) surrendered to him. When his men finally caught up with him, he attacked another pillbox with a Lewis-gun section and captured a further 35 prisoners with machine-guns.

In 1942 he was posted to Nassau in the Bahamas, where he guarded the Duke and Duchess of Windsor during the Duke's governorship of the colony.

WEALE, Henry *Lance Corporal, 14th (R) Bn., Royal Welch Fusiliers*

26 August 1918 – When an adjacent battalion was held up by enemy machine-guns at Bazentin-le-Grand, France, he was ordered to deal with the posts. When his Lewis gun failed, he rushed at the nearest post and killed the crew. He then went for the others, the crews of which fled on his approach.

CLARK-KENNEDY, William Hew *Lieutenant Colonel, commanding 24th Bn. (Victoria Rifles of Canada), Canadian Expeditionary Force*

27–28 August 1918 – When the brigade of which his battalion was part came under heavy shell and machine-gun fire, he inspired his men through sheer personality and initiative. On several occasions he led parties straight at machine-gun nests. By the afternoon his battalion had secured their objectives. Despite being severely wounded the next morning, he refused to be evacuated for several hours, by which time a position had been gained from which the advance could be continued.

He was mistakenly reported killed at the Second Battle of Ypres, 1915.

SEWELL, Cecil Harold *Lieutenant, Royal West Kent Regiment, attached 3rd (Light) Bn., Tank Corps*

29 August 1918 – Whilst in command of a section of Whippet light tanks at Fremicourt, France, he got out of his own tank and crossed open ground under heavy shell and machine-gun fire to rescue the crew of another tank which had side-slipped into a shell hole, overturned and caught fire. The door of the tank had become jammed against the side of the shell hole so he dug away the earth around the door to release it. As he was doing so, he was killed.

CARTWRIGHT, George *Private, 33rd Bn. (New South Wales), Australian Imperial Force*

31 August 1918 – When two companies were held up by machine-gun fire during the assault on Road Wood near Péronne, France, he attacked the gun, shooting three of the team, capturing the gun and taking nine prisoners. This immediately galvanized the whole line into rushing forward.

HUFFAM, James Palmer *Second Lieutenant, 5th Bn., Duke of Wellington's (West Riding) Regiment, attached 2nd Bn.*

31 August 1918 – He rushed an enemy machine-gun post with three men at St-Servin's Farm, France, and captured the position. Attacked, he withdrew fighting, carrying back a wounded comrade. Later that night, accompanied by two men, he attacked another machine-gun post, capturing eight prisoners and allowing the advance to continue.

BUCKLEY, Alexander Henry *T/Corporal, 54th Bn. (New South Wales), Australian Imperial Force*

1 September 1918 – With one other man, he rushed an enemy machine-gun nest at Péronne, France, shooting 4 of the occupants and taking 22 prisoners. Later, attempting to rush another nest, he was killed.

CURREY, William Matthew *Private, 53rd Bn. (New South Wales), Australian Imperial Force*

1 September 1918 – When his battalion suffered heavy casualties from a 77mm field gun at Péronne, France, he rushed forward under intense machine-gun fire and captured the gun single-handedly after killing its entire crew. He later engaged an enemy strongpoint with a Lewis gun before rushing the post and causing many casualties. He subsequently volunteered to carry orders for the withdrawal of an isolated company, which he succeeded in doing in spite of artillery and rifle fire.

GRANT, John Gilroy *Sergeant, 1st Bn., Wellington Infantry Regiment, New Zealand Expeditionary Force*

1 September 1918 – When his platoon reached a crest during an attack on high ground near Bancourt, France, it was found that a line of five enemy machine-gun posts offered a serious obstacle to any further advance. Grant, closely followed by a comrade, rushed forward ahead of the platoon and gained two of the posts in quick succession. His bravery took the Germans by surprise and the posts were quickly mopped up by his men.

HALL, Arthur Charles *Corporal, 54th Bn. (New South Wales), Australian Imperial Force*

1–2 September 1918 – During the attack at Péronne, France, he rushed a machine-gun post single-handed, shooting four of the occupants and capturing nine others and two machine-guns. He carried on ahead of the main party and captured many small groups of prisoners and machine-guns. The following day, during a heavy barrage, he carried a seriously wounded comrade to safety before returning to his post.

LOWERSON, Albert David *Sergeant, 21st Bn. (Victoria), Australian Imperial Force*

1 September 1918 – During the attack at Mont-St-Quentin, near Péronne, France, an attacking party was held up by a strong position defended by twelve machine-guns. He gathered seven men together and led them through sniper and machine-gun fire against the post. All twelve guns and 30 prisoners were captured. Despite being wounded in the right thigh, he refused to leave the front line until the prisoners had been dealt with and the post was consolidated.

MACTIER, Robert *Private, 23rd Bn. (Victoria), Australian Imperial Force*

1 September 1918 – After bombing patrols had failed to clear up several enemy strongpoints during the attack at Mont-St-Quentin, near Péronne, France, he jumped alone out of his trench and charged at the positions, armed with bombs and a revolver. First he attacked and killed an entire machine-gun team of eight men. Next he jumped into a post where eight men surrendered. He then disposed of a machine-gun that had been enfilading advancing troops. Finally, whilst attacking another gun, he was shot and killed.

NUNNEY, Claude Joseph Patrick *Private, 38th Bn. (Ottawa), Canadian Expeditionary Force*

1–2 September 1918 – As his battalion was preparing to advance at Vis-en-Artois, France, the enemy laid down a heavy barrage and launched a counter-attack. He went immediately from company headquarters to the outpost lines, where he encouraged the men by his fearless example. The attack was repulsed. The following day his leadership and courage helped to carry the company forward to its objective but he received a severe wound from which he died sixteen days later.

TOWNER, Edgar Thomas *Lieutenant, 2nd Bn., Australian Machine Gun Corps, Australian Imperial Force*

1 September 1918 – Whilst in charge of four Vickers guns during the attack on Mont-St-Quentin near Péronne, France, he captured a machine-gun which he turned on the enemy, inflicting great losses and capturing 25 prisoners. When short of ammunition, he secured another enemy gun, causing the Germans to retire further. Despite being wounded, he maintained the fire and carried out reconnaissance on enemy movements for thirty hours until he was evacuated. His actions contributed greatly to the success of the attack.

He was later a Fellow of the Royal Geographical Society of Australia, and received the Doctor Thomas Foundation Gold Medal in 1956 for his geographical work.

DOYLE, Martin *Company Sergeant Major, 1st Bn., Royal Munster Fusiliers*

Martin Doyle, born on 25 October 1894 in New Ross, Co. Wexford, won his Victoria Cross during fighting near Riencourt, France, on 2 September 1918. He had enlisted in the British army at the age of fifteen in 1909 (he claimed to be seventeen), and served for nine years and five months. He was demobilized in July 1919 but continued to work for the British army, and it was during this period that Doyle became a servant of two masters – he joined the IRA and began acting as an intelligence officer in the Mid-Clare Brigade. His role was to pass information on to his IRA superiors. He remained undetected by the British, and following the truce of 1922 he joined the new Irish army, which he served until 1939. Unsurprisingly perhaps, British accounts of his Victoria Cross glory neglect to mention his subsequent role in the IRA, whilst his Irish Defence Force records do not mention that he was the holder of the VC and the Military Medal. Doyle has managed to become at once a hero and an embarrassment to both the British and Irish armies.

Doyle, the only son of Larry Doyle, a 'worker of the land', and his wife Bridget, joined the 18th Royal Irish Regiment in 1909 and was immediately sent to serve in India. In December 1914, now serving with the Royal Dublin Fusiliers, he was posted to France. He fought in the Battle of Mons and was promoted sergeant in 1915. He rose to become company sergeant major and was transferred to 1st Battalion, Royal Munster Fusiliers. On 24 March 1918, at Hattenfield, France, his unit was under machine-gun fire from a barn situated in no-man's land in front of the German lines. Doyle called for volunteers and led a bayonet charge. Arriving alone at the barn, he bayoneted the gunners and seized the gun. Later in the day, he was captured and roughly treated but was released after a successful counter-attack by his regiment. For his action that day, Doyle was awarded the Military Medal.

The action for which he won the Victoria Cross took place at Riencourt on 2 September 1918. Doyle took command of his company after all his officers had become casualties and rescued a number of men who had become surrounded by the enemy. He then carried a wounded officer to safety under heavy fire, before spotting a British tank in difficulties. The tank crew were all wounded and under heavy machine-gun fire from a

German trench. Doyle ran along the trench alone until he found the machine-gun, which he knocked out, capturing 3 of its crew. He then returned to the tank. By now it was on fire and surrounded by Germans, but he managed to rescue a badly wounded sergeant, whom he brought to safety. That evening, the Germans launched an attack but the company was able to withstand the assault and to capture a large number of German prisoners, due to Doyle's inspiration and leadership.

He was presented with his Victoria Cross by King George V at Buckingham Palace on 8 May 1919. On his return to New Ross, he was given a hero's welcome by the townspeople, and on 25 November he married Charlotte Kennedy and set up home in the town.

It was at this time that his republican sympathies came to the fore. As far as the IRA were concerned his British war record would have made him the ideal candidate for work as an informant. Having been demobilized in July 1919, he continued working for the British army at their 'Home Barracks' in Ennis. He would have been party to information that would prove invaluable to the IRA. On one occasion, the British became so suspicious of his activities that he requested of his IRA superiors to be allowed to leave 'with his rifle' for the hills. He was persuaded to remain, which gives an indication of how effective his intelligence was proving. At one point, he was sent to Kilrush on a mission for the rebels during which he very nearly stepped into a trap, escaping 'only by the skin of his teeth'. On a subsequent occasion, he is known to have supplied stolen arms to local rebels.

After the truce of July 1921, Doyle joined the new Irish army, and was stationed during the Civil War in Waterford, Kilkenny and South Tipperary. In 1924, he re-enlisted into the peace-time army and was posted to 20 Infantry Battalion, where he became company sergeant major in D Company. He remained in the army for the next thirteen years, serving for part of the time in the School of Instruction as a rifle and Vickers machine-gun instructor. By 1937, with a wife and three daughters to support, he left the service (with some difficulty – the army was very reluctant to see him go) and took up a job with the Guinness Brewery as security officer. He did not sever all his links with the military, however. He joined 2 Battalion, Dublin Army Reserve, with which he remained until January 1939. Not long afterwards, on 20 November 1940, he died at the age of forty-six. He is buried at the Grangegorman British Military Cemetery in Dublin.

EVANS, Arthur Walter (also known as SIMPSON, Walter) *Lance Sergeant, 6th (S) Bn., Lincolnshire Regiment*

2 September 1918 – Whilst on daylight patrol beside a river near Étaing, France, he spotted an enemy machine-gun post on the opposite bank. He swam across the river, crept up to the rear of the post and shot the sentry and a second man who ran out. Four Germans immediately surrendered. He was then joined by other members of his patrol, but a machine-gun opened up and he was forced to cover the withdrawal of the patrol under difficult conditions.

HARVEY, Jack *Private, 1/22nd Bn., London Regiment*
2 September 1918 – When the advance of his company was held up by intense machine-gun fire near Clery, France, he dashed forward 50 yards through the fire and rushed a machine-gun, shooting two of its team and bayoneting another. Continuing along the enemy trench, he rushed a dugout which contained 37 Germans and forced them to surrender.

HUTCHESON, Bellenden Seymour *Captain, Canadian Army Medical Corps, attached 75th Bn. (Mississauga), Canadian Expeditionary Force*
2 September 1918 – In France, while advancing through the Quéant–Drocourt support line with his battalion, he remained on the field until every wounded man had been attended to. He dressed the wounds of a seriously wounded officer under terrific machine-gun and artillery fire, and with the assistance of prisoners and of his own men, succeeded in evacuating him to safety. He then rushed out to a wounded sergeant whom he placed in a shell hole and treated.

METCALF, William Henry *Lance Corporal, 16th Bn. (The Canadian Scottish), Canadian Expeditionary Force*
2 September 1918 – When his battalion was held up by enemy machine-gun posts at Arras, France, he rushed out to a passing tank. With his signal flag, he walked in front of the tank, directing it along the trench in an intense hail of bullets. The tank overcame the strongpoints and a critical situation was relieved. Later, although wounded, he continued to advance until ordered to get into a shell hole and have his wounds dressed.
He had crossed the Canadian border to enlist in 1914, very much against the wishes of his mother, who wrote repeatedly to the US Ambassador in London asking for his return.

PECK, Cyrus Wesley *Lieutenant Colonel, commanding 16th Bn. (The Canadian Scottish), Canadian Expeditionary Force*
2 September 1918 – After his command had captured its first objective at Cagnicourt, France, progress was held up by machine-gun fire on the right flank. He made a personal reconnaissance under heavy fire, before reorganizing his battalion and pushing them forward. He then went out under the most intense fire, intercepted some tanks and gave them directions which paved the way for an infantry battalion to push forward.
He was a Member of the Canadian House of Commons, 1917–21.

PROWSE, George *Chief Petty Officer, Royal Naval Volunteer Reserve (Drake Bn.)*
2 September 1918 – When heavy fire from a machine-gun position held up his company at Pronville, France, he led a party against the post,

capturing it, together with 23 prisoners and five machine-guns. He later attacked with another party two further machine-gun posts, killing 6 Germans and capturing 13 prisoners and two guns. He was the only survivor of this attack, but the action enabled the battalion to advance.

RAYFIELD, Walter Leigh *Private, 7th Bn. (1st British Columbia Regiment), Canadian Expeditionary Force*

2–4 September 1918 – Out ahead of his company near Arras, France, he rushed a trench occupied by a large party of the enemy, personally bayoneting two and taking ten prisoner. He then located and engaged an enemy sniper who was causing many casualties, and rushed the sniper's trench. He so demoralized the enemy that 30 others surrendered to him. He subsequently left cover under heavy machine-gun fire to carry in a badly wounded comrade.

WEATHERS, Lawrence Carthage *T/Corporal, 43rd Bn. (South Australia), Australian Imperial Force*

2 September 1918 – When an advanced bombing party was held up by a strongly held enemy trench near Péronne, he went forward alone and attacked the enemy with bombs. After returning for more bombs, he went forward again with three comrades and continued his attack. He mounted the enemy parapet and bombed the trench, capturing 180 prisoners and three machine-guns.

YOUNG, John Francis *Private, 87th Bn. (Canadian Grenadier Guards), Canadian Expeditionary Force*

2 September 1918 – Despite a complete absence of cover, he went out across fire-swept ground in the Dury–Arras sector, France, to attend the wounded. When he had exhausted his stock of dressings, he returned to company headquarters for a further supply. He carried on this work for over an hour. Later, when fire had somewhat slackened, he brought out stretcher parties to carry in those whose wounds he had dressed.

McNAMARA, John *Corporal, 9th (S) Bn., East Surrey Regiment*

3 September 1918 – Whilst operating a telephone in enemy trenches occupied by his battalion near Lens, France, he became aware that a determined enemy counter-attack was gaining ground. Rushing to the nearest firing position, he made effective use of a revolver taken from a wounded officer. Then, seizing a Lewis gun, he fired it until it jammed. He was now alone in the position so, having destroyed his telephone, he joined a nearby party and maintained Lewis-gun fire until reinforcements arrived.

When his regiment returned to Surrey after the war, they brought with them a thirteen-year-old French boy, 'Vignolle Serge', who had attached himself to the 2nd Battalion and refused to leave, even after he had been sent home five times under escort.

THE BATTLE OF HAVRINCOURT

The Germans had now withdrawn behind the Hindenburg Line, and the next step was to take the enemy positions around Havrincourt and Epehy, which would allow the Allies to advance within striking distance of the main line of German resistance. This was complete by 18 September, and despite stubborn and prolonged resistance in the well-organized defensive belt formed by the old British and German lines, the attack that day advanced three miles and took Epehy. After mopping-up operations in the next few days, twelve thousand Germans had been taken prisoner.

CALVERT, Laurence *Sergeant, 5th Bn., King's Own Yorkshire Light Infantry*
12 September 1918 – When his company was held up by machine-gun fire at Havrincourt, France, he rushed the enemy position alone, bayoneting three Germans and shooting four, and capturing two machine-guns. His actions enabled the ultimate objective to be achieved.

LAURENT, Harry John *Sergeant, 2nd Bn., New Zealand (Rifle) Brigade, New Zealand Expeditionary Force*
12 September 1918 – During an attack near Gouzeaucourt Wood, France, he was detailed to exploit an initial success and keep in touch with the enemy. With a party of 12 he located the strongly held enemy support line and at once charged the position followed by his men. The sudden attack completely disorganized the enemy. In the hand-to-hand fighting which followed, 30 of the enemy were killed and the remainder (1 officer and 111 other ranks) surrendered. His party suffered four casualties.

WILCOX, Alfred *Lance Corporal, 2/4th (T) Bn., Oxfordshire and Buckinghamshire Light Infantry*
12 September 1918 – Having cut through the enemy wire whilst in charge of his section's advance near Laventie, France, he discovered that all but one of his men were wounded. He proceeded to bomb his way up the enemy trench, capturing two machine-guns after hand-to-hand struggles and a third after bombing its position. By this time, his rifle was clogged with mud, so he began using German stick bombs, with which he captured a fourth gun. By the time he rejoined his platoon, he had captured one light and three heavy machine-guns and killed 12 Germans.
At an informal occasion in 1920 he described his deed in the following terms: 'I saw a lot of square-heads, as I call 'em, in front of me, and I was after 'em. If I hadn't been after 'em they'd have been after me, and I used more language than the British army ever learnt.'

HUNTER, David Ferguson *Corporal, 1/5th (T) Bn., Highland Light Infantry*
16–17 September 1918 – When his battalion relieved another unit at Moeuvres, France, he occupied an advanced post in shell holes close to the

enemy. The following day, the enemy established posts all round him, completely isolating his command. Despite shortages of food and water, he held the position and repelled frequent attacks for three days until a counter-attack relieved him. He also had to endure artillery fire from the enemy and from his own side, which came right across the position.

BUCKLEY, Maurice Vincent (also known as SEXTON, Gerald) *Sergeant, 13th Bn. (New South Wales), Australian Imperial Force*
18 September 1918 – When his company was held up by a field gun during an attack near Le Verguier, St-Quentin, France, he rushed the gun and killed its crew. He then ran across open ground under machine-gun fire and fired into some dugouts, inducing 30 Germans to surrender. When the advance was again held up by machine-gun fire, he disposed of the enemy guns. By the end of the day he had rushed a number of machine-gun positions and captured nearly a hundred Germans.

Having been declared a deserter in January 1916 when he went missing from a containment camp in Australia, he re-enlisted in May 1916 under the name Gerald Sexton. Gerald was the name of his deceased brother and Sexton was his mother's maiden name. The Gazette *of 14 December 1919 confirmed that he was permitted to reassume the name Maurice Buckley.*

LEWIS, Leonard Allan *Lance Corporal, 6th (S) Bn., Northamptonshire Regiment*
18 and 21 September 1918 – On 18 September, whilst in command of a section on the right of the attacking line at Ronssoy he was held up by two enemy machine-guns. Crawling forward alone, he successfully bombed the guns and captured the gunners, allowing the advance to continue. Three days later, having seen his company through an enemy barrage, he was struck on the head by shrapnel and killed while getting his men under cover from heavy machine-gun fire.

While suffering from jaundice in early 1918 he had been treated in a Red Cross hospital situated in Longleat House in Wiltshire where, according to the Hereford Times, *'Lord and Lady Bath ... and also Lady Kathleen displayed more than an ordinary interest in him.'*

WARING, William Herbert *Lance Corporal, 25th (T) Bn., Royal Welch Fusiliers*
18 September 1918 – At Ronssoy, France, he led an attack against enemy machine-guns holding up the advance of neighbouring troops. In the face of devastating fire, he rushed a strongpoint single-handed, bayoneting 4 of the garrison and capturing 20. He then reorganized his men, inspiring them until he fell mortally wounded.

WOODS, James Park *Private, 48th Bn. (South Australia), Australian Imperial Force*
18 September 1918 – With a weak patrol near Le Verguier, St-Quentin, France, he attacked and captured a formidable enemy post, which he held

20. Harry Christian, making separate trips, brought three wounded men to safety under heavy fire during severe fighting at Cuinchy, France, 18 October 1915 (p. 217) George V is presenting his VC.

21. *Below, left.* Francis Grenfell (on the right with his twin brother). Although wounded, he helped to save the British guns under heavy enemy fire at Audregnies, France, 24 August 1914 (p. 191).

22. Hugo Throssell, although wounded several times, refused to leave the line and so inspired his fellow Australians by his example at Gallipoli, 29–30 August 1915 (p. 228).

23. Joseph Tombs, despite his wounds, went out repeatedly to rescue wounded men, at times improvising equipment to bring them to safety at Rue de Bois, France, 16 June 1915 (p. 213).

24. Albert Jacka single-handedly attacked seven of the enemy, thereby saving the lives of four wounded comrades at Gallipoli, 19/20 May 1915 (p. 223).

25. Walter James, pictured leading a party of men in an attack. Later he led a bombing party until he was the only one left, and then held the enemy at bay until a barrier could be built at Gallipoli, 28 June and 3 July 1915 (p. 226).

26. Reginald Warneford, a naval airman, destroyed an airship, the blast of which forced his own aircraft to land in enemy territory near Ghent, Belgium, 7 June 1915 (p. 233). Effecting running repairs, he safely returned to base.

27. John Cornwell, aged just fifteen, remained at his post among the dead and dying, refusing to leave until the end of the action, although mortally wounded at the Battle of Jutland, 31 May 1916 (p. 242).

28. William Congreve, over a period of fourteen days, performed many acts of bravery in attack and in effecting the rescue of wounded men although suffering from the effects of gas and shell attacks at the Somme, France, 6–20 July 1916 (p. 248).

29. *Above, right.* Noel Chavasse (on the right with his brother) was one of only three men to be awarded a bar to his VC. An army surgeon, he distinguished himself by his unceasing care for the wounded, himself rescuing many from territory near the enemy lines in France and Flanders, 1916 and 1917 (p. 252).

30. Thomas Turrall remained with a wounded officer under heavy fire for several hours, later managing to get him to safety at the Somme, France, 3 July 1916 (p. 247).

31. *Left*. Albert Ball, the first 'ace' of the RFC, with forty-three victories. Killed in action May 1917, aged twenty. Also awarded the DSO and two bars, and the MC (p. 298).

32. *Below*. Ernest Egerton (on the left, shaking hands with William Butler VC), charged several enemy dugouts, shooting three of the enemy while under heavy fire at Ypres, Belgium, 20 September 1917. Twenty-nine further enemy surrendered soon after (p. 286). Butler won his VC when he put himself between his comrades and a live shell at Lempire, France, 1917 (p. 267).

33. John Molyneux, with a bombing party, captured an enemy machine gun, killing the crew. After hand-to-hand fighting, twenty to thirty enemy surrendered at Langemarck, Belgium, 9 October 1917 (p. 291).

34. John Hamilton, pictured in a kilt at his investiture. He repeatedly fetched ammunition to the front lines in full view and under fire on the Ypres–Menin Road, Belgium, 25–26 September 1917 (p. 287).

35. Frederick Dancox, who attacked a pillbox from the rear, threatening to bomb the enemy. He left with the machine gun and forty of the enemy as prisoners, later using the gun against the Germans, in the Boesinghe Sector, Belgium, 9 October 1917 (p. 290).

36. Karanbahadur Rana, Gurkha rifleman, engaged an enemy machine gun and silenced it, also killing enemy bombers and infantry at El Kefr, Egypt, 10 April 1918 (p. 357).

37. John Daykins charged a machine-gun post and personally killed several of the enemy. He then took out a further machine gun single-handed, taking twenty-five prisoners, at Solesmes, France, 20 October 1918 (p. 352).

38. *Left*. Henry Tandey, with a Lewis-gun team, took out an enemy machine-gun post. Later, after restoring a bridge under heavy fire, he and others drove a large number of the enemy into a trap where they were taken prisoner at Marcoing, France, 28 September 1918 (p. 346).

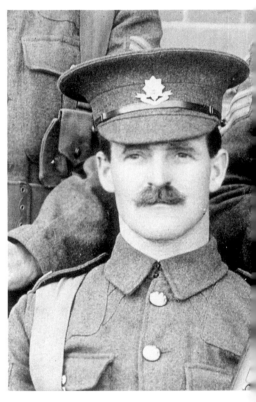

39. *Right*. John Crowe forced the crew of an enemy machine-gun post to retreat. Later with two others he attacked other machine-gun posts, killing the crews and capturing the guns, at Neuve Église, Belgium, 14 April 1918 (p. 325).

40. *Left*. Arthur Poulter, a stretcher bearer, carried wounded men on his back on ten separate occasions and later bandaged forty men while under continuous heavy fire, at Erguinghem, France, 10 April 1918 (p. 325).

with two comrades against heavy enemy counter-attacks. Although exposed to heavy fire of all kinds, he fearlessly mounted the parapet and opened fire on the attackers. He held up the enemy until help arrived.

YOUNG, Frank Edward *Second Lieutenant, 1st Bn., Hertfordshire Regiment*
18 September 1918 – During an enemy counter-attack near Havrincourt, France, he visited all his posts, encouraging the men. In the early stages of the attack he rescued two captured men and bombed and silenced an enemy machine-gun. He then drove out an enemy party assembling nearby. An officer of the battalion recalled, 'He seemed to be everywhere where most wanted.' After four hours of intense hand-to-hand fighting, he was killed.
He told a friend at the outbreak of war, 'This is war. We are now in for the real thing. We have been playing at soldiers; now we must go and be *soldiers.'*

WHITE, William Allison *T/Second Lieutenant, 38th Bn., Machine-Gun Corps*
20 September 1918 – When an advance was delayed by an enemy machine-gun at Gouzeaucourt, France, he rushed the gun position single-handed, shot the three gunners and captured the gun. Later, accompanied by two men both of whom were immediately shot down, he attacked another machine-gun, where he killed the team of five and captured the gun. He subsequently collected a small party and rushed a third position, inflicting heavy losses on the enemy.

BARRETT, John Cridlan *Lieutenant, 1/5th (T) Bn., Leicestershire Regiment*
24 September 1918 – During an attack at Pontruet, France, he collected all available men and charged a trench containing numerous machine-guns. Despite being wounded, he gained the trench, personally disposed of two machine-guns and inflicted many casualties. He was again severely wounded but climbed out of the trench to fix his position and locate the enemy. He then ordered his men to cut their way back to the battalion, which they did. He was once more wounded, so seriously that he had to be carried away.
Presenting him with a cheque from the people of Paddington, General Sir Ian Hamilton (commander of the Gallipoli expedition) said, 'We are inclined to envy those who are born with a silver spoon in their mouth, but when we come across a young man starting his career with the VC on his breast we do not envy – we admire.'

DEAN, Donald John *T/Lieutenant, 8th (S) Bn., Queen's Own Royal West Kent Regiment*
24–26 September 1918 – Holding a newly captured trench which was ill-prepared for defence near Lens, France, he worked unceasingly through the night to repulse enemy attacks. Five times in all the post was attacked, and throughout this time he inspired the command with his contempt of danger and set an example of valour, leadership and devotion to duty of the highest order.

THE BATTLE OF CAMBRAI AND THE HINDENBURG LINE

The strategic plan as outlined in Haig's despatch now involved four convergent and simultaneous offensives: by the Americans, west of the Meuse in the direction of Mezières; by the French, west of Argonne, with the same general objectives; by the British, on the St-Quentin–Cambrai front in the direction of Maubeuge; and by the Belgian and Allied forces in Flanders in the direction of Ghent. The British faced a series of defences, which 'with the numerous defended villages contained in it formed a belt of country varying from 7,000 to 10,000 yards in depth, organised by the employment of every available means into a most powerful system, well meriting the great reputation attached to it.'

On 27 September British and Canadian troops attacked on a front of 13 miles from Gouzeaucourt north to Souchy-Lestrée, supported by sixty-five tanks; they secured the crossings of the Canal du Nord, though at a heavy cost. Bridges were built under fire and thereafter the advance was rapid, assisted by a continuous bombardment that disrupted German resupply. On 5 October the Scheldt Canal was crossed between Le Catelet and Crèvecoeur, and the Hindenburg Line occupied. In Flanders an attack begun on 28 September near Ypres had reached the Lys by 1 October.

FRISBY, Cyril Hubert *A/Captain, 1st Bn., Coldstream Guards*
27 September 1918 – Whilst in command of a company detailed to capture a crossing of the Canal du Nord near Graincourt, France, he and three others (including Lance Corporal JACKSON) climbed down into the canal under point-blank fire and captured a machine-gun post. Two machine-guns and 12 men were taken. He then gave support to a company on his right which had lost all its officers and sergeants, organizing its defences and beating off a heavy counter-attack.

After the war, he worked as a jobber at the London Stock Exchange alongside his brother who had won the DSO whilst serving with the 6th Welsh Regiment. They were known by the other jobbers as 'the Cowards'.

GORT, John Standish Surtees Prendergast Vereker, Viscount *A/Lieutenant Colonel, commanding 1st Bn., Grenadier Guards*
27 September 1918 – Despite being wounded as he led his battalion near Flesquières, France, he went across open ground to obtain assistance from a tank, which he personally directed to the best advantage. He was again wounded and lay on a stretcher for a while but insisted on getting up and personally directing the continued attack during which two hundred prisoners, two batteries of field guns and numerous machine-guns were captured. Even after he collapsed from loss of blood, he refused to leave the field until success on the final objective was signalled.

Major W. P. Sidney (Viscount de L'Isle) VC was his son-in-law. As Com-

mander-in-Chief of the British Expeditionary Force 1939–40, he made the decision to retreat to Dunkirk rather than remain and fight alongside the French army. He was Governor of Gibraltar 1941–42, Governor of Malta 1942–44 and High Commissioner for Palestine and Transjordan 1944–45.

GREGG, Milton Fowler (later the Hon. Milton) *Lieutenant, Royal Canadian Regiment, Canadian Expeditionary Force*

27 September to 1 October 1918 – When the advance of the brigade near Cambrai, France, was held up by fire from both flanks and thick uncut wire, he crawled forward alone and explored the wire until he found a small gap, through which he led his men. Although wounded twice, he led his men into the enemy trenches where he personally killed or wounded 11 Germans, took 25 prisoners and captured twelve machine-guns. He remained with his company in spite of his wounds and led his men in a further attack a few days later in which he was severely wounded.

After the Second World War, he entered the Canadian parliament and was Minister for Fisheries 1947, Veterans' Affairs 1948–49 and Labour 1950–57. He then served with the United Nations' Children's Fund in Iraq 1958–59 and in Indonesia 1960–63.

HONEY, Samuel Lewis *Lieutenant, 78th Bn. (Winnipeg Grenadiers), Canadian Expeditionary Force*

27 September 1918 – When all the other officers of his company became casualties at Bourlon Wood he took command and gained the objective. An enemy machine-gun post then began enfilading his new position so he rushed the post single-handed, capturing the guns and ten prisoners. After repelling four enemy counter-attacks, he led out a party which captured another post of three guns. He died on the last day of his battalion's attack.

JACKSON, Thomas Norman *Lance Corporal, 1st Bn., Coldstream Guards*

27 September 1918 – He volunteered to follow his company commander (Captain FRISBY) across a canal near Graincourt in an attack on an enemy machine-gun post. Under point-blank fire, they climbed down the barbed-wire-festooned sides of the canal and rushed the post, capturing two guns and 12 prisoners. Later in the morning he jumped into a German trench calling 'Come on, boys!' to the other members of his platoon. He killed two Germans before he was himself killed.

KERR, George Fraser *Lieutenant, 3rd Bn. (Toronto Regiment), Canadian Expeditionary Force*

27 September 1918 – Whilst in command of the left support company in an attack at Bourlon Wood, France, he handled his company with great skill and gave timely support by outflanking a machine-gun impeding the advance. Later, far in advance of his company, with the advance held up by a strongpoint, he rushed the position single-handed, capturing four machine-guns and 31 prisoners.

LYALL, Graham Thomson *Lieutenant, 102nd (Central Ontario) Bn.,*
Canadian Expeditionary Force

27 September and 1 October 1918 – On 27 September, leading his
platoon against Bourlon Wood, Cambrai, France, he captured a strongpoint
together with 13 prisoners, one field gun and four machine-guns. He later
rushed another strongpoint alone, killing the officer in charge and capturing the position. Forty-five prisoners and five machine-guns were taken.
Four days later, whilst in command of a weak company, he captured a
strongly defended position which yielded 60 prisoners and seventeen
machine-guns.

NEELY, Thomas *Corporal, 8th (S) Bn., King's Own (Royal Lancaster*
Regiment)

27 September 1918 – When his company was held up during an advance
by heavy machine-gun fire from a flank at Flesquières, France, with 2 men
he rushed the enemy positions, disposing of the gun crews and capturing
three guns. On two subsequent occasions he rushed concrete strongpoints,
killing or capturing the occupants. His initiative and fighting spirit enabled
his company to advance 3,000 yards along the Hindenburg support line. He
was immediately promoted in the field to lance sergeant.

TANDEY, Henry *Private, 5th Bn., Duke of Wellington's (West Riding)*
Regiment

28 September 1918 – When his platoon was held up by machine-gun
fire at Marcoing, France, he crawled forward, located the gun position and
led a Lewis-gun team into a neighbouring house from which they were able
to knock out the gun. On reaching a canal, he repaired a broken plank
bridge under a hail of bullets, allowing the first crossings to be made.
When, later in the evening, he and eight comrades were surrounded by an
overwhelming number of Germans, he led a bayonet charge through them.
His small party fought so fiercely that 37 of the enemy were driven back
into the hands of the remainder of his company, where they were taken
prisoner.

When the British Prime Minister, Neville Chamberlain, visited Adolf Hitler
at Berchtesgaden in 1938, Hitler pointed to a picture on his office wall. The
picture was of Tandey at the Menin Crossroads in 1914. Hitler told Chamber-
lain that this man 'came so close to killing me that I thought I should never
see Germany again'. He explained that Tandey had been about to shoot him
dead during the Great War but had changed his mind when he realized that
Hitler was wounded and unarmed. After the war, Hitler had recognized Tan-
dey's face in the picture. He asked Chamberlain to contact Tandey and offer
him his thanks, which Chamberlain did when he returned to London. Much
doubt has since been cast on Hitler's claim. Tandey himself believed that the
incident took place as described at Marcoing but this does not seem possible
as Hitler was not in the area at the time. Perhaps the incident took place at

some other point in the war or perhaps it was an invention of Hitler's to per-
suade Chamberlain of his respect for the British. The story remains intrigu-
ingly possible.

McGREGOR, John *T/Captain, 2nd Bn. Canadian Mounted Rifles, Canadian*
Expeditionary Force

29 September to 3 October 1918 – When his company's advance was
held up by machine-guns near Cambrai, France, he located the guns, ran
forward alone and put them out of action, killing four Germans and taking
eight prisoner. As the enemy were resisting stubbornly he went along the
line organizing the platoons and taking command of the leading waves
which continued the advance. He displayed great bravery during five days
of continuous fighting.

He had enlisted in Vancouver in March 1915, after travelling 120 miles
cross-country in snowshoes to reach the recruitment office.

VANN, Bernard William *A/Lieutenant Colonel, 1/8th (T) Bn., Sherwood*
Foresters, commanding 1/6th (T) Bn.

29 September 1918 – He led his men across the Canal du Nord, France,
through thick fog whilst under heavy enemy fire. Reaching high ground,
the advance was held up by fire from both flanks so he hurried up to the
line and led it forward. He later rushed a field gun single-handed and
knocked out three of its crew, enabling the line to advance.

Ordained in 1911, he had tried to enter the army as a chaplain but was
unwilling to wait for a position to become available so enlisted in the 28th
London Regiment in 1914 as an infantryman.

WARK, Blair Anderson *Major, 32nd Bn. (South Australia and Western*
Australia), Australian Imperial Force

29 September to 1 October 1918 – During an advance from Bellicourt to
Joncourt, France, he moved fearlessly at the head of and sometimes far in
advance of his troops. Observing a battery of 77mm guns firing on his rear
companies, he collected a few of his men, rushed the battery and captured
four guns and ten of the crew. He then moved rapidly forward with two
NCOs and captured 50 Germans. He later dashed forward and silenced some
machine-guns which were causing heavy casualties.

CRICHTON, James *Private, 2nd Bn., Auckland Infantry Regiment, New*
Zealand Expeditionary Force

30 September 1918 – Although wounded in the foot, he stayed with his
unit, advancing across difficult canal and river obstacles. When his platoon
was forced back by a counter-attack, he succeeded in carrying a message,
which involved swimming a river and crossing an area swept by machine-
gun fire. He later undertook to save a bridge mined by the Germans; despite
being fired on every time he showed his head, he removed the explosives
and returned to his platoon with the charges and detonators.

RYAN, Edward John Francis (commonly known as John) *Private, 55th Bn. (New South Wales), Australian Imperial Force*

30 September 1918 – One of the first to reach the enemy trenches during an advance at the Hindenburg defences, France, he established a party at the rear of the position when the enemy counter-attacked. By skilful bayonet work, his party killed the first three Germans on the enemy's flank before he rushed alone at the remainder with bombs. The enemy were driven back across no-man's-land although he was himself wounded. Throughout this action he was an inspiration to all.

MERRIFIELD, William *Sergeant, 4th Bn. (Central Ontario), Canadian Expeditionary Force*

1 October 1918 – When his men were held up by intense fire from two machine-gun emplacements at Abancourt, France, he attacked them both single-handed. Dashing from shell hole to shell hole, he killed the occupants of the first post and, although wounded, bombed the second. He refused to be evacuated until he was again severely wounded.

RIGGS, Frederick Charles *Sergeant, 6th (S) Bn., York and Lancaster Regiment*

1 October 1918 – Having led his platoon through uncut wire under severe fire near Epinoy, France, he continued the attack. Although sustaining heavy casualties from flanking fire, the platoon succeeded in reaching its objective, where Riggs rushed and captured a machine-gun. He later brought two captured guns into action and caused the surrender of 50 men. He was killed as he encouraged his men to resist a subsequent enemy advance.

COLTMAN, William Harold *Lance Corporal, 1/6th (T) Bn., North Staffordshire Regiment*

3–4 October 1918 – Whilst acting as a stretcher bearer at Mannequin Hill, north-east of Sequehart, France, he heard that wounded men had been left behind after a retirement. He went forward alone into machine-gun fire, found the wounded, dressed their injuries and made three trips carrying them to safety on his back. He worked unceasingly for forty-eight hours.

His Christian beliefs would not allow him to kill another man so he was allowed to become a stretcher bearer shortly after enlisting. He was the most decorated NCO of the First World War, with the following awards: VC, DCM and bar, MM and bar.

JOHNSON, William Henry *Sergeant, 1/5th (T) Bn., Sherwood Foresters*

3 October 1918 – When his platoon was held up by a nest of machine-guns at Ramicort, France, he charged the nest single-handed, bayoneting several gunners and capturing two guns. Despite being severely wounded by a bomb during this attack, he later rushed another machine-gun post, bombing the garrison and putting the gun out of action.

MAXWELL, Joseph *Lieutenant, 18th Bn. (New South Wales), Australian Imperial Force*

3 October 1918 – When his company commander was severely wounded early in the advance on the Beaurevoir–Fonsomme line near St-Quentin, France, he took charge. Under heavy fire, he charged alone through the German wire and captured the most dangerous enemy machine-gun, killing three Germans and capturing four. He dashed forward alone again and silenced a gun which was holding up a flank company. He was subsequently told by an enemy prisoner that the occupants of a nearby German post wanted to surrender, so he approached the post with two men. His small party was immediately surrounded by a much larger force of Germans, but at that moment a huge barrage began. Taking advantage of the confusion, he shot two of the enemy with his pistol and led his comrades to safety.

It is said that he would have achieved higher rank had he moderated his unruly behaviour. On one occasion, whilst in England attending officer training school, he was fined £20 and sent back to his unit after military and civilian police arrested him at a party in London. He was also present when a piano was hurled through a Cairo brothel window. In 1932 he and Hugh Buggy wrote Hell's Bells and Mademoiselles, *a book of his wartime exploits.*

INGRAM, George Mawby *Lieutenant, 24th Bn. (Victoria), Australian Imperial Force*

5 October 1918 – During an advance at Montbrehain, France, his platoon was held up by a strongpoint so he rushed the position at the head of his men, capturing nine machine-guns and killing 42 Germans. Later, after his company had suffered severe casualties, he rushed another machine-gun post, shooting six Germans and capturing the gun. He displayed great dash and resource in the capture of two further posts during which 62 prisoners were taken.

THE SECOND BATTLE OF LE CATEAU

Between 6 and 12 October the Germans were forced out of Cambrai and fell back behind the River Selle. An attack on 8 October gained between three and four miles; it was counter-attacked with tanks, but after several important villages were taken the German infantry were in disorganized retreat to the east. By the 9th Cambrai was three miles behind Allied positions, and the Selle was reached on the 10th, where German positions once more showed resistance.

TOWERS, James *Private, 2nd Bn., Cameronians*

6 October 1918 – When five runners failed to deliver an important message through heavy fire at Mericourt, France, he volunteered to make another attempt despite being aware of the fate of those who had gone before him. As soon as he started out he came under heavy fire, but dodged from cover to cover and eventually delivered the message.

He said of his action, 'We were young men, old before our time ... I had been in worse situations than that before and no medals were awarded, but that's how it was.'

WILLIAMS, John Henry *Company Sergeant Major, 10th (S) Bn., South Wales Borderers*

7–8 October 1918 – His company was suffering severe casualties from an enemy machine-gun during an attack on Villers-Outreaux, France, so he ordered a Lewis gun to engage it as he rushed it single-handed. He engaged 15 of the enemy, one of whom grabbed his rifle. He managed to break away and bayoneted five Germans, whereupon the remainder surrendered. His bravery enabled his company and those on the flanks to advance.

MITCHELL, Coulson Norman *Captain, 1st Tunnelling Coy., 4th Canadian Engineers, Canadian Expeditionary Force*

8–9 October 1918 – At the Canal de l'Escaut near Cambrai, France, he led a small party to check the bridges and if possible prevent their demolition by the enemy. He found the first bridge already blown up. At the next he cut a number of wires and then dashed across the main bridge, which was heavily charged for demolition. As the enemy tried to rush this bridge and blow the charges, he killed 3 Germans, captured 12 and continued to cut wires and remove charges until he had saved the bridge from destruction.

HOLMES, William Edgar *Private, 2nd Bn., Grenadier Guards*

9 October 1918 – Acting as a stretcher bearer at Cattenières, France, he carried in two men under intense fire, and while attending to a third was severely wounded. He struggled on for a short time but was again wounded, this time with fatal results. He saved the lives of several of his comrades.

ALGIE, Wallace Lloyd *Lieutenant, 20th Bn. (Central Ontario), Canadian Expeditionary Force*

11 October 1918 – During an advance near Cambrai, France, he dashed forward with nine volunteers and shot the crew of a German machine-gun, which he turned on the enemy, enabling his unit to continue advancing. He then rushed another machine-gun, killing its crew and capturing an officer and ten men. He subsequently went back for reinforcements but was killed whilst bringing them forward.

LESTER, Frank *Private, 10th (S) Bn., Lancashire Fusiliers*

12 October 1918 – During the clearing of the village of Neuvilly, France, as he entered a house at the back, he shot two Germans leaving through the front door. A moment later, falling masonry blocked the back door. The front door was clear but was under heavy fire. Spotting an enemy sniper causing heavy casualties to a party of men in a house across the street, he ran out of the front door and shot the sniper but fell mortally wounded at the same instant. He had sacrificed his own life to save the lives of the men in the house opposite.

WOOD, Harry Blanshard *Lance Sergeant, 2nd Bn., Scots Guards*
13 October 1918 – When his sergeant was killed during an advance on St-Python, France, command of the leading platoon fell to him. Control of a bridge, from which a number of Germans were sniping, had to be gained. He boldly carried a very large brick into the open, lay down behind it and proceeded to fire at the snipers. He ordered his men to work across the bridge as he covered them with his fire. He did this until his entire party had reached their objective. Later in the day, he drove off repeated counter-attacks against his position.

McPHIE, James *Corporal, 416th Field Coy., Royal Engineers*
14 October 1918 – Whilst assisting a party of sappers with a cork-float bridge across the Canal de la Sensée near Aubencheul-au-Bac, France, the bridge began to sink under the weight of infantrymen crossing it. He jumped into the water and attempted to hold the bridge together but failed. With the words 'It is death or glory work which must be done for the sake of our patrol on the other side' he marched onto the bridge under heavy fire, axe in hand, intending to repair it. He was instantly wounded and fell partly into the water. He died after receiving further wounds.

THE BATTLE OF THE SELLE

From 17 to 25 October operations on the Le Cateau front had as their objective the Sambre–Oise Canal, which would bring Aulnoye, an important railway junction, within artillery range. By now the enemy was putting up serious resistance, and the advance met with strong opposition everywhere, but with the help of tanks the high ground to the east of the Selle was occupied on the 20th and by the 25th the line was established east of the Le Quesnoy–Valenciennes railway.

ELCOCK, Roland Edward *A/Corporal, 11th (S) Bn., Royal Scots*
15 October 1918 – Whilst in charge of a Lewis gun team near Capelle-Ste-Catherine, France, he rushed two enemy guns which were causing heavy casualties and preventing the advance. He put both guns out of action, captured five prisoners and enabled the advance to continue.

CURTIS, Horace Augustus *Sergeant, 2nd Bn., Royal Dublin Fusiliers*
18 October 1918 – When his platoon came under unexpected machine-gun fire near Le Cateau, France, he ran forward through a 'friendly' barrage and enemy fire and killed or wounded the teams of two of the enemy guns,

at which point the remaining four guns surrendered. He then captured a trainload of German reinforcements before his comrades caught up with him.

DAYKINS, John Brunton *A/Sergeant, 2/4th (T) Bn., York and Lancaster Regiment*

20 October 1918 – With the 12 remaining men of his platoon, he rushed a machine-gun and himself disposed of many of the enemy during severe hand-to-hand fighting at Solesmes, France, during which 30 prisoners were taken. He then worked forward alone to another machine-gun post holding up the company and returned with 25 prisoners and a German machine-gun.

WILKINSON, Alfred Robert *Private, 1/5th (T) Bn., Manchester Regiment*

20 October 1918 – During the attack at Marou, France, four runners from his unit were killed one after the other in attempts to deliver a message to the supporting company 600 yards away across open ground. He volunteered to carry the message and succeeded in doing so. On the same day he gave blood (which saved the life of a wounded Australian despatch rider) despite having just been hit in the face by shrapnel.

When he took time off work to attend a VC reunion dinner held in the Royal Gallery of the House of Lords in 1929, his employers docked his pay. A newspaper-led public outcry ensued, ensuring that he eventually received his wages.

GREENWOOD, Harry *A/Lieutenant Colonel, commanding 9th (S) Bn., King's Own Yorkshire Light Infantry*

23–24 October 1918 – When the advance of his battalion was checked by enemy machine-gun fire at Ovillers, France, he rushed the gun single-handed and killed the crew. He killed the occupants of another machine-gun post at the entrance to the village before he discovered that his command was almost surrounded by further machine-gun emplacements. He repelled an enemy attack and then led his troops successfully to their objective, capturing a hundred and fifty prisoners, eight machine-guns and one field gun. The following day he rushed another machine-gun post and inspired his men to such a degree that that day's objective was also taken.

MILES, Francis George *Private, 1/5th (T) Bn., Gloucestershire Regiment*

23 October 1918 – When his company was held up by a line of enemy machine-guns during an advance at Bois de l'Evêque, Landrecies, France, he went forward alone under exceptionally heavy fire, located a machine-gun, shot the gunner and put the gun out of action. Observing another nearby, he again advanced alone, shot the gunner, rushed the gun and captured the team of 8. Finally, he stood up and beckoned to his company who, acting on his signals, worked round the rear of the line and captured sixteen machine-guns, an officer and 50 other ranks.

In 1917 he had been the only survivor of 50 men buried alive by an exploding shell. It was claimed that his home village of Clearwell sent more soldiers to the war than any other village in England in proportion to its size. In 1956 he was presented to Queen Elizabeth II at a special celebration to mark the centenary of the Victoria Cross.

HEDGES, Frederick William *T/Lieutenant, Bedfordshire Regiment, attached 6th (S) Bn., Northamptonshire Regiment*

24 October 1918 – During operations north-east of Bousies, France, he led his company towards its objective under the most difficult conditions. When the advance was held up by machine-guns, he went forward with a sergeant and together they captured six guns and took 14 prisoners.

BISSETT, William Davidson *Lieutenant, 1/6th (T) Bn., Argyll and Sutherland Highlanders*

25 October 1918 – Whilst in command of his company near Maing, France, he withdrew to a railway line after a determined enemy attack had turned his left flank. The enemy continued to advance in force and his men exhausted their ammunition. Under heavy fire, he mounted the railway embankment and called upon his men to charge with bayonets. They did so, driving the enemy back with heavy loss. They then charged forward again and re-established their line.

In an article he wrote for the Daily Sketch *in 1932, he described the experiences of many who returned from the Great War: 'thousands who escaped death or disability only returned to a living hell in civilian life – jobless, destitute, well nigh hopeless. But never a regret amongst them that they answered their country's call. A generation sacrificed to the God of War.'*

THE BATTLE OF THE SAMBRE

Valenciennes was an essential preliminary to the main offensive in November, and it was taken after two days' heavy fighting. On 4 November an attack was opened on a front of 30 miles, from Valenciennes to the Sambre, north of Oisy. At this point the Sambre–Oise Canal runs approximately north–south, about five miles east of Le Cateau: although resistance was considerable it was crossed by bridges and rafts, and at the end of the day forward troops had advanced five miles. Before dawn on the 5th British troops were on the far side of the Forest of Mormal: that day Le Quesnoy surrendered, and with the capture of Wargnies-le-Grand, Bry and Eth were within two miles of the Belgian border. Around nineteen thousand prisoners had been taken. Haig's despatch notes: 'By this great victory the enemy's resistance was definitely broken. On the night 4th/5th November his troops began to fall back on practically the whole battle front. Throughout the following days, despite continuous rain, which imposed great hardships on our troops, infantry and cavalry pressed forward with scarcely a check, maintaining close touch with the rapidly retreating Germans.'

CAIRNS, Hugh *Sergeant, 46th Bn. (South Saskatchewan), Canadian Expeditionary Force*

1 November 1918 – When a machine-gun opened fire on his platoon at Valenciennes, France, he seized a Lewis gun, ran at the gun and captured it, killing its crew of five. He then rushed forward twice more, killing and capturing many Germans. After consolidating his position, he went out with a battle patrol and came upon 60 Germans. Seeing his Lewis gun, they threw up their hands but an officer among them shot him through the body, bringing him to his knees. He fired off a burst from the gun which killed the officer, but in the melee which ensued he was shot again. He continued firing, cutting down a number of the enemy, until eventually he collapsed from loss of blood and was dragged clear by his comrades. He died the following day.

In 1936, the city of Valenciennes renamed a street L'Avenue du Sergent Hugh Cairns.

CLARKE, James *Sergeant, 15th (S) Bn., Lancashire Fusiliers*

2 November 1918 – Whilst in command of a platoon at Happegarbes, France, he attacked single-handed a strongly held ridge and captured four machine-guns, bayoneting the crews. He later led the remnants of his platoon forward to capture three machine-guns and many prisoners. Later in the day, he successfully led a tank over exposed ground against enemy machine-guns.

Suffering from poor health after the war, he fell into poverty and tried his hand at many jobs, including operating a barrel-organ on the streets of London and Manchester.

AMEY, William *Lance Corporal, 1/8th (T) Bn., Royal Warwickshire Regiment*

4 November 1918 – During the attack at Landrecies, France, many hostile machine-gun nests were missed by the leading troops due to heavy fog. He led his section through heavy fire against one of these positions, driving the garrison into a nearby farm and eventually capturing 50 Germans and several guns. He later attacked a machine-gun post in a farmhouse single-handed, killing two Germans and driving the remainder into a cellar. He then rushed another post on his own, capturing 20 men.

ARCHIBALD, Adam *Sapper, 218th Field Coy., Royal Engineers*

4 November 1918 – Building a floating bridge across the Sambre–Oise Canal near Ors, France, intense machine-gun fire was directed at him from a few yards away as he worked on the cork floats. He persevered in his task and completed the bridge, which was immediately used by two platoons of infantry. As he completed his task, he collapsed from gas poisoning.

A painting depicting this action hangs in the Royal Engineers' Museum in Chatham, Kent.

FINDLAY, George de Cardonnel Elmsall *A/Major, 409th Field Coy., Royal Engineers*

4 November 1918 – During bridging operations at the lock on the Sambre–Oise Canal, France, intense fire checked the advance of the assault parties. Collecting what men he could, he tried to repair the bridge, making two unsuccessful attempts because of heavy casualties but eventually placing the bridge across the lock. He was the first man across. It was entirely due to his gallantry and devotion that the crossing was effected.

JOHNSON, Dudley Graham *A/Lieutenant Colonel, South Wales Borderers, commanding 2nd Bn., Royal Sussex Regiment*

4 November 1918 – When assault and bridging parties were repulsed by heavy artillery and machine-gun fire at the Sambre–Oise Canal, France, he personally led an attack. When the assault was again broken up by enemy fire, he reorganized the platoons and bridging parties and then led a successful crossing of the canal. He remained untouched throughout the action even though the assaulting troops were decimated.

He was ADC to King George VI, 1936–39. As General Officer Commanding 4th Division at the beginning of the Second World War, he was present at the evacuation of the BEF from Dunkirk.

KIRK, James *Second Lieutenant, 10th Bn., Manchester Regiment, attached 2nd Bn.*

4 November 1918 – During the bridging of the Sambre–Oise Canal near Ors, France, he took a Lewis gun and under intense machine-gun fire paddled across the canal on a raft, firing all his ammunition into the enemy 10 yards away. Further ammunition was ferried across to him and he maintained covering fire for the bridging party until he was killed at his gun. His actions enabled two platoons to cross the temporary bridge before it was destroyed.

MARSHALL, James Neville *A/Lieutenant Colonel, Irish Guards (Special Reserve), attached Lancashire Fusiliers, commanding 16th (S) Bn.*

4 November 1918 – When a partly constructed bridge came under severe fire during the attack on the Sambre–Oise Canal near Ors, France, he went forward and organized parties to repair the bridge. The first party was killed or wounded but further volunteers came forward instantly. He stood on the bank encouraging the men and when the bridge was repaired, rushed across at the head of his battalion but was killed as he did so.

WATERS, Arnold Horace Santo *A/Major, 218th Field Coy., Royal Engineers*

4 November 1918 – Whilst bridging the Sambre–Oise Canal near Ors, France, he learnt that all his officers had been killed or wounded so went forward and personally supervised the completion of the bridge, working on cork floats under point-blank fire. The fire was so intense that it seemed impossible he could escape, but he was shielded by the bodies of the many dead around him.

A painting depicting this action hangs in the Royal Engineers' Museum in Chatham, Kent.

CLOUTMAN, Brett *A/Major, 59th Field Coy., Royal Engineers*
6 November 1918 – At Pont-sur-Sambre, France, he found the bridge almost intact but prepared by the Germans for demolition. Leaving his party under cover, he went forward alone, swam across the river, cut the leads to the charges and returned to his party. Throughout this action the bridge and canal were under heavy artillery and machine-gun fire. Although the bridge was destroyed later in the day, the abutments remained intact.

After the war he became a barrister, taking silk in 1946. He was Senior Chairman of the War Pensions (Special Reviews) Tribunals, 1947, and Senior Official Referee of the Supreme Court of Judicature, 1954–63.

THE WAR AT SEA

Apart from the raids on Zeebrugge and Ostend, mystery ships were still engaged in the war against the U-boat menace, and the navy continued patrols in the Dardanelles, in which two roles the last two naval VCs of the war were awarded.

WHITE, Geoffrey Saxton *Lieutenant Commander, Royal Navy*
28 January 1918 – Whilst in command of HM Submarine *E.14* in the Dardanelles, he was instructed to locate a German battlecruiser, but was unable to find her. Shortly afterwards, *E.14* was hit and her controls severely damaged. When the air supply began to run out, White brought the submarine to the surface where she immediately came under fire from all sides and received so much damage that he turned her towards the shore to save the crew. He remained on deck throughout until he was killed by a shell.

AUTEN, Harold *Lieutenant Commander, Royal Naval Reserve*
30 July 1918 – Whilst he was in command of HMS *Stock Force*, a 'mystery ship', in the English Channel, she was torpedoed by a U-boat and badly damaged. Mystery ships were fitted with carefully disguised guns and were designed to attack U-boats. When the 'panic party' (sailors dressed as merchant seamen) took to the boats, the U-boat surfaced 300 yards from *Stock Force*, at which point her disguised guns opened fire and swiftly sank the U-boat. *Stock Force* sank four hours later. Auten and his crew were safely taken off by a torpedo boat.

In 'Q' Boat Adventures, an account of his experiences on the mystery ships, he recalled the civilian clothes worn on board: 'When I regarded myself in the looking-glass for the first time after donning my "Q" boat clothes, I had to confess that I had fallen in my own estimation. I had hitherto thought that I was a much better-looking fellow.'

EGYPT

WHITFIELD, Harold *Private, 10th (T) Bn., King's Shropshire Light Infantry*
10 March 1918 – During an enemy attack at Burj-el-Lisaneh, Egypt, he charged and captured a Lewis gun harassing his company. He shot or bayoneted the whole gun team before turning the gun on the Turks and driving them back with heavy casualties. He later organized and led a bombing attack which drove the enemy back and assisted in their defeat.

KARANBAHADUR RANA *Rifleman, 2nd Bn., 3rd Queen Alexandra's Own Gurkha Rifles*
10 April 1918 – At El Kefr, Egypt, he crept forward with a Lewis gun to engage an enemy machine-gun. When the leader of his team was killed, he took his place and knocked out the machine-gun crew. He kept the gun in action and when a withdrawal was later ordered assisted with covering fire until the enemy were almost upon him.

THE WAR IN THE AIR

On 1 April the RFC and RNAS combined to form the Royal Air Force. The RFC contributed about four thousand aircraft and a hundred and fourteen thousand personnel, the RNAS about three thousand aircraft and sixty-seven thousand personnel. In June the Independent Air Force under Major General Trenchard began strategic bombing of industrial and military targets inside Germany, but most units of the RAF continued their pre-1918 roles. The RAF was important in the victories in Palestine and in Salonika as well as in the fighting on the Western Front, and in July carried out a carrier-borne raid on Tondern that destroyed two Zeppelins.

McLEOD, Alan Arnett *Second Lieutenant, 2 Squadron, Royal Flying Corps*
27 March 1918 – Whilst flying an FK8 over Albert, France, at a height of 5,000 feet, eight enemy triplanes dived at him from all directions. He was hit several times but by skilful manoeuvring he enabled his observer to shoot down three of the triplanes before a bullet set his petrol tank on fire. He climbed out onto the left bottom wing and retained control by leaning across the fuselage. Keeping the flames to one side by side-stepping steeply, he crash-landed in no-man's-land. He pulled his wounded observer from the

wreckage and was dragging him to safety when a machine-gun opened up on them from the German lines. Shortly afterwards, he collapsed from exhaustion and loss of blood.

JERRARD, Alan *Lieutenant, 66 Squadron, Royal Flying Corps*
30 March 1918 – Whilst on an offensive patrol in his Sopwith Camel, he shot down an enemy aeroplane near Mansue, Italy. He then attacked an enemy aerodrome from a height of only 50 feet before engaging nineteen enemy aircraft single-handed, destroying two of them. Fresh aeroplanes continued to take off from the aerodrome, which he attacked one after the other. He only withdrew when ordered to do so by his patrol leader. He was eventually overwhelmed by numbers and driven to the ground, by which time there were 163 bullet holes in his Camel. He was captured and taken prisoner.

MANNOCK, Edward *A/Major, 85 Squadron, Royal Air Force*
Edward Mannock was born in Ballincollig, County Cork in 1887, where his father was serving as a corporal in the army. In 1893, the Mannocks moved to India, and in the heat and dust of the Indian climate, Edward, aged ten, suffered an amoebic infestation which left the sight in one eye permanently impaired.

After seeing action in the Boer War, Mannock senior returned home to England and the family settled in Canterbury. Out of the army, Mannock's father couldn't find steady work so he deserted the family, taking his savings with him, leaving Edward and his mother in serious poverty.

Edward found work with the Post Office and joined their engineering section when he was twenty-four. He was happy to go to Turkey to work on their cable-laying operations in Constantinople early in 1914, but by the end of the year, although not a combatant, he was a prisoner of war of the Germans, interned as a British national. In July 1915 he had to be repatriated due to ill health – he had suffered dreadful physical abuse and had been made to live in a tiny cage in solitary confinement – and he arrived home nursing an understandable and deep-seated hatred of the Germans.

Recuperated, he joined the Royal Engineers Signals Section in March 1916, but was irresistibly attracted by the exploits of Captain Albert Ball (p. 299) in the Royal Flying Corps. He applied for a transfer, cheated when he had to take a sight test, then completed all his pilot's tests – and joined 40 Squadron in early April 1917. At nearly thirty, maybe Mannock was more confident than his fellow pilots – whatever the reason, he certainly rubbed them up the wrong way when he first arrived. One Lieutenant Blaxland recalled, 'He seemed a boorish know-all and we all felt that the quicker he got amongst the Hun, the better. That would show him how little he knew.'

In a shaky first foray, Mannock panicked and left the formation – but watched the dogfight unfold and started to have his own ideas about aerial combat. He learned and studied – and became a brilliant fighter pilot. By September his skill and bravery were recognized with the award of the Military Cross – and promotion to captain in command of A Flight Formation. Leading by example and tactically brilliant, Mannock left those first impressions behind and was admired and loved by all under his command.

By January 1918, he had twenty 'kills' to his name and was given thirty days' leave and two months' service back in the UK – which idleness he found unbearable. He pestered his senior officers until they gave him command at 74 Training Squadron, where he taught as he led, with skill and humour. On one occasion he bombed a nearby RFC squadron with two hundred oranges – to which they responded with a bombardment of hundreds of bananas.

Trained and battle-ready, 74 Squadron accompanied Mannock back to France, to St-Omer, where, on his first patrol, Mannock shot down two enemy aircraft. To his men's amazement he shared the glory and credit with the entire squadron. He suffered personally with every loss from among his comrades – and he mourned inconsolably when he saw one of his best students, Lieutenant Dolan, shot down in flames. He saw this as the most terrible death – pilots were not allowed to use parachutes, so Dolan had to stay with his aircraft as it burned and crashed. Mannock started to carry a pistol on his patrols in case the same should befall him.

Like the shell-shock which affected the men in the trenches, combat stress and tiredness started to take their toll on Mannock, whose hatred of the Germans became increasingly obsessive. He had nightmares about being burned to death in his aircraft, often suffering from violent shaking, but liked to see German pilots go down in flames: 'Sizzle, sizzle – I sent one of the bastards to hell in flames yesterday.' But the safety of his own men was paramount, and when a novice pilot left the formation (as he himself had once done), he stripped him of his wings and had him sent home.

A considerable solace during this period of strain was music. He carried with him the only thing his father had left behind – a violin. Mannock was totally absorbed when playing the instrument. As one of his pilots described him:

> Watching Mick's expressive face as he successfully accomplished the difficult double-stopping passages in a piece such *Caprice Viennois*, I was amazed at the emotional splendour of his playing. Technique was required, but there was something greater than that, something no other violinist had ever conveyed to me. Mick had the soul of an idealist, one that can endure agonies of mind and body for his ideals, can kill for his beliefs. He told us all of this in his playing. Perhaps my appreciation was heightened by my knowledge of his emotions – but I noticed that many of the others were equally spellbound by the tall, gaunt figure standing in the half light at the far corner of the mess.

In June he was ordered to 85 Squadron, and wept to leave the men of 74 – but this new group too benefited from his skill and dedication, becoming a successful working unit. News of the death of his greatest friend, James McCudden, shook his sense of purpose and conviction, and in a week-long rampage he fought with incredible ferocity and venom – he felt he had nothing to lose. He wrote home, 'I feel that life is not worth hanging on to . . . had hopes of getting married, but?'

On his final flight, on 26 July 1918, the mechanics were surprised when he shook their hands. This he had never done before. One of them was heard to shout, 'Hope you get your seventy-third, sir.' Mannock was instructing a novice pilot, Inglis, aiming to ensure he got his first kill. Delighted when the young man shot down a German two-seater, he broke from his normal tradition of never following an enemy down. The last Inglis saw of him was his aircraft hitting the ground, wreathed in flames. Mannock's ultimate nightmare of being burned alive had become a reality. Significantly, it was not a German pilot but anti-aircraft fire which had hit his aircraft. The Germans gave him a full military funeral.

The award of the VC was made posthumously – not for a single deed, but for his entire service. George V announced, 'This highly distinguished officer, during the whole of his career in the RAF, was an outstanding example of fearless courage, remarkable skill, devotion to duty and self-sacrifice which has never been surpassed.'

At the Buckingham Palace investiture, his father returned from the past and accepted Mannock's VC, and then vanished again. It was many years before he was found and the VC was passed to his brother.

BEAUCHAMP-PROCTOR, Andrew Frederick Weatherby *A/Captain, 84 Squadron, Royal Air Force*
8 August to 8 October 1918 – Between these dates, he emerged victorious from twenty-six combats and during the entire war claimed fifty-four kills. He had a particular reputation as a 'balloon buster'. On 9 August 1918, he brought down nine observation balloons. His work attacking enemy troops on the ground and in reconnaissance during the Allied advance was almost unsurpassed. On 8 October, he landed safely at his aerodrome despite being badly wounded in the arm whilst engaging eight enemy aircraft at once.

Because of his height (he was only five feet two inches tall) his aircraft needed specially raised seats and modified controls.

WEST, Ferdinand Maurice Felix *Captain, 8 Squadron, Royal Air Force*
10 August 1918 – On the eve of the major Allied offensive of August 1918, West's squadron was ordered to establish the location, direction and movement of German reserves. On 10 August, whilst flying at 1,500 feet, West and his observer John Haslam discovered a large concentration of German troops, transport and guns. Shortly afterwards they were attacked by seven German aircraft. Three exploding bullets partially severed West's

leg, which fell powerless onto the controls. He lifted it off, twisted his underwear into an improvised tourniquet and landed in a field near some Canadian positions. He fainted, but regained consciousness for long enough to make his report. He was taken to hospital, where his leg was amputated.

Years later he said: 'I was very young and strong and healthy and had a bit of luck.' He was fitted with an aluminium leg and continued flying in the RAF. During the Second World War, he was air attaché first at the British Embassy in Rome, then at the British Legation in Berne.

BARKER, William George *A/Major, 201 Squadron, Royal Air Force*

Billy Barker, as he is better known, was born in a log cabin in Manitoba, Canada – a country lad who would become Canada's greatest and most honoured fighting hero. Fellow countryman and VC holder Billy Bishop (with whom Barker seems to have become sadly confused in the Canadian national memory) called him simply 'the deadliest air fighter that ever lived.' His was a story of derring-do – but in Barker's case it was all true.

Barker joined the Canadian Mounted Rifles in December 1914 and was quickly dispatched to the Western Front, where he spent a year in the trenches before transferring to the Royal Flying Corps in April 1916. Starting as a mechanic, he qualified in four months as an observer and scored his first kill from the rear seat of a BE2d. By January 1917 he had his pilot's certificate and was immediately brought into combat over the battlefields of France flying an RE8. His first acts of 'conspicuous gallantry' were recognized with the Military Cross in January 1917, when he flew over enemy lines at just 500 feet to gather information. On another foray he carried out crucial photographic reconnaissance, having first driven off two enemy aircraft.

By July 1917 he had added a bar to his MC – 'He has done continuous good work in co-operation with the artillery, and has carried out successful reconnaissances under most difficult and dangerous conditions.' His exploits were put on ice when he was injured by anti-aircraft fire in August and worked as a flying instructor while he recuperated. However, he was soon back on duty over the battlefields. Exactly a year after the bar to his MC, the *London Gazette* carried news of Barker being awarded the Distinguished Service Order. 'When on scouting and patrol work he has on five different occasions brought down and destroyed five enemy aeroplanes and two balloons, though on two of these occasions he was attacked by superior numbers. On each occasion, the hostile machines were observed to crash to earth, the wreckage bursting into flames. His splendid example of fearlessness and magnificent leadership have [sic] been of inestimable value to his squadron.'

This was followed quickly by a further bar to the MC. 'When leading patrols he on one occasion attacked eight hostile machines, himself shooting down two, and on another occasion seven, one of which he shot down. In two months he himself destroyed four enemy machines and drove down one and burned two balloons.' Further extraordinary aerial feats brought a bar to his DSO. 'A highly distinguished patrol leader whose courage, resource and determination has set a fine example to those around him. Up to the 20th July 1918, he had destroyed 33 enemy aircraft – 21 of these since the date of the last award (second bar to the Military Cross) was conferred on him. Major Barker has frequently led formations against greatly superior numbers of the enemy with conspicuous success.' By October 1918, Barker and his Sopwith Camel had notched up a tally of forty-six enemy aircraft destroyed. Although hostilities were not over, he was given command of Hounslow's Air Combat School. Before returning to England, he decided to fly one more foray.

He took off in a Sopwith Snipe and quickly came under attack over the Bois de Marmal by fifteen Fokker D.VIIs of Jagdgeschwader 3. In the ensuing battle he shot down three in flames before passing out from serious wounds to both legs and his left arm. Regaining consciousness and finding himself still airborne, Barker turned on the aircraft attacking him and shot it down. As he dived towards the British lines, Barker met another formation and, exhausted as he was, he broke them up and limped back into British territory to crash his Snipe in a field. Troops who rushed to the wreckage were amazed to find him still – but barely – alive. This final action brought him the award of the VC – and, with the French Croix de Guerre and the Italian Silver Medal for Military Valour awarded for other deeds of courage, Barker, promoted to lieutenant colonel, returned to Canada after the war the nation's most honoured combatant.

Here the glory ends. Barker went into the aviation business with fellow fighter ace and VC Billy Bishop, and married Bishop's fabulously rich cousin, Jean Smith, but the business failed and his marriage foundered. He suffered increasingly from depression, along with constant pain from his injuries and, previously a non-drinker, turned increasingly to the bottle over the next twelve years.

In 1930 Barker was hired to sell Fairchild aircraft to the Canadian government and prospects improved. On 12 March at Rockcliffe Aerodrome near Ottawa he decided to take the plane for a spin himself. Unfamiliar with the aircraft, he extended it beyond its capability and crashed.

A two-mile cortège followed Barker's coffin through the streets of Toronto and fifty thousand people lined the streets. As the coffin reached Mount Pleasant Cemetery, six biplanes scattered rose petals over the crowds below. A fitting send-off for a hero.

Wayne Ralph, his biographer, recognizes in Barker a superstar. 'Barker had all the traits of the great Hollywood heroes. He was disobedient, gregarious, flamboyant. He was a frontier lad – a classical figure in the American style of hero. Born in a log cabin, went on to fame and fortune and died tragically at thirty-five'. If he had been born just two hundred miles further south, he'd have been the stuff of Hollywood epics. As it is, he got a mention in a short story by Ernest Hemingway.

THE ZEEBRUGGE AND OSTEND RAIDS

In 1917 an operation was conceived to deal with the U-boat presence in the Channel and North Sea. The major base, Bruges, could not be attacked, but its eighteen U-boats and twenty-five destroyers could be trapped by sinking blockships at Zeebrugge and Ostend, its two canal exits. Zeebrugge harbour was protected by a curved mole, about 1.5 miles long, and connected to the land by a viaduct built on steel pillars. On the western (sea) side it was 27ft 10in above high water, with a 3ft wide parapet, on the harbour side of which was a ledge 12ft wide and 16ft 9in above the quay. Its height and position meant that even at high water any storming party would have to ascend to the parapet by gangplanks. The objective was to sink three old minelayers, *Intrepid*, *Iphigenia* and *Thetis*, in the canal mouth, and they were accompanied by the 6in cruiser HMS *Vindictive* and two Mersey ferry boats, HMS *Iris II* and HMS *Daffodil*, all adapted for the task. Two storming parties were embarked, 50 officers and 980 men of the Royal Navy in three companies, and 4th Battalion Royal Marines (32 officers and 718 men): the sailors would destroy the battery at the seaward end and the marines would take the fortified zone, about 150 yards to shoreward, then both would cause as much damage as they could with explosives. Two submarines, *C.1* and *C.3*, would ram the viaduct to prevent counter-attacks. The force was supported by fifteen destroyers; eight coastal motor boats would provide a smoke screen, five would support the *Vindictive*, and four would attack vessels inside the harbour; thirty-three motor launches would assist with the smoke screen and provide inshore rescue work; two monitors would deal with the batteries. The force was commanded by Rear Admiral Sir Roger Keyes in HMS *Warwick*.

As the ships approached Zeebrugge mole at about 11.40 p.m. on 22 April the harbour was attacked from the air, but the wind shifted, blowing the smoke screen clear, and the ships were fired on for the last 250–300 yards. When *Vindictive* reached the mole at 12.01, 400 yards to landward of her planned position, only two of the storming party's eighteen gangplanks were intact, but the leading company had already taken so many casualties it effectively no longer existed. At 12.04 *Daffodil* pushed *Vindictive* into the mole, and the remaining company landed, taking approximately seventy-five per cent casualties, dealt with opposition, and was followed by the second wave. *C.3* destroyed the viaduct as planned at 12.20, and Captain Bamford RMLI decided to attack the battery at the fortified seaward end, 200 yards away and the far side of the fortified zone. He had started the attack when the marines were recalled by signal at about 12.50 – tidal conditions meant *Vindictive* could not remain longer than 100 minutes. The *Iris II* had failed to grapple to the mole and was about to land the remains of her party across *Vindictive* (two shells had killed 4 officers and 75 men) when the signal sounded. A naval party had advanced on the lighthouse via a ledge on the seaward side; they had secured a lookout station and were preparing to advance when the recall sounded. One platoon was accidentally left and was taken prisoner, but the remainder of the force returned safely, as did most of the crews of the blockships.

Air reconnaissance reported blockships in the canal mouth, and contemporary accounts and the *Gazette* reported the attack as a success, but *Intrepid* was pushed from her position by *Iphigenia*, *Thetis* did not reach the canal mouth and the Germans were denied the canal for only a month.

At Ostend that night the blockships *Sirius* and *Brilliant* were supported by six monitors, eight destroyers and five French torpedo boats, with twenty-two motor launches as at Zeebrugge. The wind blew the smokescreen away at about 11.50; the blockships, misled by a moved buoy, went ashore a mile from the piers. The crews were rescued, and a second attempt was made on 9/10 May, with the *Vindictive*; she was fired on about 200 yards from the harbour entrance, and though sunk she did not close the entrance. Total casualties for the three raids were 637 killed, wounded and missing.

BAMFORD, Edward *Captain, Royal Marine Light Infantry*
22/23 April 1918 – At a time when Allied shipping was coming under increasing attack from German submarines, the Royal Navy carried out a raid which successfully blocked the entrance to the canal at Zeebrugge, Belgium. During the raid, Bamford landed with three platoons of Royal Marines on the fortified mole which guarded Zeebrugge harbour. Under heavy fire, he established a strongpoint and led an assault on a battery.
He was elected for the award under Rule 13 of the Royal Warrant.

BRADFORD, George Nicholson *Lieutenant Commander, Royal Navy*
22/23 April 1918 – At a time when Allied shipping was coming under increasing attack from German submarines, the Royal Navy carried out a raid which successfully blocked the entrance to the canal at Zeebrugge, Belgium. During the raid, Bradford commanded the naval storming parties embarked in HMS *Iris II*. Encountering difficulties placing parapet anchors alongside the fortified mole which defended Zeebrugge harbour, he climbed a derrick projecting over the mole, waited for his moment as the ship moved up and down, and jumped with an anchor which he placed in position. Within seconds, he was riddled with machine-gun bullets and fell dead into the sea.
Lieutenant Colonel R. B. Bradford VC was his brother.

CARPENTER, Alfred Francis Blakeney *Captain, Royal Navy*
22/23 April 1918 – At a time when Allied shipping was coming under increasing attack from German submarines, the Royal Navy carried out a raid which successfully blocked the entrance to the canal at Zeebrugge, Belgium. Whilst in command of HMS *Vindictive*, Carpenter navigated mined waters to arrive alongside the fortified mole which defended Zeebrugge

harbour. Under heavy artillery, machine-gun and rifle fire, Carpenter calmly walked the decks supervising the landing and encouraging his men.

He was elected for the award under Rule 13 of the Royal Warrant. He was Director of Shipping at the Admiralty 1945, and the author of The Blocking of Zeebrugge.

CRUTCHLEY, Victor Alexander Charles *Lieutenant, Royal Navy*
22/23 April and 9/10 May 1918 – Crutchley took command of HMS *Vindictive* when its senior officers had become casualties, and displayed great gallantry in both her and Motor Launch *254*, which rescued *Vindictive*'s crew after she was sunk between the piers in Ostend harbour. He then managed to keep the sinking ML *254* full of wounded afloat until HMS *Warwick* came to the rescue.

DEAN, Percy Thompson *Lieutenant, Royal Naval Volunteer Reserve*
22/23 April 1918 – At a time when Allied shipping was coming under increasing attack from German submarines, the Royal Navy carried out a raid which successfully blocked the entrance to the canal at Zeebrugge, Belgium. During the raid, Dean was in command of Motor Launch *282*, which took aboard the crews of HMS *Intrepid* and HMS *Iphigenia* after they had been scuttled. He embarked over a hundred men under deadly machine-gun fire. As he was leaving the canal, he turned back to rescue an officer stranded in the water. Shortly afterwards, the steering gear broke down, forcing him to manoeuvre using the engines. In spite of this, he steered so close to the mole that the German guns could not depress sufficiently to fire on him.
He was MP for Blackburn, 1918–22.

FINCH, Norman Augustus *Sergeant, Royal Marine Artillery*
22/23 April 1918 – At a time when Allied shipping was coming under increasing attack from German submarines, the Royal Navy carried out a raid which successfully blocked the entrance to the canal at Zeebrugge, Belgium. During the raid, Finch maintained continuous fire from the pom-poms and Lewis guns of HMS *Vindictive* until a direct hit killed or disabled all of his comrades. Even though he was severely wounded, he continued firing on the fortified mole which defended Zeebrugge harbour until another direct hit put all the guns out of action.
He was elected for the award under Rule 13 of the Royal Warrant.

HARRISON, Arthur Leyland *Lieutenant Commander, Royal Navy*
22/23 April 1918 – At a time when Allied shipping was coming under increasing attack from German submarines, the Royal Navy carried out a raid which successfully blocked the entrance to the canal at Zeebrugge, Belgium. During the raid, Harrison commanded the naval storming parties embarked in HMS *Vindictive*. As he came alongside the fortified mole which defended Zeebrugge harbour, he was struck on the head by shrapnel which

broke his jaw and knocked him senseless. He recovered consciousness and led his men in the attack on the seaward end of the mole. He was killed during the attack.

McKENZIE, Albert Edward *Able Seaman, Royal Navy*
22/23 April 1918 – At a time when Allied shipping was coming under increasing attack from German submarines, the Royal Navy carried out a raid which successfully blocked the entrance to the canal at Zeebrugge. During the raid, McKenzie was a member of the storming party commanded by Lieutenant Commander HARRISON. He landed on the fortified mole defending Zeebrugge harbour with his Lewis gun and shot about 12 Germans before the gun was shot out of his hands. Confronted by another German, McKenzie stunned him with his pistol grip before finishing him off. He was eventually reduced to 'pushing, kicking and kneeing every German who got in the way'. As he was doing so, he received such serious wounds that he had to be carried back on board his ship by a comrade.

He was elected for the award by the men of HMS Vindictive, *HMS Iris II, HMS* Daffodil *and the naval assaulting force under Rule 13 of the Royal Warrant. At his funeral, the following message was read: 'In the special circumstances of Able Seaman Albert Edward McKenzie's lamentable death, and the fact of his being a VC and the first London sailor to receive that most honourable award, you are authorised to express at the public funeral at St Mark's, Camberwell, the sympathy of their Majesties with the widowed mother and family.'*

SANDFORD, Richard Douglas *Lieutenant, Royal Navy*
22/23 April 1918 – At a time when Allied shipping was coming under increasing attack from German submarines, the Royal Navy carried out a raid which successfully blocked the entrance to the canal at Zeebrugge, Belgium. Sandford was in command of HM Submarine *C.3* during the raid. He skilfully placed *C.3* between the piles of the viaduct which connected the mole to the shore before lighting his fuse and abandoning her. He was aware that if the means of rescue failed he and his crew were certain to be killed, but he refused to use the gyro steering (which would enable him and the crew to abandon *C.3* at a safe distance) such was his determination that the mission should succeed.

He was remembered as a man of exceptionally good humour. It was said that if a submarine was the 'most cheery and most piratical of her flotilla, one may be sure that Baldy's laugh and joy in life had something to do with it'. Baldy was Sandford's nickname.

BOURKE, Rowland Richard Louis *Lieutenant, Royal Naval Volunteer Reserve*
9/10 May 1918 – During a naval raid on Ostend, he was in command of Motor Launch *276*, which followed HMS *Vindictive* into Ostend harbour and

engaged the enemy's machine-guns on both piers with Lewis guns. Hearing cries in the water, he spotted 3 badly wounded men clinging to an up-ended skiff and turned ML *276* round to rescue them, before getting her into the open sea where she was taken in tow. The launch was hit fifty-six times during the action.

DRUMMOND, Geoffrey Heneage *Lieutenant, Royal Naval Volunteer Reserve*
9/10 May 1918 – During a naval raid on Ostend, he was in command of Motor Launch *254*, which followed HMS *Vindictive* into Ostend harbour. ML *254* was hit by a shell which killed an officer and a deckhand and wounded many others including Drummond himself. Nevertheless, he placed the launch alongside HMS *Vindictive* and took off 2 officers and 38 men. He then backed ML *254* clear of the piers and into the open sea before collapsing exhausted from his wounds.
During the Second World War he served as a seaman in the River Thames Patrol Service.

PALESTINE

Having secured Jerusalem, General Allenby had two immediate objectives: to occupy the Jordan valley and threaten the railway from Damascus that supplied the Turko-German forces; and to develop his main attack along the coast, first to Haifa then Beirut. He ordered an assault on Amman in March, but before it was successful he had to send much of his force to support the collapsing Allied position on the Western Front. A second attack on Amman focused on Es Salt, about 15 miles west of Amman, and its plateau: although it was captured, a counter-attack, in which a VC was won, was successful and the force was withdrawn.

He now carried out a major reorganization, which was complete by September. Having persuaded the enemy his attack was to come in the east, at dawn on 19 September, supported by the RAF and two destroyers, the infantry drove through the defences south of Haifa and by late afternoon had captured the Turkish headquarters. The cavalry galloped north towards Haifa then to Nazareth while a smaller force made a diversionary attack on the Jordan. Nazareth was occupied on the 20th, as was Beisan on the Jordan, Haifa and Acre on the 23rd, Amman on the 25th: throughout, the advance was made with control of the air, and the RAF caused considerable casualties to the retreating enemy columns, destroyed the railway in several places and damaged headquarters and communications sites. After Damascus had fallen on 1 October only about four thousand effective Turkish soldiers remained; Beirut was occupied by a French naval squadron on the 7th, Homs by British cavalry on the 16th, and Aleppo on the 27th. On the 31st, with the Australian cavalry approaching Homs, the armistice with Turkey came into force.

CRUICKSHANK, Robert Edward *Private, 2/14th Bn., London Regiment*

1 May 1918 – When his platoon was driven into a wadi in Palestine, he volunteered to run back to company headquarters to request support. He twice rushed up the sandy slope but on both occasions was shot and rolled back into the wadi. He had his wounds dressed before making a third attempt. Once again he was shot and by now was so seriously wounded that he could only roll himself into a ball and lie helpless for the rest of the day. Whilst in this position, he was hit a fourth time by sniper fire.

NEEDHAM, Samuel *Private, 1/5th (T) Bn., Bedfordshire Regiment*

10–11 September 1918 – When his patrol came under attack from Turkish troops, artillery and machine-gun fire at Kefr Kasim, Palestine, he turned to face the enemy only 30 yards away and fired rapidly into them. His action checked their advance and gave the patrol commander time to reorganize his men. Of the 50 men in the patrol, 25 became casualties, but all the wounded were brought to safety.

BADLU SINGH *Risaldar, 14th Lancers (Scinde Horse), attached 29th Lancers*

23 September 1918 – As his squadron charged a strong enemy position at Khes Samariveh, Palestine, he noted that casualties were being caused by machine-guns and two hundred enemy infantrymen situated on a small hill. Without the slightest hesitation he collected 6 other ranks, charged and captured the position. He was mortally wounded whilst capturing one of the machine-guns single-handed, but all the guns and infantrymen had surrendered to him before he died.

ITALY

British and French forces were sent to Italy after the success of the Caporetto offensive in the Isonzo valley (in October and November 1917) had forced the Italians back to the Piave River and brought down the government. The position was stabilized through the winter after fierce fighting and the withdrawal of German units, but in the spring of 1918 the Austro-Hungarian army made a new offensive on the Asiago plateau north of Vicenza. The attack opened on 15 June, but fortunately a planned British offensive had concentrated artillery in the sector, and although there was limited penetration of the British line this had been counter-attacked and defeated by the next day. The Piave was up to 800 yards wide at the chosen point, but Papadopoli Island was taken from the Hungarians on 23/24 October and a pontoon bridge built; the Austrian line on the far bank was cleared in fifteen minutes on the 27th and the area secure by nightfall; on the 29th the River

Monticano was crossed after difficult fighting. By the 31st the British had outrun both their supplies and the Italians, and a halt was called until 1 November. The Austro-Hungarian Armistice came into effect on the 3rd.

By the autumn the Italians had reorganized under a new commander and were ready for a counter-offensive. The attack would be made by sixty Allied divisions across the Piave River, which would then turn north to the town of Vittorio Veneto, 35 miles away.

HUDSON, Charles Edward *T/Lieutenant Colonel, commanding 11th (S) Bn., Sherwood Foresters*

15 June 1918 – When the enemy penetrated the British front near Asiago, Italy, he collected together orderlies, servants and runners, led them against the attackers and drove them back. Despite being badly wounded by a bomb which exploded on his foot, he continued to organize the counter-attack, which captured a hundred prisoners and six machine-guns and averted a dangerous situation.

He was the Chief Instructor at the Royal Military College 1933–37.

YOULL, John Scott *T/Second Lieutenant, 1st Bn., Northumberland Fusiliers, attached 11th (S) Bn.*

15 June 1918 – Commanding a patrol which came under a hostile barrage near Asiago, Italy, he sent his men back to safety and remained to observe the situation. Finding himself unable to rejoin his company, he reported to a neighbouring unit. When an enemy machine-gun opened fire from behind, he rushed the gun, killed most of its team and brought the gun into action against the enemy. He then led three counter-attacks which drove the enemy back.

McNALLY, William *Sergeant, 8th (S) Bn., Yorkshire Regiment*

27 October and 29 October 1918 – On 27 October, when his company was held up by machine-gun fire at Piave, Italy, he rushed the post single-handed, killing the team and capturing the gun. Two days later, when his company came under machine-gun fire at Vazzola, he directed his platoon's fire on the danger point while he crept behind the enemy, rushed their position and captured the gun. On the same day, he frustrated an enemy counter-attack from both flanks by skilful control of his unit's fire.

WOOD, Wilfred *Private, 10th (S) Bn., Northumberland Fusiliers*

28 October 1918 – When a unit on his right flank was held up by machine-guns and snipers near Casa Vana, Italy, he worked forward with his Lewis gun, enfiladed the enemy machine-gun nest and caused 140 men to surrender. When a hidden machine-gun suddenly opened fire, he charged, firing his Lewis gun from the hip, and killed the entire enemy crew. Without further orders, he pushed on and enfiladed a ditch from which 3 officers and 160 men surrendered.

SALONIKA

The Allied C.-in-C. in the Balkans took advantage of the withdrawal of German forces in spring 1918 to plan a new offensive against Austria-Hungary. Launched in September with Serbian, French, Greek and British forces, it was an immediate success, although the British attack at Lake Doiran, a frontal uphill assault, failed at great cost and the position was only taken after the Bulgarians withdrew. The Armistice was declared on 30 September, and by the Armistice with Austria-Hungary on 3 November Allied forces had reached the Danube.

BURGES, Daniel *T/Lieutenant Colonel, Gloucestershire Regiment, commanding 7th (S) Bn., South Wales Borderers*

18 September 1918 – His reconnaissance of the enemy front line prior to an attack at Lake Doiran in the Balkans enabled his battalion to reach their assembly point safely. The battalion subsequently came under severe machine-gun fire but he encouraged and led his men forward, despite being himself wounded. Twice hit again, he became unconscious and was taken prisoner. He was later found abandoned in a dugout with his left leg shattered.

He was recovered after the Bulgarians retired on the 22nd.

THE UNKNOWN WARRIOR OF THE UNITED STATES

The United States awarded the Congressional Medal of Honor to the 'unknown, unidentified British soldier' by Act of Congress approved on 4 March 1921, and in the same spirit of comradeship a Cabinet meeting of 26 October 1921 approved the award of the Victoria Cross to the Unknown Warrior of the United States. It arrived by diplomatic bag aboard HMS *Eurydice* on 31 October, and was presented on behalf of King George V by Admiral of the Fleet Lord Beatty on 11 November 1921 at Arlington National Cemetery.

THE INTER-WAR PERIOD

THE NORTH RUSSIA RELIEF FORCE (1919)

Following the Bolshevik revolution in November 1917, which saw the overthrow of the Tsar, Russia withdrew from the First World War – leaving the way clear for Germany to move troops unhindered to the Western Front. Furthermore, under the terms of the Treaty of Brest Litovsk, Germany was allowed to occupy large areas of European Russia. The Allies had stocked up large supplies of military equipment in this area – especially in the northern ports of Murmansk and Archangel. To prevent these supplies falling into German hands, in March 1918 an Allied force was sent to Russia – not just to secure the supplies, but to train Tsarist White Russian troops to reinforce a new eastern front. These forces were drawn into action against the Bolsheviks and were not withdrawn after the Armistice was signed in November 1918. Trapped and iced in by the Russian winter, discontent grew among the troops and there was a real threat of mutiny. The British government raised the North Russia Relief Force to oversee their safe withdrawal.

Although no Australian units were involved in this operation, a number of Australians who were awaiting repatriation after the war volunteered and enlisted in the British army, joining the 45th Battalion the Royal Fusiliers and the 201st Battalion Machine-Gun Corps, and went to Russia with the relief force which arrived in June 1919.

The Bolsheviks made frequent attacks on the Allies during the evacuation. On 17 June, British coastal motor boats engaged and sank the cruiser *Olig*, during which action Lieutenant Augustine Agar earned the VC. In August, for his bravery in a rearguard action in which the troops were retreating across the Sheika River, Australian Corporal Arthur Sullivan was awarded the VC. Agar was further decorated, being awarded the DSO, when on 17/18 August eight coastal motor boats, led by Commander Claude Dobson, carried out an attack on the Bolshevik-held Kronstadt. Breaking into the inner harbour early on the morning of the 18th, the raiders sank the armoured cruiser *Pamiat Azova* and the dreadnought *Petropavlosk*, and seriously damaged the *Andrei Pervozvanni* – although three CMBs were sunk during the raid, for which Commander Claude Dobson and Lieutenant Gordon Steele were awarded the VC.

On 29 August an assault was carried out to take a Bolshevik battery position north-west of Emtsa, which was achieved with only minor casualties due to the action of Sergeant Samuel Pearse, whose self-sacrifice in taking out an enemy blockhouse earned him a posthumous VC. By September 1919, all British troops had been withdrawn.

AGAR, Augustus Willington Shelton *Lieutenant, Royal Navy*
17 June 1919 – During the attack on the Bolshevik fleet in Kronstadt Harbour, Russia, he was in command of HM Coastal Motor Boat 4. She entered the bay, penetrated a destroyer screen and was about to attack an enemy warship further inshore when she broke down. Repairs were carried out under heavy fire and twenty minutes later the attack was resumed. She sank the Russian cruiser *Oleg* and then returned to the safety of the open bay.

He had drawn Russian attention, and a reward of £5,000 was placed on his head. Undeterred, he took part in a second Kronstadt raid on 18 August, leading in one column of CMBs and remaining on patrol in the harbour mouth, for which action he was awarded the DSO.

In his earlier naval career, Agar had served on the Iphigenia *– one of the three blockships sunk in the canal mouth at Zeebrugge in the raid in 1918 (p. 363). Later in 1920, Agar was promoted to lieutenant-commander, then commander in 1925, and captain in 1933. It was while he was commanding the cruiser* Dorsetshire *in April 1942 that she and her sister ship,* Cornwall, *were attacked by fifty Japanese bombers launched from carriers in the Indian Ocean while sailing to rejoin the Eastern Fleet to the south-west of Ceylon. Both sank in minutes and Agar went down with his ship. He suffered the bends on surfacing from deep down, permanently damaging one lung; however, he managed to encourage his men and keep their spirits up during a twenty-four-hour ordeal, during which 424 lives were lost due to the extreme heat and shark attacks. 1,122 men from both ships were eventually picked up the next day.*

Agar's last appointment was as Commodore and President of the Royal Naval College, Greenwich, 1943–45, and after a failed candidacy as a conservative in the 1945 election he went home to Alton in Hampshire.

SULLIVAN, Arthur Percy *Corporal, 45th Bn., Royal Fusiliers, attached North Russia Relief Force*
10 August 1919 – When his platoon had to cross the Sheika River, Russia, by means of a narrow plank, an officer and three men fell in. Without hesitation, he jumped into the river and brought them out one by one under intense fire from 100 yards away. Without his action, his comrades would undoubtedly have drowned.

DOBSON, Claude Congreve *Commander, Royal Navy*
18 August 1919 – During the attack on Kronstadt Harbour, Russia, he was in command of the Coastal Motor Boat Flotilla, which he led through

the chain of forts to the entrance of the harbour. HM Coastal Motor Boat 31, from which he directed operations, then passed in under heavy machine-gun fire and torpedoed the battleship before returning to the open sea.

STEELE, Gordon Charles *Lieutenant, Royal Navy*
18 August 1919 – After HM Coastal Motor Boat 88 entered Kronstadt harbour, her commanding officer was shot through the head and the boat veered off course. He took the wheel, steadied her, lifted the officer away from the steering and firing position and torpedoed the battleship at a range of 100 yards. He fired a second torpedo into the battleship and then regained the entrance to the harbour and returned to the open sea, firing his machine-guns at the harbour wall on his way out.

He served as an anti-submarine commander during the Second World War and was author of The Waziristan Campaign (1919–1921).

PEARSE, Samuel George *Sergeant, 45th Bn., Royal Fusiliers, attached North Russia Relief Force*
29 August 1919 – Near Emtsa, Russia, he cut his way through barbed wire under heavy machine-gun and rifle fire and cleared a way for troops to enter a crucial battery position. Seeing that a blockhouse was stalling the advance, he charged it single-handedly, killing its occupants with bombs. He was killed a minute later but it was due to his action that the position was carried with so few casualties.

Like many Australians who wanted to stay with their mates when the fighting ended, he volunteered for the specially formed 45th Bn Royal Fusiliers.

NORTH-WEST FRONTIER

Since May 1919, British-occupied towns and military posts on India's north-western frontier had come under continual attack from Mahsud tribesmen. Following one such attack on a British convoy on 22 October, Captain Henry Adams set up an aid post to deal with the casualties and was awarded the VC for his bravery under fire. A force of sixty-three thousand was mustered to put down the growing Mahsud insurrection, and it set out in November 1919 to invade their mountain territories. One column met no opposition from the Tochi Wazir tribesmen, who accepted British terms, but the Mahsuds refused to attend talks and a second column was sent to subjugate them by force. By 28 December, after heavy fighting, the column was within four miles of Kot Kai, at which point the Mahsuds agreed to British terms – only to break the agreement almost immediately. On 2 January 1920 a lightly manned advance position came under heavy Mahsud attack and the eventual safe withdrawal was accomplished with minimum loss of life due to the leadership of Lieutenant William Kenny, who was awarded the VC following this battle.

The column moved on to take the Mahsud capital of Kaniguram on 6 March 1920, and resistance petered out by early May. However, in the wake of the uprising, the Wana-Waziris in southern Waziristan refused to accept British terms, so a column was dispatched to set up permanent garrisons in the Wana region. These came under frequent attack and between November 1920 and March 1921 over 376 British lives were lost. In April, during a three-hour battle near Haidari Kach, Sepoy Singh became the first Sikh soldier to be awarded the VC. Raids became fewer and any uprisings were quickly put down by punitive expeditions over a period lasting until March 1924.

ANDREWS, Henry John *T/Captain, Indian Medical Service*

22 October 1919 – Whilst he was the senior medical officer in charge of the Khajuri post, Waziristan, north-west India, he heard that a convoy had been attacked and men wounded. He went to the scene under heavy fire and established an aid post, which he then had to move to another position. Finally, when a van was available to move the wounded, he collected them together under fire, and placed them in it. He was killed whilst climbing into the van on completion of his task.

KENNY, William David *Lieutenant, 4th Bn., 39th Garhwal Rifles*

2 January 1920 – Whilst commanding his company near Kot Kai, North-West Frontier, India, he held an advanced position for over four hours under repeated attack from Mahsuds in greatly superior numbers. He repulsed three attacks and was foremost in the fierce hand-to-hand fighting, engaging the enemy with bomb and bayonet. During his company's subsequent withdrawal, he realized that the pursuing enemy were catching up so he turned back and led a counter-attack. He was killed with the rest of his small party, fighting to the last.

ISHAR SINGH *Sepoy, 28th Punjab Regiment*

10 April 1921 – Whilst No. 1 in a Lewis-gun section near Haidari Kach, North-West Frontier, India, he received a gunshot wound in the chest and fell beside his Lewis gun, which was seized by the enemy. He got up, charged the enemy, recovered the Lewis gun, and got it into action. He was told to retire and have his wound dressed but instead made trips to the river to fetch water for the wounded. At one point he stood in front of a medical officer as he tended a wounded man, shielding him with his own body. Three hours later and weak from loss of blood, he finally consented to be evacuated.

THE ARAB REVOLT, MESOPOTAMIA (1920)

After the First World War, lands which made up the German and Ottoman empires were shared among the victors as 'mandate' territories by the League of Nations under the Sykes Picot Agreement. Under this arrangement, the mandate lands – in Britain's case Iraq and Palestine – would remain under their guidance until they were considered able to rule themselves.

There was immediate opposition to British rule in Iraq (Mesopotamia), and Sunni and Shia Muslim clerics cooperated to incite revolt. Exhausted and financially crippled by the war, Britain was obliged to draft in troops from India to deal with the rebellion – and suppression was carried out ruthlessly, with aerial bombardment of Iraqi villages carried out to quell the widespread unrest. On 24 July near Hillah, as his company was retiring, Captain George Henderson earned the VC for holding off repeated enemy charges and rallying his men until they could reach safety – prisoners taken by the Arab rebels were treated savagely, so capture was to be avoided at all costs.

HENDERSON, George Stuart *Captain, 2nd Bn., Manchester Regiment*
24 July 1920 – Shortly after the company under his command was ordered to retire near Hillah, Mesopotamia, a large party of Arabs opened fire from the flanks causing the company to split up and waver. He at once led a charge which drove the enemy off. He led two further bayonet charges, during the second of which he fell wounded but struggled on until he was wounded again. 'I'm done now. Don't let them beat you!' he said to an NCO. He died fighting.

THE SECOND MOHMAND CAMPAIGN (1935)

After years of unrest, as the tribes near India's north-western frontier battled against British colonial expansion, continued political pressure eventually achieved the same rights and institutions for the people of the North-West Frontier Province as were enjoyed in British India. Meanwhile, across the border, Afghanistan was developing into a stable state under the rule of Nadir Shah, who was anxious to stay on friendly terms with the British government in India. Unfortunately, this, and his willingness to accept Britain's frontier policies, caused violent antagonism within Afghanistan and there was an open conspiracy to oust him and restore a former ruler, Amanullah, to the throne. Shah had the leader of the conspiracy arrested and executed in 1932, but was assassinated the following year by the son of the executed rebel. Shah's nineteen-year-old son succeeded him and also maintained cordial relations with British India – however, the hill tribes remained fiercely anti-British and embarked on a two-year rampage of robbery and murder which the Indian Army struggled to contain.

Eventually, in February 1935, the Nowshera Brigade was sent to deal with the powerful Mohmand military led by the Fakir of Alinger. Following a few minor skirmishes, the Mohmands launched a ferocious attack on the

Kila Han position, held by a company of Sikh riflemen and a Gurkha machine-gun platoon. After a night of fierce hand-to-hand fighting, the attackers were driven off, but this action prompted the British to mount a full-scale operation to quash the enemy forces to the west of Malakand and defeat the Fakir conclusively. This largely put an end to tribal revolt and order was reinforced by the presence of thirty thousand Indian troops at the three main frontier forts. However, occasional feuds broke out, and it was at such an action on 29 September 1935 that Captain Godfrey Meynell earned the VC.

MEYNELL, Godfrey *Captain, 5th Bn., Corps of Guides, 12 Frontier Force Regiment, Indian Army*

29 September 1935 – During the final phase of an attack near Mohmand, North-West Frontier, he was sent ahead to make contact with the forward companies. He found them engaged in a struggle with an enemy greatly superior in numbers. He took command and with two Lewis guns and 30 men maintained a steady fire into the enemy, whose greater numbers enabled them to advance until they reached his position and put his Lewis guns out of action. Fierce hand-to-hand fighting followed, during which he was mortally wounded. His action prevented the Mohmands from exploiting their success.

The medal was presented to his widow by Edward VIII, the only VC award during his reign.

THE SECOND WORLD WAR

1939–45

1939

In March 1939, having already taken the Sudetenland area of Czechoslovakia in 1938, Hitler ordered that Bohemia and Moravia should be occupied. On 1 September, after signing a non-aggression pact with the USSR, he ordered the invasion of Poland. Britain and France had guaranteed Poland's sovereignty and two days later declared war on Germany. The period from September 1939 to the spring of 1940 came to be known as the 'Phoney War'. Troops of the British Expeditionary Force (BEF) under Lord Gort VC arrived in France and, although patrolling activity took place, there was no all-out attack on Germany to support the Poles. Attacked by Germany from the west, Poland stood no chance and resistance effectively ended with the fall of Warsaw on 27 September. The Soviet Union then occupied eastern Poland.

LINTON, John Wallace *Commander, Royal Navy*
September 1939 to March 1943 – From the outbreak of war until HMS *Turbulent*'s last patrol, Commander Linton was constantly in command of submarines, and during that time inflicted great damage on the enemy. He sank one cruiser, one destroyer, one U-boat, twenty-eight supply ships, some 100,000 tons in all, and destroyed three trains by gunfire. In his last year he spent 254 days at sea, submerged for nearly half the time, and his ship was hunted thirteen times and had 250 depth charges aimed at her. His many and brilliant successes were due to his constant activity and skill, and the daring which never failed him when there was an enemy to be attacked. On one occasion, for instance, in HMS *Turbulent*, he sighted a convoy of two merchantmen and two destroyers in mist and moonlight. He worked round ahead of the convoy and dived to attack it as it passed through the moon's rays. On bringing his sights to bear he found himself right ahead of a destroyer. Yet he held his course till the destroyer was almost on top of him, and, when his sights came on the convoy, he fired. His great courage and determination were rewarded. He sank one merchantman and one destroyer outright, and set the other merchantman on fire so that she blew up.
Linton was lost with his crew when Turbulent *was sunk off Maddelina harbour, Italy, on 23 March 1943. His son, William, also died in a submarine, when* Affray *disappeared in the English Channel in 1951.*

1940

The German invasion of Holland, Belgium and France began on 10 May and culminated in the defeat of all three countries by 25 June. Slower-moving German troops pushed into Belgium and Holland, drawing mobile British and French troops to hold a line on the River Dyle in Belgium, while German armoured formations moved through southern Belgium to break through the French defences at Sedan. The Luftwaffe had destroyed most of the French air force in the opening hours, giving them almost complete air superiority. By concentrating its tanks into panzer divisions backed by dive-bombers, the German army achieved a local superiority in numbers and firepower and overwhelmed defences.

Despite its bravery the BEF, with French and Belgian formations, was forced back by German tanks and mechanized infantry to the Channel coast near Dunkirk. The British pushed hard to evacuate the pocket. Between 27 May and 4 June ships of the Royal Navy and merchant marine evacuated 338,226 British, French and other Allied troops to Britain. To the British it was a deliverance. Significantly it meant that there remained a core of regular soldiers, who had seen action, who would be the basis for the expanded force that was being formed in Britain. Some of these men volunteered for the commandos, the first British Special Forces formations, which took the war back to Occupied Europe in raids and reconnaissance operations. RAF Bomber Command was the only other way in which forces in Britain could strike back at Germany.

On 10 June Italy entered the war on Germany's side. On 14 June Paris fell to the advancing German forces, and following the French capitulation, southern and eastern France remained under French administration from the spa town of Vichy. Vichy France also continued to administer the French colonies and protectorates including those in North Africa and the Middle East.

In July the Luftwaffe consolidated itself along the French coast and began attacks on tactical and strategic targets in Britain. This was seen as the preliminary phase of an invasion of Britain in August or September, or a way of forcing her to accept defeat. The Battle of Britain began in July; the Luftwaffe made an all-out assault on 13 August and continued until October, when they realized they would not achieve daytime air superiority over south-east England. The Germans abandoned their invasion plan.

King George VI instituted the George Cross on 23 September, intending it for 'deeds of valour by civilian men and women in all walks of life'. The GC stood, and stands, alongside the VC. As well as to civilians it was awarded to courageous servicemen who had not been in direct contact with the enemy, including men of the bomb-disposal units that disarmed and cleared unexploded German bombs.

NORWAY

On 16 February the destroyer HMS *Cossack* intercepted the German supply ship *Altmark* in neutral Norwegian waters and released British merchant seamen captured by the *Graf Spee* in 1939 who were being held prisoner. Hitler and the German High Command realized that British naval activity threatened the supply of high-grade Swedish iron ore exported along the Norwegian coast. An invasion that would take over Denmark and Norway was set in motion on 9 April. Denmark was an easy conquest, but Norway resisted fiercely. The British, French and Polish forces sent to assist the Norwegians and at Narvik were close to victory in May 1940 when events in Belgium and France made Norway a sideshow. The Allied forces were withdrawn to France and Britain to face the new threat.

ROOPE, Gerard Broadmead *Lieutenant Commander, Royal Navy*
8 April 1940 – HMS *Glowworm* was proceeding alone in heavy weather towards a rendezvous in West Fjord when she met and engaged two enemy destroyers, scoring at least one hit on them. The enemy broke off the action and headed north, to lead the *Glowworm* onto his supporting forces. The commanding officer, correctly appreciating the intentions of the enemy, at once gave chase. The German heavy cruiser *Admiral Hipper* was sighted closing the *Glowworm* at high speed and an enemy report was sent which was received by HMS *Renown*. Because of the heavy sea, *Glowworm* could not shadow the enemy and the commanding officer therefore decided to attack with torpedoes and then to close in order to inflict as much damage as possible. Five torpedoes were fired and later the remaining five, but without success. The *Glowworm* was badly hit; one gun was out of action and her speed was much reduced, but with the other three guns still firing she closed and rammed the *Admiral Hipper*. As the *Glowworm* drew away, she opened fire again and scored one hit at a range of 400 yards. The *Glowworm*, badly stove in forward and riddled with enemy fire, heeled over to starboard, and the commanding officer gave the order to abandon her. Shortly afterwards she capsized and sank. The *Admiral Hipper* hove to for at least an hour picking up survivors but the loss of life was heavy, only 31 out of the complement of 149 being saved. Full information concerning this action has only recently been received and the Victoria Cross is bestowed in

recognition of the great valour of the commanding officer who, after fighting off a superior force of destroyers, sought out and reported a powerful enemy unit, and then fought his ship to the end against overwhelming odds, finally ramming the enemy with supreme coolness and skill.

WARBURTON-LEE, Bernard Armitage Warburton *Captain, Royal Navy*
   10 April 1940 – On being ordered to carry out an attack on Narvik, he learned that the enemy held the place in much greater force than had been thought. He signalled to the Admiralty that the enemy were reported to be holding Narvik in force, that six destroyers and one submarine were there, that the channel might be mined, and that he intended to attack at dawn, high water. The Admiralty replied that two Norwegian coast-defence ships might be in German hands, that he alone could judge whether to attack, and that whatever decision he made would have full support. Captain Warburton-Lee gave out the plan for his attack and led his flotilla of five destroyers up the fjord in heavy snowstorms, arriving off Narvik just after daybreak. He took the enemy completely by surprise and made three successful attacks on warships and merchantmen in the harbour. The last attack was made only after anxious debate. On the flotilla withdrawing, five enemy destroyers of superior gun-power were encountered and engaged. The captain was mortally wounded by a shell which hit HMS *Hardy*'s bridge. His last signal was 'Continue to engage the enemy'.

STANNARD, Richard Been *Lieutenant, Royal Naval Reserve*
   28 April to 2 May 1940 – When enemy bombing attacks had set on fire many tons of hand grenades on Namsos wharf, with no shore water supply available, Lieutenant Stannard ran HMS *Arab*'s bows against the wharf and held her there. Sending all but 2 of his crew aft, he then endeavoured for two hours to extinguish the fire with hoses from the forecastle. He persisted in this work till the attempt had to be given up as hopeless. After helping other ships against air attacks, he placed his own damaged vessel under shelter of a cliff, landed his crew and those of two other trawlers, and established an armed camp. Here those off duty could rest while he attacked enemy aircraft which approached by day, and kept anti-submarine watch during the night. When another trawler nearby was hit and set on fire by a bomb, he, with two others, boarded *Arab* and moved her 100 yards before the other vessel blew up. Finally, when leaving the fjord, he was attacked by a German bomber which ordered him to steer east or be sunk. He held on his course, reserved his fire till the enemy was within 800 yards, and then brought the aircraft down. Throughout a period of five days *Arab* was subjected to thirty-one bombing attacks and the camp and Lewis gun positions ashore were repeatedly machine-gunned and bombed; yet the defensive position was so well planned that only 1 man was wounded. Lieutenant Stannard ultimately brought his damaged ship back to an English port.

FRANCE AND BELGIUM

The German invasion of France and the Low Countries began at dawn on 10 May. The next day the BEF had arrived at the River Dyle, with its reserve on the River Escaut (the Scheldt), and was attacked on the 14th. On the night of the 17th/18th it withdrew, and on the 18th/19th had reached the Escaut. Lord Gort ordered a counter-attack near Arras, then withdrew to the Franco-Belgian border on 22/23 May. On 26 May the government authorized Operation Dynamo, the evacuation through Dunkirk.

GARLAND, Donald Edward *Flying Officer, 12 Squadron, Royal Air Force*
12 May 1940 – Flying Officer Garland was the pilot and Sergeant GRAY the observer of the leading aircraft of a formation of five that attacked a bridge over the Albert Canal which had not been destroyed and was allowing the enemy to advance into Belgium. All the air crews of the squadron concerned volunteered for the operation, and after five crews had been selected by drawing lots, the attack was delivered at low altitude against this vital target. Orders were issued that this bridge was to be destroyed at all costs. As had been anticipated, exceptionally intense machine-gun and anti-aircraft fire was encountered, and the bridge area was heavily protected by enemy fighters. In spite of this the formation success-fully delivered a dive-bombing attack from the lowest practicable altitude and British fighters in the vicinity reported that the target was obscured by the bombs bursting on it and in its vicinity. Only one aircraft returned from this mission out of the five. The pilot of this aircraft reported that in addition to the extremely heavy anti-aircraft fire, through which the aircraft dived to attack the objective, they were also attacked by a large number of enemy fighters after they had released their bombs on the target.
Flying Officer Garland and Sergeant Gray failed to return from this mission. Garland was the first of four brothers who died in the war.

GRAY, Thomas *Sergeant, 12 Squadron, Royal Air Force*
12 May 1940 – Flying Officer GARLAND was the pilot and Sergeant Gray the observer of the leading aircraft of a formation of five that attacked a bridge over the Albert Canal which had not been destroyed and was allowing the enemy to advance into Belgium. All the air crews of the squadron concerned volunteered for the operation, and after five crews had been selected by drawing lots, the attack was delivered at low altitude against this vital target. Orders were issued that this bridge was to be destroyed at all costs. As had been anticipated, exceptionally intense machine-gun and anti-aircraft fire was encountered, and the bridge area was heavily protected by enemy fighters. In spite of this the formation success-fully delivered a dive-bombing attack from the lowest practicable altitude and British fighters in the vicinity reported that the target was obscured by

the bombs bursting on it and in its vicinity. Only one aircraft returned from this mission out of the five. The pilot of this aircraft reported that in addition to the extremely heavy anti-aircraft fire, through which the aircraft dived to attack the objective, they were also attacked by a large number of enemy fighters after they had released their bombs on the target.

ANNAND, Richard Wallace

In accounts of the campaign before the evacuation of the British Expeditionary Force from the beaches of Dunkirk in the last days of May 1940, all the talk is of a rout of the British by the advancing German Blitzkrieg. But the Allied forces put up spirited resistance, and at one battle, at the River Dyle, Second Lieutenant Annand of the 2nd Battalion the Durham Light Infantry fought with tireless courage and devotion and earned the VC. His citation details how, as his platoon was camped on either side of a blown bridge over the river, a German bridging party came forward and Annand ordered an attack to drive them back. When the ammunition ran out, he advanced alone into open ground and pelted the Germans with grenades, causing severe casualties. He continued fighting, although wounded, and carried out another solo grenade attack – then when ordered back, he withdrew the platoon, only to learn that his batman had been wounded and left behind. He returned to the river alone to fetch him, bringing him to safety in a wheelbarrow before collapsing from his wounds.

That batman, Sergeant T. O'Neil, wrote his account of Annand's actions in the *Journal and Northern Mail*, and this personal view gives a more complete picture.

> On the night of 15 May, Mr Annand came to me at platoon headquarters and asked for a box of grenades as he could hear Jerry trying to repair the bridge. Off he went, and he sure must have given them a lovely time because it wasn't a great while before he was back for more. Just like giving an elephant strawberries.
>
> The previous night, while the heavy stuff of both sides were sending over their mutual regards, he realized that he had not received word from our right forward section which held a pillbox about 250 yards to our right front, so he went out to see how they were fixed. He had gone about two hours and we had come to the conclusion that they had got him when something which I found hard to recognize came crawling in. It was just Jake – that is the name by which we knew him. He looked as though he had been having an argument with a wild cat. His clothes were torn to shreds and he was cut and bruised all over. How he got there and back only he knows, because he had the fire of our own troops to contend with as well as Jerry's. I don't suppose he knows the meaning of fear. He never asked a man to do anything he could do himself. He wouldn't talk much about it. He wasn't that kind. It was just another job of work for him.

Another platoon of Royal Welch Fusiliers came to reinforce us and had been there only half an hour when one of our own mortar bombs dropped right among them. Jake came dashing up, asked me what had happened and then off he went, galloping up the hillside to stop the mortar platoon. He didn't even stop to take his steel helmet and he was under fire all the way.

Many officers were greatly respected and admired by their batmen – they were the men who probably knew them best in their platoons. The actions of Richard Annand, however, engendered something more – an unquestioning devotion to a man who had risked his own life to save him.

At the time of publication, Richard Annand is one of the surviving VC holders.

FURNESS, the Hon. Christopher *Lieutenant, 1st Bn., Welsh Guards*

17–24 May 1940 – He was in command of the carrier platoon, Welsh Guards, from 17 to 24 May 1940, when his battalion formed part of the garrison of Arras. During this time his platoon was constantly patrolling in advance of or between the widely dispersed parts of the perimeter, and fought many local actions with the enemy. During the evening of 23 May, he was wounded when on patrol but he refused to be evacuated. By this time the enemy, considerably reinforced, had encircled the town on three sides and withdrawal to Douai was ordered during the night of 23/24 May. Lieutenant Furness's platoon, together with a small force of light tanks, was ordered to cover the withdrawal of the transport, consisting of over forty vehicles. About 0230 hours the enemy attacked on both sides of the town. At one point the enemy advanced to the road along which the transport columns were withdrawing, bringing them under very heavy small-arms and anti-tank-gun fire: the whole column was blocked and placed in serious jeopardy. Immediately Lieutenant Furness, appreciating the seriousness of the situation, and in spite of his wounds, decided to attack the enemy, who were located in a strongly entrenched position behind wire. He advanced with three Bren-gun carriers, supported by the light tanks. At once the enemy opened up with very heavy fire from small arms and anti-tank guns. The light tanks were put out of action, but Furness continued to advance. He reached the enemy position and circled it several times at close range, inflicting heavy losses. All three carriers were hit and most of their crews killed or wounded. His own carrier was disabled and the driver and Bren-gunner killed. He then engaged the enemy in personal hand-to-hand combat until he was killed. His magnificent act of self-sacrifice against hopeless odds, and when already wounded, made the enemy withdraw for the time being, enabled the large column of vehicles to get clear unmolested and covered the evacuation of some of the wounded of his own carrier platoon and the light tanks.

GRISTOCK, George *Company Sergeant Major, Royal Norfolk Regiment*

21 May 1940 – His company was holding a position on the line of the River Escaut, south of Tournai. After a prolonged attack, the enemy succeeded in breaking through beyond the company's right flank, which was consequently threatened. Gristock, having organized a party of eight riflemen from company headquarters, went forward to cover the right flank. Realizing that an enemy machine-gun had moved forward to a position from which it was inflicting heavy casualties on his company, he went on, with 1 man as connecting file, to try to put it out of action. Whilst advancing, he came under heavy machine-gun fire from the opposite bank and was severely wounded in both legs, his right knee being badly smashed. He nevertheless gained his fire position, some 20 yards from the enemy machine-gun post, undetected, and by well-aimed rapid fire killed the machine-gun crew of four and put their gun out of action. He then dragged himself back to the right flank position, from which he refused to be evacuated until contact with the battalion on the right had been established and the line once more made good.

Gristock later died of his wounds.

NICHOLLS, Harry *Lance Corporal, 3rd Bn., Grenadier Guards*

21 May 1940 – Nicholls was commanding a section in the right-forward platoon of his company near the River Scheldt when the company was ordered to counter-attack. At the very start of the advance he was wounded in the arm by shrapnel, but continued to lead his section forward; as the company came over a small ridge, the enemy opened heavy machine-gun fire at close range. Nicholls, realizing the danger to the company, immediately seized a Bren gun and dashed forward towards the machine-guns, firing from the hip. He succeeded in silencing first one machine-gun and then two other machine-guns, in spite of being again severely wounded. Nicholls then went on up to a higher piece of ground and engaged the German infantry massed behind, causing many casualties, and continuing to fire until he had no more ammunition left. He was wounded at least four times in all, but absolutely refused to give in. His company reached its objective, and the enemy fell back across the River Scheldt.

He was reported killed in action, but was in fact taken prisoner. He spent the rest of the war in Stalag XXB in Poland.

ERVINE-ANDREWS, Harold Marcus *A/Captain, East Lancashire Regiment*

31 May/1 June 1940 – Captain Ervine-Andrews took over about 1,000 yards of the defences in front of Dunkirk, his line extending along the Canal de Bergues, and the enemy attacked at dawn. For over ten hours, notwithstanding intense artillery, mortar, and machine-gun fire, and in the face of vastly superior enemy forces, Ervine-Andrews and his company held their position. The enemy, however, succeeded in crossing the canal on both flanks; and, owing to superior enemy forces, a company of Ervine-Andrews' own battalion, which was despatched to protect his flanks, was unable to gain contact with him. There being danger of one of his platoons being driven in, he called for volunteers to fill the gap, and then, going forward, climbed onto the top of a straw-roofed barn, from which he engaged the enemy with rifle and light automatic fire, though, at the time, the enemy were sending mortar bombs and armour-piercing bullets through the roof. Ervine-Andrews personally accounted for 17 of the enemy with his rifle, and for many more with a Bren gun. Later, when the house which he held had been shattered by enemy fire and set alight, and all his ammunition had been expended, he sent back his wounded in the remaining carrier. He then collected the remaining 8 men of his company from this forward position, and, when almost completely surrounded, led them back to the cover afforded by the company in the rear, swimming or wading up to the chin in water for over a mile; having brought all that remained of his company safely back, he once again took up position.

STRATEGIC BOMBING

In August 1939, the RAF had fifty-five squadrons in Bomber Command and thirty-nine squadrons in Fighter Command, with about 350 and 600 operational aircraft respectively, and Coastal Command, with 96. In the first months of the war bombing operations were carried out in daylight, by aircraft flying in small groups and without a fighter escort, either on strategic targets in Germany or in cooperation with ground forces before the fall of France.

CHESHIRE, Geoffrey Leonard

At the age of seventeen, Geoffrey Leonard Cheshire was passionate about fast cars – but three years later he was drawn to aircraft, and in 1937 he joined the Oxford University Air Squadron. When war began he was commissioned into the RAFVR and later began operations in June 1940. Even at this early stage, German targets were strongly defended, but on the basis that there was no point in making raids at all if you didn't hit the target, Cheshire soon became known for accepting extra elements of risk in order to guarantee success, and occasionally, to make sure of a hit, would release his bombs at a much lower altitude than the textbooks dictated. On one occasion in November 1940 over Cologne, an anti-aircraft shell burst inside his aircraft, blowing out one side and starting a fire, but he proceeded regardless to his target, bombed it and made it back in one piece.

When he finished his first operational tour in January 1941, he immediately volunteered for a second – during which he survived missions over the major cities of the Reich. At the end of this tour he was given a posting with instructional duties, but he much preferred to lead on real missions than teach, and after six months he received his first squadron command and embarked on a third tour, which lasted from August 1942 to March 1943. This tour completed he was promoted to group captain – and given a desk job as deputy base commander. Others might have felt they had done their fair share, but Cheshire was itching to get back into the air, so he requested a return to the rank of wing commander and, having already earned the DFC, and the DSO with two bars, one of the most highly decorated men in the RAF, he returned for a fourth bombing tour in October 1943.

This was probably his most famous – and tactically influential – tour, with the now much-feted 617 Squadron. Many major targets had been effectively destroyed, but the immediate challenge was to devise a means of achieving greater accuracy over smaller targets. Cheshire developed the 'Master Bomber' technique, whereby one aircraft would fly lower than the rest and act as a marker. The theory was first put into practice with successful strikes on flying-bomb sites at the Pas de Calais, and then more ambitiously against German aircraft production sites in France. By March 1944, eleven of the twelve selected sites had been destroyed or damaged, the new technique being used in conjunction with the new 12,000lb blast bomb.

Cheshire flew the first raid using the 12,000-pounder with himself as marker – he was not one to ask his pilots and crews to do anything he would not be prepared to do himself. The target was an aero-engine factory at Limoges, to which Cheshire led his twelve Lancasters under bright moonlight. Taking his marker plane down to just 200 feet, he dropped incendiary bombs right in the centre of the target. The smoke and flames from these bombs left a mark for his deputy leader, who dropped two red-spot flares from a height of 7,000 feet. Soon the factory was ablaze for the bomb aimers of the following aircraft to pinpoint. Four out of the five 12,000lb bombs dropped were dead on target, causing complete devastation. The theory worked in practice, and with the sensible adjustment of using the more manoeuvrable Mosquito for the marker duty, it was adopted as a modus operandi for bombing in any weather conditions. Adjusting the fine details of the procedure according to the target and the visibility, Cheshire chalked up more and more successes, especially in the 'softening-up' period prior to the D-Day invasion in June.

On one such trip on 20 April, more than 250 aircraft took part in a raid on the railway marshalling yards of La Chapelle. In a finely tuned schedule, six Mosquitoes dropped strips of metallic 'window' to baffle the enemy radar, two minutes ahead of the main raid. The first wave of bombers dropped green target indicators, but three didn't function correctly, and Cheshire in the next wave had little time to mark the target accurately. Thinking quickly, he found and marked the aiming point with red-spot flares and had his deputy reinforce these points. Despite several delays and unforeseen glitches, the raid was a success, and Cheshire's planning was proved to work on a grand scale.

Two further raids in April were directed against crucial targets – this time in Germany itself. The first, employing 265 aircraft to bomb Bruns-wick, succeeded in spite of several malfunctions, including the failure of the VHF radio. At least 50 per cent of the 741 tons of bombs dropped hit the target, and only three of the aircraft were lost. It was the next raid, on Munich on 24 April, which clinched the VC award for Cheshire. Again, 265 aircraft took off, and despite the very heavy defences – a couple of hundred anti-aircraft guns – only ten failed to reach the target. Eleven Mosquitoes flew directly to the target to drop 'window' as the main bomber force fol-lowed on an oblique route, following marker flares. They arrived as planned, to drop their bombs on the positions marked by Cheshire and three other Mosquito pilots, who had to pass the heavy defences from Augsburg to Munich. At one point, Cheshire, leading, came into a cone of searchlight beams and every gun in range opened up on him, but he dived to 700 feet, spotted and marked the target and ordered the other markers to back him up. He then remained in the air over Munich, directing the attack, despite his aircraft being hit and once almost losing control due to the glare of the searchlights. Only when he was satisfied that he could do no more did he turn home – but stayed in a hail of blistering fire for a further twelve minutes before he got clear away.

The bombers gave great support to the invasion force following D-Day – now using the 14,000lb Tallboy bomb, which reached the ground faster than sound, thereby giving no tell-tale warning noise. Cheshire orchestrated these operations with painstaking precision, and achieved devastating results.

Having flown more than 100 missions, Cheshire was sent to India in July 1944, and then posted as group captain to America, from where he flew in one of the B-29s on the second atomic bomb raid on 9 August 1945, to the Japanese city of Nagasaki.

After the war he continued to make his mark, establishing the Cheshire Foundation Homes for the incurably ill – a lasting memorial to a man of courage and determination.

LEAROYD, Roderick Alastair Brook *A/Flight Lieutenant, 49 Squadron, Royal Air Force*

12/13 August 1940 – He was detailed to attack a special objective on the Dortmund–Ems Canal. He had attacked it on a previous occasion and was well aware of the risks entailed. To achieve success it was necessary to approach from a direction well known to the enemy, through a lane of especially disposed anti-aircraft defences, and in the face of the most intense point-blank fire from guns of all calibres. The reception of the preceding aircraft might well have deterred the stoutest heart, all being hit and two lost. Learoyd nevertheless made his attack at 150 feet, his aircraft being repeatedly hit and large pieces of the main planes torn away. He was almost blinded by the glare of many searchlights at close range but pressed home this attack with the greatest resolution and skill. He subsequently brought his wrecked aircraft home, and as the landing flaps were inoperative and the undercarriage indicators out of action, waited for dawn in the vicinity of his aerodrome before landing, which he accomplished without causing injury to his crew or further damage to the aircraft.

HANNAH, John *Sergeant, 83 Squadron, Royal Air Force*
15/16 September 1940 – He was the wireless operator/air gunner in an aircraft engaged in a successful attack on enemy barge concentrations at Antwerp. It was then subjected to intense anti-aircraft fire and received a direct hit from a projectile of an explosive and incendiary nature, which apparently burst inside the bomb compartment. A fire started which quickly enveloped the wireless operator's and rear gunner's cockpits, and as both the port and starboard petrol tanks had been pierced, there was grave risk of the fire spreading. Sergeant Hannah forced his way through the fire to obtain two extinguishers and discovered that the rear gunner had had to leave the aircraft. He could have acted likewise, through the bottom escape hatch or forward through the navigator's hatch, but remained and fought the fire for ten minutes with the extinguishers, beating the flames with his log book when these were empty. During this time thousands of rounds of ammunition exploded in all directions and he was almost blinded by the intense heat and fumes, but had the presence of mind to obtain relief by turning on his oxygen supply. Air admitted through the large holes caused by the projectile made the bomb compartment an inferno and all the aluminium sheet metal on the floor of this airman's cockpit was melted away, leaving only the cross bearers. Working under these conditions, which caused burns to his face and eyes, Hannah succeeded in extinguishing the fire. He then crawled forward, ascertained that the navigator had left the aircraft, and passed the latter's log and maps to the pilot, which enabled him to bring the aircraft safely to its base.
At eighteen years ten months, he was the youngest air VC.

LUFTWAFFE ATTACKS

MANTLE, Jack Foreman *A/Leading Seaman, Royal Navy*
4 July 1940 – He was in charge of the starboard pom-pom when HMS *Foylebank* was attacked by enemy aircraft during an air-raid on Portland. Early in the action his left leg was shattered by a bomb, but he stood fast at his gun and went on firing with hand-gear only, for the ship's electric power had failed. Almost at once he was wounded again in many places. Between

his bursts of fire he had time to reflect on the grievous injuries of which he was soon to die; but his great courage bore him up till the end of the fight, when he fell by the gun he had so valiantly served.

Mantle's VC was the first awarded to the Royal Navy for an act of valour on mainland Britain.

NICOLSON, Eric James Brindley

James Nicolson was born in London on 29 April 1917, but grew up in Shoreham-by-Sea in Sussex where, when he left school, he joined Ricardo Engineering to work, just prior to joining the RAF in 249 Squadron late in 1936.

In the summer of 1940, as the Battle of Britain raged in the skies over the south coast, 249 Squadron was posted to Boscombe Down in Wiltshire with the task of patrolling the area to the west of Southampton. It was on such a foray that Nicolson earned the only VC of Fighter Command awarded during the Second World War.

The citation gives only a brief account of his actions on 16 August, and although he may have dressed up his own recollection of the attack with a dash of bravado, his words provide a vivid picture. He describes how the flight commander had ordered him to chase three Junkers 88 bombers with his section of three Hurricanes – and as they did so, they drove them into range of a squadron of Spitfires, which finished them off. As he climbed to rejoin his squadron his aircraft took four hits from a Messerschmitt 110 that he had failed to notice.

> The first shell tore through the hood of the cockpit, sending splinters into my left eye, and one splinter, I discovered later, almost severed my eyelid. I couldn't see through the eye for blood. The second shell hit the spare petrol tank, setting it on fire, whilst the third shell crashed into the cockpit and tore off my right trouser leg.

Finding he could still see through his windshield and apparently not tempted to limp home, Nicolson gave chase to his attacker.

> I remember shouting loudly at him, when I first saw him, 'I'll teach you some manners, you Hun!' and I shouted other things as well! I knew that I was scoring hits on him all the time I was firing, and by this time it was pretty hot in the cockpit from the effects of the burst petrol tank. I couldn't see much flame, but I knew that it was there all right. I remember once looking at my left hand which was keeping the throttle open. It seemed to be on fire itself and I could see the skin peeling off it – yet I could feel little pain.

Nicolson watched as the Messerschmitt went down, and on the third attempt managed to lever himself out of the burning aircraft and pull the ripcord of his parachute. Playing dead to avoid further fire from a passing Messerschmitt as he descended, he assessed his injuries.

> The burns on my left hand left the knuckle showing through, and for the first time I discovered that my left foot was wounded – blood was oozing out of the lace holes and my right hand was pretty badly burned too.

Maybe the sight of his injuries awoke him to the pain – he recalled:

> The oxygen mask was still covering my face, but my hands were in too bad a state to remove it. I tried, but I couldn't manage it. I found, too, that I had lost a trouser leg and the other was badly torn. My tunic was like a lot of smouldering torn rags, so I wasn't looking very smart! Then, after a bit more of this dangling down business, I began to ache all over and my arms and legs began to hurt a lot.

Steering himself away from the sea and narrowly avoiding high-tension power cables, he managed to land in a field.

> I had a piece of good news almost immediately. One of the people who had come along and witnessed the combat said that they had seen the Messerschmitt dive straight into the sea – so it hadn't been such a bad day after all!

Nicolson's wounds were so bad that one doctor gave him only twenty-four hours to live – he had extensive third-degree burns and cannon-shell wounds and splinters of perspex all over his body, and his clothes were still smouldering as he landed. Past the critical stage and convalescing three months later in Torquay, he learned that the DFC for which his commanding officer had recommended him had been upgraded to the VC. He greeted this news with the comment, 'Now I'll have to earn it.'

It was a popular award with the public – the pilots of Fighter Command had saved Britain from invasion and it was good to see their bravery recognized with the highest award for valour – but Nicolson himself felt there were others much worthier of the honour. No one could question his bravery, but there was an undercurrent of resentment within Fighter Command. Why him and not the other heroes of the Battle of Britain – Stanford Tuck, Johnson, Lacey or Bader?

Nicolson took a year to recover from his injuries but was anxious to get back and prove his worth. In command of a squadron flying Mosquitoes he carried out many operations against Japanese ground targets, but never engaged in aerial combat again. He was awarded the DFC for this campaign, and was then posted to Bengal as Wing Commander of Training. He was itching to fly real sorties again, so persuaded one of his superiors to let him fly as an observer on a Liberator bombing mission over Rangoon in August 1943. When the outer starboard engine caught fire, the captain had to ditch the aircraft in darkness over the Bay of Bengal – the Liberator sank, and with it 10 men, one of whom was James Nicolson. It is an irony that a man who had survived against all odds in combat should die as the result of an aircraft malfunction.

In 1983 Muriel, Nicolson's widow, found herself unable to survive on the RAF pension provided and had no choice but to sell her husband's medals. The VC and DFC were expected to fetch around £25,000 at auction, the going rate at the time, but in the event they were sold for £105,000. There unfolded a dramatic bidding competition in which a representative of the RAF Museum and a coin dealer drove the price higher and higher, neither realizing that the other had the same end in view – to see Nicolson's awards saved for the nation at the RAF Museum, Hendon, where they are now on display.

BRITISH SOMALILAND

Having declared war on Britain and France on 10 June, Italy made good use of her five hundred thousand troops in East Africa: on 3 August she invaded British Somaliland with twenty-six divisions. The British garrison was only fifteen hundred men; reinforcements were in place behind the Tug Argan Gap, which controlled the main road to Berbera, the port, on the 10th. On the 11th the main Italian column attacked, and despite a determined stand had taken the key position of Observation Hill by the evening of the 15th. Withdrawal was ordered that night, covered by the 2nd Battalion, the Black Watch. The Somaliland Camel Corps were disarmed by the British and ordered to return home; the final elements were evacuated in good order on 18 August. Berbera was retaken from the sea on 16 March 1941.

WILSON, Eric Charles Twelves *A/Captain, East Surrey Regiment, attached Somaliland Camel Corps*
11–15 August 1940 – He was in command of machine-gun posts manned by Somali soldiers in the key position of Observation Hill, a defended post in the defensive organization of the Tug Argan Gap in British Somaliland. The enemy attacked Observation Hill on 11 August. Captain Wilson and Somali gunners under his command beat off the attack and opened fire on the enemy troops attacking Mill Hill, another post within his range. He inflicted such heavy casualties that the enemy, determined to put his guns out of action, brought up a pack battery to within 700 yards, and scored two direct hits through the loopholes of his defences, which, bursting within the post, wounded Captain Wilson severely in the right shoulder and in the left eye, several of his team being also wounded. His guns were blown off their stands but he repaired and replaced them and, regardless of his wounds, carried on, whilst his Somali sergeant was killed beside him. On 12 and 14 August the enemy again concentrated field artillery fire on Captain Wilson's guns, but he continued, with his wounds untended, to man them. On the 15th two of his machine-gun posts were blown to pieces, yet Wilson, now suffering from malaria in addition to wounds, still kept his own post in

action. The enemy finally overran the post at 5 p.m. on the 15th when Captain Wilson, fighting to the last, was killed.

He was not in fact killed, but was taken prisoner. He learned that he had been awarded the VC posthumously. He and his fellow prisoners had nearly completed an escape tunnel and were planning a mass breakout when the Italian guards vanished. A few hours later he was liberated. At the time of publication he is one of the few surviving VC holders.

ROYAL NAVY

FEGEN, Edward Stephen Fogarty *A/Captain, Royal Navy*
5 November 1940 – Captain Fegen, in His Majesty's Armed Merchant Cruiser *Jervis Bay*, was escorting thirty-eight merchantmen in heavy seas in the *Atlantic*. Sighting a powerful German warship, the *Admiral Scheer*, he at once drew clear of the convoy, made straight for the enemy, and brought his ship between the raider and her prey, so that they might scatter and escape. Crippled, in flames, unable to reply, for nearly an hour the *Jervis Bay* held the German's fire. So she went down: but of the merchantmen all but four or five were saved.

1941

At the start of the year Britain stood virtually alone – her army was still at home after the evacuation from Dunkirk. Hitler focused the efforts of the Luftwaffe on bombing Britain's cities and with the efforts of his U-boat wolf-packs hitting hard, stringent rationing was enforced in Britain. Only in the Western Desert was there any success.

In April, Hitler invaded Yugoslavia and Greece. Britain rushed troops to Greece, who fought bravely but were forced to evacuate to Crete.

On 24 May, in the Atlantic, the *Bismarck* sank HMS *Hood*. The chase was on to sink the *Bismarck* – which was finally achieved on the 27th.

June saw the start of Operation Barbarossa, the German invasion of the Soviet Union. Blitzkrieg finally overreached itself. As the Soviet winter set in, German supply lines disintegrated and icy conditions began to take their toll. The Russian defenders prepared for a sustained defence with winter to assist them.

In the Mediterranean, Britain moved troops in to defend Crete, with final reinforcements arriving just four days before the start of the German invasion of the strategically important island. Malta also came into the war as German raids and naval attacks threatened to starve the civilian population into submission. RAF support in the form of Spitfire squadrons was shipped in to bolster up the island's defence.

In January talks had begun on the consequences of US entry into the war, and in May German naval chief Admiral Raeder warned America that if she gave protection to British convoys it would be considered an act of war. In April, the USSR and Japan had signed a five-year Neutrality Agreement – but this became academic when on 7 December Japanese aircraft attacked the American naval base of Pearl Harbor in Hawaii, bringing the two final protagonists into the war and opening up a new front in the Far East. Japanese forces overran Hong Kong, and off the Malaysian coast, sank the *Prince of Wales* and the *Repulse*.

NORTH AFRICA

Italy had completed her East African campaign in 1940 with the occupation of French Somaliland. General Sir Archibald Wavell, C.-in-C. Middle East, planned offensives into Libya and Italian East Africa. Between 9 December 1940 and 7 February 1941 he struck westwards, capturing Sidi Barrani, Bardia and Tobruk, cutting off the Italian retreat at Beda Fomm, and taking a hundred and thirty thousand prisoners. Hitler met Mussolini on 19 January, and agreed to send him two divisions under the command of Major General Erwin Rommel. He arrived at Tripoli on 12 February with only one of his divisions, the 5th Light, in place, and with orders to wait until the 15th Panzer arrived in May before attempting to retake Benghazi: but he found the Allied positions unexpectedly weak and disorganized, and struck at once. By 11 April he had laid siege to Tobruk, and by the end of the month had reached the Egyptian border.

On 18 November Rommel, newly returned from Rome, was taken by surprise and was unable to stop the British 30th Corps from advancing 50 miles and taking the Axis airfield 10 miles from Sidi Rezegh. The feint towards Bardia also had the desired effect – believing that the British were about to surround the town, Rommel diverted the Afrika Korps away from what would be the main British attack. The British garrison at Sidi Rezegh was ordered to break out and join up with 30th Corps – but Rommel responded quickly, sending the Afrika Korps to attack at Sidi Rezegh, where he checked the British advance. The fight for the airfield would decide the battle – whoever held the ridge at Sidi Rezegh would dominate the plain in front of Tobruk. As the power of the German guns destroyed British tanks with alarming ease, the breakout from Tobruk had to be halted.

EDMONDSON, John Hurst *Corporal, 2/17th Bn. (New South Wales), Australian Military Forces*

13/14 April 1941 – A party of German infantry broke through the wire defences at Tobruk and established themselves with at least six machine-guns, mortars and two small field pieces. It was decided to attack them with bayonets and a party consisting of one officer, Corporal Edmondson and five privates took part in the charge. During the counter-attack Edmondson was wounded in the neck and stomach but continued to advance under heavy fire and killed one of the enemy with his bayonet. Later, his officer had his bayonet in one of the enemy and was grasped about the legs by him, when another attacked him from behind. He called for help, and Edmondson, who was some yards away, immediately came to his assistance and in spite of his wounds killed both of the enemy. This action undoubtedly saved his officer's life.

Edmonds, who later died of his wounds, was the first Australian to win the VC in the war.

KEYES, Geoffrey Charles Tasker *T/Lieutenant Colonel, Royal Scots Greys, Royal Armoured Corps (11 Scottish Commando)*

17/18 November 1941 – He commanded a detachment of a force which landed some 250 miles behind the enemy lines to attack headquarters, base installations and communications. From the outset he deliberately selected for himself the command of the detachment detailed to attack what was undoubtedly the most hazardous of these objectives, the residence and headquarters of the General Officer Commanding the German forces in North Africa. This attack, even if initially successful, meant almost certain death for those who took part in it. He led his detachment without guides, in dangerous and precipitous country and in pitch darkness, and maintained by his stolid determination and powers of leadership the morale of the detachment. He then found himself forced to modify his original plans in the light of fresh information elicited from neighbouring Arabs, and was left with only one officer and an NCO with whom to break into General Rommel's residence and deal with the guards and headquarters staff. At zero hour, having despatched the covering party to block the approaches to the house, he and the two others crawled forward past the guards, through the surrounding fence and so up to the house itself. Without hesitation, he boldly led his party up to the front door, beat on the door and demanded entrance. Unfortunately, when the door was opened, it was found impossible to overcome the sentry silently, and it was necessary to shoot him. The noise of the shot naturally aroused the inmates of the house and Keyes, appreciating that speed was now of the utmost importance, posted the NCO at the foot of the stairs to prevent interference from the floor above. Keyes, who instinctively took the lead, emptied his revolver with great success into the first room and was followed by the other officer who threw a grenade. Keyes with great daring then entered the second room on the ground floor but was shot almost immediately on flinging open the door and fell back into the passage mortally wounded. On being carried outside by his companions he died within a few minutes.

It was in fact Captain Campbell, a German-speaker, who knocked on the door and shot the sentry.

GUNN, George Ward *Second Lieutenant, 3rd Regiment, Royal Horse Artillery*
   21 November 1941 – At Sidi Rezegh, Second Lieutenant Gunn was in command of a troop of four anti-tank guns which was part of a battery of twelve guns attached to the Rifle Brigade Column. At 1000 hours a covering force of enemy tanks was engaged and driven off but an hour later the main attack developed by about sixty enemy tanks. Gunn drove from gun to gun during this period in an unarmoured vehicle encouraging his men and reorganizing his dispositions as first one gun and then another were knocked out. Finally only two guns remained in action and were subjected to very heavy fire. Immediately afterwards one of these guns was destroyed and the portee of another was set on fire and all the crew killed or wounded except the sergeant, though the gun itself remained undamaged. The battery commander then arrived and started to fight the flames. When he saw this, Gunn ran to his aid through intense fire and immediately got the one

remaining anti-tank gun into action on the burning portee, himself sighting it while the sergeant acted as loader. He continued to fight the gun, firing between forty and fifty rounds regardless alike of the enemy fire, which was by then concentrated on this one vehicle, and of the flames which might at any moment have reached the ammunition with which the portee was loaded. In spite of this, Gunn's shooting was so accurate at a range of about 800 yards that at least two enemy tanks were hit and set on fire and others were damaged before he fell dead, having been shot through the forehead.

BEELEY, John *Rifleman, King's Royal Rifle Corps*
   21 November 1941 – During the attack by a battalion of the King's Royal Rifle Corps at Sidi Rezegh against a strong enemy position, the company to which Rifleman Beeley belonged was pinned down by heavy fire at point-blank range from the front and flank on the flat and open ground of the aerodrome. All the officers but one of the company and many of the other ranks had been either killed or wounded. On his own initiative, and when there was no sort of cover, Beeley got to his feet carrying a Bren gun and ran forward towards a strong enemy post containing an anti-tank gun, a heavy machine-gun and a light machine-gun. He ran 30 yards and discharged a complete magazine at the post from a range of 20 yards, killing or wounding the entire crew of the anti-tank gun. The post was silenced and Beeley's platoon was enabled to advance, but Beeley fell dead across his gun, hit in at least four places. The objective was eventually captured.

CAMPBELL, John Charles *A/Brigadier, Royal Horse Artillery, commanding 7th Armoured Division*
   21–22 November 1941 – He was commanding the troops, including one regiment of tanks, in the area of Sidi Rezegh ridge and the aerodrome. His small force holding this important ground was repeatedly attacked by large numbers of tanks and infantry. Wherever the situation was most difficult and the fighting hardest he was to be seen with his forward troops, either on his feet or in his open car. In this car he carried out several reconnaissances for counter-attacks by his tanks, whose senior officers had all become casualties early in the day. Standing in his car with a blue flag, this officer personally formed up tanks under close and intense fire from all natures of enemy weapons. On the following day the enemy attacks were intensified and again he was always in the forefront of the heaviest fighting, encouraging his troops, staging counter-attacks with his remaining tanks and personally controlling the fire of his guns. On two occasions he himself manned a gun to replace casualties. During the final enemy attack on the 22nd he was wounded, but continued most actively in the foremost positions, controlling the fire of batteries which inflicted heavy losses on enemy tanks at point-blank range, and finally acted as loader to one of the guns himself. In spite of his wound he refused to be evacuated and remained with his command.

GARDNER, Philip John *A/Captain, Royal Tank Regiment, Royal Armoured Corps*

23 November 1941 – Captain Gardner was ordered to take two tanks to the assistance of two armoured cars of the King's Dragoon Guards which were out of action and under fire in close proximity to the enemy, south-east of Tobruk. He found the two cars halted 200 yards apart, being heavily fired on at close range and gradually smashed to pieces. Ordering the other tank to give him covering fire, Gardner manoeuvred his own close up to the foremost car; he then dismounted in the face of intense anti-tank and machine-gun fire and secured a tow rope to the car; seeing an officer lying beside it with his legs blown off, he lifted him into the car and gave the order to tow. The tow rope, however, broke, and he returned to the armoured car, being immediately wounded in the arm and leg: despite his wounds he lifted the other officer out of the car and carried him back to the tank, placing him on the back engine louvres and climbing alongside to hold him on. While the tank was being driven back to safety it was subjected to heavy shell fire and the loader killed.

He was taken prisoner in June 1942. He escaped from his Italian captors, but was caught by the Germans. He spent the rest of the war in a POW camp in Brunswick, where he helped organize a collection in the form of IOUs for the benefit of the poor of London. After the war, he was instrumental in using the money to found the Brunswick Boys Club in Fulham.

JACKMAN, James Joseph Bernard *T/Captain, 1st Bn., Royal Northumberland Fusiliers*

25 November 1941 – At El Duda, south-east of Tobruk, Captain Jackman was in command of a machine-gun company of the Royal Northumberland Fusiliers in the tank attack on the El Duda ridge. As the tanks reached the crest of the rise they were met by extremely intense fire from a large number of guns of all descriptions: the fire was so heavy that it was doubtful for a moment whether the brigade could maintain its hold on the position. The tanks, having slowed to hull-down positions, settled to beat down the enemy fire, during which time Jackman rapidly pushed up the ridge leading his machine-gun trucks and saw at once that anti-tank guns were firing at the flank of the tanks, as well as the rows of batteries which the tanks were engaging on their front. He immediately started to get his guns into action as calmly as though he were on manoeuvres and so secured the right flank. Then, standing up in the front of his truck, with calm determination he led his trucks across the front between the tanks and the guns – there was no other road to get them into action on the left flank. Throughout he coolly directed his guns to their positions and indicated targets to them and at times seemed to bear a charmed life, but later he was killed while inspiring everyone with the greatest confidence by his bearing.

ABYSSINIA

In General Wavell's campaign in Abyssinia, 4th and 5th Indian Divisions attacked from the Sudan and 11th and 12th African Divisions attacked from Kenya. The Italian troops under the Duke of Aosta proved to be formidable enemies – well led and motivated, they held good positions in the mountains, and Indian divisions met their greatest resistance at Keren, a mountain stronghold, where the defenders held out for fifty-three days; but the capital, Asmara, was taken on 1 April. In the south, the capital of Italian Somaliland, Mogadishu, was captured within eleven days, and Addis Ababa, the capital of Italian East Africa, on 6 April. The two forces then combined and pursued the Italians into the mountains, where they surrendered on 17 May.

PREMINDRA SINGH BHAGAT *Second Lieutenant, Corps of Indian Engineers, attached Royal Bombay Sappers and Miners*

31 January to 4 February 1941 – During the pursuit of the enemy following the capture of Metemma, Abyssinia, on the night 31 January/1 February 1941, he was in command of a section of a field company, sappers and miners, detailed to accompany the leading mobile troops (Bren carriers) to clear the road and adjacent areas of mines. For a period of four days, and over a distance of 55 miles, Bhagat in the leading carrier led the column. He detected and supervised the clearing of fifteen minefields. Speed being essential, he worked at high pressure from dawn to dusk each day. On two occasions when his carrier was blown up with casualties to others, and on a third occasion when ambushed and under close enemy fire, he carried straight on with his task. He refused relief when worn out with strain and fatigue and with one eardrum punctured by an explosion, on the grounds that he was now better qualified to continue his task to the end.

RICHPAL RAM *Subadar, 6th Rajputana Rifles*

7/8 February 1941 – During the assault on enemy positions in front of Keren, Eritrea, he was second-in-command of a leading company, and insisted on accompanying the forward platoon, leading its attack on the first objective with great dash and gallantry. His company commander being then wounded, he assumed command of the company, and led the attack of the remaining two platoons to the final objective. In face of heavy fire, some 30 men with this officer at their head rushed the objective with the bayonet and captured it. The party was completely isolated, but under his inspiring leadership it beat back six enemy counter-attacks between midnight and 0430 hours. By now, ammunition had run out, and he extricated his command and fought his way back to his battalion with a handful of survivors through the surrounding enemy. In the attack on the same position on the 12th he again led the attack of his company. He pressed on fearlessly and determinedly in the face of heavy and accurate fire, and by his personal example inspired his company with his resolute spirit until his right foot was blown off. He then suffered further wounds from which he died. While lying wounded he continued to wave his men on, and his final words were, 'We'll capture the objective.'

LEAKEY, Nigel Gray *Sergeant, 1/6th Bn., King's African Rifles*
19/20 May 1941 – Two companies of the 1/6th King's African Rifles crossed the Billate River at Colito in Abyssinia in the face of strong Italian opposition, and established a precarious bridgehead without hope of immediate reinforcement. Throughout the operation Sergeant Leakey had been supporting the crossing with 3in mortar fire, and having expended all his ammunition, he went forward to see what he could do. Suddenly, the enemy launched a surprise counter-attack with medium and light tanks which emerged from the bush threatening to overrun the two companies. Advancing from the rear, one of these tanks was bearing down on the troops, who had no anti-tank weapons for their defence. With complete disregard for his own safety, and in the face of withering machine-gun and rifle fire from the enemy's ground troops, and from more tanks in front, Leakey leaped on top of the tank which was coming in from behind the position and wrenched open the turret. With his revolver he shot the commander of this tank and the crew with the exception of the driver, whom he forced to drive in to cover. Having failed to get the cannon of this tank to fire he dismounted, calling out, 'I'll get them on foot,' and charged across ground which was being swept by machine-gun and shell fire from the other enemy tanks which were advancing and causing casualties to British infantry. In company with an African CSM and two other Askari, he proceeded to stalk these tanks. The first two tanks passed, but Leakey managed to jump onto the third and opened the turret and killed one of the crew before the fourth opened fire with a machine gun and shot him off. The position was retained.
Leakey was killed in this action.

COASTAL COMMAND

Coastal Command was nicknamed the Cinderella Command: it claimed none of the glamour of Fighter Command, nor the headlines won by Bomber Command, but its principal mission, to search and destroy U-boats, was vital for Britain's survival. In total, 10,875 members of the Command died between 1939 and 1945; 213 U-boats were sunk by 1945 (24 in joint action with surface craft), but the greatest casualties were taken not in the hunt for U-boats (see John Cruickshank VC, p. 496), but in the anti-ship strike squadrons flying Beauforts, Beaufighters and Mosquitoes in attacks on convoys and ports, destroying 366 vessels and disabling 134, in total more than a million tons of shipping.

CAMPBELL, Kenneth *Flying Officer, 22 Squadron, Royal Air Force Volunteer Reserve*

6 April 1941 – This officer was the pilot of a Beaufort aircraft in Coastal Command which was detailed to attack the battlecruiser *Gneisenau* in Brest harbour at first light on the morning of 6 April 1941. The battlecruiser was secured alongside the wall on the north shore of the harbour, protected by a stone mole bending round it from the west. On rising ground behind the ship stood protective batteries of guns. Other batteries were clustered thickly round the two arms of land which encircled the outer harbour. In this outer harbour near the mole were moored three heavily armed anti-aircraft ships, guarding the battlecruiser. Even if an aircraft succeeded in penetrating these formidable defences, it would be almost impossible, after delivering a low-level attack, to avoid crashing into the rising ground beyond. This was well known to Campbell who, despising the heavy odds, went cheerfully and resolutely to the task. He ran the gauntlet of the defences. Coming in almost at sea level, he passed the anti-aircraft ships at less than mast-height in the very mouths of their guns, and skimming over the mole launched a torpedo at point-blank range. The battlecruiser was severely damaged below the waterline, and was obliged to return to the dock whence she had come only the day before.

His battered Beaufort crashed into the harbour. He was given a full military funeral by the Germans. Gneisenau *was put out of action for nine months.*

GREECE AND CRETE

By January 1941 the British government had decided that there was a German threat to the Balkans, and honoured its guarantee of support to Greece by sending two divisions (2nd New Zealand and 6th Australian) and an armoured brigade (1st British), which were in position on the River Aliakhmon, north of Mt Olympus, when Germany invaded Yugoslavia and Greece on 6 April. The invasion of Yugoslavia was unforeseen; the Aliakhmon position would be outflanked. British evacuation was agreed on 15 April and complete on 1 May, covered by the Royal Navy.

About twenty-one thousand men were taken to Crete, where they arrived without transport or any equipment that could not be carried personally, and joined the six thousand stationed there to defend the naval base at Suda Bay. Ultra decrypts revealed that Germany was planning an airborne assault, and the British government decided to defend the island. Major General Freyberg VC was given the command. The most important defence was of the airfields, at Maleme, Retimo and Heraklion. Fliegerkorps XI's assault, on all three airfields, began on 20 May; within twenty-four hours Maleme had fallen, and by nightfall transport aircraft were landing. A counter-attack on the 23rd failed, and for the next three days there was fierce fighting in the area between Maleme and Suda Bay. On the 26th General Wavell ordered the evacuation, which was complete on 1 June. The fighting had cost the Allies 1,742 killed, and 11,835 captured.

HINTON, John Daniel *Sergeant, 20th Bn., 2nd New Zealand Expeditionary Force (Canterbury Regiment)*

28/29 April 1941 – During the fighting in Greece, a column of German armoured forces entered Kalamai; this column, which contained several armoured cars, 2in guns and 3in mortars, and two 6in guns, rapidly converged on a large force of British and New Zealand troops awaiting embarkation on the beach. When the order to retreat to cover was given, Sergeant Hinton, shouting, 'To hell with this, who'll come with me,' ran to within several yards of the nearest gun; the gun fired, missing him, and he hurled two grenades, which completely wiped out the crew. He then came on with the bayonet followed by a crowd of New Zealanders. German troops abandoned the first 6in gun and retreated into two houses. Hinton smashed the window and then the door of the first house and dealt with the garrison with the bayonet. He repeated the performance in the second house and as a result, until overwhelming German forces arrived, the New Zealanders held the guns. He then fell with a bullet wound through the lower abdomen and was taken prisoner.

He was the first New Zealander to win the VC in the war.

SEPHTON, Alfred Edward *Petty Officer, Royal Navy*

18 May 1941 – Petty Officer Sephton was director layer when HMS *Coventry* was attacked by aircraft south of Crete, whose fire grievously wounded him. In mortal pain and faint from loss of blood he stood fast doing his duty without fault until the enemy was driven off. Thereafter until his death his valiant and cheerful spirit gave heart to the wounded.

HULME, Alfred Clive *Sergeant, 23rd Bn., 2nd New Zealand Expeditionary Force (Canterbury Regiment)*

20–28 May 1941 – On ground overlooking Maleme Aerodrome on 20 and 21 May he personally led parties of his men from the area held by the forward position and destroyed enemy organized parties who had established themselves out in front of the position, from which they brought heavy rifle, machine-gun and mortar fire to bear on the defensive posts. Numerous snipers in this area were dealt with by Sergeant Hulme personally; 130 dead were counted here. On 22, 23 and 24 May Hulme was continually going out alone or with one or two men and destroying enemy snipers. On 25 May, when Hulme had rejoined his battalion, this unit counter-attacked Galatos village. The attack was partially held up by a large party of the enemy holding the school, from which they were inflicting heavy casualties. Hulme went forward alone, threw grenades into the school and so disorganized the defence that the counter-attack was able to proceed successfully. On 27 May, when Allied troops were holding a defensive line at Suda Bay during the final retirement, five enemy snipers had worked into position on the hillside overlooking the flank of the battalion line. Hulme volunteered to deal with the situation, and stalked and killed the snipers in turn. He continued similar work successfully through the day. On 28 May at Stylos, when an enemy heavy mortar was severely bombing a very important ridge held by the battalion rearguard troops, inflicting severe casualties, Hulme, on his own initiative, penetrated the enemy lines, killed the mortar crew of four, put the mortar out of action, and thus very materially assisted the withdrawal of the main body through Stylos. From the enemy mortar position he then worked to the left flank and killed three snipers who were causing concern to the rearguard. This made his score of enemy snipers 33 stalked and shot. Shortly afterwards he was severely wounded in the shoulder whilst stalking another sniper. When ordered to the rear, in spite of his wound, he directed traffic under fire and organized stragglers of various units into section groups.

UPHAM, Charles Hazlitt *Second Lieutenant, 20th Bn., 2nd New Zealand Expeditionary Force (Canterbury Regiment)*

22–30 May 1941 – He commanded a forward platoon in the attack on Maleme on 22 May and fought his way forward for over 3,000 yards unsupported by any other arms and against a defence strongly organized in depth. During this operation his platoon destroyed numerous enemy posts but on three occasions sections were temporarily held up. In the first case, under a heavy fire from a machine-gun nest he advanced to close quarters with pistol and grenades, so demoralizing the occupants that his section was able to mop up with ease. Another of his sections was then held up by two machine-guns in a house. He went in and placed a grenade through a window, destroying the crew of one machine-gun and several others, the other machine-gun being silenced by the fire of his sections. In the third case he crawled to within 15 yards of a machine-gun post and killed the gunners with a grenade. When his company withdrew from Maleme he helped to carry a wounded man out under fire, and together with another officer rallied more men together to carry other wounded men out. He was then sent to bring in a company which had become isolated. With a corporal he went through enemy territory over 600 yards, killing two Germans on the way, found the company, and brought it back to the battalion's new position. But for this action it would have been completely cut off. During the following two days his platoon occupied an exposed position on forward slopes and was continuously under fire. Upham was blown over by one mortar shell, and painfully wounded by a piece of shrapnel behind the left shoulder by another. He disregarded this wound and remained on duty. He also received a bullet in the foot which he later removed in Egypt. At Galatos on 25 May his platoon was heavily engaged and came under severe mortar and machine-gun fire. While his platoon stopped under cover of a ridge he went forward, observed the enemy and brought the platoon forward when the Germans advanced. They killed over 40 with fire and grenades and forced the remainder to fall back. When his platoon was ordered to retire he sent it back under the platoon sergeant and he went back to warn other troops that they were being cut off. When he came out himself he was fired on by two Germans. He fell and shammed dead, then crawled into a position and having the use of only one arm rested his rifle in the fork of a tree and as the Germans came forward he killed them both. The second to fall actually hit the muzzle of the rifle as he fell. On 30 May at Sphakia his platoon was ordered to deal with a party of the enemy which had advanced down a ravine to near force headquarters. Though in an exhausted condition he climbed the steep hill to the west of the ravine, placed his men in positions on the slope overlooking the ravine and himself went to the top with a Bren gun and two riflemen. By clever tactics he induced the enemy party to expose itself and then at a range of 500 yards shot 22 and caused the remainder to disperse in panic. During the whole of the operations he suffered from dysentery and was able to eat very little, in addition to being wounded and bruised.

★ On *14/15 July 1942* – Captain Upham won a bar to his VC. See p. 426.

WANKLYN, Malcolm David *Lieutenant Commander, Royal Navy*

24 May 1941 – While on patrol off the coast of Sicily, Lieutenant Commander Wanklyn, in command of His Majesty's Submarine *Upholder*, sighted a south-bound enemy troop convoy, strongly escorted by destroyers. The failing light was such that observation by periscope could not be relied on but a surface attack would have been easily seen. *Upholder*'s listening gear was out of action. In spite of these severe handicaps he decided to press home his attack at short range. He quickly steered his craft into a favourable position and closed in so as to make sure of his target. By this time the whereabouts of the escorting destroyers could not be made out. Wanklyn, while fully aware of the risk of being rammed by one of the escort, continued to press on towards the enemy troopships. As he was about to fire, one of the enemy destroyers suddenly appeared out of the darkness at high speed, and he only just avoided being rammed. As soon as he was clear, he brought his periscope sights on and fired torpedoes, which sank a large troopship. The enemy destroyers at once made a strong counter attack and during the next twenty minutes dropped thirty-seven depth charges near *Upholder*. The failure of his listening devices made it much harder for him to get away, but with the greatest courage, coolness and skill he brought *Upholder* clear of the enemy and safe back to harbour. Before this outstanding attack, and since being appointed a Companion of the Distinguished Service Order, Wanklyn had torpedoed a tanker and a merchant vessel. He carried out his attacks on enemy vessels with skill and relentless determination, and also sank one destroyer, one U-boat, two troop transports of 19,500 tons each, one tanker and three supply ships. He besides probably destroyed by torpedoes one other cruiser and one destroyer, and possibly hit another cruiser.

SYRIA

Syria was held by Vichy French forces, and was both strategically important and used by German aircraft. General de Gaulle hoped to invade with Free French troops, supported by tanks and aircraft from Wavell's command, believing that only nominal resistance would be offered. The offensive began on 8 June, with eight battalions of Free French, 7th Australian Division and British units. Resistance was strong, but the Vichy surrender was obtained on 12 July.

CUTLER, Arthur Roden *Lieutenant, 2nd/5th Field Artillery, Australian Military Forces*

19 June to 6 July 1941 – On 19 June an Allied infantry attack was checked at Merdjayoun, Syria, after suffering heavy casualties from an enemy counter-attack with tanks. Enemy machine-gun fire swept the ground but Lieutenant Cutler with another artillery officer and a small party pushed on ahead of the infantry and established an outpost in a house. The telephone line was cut and he went out and mended this line under machine-gun fire and returned to the house, from which enemy posts and a battery were successfully engaged. The enemy then attacked this outpost with infantry and tanks, killing the Bren-gunner and mortally wounding the other officer. Cutler and another manned the anti-tank rifle and Bren gun and fought back, driving the enemy infantry away. The tanks continued the attack, but under constant fire from the anti-tank rifle and Bren gun eventually withdrew. Cutler then personally supervised the evacuation of the wounded members of his party. Undaunted, he pressed for a further advance. He had been ordered to establish an outpost from which he could register the only road by which the enemy transport could enter the town. With a small party of volunteers he pressed on until finally with one other he succeeded in establishing an outpost right in the town, which was occupied by the Foreign Legion, despite enemy machine-gun fire which prevented the infantry from advancing. At this time he knew the enemy were massing on his left for a counter-attack and that he was in danger of being cut off. Nevertheless he carried out his task of registering the battery on the road and engaging enemy posts. The enemy counter-attacked with infantry and tanks and he was cut off. He was forced to go to ground, but after dark succeeded in making his way through the enemy lines. His work in registering the only road by which enemy transport could enter the town was of vital importance and a big factor in the enemy's subsequent retreat. On the night of 23/24 June he was in charge of a 25pdr sent forward into the forward defended localities to silence an enemy anti-tank gun and post which had held up the attack. This he did and next morning the recapture of Merdjayoun was completed. Later at Damour on 6 July, when forward infantry were pinned to the ground by heavy hostile machine-gun fire, Cutler, regardless of all danger, went to bring a line to his outpost when he was seriously wounded. Twenty-six hours elapsed before it was possible to rescue him, whose wound by this time had become septic necessitating the amputation of his leg.

After the war he served as Australian Ambassador to the Netherlands and Governor of New South Wales.

GORDON, James Heather *Private, 2nd/31st Bn. (Queensland and Victoria), Australian Military Forces*

10/11 July 1941 – During an attack on 'Greenhill', north of Djezzine, Syria, Private Gordon's company came under intense machine-gun fire and its advance was held up. Movement even by single individuals became almost impossible, one officer and two men being killed and two men wounded in the effort to advance. The enemy machine-gun position, which had brought the two forward platoons to a halt, was fortified and completely covered the area. Private Gordon, on his own initiative, crept forward over an area swept by machine-gun and grenade fire and succeeded in approaching close to the post; he then charged it from the front and killed the four machine-gunners with the bayonet. His action completely demoralized the enemy in this sector and the company advanced and took the position. During the remainder of the action that night and on the following day Private Gordon, who has throughout the operations shown a high degree of courage, fought with equal gallantry.

BOMBER COMMAND

In 1941 the strategic bombing offensive was still concentrated on military targets. 75 Squadron flew Wellingtons and 105 Squadron flew Bristol Blenheims, against targets in France, the Low Countries and Germany, and against shipping in the North Sea. In Malaya, 62 Squadron attacked Japanese shipping and airfields. After it lost most of its aircraft it was withdrawn to Sumatra.

EDWARDS, Hughie Idwal *A/Wing Commander, 105 Squadron, Royal Air Force*

4 July 1941 – He planned and led an important attack on the port of Bremen, one of the most heavily defended towns in Germany. This attack had to be made in daylight and there were no clouds to afford concealment.

During the approach to the German coast several enemy ships were sighted and Wing Commander Edwards knew that his aircraft would be reported and that the defences would be in a state of readiness. Undaunted by this misfortune he brought his formation 50 miles overland to the target, flying at a height of little more than 50 feet, passing under high-tension cables, carrying away telegraph wires and finally passing through a formidable balloon barrage. On reaching Bremen he was met with a hail of fire, all his aircraft being hit and four of them being destroyed. Nevertheless he made a most successful attack, and then with the greatest skill and coolness withdrew the surviving aircraft without further loss.

WARD, James Allen *Sergeant, Royal New Zealand Air Force, serving with 75 (NZ) Squadron, Royal Air Force*

7/8 July 1941 – Sergeant Ward was second pilot of a Wellington returning from an attack on Munster. When flying over the Zuider Zee at 13,000 feet, the aircraft was attacked from beneath by a Messerschmitt 110 which secured hits with cannon shell and incendiary bullets. The rear gunner was wounded in the foot but delivered a burst of fire which sent the enemy fighter down, apparently out of control. Fire then broke out near the starboard engine and, fed by petrol from a split pipe, quickly gained an alarming hold and threatened to spread to the entire wing. The crew forced a hole in the fuselage and made strenuous efforts to reduce the fire with extinguishers and even the coffee in their vacuum flasks, but without success. They were then warned to be ready to abandon the aircraft. As a last resort, Ward volunteered to make an attempt to smother the fire with an engine cover which happened to be in use as a cushion. At first he proposed to discard his parachute, to reduce wind resistance, but was finally persuaded to take it. A rope from the dinghy was tied to him, though this was of little help and might have become a danger had he been blown off the aircraft. With the help of the navigator, he then climbed through the narrow astro-hatch and put on his parachute. The bomber was flying at a reduced speed but the wind pressure must have been sufficient to render the operation one of extreme difficulty. Breaking the fabric to make hand and foot holds where necessary, and also taking advantage of existing holes in the fabric, Sergeant Ward succeeded in descending three feet to the wing and proceeding another three feet to a position behind the engine, despite the slipstream from the airscrew, which nearly blew him off the wing. Lying in this precarious position, he smothered the fire in the wing fabric and tried to push the cover into the hole in the wing and onto the leaking pipe from which the fire came. As soon as he removed his hand, however, the terrific wind blew the cover out and when he tried again it was lost. Tired as he was, he was able with the navigator's assistance to make successfully the perilous journey back into the aircraft. There was now no danger of the fire spreading from the petrol pipe, as there was no fabric left nearby, and in due course it burnt itself out. When the aircraft was nearly home some petrol which had collected in the wing blazed up furiously but died down quite suddenly. A safe landing was then made despite the damage sustained by the aircraft.

SCARF, Arthur Stewart King *Squadron Leader, 62 Squadron, Royal Air Force*

9 December 1941 – All available aircraft from RAF Butterworth, Malaya, were ordered to make a daylight attack on the advanced operational base of the Japanese air force at Singora, Thailand. From this base, the enemy fighter squadrons were supporting the landing operations. The aircraft detailed for the sortie were on the point of taking off when the enemy made a combined dive-bombing and low-level machine-gun attack on the airfield. All the aircraft were destroyed or damaged with the exception of the Blenheim piloted by Squadron Leader Scarf, which had become airborne a few seconds before the attack started. Scarf circled the airfield and witnessed the disaster. It would have been reasonable had he abandoned the projected operation which was intended to be a formation sortie. He decided, however, to press on to Singora. Although he knew that this individual action could not inflict much material damage on the enemy, he nevertheless appreciated the moral effect which it would have on the remainder of the squadron, who were helplessly watching their aircraft burning on the ground. Scarf completed his attack successfully. The opposition over the target was severe and included attacks by a considerable number of enemy fighters, in the course of which he was mortally wounded. The enemy continued to engage him in a running fight, which lasted until he had regained the Malayan border. He fought a brilliant evasive action in a valiant attempt to return to his base but was, owing to his wounds, unable to accomplish this. He made a successful forced landing at Alor Star without causing any injury to his crew. He was received into hospital as soon as possible, but died shortly after admission.

HONG KONG

Hong Kong, the headquarters of the Royal Navy's China Squadron, was attacked by air on 8 December, shortly after Pearl Harbor. On 19 December nine Japanese divisions landed on three beaches on the north of the island with artillery and air cover, and the defenders withdrew to Victoria Peak, where they held out until Christmas Day. It was the first engagement of the war for the Canadians.

OSBORN, John Robert *Warrant Officer Class II, 1st Bn., Winnipeg Grenadiers, Canadian Infantry Corps*

19 December 1941 – A company of the Winnipeg Grenadiers to which he belonged became divided during an attack on Mount Butler, a hill rising steeply above sea level at Hong Kong. A part of the company he led captured the hill at the point of the bayonet and held it for three hours when, owing to the superior numbers of the enemy and to fire from an unprotected flank, the position became untenable. Osborn and a small group covered the withdrawal and when their turn came to fall back Osborn, single-handed, engaged the enemy while the remainder successfully joined the company. He had to run the gauntlet of heavy rifle and machine-gun fire. With no consideration for his own safety he assisted and directed stragglers to the new company position, exposing himself to heavy enemy fire to cover their retirement. Wherever danger threatened he was there to encourage his men. During the afternoon the company was cut off from the battalion and completely surrounded by the enemy who were able to approach to within grenade-throwing distance of the slight depression which the company were holding. Several enemy grenades were thrown, which he picked up and threw back. The enemy threw a grenade which landed in a position where it was impossible to pick it up and return it in time. Shouting a warning to his comrades he threw himself on the grenade, which exploded killing him instantly.

A fine statue was erected to Osborn by a Hong Kong family and a plaque to those servicemen who performed acts of gallantry and self-sacrifice.

1942

On the Eastern Front, despite Soviet counter-attacks around Moscow, the German army was preparing to make further advances, and in the Far East, the Japanese drive seemed unstoppable as they over-ran Malaya, Singapore, the Philippines, Borneo and the Dutch East Indies and, with a thrust into New Guinea, stood ready to threaten Australia. The Allies would have to make a massive effort to rally their forces and begin to fight back over the coming difficult months.

Aircrews and heavy bombers of the American Army Air Forces began to arrive in Britain in strength, and the British intensified their night bombing of Germany. At sea, despite very heavy losses on the Arctic route to Russia, merchant ships were still getting through with supplies and the U-boat wolf packs were kept at bay.

German occupation of Western, Central and Eastern Europe remained unchallenged – but the Allies started to prepare for the second front. Successful raids were launched against the German radar base at Bruneval in northern France in February and a month later on the dry dock at St-Nazaire in a combined commando and naval operation – but on 19 August a disastrous landing was carried out at Dieppe, an indicator that the Allies were far from ready for a full-scale invasion.

MALAYA

Japan landed forces in Malaya on 7/8 December 1941, and by the 11th had captured the airfields and sunk HMS *Repulse* and HMS *Prince of Wales*. Having lost control of the sea and air, British forces began to withdraw, and outnumbered and outfought by experienced, well-trained and determined troops. The British retreat was rapid and disorganized, with positions taken by simultaneous encirclement and attack from the front. The action at Kuantan airfield, on the east coast, was typical of many holding actions in the retreat to Johore, the last major action being 11th Indian Division's stand with 8th Australian at the Muar River. Johore was penetrated and on 1 February the remaining forces escaped to Singapore, where they surrendered on the 15th.

CUMMING, Arthur Edward *Lieutenant Colonel, commanding*
2/12th Frontier Force Regiment, Indian Army

   3 January 1942 – Near Kuantan, Malaya, a strong force of the enemy penetrated the position while brigade headquarters and a battalion were being withdrawn. Cumming with a small party of men immediately counter-attacked and prevented any further penetration until his whole party had become casualties and he himself had received two bayonet wounds in the stomach, but thereby enabling the major portion of the men and vehicles to be withdrawn. Later, in spite of pain and weakness from his wounds, he drove in a carrier for more than an hour under very heavy fire collecting isolated detachments. He then received two further wounds, after which, and while attempting to collect a further isolated detachment, he lost consciousness and the driver of the carrier attempted to evacuate him. Cumming, however, recovered consciousness and insisted on remaining where he was until he discovered that he and his driver were the sole survivors in the locality. He then decided to retire.

ANDERSON, Charles Groves Wright *Lieutenant Colonel, commanding*
2/19th Bn. (New South Wales), Australian Military Forces

   18–22 January 1942 – While in command of a small force near the Muar River, Malaya, he was sent to restore a vital position and to assist a brigade. His force destroyed ten enemy tanks. When later cut off, he defeated persistent attacks on his position from air and ground forces, and forced his way through the enemy lines to a depth of 15 miles. He was again surrounded and subjected to very heavy and frequent attacks resulting in severe casualties. He personally led an attack with great gallantry on the enemy who were holding a bridge, and succeeded in destroying four guns. Throughout all this fighting he protected his wounded and refused to leave them. He obtained news by wireless of the enemy position and attempted to fight his way back through eight miles of enemy-occupied country. This proved to be impossible and the enemy were holding too strong a position for any attempt to be made to relieve him. On the 18th he was ordered to destroy his equipment and make his way back as best he could round the enemy position. Throughout this fighting, which lasted for four days, he set a magnificent example of brave leadership, determination and outstanding courage.

THE CHANNEL DASH

The German battlecruisers *Scharnhorst* and *Gneisenau* had spent the first years of the war as commerce raiders in the Atlantic, sinking twenty-three ships, and in the Norwegian campaign, when they accounted for the aircraft carrier HMS *Glorious*, which went down with her two escorting destroyers on 8 June 1940. In February 1942 they had been at Brest for a year, and the object of repeated attacks – the *Gneisenau* had been damaged by a torpedo attack by Kenneth Campbell VC (p. 404) – and they were transferred to the Baltic to join the *Tirpitz* and prevent an invasion of Norway in the 'Channel Dash'.

Vice Admiral Dover, Sir Bertram Ramsay, had six destroyers, six motor torpedo boats and six Swordfish torpedo bombers, with RAF fighter and bomber support. The German ships left Brest at 2245 on 11 February, and moved up-Channel in thick fog. Ramsay was informed at 1125 that they were an hour from the Straits of Dover, and ordered his Swordfish and his torpedo boats into action, covered by RAF Spitfires. The air cover for the torpedo boats did not arrive and their attack was a failure; only ten Spitfires had arrived at the Swordfish rendezvous before the German ships were out of range.

ESMONDE, Eugene *Lieutenant Commander, 825 Squadron, Fleet Air Arm, Royal Navy*

12 February 1942 – Esmonde was told that the German battlecruisers *Scharnhorst* and *Gneisenau* and the cruiser *Prinz Eugen*, strongly escorted by some thirty surface craft, were entering the Straits of Dover, and that his squadron must attack before they reached the sand-banks north-east of Calais. Soon after noon he and his squadron of six Swordfish set course for the enemy, and after ten minutes' flight were attacked by a strong force of enemy fighters, about fifteen Luftwaffe Messerschmitt 109s and Focke-Wulf 190s. Touch was lost with his fighter escort and in the action which followed all his aircraft were damaged. He flew on, cool and resolute, serenely challenging hopeless odds, to encounter the deadly fire of the battlecruisers and their escort, which shattered the port wing of his aircraft. Undismayed, he led his squadron on, straight through this inferno of fire, in steady flight towards their target. Almost at once he was shot down; but his squadron went on to launch a gallant attack, in which at least one torpedo is believed to have struck the German battlecruisers, and from which not one of the six aircraft returned.

In fact no torpedoes hit. Vice Admiral Dover, Ramsay, described the sortie as 'one of the finest exhibitions of self-sacrifice and devotion to duty this war has yet witnessed'. Gneisenau and Scharnhorst struck mines dropped by Bomber Command, but arrived safely in port.

THE WAR AT SEA

WILKINSON, Thomas *T/Lieutenant, Royal Naval Reserve*

14 February 1942 – HMS *Li Wo*, a patrol vessel of 1,000 tons, formerly a passenger steamer on the Upper Yangtse River, was on passage from Singapore to Batavia. Her ship's company consisted of 84 officers and men, including a civilian; they were mainly survivors from His Majesty's ships which had been sunk, and a few from units of the army and the Royal Air Force. Her armament was one 4in gun, for which she had only thirteen practice shells, and two machine-guns. Since leaving Singapore the previous day, the ship had beaten off four air attacks, in one of which fifty-two machines took part, and had suffered considerable damage. Late in the afternoon, she sighted two enemy convoys, the larger of which was escorted by Japanese naval units, including a heavy cruiser and some destroyers. Lieutenant Wilkinson gathered his scratch ship's company together and told them that, rather than try to escape, he had decided to engage the convoy and to fight to the last, in the hope that he might inflict damage upon the enemy. In making this decision, which drew resolute support from the whole ship's company, he knew that his ship faced certain destruction, and that his own chances of survival were small. *Li Wo* hoisted her battle ensign and made straight for the enemy. In the action which followed, the machine-guns were used with effect upon the crews of all ships in range, and a volunteer gun's crew manned the 4in gun, which they fought with such purpose that a Japanese transport was badly hit and set on fire. After a little over an hour, *Li Wo* had been critically damaged and was sinking. Wilkinson then decided to ram his principal target, the large transport, which had been abandoned by her crew. It is known that this ship burnt fiercely throughout the night following the action, and was probably sunk. *Li Wo*'s gallant fight ended when, her shells spent, and under heavy fire from the enemy cruiser, Wilkinson finally ordered abandon ship. He himself remained on board, and went down with her. There were only about 10 survivors, who were later made prisoners of war. The Victoria Cross is bestowed upon him posthumously in recognition both of his own heroism and self-sacrifice, and of that of all who fought and died with him.

GOULD, Thomas William *Petty Officer, Royal Navy*

Tommy Gould, brought up in Dover, joined the Royal Navy in 1933 aged nineteen, and went into the submarine service three years later. He loved the camaraderie of the submarine life and it was this devotion to his fellow crew and their submarine which inspired the actions which earned him the VC.

On 16 February 1942, Gould was aboard HM submarine *Thrasher*, when she sank a supply ship off the north coast of Crete. The submarine immediately came under attack from the air and was depth-charged by the escorting anti-submarine vessels for a terrifying three and a half hours. *Thrasher* survived the attack, but up on the surface to recharge later that night, the crew heard a strange banging sound. This proved to be two 100lb bombs, lying on the submarine's casing just in front of the 4in gun mounting.

Coxswain Gould and Lieutenant Peter Roberts volunteered to remove the bombs. The first was relatively easy to deal with – they wrapped it in a potato sack, tied it with rope and dropped it off the bows. *Thrasher* went full astern to get clear of any detonation and Gould and Roberts turned their attention to the second bomb. They found that this was resting in a jagged hole in the submarine's casing, on top of the pressure hull. There was no way it could be eased out the way it went in – it would have to be passed through a hinged metal-grating trapdoor. Gould explained, 'To get to the bomb we had to wiggle forward through the outer casing. In that confined space there were angle irons to hold the superstructure up, battery ventilators and drop bollards as well. When we got through I saw that it was another heavy bomb, about 100lb.'

He began a nightmare journey back through the casing – at some points there was a mere two-foot clearance from the hull.

'I picked up the bomb and passed it through to Roberts. I then laid on my back with the bomb on my stomach and held on to it while he laid on his stomach with his head to my head, pulling me by my shoulders. It was pitch dark and the bomb was making this ticking noise while the submarine was being buffeted by the waves.'

The danger was intensified with the risk of attack, at which *Thrasher* would have to dive – the pressure casing would fill with water and both Gould and Roberts would drown. After forty minutes they reached the grating with the bomb and passed it up to the forecastle, where it was wrapped in a sack and lowered over the side.

Belittling his achievement, Gould later recalled, 'When we knew it was on the surface of the water we let it go, heaving lines as well. Then we ducked and waited for the explosion, but nothing happened – it obviously could not have been primed.' Much later, when asked by the Marquess of Donegal what he was thinking while handling the bombs he replied merely, 'I was hoping the bloody things would not go off.'

It was a VC award that almost never was. Gould's VC was recommended by Commander-in-Chief Mediterranean, Admiral Sir Andrew Cunningham, but was opposed by the Honours and Awards Committee. They argued that, by definition, the VC would only be awarded for acts of bravery in the presence of the enemy – the George Cross would be more appropriate. Cunningham, however, was adamant. Two large enemy bombs in a submarine off an enemy coastline surely constituted 'enemy presence'.

Reluctantly invalided out of the Royal Navy in 1945, Gould became a Lieutenant with the Bromley branch of the Sea Cadets, and was later elected President of the International Submariners' Association of Great Britain. In this way, he kept his connections with the Royal Navy, but he also maintained a lifelong interest in the Jewish community – his VC was bought for £48,400 in 1987 by the Association of Jewish Ex-Servicemen and Women.

ROBERTS, Peter Scawen Watkinson *Lieutenant, Royal Navy*

16 February 1942 – HM Submarine *Thrasher* attacked and sank a heavily escorted supply ship in daylight. She was at once attacked by depth charges and was bombed by aircraft. The presence of two unexploded bombs in the gun-casing was discovered when after dark the submarine surfaced and began to roll. Lieutenant Roberts and Petty Officer GOULD volunteered to remove the bombs, which were of a type unknown to them. The danger in dealing with the second bomb was very great. To reach it they had to go through the casing, which was so low that they had to lie at full length to move in it. Through this narrow space, in complete darkness, they pushed and dragged the bomb for a distance of some 20 feet until it could be lowered over the side. Every time the bomb was moved there was a loud twanging noise as of a broken spring which added nothing to their peace of mind. This deed was the more gallant as *Thrasher's* presence was known to the enemy; she was close to the enemy coast, and in waters where his patrols were known to be active day and night. There was a very great chance, and they knew it, that the submarine might have to crash-dive while they were in the casing. Had this happened they must have been drowned.

MIERS, Anthony Cecil Capel *Commander, Royal Navy*

4 March 1942 – HM Submarine *Torbay* under his command made a daring and successful raid on shipping in a defended enemy harbour at Corfu, planned with full knowledge of the great hazards to be expected during seventeen hours in waters closely patrolled by the enemy. On arriving in the harbour he had to charge his batteries lying on the surface in full moonlight, under the guns of the enemy. As he could not see his target he waited several hours and attacked in full daylight in a glassy calm. When he had fired his torpedoes he was heavily counter-attacked and had to withdraw through a long channel with anti-submarine craft all round and continuous air patrols overhead.

Commander Miers attacked two transports and a destroyer with torpedoes. The transports were reported sunk. HM Submarine Torbay *landed Lieutenant Colonel Keyes and 25 commandos for the attack on Rommel's headquarters in North Africa that won him the VC. See p. 398.*

SHERBROOKE, Robert St Vincent *Captain, Royal Navy*

31 December 1942 – Captain Sherbrooke, in HMS *Onslow*, was the senior officer in command of the destroyers escorting an important convoy bound for north Russia. On the morning of 31 December, off the North Cape, he made contact with a greatly superior enemy force attempting to destroy the convoy. He led his destroyers into attack and closed the enemy. Four times the enemy tried to attack the convoy, but were forced each time to withdraw behind a smokescreen to avoid the threat of torpedoes, and each time Sherbrooke pursued and drove them outside gun range of the convoy and towards covering forces. These engagements lasted about two hours, but after the first forty minutes HMS *Onslow* was hit; Sherbrooke was seriously wounded in the face and temporarily lost the use of one eye. Nevertheless he continued to direct the ships under his command until further hits on his own ship compelled him to disengage, but not until he was satisfied that the next senior officer had assumed control. It was only then that he agreed to leave the bridge for medical attention, and until the convoy was out of danger he insisted on receiving all reports of the action. The convoy was saved from damage and was brought safely to its destination.

THE ST-NAZAIRE RAID

In March, men of No. 2 Army Commando, trained at the Achnacarry Castle Commando Basic Training Centre, undertook a raid to destroy the gates of the dry dock at St-Nazaire. This dock, built for French Atlantic liners, had been taken over by the German invaders and offered shelter to her major warships such as the *Tirpitz*. Lieutenant Colonel Newman led No. 2 Commando, while Commander Robert Ryder directed the naval element as eighteen small coastal assault craft and the ex-US Navy destroyer *Buchanan*, now renamed HMS *Campbeltown*, were sent on the sabotage mission.

Campbeltown, packed through her bows with explosives, rammed the dock gates in the early hours of 28 March. The commandos on board jumped ashore to destroy the winding gear for the gates and the U-boat pens. Despite the element of surprise, resistance was fierce and only three of the assault craft survived. In the fighting 169 officers and men were killed and 200 taken prisoner. While Ryder avoided capture, two other VC winners, Beattie and Newman, heard of their awards in a POW camp. Two more VC awards were made posthumously, along with seventy-eight other honours conferred for the raid.

As light dawned, senior German officers arrived to inspect the wreck of the *Campbeltown*. As they were doing so, the five tons of Ammanol blasting powder in the bows detonated. The officers were killed, as were two Commando officers who had been captured and taken back to the ship. Although aware of the presence of the explosives, they remained silent and died as the explosion shattered the dock gates and sent the remains of the destroyer halfway down the dock, depriving the Kriegsmarine of its French shelter. The *Tirpitz* never left Norway and was finally destroyed there by RAF bombing in November 1944.

BEATTIE, Stephen Halden *Lieutenant Commander, Royal Navy*
27/28 March 1942 – In the attack on St-Nazaire he was in command of HMS *Campbeltown*. Under intense fire directed at the bridge from point-blank range of about 100 yards, and in the face of the blinding glare of many searchlights, he steamed her into the lock gates and beached and scuttled her in the correct position. This Victoria Cross is awarded to Lieutenant Commander Beattie in recognition not only of his own valour

but also of that of the unnamed officers and men of a very gallant ship's company, many of whom have not returned.

DURRANT, Thomas Frank *Sergeant, Royal Engineers, attached*
1 Commando

27/28 March 1942 – He was in charge of a Lewis gun in HM Motor Launch 306 in the St-Nazaire raid. Motor Launch 306 came under heavy fire while proceeding up the River Loire towards the port. Durrant, in his position abaft the bridge, where he had no cover or protection, engaged enemy gun positions and searchlights on shore. During this engagement he was severely wounded in the arm but refused to leave his gun. The motor launch subsequently went down the river and was attacked by a German destroyer at 50–60 yards' range, and often closer. In this action he continued to fire at the destroyer's bridge with the greatest coolness and with complete disregard of the enemy's fire. The motor launch was illuminated by the enemy searchlight and he drew on himself the individual attention of the enemy guns, and was again wounded, in many places. Despite these further wounds he stayed in his exposed position, still firing his gun, although after a time only able to support himself by holding on to the gun mounting. After a running fight, the commander of the German destroyer called on the motor launch to surrender. Durrant's answer was a further burst of fire at the destroyer's bridge. Although now very weak he went on firing, using drums of ammunition as fast as they could be replaced. A renewed attack by the enemy vessel eventually silenced the fire of the motor launch but Durrant refused to give up until the destroyer came alongside, grappled the motor launch and took prisoner those who remained alive. His gallant fight was commended by the German officers on boarding the motor launch.

Durrant later died of his wounds.

NEWMAN, Augustus Charles *Lieutenant Colonel, Essex Regiment, attached*
2 Commando

27/28 March 1942 – He was in command of the military force detailed to land on enemy-occupied territory and destroy the dock installations of the German-controlled naval base at St-Nazaire. This important base was known to be heavily defended and bomber support had to be abandoned owing to bad weather. The operation was therefore bound to be exceedingly hazardous, but Newman, although empowered to call off the assault at any stage, was determined to carry to a successful conclusion the important task which had been assigned to him. Coolly and calmly he stood on the bridge of the leading craft, as the small force steamed up the estuary of the River Loire, although the ships had been caught in the enemy searchlights and a murderous crossfire opened from both banks, causing heavy casualties. Although he need not have landed himself, he was one of the first ashore, and during the next five hours of bitter fighting he personally entered several houses and shot up the occupants and supervised the operations in the town, utterly regardless of his own safety, and he never wavered in his resolution to carry through the operation upon which so much depended. An enemy gun position on the roof of a U-boat pen had been causing heavy casualties to the landing craft and Newman directed the fire of a mortar against this position to such effect that the gun was silenced. Still fully exposed, he then brought machine-gun fire to bear on an armed trawler in the harbour, compelling it to withdraw and thus preventing many casualties in the main demolition area. Under his brilliant leadership the troops fought magnificently and held vastly superior enemy forces at bay, until the demolition parties had successfully completed their work of destruction. By this time, however, most of the landing craft had been sunk or set on fire and evacuation by sea was no longer possible. Although the main objective had been achieved, he nevertheless was now determined to try and fight his way out into open country and so give all survivors a chance to escape. The only way out of the harbour area lay across a narrow iron bridge covered by enemy machine-guns, and although severely shaken by a German hand grenade, which had burst at his feet, he personally led the charge which stormed the position, and under his inspiring leadership the small force fought its way through the streets to a point near the open country, when, all ammunition expended, he and his men were finally overpowered by the enemy.

RYDER, Robert Edward Dudley *Commander, Royal Navy*
    27/28 March 1942 – He commanded a force of small unprotected ships in an attack on a heavily defended port and led HMS *Campbeltown* in under intense fire from short-range weapons at point-blank range. Though the main object of the expedition had been accomplished in the beaching of *Campbeltown*, he remained on the spot conducting operations, evacuating men from *Campbeltown* and dealing with strong points and close-range weapons while exposed to heavy fire for one hour and sixteen minutes, and did not withdraw till it was certain that his ship could be of no use in rescuing any of the commando troops who were still ashore. That his motor gun boat, now full of dead and wounded, should have survived and should have been able to withdraw through an intense barrage of close-range fire was almost a miracle.

SAVAGE, William Alfred *Able Seaman, Royal Navy*
    27/28 March 1942 – He was gunlayer of the pom-pom in a motor gun boat, 314, in the St-Nazaire raid. Completely exposed and under heavy fire, he engaged positions ashore with cool and steady accuracy. On the way out of the harbour he kept up the same vigorous and accurate fire against the attacking ships, until he was killed at his gun. This Victoria Cross is awarded in recognition not only of the gallantry and devotion to duty of Able Seaman Savage, but also of the valour shown by many others, unnamed, in motor launches, motor gun boats and motor torpedo boats, who gallantly carried

out their duty in entirely exposed positions against enemy fire at very close range.

BOMBER COMMAND

NETTLETON, John Dering *A/Squadron Leader, 44 Squadron, Royal Air Force*

17 April 1942 – He was the leader of one of two formations of six Lancaster heavy bombers detailed to deliver a low-level attack in daylight on the diesel engine factory at Augsburg in southern Germany. The enterprise was daring, the target of high military importance. To reach it and get back, some 1,000 miles had to be flown over hostile territory. Soon after crossing into enemy territory his formation was engaged by 25–30 fighters. A running fight ensued. His rear guns went out of action. One by one the aircraft of his formation were shot down until in the end only his own and one other remained. The fighters were shaken off but the target was still far distant. There was formidable resistance to be faced. With great spirit and almost defenceless, he held his two remaining aircraft on their perilous course and after a long and arduous flight, mostly at only 50 feet above the ground, he brought them to Augsburg. Here anti-aircraft fire of great intensity and accuracy was encountered. The two aircraft came low over the roof tops. Though fired at from point-blank range, they stayed the course to drop their bombs true on the target. The second aircraft, hit by flak, burst into flames and crash-landed. The leading aircraft, though riddled with holes, flew safely back to base, the only one of the six to return.

MANSER, Leslie Thomas *Flying Officer, 50 Squadron, Royal Air Force Volunteer Reserve*

30/31 May 1942 – He was captain and first pilot of a Manchester aircraft which took part in the mass raid on Cologne. As the aircraft was approaching its objective it was caught by searchlights and subjected to intense and accurate anti-aircraft fire. Manser held on his dangerous course and bombed the target successfully from a height of 7,000 feet. Then he set course for base. The Manchester had been damaged and was still under heavy fire. Manser took violent evasive action, turning and descending to under 1,000 feet. It was of no avail. The searchlights and flak followed him until the outskirts of the city were passed. The aircraft was hit repeatedly and the rear gunner was wounded. The front cabin filled with smoke; the port engine was overheating badly. Pilot and crew could all have escaped safely by parachute. Nevertheless, Manser, disregarding the obvious hazards, persisted in his attempt to save aircraft and crew from falling into enemy hands. He took the aircraft up to 2,000 feet. Then the port engine burst into flames. It was ten minutes before the fire was mastered, but then the engine went out of action for good, part of one wing was burnt, and the air speed became dangerously low. Despite all the efforts of pilot and crew, the Manchester began to lose height. At this critical moment, he once more disdained the alternative of parachuting to safety with his crew. Instead, with grim determination, he set a new course for the nearest base, accepting for himself the prospect of almost certain death in a firm resolve to carry on to the end. Soon, the aircraft became extremely difficult to handle and, when a crash was inevitable, he ordered the crew to bale out. A sergeant handed him a parachute but he waved it away, telling the non-commissioned officer to jump at once as he could only hold the aircraft steady for a few seconds more. While the crew were descending to safety they saw the aircraft plunge to earth and burst into flames.

MIDDLETON, Rawdon Hume *Flight Sergeant, Royal Australian Air Force, attached 149 Squadron, Royal Air Force*

28/29 November 1942 – Middleton was captain and first pilot of a Stirling aircraft detailed to attack the Fiat works at Turin. Great difficulty was experienced in climbing to 12,000 feet to cross the Alps, which led to excessive consumption of fuel. So dark was the night that the mountain peaks were almost invisible. During the crossing Middleton had to decide whether to proceed or turn back, there being barely sufficient fuel for the return journey. Flares were sighted ahead and he continued the mission and even dived to 2,000 feet to identify the target, despite the difficulty of regaining height. Three flights were made over Turin at this low altitude before the target was identified. The aircraft was then subjected to fire from light anti-aircraft guns. A large hole appeared in the port main plane which made it difficult to maintain lateral control. A shell then burst in the cockpit, shattering the windscreen and wounding both pilots. A piece of shell splinter tore into the side of Middleton's face, destroying his right eye and exposing the bone over the eye. He was probably wounded also in the body or legs. The second pilot received wounds in the head and both legs which bled profusely. The wireless operator was also wounded in the leg. Middleton became unconscious and the aircraft dived to 800 feet before control was regained by the second pilot, who took the aircraft up to 1,500 feet and released the bombs. There was still light flak, some very intense, and the aircraft was hit many times. The three gunners replied continuously until the rear turret was put out of action. Middleton had now recovered consciousness and, when clear of the target, ordered the second pilot back to receive first aid. Before this was completed the latter insisted on returning to the cockpit, as the captain could see very little and could only speak with loss of blood and great pain. Course was set for base and the crew now faced an alpine crossing and a homeward flight in a damaged aircraft with insufficient fuel. The possibilities of abandoning the aircraft or landing in northern France were discussed but Middleton expressed the intention of trying to make the English coast, so that his crew could leave the aircraft by parachute. Owing to his wounds and diminishing strength, he knew that, by then, he would have little or no chance of saving himself. After four hours, the French coast was reached and here the aircraft, flying at 6,000 feet, was once more engaged and hit by intense light anti-aircraft fire. Middleton was still at the controls and mustered sufficient strength to take evasive action. After crossing the Channel there was only sufficient fuel for minutes' flying. Middleton ordered the crew to abandon the aircraft while he flew parallel with the coast for a few miles, after which he intended to head out to sea. Five of the crew left the aircraft safely, while two remained to assist Middleton. The aircraft crashed in the sea and the bodies of the front gunner and flight engineer were recovered the following day.

WESTERN DESERT

In December 1941 Rommel had been pushed back from the Libyan–Egyptian border to the Gazala Line, from where he withdrew to Mersa Brega. Reinforced through Tripoli, he counter-attacked on 21 January, and the British fell back on the line Gazala–Bir Hacheim 50 miles west of Tobruk. On the night of 27/28 May, Rommel began what was soon to be known as the Battle of Knightsbridge (the name of a road junction). There his tanks crushed much of the resistance. Despite an initially successful counter-attack on 6 and 7 June, he took Tobruk on the 21st, and on the 23rd, crossed the Egyptian border. The British withdrew to Mersa Matruh, where their orders were to remain 'fluid and mobile'.

On 12 August Lieutenant General Bernard Montgomery assumed command of 8th Army, and at once set up a defence on the line of El Alamein, whose southern flank was secured by the Qattara depression. Rommel attacked and was defeated at the Battle of Alam Halfa; although the British failed to follow up successfully and his forces retired to a new front six miles east of his original line, Rommel never again had so good a prospect of victory. Montgomery now prepared to go on the offensive, and on 23 October he attacked Rommel's positions.

The main thrust was in the north, in the four miles between the Tell el Eisa and Miteiriya ridges, with a diversion in the south intended to hold the 21st Panzer Division, but not to advance unless the defence was weak. In the north, 9th Australian Division on the right flank reached most of its objectives but the tanks to its south and in the southern attack were slowed by minefields, so that at daylight most were still in the cleared lanes. The next night Montgomery attacked again, diverting his tanks to the north, and in the morning of the 25th four brigades deployed on the far side. The attack in the south was called off, but counter-attacks in the north were hasty and disorganized, and on the 26th the attack was renewed, but the

tanks' advance could not be exploited. Both sides now moved tank reinforcements north, and on the 28th Montgomery drove northwards from the
forward position he had gained, hoping to capture the road. This was halted,
a new attack on 2 November was also stopped by minefields and determined
resistance, and counter-attacked, but by this time Rommel had about 30
tanks and very little fuel, while Montgomery had more than 600. On the
3rd therefore Rommel began to withdraw, but was forbidden by Hitler; an
infantry attack that night between the German and Italian positions created
a gap exploited by the New Zealand Division. Rommel withdrew in disorder
along the coast road, harried on the ground and from the air, as far as
Buerat, 200 miles east of Tripoli.

FOOTE, Henry Robert Bowreman *T/Lieutenant Colonel, commanding
7th Bn., Royal Tank Regiment*
    27 May to 15 June 1942 – On 6 June, he led his battalion, which had
been subjected to very heavy artillery fire, in pursuit of a superior force of
the enemy in Libya. While changing to another tank after his own had been
knocked out, Foote was wounded in the neck. In spite of this he continued
to lead his battalion from an exposed position on the outside of a tank. The
enemy, who were holding a strongly entrenched position with anti-tank
guns, attacked his flank. As a further tank had been disabled he continued
on foot under intense fire encouraging his men by his splendid example. By
dusk, by his brilliant leadership he had defeated the enemy's attempt to
encircle two divisions. On the 13th, when ordered to delay the enemy tanks
so that the Guards Brigade could be withdrawn from the Knightsbridge
escarpment and when the first wave of British tanks had been destroyed, he
reorganized the remaining tanks, going on foot from one tank to another to
encourage the crews under intense artillery and anti-tank fire. As it was of
vital importance that his battalion should not give ground, he placed his
tank, which he had then entered, in front of the others so that he could be
plainly visible in the turret as an encouragement to the other crews, in spite
of the tank being badly damaged by shell fire and all its guns rendered
useless. By his magnificent example the corridor was kept open and the
brigade was able to march through.

SMYTHE, Quentin George Murray *Sergeant, Royal Natal Carabineers,
South African Force*
    5 June 1942 – During the attack on an enemy strongpoint in the Alem
Hamza area, in which his officer was severely wounded, Sergeant Smythe
took command of the platoon although suffering from a shrapnel wound in
the forehead. The strongpoint having been overrun, his troops came under
enfilade fire from an enemy machine-gun nest. Realizing the threat to his
position, Smythe himself stalked and destroyed the nest with hand grenades,
capturing the crew. Though weak from loss of blood, he continued to lead
the advance, and on encountering an anti-tank gun position again attacked

it single-handed and captured the crew. He was directly responsible for killing several of the enemy, shooting some and bayoneting another as they withdrew. After consolidation he received orders for a withdrawal, which he successfully executed, defeating skilfully an enemy attempt at encirclement.

WAKENSHAW, Adam Herbert *Private, 8th Bn., Durham Light Infantry*
 27 June 1942 – He was a member of the crew of a 2pdr anti-tank gun that was sited on a forward slope in front of the infantry position south of Mersa Matruh. Shortly after dawn the enemy attacked and an enemy tracked vehicle towing a light gun was brought to within short range of the position. The gun crew opened fire and succeeded in putting a round through the engine, immobilizing the enemy vehicle. Another mobile gun then came into action. All members of the crew manning the 2pdr were killed or seriously wounded and the 2pdr was silenced. In this respite the enemy moved forward towards their damaged tractor in order to get the light gun into action against the infantry. Realizing the danger to his comrades, under intense mortar and artillery fire which swept the gun site, Wakenshaw crawled back to his gun. Although his left arm was blown off above the elbow, he loaded the gun with one arm and fired five more rounds. These succeeded in setting the tractor on fire and damaged the light gun. A near miss then killed the gun aimer and blew Wakenshaw away from the gun, giving him further severe wounds. Undeterred, he slowly dragged himself back to the gun, placed a round in the breach, and was preparing to fire when a direct hit on the ammunition killed him and destroyed the gun. The company was enabled to withdraw and to embus in safety.

★ **UPHAM, Charles Hazlitt** *Captain, 20th Bn., 2nd New Zealand Expeditionary Force (Canterbury Regiment)*
 14/15 July 1942 – Captain Upham won a bar to his VC. For the first action, 22–30 May 1941, see p. 406.
 Captain Upham was commanding a company of New Zealand troops in the Western Desert during the operations which culminated in the attack on El Ruweisat Ridge. In spite of being twice wounded, once when crossing open ground swept by enemy fire to inspect his forward sections guarding the minefields and again when he completely destroyed an entire truckload of German soldiers with hand grenades, he insisted on remaining with his men to take part in the final assault. During the opening stages of the attack on the ridge, his company formed part of the reserve battalion, but when communications with the forward troops broke down and he was instructed to send up an officer to report on the progress of the attack, he went out himself armed with a Spandau gun and, after several sharp encounters with enemy machine-gun posts, succeeded in bringing back the required information. Just before dawn the reserve battalion was ordered forward, but when it had almost reached its objective very heavy fire was encountered from a strongly defended enemy locality, consisting of four machine-gun

posts and a number of tanks. Without hesitation he at once led his company in a determined attack on the two nearest strongpoints on the left flank of the sector. His voice could be heard above the din of battle cheering on his men, and in spite of the fierce resistance of the enemy and the heavy casualties on both sides the objective was captured. During the engagement he destroyed a German tank and several guns and vehicles with grenades and although he was shot through the elbow by a machine-gun bullet and had his arm broken, he went on again to a forward position and brought back some of his men who had become isolated. He continued to dominate the situation until his men had beaten off a violent enemy counter-attack and consolidated the vital position which they had won under his inspiring leadership. Exhausted by pain from his wound and weak from loss of blood he was then removed to the regimental aid post but immediately his wound had been dressed he returned to his men, remaining with them all day long under heavy enemy artillery and mortar fire, until he was again severely wounded and being now unable to move fell into the hands of the enemy when, his gallant company having been reduced to only 6 survivors, his position was finally over-run by superior enemy forces.

Captured, he was sent to Germany where he made a nuisance of himself with his repeated attempts to escape. He was transferred to Colditz Castle. He had an implacable hatred of all things German and refused to allow any German-made car on his farm.

ELLIOTT, Keith *Sergeant, 22nd Bn., New Zealand Expeditionary Force*

15 July 1942 – At Ruweisat, the battalion to which Sergeant Elliott belonged was attacked at dawn on three flanks by tanks. Under heavy tank, machine-gun and shell fire, Elliott led the platoon he was commanding to the cover of a ridge 300 yards away, during which he sustained a chest wound. Here he re-formed his men and led them to a dominating ridge a further 500 yards away where they came under heavy enemy machine-gun and mortar fire. He located enemy machine-gun posts on his front and right flank and while one section attacked on the right flank, Elliott led seven men in a bayonet charge across 500 yards of open ground in the face of heavy fire and captured four machine-gun posts and an anti-tank gun, killing a number of the enemy and taking 50 prisoners. His section then came under fire from a machine-gun post on his left flank. He immediately charged this post single-handed and succeeded in capturing it, killing several of the enemy and taking 15 prisoners. During these two assaults he sustained three more wounds in the back and legs. Although badly wounded in four places Elliott refused to leave his men until he had re-formed them, handed over his prisoners, now increased to 130, and arranged for his men to rejoin their battalion. Owing to his quick grasp of the situation, great personal courage and leadership, 19 men who were the only survivors of B Company of his battalion captured and destroyed five machine-guns and one anti-tank gun, killed a great number of the enemy and captured 130 prisoners. He sustained only one casualty among his men and brought him back to the nearest advanced dressing station.

After the war he became a minister and ran a mission for down-and-outs in Wellington.

GURNEY, Arthur Stanley *Private, 2/48th Bn. (South Australia), Australian Military Forces*

22 July 1942 – During an attack on strong German positions in the early morning, the company to which Private Gurney belonged was held up by intense machine-gun fire from posts less than a hundred yards ahead; heavy casualties were being inflicted, with all the officers killed or wounded. Grasping the seriousness of the situation and without hesitation, Gurney charged the nearest machine-gun post, bayoneted three men and silenced the post. He then continued on to a second post, bayoneted two men and sent out a third as a prisoner. At this stage a stick grenade was thrown at Gurney, which knocked him to the ground. He rose again, picked up his rifle and charged a third post using the bayonet with great vigour. He then disappeared from view; later his body was found in an enemy post. By this single-handed act of gallantry in the face of a determined enemy, he enabled his company to press forward to its objective, inflicting heavy losses upon the enemy.

KIBBY, William Henry *Sergeant, 2/48th Bn. (South Australia), Australian Military Forces*

23–31 October 1942 – On 23 October, during the initial attack at Miteiriya Ridge, the commander of 17 Platoon, to which Sergeant Kibby belonged, was killed. No sooner had Kibby assumed command than his platoon was ordered to attack strong enemy positions holding up the advance of his company. Kibby immediately realized the necessity for quick decisive action, and without thought for his personal safety he dashed forward towards the enemy posts firing his tommy gun. This rapid and courageous individual action resulted in the complete silencing of the enemy fire, by the killing of three of the enemy and the capture of twelve others. With these posts silenced, his company was then able to continue the advance. On 26 October, after the capture of Trig 29, intense enemy artillery concentrations were directed on the battalion area, which were invariably followed with counter-attacks by tanks and infantry. Throughout the attack that culminated in its capture and the reorganization period which followed, Kibby moved from section to section personally directing their fire and cheering the men, despite the fact that the platoon was suffering heavy casualties. Several times, when under intense machine-gun fire, he went out and mended the platoon line communications, thus allowing mortar concentrations to be directed effectively against the attacks on his company's front. His whole demeanour during this difficult phase in the operations was an inspiration to his platoon. On the night of 30/31

October, when the battalion attacked Ring Contour 25, behind enemy lines, it was necessary for 17 Platoon to move through the most withering enemy machine-gun fire in order to reach its objective. These conditions did not deter him from pressing forward right to the objective, despite his platoon being mown down by machine-gun fire from point-blank range. One pocket of resistance still remained and he went forward alone throwing grenades to destroy the enemy now only a few yards distant. Just as success appeared certain, he was killed by a burst of machine-gun fire. The company's objective was captured.

GRATWICK, Percival Eric *Private, 2/48th Bn. (South Australia), Australian Military Forces*

25/26 October 1942 – During the attack on Trig 29 at Miteiriya Ridge, the company to which Private Gratwick belonged met with severe opposition from strong enemy positions which delayed the capture of the company's objective and caused a considerable number of casualties. Gratwick's platoon was directed at these strong positions but its advance was stopped by intense enemy fire at short range. Withering fire of all kinds killed the platoon commander, the platoon sergeant and many other ranks, and reduced the total strength of the platoon to seven. Gratwick grasped the seriousness of the situation and acting on his own initiative, with utter disregard for his own safety at a time when the remainder of the platoon were pinned down, charged the nearest post and completely destroyed the enemy with hand grenades, killing amongst others a complete mortar crew. As soon as this task was completed, and again under heavy machine-gun fire, he charged the second post with rifle and bayonet. It was from this post that the heaviest fire had been directed. He inflicted further casualties and was within striking distance of his objective when he was killed by a burst of machine-gun fire. By his brave and determined action, which completely unnerved the enemy, and by his successful reduction of the enemy's strength, Gratwick's company was able to move forward and mop up its objective.

TURNER, Victor Buller *T/Lieutenant Colonel, 2nd Bn., Rifle Brigade*

27 October 1942 – At El Aqqaqir, he led a battalion of the Rifle Brigade at night for four thousand yards through difficult country to their objective, where 40 Germans were captured. He then organized the captured position for all-round defence. In this position he and his battalion were continuously attacked from 0530 to 0700 hours, unsupported and so isolated that replenishment of ammunition was impossible owing to the concentration and accuracy of enemy fire. During this time the battalion was attacked by not less than 90 German tanks which advanced in successive waves. All of these were repulsed with a loss to the enemy of 35 tanks which were in flames, and not less than 20 more which had been immobilized. Throughout the action Turner never ceased to go to each part of the front as it was threatened. Wherever the fire was heaviest there he was to be found. In one case, finding a solitary 6pdr gun in action (the others being casualties) and manned only by another officer and a sergeant, he acted as loader and with these two destroyed five enemy tanks. While doing this he was wounded in the head, but he refused all aid until the last tank was destroyed.

THE DIEPPE RAID

The Dieppe Raid of August 1942 was the largest amphibious raid of the war, with five thousand Canadians with a thousand British, and American Rangers supported by 237 warships and landing craft and sixty-nine squadrons of aircraft. Two battalions would land at Puits and Pourville, the headlands at each side of the port, followed by the main assault, two battalions with twenty-seven tanks covered by eight destroyers, on the beach. A third battalion would then land at Pourville, which would link up with the armour landed on the beach. Army commandos would take out coastal batteries, and Royal Marine commandos would assault the harbour, destroy installations and capture prisoners, invasion craft and intelligence.

One of the batteries was prevented from engaging by the commandos, and the other was taken. At Puits the Canadians landed late, and were not able to leave the beach; at Pourville they landed in the wrong place, but the second battalion advanced inland. The main assault was a failure: the destroyers' fire did not suppress the defences, the tanks could not advance over the shingle beach and the infantry suffered very heavy casualties. The Royal Marines did not attempt their role because the guns were still active, and were instead sent in support of one of the infantry battalions: the position on the beaches was hidden by a smoke screen, and all those who landed were killed or taken prisoner. The landed forces were withdrawn six minutes behind schedule, and the official release declared that a radio-location station and flak battery was destroyed, as well as a six-gun battery and an ammunition dump, and 'vital experience has been gained in the employment of substantial numbers of troops in an assault and in the transport and use of heavy equipment during combined operations.' Just over a thousand of the raiding force were killed, the bulk among the Canadians – 907 – as well as two thousand taken prisoner.

MERRITT, Charles Cecil Ingersoll *Lieutenant Colonel, commanding South Saskatchewan Regiment, Canadian Infantry Corps*
19 August 1942 – From the point of landing at Dieppe, his unit's advance had to be made across a bridge in Pourville which was swept by very heavy machine-gun, mortar and artillery fire. The first parties were mostly destroyed and the bridge thickly covered by their bodies. A daring lead was required; waving his helmet, Merritt rushed forward, shouting, 'Come on over! There's nothing to worry about here.' He personally led the survivors

of at least four parties in turn across the bridge. Quickly organizing these, he led them forward and when held up by enemy pillboxes he again headed rushes which succeeded in clearing them. In one case he himself destroyed the occupants of the post by throwing grenades into it. After several of his runners became casualties, he kept contact with his different positions. Although twice wounded he continued to direct the unit's operations with great vigour and determination and while organizing the withdrawal he stalked a sniper with a Bren gun and silenced him. He then coolly gave orders for the departure and announced his intention to hold off and 'get even with' the enemy. When last seen he was collecting Bren and tommy guns and preparing a defensive position which successfully covered the withdrawal from the beach.

PORTEOUS, Patrick Anthony *T/Major, Royal Artillery*
    19 August 1942 – He was detailed to act as liaison officer at Dieppe between the two detachments whose task was to assault the heavy coast defence guns. In the initial assault, Porteous, working with the smaller of the two, was shot at close range through the hand, the bullet passing through his palm and entering his upper arm. Undaunted, he closed with his assailant, succeeded in disarming him and killed him with his own bayonet thereby saving the life of a British sergeant on whom the German had turned his aim. In the meantime the larger detachment was held up, and the officer leading this detachment was killed and the troop sergeant major fell seriously wounded. Almost immediately afterwards the only other officer of the detachment was also killed. Porteous, without hesitation and in the face of a withering fire, dashed across the open ground to take over the command of this detachment. Rallying them, he led them in a charge which carried the German position at the point of the bayonet, and was severely wounded for the second time. Though shot through the thigh he continued to the final objective where he eventually collapsed from loss of blood after the last of the guns had been destroyed.

FOOTE, John Weir *The Revd Honorary Captain, Canadian Chaplain Services, attached Royal Hamilton Light Infantry, Canadian Infantry*
    19 August 1942 – Honorary Captain Foote, Canadian Chaplain Services, was regimental chaplain with the Royal Hamilton Light Infantry. Upon landing on the beach at Dieppe under heavy fire he attached himself to the regimental aid post which had been set up in a slight depression on the beach, but which was only sufficient to give cover to men lying down. During the subsequent period of approximately eight hours, while the action continued, this officer not only assisted the regimental medical officer in ministering to the wounded in the aid post, but time and again left this shelter to inject morphine, give first aid and carry wounded personnel from the open beach to the post. On these occasions, with utter disregard for his personal safety, he exposed himself to an inferno of fire and saved many

lives. During the action, as the tide went out, the aid post was moved to the shelter of a stranded landing craft. Foote continued tirelessly and courageously to carry wounded men from the exposed beach to the cover of the landing craft. He also removed wounded from inside the landing craft when ammunition had been set on fire by enemy shells. When landing craft appeared he carried wounded from the post to them through very heavy fire. On several occasions this officer had the opportunity to embark but returned to the beach as his chief concern was the care and evacuation of the wounded. He refused a final opportunity to leave the shore, choosing to suffer the fate of the men he had ministered to for over three years.

NEW GUINEA

New Guinea, which comprised Dutch New Guinea in the west and the Australian-administered North-east New Guinea and Papua, was an important objective for the Japanese advance on Australia. They landed troops in the Huon Gulf, in the south-east, in March, with the intention of advancing on Port Moresby: this was defeated in the Battle of the Coral Sea in May, and on 22 July a Japanese regiment landed at Sanananda, north of Buna. There they advanced over the Kokoda Trail within 30 miles of Port Moresby, but Allied reinforcements landed at Milne Bay managed to check them.

KINGSBURY, Bruce Steel *Private, 2/14th Bn. (Victoria), Australian Military Forces*
   29 August 1942 – In Isurava, New Guinea, the battalion to which Private Kingsbury belonged had been holding a position in the Isurava area for two days against continuous and fierce enemy attacks. On the 29th, the enemy attacked in such force that they succeeded in breaking through the battalion's right flank, creating a serious threat both to the rest of the battalion and to its headquarters. To avoid the situation becoming more desperate, it was essential to regain immediately the lost ground on the right flank. Kingsbury, who was one of the few survivors of a platoon which had been overrun and severely cut about by the enemy, immediately volunteered to join a different platoon which had been ordered to counter-attack. He rushed forward firing his Bren gun from the hip through terrific machine-gun fire and succeeded in clearing a path through the enemy. Continuing to sweep the enemy positions with his fire and inflicting an extremely high number of casualties on them, Kingsbury was then seen to fall to the ground, shot dead by a bullet from a sniper hiding in the wood.

FRENCH, John Alexander *Corporal, 2/9th Bn. (Queensland), Australian Military Forces*
   4 September 1942 – During an attack on the Japanese position east of the Buna Mission, at Milne Bay, New Guinea, the advance of the section of

which Corporal French was in command was held up by the fire from three enemy machine-gun posts. French, ordering his section to take cover, advanced and silenced one of the posts with grenades. He returned to his section for more grenades and again advanced and silenced the second post. Armed with a tommy gun, he then attacked the third post, firing from the hip as he went forward. He was seen to be badly hit by the fire from this post, but he continued to advance. The enemy gun then ceased to fire and his section pushed on to find that all members of the three enemy gun crews had been killed and that French had died in front of the third gun pit. The attack was successfully concluded.

TUNISIA: OPERATION TORCH

In July 1942 the Allies decided to occupy French North Africa, partly to prevent Germany, or possibly Spain, from doing so, partly to occupy the American armies in Europe, and partly to prepare for the eventual invasion of France. General Eisenhower was in command. Landings were made, near Casablanca, Oran and Algiers, on 8 November. HMS *Walney's* role, with her sister ship HMS *Hartland*, was to capture Oran harbour at 0245, to allow heavy equipment and supplies to be landed. Both ships carried about two hundred GIs. Although the resistance to the landings was only token, French troops defended the harbours strongly. Both ships took heavy casualties and *Hartland* blew up, but *Walney* sank an enemy destroyer.

French forces ceased opposition on 11 November. Axis reinforcements were sent to Tunis, and engaged the forward troops about 50 miles of the city on the 17th. British troops advanced within 15 miles of Tunis, but were counter-attacked and pushed back to Tebourba, where they were still held at the end of the year.

PETERS, Frederick Thornton *A/Captain, Royal Navy*

8 November 1942 – Captain Peters was in command of HMS *Walney*. He led his force into the harbour of Oran, through the boom towards the jetty in the face of point-blank fire from shore batteries, a destroyer and a cruiser. Blinded in one eye, he alone of the 17 officers and men on the bridge survived. The *Walney* reached the jetty disabled and ablaze, and went down with her colours flying.

Captain Peters was also awarded the American DSC.

MALCOLM, Hugh Gordon *Wing Commander, 18 Squadron, Royal Air Force*

17 November to 4 December 1942 – He commanded a squadron of light bombers in North Africa. On 17 November he was detailed to carry out a low-level formation attack on Bizerta airfield, taking advantage of cloud cover. Twenty miles from the target the sky became clear, but Malcolm carried on, knowing well the danger of proceeding without a fighter escort.

Despite fierce opposition, all bombs were dropped within the airfield perimeter. A Junkers 52 and a Messerschmitt 109 were shot down; many dispersed enemy aircraft were raked by machine-gun fire. Weather conditions became extremely unfavourable, and as a result two of his aircraft were lost by collision; another was forced down by enemy fighters. It was due to this officer's skilful and resolute leadership that the remaining aircraft returned safely to base. On 28 November he again led his squadron against Bizerta airfield, which was bombed from a low altitude. The airfield on this occasion was heavily defended and intense and accurate anti-aircraft fire was met. Nevertheless, after his squadron had released their bombs, Malcolm led them back again and again to attack the airfield with machine-gun fire. These were typical of every sortie undertaken by this gallant officer; each attack was pressed to an effective conclusion however difficult the task and however formidable the opposition. Finally, on 4 December, Malcolm, having been detailed to give close support to 1st Army, received an urgent request to attack an enemy fighter airfield near Chouigui. He knew that to attack such an objective without a fighter escort, which could not be arranged in the time available, would be to court almost certain disaster; but believing the attack to be necessary for the success of the army's operations, his duty was clear. He decided to attack. He took off with his squadron and reached the target unmolested, but when he had successfully attacked it his squadron was intercepted by an overwhelming force of enemy fighters. Malcolm fought back, controlling his hard-pressed squadron and attempting to maintain formation. One by one his aircraft were shot down until only his own aircraft remained. In the end he too was shot down in flames.

LE PATOUREL, Herbert Wallace *T/Major, 2nd Bn., Hampshire Regiment*
3 December 1942 – The enemy had occupied an important high feature in the Tebourba area, on the left of the company commanded by this officer. Counter-attacks by a company of another battalion and detachments of Major Le Patourel's company had been unable to regain the position. This officer then personally led four volunteers under very heavy fire to the top in a last attempt to dislodge several enemy machine-guns. The party was heavily engaged by machine-gun fire and he rallied his men several times and engaged the enemy, silencing several machine-gun posts. Finally when the remainder of his party were all killed or wounded, he went forward alone with a pistol and some grenades to attack enemy machine-guns at close quarters and from this action did not return.

1943

In the Atlantic and North Africa the Allies began to turn the tide. By May the U-boats had been effectively contained and, following the capture of Tunis, campaigns were launched to take Sicily and then to invade southern Italy. Although the Italians surrendered in September, German troops remained in Italy in large numbers and were reinforced. The Allies faced a hard slog northwards towards Rome in difficult terrain and often bad weather conditions.

Still the only means of attack on the Reich, the RAF and USAAF continued to bomb German cities and industrial centres. In Burma, Anglo-Indian forces carried out an abortive attack in Arakan, but consolidated their lines on the Imphal plain in eastern India. It was General Orde Wingate's Chindit troops who, with a guerrilla-style thrust behind Japanese lines, proved that the enemy was not invincible and could be taken on effectively with intelligent tactics.

THE BURMA CAMPAIGN

Major General Sir Archibald Wavell, C.-in-C. India (whose command had included Burma since December 1941), planned to counter the Japanese advance on India with three operations: to regain Mandalay; to retake Rangoon; and to take the airbase on Akyab island. For logistical reasons the third was the only practicable campaign in late 1942 and early 1943.

Akyab Island, in the Arakan, at the south end of the Mayu or Mayo peninsula, also controlled the mouths of two major rivers. 14th Indian Division would advance south from Chittagong to Maungelaw, and the island would be taken by amphibious assault by the British 6th Infantry Brigade. The Arakan was held by only one Japanese regiment, but the territory was very difficult: 'down the centre of the peninsula ran the Mayu range', 'steep ridges covered by dense jungle' and 'deeply cut by raging torrents', in the words of a British special service officer. The advance began in December, and by January patrols in Bren-gun carriers had reached Foul Point, the southern tip of the peninsula, but the Japanese reinforced Donbaik, on the peninsular coast, and Rathedaung, on the left bank of the Mayu River, and a month's action failed to dislodge them. A counter-attack in April made the position untenable and the division withdrew to Chittagong.

The second VC won in Burma that year was in the Chin Hills, near Imphal, the site of the battle of 1944.

PARKASH SINGH *Havildar, 8th Punjab Regiment*

6 January 1943 – On the Donbaik Mayo peninsula, Burma, when two Bren-gun carriers had been put out of action Havildar Parkash Singh drove forward in his own carrier and rescued the two crews under very heavy fire, although they had expended their ammunition and the enemy were rushing the two disabled carriers on foot. On 19 January, in the same area, three carriers were put out of action by an enemy anti-tank gun and lay on the open beach covered by enemy anti-tank and machine-gun fire. One of these carriers was carrying the survivors of another in addition to its own crew. Parkash Singh, on seeing what had happened, went out from a safe position in his own carrier, and with complete disregard for his own personal safety, rescued the combined crews from one disabled carrier, together with the weapons from the carrier. Having brought the crews to safety, he again went out on the open beach in his carrier, still under very heavy anti-tank and machine-gun fire and with the utmost disregard for his personal safety, dismounted and connected a towing chain onto a disabled carrier containing two wounded men. Still under fire, he directed the towing of the disabled carrier from under enemy fire to a place of safety.

GAJE GHALE *Havildar, 2nd Bn., 5th Royal Gurkha Rifles*

24–27 May 1943 – In order to stop an advance into the Chin Hills of greatly superior Japanese forces it was essential to capture Basha East Hill, which was the key to the enemy position. Two assaults had failed but a third was ordered to be carried out by two platoons of Havildar Gaje Ghale's company and two companies of another battalion. Gaje Ghale was in command of one platoon but had never been under fire before and the platoon consisted of young soldiers. The approach for this platoon to their objective was along a narrow knife-edge with precipitous sides and bare of jungle whereas the enemy positions were well concealed. In places, the approach was no more than five yards wide and was covered by a dozen machine-guns besides being subjected to artillery and mortar fire from the reverse slope of the hill. While preparing for the attack the platoon came under heavy mortar fire but Gaje Ghale rallied them and led them forward. Approaching to close range of the well-entrenched enemy, the platoon came under withering fire and this NCO was wounded in the arm, chest and leg by an enemy hand grenade. Without pausing to attend to his serious wounds and with no heed to the intensive fire from all sides, Gaje Ghale closed his men and led them to close grips with the enemy. A bitter hand-to-hand struggle ensued; he dominated the fight by his outstanding example of dauntless courage and superb leadership. Hurling hand grenades, covered in blood from his own neglected wounds, he led assault after assault, encouraging his platoon by shouting the Gurkha battle cry. Spurred on by the irresistible will of their leader to win, the platoon stormed and carried the hill by a magnificent all-out effort and inflicted very heavy casualties on the Japanese. He then held and consolidated this hard-won position under heavy fire and it was not until the consolidation was well in hand that he went, refusing help, to the regimental aid post, when ordered to do so by an officer.

NEW GUINEA

Fighting continued in the Huon Peninsula, in the east, in particular for the control of the area between the port of Lae and the Salamaua Isthmus. On 2–4 March, in the Battle of the Bismarck Sea, eight Japanese transports carrying seven thousand infantry and marines to Lae, with eight destroyers and air protection, were attacked by the USAAF, RAAF and US Navy: all were sunk except four destroyers, which were damaged. Only 850 men reached Lae, most without their weapons and equipment. Flight Lieutenant Newton won a VC for his part in the action.

On 4 September an amphibious assault was made with the 9th Australian Division east of Lae, and on the 5th the 503rd US Parachute Regiment dropped on and took Nadzab, an airfield to the north-west, allowing the 7th Australian Division to be flown in. 7th Division advanced down the Markham River valley to Lae, while 9th Division moved west along the coast; to avoid being cut off at Lae the Japanese withdrew to Kiari, the other side of the peninsula. With Lae taken, 7th Division moved along the Ramu valley until by October it had reached Dumpu, 80 miles north-west of Adzab. Meanwhile, a brigade of the 9th Division had landed at Finschafen to find that most of the garrison had withdrawn to Satelberg, a fortified base. The division advanced using tanks to destroy the Japanese bunkers and infantry platoons to mop up, but in the difficult terrain and wet weather the tanks were not always able to keep up; in the battle for Satelberg, they were stopped by a landslide, and it was in a four-day infantry-only battle that Sergeant Derrick, a veteran of Tobruk, won his VC.

NEWTON, William Ellis *Flight Lieutenant, 22 Squadron, Royal Australian Air Force*

16 March 1943 – Flight Lieutenant Newton served with 22 Squadron, Royal Australian Air Force, in New Guinea from May 1942 to March 1943, and completed fifty-two operational sorties. Throughout, he displayed great courage and an iron determination to inflict the utmost damage on the enemy. His splendid offensive flying and fighting were attended with brilliant success. Disdaining evasive tactics when under the heaviest fire, he always went straight to his objectives. He carried out many daring machine-gun attacks on enemy positions involving low flying over long distances in the face of continuous fire at point-blank range. On three occasions, he dived through intense anti-aircraft fire to release his bombs on important targets on the Salamaua isthmus. On one of these occasions, his starboard engine failed over the target, but he succeeded in flying back to an airfield 160 miles away. When leading an attack on an objective on 16 March 1943, he dived through intense and accurate shell fire and his aircraft was hit repeatedly. Nevertheless, he held to his course and bombed his target from a low level. The attack resulted in the destruction of many buildings and dumps, including two 40,000-gallon fuel installations. Although his aircraft was crippled, with fuselage and wing sections torn, petrol tanks pierced, main planes and engines seriously damaged, and one of the main tyres flat, Newton managed to fly it back to base and make a successful landing. Despite this harassing experience, he returned next day to the same locality. His target, this time a single building, was even more difficult but he again attacked with his usual courage and resolution, flying a steady course through a barrage of fire. He scored a hit on the building but at the same moment his aircraft burst into flames. Maintaining control, he calmly turned his aircraft away and flew along the shore, seeing it as his duty to keep the aircraft in the air as long as he could so as to take his crew as far away as possible from the enemy's positions. With great skill, he brought his blazing aircraft down on the water. Two members of the crew were able to extricate themselves and were seen swimming to the shore, but the pilot's escape hatch was not opened and his dinghy was not inflated.

The two crew members were in fact the pilot, Flight Lieutenant Newton, and Flight Sergeant John Lyon. They were captured and killed: on 29 March, Newton was beheaded and Lyon bayoneted.

KELLIHER, Richard *Private, 2nd/25th Bn. (Queensland), Australian Military Forces*

Born the sixth of seven children to cattle dealer Michael Kelliher and his wife Mary in Ballybreggan, Ireland, Richard Kelliher trained as a mechanic on leaving school. He was working in his older brother's motor works when he saw a chance of a better life on the other side of the world and emigrated with his fifteen-year-old sister to Australia in 1929. At first they lived with their uncle and Kelliher worked on his farm but in 1930 the Great Depression struck. Although he had contracted typhoid and meningitis and his health was very poor, Kelliher had to tough around in Queensland for what work he could get – farm hand on a banana plantation, cane cutter, painter/decorator – to make ends meet. He was thirty years old and working as a labourer in 1941 when the Japanese threat to Australia forced the army into a recruiting drive, and Kelliher took welcome refuge in the Australian Infantry Forces.

After training – still plagued by ill health – and postings around the Far East, his battalion, the 2nd/25th, returned to Australia for jungle training. In autumn 1942 Kelliher and the 2nd/25th were in New Guinea as the Japanese threat grew closer to the Australian homeland. It was in November, when his section was heavily engaged in battle against the Japanese, that Kelliher arrived back at Company HQ with, he said, information from his commanding officer. Unfortunately this officer was never able to corroborate his story, as he was killed in action – and doubt seemed to hang over Kelliher's honesty and motives in leaving the front line. After a brief investigation, he was charged with 'failing to get into his allotted position with his section', and allegedly saying 'It's too bloody hot for me,' and 'I am not a bloody fool.' Kelliher protested his innocence vehemently – and significantly, the officer who accused him owned that he had based his charges on hearsay and that he didn't know Kelliher personally at all. However, Kelliher was sent back to Queensland in disgrace to face court martial. In March 1943 he was found guilty of 'misbehaving before the enemy in such a way as to show cowardice' and he was given a sentence of twelve months in detention. Only in May did his appeal to the Adjutant General result in the verdict and the sentence of the court martial being quashed.

Kelliher was released to return to his battalion, which was back in Australia and preparing to return to New Guinea, where it arrived in August. Quickly engaged at the front, on 11 September it found the Japanese pinning down two Australian platoons at Nadzab. Private L. J. Brown recalled the action:

> During our attack on a Jap position at Nadzab, I witnessed the following act of bravery by Private Richard Kelliher. Eleven Platoon of B Company was pinned down by very heavy machine-gun fire, which killed 5 and wounded 3 of this platoon. Private Kelliher, without instructions, dashed down the hill to within yards of the enemy position, throwing his two grenades. He was forced back to our lines by heavy enemy fire. He then took a Bren gun and once more charged to within 30 yards of the enemy position and, firing from the hip, he succeeded in silencing the enemy stronghold. One Japanese officer and eight other ranks were found dead in this position following the battle. Four of these had been accounted for by snipers. I do not know if Kelliher killed the other five, but he silenced the position. Then straight away, still under heavy rifle fire from another Jap position, he went forward and brought in Corporal William Richards, who had been severely wounded in the arm, back and stomach.

Other members of the platoon corroborated this account, agreeing that Kelliher's action was responsible for saving Richards' life and allowing the advance to continue. Kelliher later spoke of his action:

> I wanted to bring Billy back because he was my cobber, so I jumped out from the scrub where I was sheltering, threw a few grenades over into the position where the Japanese were dug in. I did not kill them all, so I went back, got a Bren gun, and emptied the magazine into the post. That settled the Japanese. I didn't think of doing it to get a medal. I just wanted to bring Billy back, and what I did was the only way to do it.

The news of his VC reached Kelliher when he was again in hospital – and was broadcast in his homeland to a rapturous reception. The Australian Prime Minister, John Curtin, sent the first ever cablegram to Ballybeggan to tell his mother of his pride at his countryman's achievement. Even the Irish press, which had banned any mention of deeds of Irishmen serving with British or American forces, was proud to announce Kelliher's award.

Following his discharge from the army in August 1945, Kelliher was classified as 10 per cent disabled – fit for only light work due to his post-malarial illness – and he found work as a cleaner in Brisbane. Penury was deferred when he was selected to join the Australian Victory Contingent which visited London to take part in the Victory Parade on 8 June 1946 – and while the rest of the contingent set sail again for Australia, he and fellow VC winner Reg Rattey stayed on to receive their medals from the King.

Back in Australia, Kelliher married nineteen-year-old Olive Margaret Hearn and moved to Melbourne – but he still suffered from ill health. In 1955 a Sydney paper reported on Australia's VC holders: 'He is a sick man and has gone from one poor job to another. He had been employed as a cleaner at the Brisbane Town Hall before moving to Victoria, where he had worked a concrete machine for the Camberwell Council. He died after suffering a stroke on 28 January 1963 in the Heidelberg hospital – at which time he was Totally and Permanently Incapacitated – and was buried with full military honours.

Like many widows of medal-holders, Olive was driven by poverty to sell his medals. The London auctioneer Sotheby's offered the medal group to the Australian War Memorial for £1,000, but the Director of the Memorial turned it down on the grounds that it would encourage VC owners or their families to sell their medals – and they were withdrawn from sale. The Secretary of the 2nd/25th Battalion Association later launched an appeal to raise the £1,000 to secure the medals for the Australian War Memorial, to which they were donated on the twenty-third anniversary of the battle in which Kelliher had shown such selflessness and courage.

DERRICK, Thomas Currie *Sergeant, 2/48th Bn., Australian Military Forces*
24 November 1943 – In New Guinea, a company of an Australian infantry battalion was ordered to outflank a strong enemy position sited on a precipitous cliff face and then to attack a feature 150 yards from the township of Satelberg. Sergeant Derrick was in command of his platoon of the company. Due to the nature of the country, the only possible approach to the town lay through an open kunai patch situated directly beneath the top of the cliffs. Over a period of two hours many attempts were made by Australian troops to clamber up the slopes to their objective, but on each occasion the enemy prevented success with intense machine-gun fire and grenades. Shortly before last light it appeared that it would be impossible to reach the objective or even to hold the ground already occupied and the

company was ordered to retire. On receipt of this order, Derrick, displaying dogged tenacity, requested one last attempt to reach the objective. His request was granted. Moving ahead of his forward section he personally destroyed with grenades an enemy post which had been holding up this section. He then ordered his second section around on the right flank. This section came under heavy fire from light machine-guns and grenades from six enemy posts. Without regard for personal safety he clambered forward well ahead of the leading men of the section and hurled grenade after grenade, so completely demoralizing the enemy that they fled leaving weapons and grenades. By this action alone the company was able to gain its first foothold on the precipitous ground. Not content with the work already done, he returned to the first section, and together with the third section of his platoon advanced to deal with the three remaining posts in the area. On four separate occasions he dashed forward and threw grenades at a range of six to eight yards until these positions were finally silenced. In all, he reduced ten enemy posts. From the vital ground he had captured the remainder of the battalion moved on to capture Satelberg the following morning.

TUNISIA

By December 1942 the Allied advance in Tunisia had been halted at Tebourba, about 20 miles west of Tunis. Field Marshal Rommel had retreated to the Mareth Line, originally built by the French to defend against attack from Libya; Montgomery built up his supplies and logistic facilities in Tripoli and sent 7th Armoured Division to follow up the retreat. Rommel attacked it on 6 March, but Montgomery had received Ultra intelligence and reinforced it with the New Zealand Division, and Rommel lost fifty-two tanks. He left for Germany shortly afterwards and control of all Axis troops in Africa passed to Colonel General Jürgen von Arnim, who had commanded Axis forces in Tunis and had just lost a battle with the British 5th Corps at Medjez el Bab.

Montgomery's attack on the Mareth Line was launched on 20 March with a frontal advance supported by a flanking movement through the Tebaga Gap to the south. The main attack was costly and unsuccessful, and the flank attack halted; when it was reinforced on the 23rd and relaunched on the 26th the enemy were driven out, but 15th Panzer Division held the advance long enough for the garrison to fall back to Wadi Akarit. This was a series of hills linked by 10–12 miles of defences running to the sea; it was taken on 6 April after several of the important positions were captured in the night by Indian and Gurkha troops, but exploitation was slow and the Germans were able to retreat to Enfidaville, about 150 miles north and 40 miles south of Tunis, by the 11th. From 19 to 25 April the US 2nd Corps advanced north while 8th Army attacked Enfidaville, but both Italian and German forces mounted stubborn resistance, despite being almost without fuel, food and ammunition. Two of Montgomery's armoured divisions were transferred north, the attack was renewed, and the Axis forces again withdrew to a prepared line. Tunis was finally taken on 7 May after an attack preceded by concentrated artillery fire on all known strongpoints and launched in darkness at 3 a.m. on the 6th, and Bizerta the same day. At 8.15 p.m. on the 13th armed resistance ceased.

SEAGRIM, Derek Anthony *T/Lieutenant Colonel, commanding 7th Bn., Green Howards*

20/21 March 1943 – A battalion of the Green Howards was tasked to attack and capture an important feature on the left flank of the main attack on the Mareth Line, Tunisia. The defence of this feature was very strong and it was protected by an anti-tank ditch 12 feet wide and 8 feet deep with minefields on both sides. It formed a new part of the main defences of the Mareth Line and the successful capture of this feature was vital to the success of the main attack. From the time the attack was launched the battalion was subjected to the most intense fire from artillery, machine-guns and mortars and it appeared more than probable that it would be held up, entailing failure of the main attack. Realizing the seriousness of the situation, Seagrim placed himself at the head of his battalion, which was suffering heavy casualties, and led it through the hail of fire. He personally helped the team which was placing the scaling ladder over the anti-tank ditch and was himself the first to cross it. He led the assault firing his pistol, throwing grenades and personally assaulting two machine-gun posts which were holding up the advance of one of his companies. It is estimated that in this phase he killed or captured 20 Germans. This display of leadership and personal courage led directly to the capture of the objective. When dawn broke the battalion was firmly established on the position, which was of obvious importance to the enemy, who immediately made every effort to regain it. Every post was mortared and machine-gunned unmercifully and movement became practically impossible but Seagrim was quite undeterred. He moved from post to post organizing and directing the fire until the attackers were wiped out to a man.

The thirty-nine-year-old colonel died in hospital on 6 April 1943. His brother, Major H. P. Seagrim of the Indian Army, for his sacrificial courage behind Japanese lines in Burma, was posthumously awarded the George Cross. He was executed on 22 September 1944. The brothers are the only instance of the two crosses being awarded to the same family.

NGARIMU, Moana-Nui-a-Kiwa *Second Lieutenant, 28th (Maori) Bn., New Zealand Expeditionary Force*

26–27 March 1943 – During the action at the Tebaga Gap, Tunisia, he commanded a platoon in an attack upon the vital hill feature, Point 209. He was given the task of attacking and capturing a lower feature forward of Point 209 itself held in considerable strength by the enemy. He led his men with great determination straight up the face of the hill, undeterred by the intense mortar and machine-gun fire, which caused considerable casualties. He was himself first on the hill crest, personally annihilating at least two enemy machine-gun posts. In the face of such a determined attack the remainder of the enemy fled, but further advance was impossible as the reverse slope was swept by machine-gun fire from Point 209 itself. Under cover of a most intense mortar barrage the enemy counter-attacked, and Ngarimu ordered his men to stand up and engage the enemy man for man. This they did with such good effect that the attackers were mown down, Ngarimu personally killing several. He was twice wounded, once by rifle fire in the shoulder and later by shrapnel in the leg, and though urged by both his company and battalion commanders to go back, he refused to do so, saying that he would stay a little while with his men. He stayed till he met his death the following morning. Darkness found this officer and his depleted platoon lying on the rocky face of the forward slope of the hill feature, with the enemy in a similar position on the reverse slope about 20 yards distant. Throughout the night the enemy repeatedly launched fierce attacks in an attempt to dislodge Ngarimu and his men, but each counter-attack was beaten off entirely by his inspired leadership. During one of these counter-attacks the enemy, by using hand grenades, succeeded in piercing a certain part of the line. Without hesitation he rushed to the threatened area, and those of the enemy he did not kill he drove back with stones and with his tommy gun. During another determined counter-attack by the enemy, part of his line broke. Yelling orders and encouragement, he rallied his men and led them in a fierce onslaught back into their old positions. All through the night, between attacks, he and his men were heavily harassed by machine-gun and mortar fire, but he watched his line very carefully, cheering his men on and inspiring them by his gallant personal conduct. Morning found him still in possession of the hill feature, but only he and two unwounded other ranks remained. Reinforcements were sent up to him. In the morning the enemy again counter-attacked, and it was during this attack that he was killed. He was killed on his feet defiantly facing the enemy with his tommy gun at his hip. As he fell, he came to rest almost on the top of those of the enemy who had fallen, the number of whom testified to his outstanding courage and fortitude.

LALBAHADUR THAPA *Subadar, 1st Bn., 2nd Gurkha Rifles*
    5/6 April 1943 – During a silent attack on the Rass-Ez-Zouai feature, Tunisia, Subadar Lalbahadur Thapa was second in command of D Company. The commander of 16 Platoon was detached with one section to secure an isolated feature on the left of the company's objective. Lalbahadur Thapa took command of the remaining two sections and led them forward towards

the main feature on the outer ridge, in order to break through and secure the only passage by which the vital commanding feature could be seized to cover the penetration of the division into the hills. On the capture of these hills the whole success of the corps plan depended. First contact with the enemy was made at the foot of a pathway winding up a narrow cleft. This steep cleft was thickly studded with a series of enemy posts, the inner of which contained an anti-tank gun and the remainder medium machine-guns. After passing through the narrow cleft, one emerges into a small arena with very steep sides, some 200 feet in height, and in places sheer cliff. Into this arena and down its sides numbers of automatic weapons were trained and mortar fire directed. The garrison of the outer posts were all killed by Lalbahadur Thapa and his men with kukri or bayonet in the first rush and the enemy then opened very heavy fire straight down the narrow enclosed pathway and steep arena sides. Lalbahadur Thapa led his men on and fought his way up the narrow gully straight through the enemy's fire, with little room to manoeuvre, in the face of intense and sustained machine-gun concentrations and the liberal use of grenades by the enemy. The next machine-gun posts were dealt with, Lalbahadur Thapa personally killing two men with his kukri and two more with his revolver. He continued to fight his way up the narrow bullet-swept approaches to the crest, which he reached with two riflemen; there he killed another two men with his kukri, the riflemen killed two more and the rest fled. The subadar then secured the whole feature and covered his company's advance up the defile. This pathway was found to be the only practicable route up the precipitous ridge, and by securing it the company was able to deploy and mop up all enemy opposition on their objective, which was an essential feature covering the further advance of the brigade and of the division, as well as the bridgehead over the anti-tank ditch.

ANDERSON, Eric *Private, 5th Bn., East Yorkshire Regiment*
   6 April 1943 – A battalion of the East Yorkshire Regiment was making a dawn attack on a strong enemy locality on the Wadi Akarit, with A Company leading. After some progress had been made and A Company was advancing over an exposed forward slope, it suddenly came under most intense and accurate machine-gun and mortar fire from well-concealed enemy strong-points not more than 200 yards away. Further advance in that direction was impossible and A Company was able to withdraw behind the crest of a hill, with the exception of a few men who were wounded and pinned to the ground by strong and well-directed small-arms fire. Private Anderson was a stretcher bearer attached to A Company; seeing these men lying wounded in no-man's-land, he went forward alone through intense fire, quite regardless of his personal safety, and single-handed carried back a wounded soldier to a place of safety where medical attention could be given. Knowing that more men were lying wounded in the open he again went out to the bullet-

swept slope, located a second wounded man and carried him to safety, then went forward once again and safely evacuated a third casualty. Without any hesitation or consideration for himself he went out for a fourth time, but by now he was the only target the enemy had to shoot at and when he reached the fourth wounded man, and was administering such first aid as he could to prepare for the return journey, he was himself hit and mortally wounded.

CAMPBELL, Lorne MacLaine *T/Lieutenant Colonel, commanding 7th Bn., Argyll and Sutherland Highlanders*

6 April 1943 – In the attack upon the Wadi Akarit position, Tunisia, the task of breaking through the enemy minefield and anti-tank ditch to the east of the Roumana feature and of forming the initial bridgehead for a brigade of the 51st Highland Division was allotted to the battalion of the Argyll and Sutherland Highlanders commanded by Lieutenant Colonel Campbell. The attack had to form up in complete darkness and traverse the main offshoot of the Wadi Akarit at an angle to the line of advance. In spite of heavy machine-gun and shell fire in the early stages of the attack, Campbell successfully accomplished this difficult operation, captured at least 600 prisoners and led his battalion to its objective, having to cross an unswept portion of an enemy minefield in doing so. Later, upon reaching his objective he found that a gap which had been blown by the Royal Engineers in the anti-tank ditch did not correspond with the vehicle lane which had been cleared in the minefield. Realizing the vital necessity of quickly establishing a gap for the passage of anti-tank guns, he took personal charge of this operation. It was now broad daylight and, under very heavy machine-gun fire and shell fire he succeeded in making a personal reconnaissance and in conducting operations which led to the establishing of a vehicle gap. Throughout the day he held his position with his battalion in the face of extremely heavy and constant shellfire, which the enemy was able to bring to bear by direct observation. About 1630 hours determined enemy counter-attacks began to develop, accompanied by tanks. Realizing that it was imperative for the future success of the army plan to hold the bridgehead his battalion had captured, he inspired his men by his presence in the forefront of the battle, cheering them on and rallying them as he moved to those points where the fighting was heaviest. When his left forward company was forced to give ground he went forward alone into a hail of fire and personally reorganized their position, remaining with the company until the attack at this point was held. As reinforcements arrived upon the scene he was seen standing in the open directing the fight under close-range fire of enemy infantry, and he continued to do so although already painfully wounded in the neck by shell fire. It was not until the battle died down that he allowed his wound to be dressed. Even then, although in great pain, he refused to be evacuated, remaining with his battalion and continuing to inspire them by his presence on the field.

Darkness fell with the Argylls still holding their positions, though many of the officers and men had become casualties.

He was the nephew of Admiral Gordon Campbell, the First World War 'Q'-ship VC.

CHHELU RAM *Company Havildar Major, 4th Rajputana Rifles*
19/20 April 1943 – During the attack by the 5th Indian Infantry Brigade on the Djebel Garli feature, Tunisia, he was with one of the two leading companies. During the advance to the battalion's second objective, the forward troops were held up by an enemy machine-gun position on some high ground. Chhelu Ram, armed with a tommy gun, immediately rushed forward through the intense machine-gun and mortar fire and single-handedly silenced the post, killing its three or four occupants and thus enabling the advance to continue. When the leading companies were approaching their third objective the enemy brought down intense machine-gun and mortar fire on them which mortally wounded the company commander. Chhelu Ram went to the officer's assistance in a completely exposed position and attended to him, during which he himself was seriously wounded. He then took command of his own company and elements of the other leading company and quickly reorganized them. Almost immediately the enemy put in a heavy counter-attack and the troops began to run short of ammunition. During the fierce hand-to-hand fighting which followed, this NCO's bravery and determination were beyond praise. Rushing from point to point, wherever the fighting was heaviest, he rallied the men and drove back the enemy with the cry of, 'Jats and Mohammedans, there must be no withdrawal! We will advance! Advance!' He then advanced ahead of the two companies. Inspired by his fine example, the counter-attack on this vital ground was driven back with bayonets, stones and rocks. During this fighting Chhelu Ram was again wounded, this time mortally. He refused, however, to be carried back and continued to command and inspire his men until finally losing consciousness. A few minutes later he died from the effects of his wounds.

LYELL, Charles Anthony, the Lord *T/Captain, 1st Bn., Scots Guards*
22–27 April 1943 – Near Djebel Bou Arada, Tunisia, Lyell commanded his company, which had been placed under the orders of a battalion of the Grenadier Guards, with great gallantry, ability and cheerfulness. He led it down a slope under heavy mortar fire to repel a German counter-attack on 22 April, led it again under heavy fire through the battalion's first objective on 23 April in order to capture and consolidate a high point, and held this point through a very trying period of shelling, heat and shortage of water. During this period, through his energy and cheerfulness, he not only kept up the fighting spirit of his company but also managed through radio telephony, which he worked himself from an exposed position, to bring most effective artillery fire to bear on enemy tanks, vehicles and infantry

positions. At about 1800 hours on 27 April, his company was taking part in the battalion's attack on Djebel Bou Arada. The company was held up in the foothills by heavy fire from an enemy post on the left, which consisted of an 88mm gun and a heavy machine-gun in separate pits. Realizing that until this post was destroyed the advance could not proceed, Lyell collected the only available men not pinned down by fire – a sergeant, a lance corporal and two guardsmen – and led them to attack it. He was a long way in advance of the others and lobbed a hand grenade into the machine-gun pit, destroying the crew. At this point his sergeant was killed and both the guardsmen were wounded. The lance corporal got down to give covering fire to Lyell, who had run straight on towards the 88mm gun pit and was working his way round to the left of it. So quickly had this officer acted that he was in among the crew with the bayonet before they had time to fire more than one shot. He killed a number of them before being overwhelmed and killed himself. The few survivors of the gun crew then left the pit, some of them being killed while they were retiring, and both the heavy machine-gun and 88mm gun were silenced. The company was then able to advance and take its objective, which had an important bearing on the success of the battalion and of the brigade.

ANDERSON, John Thompson McKellar *A/Major, 8th Bn., Argyll and Sutherland Highlanders*

23 April 1943 – Over a period of five hours Major Anderson led the attack on 'Longstop' Hill, Tunisia, through intense enemy machine-gun and mortar fire. As leading company commander he led the assault on the battalion's first objective, in daylight, over a long expanse of open sloping hillside and most of the time without the effective cover of smoke. Enemy infantry opposition was most determined, and very heavy casualties were sustained, including all other rifle company commanders, before even the first objective was reached. On the first objective and still under continual enemy fire, Anderson reorganized the battalion and rallied men whose commanders had been either killed or wounded. The commanding officer having been killed, he took command of the battalion and led the assault on the second objective. During this assault he received a leg wound, but in spite of this he carried on and finally captured Longstop Hill with a total force of only four officers and less than forty other ranks. Fire had been so intense during this stage of the attack that the remainder of the battalion were pinned down and unable to advance until he had successfully occupied the hill. During the assault, he personally led attacks on at least three enemy machine-gun positions and in every case was the first man into the enemy pits; he also led a successful attack on an enemy mortar position of four mortars, defended by over thirty of the enemy. His force on the hill captured about two hundred prisoners and killed many more during the attack.

Anderson was killed in Italy on 5 October 1943.

SANDYS-CLARKE, Willward Alexander *Lieutenant, Loyal North Lancashire Regiment*

23 April 1943 – During the attack on the Guiriat el Atach feature, Tunisia, Lieutenant Clarke's battalion had been fully committed by dawn. B Company gained their objective but were counter-attacked and almost wiped out. The sole remaining officer was Clarke, who, already wounded in the head, gathered a composite platoon together and volunteered to attack the position again. As the platoon closed on to the objective, it was met by heavy fire from a machine-gun post. Clarke manoeuvred his platoon into position to give covering fire, and then tackled the post single-handed, killing or capturing the crew and knocking out the gun. Almost at once the platoon came under heavy fire from two more machine-gun posts. Clarke again manoeuvred his platoon into position and went forward alone, killed the crews or compelled them to surrender, and put the guns out of action. This officer then led his platoon on to the objective and ordered it to consolidate. During consolidation, the platoon came under fire from two sniper posts. Without hesitating, Clarke advanced single-handed to clear the opposition, but was killed outright within a few feet of the enemy.

KENNEALLY, John Patrick (real name Leslie Robinson) *Lance Corporal, Irish Guards*

Leslie Robinson – for such was his real name – was born the illegitimate son of eighteen-year-old Gertrude Robinson (the daughter of a Blackpool pharmacist) and a wealthy Jewish textile manufacturer. Under a cloud of disgrace, Robinson's mother changed her name to Jackson and went to live with friends in Birmingham, where she made ends meet by working as a hairdresser and as a high-class prostitute or 'dance hostess'. Maintenance support from his father ensured that Robinson could go to a good school – King Edward's in Birmingham – but he grew up in one of the roughest areas of the city and soon learned to look out for himself using his wits and fists where necessary. He was physically strong and a good athlete, he enjoyed his role as patrol leader with the Boy Scouts – and as soon as he was eighteen he joined as a territorial in the Royal Artillery.

Territorial units were mobilized when war began in 1939, and Leslie found himself in an anti-aircraft battery in Dollis Hill, North London. This was not the life of action he had hoped for when he signed up, and when he failed to return on time from leave he served a period of detention at Wellington Barracks under the supervision of the Irish Guards. To Robinson, these men embodied what soldiering was all about and on return to the gunners he asked for a transfer to join them, but was refused. He deserted and threw in his lot with a bunch of Irish labourers.

One of the men acquired for him the identity card and National Insurance number of an Irish colleague who had returned home and Robinson had a new identity – John Patrick Kenneally. This was a turning point. With a fine new Irish name he felt he was entitled to join the Irish Guards. He travelled to Manchester, invented a Tipperary childhood for himself and was accepted at once.

The Irish Guards gave Kenneally the physical challenge and, probably more importantly, the sense of belonging that he needed. He wrote in his autobiography, 'It was a hard school to learn in. Without being over-sentimental, men can love each other. It is born of mutual suffering, hardships shared, dangers encountered. It is a spiritual love and there is nothing sexual about it. It's entirely masculine, even more than brotherly love, and is called comradeship.'

In March 1943 Kenneally set sail for Tunisia with the 1st Battalion Irish Guards, and just a month later he showed the courage and dedication which earned him his VC. At the end of April, the Irish Guards were engaged in the final assault to take Tunis. In order to secure the city, they needed to capture 'the Bou' – a high ridge that dominated the approach to Tunis between Medjez el Bab and Tebourba. Kenneally's battalion were holding on grimly at the western end, coming under frequent fire. The Irish Guards, with a force reduced to just 173 men, were defending the crucial Point 212 on the Bou when Kenneally saw a company of around 100 panzer-grenadiers preparing to attack their position. He seized the moment and charged alone down the rocky slope, firing his Bren gun from the hip. The enemy were caught completely off guard by his extraordinary and totally unpredictable attack and started to retreat in disarray.

Of this action, he recalled:

> I estimated there were 100 German infantry about 50 yards in front of us. They were scattered amongst the rocks, firing rifles and semi-automatics, the nearest of them were chucking stick grenades. 'Those are the guys for me,' I thought. I put my Bren gun on single shot. I downed quite a few and the increased firepower had its effect and they began to back-pedal. Soon it was a general flight and we picked them off as they retreated. It gave us a great lift and I felt quite elated. It had been the closest we had been to the enemy, and we had beaten them.

The Germans again formed up to attack in a large gully. Kenneally observed them taking orders and charged headlong at the enemy.

> I took a deep breath and belted forward, firing from the hip. I achieved complete surprise. I hose-piped them from the top of the gully. They were being bowled over like ninepins and were diving in all directions. I had time to flip on another magazine and gave them that too. Enough was enough, and I fled back to the boulders for safety.

On the morning of 30 April the Germans launched a final and very determined attack on the Bou. This time Kenneally harassed the enemy, inflicting a number of casualties, but was hit in the calf by a bullet as he climbed back up the slope. Ignoring his wound he hopped from one firing position to another as the Germans advanced over the rocks. He flatly refused to give up his Bren gun, with the probably justified claim that no one else would be able to handle it properly, and fought on all day until the Germans withdrew, with Kenneally and the remnants of his company firing at them as they retreated. He said later,

> There was no time for fear; a strange 'don't-give-a-damn' feeling takes a grip. This is something every infantryman feels when he is constantly exposed to death in brutal and violent forms.

Perhaps it was his personal sense of rage at the loss of his comrades in a battle where the Irish Guards had sustained huge casualties that inspired him – whatever it was, his action was recognized as influencing the whole course of the battle. The Allies took Tunis – and Kenneally was promoted to sergeant, after turning down a commission to stay where he was, happy in the ranks. On hearing of his VC award, he responded with characteristic modesty, 'It was the worst thing that could have happened to me. I thought, "Now I'm bound to be rumbled."'

Kenneally was wounded again at the Anzio beachhead in February 1944 – the battalion sustained such fierce losses that it was withdrawn to England. There he trained RAF airmen transferred to the army and with them joined the 3rd Battalion in Germany in 1945, where he remained on occupation duties. Not finding his new role to his taste, he joined the newly forming 1st Guards Parachute Battalion, and was sent to Palestine.

He distinguished himself again when, after organizing the defence of a kibbutz in northern Galilee, it survived a major night attack by Arab forces in 1948. He was offered a position in the Israeli forces, but by this time he had a wife and two sons in England, and he declined; unfortunately he could not be given a home posting near them, and he bought himself out of the army in July 1948. He had a successful civilian career, running a garage, and then retired to Worcestershire.

BOMBER COMMAND

TRENT, Leonard Henry *Squadron Leader, Royal New Zealand Air Force, attached 487 (NZ) Squadron, Royal Air Force*

3 May 1943 – Squadron Leader Trent was detailed to lead a formation of Ventura aircraft in a daylight attack on the power station at Amsterdam. This operation was intended to encourage the Dutch workmen in their resistance to the enemy. The target was known to be heavily defended. The importance of bombing it, regardless of enemy fighters or anti-aircraft fire, was strongly impressed on the aircrews taking part in the operation. Before taking off, Trent told the deputy leader that he was going over the target whatever happened. All went well until the Venturas and their fighter escort were nearing the Dutch coast. Then one bomber was hit and had to turn back. Suddenly large numbers of enemy fighters appeared. The escorting fighters were hotly engaged and lost touch with the bombing force. The Venturas closed up for mutual protection and commenced their run-up to the target. Unfortunately, the fighters detailed to support them over the target had reached the area too early and had been recalled. Soon the bombers were attacked. They were at the mercy of fifteen to twenty Messerschmitts, which dived on them incessantly. Within four minutes six Venturas were destroyed. Squadron Leader Trent continued on his course with the three remaining aircraft. In a short time two more Venturas went down in flames. Heedless of the murderous attacks and of the heavy anti-aircraft fire which was now encountered, Trent completed an accurate bombing run and even shot down a Messerschmitt at point-blank range. Dropping his bombs in the target area, he turned away. The aircraft following him was shot down on reaching the target. Immediately afterwards his own aircraft was hit, went into a spin and broke up. Trent and his navigator were thrown clear and became prisoners of war. The other two members of the crew perished.

He was sent to Stalag Luft III and took part in the great escape of March 1944; he was recaptured and put in solitary confinement.

GIBSON, Guy Penrose *Wing Commander, 617 Squadron, Royal Air Force*
16–17 May 1943 – This officer served as a night bomber pilot at the beginning of the war and quickly established a reputation as an outstanding operational pilot. In addition to taking the fullest possible share in all normal operations, he made single-handed attacks during his rest nights on such highly defended objectives as the German battleship *Tirpitz*, then completing in Wilhelmshaven. When his tour of operational duty was concluded, he asked for a further operational posting and went to a night-fighter unit instead of being posted for instructional duties. In the course of his second operational tour, he destroyed at least three enemy bombers and contributed much to the raising and development of new night-fighter formations. After a short period in a training unit, he again volunteered for operational duties and returned to night bombers. Both as an operational pilot and as leader of his squadron, he achieved outstandingly successful results and his personal courage knew no bounds. Berlin, Cologne, Danzig, Gdynia, Genoa, Le Creusot, Milan, Nuremberg and Stuttgart were among the targets he attacked by day and by night. On the conclusion of his third operational tour, Wing Commander Gibson pressed strongly to be allowed to remain on operations and he was selected to command a squadron then forming for special tasks. Under his inspiring leadership, this squadron executed one of the most devastating attacks of the war, the breaching of the Moehne and Eder dams. The task was fraught with danger and difficulty. Gibson personally made the initial attack on the Möhne dam. Descending to within a few feet of the

water and taking the full brunt of the anti-aircraft defences, he delivered his attack with great accuracy. Afterwards he circled very low for 30 minutes, drawing the enemy fire on himself in order to leave as free a run as possible to the following aircraft which were attacking the dam in turn. He then led the remainder of his force to the Eder dam where, with complete disregard for his own safety, he repeated his tactics and once more drew on himself enemy fire so that the attack could be successfully developed. Wing Commander Gibson has completed over 170 sorties, involving more than 600 hours' operational flying. Throughout his operational career, prolonged exceptionally at his own request, he has shown leadership, determination and valour of the highest order.

'Bomber' Harris gave Gibson permission to fly 'one last sortie' on 19 September 1944. The raid completed, Gibson spoke to his crews by wireless: 'Nice work, chaps, now beat it home.' They were his final words. Gibson's Mosquito was brought down in flames. He was twenty-six and held the VC, DSO and bar and DFC and bar.

AARON, Arthur Louis *A/Flight Sergeant, 218 Squadron, Royal Air Force Volunteer Reserve*

12/13 August 1943 – He was captain and pilot of a Stirling aircraft detailed to attack Turin. When approaching to attack, the bomber received devastating bursts of fire from an enemy fighter. Three engines were hit, the windscreen shattered, the front and rear turrets put out of action and the elevator control damaged, causing the aircraft to become unstable and difficult to control. The navigator was killed and other members of the crew were wounded. A bullet struck Aaron in the face, breaking his jaw and tearing away part of his face. He was also wounded in the lung and his right arm was rendered useless. As he fell forward over the control column, the aircraft dived several thousand feet. Control was regained by the flight engineer at 3,000 feet. Unable to speak, Aaron urged the bomb aimer by signs to take over the controls. Course was then set southwards in an endeavour to fly the crippled bomber, with one engine out of action, to Sicily or North Africa. Aaron was assisted to the rear of the aircraft and treated with morphia. After resting for some time he rallied and, mindful of his responsibility as captain of the aircraft, insisted on returning to the pilot's cockpit, where he was lifted into his seat and had his feet placed on the rudder bar. Twice he made determined attempts to take control and hold the aircraft to its course but his weakness was evident and with difficulty he was persuaded to desist. Though in great pain and suffering from exhaustion, he continued to help by writing directions with his left hand. Five hours after leaving the target the petrol began to run low, but soon afterwards the flare path at Bone airfield was sighted. Aaron summoned his failing strength to direct the bomb aimer in the hazardous task of landing the damaged aircraft in the darkness with undercarriage retracted. Four attempts were made under his direction; at the fifth Aaron was so near to collapsing that he had to be restrained by the crew and the landing was completed by the bomb aimer. Nine hours after landing, he died from exhaustion.

REID, William *A/Flight Lieutenant, 61 Squadron, Royal Air Force Volunteer Reserve*

Although Bill Reid joined the RAF Volunteer Reserve in 1940, he didn't fly his first operational flight until August 1943 as, after initial training in America, his skills were put to use as an instructor. Flying with 61 Squadron, Reid flew nine sorties before the mission which earned him his VC.

As Reid's Lancaster crossed the Dutch coast heading for Düsseldorf, an Me110 attacked from dead astern, shattering the windscreen and cockpit and damaging both gun turrets. Reid was hit in the head and shoulder and his face was cut by shards of Perspex, but he managed to right the aircraft and flew on.

In a second attack, a Focke-Wulf 190 raked the length of the plane, killing the navigator and mortally wounding the wireless operator – and Reid too was again wounded. 'We were really hit this time and we started to spin down. Everything went dead in my ears; there was no intercom – nothing. My hands were a bit bloody – skinned, really, when the windscreen had shattered. '

Aided by the flight engineer, Norris, Reid brought the plane back under control – but with the oxygen system ruptured and the hydraulics damaged any normal pilot would have turned for home. Reid decided, however, to press on to the target, but without a navigator he had to rely on his memory of the route to reach the target. He made the target, dropped the bombs and headed for home, navigating by the stars.

Back at the Dutch coast, they again came under heavy anti-aircraft fire and suddenly all four engines cut out. The Lancaster went into a spin. By now, Reid was lapsing into unconsciousness due to loss of blood and lack of oxygen. Only his pilot's instinct reminded him to change over petrol cocks to full engine. The engines surged back to life and they headed back to England. Over the USAAF airbase at Shipham in Norfolk, Reid had to wind down the landing gear by hand – and it collapsed on contact with the ground causing the Lancaster to slither on its belly 60 feet along the runway before coming to a halt.

In hospital he was visited by Air Vice Marshal Cochrane, who asked him why he didn't turn back. Reid said that he thought it safer to go on rather than turning back among all the other planes all flying in the same direction. Cochrane told Reid that the early returns from operations had since his raid been practically nil. He then added: 'It's as if they all said, "That bugger, Jock, he went on even though he was badly wounded, so we can't turn back just because of a faulty altimeter, or something like that."'

After recovering from his wounds, Reid joined 617 Squadron with Leonard Cheshire – and on his first flight he fouled up his landing, knocking the tail off the plane. Despite Cheshire's sympathetic attitude, he had no choice but to put an endorsement in Reid's logbook. Reid recalled later being surely 'the only pilot to get a Victoria Cross on one trip and a red endorsement on the next.'

Asked how he came to terms with the stress of the endless bombing missions, he explained, 'Before a raid, I made a point of never writing letters, because you would naturally find yourself thinking, "Will this be my last ever letter?" When you lost people who were your closest friends, the danger certainly came home to you. If you'd thought it would happen to you, too, you'd simply never have been able to fly again.'

In July 1944, on a raid on a weapons store near Rheims, Reid's aircraft was hit by a bomb falling from a Lancaster 6,000 feet above him. This severed all control cables and Reid had no choice but to bale out. He landed safely, but saw out the rest of the war as a prisoner of war – at first in Stalag Luft III and then, as the Allies advanced, in a camp nearer to Berlin.

After the war Reid left the RAF to go to Glasgow University, then the West of Scotland Agricultural College, following which he worked for twenty years as national cattle and sheep adviser for Spillers Farm Feeds. A founder member of the Air Crew Association, this modest and courageous man stayed in touch throughout his life with the veterans who shared his sense of comradeship from his days in the RAF. It is a mark of Reid's modesty, too, that when he married in 1952, he never mentioned his Victoria Cross to his wife. When she found out she owned to being 'a wee bit impressed'.

COASTAL COMMAND

TRIGG, Lloyd Allan *Flying Officer, Royal New Zealand Air Force, attached 200 Squadron, Royal Air Force*

11 August 1943 – He had rendered outstanding service on convoy escort and anti-submarine duties, completing 46 operational sorties and had invariably displayed skill and courage of a very high order. One day in August 1943, he undertook, as captain and pilot, a patrol in a Liberator although he had not previously made any operational sorties in that type of aircraft. After searching for eight hours, a surfaced U-boat was sighted. He immediately prepared to attack. During the approach, the aircraft received many hits from the submarine's anti-aircraft guns and burst into flames, which quickly enveloped the tail. The moment was critical. He could have broken off the engagement and made a forced landing in the sea. But if he continued the attack, the aircraft would present a 'no deflection' target to deadly accurate anti-aircraft fire, and every second spent in the air would increase the extent and intensity of the flames and diminish his chances of survival. There could have been no hesitation or doubt in his mind. He maintained his course in spite of the already precarious condition of his aircraft and executed a masterly attack. Skimming over the U-boat at less than 50 feet with anti-aircraft fire entering his opened bomb doors, Trigg dropped his bombs on and around the U-boat where they exploded with devastating effect. A short distance further on the Liberator dived into the sea with her gallant captain and crew. The U-boat sank within twenty minutes and some of her crew were picked up later in a rubber dinghy that had broken loose from the Liberator.

Trigg and his crew were killed but there were no Allied witnesses to his exploit. However, a number of survivors of the U-boat told of Trigg's courage. On the evidence of their witness statements, Trigg was posthumously awarded a VC.

THE *TIRPITZ*

The *Tirpitz* had been stationed off Norway since 1942, and although she had rarely ventured out, a 43,000-ton 15in battleship was a dangerous threat that needed powerful capital ships to contain it – ships needed for the immense naval battles developing in the Pacific. She had survived air attacks, but in September six midget submarines were towed across the North Sea by submarines to place charges under her. One sank and one was scuttled in the North Sea: four reached the fjord: two successfully placed their charges. The *Tirpitz* was out of action for six months.

CAMERON, Donald *Lieutenant, Royal Naval Reserve*
    22 September 1943 – Lieutenants PLACE and Cameron were the commanding officers of two of HM Midget Submarines, *X.6* and *X.7*, which carried out a most daring and successful attack on the German battleship *Tirpitz*, moored in the protected anchorage of Kaafiord, north Norway. To reach the anchorage necessitated the penetration of an enemy minefield and a passage of 50 miles up the fjord, known to be vigilantly patrolled by the enemy and to be guarded by nets, gun defences and listening posts; this after a passage of at least 1,000 miles from base. Having successfully eluded all these hazards and entered the fleet anchorage, Lieutenants Place and Cameron, with a complete disregard for danger, worked their small craft past the close anti-submarine and torpedo nets surrounding the *Tirpitz*, and from a position inside these nets carried out a cool and determined attack. Whilst they were still inside the nets a fierce enemy counter-attack by guns and depth charges developed which made their withdrawal impossible. Lieutenants Place and Cameron therefore scuttled their craft to prevent them falling into the hands of the enemy. Before doing so they took every measure to ensure the safety of their crews, the

majority of whom, together with themselves, were subsequently taken prisoner.

PLACE, Basil Charles Godfrey *Lieutenant, Royal Navy*

22 September 1943 – Lieutenants Place and CAMERON were the commanding officers of two of HM Midget Submarines, *X.6* and *X.7*, which carried out a most daring and successful attack on the German battleship *Tirpitz*, moored in the protected anchorage of Kaafiord, north Norway. To reach the anchorage necessitated the penetration of an enemy minefield and a passage of 50 miles up the fjord, known to be vigilantly patrolled by the enemy and to be guarded by nets, gun defences and listening posts; this after a passage of at least 1,000 miles from base. Having successfully eluded all these hazards and entered the fleet anchorage, Lieutenants Place and Cameron, with a complete disregard for danger, worked their small craft past the close anti-submarine and torpedo nets surrounding the *Tirpitz*, and from a position inside these nets carried out a cool and determined attack. Whilst they were still inside the nets a fierce enemy counter-attack by guns and depth charges developed which made their withdrawal impossible. Lieutenants Place and Cameron therefore scuttled their craft to prevent them falling into the hands of the enemy. Before doing so they took every measure to ensure the safety of their crews, the majority of whom, together with themselves, were subsequently taken prisoner.

He became Chairman of the Victoria Cross and George Cross Association.

ITALY

Sicily was invaded on 10 July 1943. The strategic objectives were to regain control of the Mediterranean for shipping, to draw forces from the Eastern front and to begin to force Italy out of the war. In all these points it was successful, although the Germans managed to withdraw forty thousand men across the Straits of Messina. Mussolini was deposed on 25 July, and the new government proposed surrender terms; the Allies decided that it should coincide with a landing at Salerno on 9 September, six days after a landing by 8th Army at Reggio.

The German counter-attack at Salerno was nearly successful on 13 September, but was defeated by airdropping two regimental combat teams from the US 81st Airborne Division, and by lead elements from 8th Army. The German response was to hold the Allies with a succession of defence lines, starting with the Viktor line (from the River Volturno to the River Biferno), to be held until 15 October, then the Gustav line for the winter. Every effort was made to make Allied progress as difficult and costly as possible.

Naples fell on 1 October, and the Volturno was reached on the 5th, but met strong resistance, coupled with bad weather, and the river line was not secure until the 19th. On the Adriatic, the Canadians had crossed the Moro River on 8 December, but took a week to fight through Ortona. On 30 December Montgomery left Italy for Britain to prepare for the invasion of France. The Allied advance was then halfway between the Sangro and Pescara and facing the Gustav line.

WRIGHT, Peter Harold *Warrant Officer Class II (Company Sergeant Major), 3rd Bn., Coldstream Guards*
    25 September 1943 – 3rd Battalion Coldstream Guards attacked the Pagliarolli feature, a steep wooded hill near Salerno, Italy. Before it reached the crest the right-hand company was held up by heavy Spandau and mortar fire and all the officers had become casualties. Wright, seeing that his company was held up, went forward to see what could be done. Finding that there were no officers left he immediately took charge and crawled forward by himself to see what the opposition was. He returned with the information that three Spandau posts were holding them up. He collected a section and put it into a position where it could give covering fire. Single-handed he then attacked each post in turn with hand grenades and bayonet and silenced each one. He then led the company onto the crest but realizing that the enemy fire made this position untenable he led them a short way down the hill and up onto the objective from a different direction. Entirely regardless of enemy fire, which was very heavy, he then reorganized what was left of the company and placed them into position to consolidate the objective. Soon afterwards the enemy launched a counter-attack, which was successfully beaten off. Later, with complete disregard of heavy enemy shell fire on the area of company headquarters and the reverse slopes of the hill and of machine-gun fire from the commanding slopes on the left flank of the position, he brought up extra ammunition and distributed it to the company. The objective was held.
    He was originally awarded a DCM. On the recommendation of King George VI and the Military Secretary, medal history was made on 7 September when the London Gazette *published the cancellation of the DCM and the award of a VC.*

TRIQUET, Paul *Captain, Royal 22e Régiment, Canadian Army*
    14 December 1943 – The capture of the key road junction on the main Ortona–Orsogna lateral was entirely dependent on securing the hamlet of Casa Berardi. Both this and a gully in front of it had been turned by the Germans into formidable strongpoints defended by infantry and tanks. On 14 December 1943, Captain Triquet's company of the Royal 22e Régiment with the support of a squadron of a Canadian armoured regiment was given the task of crossing the gully and securing Casa Berardi. Difficulties were encountered from the outset. The gully was held in strength and on approaching it the force came under extremely heavy fire from machine-

guns and mortars. All the company officers and half the men were killed or wounded. Showing superb contempt for the enemy, Triquet went round reorganizing the remainder and encouraging them with the words, 'Never mind them, they can't shoot.' Finally, when enemy infiltration was observed on all sides, he dashed forward shouting, 'There are enemy in front of us, behind us and on our flanks, there is only one safe place that is on the objective,' and with his men following him, broke through the enemy resistance. In this action four tanks were destroyed and several enemy machine-gun posts silenced. Against the most bitter and determined defence and under heavy fire Captain Triquet and his company, in close cooperation with the tanks, forced their way on until a position was reached on the outskirts of Casa Berardi. By this time the strength of the company was reduced to 2 sergeants and 15 men. In expectation of a counter-attack Triquet at once set about organizing his handful of men into a defensive perimeter around the remaining tanks and passed the 'mot d'ordre. Nous ne passeront pas.' A fierce German counter-attack supported by tanks developed almost immediately. Triquet, ignoring the heavy fire, was everywhere encouraging his men and directing the defence, and by using whatever weapons were to hand personally accounted for several of the enemy. This and subsequent attacks were beaten off with heavy losses and Triquet and his small force held out against overwhelming odds until the remainder of the battalion took Casa Berardi and relieved them the next day.

1944

At the start of 1944 the Axis powers were on the defensive and fighting to survive as Allied efforts were stepped up in all theatres.

Four years after the evacuation of Dunkirk, Britain was ready to return to France. With American and Canadian support, the decisive strike of D-Day on 6 June marked the beginning of the end for Hitler's forces in Europe. A secondary Allied landing in southern France put the Germans in an untenable position. Despite this, resistance was fierce as the Allies fought through France to the Netherlands where on 17 September airborne troops were landed in Operation Market Garden to take Arnhem. Although overwhelmed at Arnhem bridge, Allied forces pressed on and finally crossed into Germany on 24 September. The German army chose the snowy forests of the Ardennes for their major counter-attack – the Battle of the Bulge – in December, but the Allied momentum could not be halted.

On the German home front, morale was battered by increasing bombing raids and the news from the Eastern Front that troops were no longer able to withstand the relentless Soviet counter-attacks and the effects of failed supply lines. The German soldiers, starving and without adequate equipment and clothing against the cold, could advance no further and were stretched to the limit just to hold their ground.

In Italy, the Allies landed at Anzio in January, but were denied a breakout until May. In the same month, after some of the fiercest fighting, the Germans evacuated Monte Cassino. On 5 June US troops entered Rome and on the 14th took Orvieto, but German combat skills continued to tie down Allied troops in the north.

These Allied gains in Europe were supported in the Far East by a turnaround in Burma as the Japanese were driven back from Kohima and Imphal in savage fighting, and by American successes in the Pacific islands. These gains furnished American troops with forward bases from which to strike at the heart of Japan; the first bombing raid on Tokyo was launched on 24 November.

THE BURMA CAMPAIGN: ARAKAN

Allied planners had decided that Germany must be defeated before Japan. Strategy for the Burma theatre in the campaigning season in winter 1943/ 44, therefore, was limited to what Lieutenant General William Slim, appointed to command 14th Army on 25 August 1943, called a 'four-pronged invasion'. In the north, a Nationalist Chinese army led by the American Lieutenant General Stillwell would take Myitkyina and establish a land supply route to replace the dangerous air route over the Himalayas. In the centre there would be a limited advance on the Chindwin River, the great natural barrier behind which the Allies had retreated in 1942. These two operations would be supported by an operation by Major General Orde Wingate's Chindits, the long-range penetration force that had crossed the Chindwin into Japanese-held territory in spring 1943, now greatly enlarged. In the south, there would be a second attempt to take the Maungdaw–Buthidaung road in the Arakan. The Japanese were not considering a major offensive in Burma, but planned two operations: to capture Imphal and Kohima and secure Assam, thus taking the initiative from the British and stopping the air supply over the Himalayas; and a diversion in Arakan that if successful could be developed into an invasion of India. They were to start on 15 March and 4 February respectively.

The 16-mile road from Maungdaw to Buthidaung ran west–east across the peninsula, and was the only lateral road good enough for wheeled traffic, on which the Allies (unlike the Japanese) relied, before the road from Taungap on the coast to Prome on the Irrawaddy, more than 200 miles south-east. It was heavily defended along its length and had three strongholds, at Razabil in the west and Letwedet in the east, and in the tunnels under the Mayu range. To attack Letwedet a new road over the mountains had to be made, and a footpath running through the Ngakyedauk Pass was chosen. It was ready for use by the end of January 1944, but since it ran parallel to the front it was always vulnerable to Japanese attack. Maungdaw was taken on 9 January, and Razabil by the end of the month, after a combined attack with bombers, artillery and Lee-Grant tanks brought to the theatre in great secrecy. While the assault on Buthidaung was in preparation, the Japanese Arakan offensive began, taking the British by surprise. By 1944, however, Allied tactics in Burma had evolved, and instead of retreating from defence positions, troops could hold firm, resupplied by air, while reserve forces held ready cut off the enemy advance. The siege of 7th Division's position in the Ngakyedauk Pass lasted twenty-one days, until 24 February, but the Japanese force was encircled and defeated. The battle for the Maungdaw–Buthidaung road was not over until May, after very tough fighting against some of the best Japanese formations, but Slim wrote in his autobiography that it had destroyed the 'legend of Japanese invincibility in the jungle'.

HORWOOD, Alec George *Lieutenant, 1/6th Bn., Queen's Royal Regiment, attached 1st Bn., Northamptonshire Regiment*

18 January 1944 – At Kyauchaw, Lieutenant Horwood accompanied the forward company of the Northamptonshire Regiment into action against a Japanese-defended locality with his forward mortar observation post. Throughout that day he lay in an exposed position, which had been completely cleared of cover by concentrated air bombing, and effectively shot his own mortars and those of a half troop of another unit while the company was manoeuvring to locate the exact position of the enemy bunkers and machine-gun nests. During the whole of this time he was under intense sniper, machine-gun and mortar fire, and at night he came back with most valuable information about the enemy. On 19 January he moved forward with another company and established an observation post on a precipitous ridge. From here, while under continual fire from the enemy, he directed accurate mortar fire in support of two attacks which were put in during the day. He also carried out a personal reconnaissance along and about the bare ridge, deliberately drawing the enemy fire so that the fresh company which he had led to the position and which was to carry out an attack might see the enemy positions. He remained on the ridge during the night 19/20 January and on the morning of 20 January shot the mortars again to support a fresh attack by another company put in from the rear of the enemy. He was convinced that the enemy would crack and volunteered to lead the attack planned for that afternoon. He led this attack with such calm, resolute bravery that the enemy were reached, and while standing up in the wire, directing and leading the men with complete disregard to the enemy fire which was then at point-blank range, he was mortally wounded. The position was captured on 24 January.

HOEY, Charles Ferguson *T/Major, 1st Bn., Lincolnshire Regiment*

16 February 1944 – In Burma, Major Hoey's company formed part of a force which was ordered to capture at all costs a position in the Ngakyedauk Pass. After a night march through enemy-held territory the force was met at the foot of the position by heavy machine-gun and rifle fire. Hoey personally led his company on, and although wounded at least twice in the leg and head he seized a Bren gun from one of his men and firing from the hip reached the objective. The company had difficulty in keeping up with him, and he reached the enemy post first, where he killed all the occupants before being mortally wounded.

NAND SINGH *A/Naik, 1/11th Sikh Regiment*

11/12 March 1944 – A Japanese platoon about 40 strong with medium and light machine-guns and a grenade discharger infiltrated into the battalion position covering the main Maungdaw to Buthidaung road and occupied a dominating position, where they dug foxholes and underground trenches on the precipitous sides of a hill. Naik Nand Singh commanded the leading section of the platoon which was ordered to recapture the position at all costs. He led his section up a very steep knife-edged ridge under heavy machine-gun and rifle fire. Although wounded in the thigh he rushed ahead of his section and took the first enemy trench with the bayonet by himself. He then crawled forward alone under heavy fire and though wounded again in the face and shoulder by a grenade which burst one yard in front of him, took the second trench at the point of the bayonet. A short time later, when all his section had been either killed or wounded, Nand Singh dragged himself out of the trench and captured a third trench, killing all the occupants with his bayonet. Due to the capture of these three trenches the remainder of the platoon were able to seize the top of the hill and deal with the enemy. Nand Singh personally killed seven of the enemy, and owing to his determination, outstanding dash and magnificent courage, the important position was won back from the enemy.

Nand Singh's fighting spirit was recognized by the Indian government for an action between India and Pakistan in 1947. He was given posthumously the highest award for gallantry – the Maha Vir Chakra. He remains the only holder of both the VC and the MVC and, killed in action, he is the only VC of the Second World War to be killed in a subsequent conflict.

THE BURMA CAMPAIGN: THE SECOND CHINDIT EXPEDITION

Major General Orde Wingate's second Chindit expedition, nine thousand men, thirteen hundred mules and 250 tons of stores landed over seven nights by six hundred and fifty aircraft and glider sorties, was the biggest operation behind enemy lines of the war. Its main task was to assist the operation to take Myitkyina by cutting the Japanese line of communication; its secondary tasks were to enable the Chinese army to cross the Salween and to cause as much damage as possible to Japanese operations in north Burma.

The Chindit force was divided into two waves. In the first, 16th Brigade was to march from the Ledo road and secure the airfields at Indaw, and 77th, 111th, Morrisforce and Dahforce would land by glider and Dakota. 77th would block the railway from Mandalay, on the Irrawaddy, to Myit-kyina 250 miles south-south-west, along which passed the supplies for the Japanese opposing Stilwell; 111th would protect the southern approaches of 16th Brigade with road blocks and demolition; Morrisforce would raid the road from Myitkyina to Bhoma, 80 miles downriver; and Dahforce would protect Morrisforce by raising guerrilla bands. 14th, 23rd and 3rd West African brigades were in reserve as the second wave.

77th Indian Infantry Brigade, led by Brigadier Michael Calvert, established its block quickly, though in stiff fighting in which Calvert repeatedly led charges with grenades and Lieutenant George Cairns won a VC, and dug in. 16th Brigade's attack on Indaw failed, and it was pulled back to a block called Aberdeen. On 24 March, Wingate was killed in an air crash. In May General Stillwell assumed command, and the Chindits became engaged in his battle for Mogaung and Myitkyina. 77th Brigade took Mogaung on 26 June, winning two more VCs.

CAIRNS, George Albert *Lieutenant, Somerset Light Infantry, attached 1st Bn., South Staffordshire Regiment*

13 March 1944 – On 5 March 1944, 77th Indian Infantry Brigade, of which the South Staffordshire Regiment formed a part, landed by glider at Broadway, in Burma. On 12 March, columns from the South Staffordshire Regiment and 3rd Bn., 6th Gurkha Rifles established a road and rail block across the Japanese lines of communications at Henu Block. The Japanese counter-attacked this position heavily in the early morning of 13 March, and the South Staffordshire Regiment was ordered to attack a hill which formed the basis of the Japanese attack. During this action, in which Lieutenant Cairns took a leading part, he was attacked by a Japanese officer, who with his sword hacked off Cairns's left arm. Cairns killed this officer, picked up his sword and continued to lead his men in the attack. Slashing left and right with the captured sword he killed and wounded several Japanese before he himself fell to the ground. Lieutenant Cairns subsequently died from his wounds. His actions so inspired his comrades that later the Japanese were completely routed, a very rare occurrence at the time.

Wingate was carrying the recommendation from three officers who had witnessed Cairns' remarkable act when his plane crashed and all paper work was destroyed. Cairns' regiment brought the recommendation to the War Office only to be told that two of the witnesses had been killed in Burma. In 1948 Cairns' widow took the matter to her MP who, supported by Brigadier Calvert, persuaded those in authority to award the Victoria Cross in May 1949. It was the last to be gazetted for the Second World War.

ALLMAND, Michael *A/Captain, Indian Armoured Corps, attached 3rd Bn., 6th Gurkha Rifles*

11–23 June 1944 – Captain Allmand was commanding the leading platoon of a company of the 6th Gurkha Rifles in Burma when the battalion was ordered to attack the Pin Hmi road bridge. The enemy had already succeeded in holding up the advance at this point for twenty-four hours. The approach to the bridge was very narrow as the road was banked up and the low-lying land on either side was swampy and densely covered in jungle. The Japanese, who were dug in along the banks of the road and in the jungle with machine-guns and small arms, were putting up the most desperate resistance. As the platoon came within 20 yards of the bridge, the enemy opened heavy and accurate fire, inflicting severe casualties and forcing the men to seek cover. Captain Allmand, however, with the utmost gallantry, charged on by himself, hurling grenades into the enemy gun positions and killing three Japanese himself with his kukri. Inspired by the splendid example of their platoon commander, the surviving men followed him and captured their objective. Two days later, Allmand, owing to casualties among the officers, took over command of the company and, dashing 30 yards ahead of it through long grass and marshy ground swept by machine-gun fire, personally killed a number of enemy machine-gunners then successfully led his men onto the ridge of high ground that they had been ordered to seize. Once again, on 23 June in the final attack on the railway bridge at Mogaung, Allmand, although suffering from trench foot which made it difficult for him to walk, moved forward alone through deep mud and shell holes and charged a Japanese machine-gun nest single-handed, but he was mortally wounded and died shortly afterwards.

TULBAHADUR PUN *Rifleman, 3rd Bn., 6th Gurkha Rifles*
    23 June 1944 – A battalion of the 6th Gurkha Rifles was ordered to attack the railway bridge at Mogaung, Burma. Immediately the attack developed, the enemy opened concentrated and sustained crossfire at close range from a position known as the Red House and from a strong bunker position 200 yards to the left of it. So intense was this crossfire that both the leading platoons of B Company, one of which was Rifleman Tulbahadur Pun's, were pinned to the ground and the whole of his section was wiped out with the exception of himself, the section commander and another man. The section commander immediately led the remaining two men in a charge on the Red House but was at once badly wounded. Tulbahadur Pun and his remaining companion continued the charge, but the latter too was immediately badly wounded. Tulbahadur Pun then seized the Bren gun, and firing from the hip as he went, continued the charge on this heavily bunkered position alone, in the face of the most shattering concentration of automatic fire, directed straight at him. With the dawn coming up behind him, he presented a perfect target to the Japanese. He had to move for 30 yards over open ground, ankle deep in mud, through shell holes and over fallen trees. Despite these overwhelming odds, he reached the Red House and closed with the Japanese occupants. He killed three and put five more to flight and captured two light machine-guns and much ammunition. He then gave accurate supporting fire from the bunker to the remainder of his platoon, which enabled them to reach their objective.
    At the time of publication, Tulbahadur Pun is one of the surviving VC holders.

BLAKER, Frank Gerald *T/Major, Highland Light Infantry attached 3rd Bn., 9th Gurkha Rifles*
    9 July 1944 – In Burma a company of the 9th Gurkha Rifles was ordered to carry out an encircling movement across unknown and precipitous country, through dense jungle, to attack a strong enemy position on the

summit of an important hill overlooking Taungni. Major Blaker carried out this movement with the utmost precision and took up a position with his company on the extreme right flank of the enemy, in itself a feat of considerable military skill. Another company, after bitter fighting, had succeeded in taking the forward edge of the enemy position by a frontal assault, but had failed to reach the main crest of the hill in the face of fierce opposition. At this crucial moment Blaker's company came under heavy and accurate fire at close range from a medium machine-gun and two light machine-guns, and their advance was completely stopped. Blaker then advanced ahead of his men through very heavy fire and, in spite of being severely wounded in the arm by a grenade, he located the machine-guns, which were the pivot of the enemy defence, and single-handed charged the position. When hit by a burst of three rounds through the body, he continued to cheer on his men while lying on the ground. His fearless leadership and outstanding courage so inspired his company that they captured the objective, whilst the enemy fled in terror into the jungle. Major Blaker died of wounds while being evacuated from the battlefield.

THE BURMA CAMPAIGN: KOHIMA AND IMPHAL

The epic siege of Kohima by the Japanese 31st Division from 4 to 19 April, and its defeat, was perhaps the most important engagement of the war in Burma. After a Japanese attack on the Silchar track failed at great cost to both sides in May, the Japanese commander, Mutaguchi, decided to force the Bishenpur position before the monsoon broke. On the 17th, the attack began with four light tanks on a position held by 1/7th Gurkhas, who had no anti-tank guns but did have PIATs, deployed to great effect by Rifleman Ganju Lama who destroyed two, winning the MM in a rehearsal of his VC action. Outnumbered, the British forces fought their way up the Tiddim road to Bishenpur.

On 25/26 May the monsoon broke, and in some cases 15 inches of rain fell in a single day and men lived in this mud. After the heavy rains the bushes were laden with blood-sucking leeches. But two Japanese regiments had been destroyed and the British positions at Bishenpur remained intact. On 27 May the Japanese commander of the 33rd Division issued an order of the day: 'The coming battle [for Imphal] is the turning point. It will denote the success or failure of the Greater East Asia War ... for that reason it must be expected that the division will be almost annihilated.' It concluded: 'On this battle rests the fate of the Empire. All officers and men fight courageously!'

All the Japanese attacks ended in failure, but with savage fighting and no quarter given, at great cost to both sides. An officer in the 7th Bn., 10th Baluch Regiment described the fighting on the Silchar track:

It was rather like the Western Front, dug in wired positions, with the Japs only about 50–60 yards away. Everyone was mixed up. For about three weeks there was very intensive fighting. The scrub was thicker than in the Chin Hills, and very wet. It was a very hard infantry slog. The Japs attacked then we counter-attacked. Positions changed hands several times . . .

Water Piquet, Mortar Bluff, etc, were pimples or hills occupied by companies or even platoons, and mutually supporting. Subedar Netra-bahadur Thapa on Water Piquet called for fire through me. Spoke in Gurkhali, but switched to Urdu when realised he was not talking to Gurkha officer. He was overrun – got a VC [p. 470].

Next day 2/5 RGR got another VC, Agansing Rai, only time I've seen Gurkhas go in with the kukri. An awe-inspiring sight. They were counter-attacking the position and took it back. It was the most close fighting I ever saw in Burma [p. 471].

Japanese attacks tended to come up and close the last few yards with bayonets. In a counter-attack we gave enemy positions a really good pasting, then fought our way in, clearing enemy positions with grenades, Tommy Guns, Gurkhas with kukris, and our chaps used a bayonet.

Two divisions were meanwhile fighting their way south from Kohima, and on 22 June the forward units met. It was now clear that any reconquest of Burma must come from Assam, not an amphibious assault on Rangoon as Mountbatten, Supreme Allied Commander South East Asia, had long wanted, and on 7 July Slim ordered his two corps to advance from Imphal down the Tamu and Tiddim roads. That day Mutaguchi was ordered to withdraw; on the Tiddim road, the Japanese were retreating before the 5th Indian Division, and made them pay for every yard. Subadar Ram Sarup Singh won the VC for his action in clearing part of the road called the Chocolate Staircase, thirty-seven hairpin bends which the rain had turned to the consistency of 'melted chocolate fudge'.

Twenty thousand Japanese died in the retreat to the Chindwin of malaria, dysentery and starvation. Eighty-five thousand took part in the attack on Assam: more than forty thousand died in battle. Little more than a hundred prisoners were captured. On 2 December the first elements of the British 14th Army crossed the Chindwin.

ABDUL HAFIZ *Jemadar, 9th Jat Infantry*
6 April 1944 – In the hills 10 miles north of Imphal, the enemy had attacked a standing patrol of four men and occupied a prominent feature overlooking a company position. At first light a patrol was sent out and contacted the enemy, reporting that they thought approximately 40 enemy were in position. It was not known if they had dug in during the hours of darkness. The company commander ordered Jemadar Abdul Hafiz to attack the enemy, with two sections from his platoon, at 0930 hours. An artillery

concentration was put down on the feature and Abdul Hafiz led the attack. The attack was up a completely bare slope with no cover, very steep near the crest. Prior to the attack, Abdul Hafiz assembled his sections and told them that they were invincible, and all the enemy on the hill would be killed or put to flight. He so inspired his men that from the start the attack proceeded with great dash. When a few yards below the crest the enemy opened fire with machine-guns and threw grenades. Abdul Hafiz sustained several casualties, but immediately ordered an assault, which he personally led. The assault went in without hesitation and with great dash up the last few yards of the hill. On reaching the crest Abdul Hafiz was wounded in the leg, but seeing a machine-gun firing from a flank, which had already caused several casualties, he immediately went towards it and, seizing the barrel, pushed it upwards whilst another man killed the gunner. Abdul Hafiz then took a Bren gun from a wounded man and advanced against the enemy, firing as he advanced and killing several of the enemy. So fierce was the attack, and so inspired were all his men by the determination of Abdul Hafiz to kill all enemy in sight at whatever cost, that the enemy, who were still in considerable numbers on the position, ran away down the opposite slope of the hill. Regardless of machine-gun fire from another feature a few hundred yards away, he pursued the enemy, firing at them as they retired. He was badly wounded in the chest from this machine-gun fire and collapsed holding the Bren gun and attempting to fire at the retreating enemy, and shouting at the same time, 'Reorganize on the position and I will give covering fire.' He died of his wounds shortly afterwards.

HARMAN, John Pennington *Lance Corporal, 4th Bn., Queen's Own Royal West Kent Regiment*

8–9 April 1944 – He was commanding a section of a forward platoon at Kohima, India, when under cover of darkness the enemy established a machine-gun post within 50 yards of his position which became a serious menace to the remainder of his company. Owing to the nature of the ground he was unable to bring the fire of his section on to the enemy machine-gun post. Without hesitation he went forward by himself and, using a four-second grenade which he held on to for at least two seconds after releasing the lever in order to get immediate effect, bombed the post and followed up immediately. He annihilated the post and returned to his section with the machine-gun. Early the following morning he recovered a position on a forward slope 150 yards from the enemy in order to strengthen a platoon which had been heavily attacked during the night. On occupying his position he discovered a party of enemy digging in under cover of machine-gun fire and snipers. Ordering his Bren gun to give him covering fire he fixed his bayonet and alone charged the post shooting four and bayoneting one, thereby wiping out the post. When walking back he received a burst of machine-gun fire in his side and died shortly after reaching the British lines.

He came from a wealthy family, who owned Lundy Isle. He refused to be commissioned, and was much influenced by an old Spanish sage, who introduced him to spiritualism. He was told that he would live to be seventy years old, which may have influenced his total disregard for enemy fire.

RANDLE, John Niel *T/Captain, 2nd Bn., Royal Norfolk Regiment*

4–6 May 1944 – On 4 May, a battalion of the Norfolk Regiment attacked the Japanese positions on a nearby ridge at Kohima, India. Captain Randle took over command of the company leading the attack when the company commander was severely wounded. His handling of a difficult situation in the face of heavy fire was masterly and although wounded himself in the knee by grenade splinters he continued to inspire his men by his initiative, courage and outstanding leadership, until the company had captured its objective and consolidated its position. He then went forward and brought in all the wounded men who were lying outside the perimeter. In spite of his painful wound he refused to be evacuated and insisted on carrying out a personal reconnaissance with great daring in bright moonlight prior to a further attack by his company on the positions to which the enemy had withdrawn. At dawn on 6 May the attack opened led by Captain Randle, and one of the platoons succeeded in reaching the crest of the hill held by the Japanese. Another platoon, however, ran into heavy machine-gun fire from a bunker on the reverse slope of the feature. Randle immediately appreciated that this particular bunker covered not only the rear of his new position but also the line of communication of the battalion and therefore the destruction of the enemy post was imperative if the operation was to succeed. With utter disregard of the obvious danger to himself, Randle charged the Japanese machine-gun post single-handed with rifle and bayonet. Although bleeding in the face and mortally wounded by numerous bursts of machine-gun fire he reached the bunker and silenced the gun with a grenade thrown through the bunker slit. He then flung his body across the slit so that the aperture should be completely sealed. By his self-sacrifice he saved the lives of many men. The battalion gained its objective.

He was the brother of Flying Officer Manser VC, who was shot down over Belgium on 31 May 1943. Mrs Randle therefore lost her husband and her brother, both VC holders.

TURNER, Hanson Victor *A/Sergeant, 1st Bn., West Yorkshire Regiment*

6/7 June 1944 – At Ningthoukong, south of Imphal, an attack was made by a strong force of Japanese with medium and light machine-guns soon after midnight on the night of 6/7 June. In the first instance the attack largely fell on the south-west corner of a position which was held by a weak platoon of about 20 men of which Sergeant Turner was one of the section commanders. By creeping up under cover of a nullah the enemy were able to use grenades with deadly effect against this portion of the perimeter. Three out of the four light machine-guns in the platoon were destroyed and the platoon was forced to give ground. Turner with coolness and fine leadership at once reorganized his party and withdrew 40 yards. The enemy made determined and repeated attempts to dislodge them and concentrated all the fire they could produce in an effort to reduce the position and so extend the penetration. Sustained fire was kept up on Turner and his dwindling party by the enemy for a period of two hours. The enemy, however, achieved no further success in this sector. Sergeant Turner with a doggedness and spirit of endurance of the highest order repelled all their attacks, and it was due entirely to his leadership that the position was ultimately held throughout the night. When it was clear that the enemy were attempting to outflank the position, Turner determined to take the initiative in driving the enemy off and killing them. The men left under his command were the minimum essential to maintain the position he had built up with such effect. No party for a counter-attack could therefore be mustered and speed was essential if the enemy were to be frustrated. He at once went forward from his position alone, armed with all the hand grenades he could carry, and went into the attack against the enemy single-handed. He used his weapons with devastating effect and when his supply was exhausted went back for more and returned to the offensive again. During all this time the enemy were keeping up intense small-arms and grenade fire. Sergeant Turner in all made five journeys to obtain further supplies of grenades and it was on the sixth occasion, still single-handed while throwing a grenade among a party of the enemy, that he was killed. The number of dead found the next morning was ample evidence of the deadly effect his grenade-throwing had.

GANJU LAMA *Rifleman, 1st Bn., 7th Gurkha Rifles*
    12 June 1944 – In India, the enemy put down an intense artillery barrage lasting an hour on British positions north of the village of Ningthoukhong. This heavy artillery fire knocked out several bunkers and caused heavy casualties and was immediately followed by a very strong enemy attack supported by five medium tanks. After fierce hand-to-hand fighting, the perimeter was driven in in one place and enemy infantry, supported by three medium tanks, broke through, pinning British troops to the ground with intense fire. B Company, 1st Bn. 7th Gurkha Rifles was ordered to counter-attack and restore the situation. Shortly after passing the starting line it came under heavy enemy machine-gun fire at point-blank range, which covered all lines of approach. Rifleman Ganju Lama, the No. 1 of the PIAT, on his own initiative, with great coolness and complete disregard for his own safety, crawled forward and engaged the tanks single-handed. In spite of a broken left wrist and two other wounds, one in his right hand and one in his leg, caused by withering crossfire concentrated upon him, Ganju Lama succeeded in bringing his gun into action within 30 yards of the enemy tanks and knocked out first one and then another, the third tank being

destroyed by an anti-tank gun. In spite of his serious wounds, he then moved forward and engaged with grenades the tank crews, who now attempted to escape. Not until he had killed or wounded them all, thus enabling his company to push forward, did he allow himself to be taken back to the regimental aid post to have his wounds dressed.

Ganju Lama was batman to Major Roy Gribble, MC and bar, who died on 12 February 2004. His obituary noted that on his first day as batman, a few months before his VC action, 'Ganju came into Gribble's dug-out at four o'clock in the morning carrying a mess-tin of tea. He did not bother to say "Good morning" or "Sir"; he just said, "Get up!" Gribble was surprised, but took to him instantly.'

NETRABAHADUR THAPA *A/Subadar, 2nd Bn., 5th Royal Gurkha Rifles*

25–26 June 1944 – Subadar Netrabahadur Thapa was in command of the garrison of 41 men of the 2nd Bn., 5th Royal Gurkha Rifles, which on the afternoon of 25 June took over the isolated picket known as Mortar Bluff situated on the hillside commanding the base at Bishenpur in India. The picket position, completely devoid of any cover, was situated some 400 yards from the next picket, from which it could be supported to some extent by 3in mortar fire, but was commanded by Water Piquet, a short distance away on high ground to the south, which had been overrun by strong enemy forces on the previous night and was still in enemy hands. Owing to its commanding position the retention of Mortar Bluff was vital to the safety of other positions farther down the ridge and to Bishenpur itself. The relief had been harassed by enemy snipers at close range but was completed at 1830 hours without casualties. A little more than an hour later the enemy began to attack. For this purpose a 75mm and a 37mm gun were brought up onto the high ground overlooking the position and poured shell after shell at point-blank range for ten minutes into the narrow confines of the picket, and this was followed by a determined attack by no less than a company of Japanese troops. A fierce fight ensued in which Subadar Netrabahadur Thapa's men, exhorted by their leader, held their ground against heavy odds and drove the enemy back with disproportionate losses. During this time Netrabahadur Thapa with tireless energy and contempt for his own safety moved from post to post encouraging his young NCOs and riflemen, of which the garrison was largely composed, and tending the wounded. A short lull followed during which Netrabahadur Thapa gave a clear and concise report on the telephone to his commanding officer and asked for more artillery defensive fire. Having done this he made preparations to meet the next onslaught which was not long in coming. Under cover of the pitch-dark night and torrential rain the enemy had moved round to the jungle, from the cover of which they launched their next attack. Still in considerable strength and as determined and ferocious as ever the enemy poured out from the jungle across the short space of open ground to the picket defences

41. George St G. Grogan, disregarding all danger, rode up and down the line, under fire, inspiring his men to hold the line. Shown here in action at the River Aisne, France, 27 May 1918 (p. 327).

42. Frank Roberts, over a period from 22 March to 2 April 1918, commanded his battalion with courage and skill against an enemy offensive and led numerous counter-attacks at Pargny, France (p. 319).

43. *Left*. Augustus Agar took his coastal motor boat through the enemy defences and sank a cruiser before retiring under heavy bombardment at Kronstadt, Russia, 17 June 1919 (p. 374).

44. Leonard Cheshire, from 1940 to 1944, displayed outstanding courage and determination, flying more than 100 bombing missions with a total disregard for danger (p. 389).

45. James Nicolson, unique as the only VC awarded for the Battle of Britain and the only Fighter Command VC of the Second World War. Although severely wounded and about to bale out, he sighted an enemy aircraft which he attacked and shot down before baling out over Southampton, 16 August 1940 (p. 393).

46. Geoffrey Keyes volunteered for a mission behind enemy lines to raid Rommel's HQ, but was killed in the attack at Libya, 17/18 November 1941 (p. 399).

47. Malcolm Wanklyn sank an Italian troopship in the Mediterranean then survived an enemy counter-attack and thirty-seven depth charges over a period of some twenty minutes, Sicily, 24 May 1941 (p. 407).

48. Charles Upham, one of only three double VCs. In close-quarters fighting, even when badly wounded, he personally killed over twenty of the enemy in Crete, 1941 (p. 106). In a second action, despite severe injuries, he destroyed a German tank and heavy pieces of armour and vehicles using grenades in Egypt, 1942 (p. 426).

49. Philip Gardner, responsible for recovering damaged armoured vehicles and saving a severely wounded officer from the enemy, all the time under extreme fire at Tobruk, Libya, 23 November 1941 (p. 401).

50. Quentin Smythe commanded a platoon when the officer was severely wounded, and although himself wounded attacked an enemy machine-gun post and killed the crew at Alem Hamza, Libya, 5 June 1942 (p. 425).

52. Arthur Aaron, although severely injured, managed to keep his bomber in the air after being hit by enemy fire over Italy, 12/13 August 1943 (p. 452). He landed safely in Tunisia.

51. Augustus Newman landed at the front of the raiding troops and, under intense fire, directed operations for several hours at St-Nazaire, France, 27/28 March 1942 (p. 420).

53. Richard Kelliher was personally responsible for destroying an enemy machine-gun position and killing the crew on New Guinea, 13 September 1943 (p. 438).

54. William Reid, although suffering from multiple wounds, piloted his aircraft without instruments from the Dutch coast to land safely at a UK airfield after a raid on Düsseldorf, 3/4 November 1943 (p. 153).

55. Donald Cameron, the commander of a midget submarine, carried out a raid on the German battleship *Tirpitz* in the Kaafiord, northern Norway, 22 September 1943 (p. 455).

57. Willward Sandys-Clarke, although wounded, led men against an enemy machine-gun post, causing many casualties. Later he single-handedly attacked the post and two others, knocking out the guns in Tunisia, 23 April 1943 (p. 448).

56. John Kenneally, a deserter, re-enlisted in this name. He twice charged enemy troops, inflicting many casualties in Tunisia, 28 April 1943 (p. 448).

Anti-clockwise, from top left

58. David Currie, having captured and consolidated his objective, resisted several counter-attacks by the enemy and in doing so inflicted heavy casualties at the Battle of Falaise, France, 18–20 August 1944 (p. 492).

59. Norman Jackson, at 22,000 feet, crawled along the wing of his aircraft to extinguish an engine fire during a raid on Germany, 26 April 1944 (p. 485). Badly burned, he was swept from the aircraft and landed by parachute.

60. Gerard Norton single-handedly attacked an enemy machine-gun post, killing the crew, then attacked another, killing or taking prisoner the remaining enemy in Italy, 31 August 1944 (p. 480).

61. Frank Blaker, already wounded, single-handedly charged a Japanese machine-gun post. Wounded another three times, he cheered on his men as he lay on the ground before dying of his injuries at Taungni, Burma, 9 July 1944 (p. 464).

Clockwise, from top right

62. Tulbahadur Pun, after all his comrades were killed or wounded, charged alone at an enemy position, killing three of the enemy and routing another five. He captured two machine guns, together with ammunition, then gave valuable support to subsequent attacks at Mogaung, Burma, 23 June 1944 (p. 464).

63. Richard Burton single-handedly engaged an enemy position, killing three of the crew. He then attacked two more machine-gun posts, killing their crews. His accurate firing later helped to hold the position at Monte Ceco, Italy, 8 October 1944 (p. 481).

64. Stanley Hollis, recipient of the only VC awarded during the D-Day landings, rushed a German pillbox, killing two and taking the rest prisoner. He then rushed another pillbox, taking twenty-six prisoners, and later put a field gun out of action. He then rescued two men under heavy fire in Normandy, 6 June 1944 (p. 489).

65. Namdeo Jadhao carried two wounded men to safety under heavy fire through difficult terrain, including a minefield. He then wiped out three machine-gun posts at the Senio River, Italy, 9 April 1945 (p. 532).

66. *Left.* James Magennis (on the left with Lt Ian Fraser VC, DSC) was a diver on a midget submarine skilfully commanded by Fraser, and under extremely difficult conditions attached mines to the hull of a Japanese cruiser in the Singapore Straits, 31 July 1945 (p. 534).

67. *Below, left.* Kevin Wheatley, although having a chance to escape the enemy, refused to leave a wounded comrade and was killed trying to get him to safety at Tra Bong, Vietnam, 13 November 1965 (p. 546).

68. *Below, right.* Herbert 'H' Jones, recipient of the last but one VC awarded. Leading from the front, he was killed while charging up a slope towards the enemy under heavy fire at Darwin, Falkland Islands, 28 May 1982 (p. 550).

under cover of small arms and 37mm gunfire from a flank. For a time the Gurkhas held their ground until, as ill-luck would have it, both machine-guns of one section jammed. With much reduced firepower the section were unable to hold on, and the enemy forced an entrance and overran this and another section, killing or wounding 12 out of the 16 men comprising the two sections. Having no reserve Subadar Netrabahadur Thapa himself went forward from his headquarters and stemmed any further advance with grenades. The situation was however critical. With more than half his men casualties, ammunition low, and the enemy in possession of part of his perimeter, Netrabahadur Thapa would have been justified in withdrawing, but in his next report to his commanding officer he stated that he intended holding on and asked for reinforcements and more ammunition. So efficient were his plans for defence and such was the fine example of this gallant Gurkha officer that not a man moved from his trench and not a yard more ground was gained by the enemy, despite their desperate attempts. Thus the night passed until at 0400 hours a section of eight men with grenades and small-arms ammunition arrived. Their arrival inevitably drew fire and all the eight were soon casualties. Undismayed, Netrabahadur Thapa retrieved the ammunition, and himself with his platoon headquarters took the offensive armed with grenades and kukris. Whilst so doing he received a bullet wound in the mouth followed shortly afterwards by a grenade which killed him outright. His body was found next day, kukri in hand and a dead Japanese with a cleft skull by his side.

AGANSING RAI *Naik, 2nd Bn., 5th Royal Gurkha Rifles*

26 June 1944 – In India on 24 and 25 June 1944, after fierce fighting, the enemy, with greatly superior forces, had captured two posts known as Water Piquet and Mortar Bluff. These posts were well sited and mutually supporting and their possession by the enemy threatened communications. On the morning of 26 June, a company of the 5th Royal Gurkha Rifles was ordered to recapture these positions. After a preliminary artillery concentration, the company went into the attack, but on reaching a false crest about 80 yards from its objective it was pinned down by heavy and accurate fire from a machine-gun in Mortar Bluff and a 37mm gun in the jungle, suffering many casualties. Naik Agansing Rai, appreciating that more delay would inevitably result in heavier casualties, at once led his section under withering fire directly at the machine-gun and, firing as he went, charged the position, himself killing three of the crew of four. Inspired by this cool act of bravery the section surged forward across the bullet-swept ground and routed the whole garrison of Mortar Bluff. This position was now under intense fire from the 37mm gun in the jungle and from Water Piquet. Agansing Rai at once advanced towards the gun, his section without hesitation following their gallant leader. Intense fire reduced the section to 3 men before half the distance had been covered but they pressed on to their objective. Arriving at close range, Agansing Rai killed three of the crew and his men killed the other two. The party then returned to Mortar Bluff, where the rest of their platoon were forming up for the final assault on Water Piquet. In the subsequent advance heavy machine-gun fire and showers of grenades from an isolated bunker position caused further casualties. Once more, with indomitable courage, Agansing Rai, covered by his Bren-gunner, advanced alone with a grenade in one hand and his tommy gun in the other. Through devastating fire he reached the enemy position and killed all four occupants of the bunker. The enemy, demoralized by this NCO's calm display of courage and complete contempt for danger, now fled before the onslaught on Water Piquet, and this position too was captured.

Rai also received the Military Medal, for his courage during fighting in Burma's Chill Hills. After the war, Rai stayed with his regiment as an instructor and served in the Congo with the United Nations peacekeeping force. Made an honorary captain on leaving the Gurkhas, he returned to Kathmandu where he lived for the rest of his life.

RAM SARUP SINGH *A/Subadar, 2nd Bn., 1st Punjab Regiment*
25 October 1944 – At Kennedy peak, Tiddim, India, two platoons of the 1st Punjab Regiment were ordered to put in a diversionary attack on the flank of an enemy position. This feature was of exceptional natural strength and was defended by a large force of fresh Japanese troops who had turned the hill into a fortress. Every approach was covered by medium and light machine-guns sited in bunkers. The platoon of Subadar Ram Sarup Singh at once charged the position with another section. This instantaneous action completely bewildered the enemy, who fled from the bunkered positions suffering casualties in their retreat. The subadar was wounded in the legs but took no notice of his wounds. While he was consolidating his position, the enemy opened heavy fire with grenade dischargers, and at the same time put in a strong counter-attack in three waves of 20 each from a flank. It seemed that the platoon must be overwhelmed, but Ram Sarup Singh got another light machine-gun into position and led a charge against the advancing enemy, bayoneting four himself. Although badly wounded in the thigh, he got up and, ignoring his wound, again went for the enemy shouting encouragement to his men. He bayoneted another Japanese and shot a further one, but was mortally wounded by a burst of machine-gun fire in the chest and neck.

ITALY: THE GARIGLIANO AND ANZIO

In December 1943, at a summit meeting in Teheran, Roosevelt, Churchill and Stalin decided European strategy for 1944. First in importance were the landings in France: in Normandy and a smaller landing in southern France, planned for May. In Italy, General Sir Harold Alexander would advance as far as the line Pisa–Rimini, then keep the Germans occupied while priority was switched to southern France. An attack on the Andaman Islands was cancelled, releasing fifty American landing ships to the Mediterranean, for use in Italy then France.

The year had closed with British, American, French and other Allied troops close to the Gustav Line, just north of the River Sangro and Monte Cassino. The first major operation of 1944 was the landing at Anzio, 30 miles south of Rome, 95 north-west of Naples and 60 behind the Gustav Line. On the Mediterranean coast 5th Army would drive up the Liri valley towards Rome, while on the Adriatic coast 8th Army (less three divisions in reserve for 5th Army) continued north.

On 11/12 January the French Expeditionary Corps began the attack on the Gustav Line, reaching it quickly. 10th British Corps crossed the Garigliano (the river from the confluence of the Gari/Rapido and Liri rivers to the sea) on the 17th, but was stopped by three German divisions a few miles west of the river in the foothills of the Aurunci Mountains. Upstream the assaults had not met with success – the Rapido was flooded and mined on both sides, the Garigliano swollen by water from an opened dam on the Liri – and bridgeheads on the far side were withdrawn or pinched out.

On the 22nd, the landings at Anzio achieved complete surprise. Unopposed, the lead elements secured positions between three and seven miles inland within a few hours. The German High Command decided this was a major offensive and deployed reinforcements from Germany and France, but on the 24th the British patrols on the left of the beachhead met the Hermann Goering Panzer Division and American patrols on the right met the 3rd Panzer Grenadier Division, stationed in the area. By the end of January the British had advanced almost to Campoleone on the railway from Rome, about seven miles inland and fourteen north-west of Anzio, and the Americans a mile short of Cisterna, on the far side of the railway ten miles to the east. There they were ordered to consolidate and prepare for counter-attacks, which came on 3 February as the Germans attempted to cut off the British salient. Its front was held by two battalions, its right by three and its left, in low hills, by four including 5th Bn., Grenadier Guards. The right flank was attacked and pulled back, leaving the British in possession of the villages of Aprilia and Carroceto. They were attacked on 7/8 February, and in fierce fighting, lost control of Buonriposo Ridge but held most of the main positions that night.

MITCHELL, George Allan *Private, 1st Bn., London Scottish (Gordon Highlanders)*

23/24 January 1944 – In Italy on the night of 23/24 January 1944, a company of the London Scottish was ordered to carry out a local attack to restore the situation on a portion of the main Damiano Ridge. The company attacked with two platoons forward and a composite platoon of London Scottish and Royal Berkshires in reserve. The company commander was wounded in the very early stages of the attack. The only other officer with the company was wounded soon afterwards. A section of this company was ordered by the platoon commander to carry out a right flanking movement against some enemy machine-guns which were holding up the advance. Almost as soon as he had issued the order, he was killed. There was no platoon sergeant. The section itself consisted of a lance corporal and three men, who were shortly joined by Private Mitchell, the 2in mortar crew from platoon headquarters and another private. During the advance, the enemy opened heavy machine-gun fire at point-blank range. Without hesitation, Mitchell dropped the 2in mortar which he was carrying, and, seizing a rifle and bayonet, charged alone up the hill through intense Spandau fire. He reached the enemy machine-gun unscathed, jumped into the weapon pit, shot one and bayoneted the other member of the crew, thus silencing the gun. As a result, the advance of the platoon continued, but shortly after-wards the leading section was again held up by the fire of approximately two German sections who were strongly entrenched. Private Mitchell, real-izing that prompt action was essential, rushed forward into the assault firing his rifle from his hip, completely oblivious of the bullets sweeping the area. The remainder of his section followed him and arrived in time to complete the capture of the position in which 6 Germans were killed and 12 made prisoner. As the section was reorganizing, another enemy machine-gun opened up on it at close range. Once more Mitchell rushed forward alone and with his rifle and bayonet killed the crew. The section now found itself immediately below the crest of the hill from which heavy small-arms fire was being directed and grenades were being thrown. Private Mitchell's ammunition was exhausted, but in spite of this he called on the men for one further effort and again led the assault up the steep and rocky hillside. Dashing to the front, he was again the first man to reach the enemy position and was mainly instrumental in forcing the remainder of the enemy to surrender. A few minutes later, a German who had surrendered picked up a rifle and shot Private Mitchell through the head.

SIDNEY, William Philip (later Viscount De L'Isle) *T/Major, 5th Bn., Grenadier Guards*

7/8 February 1944 – The period 6–10 February 1944 was of critical importance to the whole state of the Anzio beachhead. The Germans attacked a British division with elements of six different divisions, and a continuous series of fierce local hand-to-hand battles was fought, each one of which had its immediate reaction on the position of other troops in the neighbourhood and on the action as a whole. It was of supreme importance that every inch of ground should be doggedly, stubbornly and tenaciously fought for. The area Carroceto–Buonriposo Ridge was particularly vital.

During the night 7/8 February, Major Sidney was commanding the support company of a battalion of the Grenadier Guards, company headquarters being on the left of battalion headquarters in a gully south-west of Carroceto bridge. Enemy infantry who had bypassed the forward rifle company north-west of Carroceto heavily attacked in the vicinity of Major Sidney's company headquarters and successfully penetrated into the wadi. Major Sidney collected the crew of a 3in mortar firing nearby and personally led an attack with tommy guns and hand grenades, driving the enemy out of the gully. He then sent the detachment back to continue their mortar firing while he and a handful of men took up a position on the edge of the gully in order again to beat off the enemy who were renewing their attack in some strength. Sidney and his party succeeded in keeping the majority of the Germans out but a number reached a ditch 20 yards in front, from which they could outflank his position. Sidney – in full view and completely exposed – dashed forward without hesitation to a point whence he could engage the enemy with his tommy gun at point-blank range. As a result the enemy withdrew leaving a number of dead. On returning to his former position on the edge of the gully, Major Sidney kept two guardsmen with him and sent the remainder back for more ammunition and grenades. While they were away, the enemy vigorously renewed their attack, and a grenade struck Sidney in the face, bounced off and exploded, wounding him and one guardsman and killing the second man. Major Sidney, single-handed and wounded in the thigh, kept the enemy at bay until the ammunition party returned five minutes later, when once more they were ejected. Satisfied that no further attack would be made, he made his way to a nearby cave to have his wound dressed, but before this could be done the enemy attacked again. He at once returned to his post and continued to engage the enemy for another hour, by which time the left of the battalion position was consolidated and the enemy was finally driven off. Only then did Sidney, by that time weak from loss of blood and barely able to walk, allow his wound to be attended to. Throughout the next day contact with the enemy was so close that it was impossible to evacuate him until after dark. During that time, as before, although extremely weak, he continued to act as a tonic and inspiration to all with whom he came in contact.

Viscount De L'Isle became Governor General of Australia, 1961–65.

ITALY: MONTE CASSINO

In Churchill's famous words, 'We hoped to land a wildcat that would tear out the bowels of the Boche. Instead, we have stranded a vast, beached whale with its tail flopping about in the water'. Once the Anzio assault was stalled the beachhead became a liability, and new attempts to break the Gustav Line were attempted up the Liri valley, particularly at Monte Cassino in February and March, but were failures with high casualties. Alexander determined on a third attempt at Monte Cassino on 11 May, bringing in 8th Army to do so. The attack depended on crossing the Gari/Rapido in several places south of Cassino, where it was only about 30 feet wide but very fast flowing: the right-hand division, the 4th, got three battalions across but were without a bridge until the 13th; 8th Indian Division on the left crossed and built two bridges by 9.15 a.m. in an action that saw Sepoy Kamal Ram win a VC. On the 13th, 78th Division was moved through 4th Division's position to close the gap; it made good progress, the attack on Monte Cassino was renewed, and the Gustav Line was taken by the 18th.

The Germans were now falling back on the Hitler Line, six miles north. Canadian Corps was moved forward through 8th Indian Division to Pontecorvo, where the Hitler Line crossed the Liri valley; it attacked on 23 May, concurrently with 78th Division at Aquino, the Polish Corps at Piedimonte, and by nightfall had cleared the way for its armour, which crossed the Melfa.

KAMAL RAM *Sepoy, 3rd Bn., 8th Punjab Regiment*
12 May 1944 – In Italy, after crossing the River Gari overnight, the company advance was held up by heavy machine-gun fire from four posts on the front and flanks. As the capture of the position was essential to secure the bridgehead, the company commander called for a volunteer to get round the rear of the right post and silence it. Volunteering at once and crawling forward through the wire to a flank, Sepoy Kamal Ram attacked the post single-handed and shot the first machine-gunner; a second German tried to seize his weapon but Kamal Ram killed him with the bayonet, and then shot a German officer who, appearing from the trench with his pistol, was about to fire. Kamal Ram, still alone, at once went on to attack the second machine-gun post continuing to hold up the advance, and after shooting one machine-gunner, he threw a grenade and the remaining enemy surrendered. Seeing a havildar making a reconnaissance for an attack on the third post, Sepoy Kamal Ram joined him, and, having first covered his companion, went in and completed the destruction of this post. By his courage, initiative and disregard for personal risk, Kamal Ram enabled his company to charge and secure the ground vital to the establishment of the bridgehead and the completion of work on two bridges. When a platoon, pushed further forward to widen the position, was fired on from a house, Kamal Ram dashed towards it, shot a German in a slit trench and captured two more. His battalion attained the essential part of its objective.

WAKEFORD, Richard *T/Captain, 2/4th Bn., Hampshire Regiment*
13 May 1944 – He commanded the leading company on the right flank of an attack on two hills near Cassino, and accompanied by his orderly, and armed only with a revolver, he killed a number of the enemy and handed

over 20 prisoners when the company came forward. On the final objective a German officer and five other ranks were holding a house. After being twice driven back by grenades, Wakeford, with a final dash, reached the window and hurled in his grenades. Those of the enemy who were not killed or wounded, surrendered. Attacking another feature on the following day, a tank became bogged on the start line, surprise was lost and the leading infantry were caught in the enemy's fire so that the resulting casualties endangered the whole operation. Captain Wakeford, keeping his company under perfect control, crossed the start line and although wounded in the face and in both arms, led his men up the hill. Halfway up the hill his company came under heavy Spandau fire; in spite of his wounds, he organized and led a force to deal with this opposition so that his company could get on. By now the company was being heavily mortared and Wakeford was again wounded, in both legs, but he still went on and, reaching his objective, he organized and consolidated the remainder of his company and reported to his commanding officer before submitting to personal attention. During the seven-hour interval before stretcher bearers could reach him his unwavering high spirits encouraged the wounded men around him.

JEFFERSON, Francis Arthur *Fusilier, 2nd Bn., Lancashire Fusiliers*

16 May 1944 – During an attack on the Gustav Line, an anti-tank obstacle held up some of the tanks, leaving the leading company of Fusilier Jefferson's battalion to dig in on a hill without tanks or anti-tank guns. The enemy counter-attacked with infantry and two tanks, which opened fire at short range causing a number of casualties, and eliminating one PIAT group entirely. As the tanks advanced towards the partially dug trenches, Jefferson, entirely on his own initiative, seized a PIAT and running forward alone under heavy fire, took up a position behind a hedge. As he could not see properly, he came into the open, and standing up under a hail of bullets, fired at the leading tank which was now only 20 yards away. It burst into flames and all the crew were killed. Jefferson then reloaded the PIAT and proceeded towards the second tank, which withdrew before he could get within range. By this time tanks had arrived and the enemy counter-attack was smashed with heavy casualties.

MAHONY, John Keefer *Major, Westminster Regiment (Motor), Canadian Infantry Corps*

24 May 1944 – A Company of the Westminster Regiment (Motor), under the command of Major Mahony, was ordered to establish the initial bridgehead across the River Melfa, Italy. The enemy still had strong forces of tanks, self-propelled guns and infantry holding defensive positions on the east side. Despite this, Mahony personally led his company down to and across the river, being with the leading section. Although the crossing was made in full view of and under heavy fire from enemy machine-gun posts on the right rear and left front, he personally directed each section into its proper position on the west bank with the greatest coolness and confidence. The crossing was made and a small bridgehead was established on ground where it was only possible to dig shallow weapon pits. From 1530 hours the company maintained itself in the face of enemy fire and attack until 2030 hours, when the remaining companies and supporting weapons were able to cross the river and reinforce them. The bridgehead was enclosed on three sides by an 88mm self-propelled gun 450 yards to the right, a battery of four anti-aircraft guns 100 yards to the left, a Spandau 100 yards to the left of it, to the left of the Spandau a second 88mm self-propelled gun, and approximately a company of infantry with mortars and machine-guns on the left of the 88mm gun. From all these weapons, Major Mahony's company was constantly under fire until it eventually succeeded in knocking out the self-propelled equipment and the infantry on the left flank. Shortly after the bridgehead had been established, the enemy counter-attacked with infantry supported by tanks and self-propelled guns. The counter-attack was beaten off by the company with its PIATs, 2in mortars and grenades, due to the skill with which Mahony had organized his defences. With absolute fearlessness and disregard for his own safety, Major Mahony personally directed the fire of his PIATs throughout this action, encouraging and exhorting his men. By this time, the company strength had been reduced to 60 men, and all but one of the platoon officers had been wounded. Scarcely an hour later, enemy tanks formed up about 500 yards in front of the bridgehead and in company with about a company of infantry, launched a second counter-attack. Major Mahony, determined to hold the position at all costs, went from section to section with words of encouragement, personally directing the fire of mortars and other weapons. At one stage, a section was pinned down in the open by accurate and intense machine-gun fire. Mahony crawled forward to its position, and by throwing smoke grenades succeeded in extricating it with the loss of only one man. This counter-attack was finally beaten off with the destruction of three enemy self-propelled guns and one Panther tank. Early in the action, Mahony was wounded in the head and twice in the leg, but he refused medical aid and continued to direct the defence of the bridgehead despite the fact that movement of any kind caused him extreme pain. It was only when the remaining companies of the regiment had crossed the river to support him that he allowed his wounds to be dressed and even then refused to be evacuated, staying instead with his company. The enemy's efforts to destroy the bridgehead were all defeated.

ITALY: THE ANZIO BREAKOUT

The beachhead at Anzio was reinforced by 36th US Division, held in reserve, between 18 and 21 May, and on the 23rd four American divisions struck towards Cisterna. The Germans withdrew, and the Americans moved towards Valmontone to cut them off, but on 27 May were ordered to turn towards Rome, which they entered on 5 June. The Germans' other intermediate line, the Caesar, in the Alban Hills, was abandoned on 2/3 June.

ROGERS, Maurice Albert Wyndham *Sergeant, 2nd Bn., Wiltshire Regiment*
   3 June 1944 – At Anzio, Italy, a battalion of the Wiltshire Regiment was ordered to attack high ground held by the enemy. The leading company had taken their first objective but were unable to reach their final objective, owing to heavy enemy fire and casualties. The carrier platoon, mounted, were ordered to capture the final objective, supported by fire from the company and a troop of tanks. The objective was wired and mined and strongly defended by the enemy. The carrier platoon advanced through machine-gun and mortar fire until they reached the enemy's wire, which was 70 yards from their objective. At this point the platoon was under the intense fire of seven machine-guns firing at ranges of from 50 to 100 yards, and sustained a number of casualties. The platoon, checked by the enemy's wire and the intensity of his machine-gun fire, took cover and returned the fire preparatory to gapping the wire. Sergeant Rogers without hesitation continued to advance alone, firing his tommy gun. He got through the enemy's wire, ran across the minefield and destroyed two of the enemy machine-gun posts with his machine-gun and hand grenades. By now, Rogers was 100 yards ahead of his platoon and had penetrated 30 yards inside the enemy's defences. He had drawn on to himself the fire of nearly all the enemy's machine-guns and had thrown their defence into confusion. Inspired by the example of Sergeant Rogers, the platoon breached the enemy's wire and began the assault. Still alone and penetrating deeper into the enemy position, Rogers, whilst attempting to silence a third machine-gun post, was blown off his feet by a grenade which burst beside him and wounded him in the leg. Nothing daunted he stood up and, still firing, ran on towards the enemy post. He was shot and killed at point-blank range.

ITALY: THE GOTHIC LINE

General Alexander now hoped to transfer 8th Army back to the Adriatic coast, reach Florence by late July and attack the Gothic Line (running from 15 miles north of Pisa to 30 miles south of Rimini), which the Germans hoped to hold that winter. The Albert line (River Ombrone–Pescara) was broken at the end of July and beginning of August, but 8th Army found very strong resistance both sides of Lake Trasimene, and Naik Yeshwant Ghadge won a VC for his part in clearing a post at Città di Castello, 20 miles north of it on the Tiber. Florence was entered on 4 August and 8th Army was transferred to the Adriatic.

   Preparations completed, the attack on the line began on the 25th. The

Germans had, as planned, diverted their attention to the Allied attack on the South of France on 15 August. By 3 September, 8th Army had a bridgehead on the River Conca, five miles east of Rimini. The terrain of the country now greatly favoured defenders, being a series of ridges and deep river valleys running west–east, and the Germans contested each one, but Rimini fell on 20/21 September. On 20 October the Allies took Cesena, and on 24 November they had advanced another twenty miles to the River Lamone at Faenza. Throughout November the rains turned the battlefield into an appalling morass. However, a bridgehead was secured on 3/4 December, and held against a fierce counter-attack on the 9th, and Faenza was taken by Indian and New Zealand battalions on the 17th. Operations ended that winter with a very tired 8th Army in Ravenna and 5th Army nine miles from Bologna.

YESHWANT GHADGE *Naik, 3rd Bn., 5th Mahratta Light Infantry*
        10 July 1944 – In the Upper Tiber Valley, Italy, a company of the 5th Mahratta Light Infantry attacked a position strongly defended by the enemy. During this attack a rifle section commanded by Naik Yeshwant Ghadge came under heavy machine-gun fire at close range, which killed or wounded all members of the section except the commander. Without hesitation, and well knowing that none were left to accompany him, Yeshwant Ghadge rushed the machine-gun post. He first threw a grenade which knocked out the machine-gun and firer, after which he shot one of the gun crew with his tommy gun. Finally, having no time to change his magazine, he grasped his gun by the barrel and beat to death the remaining two men of the gun crew. Unfortunately Yeshwant Ghadge was shot in the chest and back by enemy snipers and died in the post which he had captured single-handed.

NORTON, Gerard Ross *Lieutenant, Kaffrarian Rifles, South African Forces, attached 1/4th Bn., Hampshire Regiment*
        31 August 1944 – Lieutenant Norton was commanding a platoon during the attack on the Monte Gridolfo feature, one of the strongpoints of the Gothic Line defences in Italy, and one which contained well-sited concrete gun emplacements. The leading platoon of his company was pinned down by heavy enemy fire from a valley on the right flank of the advance. On his own initiative and with complete disregard for his personal safety, Norton at once engaged a series of emplacements in this valley. Single-handed, he attacked the first machine-gun position with a grenade, killing the crew of three. Still alone, he then worked his way forward to a second position containing two machine-guns and 15 riflemen. After a fight lasting ten minutes he wiped out both machine-gun nests with his tommy gun, and killed or took prisoner the remainder of the enemy. Throughout these attacks Norton came under direct fire from an enemy self-propelled gun and, whilst still under heavy fire from this gun, he went on to clear the cellar and upper rooms of a house, taking several more prisoners and putting many of the enemy to flight. Although by this time wounded and weak from

loss of blood, he continued calmly and resolutely to lead his platoon up the valley to capture the remaining enemy positions.

He settled in Zimbabwe, and was a victim of President Mugabe's policy of evicting white farmers from their land. At the time of publication he was one of the surviving VC holders.

SHERBAHADUR THAPA *Rifleman, 1st Bn., 9th Gurkha Rifles*

18/19 September 1944 – A battalion of the 9th Gurkha Rifles was fighting its way forward into the independent state of San Marino, Italy, against bitter opposition from German prepared positions dominating the river valley and held in considerable strength in depth. Rifleman Sher Bahadur Thapa was a Bren-gunner in a rifle company which just before dawn came under heavy enemy small-arms and mortar fire. He and his section commander charged an enemy post, killing the machine-gunner and putting the rest of the post to flight. Almost immediately another party of Germans attacked the two men, and the section commander was badly wounded by a grenade but, without hesitation, this rifleman, in spite of intense fire, rushed at the attackers and reaching the crest of the ridge brought his Bren gun into action against the main body of the enemy, who were counter-attacking. Disregarding suggestions that he should withdraw to the cover of a slit trench, Sher Bahadur Thapa lay in the open under a hail of bullets, firing his Bren gun which he knew he could only bring to bear on the German emplacements from his exposed position on the crest of the hill as they would not have been visible from the slit trench. By the intensity and accuracy of the fire which he could bring to bear only from the crest this isolated Gurkha Bren-gunner silenced several enemy machine-guns and checked a number of Germans who were trying to infiltrate the ridge. At the end of two hours both forward companies had exhausted their ammunition and, as they were by then practically surrounded, they were ordered to withdraw. Sher Bahadur Thapa covered their withdrawal as they crossed the open ground to positions in the rear and himself remained alone at his post until his ammunition ran out. He then dashed forward under accurate small-arms and mortar fire and rescued two wounded men lying between him and the advancing Germans. While returning the second time he paid the price of his heroism and fell riddled by machine-gun bullets fired at point-blank range.

BURTON, Richard Henry *Private, 1st Bn., Duke of Wellington's Regiment*

8 October 1944 – In Italy, two companies of the Duke of Wellington's Regiment moved forward to take Monte Ceco, a strongly held feature 2,500 feet high. The capture of this feature was vital at this stage of the operation as it dominated all the ground on the main axis of advance. The assaulting troops made good progress to within 20 yards of the crest when they came under withering fire from Spandaus on the crest. The leading platoon was held up and the platoon commander was wounded. The company commander took another platoon, of which Private Burton was runner, through to assault the crest from which at least four Spandaus were firing. Burton rushed forward and, engaging the first Spandau position with his tommy gun, killed the crew of three. When the assault was again held up by murderous fire from two more machine-guns, Burton, again showing complete disregard for his own safety, dashed toward the first machine-gun using his tommy gun until his ammunition was exhausted. He then picked up a Bren gun and firing from the hip succeeded in killing or wounding the crews of the two machine-guns. Thanks to his outstanding courage the company was then able to consolidate on the forward slope of the feature. The enemy immediately counter-attacked fiercely but Burton, in spite of most of his comrades being either dead or wounded, once again dashed forward on his own initiative and directed such accurate fire with his Bren gun on the enemy that they retired leaving the feature firmly in British hands. The enemy later counter-attacked again on the adjoining platoon position and Burton, who had placed himself on the flank, brought such accurate fire to bear that this counter-attack also failed to dislodge the company from its position.

SMITH, Ernest Alvia *Private, Seaforth Highlanders of Canada, Canadian Infantry Corps*

21/22 October 1944 – A Canadian infantry brigade was ordered to establish a bridgehead across the Savio River, in Italy. The Seaforth Highlanders of Canada were selected as the spearhead of the attack and in weather most unfavourable to the operation they crossed the river and captured their objectives in spite of strong opposition from the enemy. Torrential rain had caused the Savio to rise six feet in five hours and as the soft vertical banks made it impossible to bridge the river no tanks or anti-tank guns could be taken across the raging stream to the support of the rifle companies. As the right-forward company was consolidating its objective it was suddenly counter-attacked by a troop of three Panther tanks supported by two self-propelled guns and about 30 infantry, and the situation appeared almost hopeless. Under heavy fire from the approaching enemy tanks, Private Smith, showing great initiative and inspiring leadership, led his PIAT group of two men across an open field to a position from which the PIAT could best be employed. Leaving one man on the weapon, Smith crossed the road with a companion and obtained another PIAT. Almost immediately an enemy tank came down the road firing its machine-guns along the line of the ditches. Smith's comrade was wounded. At a range of 30 feet and having to expose himself to the full view of the enemy, Smith fired the PIAT and hit the tank, putting it out of action. Ten German infantry immediately jumped off the back of the tank and charged him. Without hesitation Private Smith moved out onto the road and with his tommy gun at point-blank range killed four Germans and drove the remainder back. Almost immediately another tank opened fire and more enemy infantry closed in on Smith's position. Obtaining some abandoned tommy-gun magazines from a ditch, he steadfastly held his position, protecting his comrade and fighting the enemy until they finally gave up and withdrew in disorder. One tank and both self-propelled guns had been destroyed by this time, but yet another tank swept the area with fire from a longer range. Smith, still showing utter contempt for enemy fire, helped his wounded friend to cover and obtained medical aid for him behind a nearby building. He then returned to his position beside the road to await the possibility of a further enemy attack. No further immediate attack developed, and as a result the battalion was able to consolidate the bridgehead position so vital to the success of the whole operation, which led to the eventual capture of San Giorgio Di Cesena and a further advance to the Ronco River.

At the time of publication he was one of the surviving VC holders.

THAMAN GURUNG *Rifleman, 1st Bn., 5th Royal Gurkha Rifles*
   10 November 1944 – A company of the 5th Royal Gurkha Rifles was ordered to send a fighting patrol on to Monte San Bartolo, the objective of a future attack. In this patrol were two scouts, one of whom was Rifleman Thaman Gurung. By skilful stalking both scouts succeeded in reaching the base of the position undetected. Thaman Gurung then started to work his way to the summit, but suddenly the second scout attracted his attention to Germans in a slit trench just below the crest, who were preparing to fire with a machine-gun at the leading section. Realizing that if the enemy succeeded in opening fire, the section would certainly sustain heavy casualties, Thaman Gurung leapt to his feet and charged them. Completely taken by surprise, the Germans surrendered without opening fire. Thaman Gurung then crept forward to the summit of the position, from which he saw a party of Germans, well dug in on reverse slopes, preparing to throw grenades over the crest at the leading section. Although the skyline was devoid of cover and under accurate machine-gun fire at close range, Rifleman Thaman Gurung immediately crossed it, firing on the German position with his tommy gun, thus allowing the forward section to reach the summit, but due to heavy fire from the enemy machine-guns, the platoon was ordered to withdraw. Thaman Gurung then again crossed the skyline alone and although in full view of the enemy and constantly exposed to heavy fire at short range, he methodically put burst after burst of tommy-gun fire into the German slit trenches until his ammunition ran out. He then threw two grenades he had with him and, rejoining his section, collected two more grenades and again doubled over the bullet-swept crest of the hillock and hurled them at the remaining Germans. This diversion enabled both rear sections to withdraw without further loss. Meanwhile, the leading section, which had remained behind to assist the withdrawal of the remainder of the platoon, was still on the summit, so Thaman Gurung, shouting to the section to withdraw, seized a Bren gun and a number of magazines. He then yet

again ran to the top of the hill and, although he well knew that his action meant almost certain death, stood up on the bullet-swept summit in full view of the enemy and opened fire at the nearest enemy positions. It was not until he had emptied two complete magazines, and the remaining section was well on its way to safety, that Thaman Gurung was killed.

BRUNT, John Henry Cound *T/Captain, Sherwood Foresters, attached 6th Bn., Lincolnshire Regiment*

9 December 1944 – The platoon commanded by Captain Brunt was holding a vital sector of the line at Faenza, Italy. At dawn the German 90th Panzer Grenadier Division counter-attacked the battalion's forward positions in great strength with three Mark IV tanks and infantry. The house around which the platoon was dug in was destroyed and the whole area was subjected to intense mortar fire. The situation then became critical, as the anti-tank defences had been destroyed and two Sherman tanks knocked out. Brunt, however, rallied his remaining men, and, moving to an alternative position, continued to hold the enemy infantry, although outnumbered by at least three to one. Personally firing a Bren gun, Brunt killed about 14 of the enemy. His wireless set was destroyed by shell fire, but on receiving a message by runner to withdraw to a company locality some 200 yards to his left and rear, he remained behind to give covering fire. When his Bren ammunition was exhausted, he fired a PIAT and 2in mortar, left by casualties, before he himself dashed over the open ground to the new position. This aggressive defence caused the enemy to pause, so Brunt took a party back to his previous position, and although fiercely engaged by small-arms fire, carried away the wounded who had been left there. Later in the day, a further counter-attack was put in by the enemy on two axes. Brunt immediately seized a spare Bren gun and, going round his forward positions, rallied his men. Then, leaping on a Sherman tank supporting the company, he ordered the tank commander to drive from one fire position to another whilst he sat or stood on the turret, directing Besa fire at the advancing enemy regardless of the hail of small-arms fire. Then, seeing small parties of the enemy armed with bazookas trying to approach round the left flank, he jumped off the tank and, taking a Bren gun, stalked these parties well in front of the company positions, killing some and causing the enemy finally to withdraw in great haste leaving their dead behind them.

BOMBER COMMAND

BARTON, Cyril Joe *Pilot Officer, 578 Squadron, Royal Air Force Volunteer Reserve*

30/31 March 1944 – He was captain and pilot of a Halifax aircraft detailed to attack Nuremberg. When some 70 miles short of the target, the aircraft was attacked by a Junkers 88. The first burst of fire from the enemy made the intercommunication system useless. One engine was damaged when a Messerschmitt 210 joined the fight. The bomber's machine-guns were out of action and the gunners were unable to return the fire. Fighters continued to attack the aircraft as it approached the target area, and in the confusion caused by the failure of the communications system at the height of the battle, a signal was misinterpreted and the navigator, air bomber and wireless operator left the aircraft by parachute. Barton faced a situation of dire peril. His aircraft was damaged, his navigational team had gone and he could not communicate with the remainder of the crew. If he continued his mission he would be at the mercy of hostile fighters when silhouetted against the fires in the target area, and if he survived he would have to make a four-hour journey home on three engines across heavily defended territory. Determined to press home his attack at all costs, he flew on and, reaching the target, released the bombs himself. As he turned for home the propeller of the damaged engine, which was vibrating badly, flew off. It was also discovered that two of the petrol tanks had suffered damage and were leaking. He held to his course, and without navigational aids and in spite of strong head winds successfully avoided the most dangerous defence areas on his route. Eventually he crossed the English coast only 90 miles north of his base. By this time the petrol supply was nearly exhausted. Before a suitable landing place could be found, the port engines stopped. The aircraft was now too low to be abandoned successfully. Barton therefore ordered the three remaining members of his crew to take up their crash stations. Then, with only one engine working, he made a gallant attempt to land clear of the houses over which he was flying. The aircraft finally crashed and Barton lost his life, but his three comrades survived.

JACKSON, Norman Cyril *Sergeant, 106 Squadron, Royal Air Force Volunteer Reserve*

Norman Cyril Jackson was an orphan and was brought up by a family called Gunter, whose name he adopted – so when he joined the RAF just before the outbreak of war in 1939 he failed to respond to his real name at the first parade, and was duly ticked off. Being, as he recalled, 'a cheeky little sod', he went to explain to the flight sergeant that he was unused to being called by the name on his birth certificate. The flight sergeant produced two bottles of light ale and then said, 'You know, boy, I'm convinced that you will go a long way in this air force.'

After a spell in Sierra Leone, Jackson returned to Britain in November 1941 and volunteered for Bomber Command, flying first Manchesters and then Lancasters. His squadron was engaged on spoof attacks and laying flares for 617 Squadron. Losses in Bomber Command were high, but Jackson was with the same crew throughout.

It was on 26 April 1944 that the crew's team spirit was tested to its limits

– and Jackson more than earned his VC. Their bombing target had been a ball-bearing factory at Schweinfurt – they'd let their bombs go and were heading for home when they were attacked from the ground and the air. Jackson recalled,

> The flak was coming up and there were fighters all around. We all thought we were going to make it. I was sitting in the cockpit when we were hit, and I saw flames coming from the starboard inner engine, so I grabbed the fire extinguisher and put it inside my Mae West – it was smallish. We'd decided that either the bomb-aimer or myself would have to get out if there was a fire, since we were the only ones who had been trained to deal with that sort of thing. I released my parachute inside so that the bomb-aimer and navigator could hold on to it in case I slipped. It was my duty to get out. There was a hatch behind me. I got out and slid down on to the wing. We were doing about 140–160 knots and we were at 22,000 feet. I hung on to the air-intakes on the leading edge of the wing with one hand, and tried to put out the fire with the other. I'd got it under control, but the German pilot had seen me and was aiming at the engines, so the aircraft was shaking all over the place. I couldn't even jump, because they were holding on to my chute. Then I was shot off the bloody wing, and they threw my parachute out of the plane.

Jackson landed with his parachute in flames, shrapnel wounds and bullets in his leg and burns to his hands and eyes. With the exception of the pilot and the rear-gunner, who had been killed, the rest of the crew were rounded up and reunited before being sent variously to prison or hospital. After a long recuperation and a spell in a POW camp next to the horrors of Belsen, he escaped and handed himself over to an American officer with the Allied invasion force.

When Jackson received his VC from King George VI at Buckingham Palace, he was accompanied by Leonard Cheshire – the only two VCs of that day. Cheshire was familiar with Jackson's extraordinary feat of bravery and insisted that they both approach the King together. Jackson remembered, 'I can't remember what the King said to him, but Cheshire said, "This chap stuck his neck out more than I did – he should have the VC first!" Of course, the King had to keep to protocol, but I'll never forget what Cheshire said.'

The first telegram he received meant a great deal to him. It simply said, 'Well done, I knew I was right. Your ex-Flight Sergeant.'

In April 2004 his VC was sold to a private collector for a new record price of £235,250.

MYNARSKI, Andrew Charles *Pilot Officer, 419 Squadron, Royal Canadian Air Force*

12/13 June 1944 – Pilot Officer Mynarski was the mid-upper gunner of a Lancaster aircraft, detailed to attack a target at Cambrai in France.

The aircraft was attacked from below and astern by an enemy fighter and ultimately came down in flames. As an immediate result of the attack, both port engines failed. Fire broke out between the mid-upper turret and the rear turret, as well as in the port wing. The flames soon became fierce and the captain ordered the crew to abandon the aircraft. Mynarski left his turret and went towards the escape hatch. He then saw that the rear gunner was still in his turret and apparently unable to leave it. The turret was, in fact, immovable, since the hydraulic gear had been put out of action when the port engines failed and the manual gear had been broken by the gunner in his attempts to escape. Without hesitation, Mynarski made his way through the flames in an endeavour to reach the rear turret and release the gunner. Whilst so doing, his parachute and his clothing up to the waist were set on fire. All his efforts to move the turret and free the gunner were in vain. Eventually the rear gunner clearly indicated to him that there was nothing more he could do and that he should try to save his own life. Mynarski reluctantly went back through the flames to the escape hatch. There, as a last gesture to the trapped gunner, he turned towards him, stood to attention in his flaming clothing and saluted, before he jumped out of the aircraft. Mynarski's descent was seen by French people on the ground. Both his parachute and clothing were on fire. He was found eventually by the French, but was so severely burnt that he died from his injuries. The rear gunner had a miraculous escape when the aircraft crashed. He subsequently testified that, had Mynarski not attempted to save his comrade's life, he could have left the aircraft in safety and would doubtless have escaped death. Mynarski must have been fully aware that in trying to free the rear gunner he was almost certain to lose his own life. Despite this, with outstanding courage and complete disregard for his own safety, he went to the rescue.

BAZALGETTE, Ian Willoughby *A/Squadron Leader, 635 Squadron, Royal Air Force Volunteer Reserve*

4 August 1944 – Squadron Leader Bazalgette was master bomber of a Pathfinder squadron detailed to mark an important target at Trossy-St-Maximin for the main bomber force. When nearing the target his Lancaster came under heavy anti-aircraft fire. Both starboard engines were put out of action and serious fires broke out in the fuselage and the starboard main plane. The bomb aimer was badly wounded. As the deputy master bomber had already been shot down, the success of the attack depended on Squadron Leader Bazalgette, and this he knew. Despite the appalling conditions in his burning aircraft, he pressed on gallantly to the target, marking and bombing it accurately. That the attack was successful was due to his magnificent effort. After the bombs had been dropped the Lancaster dived, practically out of control. By expert airmanship and great exertion Bazalgette regained control. But the port inner engine then failed and the whole of the starboard main plane became a mass of flames. Bazalgette fought bravely to

bring his aircraft and crew to safety. The mid-upper gunner was overcome by fumes. Bazalgette then ordered those of his crew who were able to leave by parachute to do so. He remained at the controls and attempted the almost hopeless task of landing the crippled and blazing aircraft in a last effort to save the wounded bomb aimer and helpless air gunner. With superb skill, and taking great care to avoid a small French village nearby, he brought the aircraft down safely. Unfortunately, it then exploded and this gallant officer and his two comrades perished.

PALMER, Robert Anthony Maurice *Squadron Leader, 109 Squadron, Royal Air Force Volunteer Reserve*

23 December 1944 – This officer has completed 110 bombing missions. Most of them involved deep penetration of heavily defended territory; many were low-level marking operations against vital targets; all were executed with tenacity, high courage and great accuracy. He first went on operations in January 1941. He took part in the first thousand-bomber raid against Cologne in 1942. He was one of the first pilots to drop a 4,000lb bomb on the Reich. It was known that he could be relied on to press home his attack whatever the opposition and to bomb with great accuracy. He was always selected, therefore, to take part in special operations against vital targets. The finest example of his courage and determination was on 23 December 1944, when he led a formation of Lancasters to attack the marshalling yards at Cologne in daylight. He had the task of marking the target and his formation had been ordered to bomb as soon as the bombs had gone from his, the leading, aircraft. The leader's duties during the final bombing run were exacting and demanded coolness and resolution. To achieve accuracy he would have to fly at an exact height and airspeed on a steady course, regardless of opposition. Some minutes before the target was reached, his aircraft came under heavy anti-aircraft fire; shells burst all around, two engines were set on fire and there were flames and smoke in the nose and in the bomb bay. Enemy fighters now attacked in force. Squadron Leader Palmer disdained the possibility of taking avoiding action. He knew that if he diverged the least bit from his course, he would be unable to utilize the special equipment to the best advantage. He was determined to complete the run and provide an accurate and easily seen aiming point for the other bombers. He ignored the double risk of fire and explosion in his aircraft and kept on. With its engines developing unequal power, an immense effort was needed to keep the damaged aircraft on a straight course. Nevertheless, he made a perfect approach and his bombs hit the target. His aircraft was last seen spiralling to earth in flames. Such was the strength of the opposition that more than half of his formation failed to return.

D-DAY

After months of planning and delay, on 6 June an Allied Expeditionary Force of British, American, Canadian, Polish and Free French troops launched Operation Overlord. Massive naval and aerial bombardment made way for the dropping in of the British 6th Airborne Division and twelve thousand paratroopers of US airborne divisions, followed by the landing of five divisions – 156,115 men – on the beaches of Normandy. Seven battleships, accompanied by cruisers, auxiliary ships and landing craft along with air cover supported the landing. Although casualties were heavy in some areas, especially among the Americans landing on Omaha Beach, the operation caught the defenders not fully prepared and by nightfall the Allies had reached and secured most of their objectives. Extraordinarily, on a day of intense action, involving air, sea and land forces, only one VC award was made.

HOLLIS, Stanley Elton *Company Sergeant Major, 6th Bn., Green Howards*

Stan Hollis was born just before the Great War to fishmonger Alfred Edward Hollis and his wife Edith in Loftus – an ordinary lad who helped out in his father's shop until starting training when he was seventeen as a navigation officer in the merchant navy. He made regular trips to West Africa with the Elder, Dempster Line until in 1930 a bout of blackwater fever put paid to his merchant naval career.

Back at home, Hollis married and made ends meet by working as a lorry driver and in local brickworks. With war looming, he joined the 4th Battalion, the Green Howards. As a lance corporal his duties with the British Expeditionary Force in France were undistinguished – laying runways, dispatch rider for his commanding officer – until the battalion was evacuated from the beaches of Dunkirk. The Green Howards again saw action in Iraq, Palestine and Cyprus before joining up with Montgomery's 8th Army and fighting through the Western Desert, from Alamein to Tunis, and prior to the invasion of Sicily, Hollis was promoted company sergeant major. Despite showing great courage in action at Primasole Bridge, during which he was wounded, the DCM for which he was recommended was never awarded. It was on D-Day that the fishmonger's son made his mark on the pages of VC history.

Getting ashore in the early hours of 6 June 1944, Hollis' battalion was sent to clear the defensive pillbox positions which guarded the coast. Seeing two still uncleared, Hollis went with his commanding officer to deal with them, and on nearing the first, came under machine-gun fire from the slit opening. Hollis charged forward, firing his Sten gun, then, leaping on the roof of the pillbox, he kept firing into the box and then threw in a grenade, killing two Germans and taking the rest prisoner.

As the day progressed, he cleared the defenders from a trench before they could open fire on his company, then, as they pressed inland, they came up against a field-gun position. Hollis led the assault on the gun, first engaging the gun with a PIAT, firing from a house just 50 yards away. Grazed on the cheek by a sniper's bullet, Hollis watched as the gun swung round and fired on his position from point-blank range. Masonry was falling all around as he and his assault party escaped from the critical situation. The field gun was finally destroyed, but as its crew continued to rake the area with fire, Hollis realized that two of his men were still trapped inside the crumbling house. He ran forward, firing his Bren gun to create a diversion and allow the two men to make their escape. This day's actions earned him the VC – but the fighting went on for him until he was wounded in the leg in September 1944, and brought back to England.

After the war, Hollis was again in search of work – sand-blaster at the local steel works, a motor-repair business, and third engineer on a merchant ship. Eventually he took over a pub – which business he stayed in until his death in 1972, aged just fifty-nine. Ten years later his medals were auctioned at Sotheby's for a record £32,000 – but they can now be seen at the Green Howards' Regimental Museum.

NORMANDY

Six days after the Allies landed, they had linked their beachheads and held an unbroken front of 60 miles which was 15 miles deep in some places. The Germans, however, contested every inch. On 31 July, American tanks and infantry had broken through German lines and had reached Avranches. Hitler ordered what remained of ten Panzer divisions to attack through Mortain to Avranches to cut off the advancing Americans. North of Mortain the Royal Norfolks were holding the village of Sourdeval when it was attacked by the 10th Panzer Division.

The Germans withdrew eastwards through the Falaise Gap but they were attacked by the Allies, and by 16 August Hitler reluctantly accepted Normandy was lost.

BATES, Sidney *Corporal, Royal Norfolk Regiment*

6 August 1944 – The position held by a battalion of the Royal Norfolk Regiment near Sourdeval, east of Avranches, was attacked in strength by the 10th SS Panzer Division. The attack started with a heavy and accurate artillery and mortar programme on the position, which the enemy had pinpointed. Half an hour later the main attack developed and heavy machine-gun and mortar fire was concentrated on the point of junction of the two forward companies. Corporal Bates was commanding the right-forward section of the left-forward company which suffered some casualties, so he decided to move the remnants of his section to an alternative position from which he could better counter the enemy thrust. However, the enemy wedge grew still deeper, until there were about 60 Germans, supported by machine-guns and mortars, in the area occupied by the section. Seeing that the situation was becoming desperate, Bates seized a light machine-gun and charged the enemy, moving forward through a hail of bullets and splinters and firing the gun from his hip. He was almost immediately wounded by machine-gun fire and fell to the ground, but recovered himself quickly, got up and continued advancing towards the enemy, spraying bullets from his gun as he went. His action by now was having an effect on the enemy riflemen and machine-gunners but mortar bombs continued to fall all around him. He was then hit for the second time and much more seriously and painfully wounded. However, undaunted, he staggered once more to his feet and continued towards the enemy, who were now seemingly nonplussed by their inability to check him. His constant firing continued until the enemy started to withdraw before him. At this moment, he was hit for the third time by mortar-bomb splinters – a wound that was to prove mortal. He again fell to the ground but continued to fire his weapon until his strength failed him. This was not, however, until the enemy had withdrawn and the situation in this locality had been restored. Corporal Bates died shortly afterwards of the wounds he had received but, by his supreme gallantry and self-sacrifice, he had personally restored what had been a critical situation.

JAMIESON, David Auldgo *Captain, Royal Norfolk Regiment*

7–8 August 1944 – Captain Jamieson was in command of a company of the Royal Norfolk Regiment which established a bridgehead over the River Orne, south of Grimbosq in Normandy. On 7 August, the enemy made three counter-attacks which were repulsed with heavy losses. The last of these took place at 1830 hours when a German battle group with Tiger and Panther tanks attacked and the brunt of the fighting fell on Captain Jamieson's company. Continuous heavy fighting ensued for more than four hours until the enemy were driven off, after suffering severe casualties and the loss of three tanks and an armoured car accounted for by this company. Throughout these actions, Captain Jamieson displayed outstanding courage and leadership, which had a decisive influence on the course of the battle and resulted in the defeat of these determined enemy attacks. On the morning of 8 August the enemy attacked with a fresh battle group and succeeded in penetrating the defences surrounding the company on three sides. During this attack two of the three tanks in support of the company were destroyed and Captain Jamieson left his trench under close-range fire from enemy arms of all kinds and went over to direct the fire of the remaining tank, but as he could not get into touch with the commander of the tank by the outside telephone, he climbed upon it in full view of the enemy. During this period he was wounded in the right eye and left forearm but when his wounds were dressed he refused to be evacuated. By this time all the other officers had become casualties so Captain Jamieson reorganized his company, regardless of personal safety, walking amongst his men in full view of the enemy as there was no cover. After several hours of bitter and confused fighting, the last Germans were driven from the company position. The enemy counter-attacked the company three more times during that day with infantry and tanks. Captain Jamieson continued in command, arranging for artillery support over his wireless and going out into the open on each occasion to encourage his men. By the evening the Germans had withdrawn, leaving a ring of dead and burnt-out tanks round his position.

WATKINS, Tasker (later the Rt. Hon.) *Lieutenant, 1/5th Bn., Welch Regiment*
    16 August 1944 – He was commanding a company of the Welch Regiment. The battalion was ordered to attack objectives near the railway at Barfour, Normandy. Lieutenant Watkins' company had to cross open corn-fields in which booby traps had been set. It was not yet dusk and the company soon came under heavy machine-gun fire from posts in the corn and farther back, and also fire from an 88mm gun; many casualties were caused and the advance was slowed up. Watkins, the only officer left, placed himself at the head of his men and under short-range fire charged two posts in succession, personally killing or wounding the occupants with his Sten gun. On reaching his objective he found an anti-tank gun manned by a German soldier; his Sten gun jammed, so he threw it in the German's face and shot him with his pistol before he had time to recover. Lieutenant Watkins' company now had only some 30 men left and was counter-attacked by 50 enemy infantry. Lieutenant Watkins directed the fire of his men and then led a bayonet charge which resulted in the almost complete destruction of the enemy. It was now dusk and orders were given for the battalion to withdraw. These orders were not received by Watkins' company as the wireless set had been destroyed. They now found themselves alone and surrounded in depleted numbers and in failing light. Watkins decided to rejoin his battalion by passing round the flank of the enemy position through which he had advanced, but while passing through the cornfields once more he was challenged by an enemy post at close range. He ordered his men to scatter and himself charged the post with a Bren gun and silenced it. He then led the remnants of his company back to battalion headquarters.
    At the time of publication he was one of the surviving VC holders.

CURRIE, David Vivian *Major, 29th Canadian Armoured Reconnaissance Regiment (South Alberta Regiment), Canadian Armoured Corps*
    18–20 August 1944 – Major Currie was in command of a small mixed force of Canadian tanks, self-propelled anti-tank guns and infantry which was ordered to cut one of the main escape routes from the Falaise pocket, in

Normandy. This force was held up by strong enemy resistance in the village of St-Lambert-sur-Dives and two tanks were knocked out by 88mm guns. Currie immediately entered the village alone on foot at last light through the enemy outposts to reconnoitre the German defences and to extricate the crews of the disabled tanks, which he succeeded in doing in spite of heavy mortar fire. Early the following morning, without any previous artillery bombardment, Currie personally led an attack on the village in the face of fierce opposition from enemy tanks, guns and infantry and by noon had succeeded in seizing and consolidating a position halfway inside the village. During the next thirty-six hours the Germans hurled one counter-attack after another against the Canadian force but so skilfully had Currie organized his defensive position that these attacks were repulsed with severe casualties to the enemy after heavy fighting. At dusk on 20 August the Germans attempted to mount a final assault on the Canadian positions, but the attacking force was routed before it could even be deployed. Seven enemy tanks, twelve 88mm guns and forty vehicles were destroyed, 300 Germans were killed, 500 wounded and 2,100 captured. Currie then promptly ordered an attack and completed the capture of the village, thus denying the Chambois–Tijun escape route to the remnants of two German armies cut off in the Falaise pocket. Throughout three days and nights of fierce fighting, Major Currie's gallant conduct and contempt for danger set a magnificent example to all ranks of the force under his command. On one occasion he personally directed the fire of his command tank onto a Tiger tank which had been harassing his position and succeeded in knocking it out. During another attack, while the guns of his command tank were taking on other targets at longer ranges, he used a rifle from the turret to deal with individual snipers who had infiltrated to within 50 yards of his headquarters. The only time reinforcements were able to get through to his force, he himself led the 40 men forward into their positions and explained the importance of their task as a part of the defence. When, during the next attack, these new reinforcements withdrew under the intense fire brought down by the enemy, he personally collected them and led them forward into position again where, inspired by his leadership, they held for the remainder of the battle. His employment of artillery support, which became available after his original attack went in, was typical of his cool calculation of the risks involved in every situation. At one time, despite the fact that short rounds were falling within 15 yards of his own tank, he ordered fire from medium artillery to continue because of its devastating effect upon the attacking enemy in his immediate area. Throughout the operations the casualties to Major Currie's force were heavy. However, he never considered the possibility of failure or allowed it to enter the minds of his men. In the words of one of his non-commissioned officers, 'We knew at one stage that it was going to be a fight to a finish but he was so cool about it, it was impossible for us to get excited.' Since all the officers under his command were either killed or wounded during the action, Major Currie had virtually no respite from his duties and in fact obtained only one hour's sleep during the entire period. Nevertheless he did not permit his fatigue to become apparent to his troops and throughout the action took every opportunity to visit weapon pits and other defensive posts to talk to his men, to advise them as to the best use of their weapons and to cheer them with words of encouragement. When his force was finally relieved and he was satisfied that the turnover was complete he fell asleep on his feet and collapsed.

SOLOMON ISLANDS

Bougainville is the most westerly of the Solomon Islands, and in 1942 and 1943 had a Japanese garrison of about forty thousand men. It became the key point in the Japanese defence of the Solomons. The 3rd US Marine Division landed on 1 November 1943, and by January had secured a large enough area to build four airfields and station forty thousand troops. The Fijian forces landed as part of the Allies' assault on Bougainville. Large numbers of isolated Japanese remained, however, and they mounted small, unsuccessful but costly counter-attacks until 1945.

SUKANAIVALU, Sefanaia *Corporal, 3rd Bn., Fijian Infantry Regiment*
   23 June 1944 – At Mawaraka, Bougainville, in the Solomon Islands, Corporal Sukanaivalu crawled forward to rescue some men who had been wounded when their platoon was ambushed and some of the leading elements had become casualties. After two wounded men had been successfully recovered, Sukanaivalu, who was in command of the rear section, volunteered to go on farther alone to try and rescue another man in spite of machine-gun and mortar fire, but on the way back he himself was seriously wounded in the groin and thighs and fell to the ground, unable to move any farther. Several attempts were then made to rescue Corporal Sukanaivalu but without success, owing to heavy fire being encountered on each occasion, and further casualties caused. This gallant NCO then called to his men not to try and get to him as he was in a very exposed position, but they replied that they would never leave him to fall alive into the hands of the enemy. Realizing that his men would not withdraw as long as they could see that he was still alive and knowing that they were themselves all in danger of being killed or captured as long as they remained where they were, Sukanaivalu, well aware of the consequences, raised himself up in front of a Japanese machine-gun and was riddled with bullets. The remainder of the platoon retired safely.

COASTAL COMMAND

HORNELL, David Ernest *Flight Lieutenant, 162 Squadron, Royal Canadian Air Force*

24 June 1944 – Flight Lieutenant Hornell was captain and first pilot of a twin-engined amphibian aircraft engaged on an anti-submarine patrol in northern waters. The patrol had lasted for some hours when a fully surfaced U-boat was sighted, travelling at high speed on the port beam. Flight Lieutenant Hornell at once turned to the attack. The U-boat altered course. The aircraft had been seen and there could be no surprise. The U-boat opened up with anti-aircraft fire which became increasingly fierce and accurate. At a range of 1,200 yards, the front guns of the aircraft replied; then its starboard gun jammed, leaving only one gun effective. Hits were obtained on and around the conning tower of the U-boat, but the aircraft was itself hit, two large holes appearing in the starboard wing. Ignoring the enemy's fire, Hornell carefully manoeuvred for the attack. Oil was pouring from his starboard engine which was, by this time, on fire, as was the starboard wing; and the petrol tanks were endangered. Meanwhile, the aircraft was hit again and again by the U-boat's guns. Holed in many places, it was vibrating violently and very difficult to control. Nevertheless, the captain decided to press home his attack, knowing that with every moment the chances of escape for him and his gallant crew would grow more slender. He brought his aircraft down very low and released his depth charges in a perfect straddle. The bows of the U-boat were lifted out of the water; it sank and the crew were seen in the sea. Flight Lieutenant Hornell contrived, by superhuman efforts at the controls, to gain a little height. The fire in the starboard wing had grown more intense and the vibration had increased. Then the burning engine fell off. The plight of aircraft and crew was now desperate. With the utmost coolness, the captain took his aircraft into wind and, despite the manifold dangers, brought it safely down on the heavy swell. Badly damaged and blazing furiously, the aircraft rapidly settled. After ordeal by fire came ordeal by water. There was only one serviceable dinghy and this could not hold all the crew. So they took turns in the water, holding on to the sides. Once, the dinghy capsized in the rough seas and was righted only with great difficulty. Two of the crew succumbed from exposure. An airborne lifeboat was dropped to them but fell some 500 yards downwind. The men struggled vainly to reach it and Hornell, who throughout had encouraged them by his cheerfulness and inspiring leadership, proposed to swim to it though he was nearly exhausted. He was with difficulty restrained. The survivors were finally rescued after they had been in the water for twenty-one hours. By this time Hornell was blind and completely exhausted. He died shortly after being picked up.

CRUICKSHANK, John Alexander *Flying Officer, 210 Squadron, Royal Air Force Volunteer Reserve*

17/18 July 1944 – This officer was the captain and pilot of a Catalina flying boat which was recently engaged on an anti-submarine patrol over northern waters. When a U-boat was sighted on the surface, Flying Officer Cruickshank at once turned to the attack. In the face of fierce anti-aircraft fire he manoeuvred into position and ran in to release his depth charges. Unfortunately they failed to drop. Cruickshank knew that the failure of this attack had deprived him of the advantage of surprise and that his aircraft offered a good target to the enemy's determined and now heartened gunners. Without hesitation, he climbed and turned to come in again. The Catalina was met by intense and accurate fire and was repeatedly hit. The navigator/bomb aimer was killed. The second pilot and two other members of the crew were injured. Cruickshank was struck in seventy-two places, receiving two serious wounds in the lungs and ten penetrating wounds in the lower limbs. His aircraft was badly damaged and filled with the fumes of exploding shells. But he did not falter. He pressed home his attack and released the depth charges himself, straddling the submarine perfectly. The U-boat was sunk. He then collapsed and the second pilot took over the controls. He recovered shortly afterwards and, though bleeding profusely, insisted on resuming command and retaining it until he was satisfied that the damaged aircraft was under control, that a course had been set for base and that all the necessary signals had been sent. Only then would he consent to receive medical aid and have his wounds attended to. He refused morphia in case it might prevent him from carrying on. During the next five and a half hours of the return flight he several times lapsed into unconsciousness owing to loss of blood. When he came to, his first thought on each occasion was for the safety of his aircraft and crew. The damaged aircraft eventually reached base but it was clear that an immediate landing would be a hazardous task for the wounded and less experienced second pilot. Although able to breathe only with the greatest difficulty, Cruickshank insisted on being carried forward and propped up in the second pilot's seat. For a full hour, in spite of his agony and ever-increasing weakness, he gave orders as necessary, refusing to allow the aircraft to be brought down until the conditions of light and sea made this possible without undue risk. With his assistance the aircraft was safely landed on the water. He then directed the taxiing and beaching of the aircraft so that it could easily be salvaged. When the medical officer went on board, Flying Officer Cruickshank collapsed and he had to be given a blood transfusion before he could be removed to hospital.

In March 2004 the Queen unveiled the first national monument to Coastal Command at Westminster Abbey. Cruickshank said in an interview after the ceremony: 'When they told me that I was to get the VC it was unbelievable. Decorations didn't enter my head. The citation said "showed great courage" and all that nonsense, but a lot of people would have done that in the circumstances.' Four VCs were awarded to Coastal Command in the war; the others were posthumous, and he was at the time of publication the last surviving member of the RAF to hold the VC.

ARNHEM: OPERATION MARKET GARDEN

Although Brussels was liberated on 3 September and Antwerp, except the docks, on the 4th, there were large numbers of Germans still in the Pas de Calais and the Allies still had no port for resupply nearer than Cherbourg. Rather than clear the River Scheldt progressively, so that Antwerp could be taken, Montgomery proposed to cut through to the Ruhr: the Airborne Army, thirty thousand men in two American and one British divisions and the Polish Airborne Brigade, would capture key bridges at Eindhoven, Nijmegen and Arnhem. Nijmegen is 30 miles north-north-east of Eindhoven and Arnhem another 10: 30th Corps's tanks would move up this 'airborne carpet', cross the bridges and drive forward into Germany. This strike would cut off the Germans in Holland and thus clear the Scheldt.

The drops took place on 17, 18 and 19 September. The road up which 30th Corps had to travel was narrow and well defended, and it only advanced 7 miles on the 17th, but the 101st Airborne Division had taken the bridges at Eindhoven. On the 19th 30th Corps reached the 82nd Airborne Division at Nijmegen, only to find the bridge still in German hands. The 82nd Airborne crossed the Rhine, took the Nijmegen bridge and 30th Corps crossed. At Arnhem, however, events had not gone to plan. The 1st Parachute Brigade had landed eight miles from the bridge, and found two SS Panzer Divisions recuperating between it and its objective. Only the 2nd Battalion reached the bridge, and the rest were still a mile away at nightfall on the 18th. Reinforcements arrived that day in a second drop, but made little progress against well-deployed tanks and artillery. On the 20th the attempt to reach the bridge was abandoned and a defensive perimeter was established at Oosterbeek, about three miles west. On the 21st, with their three days' supplies of food and ammunition exhausted, the 2nd Battalion at the bridge surrendered: the remainder of 1st Airborne Division withdrew across the river. Approximately 10,600 men had fought at Arnhem: 2,398 escaped.

GRAYBURN, John Hollington *Lieutenant, 2nd Parachute Bn.*

17–20 September 1944 – Lieutenant Grayburn was a platoon commander of the parachute battalion which was dropped on 17 September, with the task of seizing and holding the bridge over the Rhine at Arnhem. The north end of the bridge was captured and, early in the night, Grayburn was ordered to assault and capture the southern end with his platoon. He led his platoon onto the bridge and began the attack with the utmost determination, but the platoon was met by a hail of fire from two 20mm quick-firing guns and from the machine-guns of an armoured car. Almost at once Grayburn was shot through the shoulder. Although there was no cover on the bridge, and in spite of his wound, Grayburn continued to press forward with the greatest dash and bravery until casualties became so heavy that he was ordered to withdraw. He directed the withdrawal from the bridge personally and was himself the last man to come off the embankment into comparative cover. Later, his platoon was ordered to occupy a house which was vital to the defence of the bridge and he personally organized its occupation. Throughout the next day and night the enemy made ceaseless attacks on the house, using not only infantry with mortars and machine-guns but also tanks and self-propelled guns. The house was very exposed and difficult to defend and the fact that it did not fall to the enemy must be attributed to his great courage and inspiring leadership. He constantly exposed himself to the enemy's fire while moving among his platoon, and seemed completely oblivious to danger. On 19 September, the enemy renewed his attacks, which increased in intensity, as the house was vital to the defence of the bridge. All attacks were repulsed, due to Grayburn's valour and skill in organizing and encouraging his men, until eventually the house was set on fire and had to be evacuated. Grayburn then took command of elements of all arms, including the remainder of his own company, and re-formed them into a fighting force. He spent the night organizing a defensive position to cover the approaches to the bridge. On 20 September, he extended his defence by a series of fighting patrols which prevented the enemy gaining access to the houses in the vicinity, the occupation of which would have prejudiced the defence of the bridge. This forced the enemy to bring up tanks which brought Lieutenant Grayburn's positions under such heavy fire that he was forced to withdraw to an area farther north. The enemy now attempted to lay demolition charges under the bridge and the situation was critical. Realizing this, Grayburn organized and led a fighting patrol which drove the enemy off temporarily, and gave time for the fuses to be removed. He was again wounded, this time in the back, but refused to be evacuated. Finally, an enemy tank, against which Lieutenant Grayburn had no defence, approached so close to his position that it became untenable. He then stood up in full view of the tank and personally directed the withdrawal of his men to the main defensive perimeter to which he had been ordered. He was killed that night.

CAIN, Robert Henry *T/Major, Royal Northumberland Fusiliers, attached 2nd Bn., South Staffordshire Regiment*

19–25 September 1944 – Major Cain was commanding a rifle company of the South Staffordshire Regiment during the Battle of Arnhem, Holland, when his company was cut off from the rest of the battalion and during the next six days was closely engaged with enemy tanks, self-propelled guns and infantry. The Germans made repeated attempts to break into the company position by infiltration and had they succeeded in doing so the whole situation of the airborne troops would have been jeopardized. Cain, by his outstanding devotion to duty and remarkable powers of leadership, was to a large extent personally responsible for saving a vital sector from falling into the hands of the enemy. On 20 September a Tiger tank approached the area held by his company and Cain went out alone to deal with it armed with a PIAT. Taking up a position, he held his fire until the tank was only 20 yards away. The tank immediately halted and turned its guns on him, shooting away a corner of the house near where this officer was lying. Although wounded by machine-gun bullets and falling masonry, Cain continued firing until he had scored several direct hits, immobilized the tank and supervised the bringing up of a 75mm howitzer which completely destroyed it. Only then would he consent to have his wounds dressed. The next morning this officer drove off three more tanks by the fearless use of his PIAT, on each occasion leaving cover and taking up position in open ground with complete disregard for his personal safety. During the following days, Major Cain was everywhere where danger threatened, moving amongst his men and encouraging them by his fearless example to hold out. He refused rest and medical attention in spite of the fact that his hearing had been seriously impaired because of a perforated eardrum and he was suffering from multiple wounds. On 25 September the enemy made a concerted attack on his position using self-propelled guns, flame-throwers and infantry. By this time the last PIAT had been put out of action and Major Cain was armed with only a light 2in mortar. However, by skilful use of this weapon and his daring leadership of the few men still under his command, he completely demoralized the enemy who, after an engagement lasting more than three hours, withdrew in disorder.

LORD, David Samuel Anthony *Flight Lieutenant, 271 Squadron, Royal Air Force*

19 September 1944 – Lord was pilot and captain of a Dakota aircraft detailed to drop supplies at Arnhem on the afternoon of 19 September. Allied airborne troops had been surrounded and were being pressed into a small area defended by a large number of anti-aircraft guns. Aircrews were warned that intense opposition would be met over the dropping zone. To ensure accuracy they were ordered to fly at 900 feet when dropping their containers. While flying at 1,500 feet near Arnhem the starboard wing of Flight Lieutenant Lord's aircraft was twice hit by anti-aircraft fire and the starboard engine was set on fire. He would have been justified in leaving the stream of supply aircraft and continuing at the same height or even abandoning his aircraft. But on learning that his crew were uninjured and that the dropping zone would be reached in three minutes he said he would complete his mission as the troops were in dire need of supplies. By now the starboard engine was burning furiously. Lord came down to 900 feet, where he was singled out for the concentrated fire of all the anti-aircraft guns. On reaching the dropping zone he kept the aircraft on a straight and level course while supplies were dropped. At the end of the run, he was told that two containers remained. Although he must have known that the collapse of the starboard wing could not be long delayed, Lord circled, rejoined the stream of aircraft and made a second run to drop the remaining supplies. These manoeuvres took eight minutes in all, the aircraft being continuously under heavy anti-aircraft fire. His task completed, Lord ordered his crew to abandon the Dakota, making no attempt himself to leave the aircraft, which was down to 500 feet. A few seconds later, the starboard wing collapsed and the aircraft fell in flames. There was only one survivor, who was flung out while assisting other members of the crew to put on their parachutes.

The sole survivor was Pilot Officer Harry King. He was taken prisoner and it was not until he was released at the end of the war that he was able to report Lord's extraordinary sacrifice. Lord was the only member of Transport Command to receive the VC. The Chief of the Air Staff, Lord Portal, wrote to Lord's parents: 'I have read of many great deeds for which the Victoria Cross has been awarded but I do not remember one that surpassed in gallantry the action of your son.'

QUERIPEL, Lionel Ernest *Captain, Royal Sussex Regiment, attached 10th Parachute Bn.*

19 September 1944 – Captain Queripel was acting as company commander of a composite company composed of men from three parachute battalions. At 1400 hours, his company was advancing along a main road which ran on an embankment towards Arnhem, Holland. The advance was conducted under continuous medium machine-gun fire which, at one period, became so heavy that the company became split up on either side of the road and suffered considerable losses. Queripel at once proceeded to reorganize his force, crossing and re-crossing the road whilst doing so under extremely heavy and accurate fire. During this period he carried a wounded sergeant to the regimental aid post under fire and was himself wounded in the face. Having reorganized his force, he personally led a party of men against the strongpoint holding up the advance. This strongpoint consisted of a captured British anti-tank gun and two machine-guns. Despite the extremely heavy fire directed at him, Queripel succeeded in killing the crews of the machine-guns and recapturing the anti-tank gun. As a result of this, the advance was able to continue. Later in the same day, Queripel found himself cut off with a small party of men and took up a position in a ditch. By this time he had received further wounds in both arms. Regardless of his wounds and of the very heavy mortar and Spandau fire, he continued to inspire his men to resist with hand grenades, pistols and the few remaining rifles. As, however, the enemy pressure increased, Queripel decided that it was impossible to hold the position any longer and ordered his men to withdraw. Despite their protests, he insisted on remaining behind to cover their withdrawal with his automatic pistol and a few remaining hand grenades. This is the last occasion on which he was seen.

BASKEYFIELD, John Daniel *Lance Sergeant, 2nd Bn., South Staffordshire Regiment*

20 September 1944 – During the Battle of Arnhem, Lance Sergeant Baskeyfield was the NCO in charge of a 6pdr anti-tank gun at Oosterbeek. The enemy developed a major attack on this sector with infantry, tanks and self-propelled guns with the obvious intent to break into and overrun the battalion position. During the early stage of the action the crew commanded by Baskeyfield was responsible for the destruction of two Tiger tanks and at least one self-propelled gun, thanks to the coolness and daring of this NCO, who, with complete disregard for his own safety, allowed each tank to come within 100 yards of his gun before opening fire. In the course of this preliminary engagement Baskeyfield was badly wounded in the leg and the remainder of his crew were either killed or badly wounded. During the brief respite after this engagement Baskeyfield refused to be carried to the regimental aid post and spent his time attending to his gun and shouting encouragement to his comrades in neighbouring trenches. After a short interval the enemy renewed the attack with even greater ferocity than before under cover of intense mortar and shell fire. Manning his gun quite alone Baskeyfield continued to fire round after round at the enemy until his gun was put out of action. By this time his activity was the main factor in keeping the enemy tanks at bay. The fact that the surviving men in his vicinity were held together and kept in action was undoubtedly due to his magnificent example and outstanding courage. Time after time enemy attacks were driven off. Finally, when his gun was knocked out, he crawled, under intense enemy fire, to another 6pdr gun nearby, the crew of which had been killed, and proceeded to man it single-handed. With this gun he engaged an enemy self-propelled gun which was approaching to attack. Another soldier crawled across the open ground to assist him but was killed almost at once. Baskeyfield succeeded in firing two rounds at the self-propelled gun, scoring one direct hit which rendered it ineffective. Whilst preparing to fire a third shot, however, he was killed by a shell from a supporting enemy tank.

HOLLAND

Antwerp was cleared for shipping on 28 November. The final VC in Europe that year was won in the attempt to force the Germans back over the Maas/

Meuse: in some of the fiercest fighting of the war, the small village of Overloon was taken after two weeks' struggle.

HARPER, John William *Corporal, 4th Bn York and Lancaster Regiment*

29 September 1944 – The Hallamshire Battalion of the York and Lancaster Regiment attacked the Depot de Mendicité, Antwerp, a natural defensive position surrounded by an earthen wall and then a dyke, strongly held by the enemy. Corporal Harper was commanding the leading section in the assault. The enemy were well dug in and had a perfect field of fire across 300 yards of completely flat and exposed country. With superb disregard for the hail of mortar bombs and small-arms fire which the enemy brought to bear on this open ground, Harper led his section straight up to the wall and killed or captured the enemy holding the near side. During this operation the platoon commander was seriously wounded and Harper took over control of the platoon. As the enemy on the far side of the wall were now throwing grenades over the top, Corporal Harper climbed over the wall alone, throwing grenades, and in the face of heavy, close-range small-arms fire, personally routed the Germans directly opposing him. He took 4 prisoners and shot several of the remainder of the enemy as they fled. Still completely ignoring the heavy Spandau and mortar fire which was sweeping the area, once again he crossed the wall alone to find out whether it was possible for his platoon to wade the dyke which lay beyond. He found the dyke too deep and wide to cross, and once again he came back over the wall and received orders to try and establish his platoon on the enemy side of it. For the third time he climbed over alone, found some empty German weapon pits, and providing the covering fire urged and encouraged his section to scale the wall and dash for cover. By this action he was able to bring down sufficient covering fire to enable the rest of the company to cross the open ground and surmount the wall for the loss of only 1 man. Harper then left his platoon in charge of his senior section commander and walked alone along the banks of the dyke, in the face of heavy Spandau fire, to find a crossing place. Eventually he made contact with the battalion attacking on his right, and found that they had located a ford. Back he came across the open ground, and, whilst directing his company commander to the ford, he was struck by a bullet which fatally wounded him and he died on the bank of the dyke.

EARDLEY, George Harold *A/Sergeant, 4th Bn., King's Shropshire Light Infantry*

16 October 1944 – During an attack on a wooded area east of Overloon, Holland, strong opposition was met from well-sited defensive positions in orchards. The enemy were paratroops and well equipped with machine-guns. A platoon of the King's Shropshire Light Infantry was ordered to clear the orchards and so restore the momentum of the advance, but was halted some 80 yards from its objective by automatic fire from enemy machine-gun posts. This fire was so heavy that it appeared impossible for any man to expose himself and remain unscathed. Notwithstanding this, Sergeant Eardley, who had spotted one machine-gun post, moved forward firing his Sten gun, and killed the occupants of the post with a grenade. A second machine-gun post beyond the first immediately opened up, spraying the area with fire. Eardley, who was in a most exposed position, at once charged over 30 yards of open ground and silenced both the enemy gunners. The attack was continued by the platoon but was again held up by a third machine-gun post, and a section sent in to dispose of it was beaten back, losing four casualties. Eardley, ordering the section he was with to lie down, then crawled forward alone and silenced the occupants of the post with a grenade.

For a private soldier to be an acting sergeant was rare, but Eardley, who already held an MM, had shown leadership qualities. A long campaign by his son resulted in a memorial statue being erected in Eardley's home town of Oswestry in April 2004.

THE BURMA CAMPAIGN: ARAKAN II

In the Arakan, 15th Corps was withdrawn from Buthidaung to secure positions before the monsoon broke. For the campaigning season of November 1944 to May 1945, it was placed under Lieutenant General Sir Oliver Leese, who had commanded 8th Army in Italy, and was appointed to the new position of Commander-in-Chief Allied Land Forces South East Asia. Its new role was to drive the Japanese 28th Army from Arakan and to take the airfields at Akyab and Ramree that would supply 14th Army in its drive to Rangoon, and then to join the amphibious assault on Rangoon. A VC was won by Sepoy Bhandari Ram in preparatory advances, and the offensive began on 12 December. 28th Army's orders were to delay the advance long enough to allow the main force to cross to the Irrawaddy to defend against 14th Army, and Akyab was taken on 3 January. To the east the 81st West African Division advanced down the valley of the Kaladan River, and met strong resistance in the capture of Myohaung, a river crossing and the Japanese strongpoint in the valley, where Havildar Umrao Singh won his VC.

BHANDARI RAM *Sepoy, 16th Bn., 10th Baluch Regiment*
   22 November 1944 – In East Mayu, Arakan, during a company attack on a strongly held Japanese bunker position, Sepoy Bhandari Ram was in the leading section of one of the platoons. In order to reach its objective, it was necessary to climb a precipitous slope by way of a narrow ridge with sheer sides. When 50 yards from the top of the slope, the leading section of the platoon came under heavy and accurate machine-gun fire. Three men were wounded, amongst them Bhandari Ram, who received a burst of light machine-gun fire in his left shoulder and a wound in his leg. The platoon

was pinned down by intense enemy fire. Bhandari Ram then crawled up to the Japanese light machine-gun, whilst in full view of the enemy, and approached to within 15 yards of the enemy position. The enemy then hurled grenades at him, seriously wounding him in the face and chest. Undeterred, severely wounded by bullets and grenade splinters and bespattered with blood, Bhandari Ram, with superhuman courage and determination, crawled up to within five yards of his objective. He then threw a grenade into the position, killing the enemy gunner and two other men, and continued his crawl to the post. Inspired by his example, the platoon rushed up and captured the position. It was only after the position had been taken that he lay down and allowed his wounds to be dressed.

Interviewed in 1999, he explained his gallantry: it was 'all to do with wanting to please commanding officers by doing a good job.'

UMRAO SINGH *Havildar, Royal Indian Artillery*

15–16 December – In the Kaladan Valley in Burma, Havildar Umrao Singh was in charge of one gun in an advanced section of his battery when it was subjected to heavy fire from 75mm guns and mortars for some time prior to being attacked by two companies of Japanese. When the attack came he so inspired his gun detachment by his personal example and encouragement to fight and defend their gun that they were able to beat off the attack with losses to the enemy. Though twice wounded by grenades in the first attack, he held off the second by skilful control of his detachment's small-arms fire, and by manning a Bren gun himself which he fired over the shield of his gun at the Japanese who had got to within five yards. Again the enemy were beaten off with heavy losses. Third and fourth attacks were also beaten off in the same manner by his resolute action and great courage. By this time all his gun detachment had been killed or wounded with the exception of himself and two others. When the final attack came, the other gun having been overrun and all his ammunition expended, he seized a gun bearer and, calling once again on all who remained, closed with the enemy in furious hand-to-hand fighting and was seen to strike down three Japanese in a desperate effort to save his gun until he was overwhelmed and knocked senseless. Six hours later, when a counter-attack recovered the position, he was found in an exhausted state beside his gun and almost unrecognizable with seven severe wounds and ten dead Japanese round him.

At the time of publication, Umrao Singh was one of the surviving VC holders.

1945

At the start of the year, Allied troops were still tied down in Italy. In northern Europe they needed time to regroup after the German counterattack in the Ardennes – but there was now no doubt that both Germany and Japan were on the edge of defeat.

The final objective was the complete conquest of Germany. As Russian troops advanced from the east, Allied bombers attacked Dresden on 14 February. On the ground, the advance swept through to take Remagen, Wiesbaden, Frankfurt and the Rhineland by the beginning of April. As the Allies encircled Berlin, Hitler and Eva Braun committed suicide on 30 April – perhaps hoping to avoid the fate of Mussolini and his mistress, who had been captured and killed in Italy two days before. On 2 May Hamburg surrendered to the British, and German commanders were sent to discuss peace terms with Montgomery at Lüneburg Heath. German forces in Italy surrendered with effect from 6 p.m. on 2 May. On 5 May German forces in north-west Germany, Holland and Denmark surrendered. On 7 May all remaining German forces surrendered, with effect from one minute past midnight, British time, on 8 May.

The British continued to make good progress in the Far East, as Indian divisions crossed the Irrawaddy, south of Mandalay and Allied forces pressed on to take Meiktila and Mandalay in March. The Americans delivered the final blow against the Japanese. In an island-hopping drive through the Pacific, US forces landed in the Philippines, Iwo Jima and Okinawa where fierce fighting against a well-entrenched enemy cost a high toll in lives, but on 5 July the Philippines were liberated. The Japanese fleet was destroyed in Tokyo Bay in late July by Allied air attacks. With the dropping of atomic bombs on Hiroshima and Nagasaki, the Japanese were driven to offer conditional surrender on 10 August and to accept unconditional surrender on 14 August.

BOMBER COMMAND

THOMPSON, George *Flight Sergeant, 9 Squadron, Royal Air Force Volunteer Reserve*
1 January 1945 – This airman was the wireless operator in a Lancaster aircraft which attacked the Dortmund–Ems Canal in daylight on 1 January

1945. The bombs had just been released when a heavy shell hit the aircraft in front of the mid-upper turret. Fire broke out and dense smoke filled the fuselage. The nose of the aircraft was then hit and an inrush of air, clearing the smoke, revealed a scene of utter devastation. Most of the perspex screen of the nose compartment had been shot away, gaping holes had been torn in the canopy above the pilot's head, the intercom wiring was severed, and there was a large hole in the floor of the aircraft. Bedding and other equipment were badly damaged or alight; one engine was on fire. Flight Sergeant Thompson saw that the gunner was unconscious in the blazing mid-upper turret. Without hesitation he went down the fuselage into the fire and the exploding ammunition. He pulled the gunner from his turret and, edging his way round the hole in the floor, carried him away from the flames. With his bare hands, he extinguished the gunner's burning clothing. He himself sustained serious burns on his face, hands and legs. Thompson then noticed that the rear gun turret was also on fire. Despite his own severe injuries he moved to the rear of the fuselage where he found the rear gunner with his clothing alight, overcome by flames and fumes. A second time Thompson braved the flames. With great difficulty he extricated the helpless gunner and carried him clear. Again, he used his bare hands, already burnt, to beat out flames on a comrade's clothing. Thompson, by now almost exhausted, felt that his duty was yet not done. He must report the fate of the crew to the captain. He made the perilous journey back through the burning fuselage, clinging to the sides with his burnt hands to get across the hole in the floor. The flow of cold air caused him intense pain and frostbite developed. So pitiful was his condition that his captain failed to recognize him. Still, his only concern was for the two gunners he had left in the rear of the aircraft. He was given such attention as was possible until a crash-landing was made some forty minutes later. When the aircraft was hit, Thompson might have devoted his efforts to quelling the fire and so have contributed to his own safety. He preferred to go through the fire to succour his comrades. He knew that he would then be in no position to hear or heed any order which might be given to abandon aircraft. He hazarded his own life in order to save the lives of others. Young in years and experience, his actions were those of a veteran. Three weeks later Flight Sergeant Thompson died of his injuries. One of the gunners unfortunately also died, but the other owes his life to the superb gallantry of Thompson, whose signal courage and self-sacrifice will ever be an inspiration to the service.

SWALES, Edwin *Captain, South African Air Force, serving with*
582 Squadron, Royal Air Force

23 February 1945 – Captain Swales was master bomber of a force of aircraft which attacked Pforzheim on the night of 23 February 1945. As master bomber, he had the task of locating the target area with precision and of giving aiming instructions to the main force of bombers following in his wake. Soon after he had reached the target area he was engaged by an enemy fighter and one of his engines was put out of action. His rear guns failed. His crippled aircraft was an easy prey to further attacks. Unperturbed, he carried on with his allotted task: clearly and precisely he issued aiming instructions to the main force. Meanwhile the enemy fighter closed the range and fired again. A second engine of Swales's aircraft was put out of action. Almost defenceless, he stayed over the target area issuing his aiming instructions until he was satisfied that the attack had achieved its purpose. It is now known that the attack was one of the most concentrated and successful of the war. Swales did not, however, regard his mission as completed. His aircraft was damaged. Its speed had been so much reduced that it could only with difficulty be kept in the air. The blind-flying instruments were no longer working. Determined at all costs to prevent his aircraft and crew from falling into enemy hands, he set course for home. After an hour he flew into thin-layered cloud. He kept his course by skilful flying between the layers, but later heavy cloud and turbulent air conditions were met. The aircraft, by now over friendly territory, became more and more difficult to control; it was losing height steadily. Realizing that the situation was desperate Swales ordered his crew to bale out. Time was very short and it required all his exertions to keep the aircraft steady while each of his crew moved in turn to the escape hatch and parachuted to safety. Hardly had the last crew member jumped when the aircraft plunged to earth. Captain Swales was found dead at the controls. Intrepid in the attack, courageous in the face of danger, he did his duty to the last, giving his life that his comrades might live.

THE DRIVE TO THE RHINE

December and January were spent in operations in Holland and Belgium up to and then beyond the Meuse/Maas. Once that was clear, Field Marshal Montgomery planned to move from Eindhoven as far as Wesel, about 30 miles inside Germany, securing the area north to the Meuse. 1st Commando Brigade was under command of 7th Armoured Division, engaged between the Maas and Roer. The German offensive in the Ardennes delayed the planned attack until 8 February, but the Germans had been thrown back by 10 March; at that date there were no Germans left west of the Rhine.

DONNINI, Dennis *Fusilier, 4/5th Bn., Royal Scots Fusiliers*
    18 January 1945 – On 18 January 1945, a battalion of the Royal Scots Fusiliers supported by tanks was the leading battalion in the assault of the German position between the Rivers Roer and Maas. This consisted of a broad belt of minefields and wire on the other side of a stream. As the result of a thaw the armour was unable to cross the stream and the infantry had

to continue the assault without the support of the tanks. Fusilier Donnini's platoon was ordered to attack a small village. As they left their trenches the platoon came under concentrated machine-gun and rifle fire from the houses and Donnini was hit by a bullet in the head. After a few minutes he recovered consciousness, charged down 30 yards of open road and threw a grenade into the nearest window. The enemy fled through the gardens of four houses, closely pursued by Donnini and the survivors of his platoon. Under heavy fire at 70 yards' range Fusilier Donnini and two companions crossed an open space and reached the cover of a wooden barn, 30 yards from the enemy trenches. Donnini, still bleeding profusely from his wound, went into the open under intense close-range fire and carried one of his companions, who had been wounded, into the barn. Taking a Bren gun he again went into the open, firing as he went. He was wounded a second time but recovered and went on firing until a third bullet hit a grenade which he was carrying and killed him. The superb gallantry and self-sacrifice of Fusilier Donnini drew the enemy fire away from his companions on to himself. As the result of this, the platoon were able to capture the position, accounting for 30 Germans and two machine-guns. Throughout this action, fought from beginning to end at point-blank range, the dash, determination and magnificent courage of Fusilier Donnini enabled his comrades to overcome an enemy more than twice their own number.

HARDEN, Henry Eric *Lance Corporal, Royal Army Medical Corps, attached 45 Commando Royal Marines*
     23 January 1945 – At Brachterbeek, Holland, the leading section of a Royal Marine Commando troop was pinned to the ground by intense enemy machine-gun fire from well-concealed positions. As it was impossible to engage the enemy from the open owing to lack of cover, the section was ordered to make for some nearby houses. This move was accomplished, but 1 officer and 3 other-rank casualties were left lying in the open. The whole troop position was under continuous heavy and accurate shell and mortar fire. Lance Corporal Harden, the RAMC orderly attached to the troop, at once went forward a distance of 120 yards into the open under a hail of enemy machine-gun and rifle fire directed from four positions, all within 300 yards, and with the greatest coolness and bravery remained in the open while he attended to the four casualties. After dressing the wounds of three of them, he carried one back to cover. Harden was then ordered not to go forward again and an attempt was made to bring in the other casualties with the aid of tanks, but this proved unsuccessful owing to the heavy and accurate fire of enemy anti-tank guns. A further attempt was then made to recover the casualties under a smokescreen, but this only increased the enemy fire in the vicinity of the casualties. Harden then insisted on going forward again, with a volunteer stretcher party, and succeeded in bringing back another badly wounded man. Harden went out a third time, again with

a stretcher party, and after starting on the return journey with the wounded officer, under very heavy enemy small-arms and mortar fire, he was killed. Throughout this long period Lance Corporal Harden displayed superb devotion to duty and personal courage of the very highest order, and there is no doubt that had a most steadying effect upon the other troops in the area at a most critical time. His action was directly responsible for saving the lives of the wounded brought in. His complete contempt for all personal danger and the magnificent example he set of cool courage and determination to continue with his work, whatever the odds, was an inspiration to his comrades, and will never be forgotten by those who saw it.

Harden was the only member of the RAMC to be awarded the VC in the Second World War.

COSENS, Aubrey *Sergeant, 1st Bn., Queen's Own Rifles of Canada, Canadian Infantry Corps*

25/26 February 1945 – In Holland, on the night of 25/26 February 1945, the 1st Battalion Queen's Own Rifles of Canada launched an attack on the hamlet of Mooshof, to capture ground which was considered essential for the successful development of future operations. Sergeant Cosens' platoon, with two tanks in support, attacked enemy strongpoints in three farm buildings, but was twice beaten back by fanatical enemy resistance and then fiercely counter-attacked, during which time the platoon suffered heavy casualties and the platoon commander was killed. Cosens at once assumed command of the only other four survivors of his platoon, whom he placed in a position to give him covering fire, while he himself ran across open ground under heavy mortar and shell fire to the one remaining tank, where, regardless of danger, he took up an exposed position in front of the turret and directed its fire. After a further enemy counter-attack had been repulsed, Cosens ordered the tank to attack the farm buildings, while the four survivors of his platoon followed in close support. After the tank had rammed the first building he entered it alone, killing several of the defenders and taking the rest prisoner. Single-handed he then entered the second and third buildings and personally killed or captured all the occupants, although under intense machine-gun and small-arms fire. Just after the successful reduction of these important enemy strongpoints, Sergeant Cosens was shot through the head by an enemy sniper and died almost instantly. The outstanding gallantry, initiative and determined leadership of this brave NCO, who himself killed at least 20 of the enemy and took an equal number of prisoners, resulted in the capture of a position which was vital to the success of the future operations of the brigade.

STOKES, James *Private, 2nd Bn., King's Shropshire Light Infantry*

1 March 1945 – In Holland, during the attack on Kervenheim, Private Stokes was a member of the leading section of a platoon. During the advance the platoon came under intense rifle and machine-gun fire from a farm building and was pinned down. The platoon commander began to reorganize the platoon when Stokes, without waiting for any orders, got up and, firing from the hip, dashed through the enemy fire and was seen to disappear inside the farm building. The enemy fire stopped and Stokes reappeared with 12 prisoners. During this operation he was wounded in the neck. This action enabled the platoon to continue the advance to the next objective, and Stokes was ordered back to the regimental aid post. He refused to go and continued the advance with his platoon. On approaching the second objective the platoon again came under heavy fire from a house on the left. Again without waiting for orders, Stokes rushed the house by himself, firing from the hip. He was seen to drop his rifle and fall to the ground wounded. However, a moment later he got to his feet again, picked up his rifle and continued to advance despite the most intense fire, which covered not only himself but the rest of the platoon. He entered the house and all firing from it ceased. He subsequently rejoined his platoon who, due to his gallantry, had been able to advance, bringing five more prisoners. At this stage the company was forming up for its final assault on the objective, which was a group of buildings forming an enemy strongpoint. Again without waiting for orders, Stokes, although now severely wounded and suffering from loss of blood, dashed on the remaining 60 yards to the objective, firing from the hip as he struggled through intense fire. He finally fell 20 yards from the enemy position, firing his rifle until the last, and as the company passed him in the final charge he raised his hand and shouted goodbye. Stokes was found to have been wounded eight times in the upper part of the body. Private Stokes's one object throughout this action was to kill the enemy, at whatever personal risk. His magnificent courage, devotion to duty and splendid example inspired all those round him and ensured the success of the attack at a critical moment; moreover, his self-sacrifice saved his platoon and company many serious casualties.

Stokes had been convicted of GBH during a fight in a Glasgow dance hall. The judge gave him the choice of serving a long sentence or joining a front-line infantry regiment in the invasion of Europe.

TILSTON, Frederick Albert *A/Major, Essex Scottish Regiment, Canadian Infantry Corps*

1 March 1945 – The 2nd Canadian Division had been given the task of breaking through the strongly fortified Hochwald forest defence line which covered Xanten, the last German bastion west of the Rhine protecting the vital Wesel bridge escape route. The Essex Scottish Regiment was ordered to breach the defence line north-east of Udem and to clear the northern half of the forest, through which the balance of the brigade would pass. At 0715 hours on 1 March 1945, the attack was launched but due to the softness of the ground it was found impossible to support the attack by tanks as had been planned. Across approximately 500 yards of flat open country, in the

face of intense enemy fire, Major Tilston personally led his company in the attack, keeping dangerously close to supporting bursting shells in order to get the maximum cover from the barrage. Though wounded in the head he continued to lead his men forward, through a belt of wire ten feet in depth to the enemy trenches shouting orders and encouragement and using his Sten gun with great effect. When the platoon on the left came under heavy fire from an enemy machine-gun post he dashed forward and silenced it with a grenade; he was first to reach the enemy position and took the first prisoner. Determined to maintain the momentum of the attack he ordered the reserve platoon to mop up these positions and with outstanding gallantry pressed on with his main force to the second line of enemy defences, which were on the edge of the woods. As he approached the woods he was severely wounded in the hip and fell to the ground. Shouting to his men to carry on without him and urging them to get into the wood, he struggled to his feet and rejoined them as they reached the trenches on their objective. Here an elaborate system of dugouts and trenches was manned in considerable strength and vicious hand-to-hand fighting followed. Despite his wounds, Tilston's unyielding will to close with the enemy was a magnificent inspiration to his men as he led them in, systematically clearing the trenches of the fiercely resisting enemy. In this fighting two German company headquarters were overrun and many casualties were inflicted on the fanatical defenders. Such had been the grimness of the fighting and so savage the enemy resistance that the company was now reduced to only 26 men, one quarter of its original strength. Before consolidation could be completed the enemy counter-attacked repeatedly, supported by mortar and machine-gun fire from the open flank. Tilston moved in the open from platoon to platoon quickly organizing their defence and directing fire against the advancing enemy. The enemy attacks penetrated so close to the positions that grenades were thrown into the trenches held by his troops, but this officer, by personal contact, unshakeable confidence and unquenchable enthusiasm, so inspired his men that they held firm against great odds. When the supply of ammunition became a serious problem he repeatedly crossed the bullet-swept ground to the company on his right flank to carry grenades, rifle and Bren ammunition to his troops and replace a damaged wireless set to re-establish communications with battalion headquarters. He made at least six of these hazardous trips, each time crossing a road which was dominated by intense fire from numerous enemy machine-gun posts. On his last trip he was wounded for the third time, this time in the leg. He was found in a shell crater beside the road. Although very seriously wounded and barely conscious, he would not submit to medical attention until he had given complete instructions as to the defence plan, had emphasized the absolute necessity of holding the position and had ordered his one remaining officer to take over. By his calm courage, gallant conduct and total disregard for his own safety, he fired his men with grim determination and their firm stand enabled the regiment to accomplish its object of furnishing the brigade with a solid base through which to launch further successful attacks to clear the forest, thus enabling the division to accomplish its task.

He lost both his legs, but not his sense of humour. When asked by a reporter what quality was most important to winning a VC, he replied, 'Inexperience.' When he was lying in bed after his legs had been amputated, an over-zealous Red Cross lady came fussing down the ward, asking each man what was wrong with him. When it came to his turn, Tilston eyed her cryptically and said, 'A bad case of athlete's foot, madam, both feet.'

GERMANY: THE RHINE CROSSING

The Rhine was crossed by the Americans on 22/23 March near Oppenheim and by the British and Canadians in three places near Wesel on 23/24 March. In the morning of the 24th, 6th Airborne Division parachuted in ahead of the forward troops. Although there were pockets of fanatical resistance, as shown by the VCs that continued to be won, Germany no longer had any capacity to fight a war. Hitler's order to create a desert in front of the Allied armies was not obeyed, and the Allies advanced as much as 50 miles a day. Contact was made with the Soviet Army on 18 April, and unconditional surrender was signed on 8 May.

TOPHAM, Frederick George *Corporal, 1st Canadian Parachute Battalion, Canadian Army*
24 March 1945 – Corporal Topham, a medical orderly, parachuted with his battalion on a strongly defended area east of the Rhine. At about 1100 hours, whilst treating casualties sustained in the drop, a cry for help came from a wounded man in the open. Two medical orderlies from a field ambulance went out to this man in succession but both were killed as they knelt beside the casualty. Without hesitation and on his own initiative, Topham went forward through intense fire to replace the orderlies who had been killed before his eyes. As he worked on the wounded man, he was himself shot through the nose. In spite of severe bleeding and intense pain, he never faltered in his task. Having completed immediate first aid, he carried the wounded man steadily and slowly back through continuous fire to the shelter of a wood. During the next two hours Topham refused all offers of medical help for his own wound. He worked most devotedly throughout this period to bring in wounded, showing complete disregard for the heavy and accurate enemy fire. It was only when all casualties had been cleared that he consented to his own wound being treated. His immediate evacuation was ordered, but he interceded so earnestly on his own behalf that he was eventually allowed to return to duty. On his way

back to his company he came across a carrier, which had received a direct hit. Enemy mortar bombs were still dropping around, the carrier itself was burning fiercely and its own mortar ammunition was exploding. An experienced officer on the spot had warned all not to approach the carrier. Topham, however, immediately went out alone in spite of the blasting ammunition and enemy fire, and rescued the three occupants of the carrier. He brought these men back across the open and although one died almost immediately afterwards, he arranged for the evacuation of the other two, who undoubtedly owe their lives to him.

CHAPMAN, Edward Thomas *Corporal, 3rd Bn., Monmouthshire Regiment*
   2 April 1945 – On 2 April 1945, a company of the Monmouthshire Regiment crossed the Dortmund–Ems canal and was ordered to assault the ridge of the Teutoberger Wald, which dominates the surrounding country. This ridge is steep and thickly wooded and is ideal defensive country. It was, moreover, defended by a battalion of German officer cadets and their instructors, all of them picked men and fanatical Nazis. Corporal Chapman was advancing with his section in single file along a narrow track when the enemy suddenly opened fire with machine-guns at short range, inflicting heavy casualties and causing some confusion. Chapman immediately ordered his section to take cover and, seizing the Bren gun, advanced alone, firing the gun from his hip, and mowed down the enemy at point-blank range, forcing them to retire in disorder. At this point, however, his company was ordered to withdraw but Chapman and his section were still left in their advanced position as the order could not be got forward to them. The enemy then began to close up to Chapman and his isolated section and, under cover of intense machine-gun fire, they made determined charges with the bayonet. Chapman again rose with his Bren gun to meet the assaults and on each occasion halted their advance. He had now nearly run out of ammunition. Shouting to his section for more bandoliers, he dropped into a fold in the ground and covered those bringing up the ammunition by lying on his back and firing the Bren gun over his shoulder. A party of Germans made every effort to eliminate him with grenades, but with a reloaded magazine he closed with them and once again drove the enemy back with considerable casualties. During the withdrawal of his company, the company commander had been severely wounded and left lying in the open a short distance from Chapman. Satisfied that his section was now secure, at any rate for the moment, he went out alone under withering fire and carried his company commander for 50 yards to comparative safety. On the way a sniper hit the officer again, wounding Chapman in the hip and, when he reached British lines, it was discovered that the officer had been killed. In spite of his wound, Chapman refused to be evacuated and went back to his company until the position was fully restored two hours later. Throughout the action Corporal Chapman displayed outstanding gallantry and superb

courage. Single-handed he repulsed the attacks of well-led, determined troops and gave his battalion time to reorganize on a vital piece of ground overlooking the only bridge across the canal. His magnificent bravery played a very large part in the capture of this vital ridge and in the successful development of subsequent operations.

LIDDELL, Ian Oswald *T/Captain, 5th Bn., Coldstream Guards*

3 April 1945 – In Germany Captain Liddell was commanding a company of the Coldstream Guards, which was ordered to capture intact a bridge over the River Ems near Lingen. The bridge was covered on the far bank by an enemy strongpoint, which was subsequently discovered to consist of 150 entrenched infantry supported by three 88mm and two 20mm guns. The bridge was also prepared for demolition with 500lb bombs, which could plainly be seen. Having directed his two leading platoons onto the near bank, Liddell ran forward alone to the bridge and scaled the 10-foot-high roadblock guarding it, with the intention of neutralizing the charges and taking the bridge intact. In order to achieve his objective he had to cross the whole length of the bridge by himself under intense enemy fire, which increased as his object became apparent to the Germans. Having disconnected the charges on the far side, he re-crossed the bridge and cut the wires on the near side. It was necessary for him to kneel, forming an easy target, whilst he successively cut the wires. He then discovered that there were also charges underneath the bridge, and completely undeterred he also disconnected these. His task completed, he then climbed up onto the roadblock in full view of the enemy and signalled his leading platoon to advance. Thus alone and unprotected, without cover and under heavy enemy fire, he achieved his object. The bridge was captured intact and the way cleared to the advance across the River Ems. His outstanding gallantry and superb example of courage will never be forgotten by those who saw it. This very brave officer has since died of wounds subsequently received in action.

CHARLTON, Edward Colquhoun *Guardsman, 2nd Bn., Irish Guards*

21 April 1945 – In Germany on the morning of 21 April 1945, Guardsman Charlton was co-driver in one tank of a troop which, with a platoon of infantry, seized the village of Wistedt. Shortly afterwards, the enemy attacked this position under cover of an artillery concentration and in great strength, comprising, as it later transpired, a battalion of the 15th Panzer Grenadiers supported by six self-propelled guns. All the tanks, including Charlton's, were hit; the infantry were hard-pressed and in danger of being overrun. Entirely on his own initiative, Charlton decided to counter-attack the enemy. Quickly recovering the Browning machine-gun from his damaged tank, he advanced up the road in full view of the enemy, firing the Browning from his hip. Such was the boldness of his attack and the intensity of his fire that he halted the leading enemy company, inflicting heavy casualties on them. This effort at the same time brought much-needed relief to British infantry. For ten minutes Charlton fired in this manner, until wounded in the left arm. Immediately, despite intense enemy fire, he mounted his machine-gun on a nearby fence, which he used to support his wounded left arm. He stood firing thus for a further ten minutes until he was again hit in the left arm, which fell away shattered and useless. Although twice wounded and suffering from loss of blood, Charlton again lifted his machine-gun onto the fence, now having only one arm with which to fire and reload. Nevertheless, he still continued to inflict casualties on the enemy, until finally he was hit for the third time and collapsed. He died later of his wounds in enemy hands.

THE BURMA CAMPAIGN: ARAKAN

In 1945, Lieutenant General Slim's 14th Army was told to link up with the Chinese near Maymyo, leaving the amphibious assault on Rangoon to a separate force. He decided to take Rangoon overland, and planned to destroy the Japanese army between the Chindwin and the Irrawaddy. Operations in the Arakan were designed to support this. 15th Corps was moving on Myebon: 3rd Commando Brigade was landed on 12 January and followed up by 74th Indian Brigade, and by the 16th had reached the Kantha Chaung, which divided the Myebon Peninsula from the mainland. Once over the chaung, it became clear that the Japanese had set up a series of defences from Kangaw, on the road south, to the mountains. These were encircled by a landing by 3rd Commando Brigade south-west of Kangaw, through which passed 51st Brigade to meet 74th Brigade coming from the peninsula and 82nd West African Division coming from the north. Three hills were taken by the second day, and the village was taken on 4 February, but only after 'the heaviest and most desperate attack of the entire campaign', in the words of 15th Corps's commander, a three-day battle in which two Japanese battalions were thrown in wave after wave of suicide attacks at the hill held by the Commandos. Had the Japanese taken it the British would have been cut off from the beaches and the operation failed: the Japanese lost seven hundred dead and withdrew towards the An Pass, which led to the Irrawaddy, before the Africans could cut them off. Lieutenant George Knowland of 1 Army Commando won the VC for his part in this action.

The imperative now was to cut off the An Pass before the Japanese could escape. 25th Indian Division landed at Ruywa, 33 miles south-east of Myebon, and moved north to take Tamandu, a village seven miles up the coast, where a track led east to the pass. The 3rd Battalion, 2nd Gurkha Rifles took their objective, and Rifleman Bhanbhagta Gurung won the VC, but on 7 March all aircraft were diverted to the battle in the Irrawaddy valley and 15th Corps was unable to follow the Japanese much further.

SHER SHAH *Lance Naik, 7th Bn., 16th Punjab Regiment*

19/20 January 1945 – In Burma, on the night 19/20 January 1945, at Kyeyebyin, Kaladan, Lance Naik Sher Shah commanded the left-forward section of his platoon. At 1930 hours a Japanese platoon attacked his post. Realizing that overwhelming numbers would probably destroy his section, Sher Shah, by himself, stalked the enemy from their rear and broke up their attack by firing into their midst. He killed the platoon commander and 6 other Japanese and, after their withdrawal, crawled back to his section post. At 0015 hours the Japanese, who were now reinforced with a company, started to form up for another attack. He heard their officers giving orders and bayonets being fixed prior to the assault. Again he left his section post and, in spite of Japanese covering fire from small arms and mortars, crawled forward and saw Japanese officers and men grouped together. He fired into this group and they again broke up and started to withdraw in disorder. Whilst on his way back for the second time he was hit by a mortar bomb, which shattered his right leg. He regained his position, and propping himself against the side of the trench, continued firing and encouraging his men. When asked whether he was hurt, he replied that it was only slight. Some time afterwards it was discovered that his right leg was missing. The Japanese again started forming up for another attack. In spite of his severe wounds and considerable loss of blood, and very heavy Japanese supporting fire, Sher Shah again left his section post and crawled forward, firing into their midst at point-blank range. He continued firing until for the third time the Japanese attack was broken up, and until he was shot through the head, from which he subsequently died. Twenty-three dead and four wounded Japanese, including an officer, were found at daybreak immediately in front of his position. His initiative and indomitable courage throughout this very critical situation undoubtedly averted the overrunning of his platoon, and was the deciding factor in defeating the Japanese attacks. His supreme self-sacrifice, disregard of danger and selfless devotion to duty were an inspiration to all his comrades throughout the battalion.

KNOWLAND, George Arthur *Lieutenant, Royal Norfolk Regiment, attached 1 Commando*

31 January 1945 – In Burma on 31 January 1945, near Kangaw, Lieutenant Knowland was commanding the forward platoon of a commando troop positioned on the extreme north of a hill which was subjected to very heavy and repeated enemy attacks throughout the whole day. Before the first attack started, Knowland's platoon was heavily mortared and machine-gunned, yet he moved about among his men keeping them alert and encouraging them, though under fire himself at the time. When the enemy, some 300 strong in all, made their first assault they concentrated all their efforts on his platoon of 24 men, but in spite of the ferocity of the attack he moved about from trench to trench distributing ammunition and firing his rifle and throwing grenades at the enemy, often from completely exposed positions. Later, when the crew of one of his forward Bren guns had all been wounded, he sent back to troop headquarters for another crew and ran forward to man the gun himself until they arrived. The enemy was then less than 10 yards from him in dead ground down the hill so, in order to get a better field of fire, he stood on top of the trench, firing the light machine-gun from his hip, and successfully keeping them at a distance until a medical orderly had attended and evacuated the wounded men behind him. The new Bren team also became casualties on the way up, and Knowland continued to fire the gun until another team took over. Later, when a fresh attack came in, he took over a 2in mortar and in spite of heavy fire and the closeness of the enemy, he stood up in the open to face them, firing the mortar from his hip and killing six of them with his first bomb. When all bombs were expended he went back through heavy grenade, mortar and machine-gun fire to get more, which he fired in the same way from the open in front of his platoon positions. When those bombs were finished, he went back to his own trench, and still standing up fired his rifle at them. Being hard pressed and with enemy closing in on him from only 10 yards away, he had no time to recharge his magazine. Snatching up the tommy gun of a casualty, he sprayed the enemy and was mortally wounded stemming this assault, though not before he had killed and wounded many of the enemy. Such was the inspiration of his magnificent heroism that, though 14 out of 24 of his platoon became casualties at an early stage, and six of his positions were overrun by the enemy, his men held on through twelve hours of continuous and fierce fighting until reinforcements arrived. If this northern end of the hill had fallen, the rest of the hill would have been endangered, the beachhead dominated by the enemy, and other units farther inland cut off from their source of supplies. As it was, the final successful counter-attack was later launched from the vital ground which Lieutenant Knowland had taken such a gallant part in holding.

BHANBHAGTA GURUNG *Rifleman, 3rd Bn., 2nd Gurkha Rifles*
    15 March 1945 – Near Tamandu, Burma, a company of the 2nd Gurkha Rifles attacked an enemy position known as Snowdon East. On approaching the objective one of the sections was forced to ground by very heavy machine-gun, grenade and mortar fire, and owing to the severity of this fire was unable to move in any direction. While thus pinned, the section came under accurate fire from a tree sniper some 75 yards to the south. As this sniper was inflicting casualties on the section, Rifleman Bhanbhagta Gurung, being unable to fire from the lying position, stood up fully exposed to the heavy fire and calmly killed the enemy sniper with his rifle, thus saving his section from suffering further casualties. The section then advanced again, but within 20 yards of the objective was again attacked by very heavy fire. Bhanbhagta Gurung, without waiting for any orders, dashed forward alone

and attacked the first enemy foxhole. Throwing two grenades, he killed the two occupants and without any hesitation rushed on to the next enemy foxhole and killed the Japanese in it with his bayonet. Two further enemy foxholes were still bringing fire to bear on the section and again Bhanbhagta Gurung dashed forward alone and cleared these with bayonet and grenade. During his single-handed attacks on these four enemy foxholes, Bhanbhagta Gurung was subjected to almost continuous and point-blank machine-gun fire from a bunker on the north tip of the objective. Realizing that this machine-gun would hold up not only his own platoon which was now behind him, but also another platoon which was advancing from the west, Bhanbhagta Gurung for the fifth time went forward alone in the face of heavy enemy fire to knock out this position. He doubled forward and leapt on to the roof of the bunker from where, his hand grenades being finished, he flung two smoke grenades into the bunker slit. Two Japanese rushed out of the bunker partially blinded by the smoke. Bhanbhagta Gurung promptly killed them both with his kukri. A remaining Japanese inside the bunker was still firing the machine-gun and holding up the advance of 4 Platoon, so Bhanbhagta Gurung crawled inside the bunker, killed this Japanese gunner and captured the machine-gun. Most of the objective had now been cleared by the men behind and the enemy driven off were collecting for a counter-attack beneath the north end of the objective. Bhanbhagta Gurung ordered the nearest Bren-gunner and two riflemen to take up positions in the captured bunker. The enemy counter-attack followed soon after, but under Bhanbhagta Gurung's command the small party inside the bunker repelled it with heavy loss to the enemy. Rifleman Bhanbhagta Gurung showed outstanding bravery and a complete disregard for his own safety. His courageous clearing of five enemy positions single-handed was in itself decisive in capturing the objective and his inspiring example to the rest of the company contributed to the speedy consolidation of this success.

At the time of publication, Bhanbhagta Gurung was one of the surviving VC holders.

RAYMOND, Claud *Lieutenant, Royal Engineers*

21 March 1945 – In Burma, on the afternoon of 21 March 1945, Lieutenant Raymond was second-in-command of a small patrol, which was acting in conjunction with a larger detachment of a special force, whose objective was to obtain information and create a diversion in the area of Taungup, by attacking and destroying isolated enemy posts some 40 miles in advance of an Indian infantry brigade, pushing down the road from Letpan to Taungup. The patrol was landed on the south bank of the Thinganet Chaung, an area known to be held by numerous enemy strong-points and gun positions, and marched about five miles inland. As they were nearing the village of Talaku and moving across an open stretch of ground, they were heavily fired on from the slopes of a jungle-covered hill by a strongly entrenched enemy detachment. Raymond immediately charged in the direction of the fire. As he began to climb the hill he was wounded in the right shoulder, but he ignored this wound and continued up the slope firing his rifle from the hip. He had advanced only a few yards further when a Japanese threw a grenade which burst in his face and most severely wounded him. He fell, but almost immediately picked himself up again, and, in spite of loss of blood from his wounds, which later were to prove fatal, he continued on, leading his section under intense fire. He was hit a third time, his wrist being shattered by what appeared to be an explosive bullet. In spite of this third wound, he never wavered, but carried on into the enemy position itself and, in the sharp action which followed, was largely responsible for the killing of two Japanese and the wounding of another. The remaining Japanese then fled in panic into the jungle, thus leaving the position in British hands, together with much equipment. The position was strongly fortified by foxholes and small bunkers and would have proved extremely formidable had not the attack been pressed home with great determination under the courageous leadership of Raymond. Several other men were wounded during the action and Raymond refused all treatment until they had been attended to, insisting despite the gravity of his injuries on walking back towards the landing craft in case the delay in treating his wounds and carrying him should endanger the withdrawal of the patrol. It was not until he had walked nearly a mile that he collapsed and had to allow himself to be carried on an improvised stretcher. Even then he was continually encouraging the other wounded by giving the thumbs-up sign and thus undoubtedly helping them to keep cheerful and minimize the extent of their injuries until the landing craft was reached. Soon after, he died of his wounds. The outstanding gallantry, remarkable endurance and fortitude of Lieutenant Raymond, which refused to allow him to collapse, although mortally wounded, was an inspiration to everyone and a major factor in the capture of the strongpoint. His self-sacrifice in refusing attention to his wounds undoubtedly saved the patrol by allowing it to withdraw in time before the Japanese could bring up fresh forces from neighbouring positions for a counter-attack.

BURMA: THE BATTLE OF THE IRRAWADDY SHORE

The Japanese had decided that priority must be given to southern Burma, and so withdrew behind the Irrawaddy, hoping to trap Slim's army on its east side. The Irrawaddy was crossed by 33rd Corps south-west of Mandalay and south of the confluence with the Chindwin, with a smaller crossing by 4th Corps near Mandalay which the Japanese were persuaded was the main thrust. The Irrawaddy in February is over 2,000 yards wide, and this was a tough opposed crossing, but by 26 February tanks and infantry had taken

Thabutkon airfield, 12 miles north-west of Meiktila, enabling 99th Brigade to be flown in. Meiktila itself was taken on 5 March, after a four-day battle in which two VCs were won. The road to Rangoon, up which supplies for Mandalay had to pass, was cut. Mandalay was taken between 8 and 20 March, but then the Japanese counter-attacked Meiktila. 9th Indian Infantry Brigade was flown in, and the town and airfield held, but meanwhile 4th Corps was fighting its way south, aiming for Myingyan, capture of which would allow the river to be used for supplies. Lieutenant Karamjeet Singh Judge won a VC in this action, and on 1 April the shattered remnants of the Japanese army retreated from both Mandalay and Meiktila.

It was now imperative to reach Rangoon before the monsoon broke. 4th Corps took the road and rail route, while 33rd Corps the banks of the Irrawaddy. The Japanes escaping from Arakan were too weak to stop this thrust south, but the monsoon broke thirteen days early. The Japanese attempted to fight their way out, and battles to prevent this continued until July. It was during one of these that Rifleman Lachhiman Gurung won the VC: in the attack against his single company the Japanese left more than three hundred dead.

PARKASH SINGH *Jemadar, 4/13th Frontier Force Rifles*
16/17 February 1945 – At Kanlan Ywathit in Burma, on the night of 16/17 February 1945, Jemadar Parkash Singh was in command of a platoon of a rifle company. At about 2300 hours the Japanese, in great strength and supported by artillery, mortars, medium machine-guns and subsequently flame-throwers, initiated a series of fierce attacks on the position. The main weight of the attack was directed against Parkash Singh's platoon locality. At about 2330 hours Parkash Singh was severely wounded in both ankles. His company commander, on being informed of this, ordered him to be relieved and brought into a trench beside company headquarters, from where he kept shouting encouragement to all his men. A short time afterwards, owing to his relief having been wounded, Parkash Singh crawled forward, dragging himself on his hands and knees, to his platoon sector and again took over command. At 0015 hours, when his company commander visited the platoon area, Parkash Singh was found, propped up by his batman, who had also been wounded, firing his platoon 2in mortar, the crew of which had both been killed, shouting encouragement to his men and directing the fire of his platoon. Having expended all the available 2in mortar ammunition, Parkash Singh then crawled around the position collecting ammunition for his platoon from the dead and wounded. This ammunition he distributed himself. As one complete section of his platoon had by now become casualties, Parkash Singh took over their Bren gun and held the section's sector of the perimeter single-handed until reinforcements were rushed up by the company commander. He fired the gun at this stage from a position completely in the open as he was unable to stand up in a trench.

IIc was again wounded in both legs, above the knees, by a burst of machine-gun fire. In spite of intense pain and the loss of much blood from his wounds, Parkash Singh continued firing his Bren gun and dragging himself from place to place only by the use of his hands, as his legs were now smashed and completely useless. At the same time he continued to encourage and direct his men, regrouping the remnants of his platoon around him so that they successfully held up a fierce Japanese charge which was launched against them. At 0145 hours Parkash Singh was wounded for the third time in the right leg and was so weak from loss of blood that he was unable to move. Bleeding profusely and lying on his right side with his face towards the enemy, he continued to direct the action of his men, encouraging them to stay their ground. Although it was obvious that he was now dying, Parkash Singh shouted out the Dogra war cry, which was immediately taken up by the rest of the company engaged in hand-to-hand fighting. His example and leadership at this period so inspired the company that the enemy was finally driven out from the position. At 0230 hours Parkash Singh was wounded for a fourth time, this time in the chest, by a Japanese grenade. He died a few minutes later after telling his company commander not to worry about him for he could easily look after himself. Throughout the period of intense hand-to-hand fighting and heavy machine-gun and grenade fire from 2300 hours until the time of his death at 0230 hours, Jemadar Parkash Singh conducted himself with conspicuous bravery and complete disregard of his severe wounds, and there is no doubt that his ceaseless encouragement of his platoon, his inspired leadership and outstanding devotion to duty, though himself mortally wounded, played an outstanding part in finally repelling the Japanese with heavy casualties.

FAZAL DIN *A/Naik, 7th Bn., 10th Baluch Regiment*
2 March 1945 – Near Meiktila, Burma, Naik Fazal Din was commanding a section during a company attack on a Japanese bunkered position. During this attack, the section found itself in an area flanked by three bunkers on one side and a house and one bunker on the other side. This was the key to the enemy position and had held up a company attack made earlier. Fazal Din's section was accompanied by a tank but, at the time of entering the area, it had gone on ahead. On reaching the area, the section was held up by machine-gun fire and grenades from the bunkers. Unhesitatingly Fazal Din personally attacked the nearest bunker with grenades and silenced it. He then led his section under heavy fire against the other bunkers. Suddenly six Japanese, led by two officers wielding swords, rushed from the house. The Bren-gunner shot an officer and a Japanese other rank but by then had expended the magazine of the gun. He was almost simultaneously attacked by the second Japanese officer, who killed him with his sword. Fazal Din went to the Bren-gunner's assistance immediately but, in doing so, was run

through the chest by the officer, the sword point appearing through his back. On the Japanese officer withdrawing his sword, Fazal Din, despite his terrible wound, tore the sword from the officer and killed him with it. He then attacked a Japanese other rank and also killed him. He then went to the assistance of a sepoy of his section who was struggling with another Japanese and killed the latter with the sword. Then, waving the sword, he continued to encourage his men. He staggered to platoon headquarters, about 25 yards away, to make a report and collapsed. He died soon after reaching the regimental aid post. Naik Fazal Din's action was seen by almost the whole platoon who, undoubtedly inspired by his gallantry and taking advantage of the bewilderment created amongst the enemy by the loss of its leaders, continued the attack and annihilated the garrison, which numbered 55.

GIAN SINGH *Naik, 4th Bn., 15th Punjab Regiment*
    2 March 1945 – In Burma the Japanese were holding a strong position astride the Kamye–Myingyan road. Two companies of the 15th Punjab Regiment carried out successfully an encircling movement and established themselves on some high ground about one and a half miles in the rear of this enemy position. As all water supply points were within the enemy position it was vital that they should be dislodged. The attack on the first objective was successful and one platoon was ordered to attack a village to the right. This platoon's attack, with the aid of tanks, advanced slowly under very heavy enemy fire. Naik Gian Singh was in command of the leading section. The enemy were well concealed in foxholes along cactus hedges and Gian Singh soon observed enemy some 20 yards ahead. Ordering his light machine-gunner to cover him, he alone rushed the enemy foxholes, firing his tommy gun. He was met by a hail of fire and wounded in the arm. In spite of this he continued his advance alone, hurling grenades. He killed several Japanese including four in one of the enemy main weapon pits. By this time a troop of tanks moved up in support of this platoon and came under fire from a cleverly concealed enemy anti-tank gun. Gian Singh quickly saw the danger to the tanks and, ignoring the danger to himself and in spite of his wounds, again rushed forward, killed the crew and captured the gun single-handed. His section followed him and he then led them down a lane of cactus hedges, clearing all enemy positions. Some 20 enemy bodies were found in this area, the majority of which fell to Gian Singh and his section. After this action, the company re-formed to take the enemy positions to the rear. Gian Singh was ordered to the regimental aid post but, in spite of his wounds, requested permission to lead his section until the whole action had been completed. This was granted. There is no doubt that these acts of supreme gallantry saved Naik Gian Singh's platoon many casualties and enabled the whole operation to be carried out successfully with severe losses to the enemy.

WESTON, William Basil *Lieutenant, Green Howards, attached 1st Bn., West Yorkshire Regiment*

3 March 1945 – In Burma, during the battalion's attack on the town of Meiktila, this officer was commanding a platoon. The task of his company was to clear through the town from the north to the water's edge in the south, a distance of about 1,600 yards, of which the last 800 yards was not only very strongly held but was a labyrinth of minor roads and well-constructed buildings. The company was working with tanks and Lieutenant Weston's platoon was one of the two platoons leading the attack. The clearing of the final 800 yards was commenced at 1330 hours and was to be completed by dusk. Practically every man in Weston's platoon was seeing active service for the first time and under the most difficult conditions. From the start Weston realized that only by the highest personal example on his part could he hope to carry out his task within the time given. As the advance continued the already determined opposition increased until in the final stages it reached a stage when it can only be described as fanatical. Fire from guns and light automatics was heavy from well-bunkered positions and concrete emplacements. Each bunker position had to be dealt with separately, and superimposed on the enemy's fire from the front was accurate sniping from well-selected positions on the flanks. The fighting throughout the day was at very close quarters and at times was hand-to-hand. With magnificent bravery Weston inspired the men of his platoon to superb achievements. Without thought of his own personal safety he personally led his men into position after position, exterminating the enemy wherever found. Throughout, the leadership was superb, encouraging his platoon to the same fanatical zest as that shown by the enemy. His bravery, his coolness under fire and enthusiasm inspired his platoon. There was no hesitation on his part and no matter how heavy or sustained the enemy's fire he boldly and resolutely led his men on from bunker position to bunker position. It was at 1700 hours, within sight of the water's edge which marked the completion of the platoon's task, that he was held up by a very strong bunker position. Weston, appreciating the limited time now at his disposal and the necessity of clearing the area before nightfall, quickly directed the fire of the tanks with him on to the position. He then led a party with bayonets and grenades to eliminate the enemy within the bunker. As on many occasions before, he was the first into the bunker. At the entrance to the bunker he was shot at by the enemy inside and fell forward wounded. As he lay on the ground and still fired by the undaunted courage that he had shown throughout the day, he withdrew the pin from a grenade in his hand and by doing so killed himself and most of the enemy in the bunker. It is possible that he could have attempted to reach safety but to do so would have endangered the lives of his men who were following him into the bunker. Throughout the final three hours of battle Lieutenant Weston set an example which seldom can have been equalled. His bravery and inspiring leadership was beyond question. At no time during the day did he relax and inspired by the deeds of valour which he continually performed, he personally led on his men as an irresistible force.

KARAMJEET SINGH JUDGE *Lieutenant, 4th Bn., 15th Punjab Regiment*

18 March 1945 – Near Meiktila, Burma, a company of the 15th Punjab Regiment, in which Lieutenant Karamjeet Singh Judge was a platoon commander, was ordered to capture the Cotton Mill area on the outskirts of Myingyan. In addition to numerous bunkers and stiff enemy resistance a total of almost two hundred enemy shells fell around the tanks and infantry during the attack. The ground over which the operation took place was very broken and in parts was unsuitable for tanks. Except for the first two hours of this operation, Karamjeet Singh Judge's platoon was leading in the attack, and up to the last moment Karamjeet Singh Judge dominated the entire battlefield by his numerous and successive acts of superb gallantry. Time and again the infantry were held up by heavy machine-gun and small-arms fire from bunkers not seen by the tanks. On every such occasion Karamjeet Singh Judge, without hesitation and with a complete disregard for his own personal safety, coolly went forward through heavy fire to recall the tanks by means of the house telephone. Cover around the tanks was non-existent, but Karamjeet Singh Judge remained completely regardless not only of the heavy small-arms fire directed at him, but also of the extremely heavy shelling directed at the tanks. Karamjeet Singh Judge succeeded in recalling the tanks to deal with bunkers which he personally indicated to the tanks, thus allowing the infantry to advance. In every case Karamjeet Singh Judge personally led the infantry in charges against the bunkers and was invariably first to arrive. In this way ten bunkers were eliminated by this brilliant and courageous officer. On one occasion, while he was going into the attack, two Japanese suddenly rushed at him from a small nullah with fixed bayonets. At a distance of only 10 yards he killed both. About fifteen minutes before the battle finished, a last nest of three bunkers was located, which were very difficult for the tanks to approach. An enemy light machine-gun was firing from one of them and holding up the advance of the infantry. Undaunted, Karamjeet Singh Judge directed one tank to within 20 yards of the bunker at great personal risk and then threw a smoke grenade as a means of indication. After some minutes of fire, Karamjeet Singh Judge, using the house telephone again, asked the tank commander to cease fire while he went in with a few men to mop up. He then went forward and got within 10 yards of the bunker, when the enemy light machine-gun opened fire again, mortally wounding Karamjeet Singh Judge in the chest. By this time, however, the remaining men of the section were able to storm this strongpoint, and so complete a long and arduous task.

LACHHIMAN GURUNG *Rifleman, 4th Bn., 8th Gurkha Rifles*

12/13 May 1945 – At Taungdaw in Burma, on the west bank of the Irrawaddy on the night of 12/13 May 1945, Rifleman Lachhiman Gurung was manning the most forward post of his platoon. At 0120 hours at least 200 enemy assaulted his company position. The brunt of the attack was borne by Lachhiman Gurung's section and by his own post in particular. This post dominated a jungle path leading up into his platoon locality. Before assaulting, the enemy hurled innumerable grenades at the position from close range. One grenade fell on the lip of Lachhiman Gurung's trench; he at once grasped it and hurled it back at the enemy. Almost immediately another grenade fell directly inside the trench. Again this rifleman snatched it up and threw it back. A third grenade then fell just in front of the trench. He attempted to throw it back, but it exploded in his hand, blowing off his fingers, shattering his right arm and severely wounding him in the face, body and right leg. His two comrades were also badly wounded and lay helpless in the bottom of the trench. The enemy, screaming and shouting, now formed up and attempted to rush the position by sheer weight of numbers. Lachhiman Gurung, regardless of his wounds, fired and loaded his rifle with his left hand, maintaining a continuous and steady rate of fire. Wave after wave of fanatical attacks were thrown in by the enemy and all were repulsed with heavy casualties. For four hours after being severely wounded Lachhiman Gurung remained alone at his post, waiting with perfect calm for each attack, which he met with fire at point-blank range from his rifle, determined not to give one inch of ground. Of the 87 enemy dead counted in the immediate vicinity of the company locality, 31 lay in front of this rifleman's section, the key to the whole position. Had the enemy succeeded in overrunning and occupying Lachhiman Gurung's trench, the whole of the reverse slope position would have been completely dominated and turned. This rifleman, by his magnificent example, so inspired his comrades to resist the enemy to the last, that, although surrounded and cut off for three days and two nights, they held and smashed every attack. His outstanding gallantry and extreme devotion to duty in the face of almost overwhelming odds were the main factors in the defeat of the enemy.

At the time of publication, Lachhiman Gurung was one of the surviving VC holders.

THE SOLOMON ISLANDS

By the spring of 1945 the Japanese on Bougainville had been long cut off, but were still resisting.

RATTEY, Reginald Roy *Corporal, 25th Infantry Bn., 7th Brigade, 3rd Division, Australian Military Forces*
22 March 1945 – In the south-west Pacific a company of an Australian infantry battalion was ordered to capture a strongly held enemy position astride Buin Road, South Bougainville. The attack was met by extremely

heavy fire from advanced enemy bunkers, slit trenches and foxholes sited on strong ground, and all forward movement was stopped with casualties mounting rapidly among British troops. Corporal Rattey quickly appreciated that the serious situation delaying the advance could only be averted by silencing enemy fire from automatic weapons in bunkers, which dominated all lines of approach by our troops. He calculated that a forward move by his section would be halted by fire with heavy casualties and he determined that a bold rush by himself alone would surprise the enemy and offered the best chance for success. With amazing courage he rushed forward firing his Bren gun from the hip into the openings under the head cover of three forward bunkers. This completely neutralized enemy fire from these positions. On gaining the nearest bunker he hurled a grenade among the garrison, which completely silenced further enemy aggressive action. Rattey was now without grenades but without hesitation he raced back to his section under extremely heavy fire and obtained two grenades with which he again rushed the remaining bunkers and effectively silenced all opposition by killing seven of the enemy garrison. This led to the flight of the remaining enemy troops, which enabled his company to continue its advance. A little later the advance of his company was again held up by a heavy machine-gun, firing across the front. Without hesitation Rattey rushed the gun and silenced it with fire from his Bren gun used from his hip. When one had been killed and another wounded, the remainder of the enemy gun crew broke and fled. The machine-gun and 2,000 rounds of ammunition were captured and the company again continued its advance and gained its objective, which was consolidated. The serious situation was turned into a brilliant success, entirely by Rattey's courage, cool planning and stern determination.

PARTRIDGE, Frank John *Private, 8th Infantry Bn. (Victoria), Australian Military Forces*

24 July 1945 – In the Solomon Islands, two fighting patrols of the 8th Australian Infantry Battalion were given the task of eliminating an enemy outpost in Bougainville which denied any forward movement to Australian troops. The preliminary artillery concentration caused the enemy bunkers to be screened by a litter of felled banana plants, and from these well-concealed positions to their front and left, one of the Australian platoons came under extremely fierce machine-gun, grenade and rifle fire. The forward section at once suffered casualties and was pinned down together with two other sections. Private Partridge was a rifleman in a section which, in carrying out an encircling movement, came under heavy machine-gun fire. He was hit twice in the left arm and again in the left thigh, whilst the Bren-gunner was killed and two others seriously wounded, leaving only the section leader unwounded, but another soldier began to move up from another position. Partridge quickly appreciated the extreme gravity of the situation and decided that the only possible solution was personal action by himself. Despite wounds and with complete disregard to his own safety, Partridge rushed forward under a terrific burst of enemy fire and retrieved the Bren gun from alongside the dead gunner, when he challenged the enemy to come out and fight. He handed the Bren gun to the newly arrived man to provide covering fire while he rushed this bunker, into which he threw a grenade and silenced the machine-gun. Under cover of the grenade burst, he dived into the bunker and, in a fierce hand-to-hand fight, he killed the only living occupant with his knife. Partridge then cleared the enemy dead from the entrance to the bunker and attacked another bunker in the rear; but weakness from loss of blood compelled him to halt, when he shouted to his section commander that he was unable to continue. With the way clear by Partridge's silencing of the enemy machine-gun, the platoon moved forward and established a defence perimeter in the vicinity of the spot where Partridge lay wounded. Heavy enemy machine-gun and rifle fire both direct and enfilade from other bunkers soon created an untenable situation for the platoon, which withdrew under its own covering fire. Despite his wounds and weakness due to loss of blood, Partridge joined in this fight and remained in action until the platoon had withdrawn after recovering their casualties. The information gained by both patrols, and particularly from Partridge, enabled an attack to be mounted later. This led to the capture of a vital position sited on strong defensive ground and strengthened by numerous bunkers and other dug-in positions from which the enemy fled in panic. The serious situation during the fight of the two patrols was retrieved only by the outstanding gallantry and devotion to duty displayed by Partridge, which inspired his comrades to heroic action, leading to a successful withdrawal which saved the small force from complete annihilation.

NEW GUINEA

General MacArthur took New Guinea in spring and summer 1944 and moved on, leaving five weak Japanese divisions cut off. 6th Australian Division was sent to clear the island. Wewak was taken in May but Japanese troops in the interior held out until the surrender.

CHOWNE, Albert *Lieutenant, 2/2nd Infantry Bn. (New South Wales), Australian Military Forces*

25 March 1945 – After the capture of Dagua, the main enemy force withdrew southwards from the beach to previously prepared positions on the flank of the division. Further movement towards Wewak was impossible while this threat to the flank existed, and the battalion was ordered to destroy the enemy force. A Company, after making contact with the enemy on a narrow ridge, was ordered to attack the position. The leading platoon in the attack came under heavy fire from concealed enemy machine-guns sited on a small rise dominating the approach. In the initial approach one member of this platoon was killed and nine wounded, including the platoon commander, and the enemy continued to inflict casualties. Without awaiting orders, Lieutenant Chowne, whose platoon was in reserve, instantly appreciated the plight of the leading platoon and rushed the enemy's position. Running up a steep narrow track, he hurled grenades which knocked out two enemy machine-guns. Then, calling on his men to follow him and firing his sub-machine-gun from the hip, he charged the enemy's position. Although he sustained two serious wounds in the chest, the impetus of his charge carried him 50 yards forward under the most intense machine-gun and rifle fire. Chowne accounted for two more Japanese before he was killed standing over three foxholes occupied by the enemy. The superb heroism and self-sacrifice of this officer, culminating in his death, resulted in the capture of this strongly held enemy position, ensured the further immediate success of his company in this area and paved the way directly for the continuance of the division's advance to Wewak.

KENNA, Edward *Private, 2/4th Infantry Bn. (New South Wales), Australian Military Forces*

15 May 1945 – In the south-west Pacific at Wewak on 15 May 1945, during the attack on the Wirui Mission feature, Private Kenna's company had the task of capturing certain enemy positions. The only position from which observation for supporting fire could be obtained was continuously swept by enemy heavy machine-gun fire and it was not possible to bring artillery or mortars into action. Private Kenna's platoon was ordered forward to deal with the enemy machine-gun post, so that the company operation could proceed. His section moved as close as possible to the bunker in order to harass any enemy seen, so that the remainder of the platoon could attack from the flank. When the attacking sections came into view of the enemy they were immediately engaged at very close range by heavy automatic fire from a position not previously disclosed. Casualties were suffered and the attackers could not move further forward. Kenna endeavoured to put his Bren gun into a position where he could engage the bunker, but was unable to do so because of the nature of the ground. On his own initiative and without orders Kenna immediately stood up in full view of the enemy less than 50 yards away and engaged the bunker, firing his Bren gun from the hip. The enemy machine-gun immediately returned Kenna's fire and with such accuracy that bullets actually passed between his arms and his body. Undeterred, he remained completely exposed and continued to fire at the enemy until his magazine was exhausted. Still making a target of himself, Kenna discarded his Bren gun and called for a rifle. Despite the intense machine-gun fire, he seized the rifle and, with amazing coolness, killed the gunner with his first round. A second automatic opened fire on Kenna from a different position and another of the enemy immediately tried to move into position behind the first machine-gun, but Kenna remained standing and killed him with his next round. The result of Kenna's magnificent bravery in the face of concentrated fire was that the bunker was captured without further loss, and the company attack proceeded to a successful conclusion, many enemy being killed and numerous automatic weapons captured. There is no doubt that the success of the company attack would have been seriously endangered and many casualties sustained but for Private Kenna's magnificent courage and complete disregard for his own safety.

At the time of publication, Edward Kenna was one of the surviving VC holders.

ITALY: LAKE COMACCHIO

In spring 1945, 8th Army was planning to advance along Route 16, through Argenta. 2nd Commando Brigade carried out an operation to cross Lake Comacchio, between it and the sea, and clear the Germans from the area. The lake was separated from the Adriatic by a spit of land one to two miles wide, so the defences were intended to protect against a seaborne attack. In their attack the Commandos moved across the lake in boats and dinghies, with artillery and tank support. By the end of the first day the spit was held as far as the first canal. 43 RM Commando's advance the next day was on sand, unsuitable for tanks, but there were no enemy to be seen until they reached Porto Garibaldi, when they came under machine-gun fire. This was dealt with by an airstrike by Hurricane fighter-bombers, and artillery, and the following night the Commandos were relieved by 24th Guards Brigade. They had taken 946 prisoners and much equipment.

Islands in the southern part of the lake were taken a few days later, in an operation intended to distract the Germans from the crossing of the Senio River.

HUNTER, Thomas Peck *Corporal, 43 Royal Marine Commando, attached Special Service Troops*

3 April 1945 – In Italy during the advance by the Commando to its final objective, Corporal Hunter of C Troop was in charge of a Bren group of the leading sub-section of the Commando. Having advanced to within 400 yards of the canal, he observed the enemy were holding a group of houses south of the canal. Realizing that his troop behind him were in the open, as the country there was completely devoid of cover, and that the enemy would cause heavy casualties as soon as they opened fire, Corporal Hunter seized the Bren gun and charged alone across 200 yards of open ground. Three Spandaus from the houses and at least six from the north bank of the canal opened fire and at the same time the enemy mortars started to fire at the troop. Hunter attracted most of the fire, and so determined was his charge and his firing from the hip that the enemy in the houses became demoralized. Showing complete disregard for the intense enemy fire, he ran through the houses, changing magazines as he ran, and alone cleared the houses. Six Germans surrendered to him and the remainder fled across a footbridge onto the north bank of the canal. The troop dashing up behind Hunter now became the target for all the Spandaus on the north of the canal. Again offering himself as a target, he lay in full view of the enemy on a heap of rubble and fired at the concrete pillboxes on the other side. He again drew most of the fire, but by now the greater part of the troop had made the safety of the houses. During this period he shouted encouragement to the remainder, and called only for more Bren magazines with which he could engage the Spandaus. Firing with great accuracy up to the last, Hunter was finally hit in the head by a burst of Spandau fire and killed instantly. There can be no doubt that Corporal Hunter offered himself as a target in order to save his troop, and only the speed of his movement prevented him being hit earlier. The skill and accuracy with which he used his Bren gun is proved by the way he demoralized the enemy, and later did definitely silence many of the Spandaus firing on his troop as they crossed open ground, so much so that under his covering fire elements of the troop made their final objective before he was killed. Throughout the operation his magnificent courage, leadership and cheerfulness had been an inspiration to his comrades.

His was the only Royal Marine VC of the war.

LASSEN, Anders Frederik Emil Victor Schau *T/Major, General List, attached Special Boat Service, 1st Special Air Service Regiment*

8/9 April 1945 – In Italy, on the night of 8/9 April 1945, Major Lassen was ordered to take out a patrol of 1 officer and 17 other ranks to raid the north shore of Lake Comacchio. His tasks were to cause as many casualties and as much confusion as possible, to give the impression of a major landing, and to capture prisoners. No previous reconnaissance was possible, and the party found itself on a narrow road flanked on both sides by water. Preceded by two scouts, Lassen led his men along the road towards the town. They were challenged after approximately 500 yards from a position on the side of the road. An attempt to allay suspicion by answering that they were fishermen returning home failed, for when moving forward again to overpower the sentry, machine-gun fire started from the position, and also from two other blockhouses to the rear. Lassen himself then attacked with grenades, and annihilated the first position containing four Germans and two machine-guns. Ignoring the hail of bullets sweeping the road from three enemy positions, an additional one having come into action from 300 yards down the road, he raced forward to engage the second position under covering fire from the remainder of the force. Throwing in more grenades, he silenced this position which was then overrun by his patrol. Two enemy were killed, two captured and two more machine-guns silenced. By this time the force had suffered casualties and its firepower was very considerably reduced. Still under a heavy cone of fire, Major Lassen rallied and reorganized his force and brought his fire to bear on the third position. Moving forward himself he flung in more grenades which produced a cry of, '*Kamerad.*' He then went forward to within three or four yards of the position to order the enemy outside, and to take their surrender. Whilst shouting to them to come out he was hit by a burst of Spandau fire from the left of the position and he fell mortally wounded, but even whilst falling he flung a grenade, wounding some of the occupants, and enabling his patrol to dash in and capture this final position. Lassen refused to be evacuated as he said it would impede the withdrawal and endanger further lives, and as ammunition was nearly exhausted the force had to withdraw. By his magnificent leadership and complete disregard for his personal safety, Lassen had, in the face of overwhelming superiority, achieved his objects. Three positions were wiped out, accounting for six machine-guns, killing eight and wounding others of the enemy, and two prisoners were taken.

Lassen remains the only member of the SAS to be awarded the VC and is one of three Danes to hold the medal.

ITALY: SENIO RIVER

The Senio River was the point chosen to launch 8th Army's attack north through the Argenta Gap. On 9 April, after strategic, medium and fighter bombers had destroyed the reserve areas, the gun batteries and the forward defences respectively, the infantry crossed with tank support, 8th Indian Division on the right and the New Zealand Division on the left, with a feint in the centre by the 78th.

ALI HAIDAR *Sepoy, 13th Frontier Force Rifles*
    9 April 1945 – In Italy, during the crossing of the River Senio, near Fusignano, in daylight on 9 April 1945, a company of the 13th Frontier Force Rifles was ordered to assault enemy positions strongly dug in on the far bank. These positions had been prepared and improved over many months and were mainly on the steep flood banks, some 25 feet high. Sepoy Ali Haidar was a member of the left-hand section of the left-hand platoon. As soon as the platoon started to cross, it came under heavy and accurate machine-gun fire from two enemy posts strongly dug in about 60 yards away. Ali Haidar's section suffered casualties and only three men, including himself, managed to get across. The remainder of the company was temporarily held up. Without orders, and on his own initiative, Ali Haidar, leaving the other two to cover him, charged the nearest post which was about 30

yards away. He threw a grenade and almost at the same time the enemy threw one at him, wounding him severely in the back. In spite of this he kept on and the enemy post was destroyed and four of the enemy surrendered. With utter disregard of his own wounds he continued and charged the next post in which the enemy had one Spandau and three automatics, which were still very active and preventing movement on both banks. He was again wounded, this time in the right leg and right arm. Although weakened by loss of blood, with great determination Ali Haidar crawled closer and in a final effort raised himself from the ground, threw a grenade, and charged into the second enemy post. Two enemy were wounded and the remaining two surrendered. Taking advantage of the outstanding success of Ali Haidar's dauntless attacks, the rest of the company charged across the river and carried out their task of making a bridgehead. Ali Haidar was picked up and brought back from the second position seriously wounded. His heroism had saved an ugly situation which would – but for his personal bravery – have caused the battalion a large number of casualties at a critical time and seriously delayed the crossing of the river and the building of a bridge. With the rapid advance which it was possible to make the battalion captured 3 officers and 217 other ranks and gained their objectives.

NAMDEO JADHAO *Sepoy, 5th Mahratta Light Infantry*
    9 April 1945 – In Italy, on the evening of 9 April 1945, a company of the 5th Mahratta Light Infantry assaulted the east bank of the Senio River, north of San Polito. Three minutes afterwards another company was to pass through and assault the west bank. In this sector the Senio River is about 15 feet broad, 4–5 feet deep and flows between precipitous banks 30–35 feet high. Both banks were honeycombed with an intricate system of German dugouts and defence posts, with a mine belt on the inner face of the east bank above the dugout entrances. Sepoy Namdeo Jadhao was a company runner and when his company crossed the river he was with his company commander close behind one of the leading sections. When wading the river and emerging on the west bank the party came under heavy fire from at least three German posts on the inner face of the east bank. The company commander and two men were wounded and the rest, with the exception of Namdeo Jadhao, were killed. This gallant sepoy immediately carried one of the wounded men through the deep water and up the precipitous slope of the bank through the mine belt to safety. He then made a second trip to bring back the other wounded man. Both times he was under heavy mortar and machine-gun fire. He then determined to eliminate the machine-gun posts, which had pinned down the companies, and to avenge his dead comrades, so, crossing the exposed east bank a third time, he dashed at the nearest enemy post and silenced it with his tommy gun. He was, however, wounded in the hand and, being unable to fire his gun any further, threw it away and resorted to grenades. With these he successively charged and

wiped out two more enemy posts, at one time crawling to the top of the bank to replenish his stock of grenades from his comrades on the reverse slope. Having silenced all machine-gun fire from the east bank, he then climbed on to the top of it and, in spite of heavy mortar fire, stood in the open shouting the Mahratta war cry and waving the remainder of the companies across the river. This sepoy not only saved the lives of his comrades, but his outstanding gallantry and personal bravery enabled the two companies to hold the river banks firmly, and eventually the battalion to secure a deeper bridgehead, which in turn ultimately led to the collapse of all German resistance in the area.

NORTH BORNEO

Borneo was invaded by the Australian 2nd Corps. The first objective was the island of Tarakan, off the north-east coast, in May, then on 10 June Brunei Bay was taken. Operations continued into July, with an amphibious capture of Balikpapan.

MACKEY, John Bernard *Corporal, 2nd/3rd Pioneer Bn., Australian Military Forces*

12 May 1945 – Corporal Mackey was in charge of a section of the 2nd/ 3rd Australian Pioneer Battalion in the attack on the feature known as Helen, east of Tarakan town. Led by Mackey the section moved along a narrow spur with scarcely width for more than one man when it came under fire from three well-sited positions near the top of a very steep razor-backed ridge. The ground fell away almost sheer on each side of the track, making it almost impossible to move to a flank, so Mackey led his men forward. He charged the first machine-gun position but slipped and after wrestling with an enemy, bayoneted him, and charged straight on to the heavy machine-gun which was firing from a bunker position six yards to his right. He rushed this post and killed the crew with grenades. He then jumped back and changing his rifle for a sub-machine-gun he attacked farther up the steep slope another light machine-gun position which was firing on his platoon. Whilst charging he fired his gun and reached within a few feet of the enemy position when he was killed by machine-gun fire, but not before he had killed two more of the enemy. By his exceptional bravery and complete disregard for his own life Corporal Mackey was largely responsible for the killing of seven Japanese and the elimination of two machine-gun posts which enabled his platoon to gain its objective, from which the company continued to engage the enemy.

STARCEVICH, Leslie Thomas *Private, 2nd/43rd Australian Infantry Bn. (South Australia), Australian Military Forces*

25 May 1945 – Private Starcevich was a member of the 2nd/43rd Australian Infantry Battalion during the capture of Beaufort, North Borneo.

During the approach along a thickly wooded spur, the enemy was encountered at a position where movement off the single track leading into the enemy defences was difficult and hazardous. When the leading section came under fire from two enemy machine-gun posts and suffered casualties, Starcevich, who was Bren-gunner, moved forward and assaulted each post in turn. He rushed each post, firing his Bren gun from the hip, killed five enemy and put the remaining occupants of the posts to flight. The advance progressed until the section came under fire from two more machine-gun posts, which halted the section temporarily. Starcevich again advanced fearlessly firing his Bren gun from the hip, and ignoring the hostile fire captured both posts single-handed, disposing of seven enemy in this assault.

THE WAR AT SEA

FRASER, Ian Edward *Lieutenant, Royal Naval Reserve*
31 July 1945 – Lieutenant Fraser commanded HM Midget Submarine *XE.3* in a successful attack on a Japanese heavy cruiser, the *Takao*, at her moorings in Johore Strait, Singapore. During the long approach up the Singapore Straits *XE.3* deliberately left the believed safe channel and entered mined waters to avoid suspected hydrophone posts. The target was aground, or nearly aground, both fore and aft, and only under the midship portion was there sufficient water for *XE.3* to place herself under the cruiser. For forty minutes *XE.3* pushed her way along the seabed until finally Fraser managed to force her under the centre of the cruiser. Here he placed the limpets and dropped his main side charge. Great difficulty was experienced in extricating the craft after the attack had been completed, but finally *XE.3* was clear, and commenced her long return journey out to sea. The courage and determination of Lieutenant Fraser are beyond all praise. Any man not possessed of his relentless determination to achieve his object in full, regardless of all consequences, would have dropped his side charge alongside the target instead of persisting until he had forced his submarine right under the cruiser. The approach and withdrawal entailed a passage of 80 miles through water which had been mined by both the enemy and the Royal Navy, past hydrophone positions, over loops and controlled minefields, and through an anti-submarine boom.
At the time of publication, Ian Fraser was one of the surviving VC holders.

MAGENNIS, James Joseph *A/Leading Seaman, Royal Navy*
31 July 1945 – Leading Seaman Magennis served as diver in HM Midget Submarine *XE.3* for her attack on a Japanese cruiser, the *Takao*, in Johore Strait, Singapore. Owing to the fact that it was tightly jammed under the target the diver's hatch could not be fully opened, and Magennis had to squeeze himself through the narrow space available. He experienced great

difficulty in placing his limpets on the bottom of the cruiser owing both to the foul state of the bottom and to the pronounced slope upon which the limpet mines would not hold. Before a limpet could be placed, therefore, Magennis had thoroughly to scrape the area clear of barnacles, and in order to secure the limpets he had to tie them in pairs by a line passing under the cruiser keel. This was very tiring work for a diver, and he was moreover handicapped by a steady leakage of oxygen which was ascending in bubbles to the surface. A lesser man would have been content to place a few limpets and then to return to the craft. Magennis, however, persisted until he had placed his full outfit before returning to the craft in an exhausted condition. Shortly after withdrawing, Lieutenant FRASER endeavoured to jettison his limpet carriers, but one of these would not release itself and fell clear of the craft. Despite his exhaustion, his oxygen leak and the fact that there was every probability of his being sighted, Magennis at once volunteered to leave the craft and free the carrier rather than allow a less experienced diver to undertake the job. After seven minutes of nerve-racking work he succeeded in releasing the carrier. Magennis displayed very great courage and devotion to duty and complete disregard for his own safety.

He was the only native of Northern Ireland to be awarded the VC during the Second World War. He fell foul of Ulster's sectarianism and settled in Bradford, where he died in 1986. Belatedly, Belfast City Council voted to erect a suitable memorial in 1995 to the city's only VC.

GRAY, Robert Hampton *T/Lieutenant, Royal Canadian Naval Volunteer Reserve, serving with 1841 Squadron, Fleet Air Arm*

9 August 1945 – In the face of fire from shore batteries and a heavy concentration of fire from some five warships Lieutenant Gray pressed home his attack, flying very low in order to ensure success, and, although he was hit and his aircraft was in flames, he obtained at least one direct hit, sinking the destroyer. Lieutenant Gray has consistently shown a brilliant fighting spirit and most inspiring leadership.

FROM KOREA TO THE FALKLANDS

1950–82

THE KOREAN WAR (1950–53)

After the Second World War, Korea was divided up, by American and Soviet agreement, into the communist Democratic People's Republic of Korea in the north, which remained under Soviet influence, and the pro-Western Republic of Korea in the south.

On 25 June 1950, communist troops invaded South Korea and the United Nations Security Council summoned the aid of all member nations in halting the attack. Despite early reverses, Allied reinforcements drove the North Koreans back, assisted by an amphibious landing by an American amphibious corps under the overall command of General Douglas MacArthur which cut the communists' lines of supply north of the main battle ground.

China threatened to intervene if troops other than those of the Republic of Korea crossed into North Korea; US troops did so with the approval of the UN on 7 October; on the 21st Pyongyang fell and US and Commonwealth troops headed for the Yalu River. The Chinese assembled an army of three hundred and thirty thousand men, and a massive attack began on 27 November. The Allied troops were then engaged in bitter fighting as they were forced south, and on 31 December the combined communist forces of China and North Korea again invaded South Korea.

In retaliation the Allies put down a constant aerial bombardment which halted the advance and established a front line along the 38th Parallel, where fighting continued until July 1951 – at which time truce negotiations were started. There was a brief outbreak of fighting in June 1953, but by the end of July an armistice laid down the front line as the north–south boundary.

Although aerial bombardment played a major role, there was much close-quarters fighting. In an early action near Songiu in central South Korea, Major Kenneth Muir was awarded the VC for his initiative in carrying out attacks on enemy positions, and a further two VCs were awarded, to Lieutenant Colonel James Carne and Lieutenant Philip Curtis for their actions near the Imjin River against vastly superior enemy numbers. On 4 November 1951 Private William Speakman was also involved in close fighting as he made charging attacks with grenades – for which he too was awarded the VC.

The conflict involved over sixty thousand British troops, including many National Servicemen, most serving in independent brigades alongside the Americans and, from July 1951, in the 1st Commonwealth Division, made up of British, Canadian, Australian, New Zealand and Indian troops.

MUIR, Kenneth *Major, 1st Bn., Argyll and Sutherland Highlanders*
23 September 1950 – B and C Companies of the 1st Battalion Argyll and Sutherland Highlanders attacked an enemy-held feature, Hill 282, and by 0800 hours had consolidated upon it. Some difficulty was experienced in evacuating the wounded from the position and demands were made for stretcher parties to be sent forward by the battalion. At this juncture the position came under mortar and shell fire. At approximately 0900 hours small parties of the enemy started to infiltrate on the left flank, necessitating the reinforcement of the forward platoon. For the next hour this infiltration increased, as did the shelling and mortaring, causing further casualties within the two companies. By 1100 hours casualties were moderately severe and some difficulty was being experienced in holding the enemy. In addition, due to reinforcing the left flank and to providing personnel to assist with the wounded, both companies were so inextricably mixed that it was obvious that they must come under a unified command. Major Muir, although only visiting the position, automatically took over command and with complete disregard for his own personal safety started to move around the forward element, cheering on and encouraging the men to greater efforts despite the fact that ammunition was running low. He was continually under enemy fire, and, despite entreaties from officers and men alike, refused to take cover. An air strike against the enemy was arranged and air-recognition panels were put out on the ground. At approximately 1215 hours the air strike came in, but unfortunately the aircraft hit the companies' position instead of that of the enemy. The main defensive position was hit with fire bombs and machine-gun fire, causing more casualties and necessitating the withdrawal of the remaining troops to a position some 50 feet below the crest. There is no doubt that a complete retreat from the hill would have been fully justified at this time. Only some 30 fighting men remained and ammunition was extremely low. Muir, however, realized that the enemy had not taken immediate advantage of the unfortunate incident and that the crest was still unoccupied although under fire. With the assistance of the three remaining officers, he immediately formed a small force of some 30 all ranks and personally led a counter-attack on the crest. To appreciate fully the implication of this, it is necessary to realize how demoralizing the effect of the air strike had been and it was entirely due to the courage, determination and splendid example of this officer that such a counter-attack was possible. All ranks responded magnificently and the crest was retaken. From this moment on, Muir's actions were beyond all possible praise. He was determined the wounded

would have adequate time to be taken out and he was just as determined that the enemy would not take the crest. Grossly outnumbered and under heavy automatic fire, Major Muir moved about his small force, redistributing fast-diminishing ammunition, and when the ammunition for his own weapon was spent he took over a 2in mortar, which he used with very great effect against the enemy. While firing the mortar he was still shouting encouragements and advice to his men, and for a further five minutes the enemy were held. Finally, Muir was hit with two bursts of automatic fire which mortally wounded him, but even then he retained consciousness and was still determined to fight on. His last words were, 'The gooks will never drive the Argylls off this hill.' The effect of his splendid leadership on the men was nothing short of amazing and it was entirely due to his magnificent courage and example and the spirit which he imbued in those about him that all the wounded were evacuated from the hill, and, as was subsequently discovered, very heavy casualties inflicted on the enemy in defence of the crest.

CARNE, James Power *Lieutenant Colonel, 1st Bn., Gloucestershire Regiment*
    22/23 April 1951 – On the night 22/23 April 1951, Lieutenant Colonel Carne's battalion was heavily attacked, and the enemy on the Imjin River were repulsed, having suffered heavy casualties. On 23, 24 and 25 April 1951, the battalion was heavily and incessantly engaged by vastly superior numbers of enemy, who repeatedly launched mass attacks but were stopped at close quarters. During 24 and 25 April 1951, the battalion was completely cut off from the rest of the brigade, but remained a fighting entity, in face of almost continual onslaughts from an enemy who were determined at all costs and regardless of casualties to overrun it. Throughout, Lieutenant Colonel Carne's manner remained coolness itself, and on the wireless, the only communication he still had with brigade, he repeatedly assured the brigade commander that all was well with his battalion, that they could hold on and that everyone was in good heart. Throughout the entire engagement Carne, showing a complete disregard for his own safety, moved among the whole battalion under very heavy mortar and machine-gun fire, inspiring the utmost confidence and the will to resist amongst his troops. On two separate occasions, armed with a rifle and grenades, he personally led assault parties which drove back the enemy and saved important situations. Carne's example of courage, coolness and leadership was felt not only in his own battalion, but throughout the whole brigade. He fully realized that his flanks had been turned, but he also knew that the abandonment of his position would clear the way for the enemy to make a major breakthrough, and this would have endangered the corps. When at last it was apparent that his battalion would not be relieved, on orders from higher authority he organized his battalion into small, officer-led parties who then broke out, while he himself in charge of a small party fought his way out, but was captured. He

inspired his officers and men to fight beyond the normal limits of human endurance, in spite of overwhelming odds and ever-increasing casualties, shortage of ammunition and of water.

CURTIS, Philip Kenneth Edward *Lieutenant, Duke of Cornwall's Light Infantry, attached 1st Bn., Gloucestershire Regiment*
   22/23 April 1951 – During the first phase of the Battle of the Imjin River on the night of 22/23 April 1951, A Company, 1st Gloucesters, was heavily attacked by a large enemy force. By dawn on 23 April the enemy had secured a footing on the 'Castle Hill' site in very close proximity to 2 Platoon's position. The company commander ordered 1 Platoon, under the command of Lieutenant Curtis, to carry out a counter-attack with a view to dislodging the enemy from the position. Under the covering fire of medium machine-guns the counter-attack, gallantly led by Curtis, gained initial success but was eventually held up by heavy fire and grenades. Enemy from just below the crest of the hill were rushed to reinforce the position and a fierce firefight developed. Curtis ordered some of his men to give him covering fire while he himself rushed the main position of resistance; in this charge Curtis was severely wounded by a grenade. Several of his men crawled out and pulled him back under cover, but recovering himself, Curtis insisted on making a second attempt. Breaking free from the men who wished to restrain him, he made another desperate charge, hurling grenades as he went, but was killed by a burst of fire when within a few yards of his objective. Although the immediate objective of this counter-attack was not achieved, it had a great effect on the subsequent course of the battle; for although the enemy had gained a footing on a position vital to the defence of the whole company area, this success had resulted in such furious action that they made no further effort to exploit their success in this immediate area; had they done so, the eventual withdrawal of the company might well have proved impossible.

SPEAKMAN, William *Private, Black Watch, attached 1st Bn., King's Own Scottish Borderers*
   Born in 1927 in Altrincham near Manchester, at the age of fifteen Speakman joined the Army Cadet Corps as a drummer boy, then in 1945, aged eighteen, joined the army. Although a Cheshire lad, Big Bill (he topped six feet seven inches tall) had dark, Scottish looks, and it was appropriate that he enlisted with the Black Watch. After serving in Trieste, Hong Kong and post-war Germany, he volunteered for duty in Korea – where he was one of just four men awarded the VC. Much was made of the fact that when out of ammunition, Speakman continued to bombard the enemy position with cans, stones and beer bottles – hence the name 'the Beer-bottle VC' – but his own account of events at United Hill, recalled fifty years after the end of the Korean War, was less colourful.

We were out reinforcing the wire and had a funny feeling that something was going to happen. Two or three hours later, all hell broke loose. There were thousands of Chinese – they must have concealed themselves like rabbits in the ground. They were very skilful at it. It was getting dark and we could only just pick them out. They came at us in a rush all along the front. There was a lot of hand-to-hand.

There were three waves – the cannon fodder who flattened the wire, the second and then the third are the really tough ones, and you have to mix it with them. There were so many of them, you just had to get on with it.

They were milling around you – you can't even pull your bolt back, so you fight with the butt of your rifle and bayonet. The battle went on for six hours. When we ran out of ammunition we started to throw rocks and stones and anything we could lay our hands on. I led up to fifteen counter-charges – we had to get our wounded. We couldn't just give in – we'd fought for so long we just couldn't give up that bloody hill. You are fighting for your life and it's your job to hold the line. If you give in they'll attack the other units from the rear.

We were told to withdraw, and that's when we went forward to clear the hill – to get our wounded off. Eventually the fighting died down and we could get our people off the hill. I was wounded by shrapnel in the shoulder and the leg. To be honest, you get hit and you don't realize it – you're a bit busy – and someone says, 'Bill, you've been hit in the back!' I was ordered off the hill to get my wounds dressed. The medical orderly tending me was caught in a burst and I said 'stuff it' and went forward again. It was only later I flaked out unconscious for a while – finished up in hospital in Japan.

Although his award was made by King George VI, Speakman was the first VC to be invested by Queen Elizabeth II – and was also honoured with a civic reception at home in Altrincham. Speakman married while serving in Singapore and had six children, but returned home to England when he retired from the army aged forty. Civilian life didn't really suit him and work was hard to find – so much so that he sold his medals for £1,500 to pay for repairs to his house (these were later sold in 1982 for £20,000, but are now in the War Museum of Scotland).

At the time of publication, William Speakman was a surviving holder of the VC.

THE MALAYSIA–INDONESIA CONFRONTATION (1963–66)

In September 1963 the Federation of Malaysia was officially recognized. It comprised the former British colonies of the Malay Peninsula, Singapore, Sabah and Sarawak in North Borneo, and was now governed by Prime

Minister Tengku Abdul Rahman, who agreed to the continued presence of British armed forces in the country.

President Sukarno of Indonesia, to the south, regarded this military presence as a thinly disguised attempt to continue colonial rule and was concerned that the new federation would be used as a base from which troops could move to subvert the course of the revolution in his own country.

The so-called 'Confrontation' began with the aim of destabilizing the Malaysian federations, and raids were launched into Malaysian territory, even before its official recognition. At first, small parties of armed Indonesians crossed into Malaysia on propaganda and sabotage missions, but by 1964, regular units of the Indonesian army were involved. British military presence had hitherto consisted of border-based companies which were tasked with protecting the local populace from Indonesian attack, but by 1965, Britain was prepared to take more aggressive measures. British troops now made offensive forays across the border, keeping the Indonesians on the defensive in their own territory, drastically reducing their incursions into Malaysia.

The only VC of the campaign was awarded to Lance Corporal Rambahadur Limbu, following action in Sarawak on 21 November 1965.

Eventually Indonesia ended hostilities on 11 August 1966, and rejoined the UN in September.

RAMBAHADUR LIMBU *Lance Corporal, 2nd/10th Gurkha Rifles*

21 November 1965 – On 21 November 1965 in the Bau District of Sarawak, Lance Corporal Rambahadur Limbu was with his company when they discovered and attacked a strong enemy force located in the border area. The enemy were strongly entrenched in platoon strength on top of a sheer hill, the only approach to which was along a knife-edge ridge allowing only three men to move abreast. Leading his support group in the van of the attack, Rambahadur Limbu could see the nearest trench and in it a sentry manning a machine-gun. Determined to gain first blood he inched himself forward until, still 10 yards from his enemy, he was seen and the sentry opened fire, immediately wounding a man to his right. Rushing forward he reached the enemy trench in seconds and killed the sentry, thereby gaining for the attacking force a first but firm foothold on the objective. The enemy were now fully alerted and, from their positions in depth, brought down heavy automatic fire on the attacking force, concentrating this onto the area of the trench held alone by Rambahadur Limbu. Appreciating that he could not carry out his task of supporting his platoon from this position he courageously left the comparative safety of his trench and, with a complete disregard for the hail of fire being directed at him, he got together and led his group to a better fire position some yards ahead. He now attempted to indicate his intentions to his platoon commander by shouting and hand signals but failing to do so in the deafening noise of exploding grenades and continuous automatic fire he again moved out into the open and reported personally, despite the extreme dangers of being hit by the fire not only from the enemy but by his own comrades. It was at the moment of reporting that he saw both men of his own group seriously wounded. Knowing that their only hope of survival was immediate first aid, that evacuation from their very exposed position so close to the enemy was vital, he immediately commenced the first of his three supremely gallant attempts to rescue his comrades. Using what little cover he could find he crawled forward, in full view of at least two enemy machine-gun posts which concentrated their fire on him and which, at this stage of the battle, could not be effectively subdued by the rest of his platoon. For three full minutes he continued to move forward but when almost able to touch the nearest casualty he was driven back by the accurate and intense weight of fire covering his line of approach. After a pause he again started to crawl forward but he soon realized that only speed would give him the cover which the ground could not. Rushing forward he hurled himself on the ground beside one of the wounded and, calling for support from two machine-guns which had now come up to his right in support, he picked up the man and carried him to safety out of the line of fire. Without hesitation he immediately returned to the top of the hill determined to complete his self-imposed task of saving those for whom he felt personally responsible. It was now clear, from the increased weight of fire being concentrated on the approaches to and in the immediate vicinity of the remaining casualty, the enemy were doing all they could to prevent any further attempts at rescue. However, despite this, Rambahadur Limbu again moved out into the open for his final effort. In a series of short forward rushes, and once being pinned down for some minutes by the intense and accurate automatic fire which could be seen striking the ground all round him, he eventually reached the wounded man. Picking him up and unable now to seek cover he carried him back as fast as he could, through the hail of enemy bullets. It had taken twenty minutes to complete this gallant action and the events leading up to it. For all but a few seconds this young NCO had been moving alone in full view of the enemy and under the continuous aimed fire of their automatic weapons. That he was able to achieve what he did against such overwhelming odds without being hit, was miraculous. His outstanding personal bravery, selfless conduct, complete contempt of the enemy and determination to save the lives of the men of his fire group set an incomparable example and inspired all who saw him. Finally rejoining his section on the left flank of the attack, Lance Corporal Rambahadur Limbu was able to recover the machine-gun abandoned by the wounded and with it won his revenge, initially giving support during the later stage of the prolonged assault and finally being responsible for killing four more enemy as they attempted to escape across the border. This hour-long battle which had throughout been fought at point-blank range and with the utmost ferocity by both sides was finally won. At least 24 enemy are known to have died at a cost to the attacking force of three killed and two wounded. In scale and in achievement this engagement stands out as one of the first importance and there is no doubt that, but for the inspired conduct and example set by Lance Corporal Rambahadur Limbu at the most vital stage of the battle, much less would have been achieved and greater casualties caused.

At the time of publication, Rambahadur Limbu was a surviving holder of the VC.

THE VIETNAM WAR (1959–75)

Australian troops (to whom all four VCs of the war were awarded) became increasingly involved in the Vietnam War in the course of enforcing Australia's 'forward defence' planning policy. This complemented the United States' determination to contain the threat of communism in South-East Asia while also fulfilling Australia's obligations as a member of the South-East Asia Treaty Organization. In August 1962, Australian army advisers arrived to work with the US planners, assisting in training South Vietnamese troops for action – but without the mandate to take part in actual operations.

By early 1965, there were 100 Australians working with the US advisory team, and when the first US combat troops arrived in Vietnam in March, the Australian premier, Robert Menzies, committed a force totalling 1,100 to the conflict, working in counter-insurgency operations. In March 1966 an Australian Task Force of 4,500 was in action over an expanding area, but popular support for the war was falling in Australia and troops were finally withdrawn by June 1973.

The Australian Army Training Team Vietnam – known as 'The Team' – was the first and last Australian unit serving in Vietnam, and all four VC awards were made to Team men. The unit was also honoured with the American Meritorious Unit Commendation and the Vietnamese Cross of Gallantry with Palm Unit Citation.

WHEATLEY, Kevin Arthur *Warrant Officer Class II, Australian Army Training Team Vietnam*
13 November 1965 – At approximately 1300 hours, a Vietnamese Civil Irregular Defence Group company commenced a search-and-destroy operation in the Tra Bong valley, 15 kilometres east of Tra Bong Special Forces camp in Quang Ngai province. Accompanying the force were Captain Fazekas with the centre platoon, and Warrant Officers Wheatley and Swanton with the right-hand platoon. At about 1340 hours, Wheatley reported contact with Viet Cong elements. The Viet Cong resistance increased in strength until finally Wheatley asked for assistance. Captain Fazekas

immediately organized the centre platoon to help and personally led and fought it towards the action area. While moving towards this area he received another radio message from Wheatley to say that Warrant Officer Swanton had been hit in the chest, and requested an air strike and an aircraft for the evacuation of casualties. At about this time the right platoon broke in the face of heavy Viet Cong fire and began to scatter. Although told by the Civil Irregular Defence Group medical assistant that Swanton was dying, Wheatley refused to abandon him. He discarded his radio to enable him to half drag, half carry Swanton, under heavy machine-gun and automatic rifle fire, out of the open rice paddies into the comparative safety of a wooded area some 200 metres away. He was assisted by a Civil Irregular Defence Group member, Private Dinh Do who, when the Viet Cong were only some 10 metres away, urged him to leave his dying comrade. Again he refused, and was seen to pull the pins from two grenades and calmly await the Viet Cong, holding one grenade in each hand. Shortly afterwards, two grenade explosions were heard, followed by several bursts of fire. The two bodies were found at first light next morning after the fighting had ceased, with Wheatley lying beside Swanton. Both had died of gunshot wounds. Warrant Officer Wheatley displayed magnificent courage in the face of an over-whelming Viet Cong force which was later estimated at more than a company. He had the clear choice of abandoning a wounded comrade and saving himself by escaping through the dense timber or of staying with Warrant Officer Swanton and thereby facing certain death. He deliberately chose the latter course.

BADCOE, Peter John *Major, Australian Army Training Team Vietnam*
23 February, 7 March and 7 April 1967 – On 23 February 1967 he was acting as an adviser to a Regional Force company in support of a sector operation in Phu Thu district. He monitored a radio transmission which stated that the subsector adviser, an American officer, had been killed and that his body was within 50 metres of an enemy machine-gun position. An American medic had also been wounded and was in immediate danger from the enemy. Major Badcoe, with complete disregard for his own safety, moved alone across 600 metres of fire-swept ground and reached the wounded medic, attended to him and ensured his future safety. He then organized a force of one platoon and led them towards the enemy post. His personal leadership, words of encouragement, and actions in the face of hostile enemy fire forced the platoon to successfully assault the enemy position and capture it, where he personally killed the machine-gunners directly in front of him. He then picked up the body of the dead officer and ran back to the command post over open ground still covered by enemy fire. On 7 March 1967, at approximately 0645 hours, the sector reaction company was deployed to Quang Dien subsector to counter an attack by the Viet Cong on the headquarters. Badcoe left the command group after their vehicle broke

down and a US officer was killed. He joined the company headquarters and personally led the company in an attack over open terrain to assault and capture a heavily defended enemy position. His personal courage and leadership turned defeat into victory and prevented the enemy from capturing the district headquarters. On 7 April 1967, on an operation in Huong Tra district, Badcoe was with the 1st ARVN Division reaction company and some armoured personnel carriers. During the move forward to an objective the company came under heavy small-arms fire and withdrew to a cemetery for cover. This left Badcoe and his radio operator about 50 metres in front of the leading elements, under heavy mortar fire. Seeing this withdrawal, Badcoe ran back to them and by encouragement and example got them moving forward again. He then set out in front of the company to lead them on. The company stopped again under heavy fire but Badcoe continued on and prepared to throw grenades. When he rose to throw a grenade, his radio operator pulled him down as heavy small-arms fire was being brought to bear on them. He later got up again to throw a grenade and was hit and killed by a burst of machine-gun fire. Soon after, friendly artillery fire was called in and the position was assaulted and captured. Major Badcoe's conspicuous gallantry and leadership on all these occasions was an inspiration to all. Each action, ultimately, was successful, due entirely to his efforts, the final one ending in his death.

SIMPSON, Rayene Stewart *Warrant Officer Class II, Australian Army Training Team Vietnam*

6 and 11 May 1969 – On 6 May 1969, Warrant Officer Simpson was serving as commander of 232nd Mobile Strike Force Company of 5th Special Forces Group on a search-and-clear operation in Kontum province, near the Laotian border. When one of his platoons became heavily engaged with the enemy, he led the remainder of his company to its assistance. Disregarding the dangers involved, he placed himself at the front of his troops, thus becoming a focal point of enemy fire, and personally led the assault on the left flank of the enemy position. As the company moved forward an Australian warrant officer commanding one of the platoons was seriously wounded and the assault began to falter. Simpson, at great personal risk and under heavy fire, moved across open ground, reached the wounded warrant officer and carried him to a position of safety. He then returned to his company where, with complete disregard for his safety, he crawled forward to within 10 metres of the enemy and threw grenades into their positions. As darkness fell, and being unable to break into the enemy position, Simpson ordered his company to withdraw. He then threw smoke grenades and, carrying a wounded platoon leader, covered the withdrawal of the company together with five indigenous soldiers. On 11 May 1969, in the same operation, Warrant Officer Simpson's battalion commander was killed and an Australian warrant officer and several indigenous soldiers were wounded.

In addition, another Australian warrant officer who had been separated from the majority of his troops was contained in the area by enemy fire. Simpson quickly organized two platoons of indigenous soldiers and several advisers and led them to the position of the contact. On reaching the position the element with Simpson came under heavy fire and all but a few of the soldiers with him fell back. Disregarding his own safety, he moved forward in the face of accurate enemy machine-gun fire in order to cover the initial evacuation of the casualties. The wounded were eventually moved out of the line of enemy fire, which all this time was directed at Simpson from close range. At the risk of almost certain death, he made several attempts to move further towards his battalion commander's body, but on each occasion he was stopped by heavy fire. Realizing the position was becoming untenable and that priority should be given to extricating other casualties as quickly as possible, Simpson, alone and still under enemy fire, covered the withdrawal of the wounded by personally placing himself between the wounded and the enemy. From this position, he fought on and by outstanding courage and valour was able to prevent the enemy advance until the wounded were removed from the immediate vicinity. Simpson's gallant and individual action and his coolness under fire were exceptional and were instrumental in achieving the successful evacuation of the wounded to the helicopter evacuation pad.

PAYNE, Keith *Warrant Officer Class II, Australian Army Training Team Vietnam*

24 May 1969 – On 24 May 1969, in Kontum province, Warrant Officer Payne was commanding 212th Company of 1st Mobile Strike Force Battalion when the battalion was attacked by a North Vietnamese force of superior strength. The enemy isolated the two leading companies, one of which was Payne's, and with heavy mortar and rocket support assaulted their position from three directions simultaneously. Under this heavy attack, the indigenous soldiers began to fall back. Directly exposing himself to the enemy's fire, Payne, through his own efforts, temporarily held off the assaults by alternately firing his weapon and running from position to position collecting grenades and throwing them at the assaulting enemy. While doing this, he was wounded in the hands and arms. Despite his outstanding efforts, the indigenous soldiers gave way under the enemy's increased pressure and the battalion commander, together with several advisers and a few soldiers, withdrew. Paying no attention to his wounds and under extremely heavy enemy fire, Payne covered this withdrawal by again throwing grenades and firing his own weapon at the enemy who were attempting to follow up. Still under fire, he then ran across exposed ground to head off his own troops who were withdrawing in disorder. He successfully stopped them and organized the remnants of his and the second company into a temporary defensive perimeter by nightfall. Having achieved this, Payne, of his own accord and at great personal risk, moved out of the perimeter into the darkness alone in an attempt to find the wounded and other indigenous soldiers. Some had been left on the position and others were scattered in the area. Although the enemy were still occupying the previous position, Payne, with complete disregard for his own life, crawled back on to it and extricated several wounded soldiers. He then continued to search the area, in which the enemy were also moving and firing, for some three hours. He finally collected 40 lost soldiers, some of whom had been wounded, and returned with this group to the temporary defensive perimeter he had left, only to find that the remainder of the battalion had moved back. Undeterred by this setback and personally assisting a seriously wounded American soldier, he led the group through the enemy to the safety of his battalion base. His sustained and heroic personal efforts in this action were outstanding and undoubtedly saved the lives of a large number of his indigenous soldiers and several of his fellow advisers.

At the time of publication, Keith Payne was a surviving holder of the VC.

THE FALKLANDS WAR (1982)

On 2 April 1982 Argentina invaded the Falkland Islands – the Malvinas – to reclaim what they saw as their own territory. The following day Argentine troops invaded the British-held island of South Georgia, and on 6 April the Task Force set out from the UK to repel the invaders.

During the next two months concentrated air, sea and land operations were carried out in the harsh and inhospitable climate of the South Atlantic. May saw the sinking of the Argentine ship *General Belgrano*, an Exocet attack on HMS *Sheffield* and the sinking of HMS *Ardent, Antelope* and *Coventry* and the container ship *Atlantic Conveyor*. British troops landed at San Carlos and were engaged in fierce fighting with well-entrenched Argentine forces, 2nd Bn., Parachute Regiment eventually retaking Goose Green on 28 May, during which attack at nearby Darwin, Lieutenant Colonel Herbert Jones won the VC. The Argentine troops were systematically removed from Mount Harriet, Two Sisters and Mount Longdon on the night of 11/12 June. A VC was awarded to Sergeant Ian McKay for his action on Mount Longdon. The following night 3rd Commando Brigade and 7th Infantry Brigade cleared Tumbledown, Wireless Ridge and Mount William, following which the Argentinians surrendered.

JONES, Herbert *Lieutenant Colonel, commanding 2nd Bn., Parachute Regiment*
    28 May 1982 – Lieutenant Colonel Jones was commanding 2nd Bn., Parachute Regiment on operations on the Falklands Islands. The battalion was ordered to attack enemy positions in and around the settlements of

Darwin and Goose Green. During the attack against the Argentinians, who were well dug-in with mutually supporting positions sited in depth, the battalion was held up just south of Darwin by a particularly well-prepared and resilient enemy position of at least eleven trenches on an important ridge. A number of casualties were taken. In order to read the battle fully and to ensure that the momentum of his attack was not lost, Lieutenant Colonel Jones took forward his reconnaissance party to the foot of a re-entrant which a section of his battalion had just secured. Despite persistent, heavy and accurate fire the reconnaissance party gained the top of the re-entrant at approximately the same height as the enemy positions. However, these had been well prepared and continued to pour effective fire onto the battalion advance, which, by now held up for over an hour and under increasingly heavy artillery fire, was in danger of faltering. In his effort to gain a good viewpoint Jones was now at the very front of his battalion. It was clear to him that desperate measures were needed in order to overcome the enemy position and rekindle the attack, and that unless these measures were taken promptly the battalion would sustain increasing casualties and the attack perhaps fail. It was time for personal leadership and action. He immediately seized a sub-machine-gun and, calling on those around him and with total disregard for his own safety, charged the nearest enemy position. This action exposed him to fire from a number of trenches. As he charged up a short slope at the enemy position he was seen to fall and roll back downhill. He immediately picked himself up, and again charged the enemy trench, firing his sub-machine-gun and seemingly oblivious to the intense fire directed at him. He was hit by fire from another trench which he outflanked, and fell dying only a few feet from the enemy he had assaulted. A short time later a company of the battalion attacked the enemy, who quickly surrendered. The devastating display of courage by Lieutenant Colonel Jones had completely undermined their will to fight further. There-after, the momentum of the attack was rapidly regained, Darwin and Goose Green were liberated, and the battalion released the local inhabitants unhar-med and forced the surrender of some 1,200 of the enemy. The achieve-ments of 2nd Bn., Parachute Regiment at Darwin and Goose Green set the tone for the subsequent land victory on the Falklands. They achieved such a moral superiority over the enemy in this first battle that, despite the advantages of numbers and selection of ground, the Argentinians never thereafter doubted either the superior fighting qualities of the British troops or their own inevitable defeat. This was an action of the utmost gallantry by a commanding officer whose dashing leadership and courage throughout the battle were an inspiration to all about him.

McKAY, Ian *Sergeant, 3rd Bn., Parachute Regiment*
    12 June 1982 – During the night of 11/12 June 1982, 3rd Bn., Parachute Regiment mounted a silent attack on an enemy battalion position on Mount

Longdon, an important objective in the battle for Port Stanley in the Falkland Islands. Sergeant McKay was platoon sergeant of 4 Platoon, B Company which, after the initial objective had been secured, was ordered to clear the northern side of the long east–west ridge feature held by the enemy in depth, with strong, mutually supporting positions. By now the enemy were fully alert and resisting fiercely. As 4 Platoon's advance continued it came under increasingly heavy fire from a number of well-sited enemy machine-gun positions on the ridge, and took casualties. Realizing that no further advance was possible, the platoon commander ordered the platoon to move from its exposed position to seek shelter among the rocks of the ridge itself. Here it met up with part of 5 Platoon. The enemy fire was still both heavy and accurate and the position of the platoons was becoming increasingly hazardous. Taking Sergeant McKay, a corporal and a few others, and covered by supporting machine-gun fire, the platoon commander moved forward to reconnoitre the enemy positions but was hit by a bullet in the leg and command devolved upon Sergeant McKay. It was clear that instant action was needed if the advance was not to falter and increasing casualties to ensue. McKay decided to convert this reconnaissance into an attack in order to eliminate the enemy positions. He was in no doubt of the strength and deployment of the enemy as he undertook this attack. He issued orders and taking three men with him broke cover and charged the enemy position. The assault was met by a hail of fire. The corporal was seriously wounded, a private killed and another wounded. Despite these losses Sergeant McKay, with complete disregard for his own safety, continued to charge the enemy position alone. On reaching it he dispatched the enemy with grenades, thereby relieving the position of the beleaguered 4 and 5 Platoons, who were now able to redeploy with relative safety. McKay, however, was killed at the moment of victory, his body falling on the bunker. Without doubt Sergeant McKay's action retrieved a most dangerous situation and was instrumental in ensuring the success of the attack. His was a coolly calculated act, the dangers of which must have been apparent to him beforehand. Undeterred, he acted with outstanding selflessness, perseverance and courage. With a complete disregard for his own safety, he displayed courage and leadership of the highest order, and was an inspiration to all those around him.

Glossary

INDIAN ARMY RANKS

Indian Army	British army equivalent (*or role, in italics*)
Risaldar	Lieutenant
Jemadar	Second Lieutenant
Subadar Major	*Company second-in-command*
Subadar	*Platoon commander*
Jemadar	*Platoon commander*
Havildar Major	Company Sergeant Major
Havildar (infantry) *or* Duffadar (cavalry)	Sergeant
Naik (infantry) *or* Lance Duffadar (cavalry)	Corporal
Lance Naik (infantry) *or* Acting Lance Duffadar (cavalry)	Lance Corporal
Sepoy/Rifleman (infantry) *or* Sowar (cavalry)	Private (infantry) *or* Trooper (cavalry)

ORDERS AND DECORATIONS

AFC	Air Force Cross
AK	Knight of the Order of Australia
BEM	British Empire Medal
CB	Companion of the Most Honourable Order of the Bath
CBE	Companion of the Order of the British Empire
CD	Canadian Forces Decoration
CGM	Conspicuous Gallantry Medal
CIE	Companion of the Most Eminent Order of the Indian Empire

CMG	Companion of the Most Distinguished Order of St Michael and St George
CSI	Companion of the Most Exalted Order of the Star of India
CVO	Companion of the Royal Victorian Order
DCM	Distinguished Conduct Medal
DFC	Distinguished Flying Cross
DFM	Distinguished Flying Medal
DSC	Distinguished Service Cross
DSM	Distinguished Service Medal
DSO	Distinguished Service Order
ED	Efficiency Decoration
GCB	Knight Grand Cross of the Most Honourable Order of the Bath
GCMG	Knight Grand Cross of the Most Distinguished Order of St Michael and St George
GCVO	Knight Grand Cross of the Royal Victorian Order
IOM	Indian Order of Merit
ISM	Indian Service Medal
KBE	Knight Commander of the Order of the British Empire
KCB	Knight Commander of the Most Honourable Order of the Bath
KCIE	Knight Commander of the Most Eminent Order of the Indian Empire
KCMG	Knight Commander of the Most Distinguished Order of St Michael and St George
KCSI	Knight Commander of the Most Exalted Order of the Star of India
KCVO	Knight Commander of the Royal Victorian Order
MBE	Member of the British Empire
MC	Military Cross
MM	Military Medal
MSM	Meritorious Service Medal
MVA	Maha Vir Chakra
MVO	Member of the Royal Victorian Order
OBE	Order of the British Empire
OBI	Order of British India
OM	Order of Merit
PVSM	Pararn Vishishe Seva Medal (India)
RD	Reserve Decoration

RVM   Royal Victorian Medal

SGM   Sea Gallantry Medal

TD   Territorial Decoration

VD   Volunteer Decoration

ACRONYMS AND SPECIALIST TERMS

AIF   Australian Imperial Forces

AMF   Australian Military Forces

Besa   a machine-gun, originally Czech, used in British armoured cars and tanks in the Second World War in 7.92mm and 15mm forms.

Bn.   Battalion

brevet   Until the Second World War, an officer could have a rank in the army separate from his rank in his regiment. The officer took his army rank when he served outside his regiment or when his unit was brigaded with another.

Bty.   Battery

CEF   Canadian Expeditionary Force

chaung   watercourse or minor river

colour sergeant   the senior sergeant of an infantry company (cf. staff sergeant)

CSM   company sergeant major

dhoolie   'rudimentary litter or palanquin used by the lower classes in India, and as an army ambulance' (*OED*)

dorp   village

(ER)   Extra Reserve

gabion   basket or container filled with stones, rubble, etc.

Ghazis   'Muslim fanatics who have devoted themselves to the destruction of infidels' (*OED*)

kop, kopje   small isolated hill

nek   pass

NZEF   New Zealand Expeditionary Force

PIAT   Projectile Infantry Anti-Tank: British shoulder-fired weapon issued from mid-1942, effective up to 100 yards, consisting of a tube containing a powerful spring that threw a hollow-charge projectile

QGO   Queen's Gurkha Officer

(R)	Regular battalion. See also (S) and (T)
Regt.	Regiment
RSM	regimental sergeant major
(S)	Service battalion, i.e. a battalion of New Army volunteers. See also (R) and (T)
sangar	breastwork of stone
sap	a trench or a tunnel that conceals an approach to a defended position
sowar	'a native horseman or mounted orderly, policeman, etc.; a native trooper, esp. one belonging to the irregular cavalry' (*OED*)
Spandau	Allied name for the German MG34 and MG42 infantry machine guns, and by extension any machine gun
spruit	stream or watercourse
SR	Special Reserve
staff sergeant	the senior sergeant of a non-infantry company (cf. colour sergeant)
(T)	Territorial battalion. See also (R) and (S)
TM	trench mortar
traverse	'a pair of right-angled bends incorporated in a trench to avoid enfilading fire' (*COD*)
tulwar	Indian sabre
veld	open country

Bibliography

Bancroft, James W., *Deeds of Valour: A Victorian Military and Naval History Trilogy* (The House of Heroes, 1994)
— *Local Heroes: Boer War VCs* (The House of Heroes, 2003)
— *The Victoria Cross Roll of Honour* (Aim High Productions, 1989)
— *Zulu War Heroes: The Defence of Rorke's Drift* (James W. Bancroft, 2004)
Batchelor, Peter F. and Christopher Matson, *VCs of the First World War: The Western Front 1915* (Wrens Park Publishing, 1999)
Bond, Brian.(ed.), *Victorian Military Campaigns* (Hutchinson, 1967)
Braddon, Russell, *Cheshire V.C.* (Evans Brothers, 1954)
Cooksley, Peter G., *VCs of the First World War: The Air VCs* (Wrens Park Publishing, 1999)
Crook, M. J., *The Evolution of the Victorian Cross* (Midas Books, 1975)
Doherty, Richard and David Truesdale, *Irish Winners of the Victoria Cross* (Four Courts Press, 2000)
Farwell, Byron, *Queen Victoria's Little Wars* (Allen Lane, 1973; repr. Wordsworth, 1999)
Featherstone, Donald, *Victoria's Enemies: An A–Z of British Colonial Warfare* (Blandford Press, 1989)
Giddings, Robert *Imperial Echoes: Eye-Witness Accounts of Victoria's Little Wars* (Leo Cooper, 1996)
Gilbert, Martin, *The Second World War* (Weidenfeld and Nicolson, 1989)
Gliddon, Gerald, *VCs of the First World War: Arras & Messines 1917* (Wrens Park Publishing, 2000)
— *VCs of the First World War: 1914* (Budding Books, 1997)
— *VCs of the First World War: Spring Offensive 1918* (Sutton Publishing, 1997)
— *VCs of the First World War: The Final Days 1918* (Sutton Publishing, 2000)
— *VCs of the First World War: The Road to Victory 1918* (Sutton Publishing, 2000)
— *VCs of the First World War: The Somme* (Budding Books, 1997)
Gordon, Lawrence and Edward Joslin (eds), *British Battles and Medals* (Spink & Son, 1971)
Harvey, David, *Monuments to Courage: Victoria Cross Headstones and Memorials Vols. I and II* (Kevin and Kay Patience, 1999; repr. The Naval & Military Press, 1999)
Haydon, A. L., *The Book of the V.C.* (Andrew Melrose, 1906)

Haythornthwaite, Philip J., *The Colonial Wars Source Book* (Arms and Armour Press, 1997)

Laffin, John, *British VCs of World War 2: A Study in Heroism* (Budding Books, 2000)

Magor, R. B., *African General Service Medals* (R. B. Magor, 1979; repr. The Naval & Military Press, 1993)

Massie, Alastair, *The National Army Museum Book of the Crimean War: The Untold Stories* (Sidgwick & Jackson, 2004)

Pakenham, Thomas, *The Boer War* (Weidenfeld and Nicolson, 1979; Avon Books, 1979)

— *The Scramble for Africa* (Weidenfeld & Nicolson, 1991; Abacus, 2002)

Pemberton, W. Baring, *Battles of the Boer War* (B. T. Batsford, 1964; Pan Books Ltd., 1969)

Ralph, Wayne, *Barker VC: The Life, Death and Legend of Canada's Most Decorated War Hero* (Grub Street, 1997)

Richards, D. S., *The Savage Frontier: A History of the Anglo-Afghan Wars* (Macmillan, 1990; Pan Books, 2003)

Roe, F. Gordon, *The Bronze Cross: A Tribute to Those who Won the Supreme Award for Valour in the years 1940–45* (P.R. Gawthorn, 1945)

Sandford, Kenneth, *Mark of the Lion: The Story of Capt. Charles Upham, V.C. and Bar* (Hutchinson, 1962)

Snelling, Stephen, *VCs of the First World War: Gallipoli* (Wrens Park Publishing, 1999)

— *VCs of the First World War: Passchendaele 1917* (Sutton Publishing, 1998)

The Journal of The King's Royal Rifle Corps Association, ed. Richard Frost (The King's Royal Rifle Corps Association, 2001)

The Journal of The Victoria Cross Society, Editions 1–4, ed. Brian Best (The Victoria Cross Society, 2004)

The Regiment of Fusiliers (English Life Publications, 1999)

The Register of the Victoria Cross (This England Books, 1988)

The V.C. and D.S.O. Book: The Victoria Cross 1856–1920, ed. The Late Sir O'Moore Creagh and E. M. Humphris (The Naval & Military Press)

Turner, John Frayn, *VCs of the Air* (Wrens Park Publishing, 2001)

Victoria Cross Research Group, John Mulholland and Alan Jordan (eds), *Victoria Cross Bibliography* (Spink and Son, 1999)

Appendix

VICTORIA CROSS RECIPIENTS AND THE *LONDON GAZETTE*

It has often been noticed that in different publications on the VC and its recipients discrepancies occur in the date on which an award was promulgated in the *London Gazette*. This is because awards were published in either the first issue of a particular *Gazette* or in a subsequent supplement or supplements. Many authors and publishers quote the original date of the *Gazette*, even though the actual award of the VC was not published until a later supplement. Up to twelve supplements are known for some issues of the *Gazette*.

In the following list *London Gazettes* and their Supplements have been checked and the particular issue in which an award was *first* promulgated whether it be an original *Gazette* or its Supplement has been noted.

London Gazette 31259, 31 Mar 1919, pp. 4153–4163 (4th Supplement to LG 31255, 28 Mar 1919) contains a consolidated list of action dates and locations for 346 VC recipients, this information not being promulgated with the original citation for security reasons.

Many of these entries contained errors and were corrected by *London Gazette* 31340, 15 May 1919, pp. 6084–6085 (4th Supplement to *London Gazette* 31336, 13 May 1919).

	London Gazette	Date	Page	Supplement (if any)	Release Date
Aaron, AL	36235	5 Nov 1943	4859	4th Supp. to LG 36231 2 Nov 1943	Air Min. 26 Oct 1943
Abdul Hafiz	36627	27 Jul 1944	3501/2	Supp. to LG 36626 25 Jul 1944	WO 27 Jul 1944
Ablett, A	21971	24 Feb 1857	657	Supp. to LG 21970 24 Feb 1857	WO 24 Feb 1857
Ackroyd, H	30272	6 Sep 1917	9259	5th Supp. to LG 30267 4 Sep 1917	WO 6 Sep 1917
Acton, A	29074	18 Feb 1915	1700	4th Supp. to LG 29070 16 Feb 1915	WO 18 Feb 1915
Adams, JW	25008	26 Aug 1881	4393	Gazette	WO 24 Aug 1881
Adams, RB	26908	9 Nov 1897	6143	Gazette	WO 9 Nov 1897
Addison, H	22303	2 Sep 1859	3302	Gazette	WO 2 Sep 1859
Addison, WRF	29765	26 Sep 1916	9417	Supp. to LG 29764 26 Sep 1916	WO 26 Sep 1916
Adlam, TE	29836	25 Nov 1916	11525/6	Supp. to LG 29835 24 Nov 1916	WO 25 Nov 1916
Agansing Rai	36730	5 Oct 1944	4569	Supp. to LG 36729 3 Oct 1944	WO 5 Oct 1944
Agar, AWS	31516	22 Aug 1919	10631	6th Supp. to LG 31510 19 Aug 1919	Adm. 22 Aug 1919
Aikman, FR	22179	3 Sep 1858	4014	Gazette	WO 3 Sep 1858
Aitken, RHM	22727	17 Apr 1863	2070	Gazette	WO 16 Apr 1863
Albrecht, H	27462	8 Aug 1902	5085	Gazette	WO 8 Aug 1902
Alexander, EW	29074	18 Feb 1915	1699	4th Supp. to LG 29070 16 Feb 1915	WO 18 Feb 1915
Alexander, J	21971	24 Feb 1857	661	Supp. to LG 21970 24 Feb 1857	WO 24 Feb 1857
Algie, WL	31155	31 Jan 1919	1504	8th Supp. to LG 31147 28 Jan 1919	WO 31 Jan 1919
Ali Haidar	37156	3 Jul 1945	3439	Supp. to LG 37155 29 Jun 1945	WO 3 Jul 1945
Allan, HM Havelock-	See Havelock, HM				
Allan, WW	24717	2 May 1879	3178	Supp. to LG 24716 2 May 1879	WO 2 May 1879
Allen, WB	29802	26 Oct 1916	10394	4th Supp. to LG 29798 24 Oct 1916	WO 26 Oct 1916
Allmand, M	36764	26 Oct 1944	4900	Supp. to LG 36763 24 Oct 1944	WO 26 Oct 1944

	London Gazette	Date	Page	Supplement (if any)	Release Date
Amey, W	31155	31 Jan 1919	1505	8th Supp. to LG 31147 28 Jan 1919	WO 31 Jan 1919
Anderson, C	22680	11 Nov 1862	5346	Gazette	WO 11 Nov 1862
Anderson, CGW	35456	13 Feb 1942	749	Supp. to LG 35455 13 Feb 1942	WO 13 Feb 1942
Anderson, E	36110	29 Jul 1943	3421	Supp. to LG 36109 27 Jul 1943	WO 29 Jul 1943
Anderson, JTMcK	36071	29 Jun 1943	2937/8	2nd Supp. to LG 36069 25 Jun 1943	WO 9 Jun 1943
Anderson, W	29170	22 May 1915	4989	Supp. to LG 29169 21 May 1915	WO 22 May 1915
Anderson, WH	30667	3 May 1918	5353/4	7th Supp. to LG 30660 30 Apr 1918	WO 3 May 1918
Andrew, LW	30272	6 Sep 1917	9260	5th Supp. to LG 30267 4 Sep 1917	WO 6 Sep 1917
Andrews, HJ	32046	9 Sep 1920	9133	3rd Supp. to LG 32043 7 Sep 1920	WO 9 Sep 1920
Andrews, HM Ervine-	See Ervine-Andrews, HM				
Angus, W	29210	29 Jun 1915	6269	Gazette	WO 29 Jun 1915
Annand, RW	34928	23 Aug 1940	5137	Supp. to LG 34927 20 Aug 1940	WO 23 Aug 1940
Anson, AHA	22212	24 Dec 1858	5513	Gazette	WO 24 Dec 1858
Archibald, A	31108	6 Jan 1919	308	4th Supp. to LG 31104 3 Jan 1919	WO 6 Jan 1919
Arthur, T (McArthur)	21971	24 Feb 1857	656	Supp. to LG 21970 24 Feb 1857	WO 24 Feb 1857
Ashford, TE	25023	7 Oct 1881	4990	Gazette	WO 4 Oct 1881
Atkinson, A	27462	8 Aug 1902	5086	Gazette	WO 8 Aug 1902
Auten, H	30900	14 Sep 1918	10847	2nd Supp. to LG 30898 13 Sep 1918	Adm. 14 Sep 1918
Auten, H	31021	20 Nov 1918	13695	2nd Supp. to LG 31019 19 Nov 1918	Adm. 20 Nov 1918
Axford, TL	33849	17 Aug 1918	9660	3rd Supp. to LG 30846 16 Aug 1918	WO 17 Aug 1918
Aylmer, FJ	25306	12 Jul 1892	4006	Gazette	WO 12 Jul 1892
Babtie, W	27184	20 Apr 1900	2547	Gazette	WO 20 Apr 1900

	London Gazette	Date	Page	Supplement (if any)	Release Date
Badcoe, PJ	44431	17 Oct 1967	11273	2nd Supp. to LG 44429 13 Oct 1967	None
Badlu Singh	31034	27 Nov 1918	14040/1	2nd Supp. to LG 31032 26 Nov 1918	WO 27 Nov 1918
Baker, CG	22601	25 Feb 1862	956/957	Gazette	WO 25 Feb 1862
Ball, A	30122	8 Jun 1917	5702	2nd Supp. to LG 30120 8 Jun 1917	WO 8 Jun 1917
Bambrick, V	22212	24 Dec 1858	5513	Gazette	WO 24 Dec 1858
Bamford, E	30807	23 Jul 1918	8586	4th Supp. to LG 30803 19 Jul 1918	Adm. 23 Jul 1918
Bankes, WGH	22212	24 Dec 1858	5519	Gazette	WO 24 Dec 1858
Barber, E	29135	19 Apr 1915	3815	2nd Supp. to LG 29133 16 Apr 1915	WO 19 Apr 1915
Barker, WG	31042	30 Nov 1918	14203/4	2nd Supp. to LG 31040 29 Nov 1918	Air Min. 30 Nov 1918
Barratt, T	30272	6 Sep 1917	9260	5th Supp. to LG 30267 4 Sep 1917	WO 6 Sep 1917
Barrett, JC	31067	14 Dec 1918	14774/5	2nd Supp. to LG 31065 13 Dec 1918	WO 14 Dec 1918
Barron, CF	30471	11 Jan 1918	723	6th Supp. to LG 30465 8 Jan 1918	WO 11 Jan 1918
Barry, J	27462	8 Aug 1902	5086	Gazette	WO 8 Aug 1902
Barry, M	See Magner, M				
Barter, F	29210	29 Jun 1915	6269	Gazette	WO 29 Jun 1915
Barton, CJ	36584	27 Jun 1944	3041	5th Supp. to LG 36579 23 Jun 1944	Air Min. 27 Jun 1944
Baskeyfield, JD	36807	23 Nov 1944	5375	Supp. to LG 36806 21 Nov 1944	WO 23 Nov 1944
Bassett, CRG	29328	15 Oct 1915	10154	Gazette	WO 15 Oct 1915
Bates, S	36774	2 Nov 1944	5016	Supp. to LG 36773 31 Oct 1944	WO 2 Nov 1944
Batten-Pooll, AHH	29695	5 Aug 1916	7743	Supp. to LG 29694 4 Aug 1916	WO 5 Aug 1916
Baxter, EF	29765	26 Sep 1916	9417	Supp. to LG 29764 26 Sep 1916	WO 26 Sep 1916
Baxter, FW	26850	7 May 1897	2535	Gazette ('Had he survived')	WO 7 May 1897
Baxter, FW	27986	15 Jan 1907	325	Gazette	WO 15 Jan 1907

	London Gazette	Date	Page	Supplement (if any)	Release Date
Bazalgette, IW	37228	17 Aug 1945	4185	6th Supp. to LG 37222 14 Aug 1945	Air Min. 17 Aug 1945
Beach, T	21971	24 Feb 1857	660	Supp. to LG 21970 24 Feb 1857	WO 24 Feb 1857
Beak, DMW	31012	15 Nov 1918	13471/2	7th Supp. to LG 31005 12 Nov 1918	WO 15 Nov 1918
Beal, EF	30726	4 Jun 1918	6572	12th Supp. to LG 30714 31 May 1918	WO 4 Jun 1918
Beatham, RM	31067	14 Dec 1918	14779	2nd Supp. to LG 31065 13 Dec 1918	WO 14 Dec 1918
Beattie, SH	35566	21 May 1942	2225	Supp. to LG 35565 19 May 1942	Adm. 21 May 1942
Beauchamp-Proctor, AFW	31042	30 Nov 1918	14204	2nd Supp. to LG 31040 29 Nov 1918	Air Min. 30 Nov 1918
Beeley, J	35530	21 Apr 1942	1741	2nd Supp. to LG 35528 17 Apr 1942	WO 21 Apr 1942
Bees, W	27388	17 Dec 1901	8915	Gazette	WO 17 Dec 1901
Beesley, W	30770	28 Jun 1918	7619/20	6th Supp. to LG 30764 25 Jun 1918	WO 28 Jun 1918
Beet, HC	27283	12 Feb 1901	1059	Gazette	WO 12 Feb 1901
Belcher, DW	29202	23 Jun 1915	6115	Supp. to LG 29201 22 Jun 1915	WO 23 Jun 1915
Bell, D	23333	17 Dec 1867	6878	Gazette	WO 17 Dec 1867
Bell, DS	29740	9 Sep 1916	8870	Supp. to LG 29739 8 Sep 1916	WO 9 Sep 1916
Bell, ENF	29765	26 Sep 1916	9417/18	Supp. to LG 29764 26 Sep 1916	WO 26 Sep 1916
Bell, EWD	21971	24 Feb 1857	659	Supp. to LG 21970 24 Feb 1857	WO 24 Feb 1857
Bell, FW	27362	4 Oct 1901	6481	Gazette	WO 4 Oct 1901
Bell, MS	24153	20 Nov 1874	5469	Gazette	WO 20 Nov 1874
Bell-Davies, R	29423	1 Jan 1916	86	2nd Supp. to LG 29421 31 Dec 1915	Adm. 1 Jan 1916
Bellew, ED	31340	15 May 1919	6083/4	4th Supp. to LG 31336 13 May 1919	WO 15 May 1919
Bennett, EP	29885	30 Dec 1916	12736	2nd Supp. to LG 29883 29 Dec 1916	WO 30 Dec 1916
Bent, PE	30471	11 Jan 1918	722/3	6th Supp. to LG 30465 8 Jan 1918	WO 11 Jan 1918
Bent, SJ	29001	9 Dec 1914	10533	Supp. to LG 29000 8 Dec 1914	WO 9 Dec 1914

	London Gazette	Date	Page	Supplement (if any)	Release Date
Beresford, WL de la P	24760	9 Sep 1879	5395	Gazette	WO 23 Aug 1879
Bergin, J	23405	28 Jul 1868	4187	Gazette	WO 28 Jul 1868
Berryman, J	21971	24 Feb 1857	655	Supp. to LG 21970 24 Feb 1857	WO 24 Feb 1857
Best-Dunkley, B	30272	6 Sep 1917	9259/60	5th Supp. to LG 30267 4 Sep 1917	WO 6 Sep 1917
Bhagat, PS	see Premindra Singh Bhagat				
Bhanbhagta Gurung	37107	5 Jun 1945	2831	Supp. to LG 37106 1 Jun 1945	WO 5 Jun 1945
Bhandari Ram	36928	8 Feb 1945	792	Supp. to LG 36927 6 Feb 1945	WO 8 Feb 1945
Bingham, EBS	29751	15 Sep 1916	9070	Supp. to LG 29750 15 Sep 1916	Adm. 15 Sep 1916
Birks, F	30372	8 Nov 1917	11568	3rd Supp. to LG 30369 6 Nov 1917	WO 8 Nov 1917
Bisdee, JH	27246	13 Nov 1900	6927	Gazette	WO 13 Nov 1900
Bishop, WA	30228	11 Aug 1917	8211/2	4th Supp. to LG 30224 10 Aug 1917	WO 11 Aug 1917
Bissett, WD	31108	6 Jan 1919	306	4th Supp. to LG 31104 3 Jan 1919	WO 6 Jan 1919
Bissett-Smith, A	31354	24 May 1919	6446	2nd Supp. to LG 31352 23 May 1919	Adm. 24 May 1919
Blackburn, AS	29740	9 Sep 1916	8870	Supp. to LG 29739 8 Sep 1916	WO 9 Sep 1916
Blair, J	22601	25 Feb 1862	956	Gazette	WO 25 Feb 1862
Blair, R	22154	18 Jun 1858	2960	Gazette	WO 18 Jun 1858
Blaker, FG	36715	26 Sep 1944	4423	Supp. to LG 36714 22 Sep 1944	WO 26 Sep 1944
Bloomfield, WA	29885	30 Dec 1916	12735/6	2nd Supp. to LG 29883 29 Dec 1916	WO 30 Dec 1916
Bogle, AC	22303	2 Sep 1859	3302	Gazette	WO 2 Sep 1859
Boisragon, GH	26306	12 Jul 1892	4006	Gazette	WO 12 Jul 1892
Bonner, CG	30363	2 Nov 1917	11315	5th Supp. to LG 30358 30 Oct 1917	Adm. 2 Nov 1917
Bonner, CG	31021	20 Nov 1918	13694/5	2nd Supp. to LG 31019 19 Nov 1918	Adm. 20 Nov 1918
Booth, AC	24814	24 Feb 1880	832	Gazette	WO 23 Feb 1880

	London Gazette	Date	Page	Supplement (if any)	Release Date
Booth, FC	30122	8 Jun 1917	5704	2nd Supp. to LG 30120 8 Jun 1917	WO 8 Jun 1917
Borella, AC	30903	16 Sep 1918	11075	5th Supp. to LG 30898 13 Sep 1918	WO 16 Sep 1918
Borton, AD	30433	18 Dec 1917	13221	5th Supp. to LG 30428 14 Dec 1917	WO 18 Dec 1917
Boughey, SHP	30523	13 Feb 1918	2004	Supp. to LG 30522 12 Feb 1918	WO 13 Feb 1918
Boulger, A	22154	18 Jun 1858	2957	Gazette	WO 18 Jun 1858
Boulter, WE	29802	26 Oct 1916	10394	4th Supp. to LG 29798 24 Oct 1916	WO 26 Oct 1916
Bourchier, CT	21971	24 Feb 1857	662	Supp. to LG 21970 24 Feb 1857	WO 24 Feb 1857
Bourke, RRL	30870	28 Aug 1918	10088	2nd Supp. to LG 30868 27 Aug 1918	Adm. SW 28 Aug 1918
Boyd-Rochfort, GA	29281	1 Sep 1915	8700	Supp. to LG 29280 31 Aug 1915	WO 1 Sep 1915
Boyes, DG	22960	21 Apr 1865	2130	Gazette	WO 21 Apr 1865
Boyle, EC	29169	21 May 1915	4894	Gazette	Adm. 21 May 1915
Bradbury, EK	28985	25 Nov 1914	9958	Supp. to LG 28984 24 Nov 1914	WO 25 Nov 1914
Bradford, GN	31236	17 Mar 1919	3590	6th Supp. to LG 31230 14 Mar 1919	Adm. 17 Mar 1919
Bradford, RB	29836	25 Nov 1916	11525	Supp. to LG 29835 24 Nov 1916	WO 25 Nov 1916
Bradley, FH	27391	27 Dec 1901	9147	Gazette	WO 27 Dec 1901
Bradshaw, J	21971	24 Feb 1857	663	Supp. to LG 21970 24 Feb 1857	WO 24 Feb 1857
Bradshaw, W	22154	18 Jun 1858	2959	Gazette	WO 18 Jun 1858
Brennan, JC	22324	11 Nov 1859	4032	Gazette	WO 11 Nov 1859
Brereton, AP	30922	27 Sep 1918	11430	4th Supp. to LG 30918 24 Sep 1918	WO 27 Sep 1918
Brillant, J	30922	27 Sep 1918	11429/30	4th Supp. to LG 30918 24 Sep 1918	WO 27 Sep 1918
Brodie, WL	29005	12 Dec 1914	10661	2nd Supp. to LG 29003 11 Dec 1914	WO 12 Dec 1914
Bromhead, G	24717	2 May 1879	3177	Supp. to LG 24716 2 May 1879	WO 2 May 1879
Bromley, C	29985	15 Mar 1917	2619	3rd Supp. to LG 29982 13 Mar 1917	WO 15 Mar 1917

	London Gazette	Date	Page	Supplement (if any)	Release Date
Brooke, JAO	29074	18 Feb 1915	1700	4th Supp. to LG 29070 16 Feb 1915	WO 18 Feb 1915
Brooks, E	30154	27 Jun 1917	6381	4th Supp. to LG 30150 26 Jun1917	WO 27 Jun 1917
Brooks, O	29342	28 Oct 1915	10629	2nd Supp. to LG 29340 26 Oct 1915	WO 28 Oct 1915
Brown, DF	30130	14 Jun 1917	5866	4th Supp. to LG 30126 12 Jun 1917	WO 14 Jun 1917
Brown, ED	27266	15 Jan 1901	308	Gazette	WO 15 Jan 1901
Brown, FDM	22357	17 Feb 1860	557	Gazette	WO 17 Feb 1860
Brown, HG Gore-	See Gore-Browne, HG				
Brown, HW	30338	17 Oct 1917	10678	2nd Supp. to LG 30336 16 Oct 1917	WO 17 Oct 1917
Brown, P	24833	13 Apr 1880	2510	Gazette	WO 12 Apr 1880
Brown, WE	30849	17 Aug 1918	9659/60	3rd Supp. to LG 30846 16 Aug 1918	WO 17 Aug 1918
Browne, ES	24734	17 Jun 1879	3966	Gazette	WO 17 Jun 1879
Browne, SJ	22485	1 Mar 1861	1007	Gazette	WO 1 Mar 1861
Bruce, WA McC	31536	4 Sep 1919	11206	4th Supp. to LG 31532 2 Sep 1919	WO 4 Sep 1919
Brunt, JHC	36928	8 Feb 1945	791	Supp. to LG 36927 6 Feb 1945	WO 8 Feb 1945
Bryan, T	30122	8 Jun 1917	5705	2nd Supp. to LG 30120 8 Jun 1917	WO 8 Jun 1917
Buchan, JC	30697	22 May 1918	6058	3rd Supp. to LG 30694 21 May 1918	WO 22 May 1918
Buchanan, A	29765	26 Sep 1916	9418	Supp. to LG 29764 26 Sep 1916	WO 26 Sep 1916
Buckingham, W	29146	28 Apr 1915	4143	Supp. to LG 29145 27 Apr 1915	WO 28 Apr 1915
Buckley, AH	31067	14 Dec 1918	14778	2nd Supp. to LG 31065 13 Dec 1918	WO 14 Dec 1918
Buckley, CW	21971	24 Feb 1857	649	Supp. to LG 21970 24 Feb 1857	WO 24 Feb 1857
Buckley, J	22154	18 Jun 1858	2959	Gazette	WO 18 Jun 1858
Buckley, MV (as Sexton, G)	31067	14 Dec 1918	14777	2nd Supp. to LG 31065 13 Dec 1918	WO 14 Dec 1918
Buckley, MV (as Buckley, MV)	31494	8 Aug 1919	10078	5th Supp. to LG 31489 5 Aug 1919	WO 8 Aug 1919

	London Gazette	Date	Page	Supplement (if any)	Release Date
Bugden, PJ	30400	26 Nov 1917	12329/30	4th Supp. to LG 30396 23 Nov 1917	WO 26 Nov 1917
Buller, RH	24734	17 Jun 1879	3966	Gazette	WO 17 Jun 1879
Burges, D	31067	14 Dec 1918	14774	2nd Supp. to LG 31065 13 Dec 1918	WO 14 Dec 1918
Burgoyne, HT	21971	24 Feb 1857	650	Supp. to LG 21970 24 Feb 1857	WO 24 Feb 1857
Burman, WF	30400	26 Nov 1917	12327/8	4th Supp. to LG 30396 23 Nov 1917	WO 26 Nov 1917
Burslem, NG	22538	13 Aug 1861	3363	Gazette	WO 13 Aug 1861
Burt, AA	29447	22 Jan 1916	945	2nd Supp. to LG 29445 21 Jan 1916	WO 22 Jan 1916
Burton, AS	29328	15 Oct 1915	10154	Gazette	WO 15 Oct 1915
Burton, RH	35876	4 Jan 1945	207	Supp. to LG 36875 2 Jan 1945	WO 4 Jan 1945
Bushell, C	30667	3 May 1918	5353	7th Supp. to LG 30660 30 Apr 1918	WO 3 May 1918
Butler, JFP	29272	23 Aug 1915	8373	3rd Supp. to LG 29269 20 Aug 1915	WO 23 Aug 1915
Butler, TA	22260	6 May 1859	1867	Gazette	WO 6 May 1859
Butler, WB	30338	17 Oct 1917	10678	2nd Supp. to LG 30336 16 Oct 1917	WO 17 Oct 1917
Bye, RJ	30272	6 Sep 1917	9260	5th Supp. to LG 30267 4 Sep 1917	WO 6 Sep 1917
Byrne, James	22324	11 Nov 1859	4032	Gazette	WO 11 Nov 1859
Byrne, John	21971	24 Feb 1857	661	Supp. to LG 21970 24 Feb 1857	WO 24 Feb 1857
Byrne, T	27023	15 Nov 1898	6688	Gazette	WO 15 Nov 1898
Bythesea, J	21971	24 Feb 1857	653	Supp. to LG 21970 24 Feb 1857	WO 24 Feb 1857
Cadell, T	22621	29 Apr 1862	2229	Gazette	WO 29 Apr 1862
Cafe, WM	22357	17 Feb 1860	557	Gazette	WO 17 Feb 1860
Caffrey, JJ	29447	22 Jan 1916	945	2nd Supp. to LG 29445 21 Jan 1916	WO 22 Jan 1916
Cain, RH	36774	2 Nov 1944	5015	Supp. to LG 36773 31 Oct 1944	WO 2 Nov 1944

	London Gazette	Date	Page	Supplement (if any)	Release Date
Cairns, GA	38615	20 May 1949	2461	Supp. to LG 38614 17 May 1949	WO 20 May 1949
Cairns, H	31155	31 Jan 1919	1504	8th Supp. to LG 31147 28 Jan 1919	WO 31 Jan 1919
Caldwell, T	31108	6 Jan 1919	307	4th Supp. to LG 31104 3 Jan 1919	WO 6 Jan 1919
Calvert, L	31012	15 Nov 1918	13472	7th Supp. to LG 31005 12 Nov 1918	WO 15 Nov 1918
Cambridge, D	22014	23 Jun 1857	2165	Gazette	WO 23 Jun 1857
Cameron, AS	22324	11 Nov 1859	4032	Gazette	WO 11 Nov 1859
Cameron, D	36390	22 Feb 1944	901/2	3rd Supp. to LG 36387 18 Feb 1944	Adm. 22 Feb 1944
Campbell, FW	29272	23 Aug 1915	8374	3rd Supp. to LG 29269 20 Aug 1915	WO 23 Aug 1915
Campbell, G	30029	21 Apr 1917	3819	Supp. to LG 30028 20 Apr 1917	Adm. 21 Apr 1917
Campbell, G	31021	20 Nov 1918	13693	2nd Supp. to LG 31019 19 Nov 1918	Adm. 20 Nov 1918
Campbell, JC	35442	3 Feb 1942	545	2nd Supp. to LG 35440 30 Jan 1942	WO 3 Feb 1942
Campbell, JV	29802	26 Oct 1916	10393	4th Supp. to LG 29798 24 Oct 1916	WO 26 Oct 1916
Campbell, K	35486	13 Mar 1942	1163	3rd Supp. to LG 35483 10 Mar 1942	Air Min. 13 Mar 1942
Campbell, L MacL	36045	8 Jun 1943	2623	3rd Supp. to LG 36042 4 Jun 1943	WO 8 Jun 1943
Carless, JH	30687	17 May 1918	5857	4th Supp. to LG 30683 14 May 1918	Adm. 17 May 1918
Carlin, P	22194	26 Oct 1858	4574	Gazette	WO 26 Oct 1858
Carmichael, J	30338	17 Oct 1917	10677	2nd Supp. to LG 30336 16 Oct 1917	WO 17 Oct 1917
Carne, JP	39994	27 Oct 1953	5693	Supp. to LG 39993 23 Oct 1953	WO 27 Oct 1953
Carpenter, AFB	30807	23 Jul 1918	8585	4th Supp. to LG 30803 19 Jul 1918	Adm. 23 Jul 1918
Carroll, J	30215	2 Aug 1917	7906/7	4th Supp. to LG 30211 31 Jul 1917	WO 2 Aug 1917
Carter, HA	27742	9 Dec 1904	8449	Gazette	WO 9 Dec 1904
Carter, NV	29740	9 Sep 1916	8870	Supp. to LG 29739 8 Sep 1916	WO 9 Sep 1916
Carton de Wiart, A	29740	9 Sep 1916	8869	Supp. to LG 29739 8 Sep 1916	WO 9 Sep 1916

	London Gazette	Date	Page	Supplement (if any)	Release Date
Cartwright, G	31067	14 Dec 1918	14779	2nd Supp. to LG 31065 13 Dec 1918	WO 14 Dec 1918
Cassidy, BM	30667	3 May 1918	5354	7th Supp. to LG 30660 30 Apr 1918	WO 3 May 1918
Castleton, CC	29765	26 Sep 1916	9418	Supp. to LG 29764 26 Sep 1916	WO 26 Sep 1916
Cates, GE	30064	11 May 1917	4587	2nd Supp. to LG 30062 11 May 1917	WO 11 May 1917
Cather, GStGS	29740	9 Sep 1916	8869	Supp. to LG 29739 8 Sep 1916	WO 9 Sep 1916
Cator, H	30122	8 Jun 1917	5704	2nd Supp. to LG 30120 8 Jun 1917	WO 8 Jun 1917
Chafer, GW	29695	5 Aug 1916	7744	Supp. to LG 29694 4 Aug 1916	WO 5 Aug 1916
Champion, J	22347	20 Jan 1860	178	Gazette	WO 20 Jan 1860
Channer, GN	24314	14 Apr 1876	2476	Gazette	WO 12 Apr 1876
Chaplin, JW	22538	13 Aug 1861	3363	Gazette	WO 13 Aug 1861
Chapman, ET	37173	13 Jul 1945	3599	2nd Supp. to LG 37171 10 Jul 1945	WO 13 Jul 1945
Chard, JRM	24717	2 May 1879	3177	Supp. to LG 24716 2 May 1879	WO 2 May 1879
Charlton, EC	37551	2 May 1946	2119	Supp. to LG 37550 30 Apr 1946	WO 2 May 1946
Chase, W StL	25023	7 Oct 1881	4990	Gazette	WO 4 Oct 1881
Chatta Singh	29633	21 Jun 1916	6191	4th Supp. to LG 29629 20 Jun 1916	WO 21 Jun 1916
Chavasse, NG	29802	26 Oct 1916	10394	4th Supp. to LG 29798 24 Oct 1916	WO 26 Oct 1916
Chavasse, NG, VC	30284	14 Sep 1917	9531	2nd Supp. to LG 30282 14 Sep 1917	WO 14 Sep 1917
Cherry, PH	30064	11 May 1917	4587	2nd Supp. to LG 30062 11 May 1917	WO 11 May 1917
Cheshire, GL	35693	8 Sep 1944	4175/6	5th Supp. to LG 36688 5 Sep 1944	Air Min. 8 Sep 1944
Chhelu Ram	35107	27 Jul 1943	3373	2nd Supp. to LG 36105 23 Jul 1943	WO 27 Jul 1943
Chicken, GB	22380	27 Apr 1860	1596	Gazette	WO 27 Apr 1860
Chowne, A	37253	6 Sep 1945	4467	Supp. to LG 37252 4 Sep 1945	WO 6 Sep 1945
Christian, H	29496	3 Mar 1916	2349	Gazette	WO 3 Mar 1916

	London Gazette	Date	Page	Supplement (if any)	Release Date
Christie, JA	30548	27 Feb 1918	2589/90	4th Supp. to LG 30544 26 Feb 1918	WO 27 Feb 1918
Clamp, W	30433	18 Dec 1917	13223	5th Supp. to LG 30428 14 Dec 1917	WO 18 Dec 1917
Clare, GWB	30471	11 Jan 1918	724	6th Supp. to LG 30465 8 Jan 1918	WO 11 Jan 1918
Clarke, J	31108	6 Jan 1919	307	4th Supp. to LG 31104 3 Jan 1919	WO 6 Jan 1919
Clarke, L	29802	26 Oct 1916	10395	4th Supp. to LG 29798 24 Oct 1916	WO 26 Oct 1916
Clarke, WAS	See Sandys-Clarke, WA				
Clark-Kennedy, WH	31067	14 Dec 1918	14773/4	2nd Supp. to LG 31065 13 Dec 1918	WO 14 Dec 1918
Clements, JJ	27320	4 Jun 1901	3769	Gazette	WO 4 Jun 1901
Clifford, HH	21971	24 Feb 1857	662	Supp. to LG 21970 24 Feb 1857	WO 24 Feb 1857
Clogstoun, HM	22318	21 Oct 1859	3792	Gazette	WO 21 Oct 1859
Cloutman, BM	31155	31 Jan 1919	1503	8th Supp. to LG 31147 28 Jan 1919	WO 31 Jan 1919
Cobbe, AS	27517	20 Jan 1903	385	Gazette	WO 20 Jan 1903
Cochrane, HS	22212	24 Dec 1858	5518	Gazette	WO 24 Dec 1853
Cockburn, HZC	27307	23 Apr 1901	2775	Gazette	WO 23 Apr 1901
Coffey, W	21971	24 Feb 1857	659	Supp. to LG 21970 24 Feb 1857	WO 24 Feb 1857
Coffin, C	30284	14 Sep 1917	9531/2	2nd Supp. to LG 30282 14 Sep 1917	WO 14 Sep 1917
Coghill, NJA	24717	2 May 1879	3178	Supp. to LG 24716 2 May 1879	WO 2 May 1879
Coghill, NJA	27986	15 Jan 1907	325	Gazette	WO 15 Jan 1907
Coghlan, C	See Coughlan, C				
Coleman, J	21971	24 Feb 1857	662	Supp. to LG 21970 24 Feb 1857	WO 24 Feb 1857
Colley, HJ	30967	22 Oct 1918	12488	9th Supp. to LG 30958 18 Oct 1918	WO 22 Oct 1918
Collin, JH	30770	28 Jun 1918	7618	6th Supp. to LG 30764 25 Jun 1918	WO 28 Jun 1918
Collings-Wells, JS	30648	24 Apr 1918	4967	2nd Supp. to LG 30646 23 Apr 1918	WO 24 Apr 1918

	London Gazette	Date	Page	Supplement (if any)	Release Date
Collins, J	30433	18 Dec 1917	13223	5th Supp. to LG 30428 14 Dec 1917	WO 18 Dec 1917
Collis, J	24973	17 May 1881	2553	Gazette	WO 16 May 1881
Coltman, WH	31108	6 Jan 1919	308	4th Supp. to LG 31104 3 Jan 1919	WO 6 Jan 1919
Columbine, HG	30667	3 May 1918	5354	7th Supp. to LG 30660 30 Apr 1918	WO 3 May 1918
Colvin, H	30372	8 Nov 1917	11568	3rd Supp. to LG 30369 6 Nov 1917	WO 8 Nov 1917
Colvin, JMC	26968	20 May 1898	3165	Gazette	WO 20 May 1898
Colyer-Fergusson, TR	30272	6 Sep 1917	9260	5th Supp. to LG 30267 4 Sep 1917	WO 6 Sep 1917
Combe, RG	30154	27 Jun 1917	6381	4th Supp. to LG 30150 25 Jun 1917	WO 27 Jun 1917
Commerell, JE	21971	24 Feb 1857	651	Supp. to LG 21970 24 Feb 1857	WO 24 Feb 1857
Congreve, W La T	29802	26 Oct 1916	10393/4	4th Supp. to LG 29798 24 Oct 1916	WO 26 Oct 1916
Congreve, WN	27160	2 Feb 1900	689	Gazette	WO 2 Feb 1900
Conker, F	See Whirlpool, F				
Connolly, W	22179	3 Sep 1858	4014/15	Gazette	WO 3 Sep 1858
Connors, J	21971	24 Feb 1857	658	Supp. to LG 21970 24 Feb 1857	WO 24 Feb 1857
Conolly, JA	21997	5 May 1857	1579	Gazette	WO 5 May 1857
Cook, J	24697	18 Mar 1879	2241	Gazette	WO 18 Mar 1879
Cook, W	22278	21 Jun 1859	2420	Gazette	WO 18 Jun 1859
Cooke, T	29740	9 Sep 1916	8870	Supp. to LG 29739 8 Sep 1916	WO 9 Sep 1916
Cookson, EC	29446	21 Jan 1916	943	Supp. to LG 29445 21 Jan 1916	Adm. 21 Jan 1916
Cooper, E	30284	14 Sep 1917	9532	2nd Supp. to LG 30282 14 Sep 1917	WO 14 Sep 1917
Cooper, H	21971	24 Feb 1857	650	Supp. to LG 21970 24 Feb 1857	WO 24 Feb 1857
Cooper, J	23333	17 Dec 1867	6878	Gazette	WO 17 Dec 1867
Cooper, NB Elliott-	See Elliott-Cooper, NB				

	London Gazette	Date	Page	Supplement (if any)	Release Date
Coppins, FG	30922	27 Sep 1918	11430	4th Supp. to LG 30918 24 Sep 1918	WO 27 Sep 1918
Corbett, F (Embleton)	25199	16 Feb 1883	859	Gazette	WO 16 Feb 1883
Cornwell, JT	29752	15 Sep 1916	9085	2nd Supp. to LG 29750 15 Sep 1916	Adm. 15 Sep 1916
Cosens, A	37086	22 May 1945	2607/8	Supp. to LG 37085 18 May 1945	DoND Ottawa 22 May 1945
Cosgrove, W	29272	23 Aug 1915	8374	3rd Supp. to LG 29269 20 Aug 1915	WO 23 Aug 1915
Costello, EW	26908	9 Nov 1897	6143	Gazette	WO 9 Nov 1897
Cotter, WR	29527	30 Mar 1916	3410	4th Supp. to LG 29523 28 Mar 1916	WO 30 Mar 1916
Coughlan, C	22680	11 Nov 1862	5346	Gazette	WO 11 Nov 1862
Coulson, GHB	27462	8 Aug 1902	5085/6	Gazette	WO 8 Aug 1902
Counter, JT	30697	22 May 1918	6059	3rd Supp. to LG 30694 21 May 1918	WO 22 May 1918
Coury, GG	29802	26 Oct 1916	10394	4th Supp. to LG 29798 24 Oct 1916	WO 26 Oct 1916
Coverdale, CH	30433	18 Dec 1917	13222	5th Supp. to LG 30428 14 Dec 1917	WO 18 Dec 1917
Cowley, CH	29928	2 Feb 1917	1160	Gazette	Adm. 31 Jan 1917
Cox, CA	30064	11 May 1917	4587/8	2nd Supp. to LG 30062 11 May 1917	WO 11 May 1917
Craig, J	22065	20 Nov 1857	3920	Gazette	WO 18 Nov 1857
Craig, JM	30215	2 Aug 1917	7905/6	4th Supp. to LG 30211 31 Jul 1917	WO 2 Aug 1917
Crandon, HG	27366	18 Oct 1901	6779	Gazette	WO 18 Oct 1901
Creagh, O'M	24784	18 Nov 1879	6494	Gazette	WO 17 Nov 1879
Crean, TJ	27405	11 Feb 1902	843	Gazette	WO 11 Feb 1902
Crichton, J	31012	15 Nov 1918	13474	7th Supp. to LG 31005 12 Nov 1918	WO 15 Nov 1918
Crimmin, J	25975	17 Sep 1889	4989	Gazette	WO 17 Sep 1889
Crisp, T	30363	2 Nov 1917	11315	5th Supp. to LG 30358 30 Oct 1917	Adm. 2 Nov 1917
Crisp, T	31021	20 Nov 1918	13695	2nd Supp. to 31019 19 Nov 1918	Adm. 20 Nov 1918

	London Gazette	Date	Page	Supplement (if any)	Release Date
Croak, JB	30922	27 Sep 1918	11430	4th Supp. to LG 30918 24 Sep 1918	WO 27 Sep 1918
Cross, AH	30726	4 Jun 1918	6572	12th Supp. to LG 30714 31 May 1918	WO 4 Jun 1918
Crowe, JJ	30770	28 Jun 1918	7618/19	6th Supp. to LG 30764 25 Jun 1918	WO 28 Jun 1918
Crowe, JPH	22083	15 Jan 1858	178	Gazette	WO 15 Jan 1858
Cruickshank, JA	36682	1 Sep 1944	4073	4th Supp. to LG 36678 29 Aug 1944	Air Min. 1 Sep 1944
Cruickshank, RE	30757	21 Jun 1918	7307	5th Supp. to LG 30752 18 Jun 1918	WO 21 Jun 1918
Crutchley, VAC	30870	28 Aug 1918	10088	2nd Supp. to LG 30868 27 Aug 1918	Adm. SW 28 Aug 1918
Cubitt, WG	22278	21 Jun 1859	2420	Gazette	WO 18 Jun 1859
Cumming, AE	35462	20 Feb 1942	833	2nd Supp. to LG 35460 17 Feb 1942	WO 20 Feb 1942
Cunningham, J (Cpl)	30122	8 Jun 1917	5704/5	2nd Supp. to LG 30120 8 Jun 1917	WO 8 Jun 1917
Cunningham, J (Pte)	29901	13 Jan 1917	559	Supp. to LG 29900 12 Jan 1917	WO 13 Jan 1917
Cunninghame, WJM	21971	24 Feb 1857	662	Supp. to LG 21970 24 Feb 1857	WO 24 Feb 1857
Cunyngham, WH Dick-	See Dick-Cunyngham, WH				
Currey, WM	31067	14 Dec 1918	14779	2nd Supp. to LG 31065 13 Dec 1918	WO 14 Dec 1918
Currie, DV	36812	27 Nov 1944	5433/4	Supp. to LG 36811 27 Nov 1944	D of Nat Def. 27 Nov 1944
Curtis, AE	27266	15 Jan 1901	308	Gazette	WO 15 Jan 1901
Curtis, H	21971	24 Feb 1857	653	Supp. to LG 21970 24 Feb 1857	WO 24 Feb 1857
Curtis, HA	31108	6 Jan 1919	307	4th Supp. to LG 31104 3 Jan 1919	WO 6 Jan 1919
Curtis, PKE	40029	1 Dec 1953	6513	Supp. to LG 40028 27 Nov 1953	WO 1 Dec 1953
Cutler, AR	35360	28 Nov 1941	6825	2nd Supp. to LG 35358 25 Nov 1941	WO 28 Nov 1941
Dalton, JL	24784	18 Nov 1879	6494	Gazette	WO 17 Nov 1879
Dalziel, H	30849	17 Aug 1918	9660	3rd Supp. to LG 30846 16 Aug 1918	WO 17 Aug 1918

	London Gazette	Date	Page	Supplement (if any)	Release Date
Danaher, J (Danagher)	25084	14 Mar 1882	1130	Gazette	WO 13 Mar 1882
Dancox, FG	30400	26 Nov 1917	12330	4th Supp. to LG 30396 23 Nov 1917	WO 26 Nov 1917
Daniel, EStJ	21971	24 Feb 1857	652	Supp. to LG 21970 24 Feb 1857	WO 24 Feb 1857
Daniels, H	29146	28 Apr 1915	4143	Supp. to LG 29145 27 Apr 1915	WO 28 Apr 1915
D'Arcy, HCD	24769	10 Oct 1879	5830	Gazette	WO 9 Oct 1879
Dartnell, WT	29414	23 Dec 1915	12797	5th Supp. to LG 29409 21 Dec 1915	WO 23 Dec 1915
Darwan Sing Negi	28999	7 Dec 1914	10425	4th Supp. to LG 28995 4 Dec 1914	WO 7 Dec 1914
Daunt, JCC	22601	25 Feb 1862	957	Gazette	WO 25 Feb 1862
Davey, P	30849	17 Aug 1918	9659	3rd Supp. to LG 30846 16 Aug 1918	WO 17 Aug 1918
Davies, JJ	29765	26 Sep 1916	9418	Supp. to LG 29764 26 Sep 1916	WO 26 Sep 1916
Davies, JL	30272	6 Sep 1917	9260	5th Supp. to LG 30267 4 Sep 1917	WO 6 Sep 1917
Davies, JT	30697	22 May 1918	6058	3rd Supp. to LG 30694 21 May 1918	WO 22 May 1918
Davies, LAE Price-	See Price-Davies, LAE				
Davies, R Bell-	See Bell-Davies, R				
Davis, G	22014	23 Jun 1857	2165	Gazette	WO 23 Jun 1857
Davis, J (Kelly, JD)	22268	27 May 1859	2106	Gazette	WO 27 May 1859
Dawson, JL	29394	7 Dec 1915	12281	Supp. to LG 29393 7 Dec 1915	WO 7 Dec 1915
Day, GF	21971	24 Feb 1857	650/51	Supp. to LG 21970 24 Feb 1857	WO 24 Feb 1857
Day, SJ	30338	17 Oct 1917	10678	2nd Supp. to LG 30336 16 Oct 1917	WO 17 Oct 1917
Daykins, JB	31108	6 Jan 1919	308	4th Supp. to LG 31104 3 Jan 1919	WO 6 Jan 1919
Dean, DJ	31067	14 Dec 1918	14775/6	2nd Supp. to LG 31065 13 Dec 1918	WO 14 Dec 1918
Dean, PT	30807	23 Jul 1918	8586	4th Supp. to LG 30803 19 Jul 1918	Adm. 23 Jul 1918
Dease, MJ	28976	16 Nov 1914	9374	3rd Supp. to LG 28973 13 Nov 1914	WO 16 Nov 1914

	London Gazette	Date	Page	Supplement (if any)	Release Date
De L'Isle, Viscount	See Sidney, WP				
de Montmorency, RHJ	27023	15 Nov 1898	6688	Gazette	WO 15 Nov 1898
Dempsey, D	22357	17 Feb 1860	557	Gazette	WO 17 Feb 1860
de Pass, FA	29074	18 Feb 1915	1700	4th Supp. to LG 29070 16 Feb 1915	WO 18 Feb 1915
Derrick, TC	35436	23 Mar 1944	1301	Supp. to LG 36435 21 Mar 1944	Govt. Ho. 23 Mar 1944
Devereux, J	See Gorman, J				
Devine, J	See Divane, J				
de Wind, E	31340	15 May 1919	6084	4th Supp. to LG 31336 13 May 1919	WO 15 May 1919
Diamond, B	22131	27 Apr 1858	2051	Gazette	WO 24 Apr 1858
Diarmid, AMC McReady-	See McReady-Diarmid, AMC				
Dick-Cunyngham, WH	25027	18 Oct 1881	5140	Gazette	WO 15 Oct 1881
Dickson, C	22014	23 Jun 1857	2165	Gazette	WO 23 Jun 1857
Digby-Jones, RJT	27462	8 Aug 1902	5085	Gazette	WO 8 Aug 1902
Dimmer, JHS	28980	19 Nov 1914	9513	3rd Supp. to LG 28977 17 Nov 1914	WO 19 Nov 1914
Dinesen, T	30975	26 Oct 1918	12670	2nd Supp. to LG 30973 25 Oct 1918	WO 26 Oct 1918
Divane, J (Devine)	22347	20 Jan 1860	178	Gazette	WO 20 Jan 1860
Dixon, MC	21971	24 Feb 1857	655	Supp. to LG 21970 24 Feb 1857	WO 24 Feb 1857
Dobson, CC	31638	11 Nov 1919	13743	Supp. to LG 31637 11 Nov 1919	Adm. 11 Nov 1919
Dobson, FW	29001	9 Dec 1914	10533	Supp. to LG 29000 8 Dec 1914	WO 9 Dec 1914
Donnini, D	36988	20 Mar 1945	1485	Supp. to LG 36987 16 Mar 1945	WO 20 Mar 1945
Donohoe, P	22212	24 Dec 1858	5517	Gazette	WO 24 Dec 1858
Doogan, J	25084	14 Mar 1882	1130	Gazette	WO 13 Mar 1882
Dorrell, GT	28976	16 Nov 1914	9374	3rd Supp. to LG 28973 13 Nov 1914	WO 16 Nov 1914

	London Gazette	Date	Page	Supplement (if any)	Release Date
Dougall, ES	30726	4 Jun 1918	6571	12th Supp. to LG 30714 31 May 1918	WO 4 Jun 1918
Doughty-Wyllie, CHM	29202	23 Jun 1915	6115	Supp. to LG 29201 22 Jun 1915	WO 23 Jun 1915
Douglas, CM	23333	17 Dec 1867	6878	Gazette	WO 17 Dec 1867
Douglas, HEM	27300	29 Mar 1901	2193	Gazette	WO 29 Mar 1901
Douglas-Hamilton, AF	29371	18 Nov 1915	11447	3rd Supp. to LG 29368 16 Nov 1915	WO 18 Nov 1915
Dowell, GD	21971	24 Feb 1857	654	Supp. to LG 21970 24 Feb 1857	WO 24 Feb 1857
Dowling, W	22328	22 Nov 1859	4193	Gazette	WO 21 Nov 1859
Down, JT	22986	23 Sep 1864	4552	Gazette	WO 22 Sep 1864
Downie, R	29836	25 Nov 1916	11526	Supp. to LG 29835 24 Nov 1916	WO 25 Nov 1916
Doxat, AC	27266	15 Jan 1901	308	Gazette	WO 15 Jan 1901
Doyle, M	31155	31 Jan 1919	1504	8th Supp. to LG 31147 28 Jan 1919	WO 31 Jan 1919
Drain, JHC	28985	25 Nov 1914	9957	Supp. to LG 28984 24 Nov 1914	WO 25 Nov 1914
Drake, AG	29447	22 Jan 1916	946	2nd Supp. to LG 29445 21 Jan 1916	WO 22 Jan 1916
Dresser, T	30154	27 Jun 1917	6382	4th Supp. to LG 30150 26 Jun 1917	WO 27 Jun 1917
Drew, AMC McReady	See McReady-Diarmid, AMC				
Drewry, GL	29264	16 Aug 1915	8132	2nd Supp. to LG 29262 13 Aug 1915	Adm. 16 Aug 1915
Drummond, GH	30870	28 Aug 1918	10088	2nd Supp. to LG 30868 27 Aug 1918	Adm. SW 28 Aug 1918
Duffy, J	30548	27 Feb 1918	2590	4th Supp. to LG 30544 26 Feb 1918	WO 27 Feb 1918
Duffy, T	22154	18 Jun 1858	2958	Gazette	WO 18 Jun 1858
Dugdale, FB	27356	17 Sep 1901	6101	Gazette	WO 17 Sep 1901
Dunbar-Nasmith, ME	29206	25 Jun 1915	6166	Gazette	Adm. 24 Jun 1915
Dundas, J	23338	31 Dec 1867	7107	Gazette	WO 31 Dec 1867
Dunkley, B Best-	See Best-Dunkley, B				

	London Gazette	Date	Page	Supplement (if any)	Release Date
Dunlay, J (Dunlea, Dunley)	22212	24 Dec 1858	5514	Gazette	WO 24 Dec 1858
Dunkley, B Best-	See Best-Dunkley, B				
Dunmore, Earl of	See Fincastle, Viscount				
Dunn, AR	21971	24 Feb 1857	655	Supp. to LG 21970 24 Feb 1857	WO 24 Feb 1857
Dunsire, R	29371	18 Nov 1915	11449	3rd Supp. to LG 29368 16 Nov 1915	WO 18 Nov 1915
Dunstan, W	29328	15 Oct 1915	10154	Gazette	WO 15 Oct 1915
Dunville, JS	30215	2 Aug 1917	7906	4th Supp. to LG 30211 31 Jul 1917	WO 2 Aug 1917
Durrant, AE	27366	18 Oct 1901	6779	Gazette	WO 18 Oct 1901
Durrant, TF	37134	19 Jun 1945	3171/2	Supp. to LG 37133 15 Jul 1945	WO 19 Jun 1945
Dwyer, E	29170	22 May 1915	4989/90	Supp. to LG 29169 21 May 1915	WO 22 May 1915
Dwyer, JJ	30400	26 Nov 1917	12328	4th Supp. to LG 30396 23 Nov 1917	WO 26 Nov 1917
Dynon, D	22601	25 Feb 1862	957	Gazette	WO 25 Feb 1862
Eardley, GH	36870	2 Jan 1945	139	5th Supp. to LG 36865 29 Dec 1944	WO 2 Jan 1945
Edmonson, JH	35207	4 Jul 1941	3807/8	Supp. to LG 35206 1 Jul 1941	WO 4 Jul 1941
Edwards, A	30284	14 Sep 1917	9532	2nd Supp. to LG 30282 14 Sep 1917	WO 14 Sep 1917
Edwards, FJ	29836	25 Nov 1916	11526	Supp. to LG 29835 24 Nov 1916	WO 25 Nov 1916
Edwards, HI	35225	22 Jul 1941	4213/14	Gazette	Air Min. 22 Jul 1941
Edwards, T	25356	21 May 1884	2278	Supp. to LG 25355 20 May 1884	WO 21 May 1884
Edwards, W	30284	14 Sep 1917	9533	2nd Supp. to LG 30282 14 Sep 1917	WO 14 Sep 1917
Edwards, WMM	25198	13 Feb 1883	792	Gazette	WO 13 Feb 1883
Egerton, EA	30400	26 Nov 1917	12328/9	4th Supp. to LG 30396 23 Nov 1917	WO 26 Nov 1917
Elcock, RE	31082	26 Dec 1918	15118	Supp. to LG 31081 24 Dec 1918	WO 26 Dec 1918

	London Gazette	Date	Page	Supplement (if any)	Release Date
Elliott, K	35715	24 Sep 1942	4153	Supp. to LG 35714 22 Sep 1942	WO 24 Sep 1942
Elliott-Cooper, NB	30523	13 Feb 1918	2003	Supp. to LG 30522 12 Feb 1918	WO 13 Feb 1918
Elphinstone, HC	22149	4 Jun 1858	2757	Gazette	WO 2 Jun 1858
Elstob, W	31395	9 Jun 1919	7419	4th Supp. to LG 31391 6 Jun 1919	WO 9 Jun 1919
Elton, FC	21971	24 Feb 1857	660	Supp. to LG 21970 24 Feb 1857	WO 24 Feb 1857
Embleton, D	See Corbett, F				
Emerson, JS	30523	13 Feb 1918	2004	Supp. to LG 30522 12 Feb 1918	WO 13 Feb 1918
Engleheart, HW	27235	5 Oct 1900	6126	Gazette	WO 5 Oct 1900
English, WJ	27362	4 Oct 1901	6481	Gazette	WO 4 Oct 1901
Erskine, J	29695	5 Aug 1916	7744	Supp. to LG 29694 4 Aug 1916	WO 5 Aug 1916
Ervine-Andrews, HM	34909	30 Jul 1940	4659	3rd Supp. to LG 34906 26 Jul 1940	WO 30 Jul 1940
Esmonde, EK	35474	3 Mar 1942	1007	3rd Supp. to LG 35471 27 Feb 1942	Wh. 3 Mar 1942
Esmonde, T	22043	25 Sep 1857	3194	Gazette	WO 25 Sep 1857
Evans, A (aka Simpson, W)	30982	30 Oct 1918	12802	2nd Supp. to LG 30980 29 Oct 1918 (Simpson)	WO 30 Oct 1918
Evans, LP	30400	26 Nov 1917	12327	4th Supp. to LG 30396 23 Nov 1917	WO 26 Nov 1917
Evans, S	22014	23 Jun 1857	2165	Gazette	WO 23 Jun 1857
Evans, WJG	31759	30 Jan 1920	1217	4th Supp. to LG 31755 27 Jan 1920	WO 30 Jan 1920
Farmer, DD	27304	12 Apr 1901	2529	Gazette	WO 12 Apr 1901
Farmer, JJ	24973	17 May 1881	2553	Gazette	WO 16 May 1881
Farquharson, FEH	22278	21 Jun 1859	2420	Gazette	WO 18 Jun 1859
Farrell, J	22065	20 Nov 1857	3920	Gazette	WO 18 Nov 1857

	London Gazette	Date	Page	Supplement (if any)	Release Date
Faulds, WF	29740	9 Sep 1916	8870	Supp. to LG 29739 8 Sep 1916	WO 9 Sep 1916
Fazal Din	37091	24 May 1945	2647	Supp. to LG 37090 22 May 1945	WO 24 May 1945
Fegen, ESF	34999	22 Nov 1940	6743	Supp. to LG 34998 22 Nov 1940	Adm. 22 Nov 1940
Fergusson, TR Colyer-	See Colyer-Fergusson, TR				
Ffrench, AK	22212	24 Dec 1858	5513	Gazette	WO 24 Dec 1858
Fielding, John	See Williams, John				
Fincastle, AEM	26908	9 Nov 1897	6143	Gazette	WO 9 Nov 1897
Finch, NA	30807	23 Jul 1918	8586	4th Supp. to LG 30803 19 Jul 1918	Adm. 23 Jul 1918
Findlater, G	26968	20 May 1898	3165	Gazette	WO 20 May 1898
Findlay, G de CE	31340	15 May 1919	6083	4th Supp. to LG 31336 13 May 1919	WO 15 May 1919
Finlay, D	29210	29 Jun 1915	6269/70	Gazette	WO 29 Jun 1915
Finn, JH	See Fynn, JH				
Firman, HOB	29928	2 Feb 1917	1160	Gazette	Adm. 31 Jan 1917
Firth, J	27322	11 Jun 1901	3933	Gazette	WO 11 Jun 1901
Fisher, F	29202	23 Jun 1915	6115/16	Supp. to LG 29201 22 Jun 1915	WO 23 Jun 1915
Fitzclarence, C	27208	6 Jul 1900	4196	Gazette	WO 6 Jul 1900
Fitzgerald, R	22131	27 Apr 1858	2051	Gazette	WO 24 Apr 1858
Fitzgibbon, A	22538	13 Aug 1861	3363	Gazette	WO 13 Aug 1861
Fitzpatrick, F	24814	24 Feb 1880	832	Gazette	WO 23 Feb 1880
Flawn, T	24814	24 Feb 1880	832	Gazette	WO 23 Feb 1880
Fleming-Sandes, AJT	29371	18 Nov 1915	11448	3rd Supp. to LG 29368 16 Nov 1915	WO 18 Nov 1915
Flinn, T	22248	12 Apr 1859	1483	Gazette	WO 12 Apr 1859
Flowerdew, GM	30648	24 Apr 1918	4968	2rd Supp. to LG 30646 23 Apr 1918	WO 24 Apr 1918

	London Gazette	Date	Page	Supplement (if any)	Release Date
Foote, HRB	36518	18 May 1944	2269	Supp. to LG 36517 16 May 1944	WO 18 May 1944
Foote, JW	37466	14 Feb 1946	941	Supp. to LG 37465 12 Feb 1946	Ottawa 14 Feb 1946
Forbes-Robertson, J	30697	22 May 1918	6057	3rd Supp. to LG 30694 21 May 1918	WO 22 May 1918
Forrest, G	22154	18 Jun 1858	2959	Gazette	WO 18 Jun 1858
Forshaw, WT	29289	9 Sep 1915	8971	2nd Supp. to LG 29287 7 Sep 1915	WO 9 Sep 1915
Forsyth, S	30967	22 Oct 1918	12487/8	9th Supp. to LG 30958 18 Oct 1918	WO 22 Oct 1918
Fosbery, GV	22988	7 Jul 1865	3425	Gazette	WO 7 Jul 1865
Foss, CC	29272	23 Aug 1915	8373	3rd Supp. to LG 29269 20 Aug 1915	WO 23 Aug 1915
Foster, E	30154	27 Jun 1917	6382	4th Supp. to LG 30150 26 Jun 1917	WO 27 Jun 1917
Fowler, EJ	25093	7 Apr 1882	1586	Gazette	WO 5 Apr 1882
Fraser, CC	22445	9 Nov 1860	4126	Gazette	WO 8 Nov 1860
Fraser, IE	37346	13 Nov 1945	5529	3rd Supp. to LG 37343 9 Nov 1945	Adm. 13 Nov 1945
Freeman, J	22212	24 Dec 1858	5517	Gazette	WO 24 Dec 1858
French, JA	35862	14 Jan 1943	319	Supp. to LG 35861 12 Jan 1943	WO 14 Jan 1943
Freyberg, BC	29866	15 Dec 1916	12307	Supp. to LG 29865 15 Dec 1916	WO 15 Dec 1916
Frickleton, S	30215	2 Aug 1917	7906	4th Supp. to LG 30211 31 Jul 1917	WO 2 Aug 1917
Frisby, CH	31034	27 Nov 1918	14039/40	2nd Supp. to LG 31032 26 Nov 1918	WO 27 Nov 1918
Fuller, WC	28983	23 Nov 1914	9663	2nd Supp. to LG 28981 20 Nov 1914	WO 23 Nov 1914
Fuller, WD	29135	19 Apr 1915	3815	2nd Supp. to LG 29133 16 Apr 1915	WO 19 Apr 1915
Furness, C	37458	7 Feb 1946	847	Supp. to LG 37457 5 Feb 1946	WO 7 Feb 1946
Fynn, JH (Finn)	29765	26 Sep 1916	9418	Supp. to LG 29764 26 Sep 1916	WO 26 Sep 1916
Gaby, AE	30982	30 Oct 1918	12802	2nd Supp. to LG 30980 29 Oct 1918	WO 30 Oct 1918

	London Gazette	Date	Page	Supplement (if any)	Release Date
Gaje Ghale	36190	30 Sep 1943	4347	Supp. to LG 36189 28 Sep 1943	WO 30 Sep 1943
Ganju Lama	36690	7 Sep 1944	4157/8	2nd Supp. to LG 36688 7 Sep 1944	WO 7 Sep 1944
Gardiner, G	22149	4 Jun 1858	2756	Gazette	WO 2 Jun 1858
Gardner, PJ	35448	10 Feb 1942	645	2nd Supp. to LG 35446 6 Feb 1942	WO 10 Feb 1942
Gardner, W	22176	24 Aug 1858	3903	Gazette	WO 23 Aug 1858
Garforth, CE	28976	16 Nov 1914	9374	3rd Supp. to LG 28973 13 Nov 1914	WO 16 Nov 1914
Garland, DE	34870	11 Jun 1940	3516	Gazette	Air Min. 11 Jun 1940
Garvin, S	22347	20 Jun 1860	178	Gazette	WO 20 Jan 1860
Geary, BH	29328	15 Oct 1915	10154	Gazette	WO 15 Oct 1915
Gee, R	30471	11 Jan 1918	722	6th Supp. to LG 30465 8 Jan 1918	WO 11 Jan 1918
Gian Singh	37086	22 May 1945	2607	Supp. to LG 37085 18 May 1945	WO 22 May 1945
Gibson, GP	36030	28 May 1943	2361	Supp. to LG 36029 25 May 1943	Air Min. 28 May 1943
Gifford, EF	24082	31 Mar 1874	1921	Gazette	WO 28 Mar 1874
Gill, A	29802	26 Oct 1916	10395	4th Supp. to LG 29798 24 Oct 1916	WO 26 Oct 1916
Gill, P	22176	24 Aug 1858	3903	Gazette	WO 23 Aug 1858
Glasock, HH	27205	26 Jun 1900	3965	Gazette	WO 26 Jun 1900
Glenn, JA	See Smith, James (*Pte*)				
Goate, W	22212	24 Dec 1858	5512	Gazette	WO 24 Dec 1858
Gobar Sing Negi	29146	28 Apr 1915	4143	Supp. to LG 29145 27 Apr 1915	WO 28 Apr 1915
Gobind Singh	30471	11 Jan 1918	725	6th Supp. to LG 30465 8 Jan 1918	WO 11 Jan 1918
Godley, SF	28985	25 Nov 1914	9957	Supp. to LG 28984 24 Nov 1914	WO 25 Nov 1914
Good, HJ	30922	27 Sep 1918	11430	4th Supp. to LG 30918 24 Sep 1918	WO 27 Sep 1918
Goodfellow, CA	22727	17 Apr 1863	2071	Gazette	WO 16 Apr 1863

	London Gazette	Date	Page	Supplement (if any)	Release Date
Goodlake, GL	21971	24 Feb 1857	657	Supp. to LG 21970 24 Feb 1857	WO 24 Feb 1857
Gordon, BS	31082	26 Dec 1918	15118	Supp. to LG 31081 24 Dec 1918	WO 26 Dec 1918
Gordon, JH	35325	28 Oct 1941	6237	2nd Supp. to LG 35323 24 Oct 1941	WO 28 Oct 1941
Gordon, WE	27233	28 Sep 1900	5966	Gazette	WO 28 Sep 1900
Gordon, WJ	26352	9 Dec 1892	7217	Gazette	WO 9 Dec 1892
Gore-Browne, HG	22636	20 Jun 1862	3152	Gazette	WO 20 Jun 1862
Gorle, RV	31067	14 Dec 1918	14775	2nd Supp. to LG 31065 13 Dec 1918	WO 14 Dec 1918
Gorman, J	21971	24 Feb 1857	653	Supp. to LG 21970 24 Feb 1857	WO 24 Feb 1857
Gort, JSSPV	31034	27 Nov 1918	14039	2nd Supp. to LG 31032 26 Nov 1918	WO 27 Nov 1918
Gosling, W	30130	14 Jun 1917	5866	4th Supp. to LG 30126 12 Jun 1917	WO 14 Jun 1917
Gough, CJS	22318	21 Oct 1859	3792	Gazette	WO 21 Oct 1859
Gough, HH	22212	24 Dec 1858	5516	Gazette	WO 24 Dec 1858
Gough, JE	27636	15 Jan 1904	331	Gazette	WO 15 Jan 1904
Gould, TW	35591	9 Jun 1942	2548	7th Supp. to LG 35584 5 Jun 1942	Wh. 9 Jun 1942
Gourley, CE	30523	13 Feb 1918	2004/5	Supp. to LG 30522 12 Feb 1918	WO 13 Feb 1918
Gowrie, Earl of	See Hore-Ruthven, AGA				
Grady, T	22014	23 Jun 1857	2165	Gazette	WO 23 Jun 1857
Graham, G	21971	24 Feb 1857	656	Supp. to LG 21970 24 Feb 1857	WO 24 Feb 1857
Graham, JRN	30284	14 Sep 1917	9532	2nd Supp. to LG 30282 14 Sep 1917	WO 14 Sep 1917
Graham, P	22212	24 Dec 1858	5514	Gazette	WO 24 Dec 1858
Grant, CJW	26165	26 May 1891	2805	Gazette	WO 26 May 1891
Grant, JD	27758	24 Jan 1905	574	Gazette	WO 24 Jan 1905
Grant, JG	31034	27 Nov 1918	14040	2nd Supp. to LG 31032 26 Nov 1918	WO 27 Nov 1918

	London Gazette	Date	Page	Supplement (if any)	Release Date
Grant, P	22212	24 Dec 1858	5515	Gazette	WO 24 Dec 1858
Grant, R	22396	19 Jun 1860	2316	Gazette (Gazetted as EWART)	WO 19 Jun 1860
Gratwick, PE	35879	28 Jan 1943	523/4	Supp. to LG 35878 26 Jan 1943	WO 28 Jan 1943
Gray, RH	37346	13 Nov 1945	5529	3rd Supp. to LG 37343 9 Nov 1945	Adm. 13 Nov 1945
Gray, T	34870	11 Jun 1940	3516	Gazette	Air Min. 11 Jun 1940
Grayburn, JH	35907	25 Jan 1945	561/2	Supp. to LG 36906 23 Jan 1945	WO 25 Jan 1945
Greaves, F	30400	26 Nov 1917	12329	4th Supp. to LG 30396 23 Nov 1917	WO 26 Nov 1917
Green, JL	29695	5 Aug 1916	7743	Supp. to LG 29694 4 Aug 1916	WO 5 Aug 1916
Green, P	22194	26 Oct 1858	4574	Gazette	WO 26 Oct 1858
Greenwood, H	31082	26 Dec 1918	15117	Supp. to LG 31081 24 Dec 1918	WO 26 Dec 1918
Gregg, MF	31108	6 Jan 1919	306	4th Supp. to LG 31104 3 Jan 1919	WO 6 Jan 1919
Gregg, W	30770	28 Jun 1918	7619	6th Supp. to LG 30764 25 Jun 1918	WO 28 Jun 1918
Grenfell, FO	28976	16 Nov 1914	9373	3rd Supp. to LG 28973 13 Nov 1914	WO 16 Nov 1914
Gribble, JR	30770	28 Jun 1918	7617	6th Supp. to LG 30764 25 Jun 1918	WO 28 Jun 1918
Grieve, J	21971	24 Feb 1857	655	Supp. to LG 21970 24 Feb 1857	WO 24 Feb 1857
Grieve, RC	30215	2 Aug 1917	7905	4th Supp. to LG 30211 31 Jul 1917	WO 2 Aug 1917
Griffiths, W	23333	17 Dec 1867	6878	Gazette	WO 17 Dec 1867
Grimbaldeston, WH	30284	14 Sep 1917	9532	2nd Supp. to LG 30282 14 Sep 1917	WO 14 Sep 1917
Grimshaw, JE	29985	15 Mar 1917	2619	3rd Supp. to LG 29982 13 Mar 1917	WO 15 Mar 1917
Gristock, G	34928	23 Aug 1940	5137	Supp. to LG 34927 20 Aug 1940	WO 23 Aug 1940
Grogan, GWStG	30811	25 Jul 1918	8723	3rd Supp. to LG 30808 23 Jul 1918	WO 25 Jul 1918
Guise, JC	22212	24 Dec 1858	5514	Gazette	WO 24 Dec 1858
Gunn, GW	35530	21 Apr 1942	1741	2nd Supp. to LG 35528 17 Apr 1942	WO 21 Apr 1942

	London Gazette	Date	Page	Supplement (if any)	Release Date
Gurney, AS	35698	11 Sep 1942	3953	2nd Supp. to LG 35696 8 Sep 1942	WO 11 Sep 1942
Guy, BJD	27262	1 Jan 1901	3	Gazette	WO 1 Jan 1901
Hackett, TB	22248	12 Apr 1859	1482	Gazette	WO 12 Apr 1859
Hackett, W	29695	5 Aug 1916	7744	Supp. to LG 29694 4 Aug 1916	WO 5 Aug 1916
Haine, RL	30122	8 Jun 1917	5703	2nd Supp. to LG 30120 8 Jun 1917	WO 8 Jun 1917
Hale, TE	21997	5 May 1857	1578	Gazette	WO 5 May 1857
Hall, AC	31067	14 Dec 1918	14778	2nd Supp. to LG 31065 13 Dec 1918	WO 14 Dec 1918
Hall, FW	29202	23 Jun 1915	6115	Supp. to LG 29201 22 Jun 1915	WO 23 Jun 1915
Hall, W	22225	1 Feb 1859	414	Gazette	WO 1 Feb 1859
Halliday, LST	27262	1 Jan 1901	3	Gazette	WO 1 Jan 1901
Halliwell, J	30811	25 Jul 1918	8724	3rd Supp. to LG 30808 23 Jul 1918	WO 25 Jul 1918
Hallowes, RP	29371	18 Nov 1915	11448	3rd Supp. to LG 29368 16 Nov 1915	WO 18 Nov 1915
Halton, A	30400	26 Nov 1917	12330	4th Supp. to LG 30396 23 Nov 1917	WO 26 Nov 1917
Hamilton, AF Douglas-	See Douglas-Hamilton, AF				
Hamilton, JB	30400	26 Nov 1917	12330	4th Supp. to LG 30396 23 Nov 1917	WO 26 Nov 1917
Hamilton, JP	29328	15 Oct 1915	10154	Gazette	WO 15 Oct 1915
Hamilton, T de C	21971	24 Feb 1857	661	Supp. to LG 21970 24 Feb 1857	WO 24 Feb 1857
Hamilton, WRP	24768	7 Oct 1879	5777	Gazette	WO 1 Sep 1879
Hammond, AG	25027	18 Oct 1881	5140	Gazette	WO 15 Oct 1881
Hampton, H	27366	18 Oct 1901	6779	Gazette	WO 18 Oct 1901
Hancock, T	22083	15 Jan 1858	178	Gazette	WO 15 Jan 1858
Hanna, RH	30372	8 Nov 1917	11568	3rd Supp. to LG 30369 6 Nov 1917	WO 8 Nov 1917

	London Gazette	Date	Page	Supplement (if any)	Release Date
Hannah, J	34958	1 Oct 1940	5788/9	Gazette	Air Min. 1 Oct 1940
Hansen, PH	29312	1 Oct 1915	9641	Gazette	WO 1 Oct 1915
Harden, HE	36972	8 Mar 1945	1297	Supp. to LG 36971 6 Mar 1945	WO 8 Mar 1945
Hardham, WJ	27362	4 Oct 1901	6481	Gazette	WO 4 Oct 1901
Harding, I	25147	15 Sep 1882	4260	Gazette	WO 15 Sep 1882
Hardy, TB	30790	11 Jul 1918	8155/6	3rd Supp. to LG 30787 9 Jul 1918	WO 11 Jul 1918
Harington, HE	22212	24 Dec 1858	5516	Gazette	WO 24 Dec 1858
Harlock, EG	See Horlock, EG				
Harman, JP	36574	22 Jun 1944	2901	Supp. to LG 36573 20 Jun 1944	WO 22 Jun 1944
Harper, JW	36870	2 Jan 1945	139/40	5th Supp. to LG 36865 29 Dec 1944	WO 2 Jan 1945
Harris, TJ	30967	22 Oct 1918	12487	9th Supp. to LG 30958 18 Oct 1918	WO 22 Oct 1918
Harrison, AL	31236	17 Mar 1919	3590/1	6th Supp. to LG 31230 14 Mar 1919	Adm. 17 Mar 1919
Harrison, John (*Ldg Smn*)	22212	24 Dec 1858	5512	Gazette	WO 24 Dec 1858
Harrison, John (*Second Lt*)	30130	14 Jun 1917	5866	4th Supp. to LG 30126 12 Jun 1917	WO 14 Jun 1917
Hart, RC	24732	10 Jun 1879	3830	Gazette	WO 10 Jun 1879
Hartigan, H	22396	19 Jun 1860	2316	Gazette	WO 19 Jun 1860
Hartley, EB	25023	7 Oct 1881	4990	Gazette	WO 4 Oct 1881
Harvey, FJW	29751	15 Sep 1916	9070	Supp. to LG 29750 15 Sep 1916	Adm. 15 Sep 1916
Harvey, FMW	30122	8 Jun 1917	5702	2nd Supp. to LG 30120 8 Jun 1917	WO 8 Jun 1917
Harvey, J	31012	15 Nov 1918	13473	7th Supp. to LG 31005 12 Nov 1918	WO 15 Nov 1918
Harvey, N	31108	6 Jan 1919	308	4th Supp. to LG 31104 3 Jan 1919	WO 6 Jan 1919
Harvey, S	29371	18 Nov 1915	11449	3rd Supp. to LG 29368 16 Nov 1915	WO 18 Nov 1915
Havelock, HM	22083	15 Jan 1858	178	Gazette	WO 15 Jan 1858

	London Gazette	Date	Page	Supplement (if any)	Release Date
Havelock-Allan, HM	See Havelock, HM				
Hawker, LG	29273	24 Aug 1915	8395	Gazette	WO 24 Aug 1915
Hawkes, D	22212	24 Dec 1858	5515	Gazette	WO 24 Dec 1858
Hawthorne, R	22131	27 Apr 1858	2051	Gazette	WO 24 Apr 1858
Hayward, RFJ	30648	24 Apr 1918	4967/8	2nd Supp. to LG 30646 23 Apr 1918	WO 24 Apr 1918
Heaphy, C	23217	8 Feb 1867	696	Gazette	WO 8 Feb 1867
Heathcote, AS	22347	20 Jan 1860	178	Gazette	WO 20 Jan 1860
Heaton, WE	27267	18 Jan 1901	394	Gazette	WO 18 Jan 1901
Heaviside, MW	30122	8 Jun 1917	5705	2nd Supp. to LG 30120 8 Jun 1917	WO 8 Jun 1917
Hedges, FW	31155	31 Jan 1919	1503	8th Supp. to LG 31147 28 Jan 1919	WO 31 Jan 1919
Henderson, A	30167	5 Jul 1917	6697	6th Supp. to LG 30161 3 Jul 1917	WO 5 Jul 1917
Henderson, EED	30122	8 Jun 1917	5701	2nd Supp. to LG 30120 8 Jun 1917	WO 8 Jun 1917
Henderson, GS	32106	29 Oct 1920	10579	Supp. to LG 32105 29 Oct 1920	WO 29 Oct 1920
Henderson, HS	26850	7 May 1897	2535	Gazette	WO 7 May 1897
Heneage-Walker, C	22223	28 Jan 1859	294	Gazette	WO 26 Jan 1859
Henry, A	21971	24 Feb 1857	655	Supp. to LG 21970 24 Feb 1857	WO 24 Feb 1857
Herring, AC	30733	7 Jun 1918	6775/6	6th Supp. to LG 30727 4 Jun 1918	WO 7 Jun 1918
Hewett, WNW	21971	24 Feb 1857	652	Supp. to LG 21970 24 Feb 1857	WO 24 Feb 1857
Hewitson, J	30770	28 Jun 1918	7619	6th Supp. to LG 30764 25 Jun 1918	WO 28 Jun 1918
Hewitt, DGW	30284	14 Sep 1917	9532	2nd Supp. to LG 30282 14 Sep 1917	WO 14 Sep 1917
Hewitt, WH	30400	26 Nov 1917	12329	4th Supp. to LG 30396 23 Nov 1917	WO 26 Nov 1917
Hill, A	29765	26 Sep 1916	9418	Supp. to LG 29764 26 Sep 1916	WO 26 Sep 1916
Hill, AR	25084	14 Mar 1882	1130	Gazette	WO 13 Mar 1882

	London Gazette	Date	Page	Supplement (if any)	Release Date
Hill, S	22212	24 Dec 1858	5514	Gazette	WO 24 Dec 1858
Hill-Walker, AR	See Hill, AR				
Hills, J (Hills-Johnes)	22131	27 Apr 1858	2050	Gazette	WO 24 Apr 1858
Hinckley, G	22705	6 Feb 1863	642	Gazette	WO 6 Feb 1863
Hinton, JD	35311	17 Oct 1941	6027	2nd Supp. to LG 35309 14 Oct 1941	WO 17 Oct 1941
Hirsch, DP	30130	14 Jun 1917	5865/6	4th Supp. to LG 30126 12 Jun 1917	WO 14 Jun 1917
Hitch, F	24717	2 May 1879	3178	Supp. to LG 24716 2 May 1879	WO 2 May 1879
Hobson, F	30338	17 Oct 1917	10677/8	2nd Supp. to LG 30336 16 Oct 1917	WO 17 Oct 1917
Hodge, S	22205	4 Jan 1867	84	Gazette	WO 4 Jan 1867
Hoey, CF	36518	18 May 1944	2269	Supp. to LG 36517 16 May 1944	WO 18 May 1944
Hogan, J	29015	22 Dec 1914	10920	Gazette	WO 22 Dec 1914
Holbrook, ND	29015	22 Dec 1914	10920	Gazette	WO 22 Dec 1914
Holland, EJG	27307	23 Apr 1901	2775	Gazette	WO 23 Apr 1901
Holland, JV	29802	26 Oct 1916	10394	4th Supp. to LG 29798 24 Oct 1916	WO 26 Oct 1916
Hollis, G	22223	28 Jan 1859	294	Gazette	WO 26 Jan 1859
Hollis, SE	36658	17 Aug 1944	3807/8	Supp. to LG 36657 15 Aug 1944	WO 17 Aug 1944
Hollowell, J (Holliwell)	22154	18 Jun 1858	2958	Gazette	WO 18 Jun 1858
Holmes, FW	28985	25 Nov 1914	9958	Supp. to LG 28984 24 Nov 1914	WO 25 Nov 1914
Holmes, J	22154	18 Jun 1858	2958	Gazette	WO 18 Jun 1858
Holmes, TW	30471	11 Jan 1918	724	6th Supp. to LG 30465 8 Jan 1918	WO 11 Jan 1918
Holmes, WE	30182	26 Dec 1918	15118/19	Supp. to LG 30181 24 Dec 1918	WO 26 Dec 1918
Home, AD	22154	18 Jun 1858	2959	Gazette	WO 18 Jun 1858
Home, DC	22154	18 Jun 1858	2961	Gazette ('Had he survived')	WO 18 Jun 1858

	London Gazette	Date	Page	Supplement (if any)	Release Date
Honey, SL	31108	6 Jan 1919	306	4th Supp. to LG 31104 3 Jan 1919	WO 6 Jan 1919
Hook, AH	24717	2 May 1879	3178	Supp. to LG 24716 2 May 1879	WO 2 May 1879
Hope, W	21997	5 May 1857	1578	Gazette	WO 5 May 1857
Hore-Ruthven, AGA	27057	28 Feb 1899	1254	Gazette	WO 28 Feb 1899
Horlock, EG (Harlock, EG)	28985	25 Nov 1914	9958	Supp. to LG 28984 24 Nov 1914	WO 25 Nov 1914
Hornby, EJ Phipps-	See Phipps-Hornby, EJ				
Hornell, DE	36630	28 Jul 1944	3523	4th Supp. to LG 36626 25 Jul 1944	Air Min. 28 Jul 1944
Horsfall, BA	30697	22 May 1918	6058	3rd Supp. to LG 30694 21 May 1918	WO 22 May 1918
Horwood, AG	36445	30 Mar 1944	1478	Supp. to LG 36444 28 Mar 1944	WO 30 Mar 1944
House, W	27480	7 Oct 1902	6341	Gazette	WO 7 Oct 1902
Howell, GJ	30154	27 Jun 1917	6382	4th Supp. to LG 30150 26 Jun 1917	WO 27 Jun 1917
Howse, NR	27320	4 Jun 1901	3769	Gazette	WO 4 Jun 1901
Hudson, CE	30790	11 Jul 1918	8155	3rd Supp. to LG 30787 9 Jul 1918	WO 11 Jul 1918
Huffam, JP	31082	26 Dec 1918	15118	Supp. to LG 31081 24 Dec 1918	WO 26 Dec 1918
Hughes, M	21971	24 Feb 1857	658	Supp. to LG 21970 24 Feb 1857	WO 24 Feb 1857
Hughes, T	29802	26 Oct 1916	10395	4th Supp. to LG 29798 24 Oct 1916	WO 26 Oct 1916
Hull, C	29496	3 Mar 1916	2349	Gazette	WO 3 Mar 1916
Hulme, AC	35306	14 Oct 1941	5936	2nd Supp. to LG 35304 10 Oct 1941	WO 14 Oct 1941
Humpston, R	21971	24 Feb 1857	662	Supp. to LG 21970 24 Feb 1857	WO 24 Feb 1857
Hunter, DF	30970	23 Oct 1918	12563	2nd Supp. to LG 30968 22 Oct 1918	WO 23 Oct 1918
Hunter, TP	37127	12 Jun 1945	3087	9th Supp. to LG 37118 8 Jun 1945	Adm. 12 Jun 1945
Hutcheson, BS	31067	14 Dec 1918	14774	2nd Supp. to LG 31065 13 Dec 1918	WO 14 Dec 1918
Hutchinson, J	29740	9 Sep 1916	8870	Supp. to LG 29739 8 Sep 1916	WO 9 Sep 1916

	London Gazette	Date	Page	Supplement (if any)	Release Date
Hutt, A	30400	26 Nov 1917	12330	4th Supp. to LG 30396 23 Nov 1917	WO 26 Nov 1917
Ind, AE	27465	15 Aug 1902	5328	Gazette	WO 15 Aug 1902
Ingham, S	See Meekosha, S				
Ingouville, G	21971	24 Feb 1857	653	Supp. to LG 21970 24 Feb 1857	WO 24 Feb 1857
Ingram, GM	31108	6 Jan 1919	306/7	4th Supp. to LG 31104 3 Jan 1919	WO 6 Jan 1919
Inkson, ET	27266	15 Jan 1901	308	Gazette	WO 15 Jan 1901
Innes, JJ McL	22212	24 Dec 1858	5518	Gazette	WO 24 Dec 1858
Insall, GSM	29414	23 Dec 1915	12797/8	5th Supp. to LG 29409 21 Dec 1915	WSO 23 Dec 1915
Inwood, RR	30400	26 Nov 1917	12330	4th Supp. to LG 30396 23 Nov 1917	WO 26 Nov 1917
Irwin, C	22212	24 Dec 1858	5513	Gazette	WO 24 Dec 1858
Ishar Singh	32530	25 Nov 1921	9609	Supp. to LG 32529 25 Nov 1921	WO 25 Nov 1921
Jacka, A	29240	24 Jul 1915	7279	Supp. to LG 29239 23 Jul 1915	WO 24 Jul 1915
Jackman, JJB	35505	31 Mar 1942	1437	2nd Supp. to LG 35503 27 Mar 1942	WO 31 Mar 1942
Jackson, H	30675	8 May 1918	5556	2nd Supp. to LG 30673 7 May 1918	WO 8 May 1918
Jackson, NC	37324	26 Oct 1945	5233	4th Supp. to LG 37320 23 Oct 1945	Air Min. 26 Oct 1945
Jackson, TN	31034	27 Nov 1918	14040	2nd Supp. to LG 31032 26 Nov 1918	WO 27 Nov 1918
Jackson, W	29740	9 Sep 1916	8870/1	Supp. to LG 29739 8 Sep 1916	WO 9 Sep 1916
James, MA	30770	28 Jun 1918	7617/18	6th Supp. to LG 30764 25 Jun 1918	WO 28 Jun 1918
James, WH	29281	1 Sep 1915	8700	Supp. to LG 29280 31 Aug 1915	WO 1 Sep 1915
Jamieson, DA	36764	26 Oct 1944	4899	Supp. to LG 36763 24 Oct 1944	WO 26 Oct 1944
Jarratt, G	30122	8 Jun 1917	5705	2nd Supp. to LG 30120 8 Jun 1917	WO 8 Jun 1917

	London Gazette	Date	Page	Supplement (if any)	Release Date
Jarrett, HCT	22278	21 Jun 1859	2420	Gazette	WO 18 Jun 1859
Jarvis, CA	28976	16 Nov 1914	9374	3rd Supp. to LG 28973 13 Nov 1914	WO 16 Nov 1914
Jee, J	22445	9 Nov 1860	4126	Gazette	WO 8 Nov 1860
Jefferson, FA	36605	13 Jul 1944	3273	Supp. to LG 36604 11 Jul 1944	WO 13 Jul 1944
Jeffries, CS	30433	18 Dec 1917	13222	5th Supp. to LG 30428 14 Dec 1917	WO 18 Dec 1917
Jennings, E	22212	24 Dec 1858	5516	Gazette	WO 24 Dec 1858
Jensen, JC	30122	8 Jun 1917	5705	2nd Supp. to LG 30120 8 Jun 1917	WO 8 Jun 1917
Jerome, HE	22324	11 Nov 1859	4032	Gazette	WO 11 Nov 1859
Jerrard, A	30663	1 May 1918	5287	3rd Supp. to LG 30660 30 Apr 1918	Air Min. 1 May 1918
Johnson, DG	31108	6 Jan 1919	305	4th Supp. to LG 31104 3 Jan 1919	WO 6 Jan 1919
Johnson, FH	29371	18 Nov 1915	11448	3rd Supp. to LG 29368 16 Nov 1915	WO 18 Nov 1915
Johnson, JB	31082	26 Dec 1918	15118	Supp. to LG 31081 24 Dec 1918	WO 26 Dec 1918
Johnson, WH	31067	14 Dec 1918	14776	2nd Supp. to LG 31065 13 Dec 1918	WO 14 Dec 1918
Johnston, R	27283	12 Feb 1901	1059	Gazette	WO 12 Feb 1901
Johnston, WH	28985	25 Nov 1914	9958	Supp. to LG 28984 24 Nov 1914	WO 25 Nov 1914
Johnstone, W	21971	24 Feb 1857	654	Supp. to LG 21970 24 Feb 1857	WO 24 Feb 1857
Jones, AS	22154	18 Jun 1858	2960	Gazette	WO 18 Jun 1858
Jones, C Mansel-	See Mansel-Jones, C				
Jones, D	29802	26 Oct 1916	10395	4th Supp. to LG 29798 24 Oct 1916	WO 26 Oct 1916
Jones, H	49134	11 Oct 1982	12831	Supp. to LG 49133 8 Oct 1982	MOD (Army) 11 Oct 1982
Jones, HM	22043	25 Sep 1857	3194	Gazette	WO 25 Sep 1857
Jones, LW	29972	6 Mar 1917	2254	Gazette	Adm. 6 Mar 1917
Jones, R	24717	2 May 1879	3178	Supp. to LG 24716 2 May 1879	WO 2 May 1879

	London Gazette	Date	Page	Supplement (if any)	Release Date
Jones, RBB	29695	5 Aug 1916	7743/4	Supp. to LG 29694 4 Aug 1916	WO 5 Aug 1916
Jones, RJT Digby-	See Digby-Jones, RJT				
Jones, TA	29802	26 Oct 1916	10395	4th Supp. to LG 29798 24 Oct 1916	WO 26 Oct 1916
Jones, W	24717	2 May 1879	3178	Supp. to LG 24716 2 May 1879	WO 2 May 1879
Jotham, E	29240	24 Jul 1915	7279	Supp. to LG 29239 23 Jul 1915	WO 24 Jul 1915
Joynt, WD	31034	27 Nov 1918	14040	2nd Supp. to LG 31032 26 Nov 1918	WO 27 Nov 1918
Judson, RS	30982	30 Oct 1918	12802	2nd Supp. to LG 30980 29 Oct 1918	WO 30 Oct 1918
Kaeble, J	30903	16 Sep 1918	11076	5th Supp. to LG 30898 13 Sep 1918	WO 16 Sep 1918
Kamal Ram	36627	27 Jul 1944	3501	Supp. to LG 36626 25 Jul 1944	WO 27 Jul 1944
Karamjeet Singh Judge	37156	3 Jul 1945	3439/40	Supp. to LG 37155 29 Jun 1945	WO 3 Jul 1945
Karanbahadur Rana	30757	21 Jun 1918	7307/8	5th Supp. to LG 30752 18 Jun 1918	WO 21 Jun 1918
Kavanagh, TH	22283	8 Jul 1859	2629	Gazette	WO 6 Jul 1859
Keatinge, RH	22601	25 Feb 1862	956	Gazette	WO 25 Feb 1862
Kellaway, J	21971	24 Feb 1857	650	Supp. to LG 21970 24 Feb 1857	WO 24 Feb 1857
Kelliher, R	36305	30 Dec 1943	5649	Supp. to LG 36304 28 Dec 1943	Canberra 30 Dec 1943
Kells, R	22212	24 Dec 1858	5517	Gazette	WO 24 Dec 1858
Kelly, H	29836	25 Nov 1916	11526	Supp. to LG 29835 24 Nov 1916	WO 25 Nov 1916
Kelly, JD	See Davis, J				
Kelly, J Sherwood-	See Sherwood-Kelly, J				
Keneally, WS	29273	24 Aug 1915	8395	Gazette	WO 24 Aug 1915
Kenna, E	37253	6 Sep 1945	4467/8	Supp. to LG 37252 4 Sep 1945	WO 6 Sep 1945
Kenna, PA	27023	15 Nov 1898	6688	Gazette	WO 15 Nov 1898

	London Gazette	Date	Page	Supplement (if any)	Release Date
Kenneally, JP	36136	17 Aug 1943	3689	3rd Supp. to LG 36133 13 Aug 1943	WO 17 Aug 1943
Kennedy, CT	27366	18 Oct 1901	6779	Gazette	WO 18 Oct 1901
Kennedy, WH Clark-	See Clark-Kennedy, WH				
Kenny, HE	29527	30 Mar 1916	3410	4th Supp. to LG 29523 28 Mar 1916	WO 30 Mar 1916
Kenny, J	22212	24 Dec 1858	5513	Gazette	WO 24 Dec 1858
Kenny, T	29394	7 Dec 1915	12281/2	Supp. to LG 29393 7 Dec 1915	WO 7 Dec 1915
Kenny, TJB	30122	8 Jun 1917	5705	2nd Supp. to LG 30120 8 Jun 1917	WO 8 Jun 1917
Kenny, W	29074	18 Feb 1915	1699	4th Supp. to LG 29070 16 Feb 1915	WO 18 Feb 1915
Kenny, WD	32046	9 Sep 1920	9133/4	3rd Supp. to LG 32043 7 Sep 1920	WO 9 Sep 1920
Ker, AE	31536	4 Sep 1919	11205	4th Supp. to LG 31532 2 Sep 1919	WO 4 Sep 1919
Kerr, GF	31108	6 Jan 1919	306	4th Supp. to LG 31104 3 Jan 1919	WO 6 Jan 1919
Kerr, JC	29802	26 Oct 1916	10395	4th Supp. to LG 29798 24 Oct 1916	WO 26 Oct 1916
Kerr, WA	22131	27 Apr 1858	2050	Gazette	WO 24 Apr 1858
Keyes, GCT	35600	19 Jun 1942	2699	2nd Supp. to LG 35598 16 Jun 1942	WO 19 Jun 1942
Keysor, LM (Keyzor)	29328	15 Oct 1915	10154	Gazette	WO 15 Oct 1915
Keyworth, LJ	29215	3 Jul 1915	6533	Supp. to LG 29214 2 Jul 1915	WO 3 Jul 1915
Keyzor, LM	See Keysor, LM				
Khudadad Khan	28999	7 Dec 1914	10425	4th Supp. to LG 28995 4 Dec 1914	WO 7 Dec 1914
Kibby, WH	35879	28 Jan 1943	523	Supp. to LG 35878 26 Jan 1943	WO 28 Jan 1943
Kilby, AFG	29527	30 Mar 1916	3409	4th Supp. to LG 29523 28 Mar 1916	WO 30 Mar 1916
Kingsbury, BS	35893	9 Feb 1943	695	Supp. to LG 35892 5 Feb 1943	WO 9 Feb 1943
Kinross, CJ	30471	11 Jan 1918	724	6th Supp. to LG 30465 8 Jan 1918	WO 11 Jan 1918
Kirby, FH	27235	5 Oct 1900	6126	Gazette	WO 5 Oct 1900

	London Gazette	Date	Page	Supplement (if any)	Release Date
Kirk, James	31108	6 Jan 1919	307	4th Supp. to LG 31104 3 Jan 1919	WO 6 Jan 1919
Kirk, John	22347	20 Jan 1860	179	Gazette	WO 20 Jan 1860
Knight, AG	31012	15 Nov 1918	13472	7th Supp. to LG 31005 12 Nov 1918	WO 15 Nov 1918
Knight, AJ	30372	8 Nov 1917	11568/9	3rd Supp. to LG 30369 6 Nov 1917	WO 8 Nov 1917
Knight, HJ	27263	4 Jan 1901	81	Gazette	WO 4 Jan 1901
Knowland, GA	37027	12 Apr 1945	1939	Supp. to LG 37026 10 Apr 1945	WO 12 Apr 1945
Knox, CL	30726	4 Jun 1918	6571/2	12th Supp. to LG 30714 31 May 1918	WO 4 Jun 1918
Knox, JS	21971	24 Feb 1857	662	Supp. to LG 21970 24 Feb 1857	WO 24 Feb 1857
Konowal, F	30400	26 Nov 1917	12329	4th Supp. to LG 30396 23 Nov 1917	WO 26 Nov 1917
Kulbir Thapa	29371	18 Nov 1915	11450	3rd Supp. to LG 29368 16 Nov 1915	WO 18 Nov 1915
Lachhiman Gurung	37195	27 Jul 1945	3861	2nd Supp. to LG 37193 24 Jul 1945	WO 27 Jul 1945
Lafone, AM	30433	18 Dec 1917	13222	5th Supp. to LG 30428 14 Dec 1917	WO 18 Dec 1917
Laidlaw, DL	29371	18 Nov 1915	11449/50	3rd Supp. to LG 29368 16 Nov 1915	WO 18 Nov 1915
Lala	29579	13 May 1916	4809	Supp. to LG 29578 12 May 1916	WO 13 May 1916
Lalbahadur Thapa	35053	15 Jun 1943	2719	Supp. to LG 36052 11 Jun 1943	WO 15 Jun 1943
Lambert, G	22154	18 Jun 1858	2957	Gazette	WO 18 Jun 1858
Lane, T	22538	13 Aug 1861	3363	Gazette	WO 13 Aug 1861
Lascelles, AM	30471	11 Jan 1918	723	6th Supp. to LG 30465 8 Jan 1918	WO 11 Jan 1918
Lassen, AFEVS	37254	7 Sep 1945	4469	2nd Supp. to LG 37252 4 Sep 1945	WO 7 Sep 1945
Lauder, DR	29901	13 Jan 1917	559	Supp. to LG 29900 12 Jan 1917	WO 13 Jan 1917
Laughnan, T	22212	24 Dec 1858	5516	Gazette	WO 24 Dec 1858
Laurent, HJ	31012	15 Nov 1918	13472	7th Supp. to LG 31005 12 Nov 1918	WO 15 Nov 1918

	London Gazette	Date	Page	Supplement (if any)	Release Date
Lawrence, BTT	27266	15 Jan 1901	308	Gazette	WO 15 Jan 1901
Lawrence, SH	22328	22 Nov 1859	4193	Gazette	WO 21 Nov 1859
Lawson, E	26968	20 May 1898	3165	Gazette	WO 20 May 1898
Leach, EP	24790	9 Dec 1879	7265	Gazette	WO 6 Dec 1879
Leach, J	29015	22 Dec 1914	10920	Gazette	WO 22 Dec 1914
Leak, J	29740	9 Sep 1916	8871	Supp. to LG 29739 8 Sep 1916	WO 9 Sep 1916
Leake, A Martin-	See Martin-Leake, A				
Leakey, NG	37349	15 Nov 1945	5571	Supp. to LG 37348 13 Nov 1945	WO 13 Nov 1945
Learmonth, OM	30372	8 Nov 1917	11567	3rd Supp. to LG 30369 6 Nov 1917	WO 8 Nov 1917
Learoyd, RAB	34923	20 Aug 1940	5090	Gazette	Air Min. 20 Aug 1940
Lee, BAW Warburton-	See Warburton-Lee, BAW				
Leet, WK	24734	17 Jun 1879	3966	Gazette	WO 17 Jun 1879
Leitch, P	22149	4 Jun 1858	2757	Gazette	WO 2 Jun 1858
Leith, JE	22212	24 Dec 1858	5517	Gazette	WO 24 Dec 1858
Lendrim, WJ	21971	24 Feb 1857	656	Supp. to LG 21970 24 Feb 1857	WO 24 Feb 1857
Lennox, WO	21971	24 Feb 1857	656	Supp. to LG 21970 24 Feb 1857	WO 24 Feb 1857
Lenon, EH	22538	13 Aug 1861	3363	Gazette	WO 13 Aug 1861
Le Patourel, HW	35929	9 Mar 1943	1117	Supp. to LG 35928 5 Mar 1943	WO 9 Mar 1943
Le Quesne, FS	25988	29 Oct 1889	5721	Gazette	WO 29 Oct 1889
Lester, F	31067	14 Dec 1918	14778	2nd Supp. to LG 31065 13 Dec 1918	WO 14 Dec 1918
Lewis, HW	29866	15 Dec 1916	12307/8	Supp. to LG 29865 15 Dec 1916	WO 15 Dec 1916
Lewis, LA	31155	31 Jan 1919	1505	8th Supp. to LG 31147 28 Jan 1919	WO 31 Jan 1919
Liddell, IO	37112	7 Jun 1945	2877	Supp. to LG 37111 5 Jun 1945	WO 7 Jun 1945

	London Gazette	Date	Page	Supplement (if any)	Release Date
Liddell, JA	29272	23 Aug 1915	8373/4	3rd Supp. to LG 29269 20 Aug 1915	WO 23 Aug 1915
Lindsay, RJ Loyd-	See Loyd-Lindsay, RJ				
Linton, JW	36028	25 May 1943	2329	4th Supp. to LG 36024 21 May 1943	Wh. 25 May 1943
Lisle-Phillipps, EA	22318	21 Oct 1859	3793	Gazette ('Had he survived')	WO 21 Oct 1859
Lisle-Phillipps, EA	27986	15 Jan 1907	325	Gazette	WO 15 Jan 1907
Lister, J	30400	26 Nov 1917	12328	4th Supp. to LG 30396 23 Nov 1917	WO 26 Nov 1917
Lloyd, OEP	26472	2 Jan 1894	1	Gazette	WO 2 Jan 1894
Lodge, I	27205	26 Jun 1900	3965	Gazette	WO 26 Jun 1900
Loosemore, A	30284	14 Sep 1917	9533	2nd Supp. to LG 30282 14 Sep 1917	WO 14 Sep 1917
Lord, DSA	37347	13 Nov 1945	5533	4th Supp. to LG 37343 9 Nov 1945	Air Min. 13 Nov 1945
Loudoun-Shand, SW	29740	9 Sep 1916	8869	Supp. to LG 29739 8 Sep 1916	WO 9 Sep 1916
Lowerson, AD	31067	14 Dec 1918	14777	2nd Supp. to LG 31065 13 Dec 1918	WO 14 Dec 1918
Loyd-Lindsay, RJ	21971	24 Feb 1857	657	Supp. to LG 21970 24 Feb 1857	WO 24 Feb 1857
Lucas, CD	21971	24 Feb 1857	654	Supp. to LG 21970 24 Feb 1857	WO 24 Feb 1857
Lucas, J	22531	19 Jul 1861	2962	Gazette	WO 17 Jul 1861
Luke, F	23985	25 Nov 1914	9957	Supp. to LG 28984 24 Nov 1914	WO 25 Nov 1914
Lumley, C	21971	24 Feb 1857	661	Supp. to LG 21970 24 Feb 1857	WO 24 Feb 1857
Lumsden, FW	30122	8 Jun 1917	5701/2	2nd Supp. to LG 30120 8 Jun 1917	WO 8 Jun 1917
Lyall, GT	31067	14 Dec 1918	14775	2nd Supp. to LG 31065 13 Dec 1918	WO 14 Dec 1918
Lyell, CA	35129	12 Aug 1943	3625	Supp. to LG 36128 10 Aug 1943	WO 12 Aug 1943
Lynn, J	29210	29 Jun 1915	6270	Gazette	WO 29 Jun 1915
Lyons, J	21971	24 Feb 1857	659	Supp. to LG 21970 24 Feb 1857	WO 24 Feb 1857
Lysons, H	25093	7 Apr 1882	1586	Gazette	WO 5 Apr 1882

	London Gazette	Date	Page	Supplement (if any)	Release Date
Lyster, HH	22318	21 Oct 1859	3792	Gazette	WO 21 Oct 1859
MacArthur, T	See Arthur, T				
McAulay, J	30471	11 Jan 1918	723	6th Supp. to LG 30465 8 Jan 1918	WO 11 Jan 1918
McBean, W	22212	24 Dec 1858	5515	Gazette	WO 24 Dec 1858
McBeath, RG	30471	11 Jan 1918	723/4	6th Supp. to LG 30465 8 Jan 1918	WO 11 Jan 1918
McCarthy, LD	31067	14 Dec 1918	14776	2nd Supp. to LG 31065 13 Dec 1918	WO 14 Dec 1918
McCorrie, C (McCurry)	21971	24 Feb 1857	661	Supp. to LG 21970 24 Feb 1857	WO 24 Feb 1857
McCrea, JF	24989	28 Jun 1881	3239	Gazette	WO 27 Jun 1881
McCudden, JTB	30604	2 Apr 1918	3997/8	Supp. to LG 30603 29 Mar 1918	WO 2 Apr 1918
McCurry, C	See McCorrie, C				
McDermond, J	21971	24 Feb 1857	660	Supp. to LG 21970 24 Feb 1857	WO 24 Feb 1857
MacDonald, H	22149	4 Jun 1858	2757	Gazette	WO 2 Jun 1858
McDonell, WF	22357	17 Feb 1860	557	Gazette	WO 17 Feb 1860
McDougall, J	22538	13 Aug 1861	3363	Gazette	WO 13 Aug 1861
McDougall, SR	30667	3 May 1918	5354	7th Supp. to LG 30660 30 Apr 1918	WO 3 May 1918
MacDowell, TW	30122	8 Jun 1917	5702	2nd Supp. to LG 30120 8 Jun 1917	WO 8 Jun 1917
McFadzean, WF	29740	9 Sep 1916	8871	Supp. to LG 29739 8 Sep 1916	WO 9 Sep 1916
McGaw, S	24082	31 Mar 1874	1921	Gazette	WO 28 Mar 1874
McGee, L	30400	26 Nov 1917	12328	4th Supp. to LG 30396 23 Nov 1917	WO 26 Nov 1917
McGovern, J	22278	21 Jun 1859	2420	Gazette	WO 18 Jun 1859
McGregor, DS	31067	14 Dec 1918	14774	2nd Supp. to LG 31065 13 Dec 1918	WO 14 Dec 1918
MacGregor, J	31108	6 Jan 1919	305/6	4th Supp. to LG 31104 3 Jan 1919	WO 6 Jan 1919

	London Gazette	Date	Page	Supplement (if any)	Release Date
McGregor, R	21971	24 Feb 1857	662	Supp. to LG 21970 24 Feb 1857	WO 24 Feb 1857
McGuffie, L	31067	14 Dec 1918	14777	2nd Supp. to LG 31065 13 Dec 1918	WO 14 Dec 1918
McGuire, J	22212	24 Dec 1858	5519	Gazette	WO 24 Dec 1858
McHale, P	22396	19 Jun 1860	2316	Gazette	WO 19 Jun 1860
McInnes, H	22212	24 Dec 1858	5516	Gazette	WO 24 Dec 1858
McIntosh, GI	30272	6 Sep 1917	9260/1	5tł Supp. to LG 30267 4 Sep 1917	WO 6 Sep 1917
MacIntyre, D	23902	27 Sep 1872	4489	Gazette	WO 27 Sep 1872
MacIntyre, DL	30975	26 Oct 1918	12669	2nd Supp. to LG 30973 25 Oct 1918	WO 26 Oct 1918
McIver, H	31012	15 Nov 1918	13473	7th Supp. to LG 31005 12 Nov 1918	WO 15 Nov 1918
Mackay, D	22212	24 Dec 1858	5515	Gazette	WO 24 Dec 1858
McFay, JJ	49134	11 Oct 1982	12831/2	Supp. to LG 49133 8 Oct 1982	MOD (Army) 11 Oct 1982
Mackay, JF (Gaz. as Mackay, F)	27219	10 Aug 1900	4944	Gazette	WO 10 Aug 1900
McKean, GB	30770	28 Jun 1918	7618	6th Supp. to LG 30764 25 Jun 1918	WO 28 Jun 1918
McKechnie, J	21971	24 Feb 1857	657	Supp. to LG 21970 24 Feb 1857	WO 24 Feb 1857
McKenna, E (MacKenna)	22809	19 Jan 1864	261	Gazette	WO 16 Jan 1864
McKenzie, AE	30807	23 Jul 1918	8586	4th Supp. to LG 30803 19 Jul 1918	Adm. 23 Jul 1918
McKenzie, H McD	30523	13 Feb 1918	2003/4	Supp. to LG 30522 12 Feb 1918	WO 13 Feb 1918
Mackenzie, James	29074	18 Feb 1915	1700	4th Supp. to LG 29070 16 Feb 1915	WO 18 Feb 1915
Mackenzie, John	27266	15 Jan 1901	307	Gazette	WO 15 Jan 1901
Mackey, JB	37340	8 Nov 1945	5431	Supp. to LG 37339 6 Nov 1945	WO 8 Nov 1945
Mackintosh, D	30122	8 Jun 1917	5703	2nd Supp. to LG 30120 8 Jun 1917	WO 8 Jun 1917
Maclean, HLS	26908	9 Nov 1897	6143	Gazette ('Had he survived')	WO 9 Nov 1897
Maclean, HLS	27986	15 Jan 1907	325	Gazette	WO 15 Jan 1907

	London Gazette	Date	Page	Supplement (if any)	Release Date
McLeod, AA	30663	1 May 1918	5287/8	3rd Supp. to LG 30660 30 Apr 1918	Air Min. 1 May 1918
McManus, P	22154	18 Jun 1858	2958	Gazette	WO 18 Jun 1858
McMaster, VM	22154	18 Jun 1858	2957	Gazette	WO 18 Jun 1858
McNair, EA	29527	30 Mar 1916	3409	4th Supp. to LG 29523 28 Mar 1916	WO 30 Mar 1916
McNally, W	31067	14 Dec 1918	14776	2nd Supp. to LG 31065 13 Dec 1918	WO 14 Dec 1918
McNamara, FH	30122	8 Jun 1917	5703	2nd Supp. to LG 30120 8 Jun 1917	WO 8 Jun 1917
McNamara, J	31012	15 Nov 1918	13473	7th Supp. to LG 31005 12 Nov 1918	WO 15 Nov 1918
McNeill, JC	22885	16 Aug 1864	4027	Gazette	WO 16 Aug 1864
McNess, F	29802	26 Oct 1916	10395	4th Supp. to LG 29798 24 Oct 1916	WO 26 Oct 1916
Macpherson, HT	22154	18 Jun 1858	2957	Gazette	WO 18 Jun 1858
McPherson, S	22248	12 Apr 1859	1483	Gazette	WO 12 Apr 1859
McPhie, J	31155	31 Jan 1919	1504/5	8th Supp. to LG 31147 28 Jan 1919	WO 31 Jan 1919
McQuirt, B	22324	11 Nov 1859	4032	Gazette	WO 11 Nov 1859
McReady-Diarmid, AMC	30578	15 Mar 1918	3305	7th Supp. to LG 30571 12 Mar 1918	WO 15 Mar 1918
McReady-Drew, AMC	See McReady-Diarmid, AMC				
Mactier, R	31067	14 Dec 1918	14778/9	2nd Supp. to LG 31065 13 Dec 1918	WO 14 Dec 1918
McWheeney, W (McWhiney)	21971	24 Feb 1857	660	Supp. to LG 21970 24 Feb 1857	WO 24 Feb 1857
Madden, A	21971	24 Feb 1857	659	Supp. to LG 21970 24 Feb 1857	WO 24 Feb 1857
Magennis, JJ	37346	13 Nov 1945	5529/30	3rd Supp. to LG 37343 9 Nov 1945	Adm. 13 Nov 1945
Magner, M	23405	28 Jul 1868	4187	Gazette	WO 28 Jul 1868
Mahoney, P	22154	18 Jun 1858	2957	Gazette	WO 18 Jun 1858
Mahony, JK	36605	13 Jul 1944	3274	Supp. to LG 36604 11 Jun 1944	D of Nat Def. 13 Jul 1944
Maillard, WJ	27029	2 Dec 1898	7816	Gazette	WO 2 Dec 1898

	London Gazette	Date	Page	Supplement (if any)	Release Date
Malcolm, HG	35992	27 Apr 1943	1905	2nd Supp. to LG 35990 23 Apr 1943	Air Min. 27 Apr 1943
Malcolmson, JG	22409	3 Aug 1860	2860	Gazette	WO 3 Aug 1860
Maling, GA	29371	18 Nov 1915	11448	3rd Supp. to LG 29368 16 Nov 1915	WO 18 Nov 1915
Malleson, WStA	29264	16 Aug 1915	8132	2nd Supp. to LG 29262 13 Aug 1915	Adm. 16 Aug 1915
Malone, J	22043	25 Sep 1857	3194	Gazette	WO 25 Sep 1857
Mangles, RL	22283	8 Jul 1859	2629	Gazette	WO 6 Jul 1859
Manley, WGN	22986	23 Sep 1864	4552	Gazette	WO 22 Sep 1864
Manners-Smith, J	See Smith, John Manners				
Mannock, E	31463	18 Jul 1919	9136	Gazette	Air Min. 18 Jul 1919
Mansel-Jones, C	27214	27 Jul 1900	4653	Gazette	WO 27 Jul 1900
Manser, LT	35755	23 Oct 1942	4593	3rd Supp. to LG 35752 20 Oct 1942	Air Min. 23 Oct 1942
Mantle, JF	34938	3 Sep 1940	5385	Supp. to LG 34937 3 Sep 1940	Adm. 3 Sep 1940
Mariner, W	29202	23 Jun 1915	6116	Supp. to LG 29201 22 Jun 1915	WO 23 Jun 1915
Marling, PS	25356	21 May 1884	2278	Supp. to LG 25355 20 May 1884	WO 21 May 1884
Marshall, JN	31178	13 Feb 1919	2249/50	4th Supp. to LG 31174 11 Feb 1919	WO 13 Feb 1919
Marshall, WT	25356	21 May 1884	2278	Supp. to LG 25355 20 May 1884	WO 21 May 1884
Martin, CG	29135	19 Apr 1915	3815	2nd Supp. to LG 29133 16 Apr 1915	WO 19 Apr 1915
Martineau, HR	27208	6 Jul 1900	4197	Gazette	WO 6 Jul 1900
Martin-Leake, A	27433	13 May 1902	3176	Gazette	WO 13 May 1902
Martin-Leake, A, VC	29074	18 Feb 1915	1700	4th Supp. to LG 29070 16 Feb 1915	WO 18 Feb 1915
Masters, RG	30675	8 May 1918	5556	2nd Supp. to LG 30673 7 May 1918	WO 8 May 1918
Masterson, JEI	27320	4 Jun 1901	3769	Gazette	WO 4 Jun 1901
Maude, FC	22154	18 Jun 1858	2957	Gazette	WO 18 Jun 1858

	London Gazette	Date	Page	Supplement (if any)	Release Date
Maude, FF	21971	24 Feb 1857	658	Supp. to LG 29170 24 Feb 1857	WO 24 Feb 1857
Maufe, THB	30215	2 Aug 1917	7906	4th Supp. to LG 30211 31 Jul 1917	WO 2 Aug 1917
Maxwell, FA	27292	8 Mar 1901	1649	Gazette	WO 8 Mar 1901
Maxwell, J	31108	6 Jan 1919	307	4th Supp. to LG 31104 3 Jan 1919	WO 6 Jan 1919
May, H	29135	19 Apr 1915	3815	2nd Supp. to LG 29133 16 Apr 1915	WO 19 Apr 1915
Maygar, LC	27405	11 Feb 1902	843	Gazette	WO 11 Feb 1902
Mayo, A	22601	25 Feb 1862	958	Gazette	WO 25 Feb 1862
Mayson, TF	30284	14 Sep 1917	9533	2nd Supp. to LG 30282 14 Sep 1917	WO 14 Sep 1917
Meekosha, S	29447	22 Jan 1916	946	2nd Supp. to LG 29445 21 Jan 1916	WO 22 Jan 1916
Meikle, J	30903	16 Sep 1918	11075	5th Supp. to LG 30898 13 Sep 1918	WO 16 Sep 1918
Meiklejohn, MFM	27212	20 Jul 1900	4509	Gazette	WO 20 Jul 1900
Mellish, EN	29555	20 Apr 1916	4119	3rd Supp. to LG 29552 18 Apr 1916	WO 20 Apr 1916
Melliss, CJ	27266	15 Jan 1901	307	Gazette	WO 15 Jan 1901
Melvill, T	24717	2 May 1879	3178	Supp. to LG 24716 2 May 1879	WO 2 May 1879
Melvill, T	27986	15 Jan 1907	325	Gazette	WO 15 Jan 1907
Melvin, C	30400	26 Nov 1917	12330/1	4th Supp. to LG 30396 23 Nov 1917	WO 26 Nov 1917
Merrifield, W	31108	6 Jan 1919	308	4th Supp. to LG 31104 3 Jan 1919	WO 6 Jan 1919
Merritt, CCI	35729	2 Oct 1942	4323/4	Supp. to LG 35728 2 Oct 1942	D of Nat Def. 2 Oct 1942
Metcalf, WH	31012	15 Nov 1918	13473	7th Supp. to LG 31005 12 Nov 1918	WO 15 Nov 1918
Meynell, G	34235	24 Dec 1935	8291	Gazette	WO 24 Dec 1935
Middleton, RH	35864	15 Jan 1943	329/30	3rd Supp. to LG 35861 12 Jan 1943	Air Min. 15 Jan 1943
Miers, ACC	35622	7 Jul 1942	2983	4th Supp. to LG 35618 3 Jul 1942	Wh. 7 Jul 1942
Milbanke, JP	27208	6 Jul 1900	4196	Gazette	WO 6 Jul 1900

	London Gazette	Date	Page	Supplement (if any)	Release Date
Miles, FG	31108	6 Jan 1919	308	4th Supp. to LG 31104 3 Jan 1919	WO 6 Jan 1919
Millar, D (Miller)	22278	21 Jun 1859	2420	Gazette	WO 18 Jun 1859
Miller, F	22260	6 May 1859	1867	Gazette	WO 6 May 1859
Miller, J	29740	9 Sep 1916	8871	Supp. to LG 29739 8 Sep 1916	WO 9 Sep 1916
Miller, JW	22601	25 Feb 1862	957	Gazette	WO 25 Feb 1862
Mills, W	30523	13 Feb 1918	2005	Supp. to LG 30522 12 Feb 1918	WO 13 Feb 1918
Milne, WJ	30122	8 Jun 1917	5705	2nd Supp. to LG 30120 8 Jun 1917	WO 8 Jun 1917
Miner, HGB	30975	26 Oct 1918	12670	2nd Supp. to LG 30973 25 Oct 1918	WO 26 Oct 1918
Mir Dast	29210	29 Jun 1915	6269	Gazette	WO 29 Jun 1915
Mitchell, CN	3: 155	31 Jan 1919	1503/4	8th Supp. to LG 31147 28 Jan 1919	WO 31 Jan 1919
Mitchell, GA	36646	10 Aug 1944	3695/6	Supp. to LG 36645 8 Aug 1944	WO 10 Aug 1944
Mitchell, S	22879	26 Jul 1864	3711	Gazette	WO 23 Jul 1864
Moffat, MJ	3:082	26 Dec 1918	15119	Supp. to LG 31081 24 Dec 1918	WO 26 Dec 1918
Molyneux, J	30400	26 Nov 1917	12328	4th Supp. to LG 30396 23 Nov 1917	WO 26 Nov 1917
Monaghan, T	22680	11 Nov 1862	5346	Gazette	WO 11 Nov 1862
Monger, G	22248	12 Apr 1859	1482	Gazette	WO 12 Apr 1859
Moon, RV	30130	14 Jun 1917	5865	4th Supp. to LG 30126 12 Jun 1917	WO 14 Jun 1917
Moor, GRD	29240	24 Jul 1915	7279	Supp. to LG 29239 23 Jul 1915	WO 24 Jul 1915
Moore, AT	22409	3 Aug 1860	2860	Gazette	WO 3 Aug 1860
Moore, HG	24738	27 Jun 1879	4143	Gazette	WO 27 Jun 1879
Moore, MSS	33372	8 Nov 1917	11568	3rd Supp. to LG 30369 6 Nov 1917	WO 8 Nov 1917
Moorhouse, WB Rhodes-	See Rhodes-Moorhouse, WB				
Morley, S	22411	7 Aug 1860	2934	Gazette	WO 7 Aug 1860

	London Gazette	Date	Page	Supplement (if any)	Release Date
Morrell, T	See Young, T				
Morrow, R	29170	22 May 1915	4990	Supp. to LG 29169 21 May 1915	WO 22 May 1915
Mott, EJ	29978	10 Mar 1917	2451	2nd Supp. to LG 29976 9 Mar 1917	WO 10 Mar 1917
Mottershead, T	29937	12 Feb 1917	1445	2nd Supp. to LG 29935 9 Feb 1917	WO 12 Feb 1917
Mouat, J	22149	4 Jun 1858	2756	Gazette	WO 2 Jun 1858
Mountain, A	30733	7 Jun 1918	6776	6th Supp. to LG 30727 4 Jun 1918	WO 7 Jun 1918
Moyney, J	30338	17 Oct 1917	10678	2nd Supp. to LG 30336 16 Oct 1917	WO 17 Oct 1917
Moynihan, A	21971	24 Feb 1857	658	Supp. to LG 21970 24 Feb 1857	WO 24 Feb 1857
Mugford, HS	30400	26 Nov 1917	12329	4th Supp. to LG 30396 23 Nov 1917	WO 26 Nov 1917
Muir, K	39115	5 Jan 1951	133/4	3rd Supp. to LG 39112 2 Jan 1951	WO 5 Jan 1951
Mullane, P	24973	17 May 1881	2553	Gazette	WO 16 May 1881
Mullin, GH	30471	11 Jan 1918	723	6th Supp. to LG 30465 8 Jan 1918	WO 11 Jan 1918
Mullins, CH	27283	12 Feb 1901	1059	Gazette	WO 12 Feb 1901
Munro, J	22445	9 Nov 1860	4126	Gazette	WO 8 Nov 1860
Murphy, M	22268	27 May 1859	2106	Gazette	WO 27 May 1859
Murphy, T	23333	17 Dec 1867	6878	Gazette	WO 17 Dec 1867
Murray, HW	29978	10 Mar 1917	2451	2nd Supp. to LG 29976 9 Mar 1917	WO 10 Mar 1917
Murray, James	25084	14 Mar 1882	1130	Gazette	WO 13 Mar 1882
Murray, John	22908	4 Nov 1864	5187	Gazette	WO 4 Nov 1864
Myles, EK	29765	26 Sep 1916	9418	Supp. to LG 29764 26 Sep 1916	WO 26 Sep 1916
Mylott, P	22212	24 Dec 1858	5513	Gazette	WO 24 Dec 1858
Mynarski, AC	37754	11 Oct 1946	5035	2nd Supp. to LG 37752 8 Oct 1946	Air Min. 11 Oct 1946

	London Gazette	Date	Page	Supplement (if any)	Release Date
Namdeo Jadhao	37134	19 Jun 1945	3172	Supp. to LG 37133 15 Jun 1945	WO 19 Jun 1945
Nand Singh	36548	6 Jun 1944	2683	5th Supp. to LG 36543 2 Jun 1944	WO 6 Jun 1944
Napier, W	22212	24 Dec 1858	5517	Gazette	WO 24 Dec 1858
Nash, W	22212	24 Dec 1858	5515	Gazette	WO 24 Dec 1858
Nasmith, ME Dunbar-	See Dunbar-Nasmith, ME				
Neame, P	29074	18 Feb 1915	1700	4th Supp. to LG 29070 16 Feb 1915	WO 18 Feb 1915
Needham, S	30982	30 Oct 1918	12803	2nd Supp. to LG 30980 29 Oct 1918	WO 30 Oct 1918
Neely, T	31067	14 Dec 1918	14777	2nd Supp. to LG 31065 13 Dec 1918	WO 14 Dec 1918
Nelson, D	28276	16 Nov 1914	9374	3rd Supp. to LG 28973 13 Nov 1914	WO 16 Nov 1914
Nesbitt, RC	26350	7 May 1897	2535	Gazette	WO 7 May 1897
Netrabahadur Thapa	36742	12 Oct 1944	4673/4	Supp. to LG 36741 10 Oct 1944	WO 12 Oct 1944
Nettleton, JD	35539	28 Apr 1942	1851	3rd Supp. to LG 35536 24 Apr 1942	Air Min. 28 Apr 1942
Newell, R	22212	24 Dec 1858	5512	Gazette	WO 24 Dec 1858
Newland, JE	30122	8 Jun 1917	5702	2nd Supp. to LG 30120 8 Jun 1917	WO 8 Jun 1917
Newman, AC	37134	19 Jun 1945	3171	Supp. to LG 37133 15 Jun 1945	WO 19 Jun 1945
Newton, WE	36215	19 Oct 1943	4617	3rd Supp. to LG 36212 15 Oct 1943	Air Min. 19 Oct 1943
Ngarimu, MN-a-K	36040	4 Jun 1943	2559	Supp. to LG 36039 1 Jun 1943	WO 4 Jun 1943
Nicholas, HJ	30471	11 Jan 1918	724	6th Supp. to LG 30465 8 Jan 1918	WO 11 Jan 1918
Nicholls, H	34909	30 Jul 1940	4659/60	3rd Supp. to LG 34906 26 Jul 1940	WO 30 Jul 1940
Nickerson, WHS	27283	12 Feb 1901	1059	Gazette	WO 12 Feb 1901
Nicolson, EJB	34993	15 Nov 1940	6569	Gazette	Air Min. 15 Nov 1940
Noble, CR	29146	28 Apr 1915	4143	Supp. to LG 29145 27 Apr 1915	WO 28 Apr 1915
Norman, W	21971	24 Feb 1857	658	Supp. to LG 21970 24 Feb 1857	WO 24 Feb 1857

	London Gazette	Date	Page	Supplement (if any)	Release Date
Norton, GR	36764	26 Oct 1944	4899/900	Supp. to LG 36763 24 Oct 1944	WO 26 Oct 1944
Norwood, J	27212	20 Jul 1900	4509	Gazette	WO 20 Jul 1900
Nunney, CJP	31067	14 Dec 1918	14779/80	2nd Supp. to LG 31065 13 Dec 1918	WO 14 Dec 1918
Nurse, GE	27160	2 Feb 1900	689	Gazette	WO 2 Feb 1900
Ockendon, J	30372	8 Nov 1917	11569	3rd Supp. to LG 30369 6 Nov 1917	WO 8 Nov 1917
O'Connor, L	21971	24 Feb 1857	659	Supp. to LG 21970 24 Feb 1857	WO 24 Feb 1857
Odgers, W	22409	3 Aug 1860	2861	Gazette	WO 3 Aug 1860
O'Hea, T	23204	1 Jan 1867	22	Gazette	WO 1 Jan 1867
O'Kelly, CPJ	30471	11 Jan 1918	722	6th Supp. to LG 30465 8 Jan 1918	WO 11 Jan 1918
O'Leary, MJ	29074	18 Feb 1915	1700	4th Supp. to LG 29070 16 Feb 1915	WO 18 Feb 1915
Olpherts, W	22154	18 Jun 1858	2957	Gazette	WO 18 Jun 1858
O'Meara, M	29740	9 Sep 1916	8871	Supp. to LG 29739 8 Sep 1916	WO 9 Sep 1916
O'Neill, J (O'Niell)	31082	26 Dec 1918	15118	Supp. to LG 31081 24 Dec 1918	WO 26 Dec 1918
Onions, G	31067	14 Dec 1918	14778	2nd Supp. to LG 31065 13 Dec 1918	WO 14 Dec 1918
Ormsby, JW	30122	8 Jun 1917	5704	2nd Supp. to LG 30120 8 Jun 1917	WO 8 Jun 1917
O'Rourke, MJ	30372	8 Nov 1917	11569	3rd Supp. to LG 30369 6 Nov 1917	WO 8 Nov 1917
Osborn, JR	37517	2 Apr 1946	1617	Supp. to LG 37516 29 Mar 1946	Ottawa 2 Apr 1946
Osborne, J	25084	14 Mar 1882	1130	Gazette	WO 13 Mar 1882
O'Sullivan, GR	29281	1 Sep 1915	8699/700	Supp. to LG 29280 31 Aug 1915	WO 1 Sep 1915
O'Toole, E	24769	10 Oct 1879	5830	Gazette	WO 9 Oct 1879
Owens, J	21971	24 Feb 1857	660	Supp. to LG 21970 24 Feb 1857	WO 24 Feb 1857
Oxenham, W	22328	22 Nov 1859	4193	Gazette	WO 21 Nov 1859

	London Gazette	Date	Page	Supplement (if any)	Release Date
Palmer, A	21971	24 Feb 1857	656	Supp. to LG 21970 24 Feb 1857	WO 24 Feb 1857
Palmer, FW	30008	3 Apr 1917	3207	Gazette	WO 3 Apr 1917
Palmer, RAM	36997	23 Mar 1945	1593	4th Supp. to LG 36993 20 Mar 1945	Air Min. 23 Mar 1945
Park, James	22212	24 Dec 1858	5516	Gazette	WO 24 Dec 1858
Park, John	21971	24 Feb 1857	661	Supp to LG 21970 24 Feb 1857	WO 24 Feb 1857
Parkash Singh (Havildar)	36013	13 May 1943	2141/2	Supp. to LG 36012 11 May 1943	WO 13 May 1943
Parkash Singh (Jemadar)	See Prakash Singh				
Parker, CEH	27225	26 Jun 1900	3965	Gazette	WO 26 Jun 1900
Parker, WR	30147	22 Jun 1917	6253	2nd Supp. to LG 30145 22 Jun 1917	Adm. 22 Jun 1917
Parkes, S	21971	24 Feb 1857	655	Supp. to LG 21970 24 Feb 1857	WO 24 Feb 1857
Parslow, FD	31354	24 May 1919	6445/6	2nd Supp. to LG 31352 23 May 1919	Adm. 24 May 1919
Parsons, FN	27248	20 Nov 1900	7136	Gazette	WO 20 Nov 1900
Parsons, HF	30338	17 Oct 1917	10677	2nd Supp. to LG 30336 16 Oct 1917	WO 17 Oct 1917
Partridge, FJ	37439	22 Jan 1946	571	3rd Supp. to LG 37436 18 Jan 1946	Canberra 22 Jan 1946
Paton, GHT	30523	13 Feb 1918	2004	Supp. to LG 30522 13 Feb 1918	WO 13 Feb 1918
Paton, J	22212	24 Dec 1858	5514	Gazette	WO 24 Dec 1858
Pattison, JG	30215	2 Aug 1917	7907	4th Supp. to LG 30211 31 Jul 1917	WO 2 Aug 1917
Payne, K	44938	19 Sep 1969	9703	Supp. to LG 44937 19 Sep 1969	St James's Palace 19 Sep 1969
Peachment, GS	29371	18 Nov 1915	11450	3rd Supp. to LG 29368 16 Nov 1915	WO 18 Nov 1915
Pearkes, GR	30471	11 Jan 1918	722	6th Supp. to LG 30465 8 Jan 1918	WO 11 Jan 1918
Pearse, SG	31613	23 Oct 1919	12979	3rd Supp. to LG 31610 21 Oct 1919	WO 23 Oct 1919
Pearson, James	22381	1 May 1860	1642	Gazette	WO 28 Apr 1860
Pearson, John	22223	28 Jan 1859	294	Gazette	WO 26 Jan 1859

	London Gazette	Date	Page	Supplement (if any)	Release Date
Peck, CW	31012	15 Nov 1918	13471	7th Supp. to LG 31005 12 Nov 1918	WO 15 Nov 1918
Peel, W	21971	24 Feb 1857	651/2	Supp. to LG 21970 24 Feb 1857	WO 24 Feb 1857
Peeler, W	30400	26 Nov 1917	12329	4th Supp. to LG 30396 23 Nov 1917	WO 26 Nov 1917
Pennell, HS	26968	20 May 1898	3165	Gazette	WO 20 May 1898
Percy, HHM	21997	5 May 1857	1578	Gazette	WO 5 May 1857
Perie, J	21971	24 Feb 1857	656	Supp. to LG 29170 24 Feb 1857	WO 24 Feb 1857
Peters, FT	36019	18 May 1943	2215	3rd Supp. to LG 36016 14 May 1943	Wh. 18 May 1943
Phillipps, EA Lisle-	See Lisle-Phillipps, EA				
Phillips, RE	30122	8 Jun 1917	5703	2nd Supp. to LG 30120 8 Jun 1917	WO 8 Jun 1917
Phipps-Hornby, EJ	27205	26 Jun 1900	3964	Gazette	WO 26 Jun 1900
Pickard, AF	22986	23 Sep 1864	4552	Gazette	WO 22 Sep 1864
Pitcher, EH	30363	2 Nov 1917	11315	5th Supp. to LG 30358 30 Oct 1917	Adm. 2 Nov 1917
Pitcher, EH	31021	20 Nov 1918	13694/5	2nd Supp. to LG 31019 19 Nov 1918	Adm. 20 Nov 1918
Pitcher, HW	22876	19 Jul 1864	3618	Gazette	WO 16 Jul 1864
Pitts, J	27338	26 Jul 1901	4949	Gazette	WO 26 Jul 1901
Place, BCG	36390	22 Feb 1944	901/2	3rd Supp. to LG 36387 18 Feb 1944	Adm. 22 Feb 1944
Pollard, AO	30122	8 Jun 1917	5703/4	2nd Supp. to LG 30120 8 Jun 1917	WO 8 Jun 1917
Pollock, JD	29371	18 Nov 1915	11449	3rd Supp. to LG 29368 16 Nov 1915	WO 18 Nov 1915
Pooll, AHH Batten-	See Batten-Pooll, AHH				
Pope, C	30122	8 Jun 1917	5703	2nd Supp. to LG 30120 8 Jun 1917	WO 8 Jun 1917
Porteous, PA	35729	2 Oct 1942	4323	Supp. to LG 35728 2 Oct 1942	WO 2 Oct 1942
Potts, FWO	29312	1 Oct 1915	9641/2	Gazette	WO 1 Oct 1915
Poulter, A	30770	28 Jun 1918	7620	6th Supp. to LG 30764 25 Jun 1918	WO 28 Jun 1918

	London Gazette	Date	Page	Supplement (if any)	Release Date
Prakash Singh	37056	1 May 1945	2281/2	Supp. to LG 37055 27 Apr 1945	WO 1 May 1945
Premindra Singh Bhagat	35136	10 Jun 1941	3307	3rd Supp. to LG 35183 6 Jun 1941	WO 10 Jun 1941
Prendergast, HND	22318	21 Oct 1859	3793	Gazette	WO 21 Oct 1859
Prettyjohn, J	21971	24 Feb 1857	654	Supp. to LG 21970 24 Feb 1857	WO 24 Feb 1857
Price-Davies, LAE	27381	29 Nov 1901	8409	Gazette	WO 29 Nov 1901
Pride, T	22560	21 Apr 1865	2130	Gazette	WO 21 Apr 1865
Probyn, D MacN	22154	18 Jun 1858	2960	Gazette	WO 18 Jun 1858
Procter, AH	29695	5 Aug 1916	7744	Supp. to LG 29694 4 Aug 1916	WO 5 Aug 1916
Proctor, AFW Beauchamp-	See Beauchamp-Proctor, AFW				
Prosser, J	21971	24 Feb 1857	657	Supp. to LG 21970 24 Feb 1857	WO 24 Feb 1857
Prowse, G	30982	30 Oct 1918	12802	2nd Supp. to LG 30980 29 Oct 1918	WO 30 Oct 1918
Pryce, TT	30697	22 May 1918	6057/8	3rd Supp to LG 30694 21 May 1918	WO 22 May 1918
Purcell, J	22083	15 Jan 1858	178	Gazette	WO 15 Jan 1858
Pye, CC	22212	24 Dec 1858	5513	Gazette	WO 24 Dec 1858
Queripel, LE	36917	1 Feb 1945	669	Supp. to LG 36916 30 Jan 1945	WO 1 Feb 1945
Quigg, R	29740	9 Sep 1916	8871	Supp. to LG 29739 8 Sep 1916	WO 9 Sep 1916
Raby, HJ	21971	24 Feb 1857	553	Supp. to LG 21970 24 Feb 1857	WO 24 Feb 1857
Ram Sarup Singh	36928	8 Feb 1945	791/2	Supp. to LG 36927 6 Feb 1945	WO 8 Feb 1945
Ramage, H	22149	4 Jun 1858	2756	Gazette	WO 2 Jun 1858
Rambahadur Limbu	43959	22 Apr 1966	4947/8	2nd Supp. to LG 43957 21 Apr 1966	MOD (Army) 22 Apr 1966
Ramsden, HE	27208	6 Jul 1900	4197	Gazette	WO 6 Jul 1900

	London Gazette	Date	Page	Supplement (if any)	Release Date
Randle, JN	36833	12 Dec 1944	5673	Supp. to LG 36832 8 Dec 1944	WO 12 Dec 1944
Ranken, HS	28976	16 Nov 1914	9374	3rd Supp. to LG 28973 13 Nov 1914	WO 16 Nov 1914
Ratcliffe, W	30215	2 Aug 1917	7907	4th Supp. to LG 30211 31 Jul 1917	WO 2 Aug 1917
Rattey, RR	37194	26 Jul 1945	3857	Supp. to LG 37193 24 Jul 1945	WO 26 Jul 1945
Ravenhill, G	27320	4 Jun 1901	3769	Gazette	WO 4 Jun 1901
Rayfield, WL	31067	14 Dec 1918	14779	2nd Supp. to LG 31065 13 Dec 1918	WO 14 Dec 1918
Raymond, C	37151	28 Jun 1945	3365	Supp. to LG 37150 26 Jun 1945	WO 28 Jun 1945
Raynes, JC	29371	18 Nov 1915	11449	3rd Supp. to LG 29368 16 Nov 1915	WO 18 Nov 1915
Raynor, W	22154	18 Jun 1858	2959	Gazette	WO 18 Jun 1858
Read, AM	29371	18 Nov 1915	11447	3rd Supp. to LG 29368 16 Nov 1915	WO 18 Nov 1915
Reade, HT	22477	5 Feb 1861	449	Gazette	WO 5 Feb 1861
Readitt, J	30167	5 Jul 1917	6697/8	6th Supp. to LG 30161 3 Jul 1917	WO 5 Jul 1917
Reed, HL	27160	2 Feb 1900	689	Gazette	WO 2 Feb 1900
Rees, I	30284	14 Sep 1917	9532/3	2nd Supp. to LG 30282 14 Sep 1917	WO 14 Sep 1917
Rees, LWB	29695	5 Aug 1916	7744	Supp. to LG 29694 4 Aug 1916	WO 5 Aug 1916
Reeves, T	21971	24 Feb 1857	653	Supp. to LG 21970 24 Feb 1857	WO 24 Feb 1857
Reid, OA	30122	8 Jun 1917	5702	2nd Supp. to LG 30120 8 Jun 1917	WO 8 Jun 1917
Reid, W	36285	14 Dec 1943	5435	3rd Supp. to LG 36282 10 Dec 1943	Air Min. 14 Dec 1943
Rendle, TE	29037	11 Jan 1915	365	2nd Supp. to LG 29035 8 Jan 1915	WO 11 Jan 1915
Rennie, W	22212	24 Dec 1858	5518	Gazette	WO 24 Dec 1858
Renny, GA	22248	12 Apr 1859	1483	Gazette	WO 12 Apr 1859
Reynolds, D	28976	16 Nov 1914	9373	3rd Supp. to LG 28973 13 Nov 1914	WO 16 Nov 1914
Reynolds, H	30372	8 Nov 1917	11567/8	3rd Supp. to LG 30369 6 Nov 1917	WO 8 Nov 1917

	London Gazette	Date	Page	Supplement (if any)	Release Date
Reynolds, JH	24734	17 Jun 1879	3966	Gazette	WO 17 Jun 1879
Reynolds, W	21971	24 Feb 1857	657	Supp. to LG 21970 24 Feb 1857	WO 24 Feb 1857
Rhodes, JH	30430	26 Nov 1917	12328	4th Supp. to LG 30396 23 Nov 1917	WO 26 Nov 1917
Rhodes-Moorhouse, WB	29170	22 May 1915	4990	Supp. to LG 29169 21 May 1915	WO 22 May 1915
Richards, AJ	29273	24 Aug 1915	8395	Gazette	WO 24 Aug 1915
Richardson, AHL	27229	14 Sep 1900	5688	Gazette	WO 14 Sep 1900
Richardson, G	22324	11 Nov 1859	4042	Gazette	WO 11 Nov 1859
Richardson, JC	30967	22 Oct 1918	12488	9th Supp. to LG 30958 18 Oct 1918	WO 22 Oct 1918
Richhpal Ram	35207	4 Jul 1941	3807	Supp. to LG 35206 1 Jul 1941	WO 4 Jul 1941
Rickard, WT	21971	24 Feb 1857	651	Supp. to LG 21970 24 Feb 1857	WO 24 Feb 1857
Ricketts, T	31108	6 Jan 1919	309	4th Supp. to LG 31104 3 Jan 1919	WO 6 Jan 1919
Ridgeway, RK	24843	11 May 1880	2968	Gazette	WO 8 May 1880
Riggs, FC	31108	6 Jan 1919	307/8	4th Supp. to LG 31104 3 Jan 1919	WO 6 Jan 1919
Ripley, J	29210	29 Jun 1915	6270	Gazette	WO 29 Jun 1915
Ritchie, HP	29123	10 Apr 1915	3549	Supp. to LG 29122 9 Apr 1915	Adm. 10 Apr 1915
Ritchie, WP	29740	9 Sep 1916	8871	Supp. to LG 29739 8 Sep 1916	WO 9 Sep 1916
Rivers, J	25146	28 Apr 1915	4143	Supp. to LG 29145 27 Apr 1915	WO 28 Apr 1915
Roberts, J	21971	24 Feb 1857	650	Supp. to LG 21970 24 Feb 1857	WO 24 Feb1857
Roberts, FC	30675	8 May 1918	5555/6	2nd Supp. to LG 30673 7 May 1918	WO 8 May 1918
Roberts, FHS	27160	2 Feb 1900	689	Gazette	WO 2 Feb 1900
Roberts, FS	22212	24 Dec 1858	5516	Gazette	WO 24 Dec 1858
Roberts, JR	22212	24 Dec 1858	5517	Gazette	WO 24 Dec 1858
Roberts, PSW	35591	9 Jun 1942	2548	7th Supp. to LG 35584 5 Jun 1942	Wh. 9 Jun 1942

	London Gazette	Date	Page	Supplement (if any)	Release Date
Robertson, C	30433	18 Dec 1917	13222	5th Supp. to LG 30428 14 Dec 1917	WO 18 Dec 1917
Robertson, CG	30619	9 Apr 1918	4297	6th Supp. to LG 30613 5 Apr 1918	WO 9 Apr 1918
Robertson, J Forbes-	See Forbes-Robertson, J				
Robertson, JP	30471	11 Jan 1918	724/5	6th Supp. to LG 30465 8 Jan 1918	WO 11 Jan 1918
Robertson, W	27212	20 Jul 1900	4509	Gazette	WO 20 Jul 1900
Robinson, E	22212	24 Dec 1858	5512	Gazette	WO 24 Dec 1858
Robinson, EG	29264	16 Aug 1915	8132	2nd Supp. to LG 29262 13 Aug 1915	Adm. 16 Aug 1915
Robinson, WL	29735	5 Sep 1916	8704	Gazette	WO 5 Sep 1916
Robson, HH	29074	18 Feb 1915	1700	4th Supp. to LG 29070 16 Feb 1915	WO 18 Feb 1915
Rochfort, GA Boyd-	See Boyd-Rochfort, GA				
Roddy, P	22248	12 Apr 1859	1483	Gazette	WO 12 Apr 1859
Rodgers, G	22324	11 Nov 1859	4033	Gazette	WO 11 Nov 1859
Rogers, J	27426	18 Apr 1902	2600	Gazette	WO 18 Apr 1902
Rogers, MAW	36646	10 Aug 1944	3695	Supp. to LG 36645 8 Aug 1944	WO 10 Aug 1944
Rogers, RM	22538	13 Aug 1861	3363	Gazette	WO 13 Aug 1861
Rolland, GM	27584	7 Aug 1903	4981	Gazette	WO 7 Aug 1903
Room, FG	30338	17 Oct 1917	10678	2nd Supp. to LG 30336 16 Oct 1917	WO 17 Oct 1917
Roope, GB	37170	10 Jul 1945	3557	4th Supp. to LG 37166 6 Jul 1945	Adm. 10 Jul 1945
Rosamund, M	22176	24 Aug 1858	3903	Gazette	WO 23 Aug 1858
Ross, J	21971	24 Feb 1857	656	Supp. to LG 21970 24 Feb 1857	WO 24 Feb 1857
Roupell, GRP	29202	23 Jun 1915	6115	Supp. to LG 29201 22 Jun 1915	WO 23 Jun 1915
Rowlands, H	21971	24 Feb 1857	659	Supp. to LG 21970 24 Feb 1857	WO 24 Feb 1857
Rushe, D	22212	24 Dec 1858	5512	Gazette	WO 24 Dec 1858

	London Gazette	Date	Page	Supplement (if any)	Release Date
Russell, C	21971	24 Feb 1857	656	Supp. to LG 21970 24 Feb 1857	WO 24 Feb 1857
Russell, JF	30471	11 Jan 1918	722	6th Supp. to LG 30465 8 Jan 1918	WO 11 Jan 1918
Rutherford, CS	31012	15 Nov 1918	13472	7th Supp. to LG 31005 12 Nov 1918	WO 15 Nov 1918
Ruthven, AGA Hore-	See Hore-Ruthven, AGA				
Ruthven, W	30790	11 Jul 1918	8156	3rd Supp. to LG 30787 9 Jul 1918	WO 11 Jul 1918
Ryan, EJF	31082	26 Dec 1918	15119	Supp. to LG 31081 24 Dec 1918	WO 26 Dec 1918
Ryan, John (L/Cpl)	22809	19 Jan 1864	261	Gazette	WO 16 Jan 1864
Ryan, John (Pte)	22154	18 Jun 1858	2958	Gazette	WO 18 Jun 1858
Ryan, M	22212	24 Dec 1858	5519	Gazette	WO 24 Dec 1858
Ryder, RE	29836	25 Nov 1916	11526	Supp. to LG 29835 24 Nov 1916	WO 25 Nov 1916
Ryder, RED	35566	21 May 1942	2225	Supp. to LG 35565 19 May 1942	Adm. 21 May 1942
Sadlier, CWK	30790	11 Jul 1918	8156	3rd Supp. to LG 30787 9 Jul 1918	WO 11 Jul 1918
Sage, TH	30433	18 Dec 1917	13223	5th Supp. to LG 30428 14 Dec 1917	WO 18 Dec 19
Salkeld, P	22154	18 Jun 1858	2961	Gazette ('Had he survived')	
Salmon, N	22212	24 Dec 1858	5512	Gazette	WO 24 Dec 1858
Samson, G McK	29264	16 Aug 1915	8132	2nd Supp. to LG 29262 13 Aug 1915	Adm. 16 Aug 1915
Sanders, G	29740	9 Sep 1916	8870	Supp. to LG 29739 8 Sep 1916	WO 9 Sep 1916
Sanders, WE	30147	22 Jun 1917	6253	2nd Supp. to LG 30145 22 Jun 1917	Adm. 22 Jun 1917
Sanders, WE	31021	20 Nov 1918	13693/4	2nd Supp. to LG 31019 19 Nov 1918	Adm. 20 Nov 1918
Sandes, AJT Fleming-	See Fleming-Sandes, AJT				
Sandford, RD	30807	23 Jul 1918	8585/6	4th Supp. to LG 30803 19 Jul 1918	Adm. 23 Jul 1918
Sandys-Clarke, WA	35071	29 Jun 1943	2937	2nd Supp. to LG 36069 25 Jun 1943	WO 29 Jun 1943

	London Gazette	Date	Page	Supplement (if any)	Release Date
Sartorius, EH	24973	17 May 1881	2553	Gazette	WO 16 May 1881
Sartorius, RW	24145	27 Oct 1874	5113	Gazette	WO 26 Oct 1874
Saunders, AF	29527	30 Mar 1916	3409/10	4th Supp. to LG 29523 28 Mar 1916	WO 30 Mar 1916
Savage, DC	See Travis, RC				
Savage, WA	35566	21 May 1942	2225	Supp. to LG 35565 19 May 1942	Adm. 21 May 1942
Sayer, JW	31395	9 Jun 1919	7419/20	4th Supp. to LG 31391 6 Jun 1919	WO 9 Jun 1919
Scarf, ASK	37623	21 Jun 1946	3211	Supp. to LG 37622 21 Jun 1946	Air Min. 21 Jun 1946
Schiess, FC	24788	2 Dec 1879	7148	Gazette	WO 29 Nov 1879
Schofield, HN	27350	30 Aug 1901	5737	Gazette	WO 30 Aug 1901
Schofield, J	30770	28 Jun 1918	7618	6th Supp. to LG 30764 25 Jun 1918	WO 28 Jun 1918
Scholefield, M	21971	24 Feb 1857	653	Supp. to LG 21970 24 Feb 1857	WO 24 Feb 1857
Scott, A	24544	18 Jan 1878	272	Gazette	WO 16 Jan 1878
Scott, R	27338	26 Jul 1901	4949	Gazette	WO 26 Jul 1901
Scott, RG	24887	1 Oct 1880	5113	Gazette	WO 1 Oct 1880
Scrimger, FAC	29202	23 Jun 1915	6115	Supp. to LG 29201 22 Jun 1915	WO 23 Jun 1915
Seagrim, DA	36013	13 May 1943	2141	Supp. to LG 36012 11 May 1943	WO 13 May 1943
Seaman, E	31012	15 Nov 1918	13473	7th Supp. to LG 31005 12 Nov 1918	WO 15 Nov 1918
Seeley, WHH	22960	21 Apr 1865	2130	Gazette	WO 21 Apr 1865
Sellar, G	25027	18 Oct 1881	5140	Gazette	WO 15 Oct 1881
Sephton, AE	35365	2 Dec 1941	6889	4th Supp. to LG 35361 28 Nov 1941	Wh. 2 Dec 1941
Sewell, CH	30982	30 Oct 1918	12801/2	2nd Supp. to LG 30980 29 Oct 1918	WO 30 Oct 1918
Sexton, G	See Buckley, MV				
Shahamad Khan	29765	26 Sep 1916	9418/19	Supp. to LG 29764 26 Sep 1916	WO 26 Sep 1916

	London Gazette	Date	Page	Supplement (if any)	Release Date
Shand, SW Loudoun-	See Loudoun-Shand, SW				
Shankland, R	30433	18 Dec 1917	13222	5th Supp. to LG 30428 14 Dec 1917	WO 18 Dec 1917
Sharpe, CR	29210	29 Jun 1915	6270	Gazette	WO 29 Jun 1915
Shaul, JDF	27233	28 Sep 1900	5966	Gazette	WO 28 Sep 1900
Shaw, H	23044	28 Nov 1865	5005	Gazette	WO 28 Nov 1865
Shaw, S (J) J	22194	26 Oct 1858	4574/5	Gazette	WO 26 Oct 1858
Shebbeare, RH	22318	21 Oct 1859	3792	Gazette	WO 21 Oct 1859
Shepherd, AE	30523	13 Feb 1918	2005	Supp. to LG 30522 12 Feb 1918	WO 13 Feb 1918
Sheppard, J (Shepherd)	21971	24 Feb 1857	652/3	Supp. to LG 21970 24 Feb 1857	WO 24 Feb 1857
Sherbahadur Thapa	36860	28 Dec 1944	5933	Supp. to LG 36859 26 Dec 1944	WO 28 Dec 1944
Sherbrooke, RStV	35859	12 Jan 1943	283/4	3rd Supp. to LG 35856 8 Jan 1943	Adm. No date
Sher Shah	37066	8 May 1945	2393	Supp. to LG 37065 4 May 1945	WO 8 May 1945
Sherwood-Kelly, J	30471	11 Jan 1918	722	6th Supp. to LG 30465 8 Jan 1918	WO 11 Jan 1918
Shields, R	21971	24 Feb 1857	659	Supp. to LG 21970 24 Feb 1857	WO 24 Feb 1857
Short, WH	29740	9 Sep 1916	8871	Supp. to LG 29739 8 Sep 1916	WO 9 Sep 1916
Short, AJ	29328	15 Oct 1915	10153	Gazette	WO 15 Oct 1915
Sidney, WP	36445	30 Mar 1944	1477/8	Supp. to LG 36444 28 Mar 1944	WO 30 Mar 1944
Sifton, EW	30122	8 Jun 1917	5704	2nd Supp. to LG 30120 8 Jun 1917	WO 8 Jun 1917
Simpson, J	22268	27 May 1859	2106	Gazette	WO 27 May 1859
Simpson, RS	44925	29 Aug 1969	8873	Supp. to LG 44924 26 Aug 1969	St James's Palace 29 Aug 1969
Simpson, W	See Evans, A				
Sims, JJ	21971	24 Feb 1857	659	Supp. to LG 21970 24 Feb 1857	WO 24 Feb 1857
Sinnott, J	22212	24 Dec 1858	5514	Gazette	WO 24 Dec 1858

	London Gazette	Date	Page	Supplement (if any)	Release Date
Sinton, JA	29633	21 Jun 1916	6191	4th Supp. to LG 29629 20 Jun 1916	WO 21 Jun 1916
Skinner, JK	30284	14 Sep 1917	9533	2nd Supp. to LG 30282 14 Sep 1917	WO 14 Sep 1917
Sleavon, M	22324	11 Nov 1859	4032	Gazette	WO 11 Nov 1859
Smith, A	25469	12 May 1885	2156	Gazette	WO 12 May 1885
Smith, A Bissett-	See Bissett-Smith, A				
Smith, AV	29496	3 Mar 1916	2349	Gazette	WO 3 Mar 1916
Smith, CL	27683	7 Jun 1904	3636	Gazette	WO 7 Jun 1904
Smith, EA	36849	20 Dec 1944	5841	Supp. to LG 36848 19 Dec 1944	D of Nat Def. 19 Dec 1944
Smith, EB	30967	22 Oct 1918	12488	9th Supp. to LG 30958 18 Oct 1918	WO 22 Oct 1918
Smith, FA	22908	4 Nov 1864	5187	Gazette	WO 4 Nov 1864
Smith, FP	21971	24 Feb 1857	658	Supp. to LG 21970 24 Feb 1857	WO 24 Feb 1857
Smith, H	22131	27 Apr 1858	2051	Gazette	WO 24 Apr 1858
Smith, I	29272	23 Aug 1915	8374	3rd Supp. to LG 29269 20 Aug 1915	WO 23 Aug 1915
Smith, James	27073	21 Apr 1899	2545	Gazette	WO 21 Apr 1899
Smith, James Alexander Glenn	29074	18 Feb 1915	1700	4th Supp. to LG 29070 16 Feb 1915	WO 18 Feb 1915
Smith, John (*Pte*)	22212	24 Dec 1858	5515	Gazette	WO 24 Dec 1858
Smith, John (*Sgt*)	22131	27 Apr 1858	2051	Gazette	WO 24 Apr 1858
Smith, John Manners	26306	12 Jul 1892	4006	Gazette	WO 12 Jul 1892
Smyth, JG	29210	29 Jun 1915	6269	Gazette	WO 29 Jun 1915
Smyth, NM	27023	15 Nov 1898	6688	Gazette	WO 15 Nov 1898
Smythe, QGM	35698	11 Sep 1942	3954	2nd Supp. to LG 35696 8 Sep 1942	WO 11 Sep 1942
Somers, J	29281	1 Sep 1915	8700	Supp. to LG 29280 31 Aug 1915	WO 1 Sep 1915
Spackman, CE	30471	11 Jan 1918	723	6th Supp. to LG 30465 8 Jan 1918	WO 11 Jan 1918

	London Gazette	Date	Page	Supplement (if any)	Release Date
Spall, R	30975	26 Oct 1918	12670	2nd Supp. to LG 30973 25 Oct 1918	WO 26 Oct 1918
Speakman, W	39418	28 Dec 1951	6731	Supp. to LG 39417 25 Dec 1951	WO 28 Dec 1951
Spence, D	22212	24 Dec 1858	5512	Gazette	WO 24 Dec 1858
Spence, E	27986	15 Jan 1907	325	Gazette	WO 15 Jan 1907
Spence, E	22268	27 May 1859	2106	Gazette (Had he survived?)	WO 27 May 1859
Stagpoole, D	22986	23 Sep 1864	4552	Gazette	WO 22 Sep 1864
Stanlake, W (Stanlock)	21971	24 Feb 1857	657	Supp. to LG 21970 24 Feb 1857	WO 24 Feb 1857
Stannard, RB	34924	16 Aug 1940	5059/60	Supp. to LG 34923 16 Aug 1940	Adm. 16 Aug 1940
Starcevich, LT	37340	8 Nov 1945	5431/2	Supp. to LG 37339 6 Nov 1945	WO 8 Nov 1945
Statton, PC	30922	27 Sep 1918	11430/1	4th Supp. to LG 30918 24 Sep 1918	WO 27 Sep 1918
Steele, GC	31638	11 Nov 1919	13743	Supp. to LG 31637 11 Nov 1919	Adm. 11 Nov 1919
Steele, T	30122	8 Jun 1917	5704	2nd Supp. to LG 30120 8 Jun 1917	WO 8 Jun 1917
Stewart, WGD (Steuart)	22212	24 Dec 1858	5514	Gazette	WO 24 Dec 1858
Stokes, J	37033	17 Apr 1945	2011	Supp. to LG 37032 13 Apr 1945	WO 17 Apr 1945
Stone, CE	30697	22 May 1918	6058/9	3rd Supp. to LG 30694 21 May 1918	WO 22 May 1918
Stone, WN	30523	13 Feb 1918	2004	Supp. to LG 30522 12 Feb 1918	WO 13 Feb 1918
Storkey, PV	30733	7 Jun 1918	6775	6th Supp. to LG 30727 4 Jun 1918	WO 7 Jun 1918
Strachan, H	30433	18 Dec 1917	13222	5th Supp. to LG 30428 14 Dec 1917	WO 18 Dec 1917
Stringer, G	29695	5 Aug 1916	7744	Supp. to LG 29694 4 Aug 1916	WO 5 Aug 1916
Strong, G	21971	24 Feb 1857	657	Supp. to LG 21970 24 Feb 1857	WO 24 Feb 1857
Stuart, RN	30194	20 Jul 1917	7424	2nd Supp. to LG 30192 20 Jul 1917	Adm. 20 Jul 1917
Stuart, RN	31021	20 Nov 1918	13694	2nd Supp. to LG 31019 19 Nov 1918	Adm. 20 Nov 1918
Stubbs, FE	29985	15 Mar 1917	2619	3rd Supp. to LG 29982 13 Mar 1917	WO 15 Mar 1917

	London Gazette	Date	Page	Supplement (if any)	Release Date
Sukanaivalu, S	36774	2 Nov 1944	5016/17	Supp. to LG 36773 31 Oct 1944	WO 2 Nov 1944
Sullivan, AP	31572	29 Sep 1919	11997	3rd Supp. to LG 31569 26 Sep 1919	WO 29 Sep 1919
Sullivan, J	21971	24 Feb 1857	652	Supp. to LG 21970 24 Feb 1857	WO 24 Feb 1857
Sutton, W	22347	20 Jan 1860	178	Gazette	WO 20 Jan 1860
Swales, E	37049	24 Apr 1945	2173	5th Supp. to LG 37044 20 Apr 1945	Air Min. 24 Apr 1945
Sykes, E	30122	8 Jun 1917	5705/6	2nd Supp. to LG 30120 8 Jun 1917	WO 8 Jun 1917
Sylvester, WHT	22065	20 Nov 1857	3920	Gazette	WO 18 Nov 1857
Symons, G	22065	20 Nov 1857	3920	Gazette	WO 18 Nov 1857
Symons, WJ	29328	15 Oct 1915	10153/4	Gazette	WO 15 Oct 1915
Tait, JE	30922	27 Sep 1918	11429	4th Supp. to LG 30918 24 Sep 1918	WO 27 Sep 1918
Tandey, H	31067	14 Dec 1918	14778	2nd Supp. to LG 31065 13 Dec 1918	WO 14 Dec 1918
Taylor, J	21971	24 Feb 1857	653	Supp. to LG 21970 24 Feb 1857	WO 24 Feb 1857
Teesdale, CC	22043	25 Sep 1857	3194	Gazette	WO 25 Sep 1857
Temple, W	22986	23 Sep 1864	4552	Gazette	WO 22 Sep 1864
Thackeray, ET	22621	29 Apr 1862	2229	Gazette	WO 29 Apr 1862
Thaman Gurung	36950	22 Feb 1945	1039	Supp. to LG 36949 20 Feb 1945	WO 22 Feb 1945
Thomas, Jacob	22212	24 Dec 1858	5519	Gazette	WO 24 Dec 1858
Thomas, John	30523	13 Feb 1918	2005	Supp. to LG 30522 12 Feb 1918	WO 13 Feb 1918
Thompson, A	22268	27 May 1859	2106	Gazette	WO 27 May 1859
Thompson, G	36948	20 Feb 1945	999	5th Supp. to LG 36943 16 Feb 1945	Air Min. 20 Feb 1945
Thompson, J	22347	20 Jan 1860	179	Gazette	WO 20 Jan 1860
Throssell, HVH	29328	15 Oct 1915	10154	Gazette	WO 15 Oct 1915

	London Gazette	Date	Page	Supplement (if any)	Release Date
Tilston, FA	37086	22 May 1945	2608	Supp. to LG 37085 18 May 1945	DoND Ottawa 22 May 1945
Tisdall, AWStC	29530	31 Mar 1916	3515/6	Supp. to LG 29529 31 Mar 1916	Adm. SW 31 Mar 1916
Tollerton, R	29135	19 Apr 1915	3816	2nd Supp. to LG 29133 16 Apr 1915	WO 19 Apr 1915
Tombs, H	22131	27 Apr 1858	2050	Gazette	WO 24 Apr 1858
Tombs, JH	29240	24 Jul 1915	7280	Supp. to LG 29239 23 Jul 1915	WO 24 Jul 1915
Topham, FG	37205	3 Aug 1945	3965	2nd Supp. to LG 37203 31 Jul 1945	DoND Ottawa 3 Aug 1945
Towers, J	31108	6 Jan 1919	308/9	4th Supp. to LG 31104 3 Jan 1919	WO 6 Jan 1919
Towner, ET	31067	14 Dec 1918	14775	2nd Supp. to LG 31065 13 Dec 1918	WO 14 Dec 1918
Towse, EBB	27208	6 Jul 1900	4196	Gazette	WO 6 Jul 1900
Toye, AM	30675	8 May 1918	5556	2nd Supp. to LG 30673 7 May 1918	WO 8 May 1918
Train, CW	30548	27 Feb 1918	2589	4th Supp. to LG 30544 26 Feb 1918	WO 27 Feb 1918
Travers, J	22485	1 Mar 1861	1007	Gazette	WO 1 Mar 1861
Travis, RC (Savage, DC)	30922	27 Sep 1918	11431	4th Supp. to LG 30918 24 Sep 1918	WO 27 Sep 1918
Traynor, WB	27356	17 Sep 1901	6101	Gazette	WO 17 Sep 1901
Trent, LH	37486	1 Mar 1946	1179	3rd Supp. to LG 37483 26 Feb 1946	Air Min. 1 Mar 1946
Trevor, WS	23338	31 Dec 1867	7107	Gazette	WO 31 Dec 1867
Trewavas, J	21971	24 Feb 1857	650	Supp. to LG 21970 24 Feb 1857	WO 24 Feb 1857
Trigg, LA	35230	2 Nov 1943	4813	3rd Supp. to LG 36227 29 Oct 1943	Air Min. 2 Nov 1943
Tricuet, P	35408	6 Mar 1944	1097	Supp. to LG 36407 3 Mar 1944	DoND Ottawa 6 Mar 1944
Tubb, FH	29328	15 Oct 1915	10154	Gazette	WO 15 Oct 1915
Tulbahadur Pun	36785	9 Nov 1944	5129	Supp. to LG 36784 7 Nov 1944	WO 9 Nov 1944
Turnbull, JY	29836	25 Nov 1916	11526	Supp. to LG 29835 24 Nov 1916	WO 25 Nov 1916
Turner, AB	29371	18 Nov 1915	11448	3rd Supp. to LG 29368 16 Nov 1915	WO 18 Nov 1915

	London Gazette	Date	Page	Supplement (if any)	Release Date
Turner, HV	36658	17 Aug 1944	3807	Supp. to LG 36657 15 Aug 1944	WO 17 Aug 1944
Turner, REW	27307	23 Apr 1901	2775	Gazette	WO 23 Apr 1901
Turner, S	22347	20 Jan 1860	179	Gazette	WO 20 Jan 1860
Turner, VB	35790	20 Nov 1942	5023	Supp. to LG 35789 17 Nov 1942	WO 20 Nov 1942
Turrall, TG	29740	9 Sep 1916	8871	Supp. to LG 29739 8 Sep 1916	WO 9 Sep 1916
Tytler, JA	22176	24 Aug 1858	3903	Gazette	WO 23 Aug 1858
Umrao Singh	37101	31 May 1945	2741	Supp. to LG 37100 29 May 1945	WO 31 May 1945
Unwin, E	29264	16 Aug 1915	8132	2nd Supp. to LG 29262 13 Aug 1915	Adm. 16 Aug 1915
Upham, CH	35306	14 Oct 1941	5935/6	2nd Supp. to LG 35304 10 Oct 1941	WO 14 Oct 1941
Upham, CH, VC	37283	26 Sep 1945	4779	Supp. to LG 37282 25 Sep 1945	WO 26 Sep 1945
Upton, J	29210	29 Jun 1915	6270	Gazette	WO 29 Jun 1915
Vallentin, JF	29074	18 Feb 1915	1700	4th Supp. to LG 29070 16 Feb 1915	WO 18 Feb 1915
Vann, BW	31067	14 Dec 1918	14774	2nd Supp. to LG 31065 13 Dec 1918	WO 14 Dec 1918
Veale, TWH	29740	9 Sep 1916	8871/2	Supp. to LG 29739 8 Sep 1916	WO 9 Sep 1916
Vickers, A	29371	18 Nov 1915	11450	3rd Supp. to LG 29368 16 Nov 1915	WO 18 Nov 1915
Vickers, CG	29371	18 Nov 1915	11448	3rd Supp. to LG 29368 16 Nov 1915	WO 18 Nov 1915
Vickery, S	26968	20 May 1898	3165	Gazette	WO 20 May 1898
Vousden, WJ	25027	18 Oct 1881	5140	Gazette	WO 15 Oct 1881
Wadeson, R	22212	24 Dec 1858	5518	Gazette	WO 24 Dec 1858
Wain, RWL	30523	13 Feb 1918	2004	Supp. to LG 30522 12 Feb 1918	WO 13 Feb 1918

	London Gazette	Date	Page	Supplement (if any)	Release Date
Wakeford, R	36605	13 Jul 1944	3273/4	Supp. to LG 36604 11 Jul 1944	WO 13 Jul 1944
Wakenshaw, AH	35698	11 Sep 1942	3953	2nd Supp. to LG 35696 8 Sep 1942	WO 11 Sep 1942
Walford, GN	29202	23 Jun 1915	6115	Supp. to LG 29201 22 Jun 1915	WO 23 Jun 1915
Walker, M	22149	4 Jun 1858	2756	Gazette	WO 2 Jun 1858
Walker, WG	27584	7 Aug 1903	4981	Gazette	WO 7 Aug 1903
Walker-Heneage, C	See Heneage-Walker, C				
Wallace, STD	30523	13 Feb 1918	2004	Supp. to LG 30522 12 Feb 1918	WO 13 Feb 1918
Waller, G	22347	20 Jan 1860	178	Gazette	WO 20 Jan 1860
Waller, H	30122	8 Jun 1917	5706	2nd Supp. to LG 30120 8 Jun 1917	WO 8 Jun 1917
Waller, WFF	22601	25 Feb 1862	957	Gazette	WO 25 Feb 1862
Walters, G	21971	24 Feb 1857	660	Supp. to LG 21970 24 Feb 1857	WO 24 Feb 1857
Wanklyn, MD	35382	16 Dec 1941	7103	3rd Supp. to LG 35379 12 Dec 1941	Adm. 16 Dec 1941
Wantage, Lord	See Loyd-Lindsay, RJ				
Warburton-Lee, BAW	34868	7 Jun 1940	3501/2	2nd Supp. to LG 34866 7 Jun 1940	Adm. 7 Jun 1940
Ward, CB	27233	28 Sep 1900	5966	Gazette	WO 28 Sep 1900
Ward, H	22154	18 Jun 1858	2958	Gazette	WO 18 Jun 1858
Ward, J	22223	28 Jan 1859	294	Gazette	WO 26 Jan 1859
Ward, JA	35238	5 Aug 1941	4515	Gazette	Air Min. 5 Aug 1941
Ware, SW	29765	26 Sep 1916	9418	Supp. to LG 29764 26 Sep 1916	WO 26 Sep 1916
Waring, WH	31155	31 Jan 1919	1504	8th Supp. to LG 31147 28 Jan 1919	WO 31 Jan 1919
Wark, BA	31082	26 Dec 1918	13117/18	Supp. to LG 31081 24 Dec 1918	WO 26 Dec 1918
Warneford, RAJ	29189	11 Jun 1915	5635	Gazette	Adm. 10 Jun 1915
Warner, E	29210	29 Jun 1915	6270	Gazette	WO 29 Jun 1915

	London Gazette	Date	Page	Supplement (if any)	Release Date
Wassall, S	24734	17 Jun 1879	3966	Gazette	WO 17 Jun 1879
Waters, AHS	31178	13 Feb 1919	2249	4th Supp. to LG 31174 11 Feb 1919	WO 13 Feb 1919
Watkins, T	36774	2 Nov 1944	5015/16	Supp. to LG 36773 31 Oct 1944	WO 2 Nov 1944
Watson, J	22154	18 Jun 1858	2960/1	Gazette	WO 18 Jun 1858
Watson, OCS	30675	8 May 1918	5555	2nd Supp. to LG 30673 7 May 1918	WO 8 May 1918
Watson, TC	26968	20 May 1898	3165	Gazette	WO 20 May 1898
Watt, J	30258	29 Aug 1917	8985	3rd Supp. to LG 30255 28 Aug 1917	Adm. 29 Aug 1917
Weale, H	31012	15 Nov 1918	13473	7th Supp. to LG 31005 12 Nov 1918	WO 15 Nov 1918
Wearne, FB	30215	2 Aug 1917	7906	4th Supp. to LG 30211 31 Jul 1917	WO 2 Aug 1917
Weathers, LC	31082	26 Dec 1918	15118	Supp. to LG 31081 24 Dec 1918	WO 26 Dec 1918
Welch, J	30154	27 Jun 1917	6382	4th Supp. to LG 30150 26 Jun 1917	WO 27 Jun 1917
Wells, H	29371	18 Nov 1915	11448/9	3rd Supp. to LG 29368 16 Nov 1915	WO 18 Nov 1915
Wells, JS Collings-	See Collings-Wells, JS				
West, FMF	30999	8 Nov 1918	13199	7th Supp. to LG 30992 5 Nov 1918	Air Min. 8 Nov 1918
West, RA	30982	30 Oct 1918	12801	2nd Supp. to LG 30980 29 Oct 1918	WO 30 Oct 1918
Weston, WB	37077	15 May 1945	2503	Supp. to LG 37076 11 May 1945	WO 15 May 1945
Wheatley, F	29171	24 Feb 1857	662	Supp. to LG 21970 24 Feb 1857	WO 24 Feb 1857
Wheatley, KA	44198	15 Dec 1966	13567	Supp. to LG 44197 13 Dec 1966	None
Wheeler, GC	30122	8 Jun 1917	5702	2nd Supp. to LG 30120 8 Jun 1917	WO 8 Jun 1917
Wheeler, GGM	29281	1 Sep 1915	8699	Supp. to LG 29280 31 Aug 1915	WO 1 Sep 1915
Whirlpool, F (Conker)	22318	21 Oct 1859	3793	Gazette	WO 21 Oct 1859
Whitchurch, HF	26644	16 Jul 1895	4021	Gazette	WO 16 Jul 1895
White, A	30154	27 Jun 1917	6382	4th Supp. to LG 30150 26 Jun 1917	WO 27 Jun 1917

	London Gazette	Date	Page	Supplement (if any)	Release Date
White, ACT	29802	26 Oct 1916	10394	4th Supp. to LG 29798 24 Oct 1916	WO 26 Oct 1916
White, Geoffrey Saxton	31354	24 May 1919	6445	2nd Supp. to LG 31352 23 May 1919	Adm. 24 May 1919
White, George Stuart	24981	3 Jun 1881	2859	Gazette	WO 2 Jun 1881
White, J	30154	27 Jun 1917	6382	4th Supp. to LG 30150 26 Jun 1917	WO 27 Jun 1917
White, WA	31012	15 Nov 1918	13472	7th Supp. to LG 31005 12 Nov 1918	WO 15 Nov 1918
Whitfield, H	30675	8 May 1918	5556	2nd Supp. to LG 30673 7 May 1918	WO 8 May 1918
Whitham, T	30272	6 Sep 1917	9261	5th Supp. to LG 30267 4 Sep 1917	WO 6 Sep 1917
Whittle, JW	30122	8 Jun 1917	5704	2nd Supp. to LG 30120 8 Jun 1917	WO 8 Jun 1917
Wilcox, A	31012	15 Nov 1918	13473	7th Supp. to LG 31005 12 Nov 1918	WO 15 Nov 1918
Wilkinson, AR	31108	6 Jan 1919	309	4th Supp. to LG 31104 3 Jan 1919	WO 6 Jan 1919
Wilkinson, Thomas (Bdr)	21971	24 Feb 1857	654	Supp. to LG 21970 24 Feb 1857	WO 24 Feb 1857
Wilkinson, Thomas (Lt)	37819	17 Dec 1946	6125	3rd Supp. to LG 37816 13 Dec 1946	Adm. 17 Dec 1946
Wilkinson, Thomas OL	29765	26 Sep 1916	9418	Supp. to LG 29764 26 Sep 1916	WO 26 Sep 1916
Williams, John	24717	2 May 1879	3177	Supp. to LG 24716 2 May 1879	WO 2 May 1879
Williams, John Henry	31067	14 Dec 1918	14776	2nd Supp. to LG 31065 13 Dec 1918	WO 14 Dec 1918
Williams, W	30194	20 Jul 1917	7424	2nd Supp. to LG 30192 20 Jul 1917	Adm. 20 Jul 1917
Williams, W	31201	20 Nov 1918	13694	2nd Supp. to LG 30199 19 Nov 1918	Adm. 20 Nov 1918
Williams, WC	29264	16 Aug 1915	8132	2nd Supp. to LG 29262 13 Aug 1915	Adm. 16 Aug 1915
Willis, RR	29273	24 Aug 1915	8395	Gazette	WO 24 Aug 1915
Wilmot, H	22212	24 Dec 1858	5515	Gazette	WO 24 Dec 1858
Wilson, AK	25356	21 May 1884	2277	Supp. to LG 25355 20 May 1884	WO 21 May 1884
Wilson, ECT	34968	14 Oct 1940	5993	2nd Supp. to LG 34966 11 Oct 1940	WO 11 Oct 1940
Wilson, G	28998	5 Dec 1914	10411	3rd Supp. to LG 28995 4 Dec 1914	WO 5 Dec 1914

	London Gazette	Date	Page	Supplement (if any)	Release Date
Wood, HB	31067	14 Dec 1918	14777	2nd Supp. to LG 31065 13 Dec 1918	WO 14 Dec 1918
Wood, HE	22419	4 Sep 1860	3257	Gazette	WO 4 Sep 1860
Wood, JA	22409	3 Aug 1860	2860	Gazette	WO 3 Aug 1860
Wood, W	31034	27 Nov 1918	14040	2nd Supp. to LG 31032 26 Nov 1918	WO 27 Nov 1918
Woodall, JE	30770	28 Jun 1918	7619	6th Supp. to LG 30764 25 Jun 1918	WO 28 Jun 1918
Woodcock, T	30338	17 Oct 1917	10678/9	2nd Supp. to LG 30336 16 Oct 1917	WO 17 Oct 1917
Wooden, C	22194	26 Oct 1858	4575	Gazette	WO 26 Oct 1858
Woodroffe, SC	29286	6 Sep 1915	8839	3rd Supp. to LG 29283 3 Sep 1915	WO 6 Sep 1915
Woods, JP	31082	26 Dec 1918	15119	Supp. to LG 31081 24 Dec 1918	WO 26 Dec 1918
Woolley, GH	29170	22 May 1915	4990	Supp. to LG 29169 21 May 1915	WO 22 May 1915
Wright, A	21971	24 Feb 1857	661	Supp. to LG 21970 24 Feb 1857	WO 24 Feb 1857
Wright, PH	36690	7 Sep 1944	4157	2nd Supp. to LG 36688 5 Sep 1944	WO 7 Sep 1944
Wright, T	28976	16 Nov 1914	9374	3rd Supp. to LG 28973 13 Nov 1914	WO 16 Nov 1914
Wright, WD	27596	11 Sep 1903	5663	Gazette	WO 11 Sep 1903
Wyatt, GH	29371	18 Nov 1915	11449	3rd Supp. to LG 29368 16 Nov 1915	WO 18 Nov 1915
Wylie, CHM Doughty	See Doughty-Wylie, CHM				
Wylly, GGE	27249	23 Nov 1900	7385	Gazette	WO 23 Nov 1900
Yate, CAL	28985	25 Nov 1914	9957	Supp. to LG 28984 24 Nov 1914	WO 25 Nov 1914
Yeshwant Ghadge	36774	2 Nov 1944	5016	Supp. to LG 36773 31 Oct 1944	WO 2 Nov 1944
Youens, F	30215	2 Aug 1917	7906	4th Supp. to LG 30211 31 Jul 1917	WO 2 Aug 1917
Youll, JS	30811	25 Jul 1918	8723/4	3rd Supp. to LG 30808 23 Jul 1918	WO 25 Jul 1918
Young, A	27373	8 Nov 1901	7221	Gazette	WO 8 Nov 1901

	London Gazette	Date	Page	Supplement (if any)	Release Date
Young, FE	31067	14 Dec 1918	14776	2nd Supp. to LG 31065 13 Dec 1918	WO 14 Dec 1918
Young, JF	31067	14 Dec 1918	14779	2nd Supp. to LG 31065 13 Dec 1918	WO 14 Dec 1918
Young, T (Morrell)	30726	4 Jun 1918	6572	12th Supp. to LG 30714 31 May 1918	WO 4 Jun 1918
Young, TJ	22225	1 Feb 1859	414	Gazette	WO 1 Feb 1859
Young, W	29527	30 Mar 1916	3410	4th Supp. to LG 29523 28 Mar 1916	WO 30 Mar 1916
Younger, DR	27462	8 Aug 1902	5085	Gazette	WO 8 Aug 1902
Younger, DR	27233	28 Sep 1900	5966	Gazette ('Had he survived')	WO 28 Sep 1900
Zengel, RL	30922	27 Sep 1918	11430	4th Supp. to LG 30918 24 Sep 1918	WO 27 Sep 1918

Biographical Index of Award-Winners

Alphabetical order is letter-by-letter, and reference is to page number. The rank held at the time of the deed is given in the main text; the ranks given here are the last known to be held. British, Empire and Commonwealth orders and decorations are listed at the end of the entry, and are those held at death, or awarded posthumously if stated.

AARON, Arthur Louis 452 BORN 5 March 1922, Gledhow, Leeds, Yorkshire. DIED 13 August 1943, as a result of wounds received during VC action, Bone, Tunisia. BURIED Bone War Cemetery. O&D DFM.

ABDUL HAFIZ 466 BORN 4 September 1915, Kalanaur Village, Rohtak District, Punjab, India. DIED 6 April 1944, during VC action, near Imphal, India. BURIED Imphal Indian Army War Cemetery, Manipur State, India.

ABLETT, Alfred 38 BORN 3 August 1830, Weybread, Suffolk. DIED 12 March 1897, Poplar, London. BURIED St Andrew's Parish Churchyard, Weybread. Grave not marked. RANK Sergeant. O&D DCM.

ACKROYD, Harold 280 BORN 13 July 1877, Southport, Lancashire. DIED 11 August 1917. He was killed in action, Jargon Trench, Glencourse Wood, Ypres, Belgium. BURIED Birr Cross Roads Cemetery, Belgium. O&D MC.

ACTON, Abraham 199 BORN 17 December 1892, Whitehaven, Cumbria. DIED 16 May 1915, in action, Festubert, France. No known grave.

ADAMS, James William 117 BORN 24 November 1839, Cork, Ireland. DIED 20 October 1903, Ashwell, Rutland. BURIED Ashwell Churchyard.

ADAMS, Robert Bellew 147 BORN 26 July 1856, Murree, India. DIED 13 February 1928, Inverness, Scotland. CREMATED Maryhill Crematorium, Glasgow. RANK Major General. O&D KCB.

ADDISON, Henry 93 BORN February 1821, Bardwell, Suffolk. DIED 18 June 1887, Bardwell. BURIED Bardwell Parish Churchyard.

ADDISON, William Robert Fountains 237 BORN 18 September 1883, Cranbrook, Kent. DIED 7 January 1962, St Leonards-on-Sea, Sussex. BURIED Brookwood Cemetery, near Woking, Surrey.

ADLAM, Tom Edwin 258 BORN 21 October 1893, Salisbury, Wiltshire. DIED 28 May 1975, Hayling Island, Hampshire. BURIED St Matthew's Churchyard, Blackmoor, Hampshire. RANK Lieutenant Colonel.

AGANSING RAI 471 BORN 24 April 1920, Amsara Village, Chisankkhu, Okhaldunga District, Nepal. DIED 27 May 2000, Kathmandu, Nepal. CREMATED Dharan, Nepal. RANK Hon. Captain. O&D MM.

AGAR, Augustus Willington Shelton 374 BORN 4 January 1890, Kandy, Ceylon. DIED 30 December 1968, Alton, Hampshire. BURIED Alton Cemetery. RANK Commodore. O&D DSO.

AIKMAN, Frederick Robertson 84 BORN 6 February 1828, Ross, Lanarkshire, Scotland. DIED 5 October 1888. He dropped dead whilst attending a ball, Hamilton, Lanarkshire. BURIED Kensal Green Cemetery, London. RANK Colonel.

AITKEN, Robert Hope Moncrieff 68 BORN 6 February 1826, Cupar, Scotland. DIED 18 September 1887, St Andrews, Scotland. BURIED Eastern Cemetery, St Andrews. RANK Colonel. O&D CB.

ALBRECHT, Herman 165 BORN c. 1876, Burghersdorp, South Africa. DIED 6 January 1900, Waggon Hill, South Africa. BURIED Waggon Hill Cemetery.

ALEXANDER, Ernest Wright 191 BORN 2 October 1870, Woolton, Liverpool. DIED 25 August 1934, Kingsbridge, Devon. Ashes interred Putney Vale Cemetery, London. RANK Major General. O&D CB, CMG.

ALEXANDER, John 33 BORN date unknown, Mullingar, Co. Westmeath, Ireland. DIED 24 September 1857. He was killed in action during the Indian Mutiny, Lucknow, India. No known grave.

attended the VC centenary celebrations. CREMATED Karrakatta Crematorium, Perth, Western Australia. RANK Corporal. O&D MM.

AYLMER, Fenton John 140 BORN 5 April 1862, Hastings, Sussex. DIED 3 September 1935, Wimbledon, London. CREMATED Golders Green Crematorium, London. RANK Lieutenant General. O&D KCB.

BABTIE, William 164 BORN May 1859, Dumbarton, Scotland. DIED 11 September 1920, Knocke, Belgium. BURIED Stoke Cemetery, Guildford, Surrey. RANK Lieutenant General. O&D KCB, KCMG.

BADCOE, Peter John 547 BORN 11 January 1934, Adelaide, South Australia. DIED 7 April 1967, during VC action, near An Thuan Village, north-west of Hue, South Vietnam. BURIED Terendak Garrison Camp Cemetery, Malaysia.

BADLU SINGH 368 BORN November 1876, Dhakla Village, Rohtak District, Punjab, India. DIED 23 September 1918, from wounds sustained during VC action, Khes Samariveh, Palestine. CREMATED near where he fell.

BAKER, Charles George 92 BORN 8 December 1830, Neocolly, Bengal, India. DIED 19 February 1906, Southbourne, Dorset. BURIED Christchurch Cemetery.

BALL, Albert 299 BORN 14 August 1896, Nottingham, Nottinghamshire. DIED 7 May 1917, from wounds received after his aircraft was brought down by anti-aircraft guns, Annoeullin, France. BURIED Annoeullin Communal Cemetery, German Extension, France. O&D DSO and two bars, MC.

BAMBRICK, Valentine 87 BORN 13 April 1837, Cawnpore, India. DIED 1 April 1864. He hanged himself in Pentonville Prison whilst suffering from a deep depression, Islington, London. BURIED St Pancras and Islington Cemetery, London. Memorial dedicated 2002.

BAMFORD, Edward 364 BORN 28 May 1897, Highgate, London. DIED 30 September 1928, Shanghai, China. BURIED Bubbling Road Cemetery, Shanghai. RANK Major. O&D DSO.

BANKES, William George Hawtry 85 BORN 11 September 1836, Kingston Lacey, Dorset. DIED 6 April 1858, as a result of wounds sustained during VC action, Lucknow, India. No known grave.

BARBER, Edward 204 BORN 10 June 1893, Tring. Hertfordshire. DIED 12 March 1915, during VC action, Neuve-Chapelle, France. No known grave.

BARKER, William George 361 BORN 3 November 1894, Dauphin, Manitoba, Canada. DIED 12 March 1930, killed demonstrating a new two-seater aircraft, Rockville, Ontario, Canada. BURIED Mount Pleasant Cemetery, Toronto, Ontario. RANK Lieutenant Colonel. O&D DSO and bar, MC and two bars.

BARRATT, Thomas 267 BORN 5 May 1895, Coseley, Worcestershire. DIED 27 July 1917, shortly after VC action, near Ypres, Belgium. BURIED Essex Farm Cemetery, Belgium.

BARRETT, John Cridlan 343 BORN 10 August 1897, Royal Leamington Spa, Warwickshire. DIED 7 March 1977, Leicester. CREMATED Gilroes Crematorium, Leicester. RANK Colonel. O&D TD.

BARRON, Colin Fraser 293 BORN 20 September 1895, Boyndie, Banffshire, Scotland. DIED 15 August 1959, Toronto, Canada. BURIED Prospect Cemetery, Toronto. RANK Sergeant.

BARRY, John 173 BORN 1 February 1873, Kilkenny, Ireland. DIED 8 January 1901. He died as a result of wounds sustained during VC action, Monument Hill, South Africa. BURIED Belfast Cemetery, South Africa.

BARTER, Frederick 210 BORN 17 January 1891, Cardiff. DIED 15 May 1953, Poole, Dorset. CREMATED Bournemouth Crematorium, Dorset. RANK Captain.

BARTON, Cyril Joe 484 BORN 5 June 1921, Elveden, Suffolk. DIED 31 March 1944, as a result of crash-landing his aircraft after VC action, Ryhope, Co. Durham. BURIED Bonner Hill Road Cemetery, Kingston-upon-Thames, Surrey.

BASKEYFIELD, John Daniel 501 BORN 18 November 1922, Burslem, Staffordshire. DIED 20 September 1944, during VC action, near Arnhem, Holland. No known grave.

BASSETT, Cyril Royston Guyton 326 BORN 3 January 1892, Mount Eden, New Zealand. DIED 9 January 1983, Stanley Point, New Zealand. CREMATED North Shore Crematorium, Albany, New Zealand. RANK Lieutenant Colonel.

BATES, Sidney 490 BORN 14 June 1921, Camberwell, London. DIED 8 August 1944, as a result of wounds received during VC action, near Sourdeval, France. BURIED Bayeux War Cemetery, Normandy, France.

BATTEN-POOLL, Arthur Hugh Henry 240 BORN 25 October 1891, Knightsbridge, London. DIED 21 January 1971, Ivybridge, Devon. BURIED St Lawrence's Parish Churchyard, Woolverton, Avon. RANK Captain. O&D MC.

BAXTER, Edward Felix 239 BORN 18 September 1885, Stourbridge, Worcestershire. DIED 18 April 1916, during VC action, near Blairville, France. BURIED Fillièvres British Cemetery, France.

BAXTER, Frank William 143 BORN 29 December 1869, Woolwich, London. DIED 22 April 1896, Umguza, Zimbabwe. BURIED Bulawayo Town Cemetery.

BAZALGETTE, Ian Willoughby 487 BORN 19 October 1918, Alberta, Canada. DIED 4 August 1944, during VC action, Senantes, France. BURIED Senantes Churchyard. O&D DFC.

BEACH, Thomas 20 BORN January 1824, Dundee, Scotland. DIED 24 August 1864, Dundee. BURIED Eastern Necropolis, Dundee. Grave not marked.

BEAK, Daniel Marcus William 331 BORN 27 July 1891, Southampton, Hampshire. DIED 3 May 1967, Swindon, Wiltshire. BURIED Brookwood Cemetery, Woking, Surrey. RANK Major General. O&D DSO, MC and bar.

BEAL, Ernest Frederick 316 BORN 27 January 1885, Brighton, Sussex. DIED 22 March 1918, during VC action, St Leger, France. No known grave.

BEATHAM, Robert Matthew 329 BORN 16 June 1894, Glassonby, Penrith, Cumberland. DIED 11 August 1918, during VC action at Rosière, France. BURIED Heath Cemetery, Harbonnières, France.

BEATTIE, Stephen Halden 419 BORN 29 March 1908, Leighton, Wales. DIED 24 April 1975, Cornwall. BURIED Ruan Minor Churchyard, Helston, Cornwall. RANK Captain.

BEAUCHAMP-PROCTOR, Andrew Frederick Weatherby 360 BORN 4 September 1894, Mossel Bay, Cape Province, South Africa. DIED 21 June 1921, killed whilst flying in an RAF display, Upavon, Wiltshire. BURIED Mafeking Cemetery, South Africa. O&D DSO, MC and bar, DFC.

BEELEY, John 404 BORN 8 February 1918, Lower Openshaw, Manchester. DIED 21 November 1941, during VC action, Sidi Rezegh Airfield, Libya. BURIED Knightsbridge War Cemetery, Acroma, Libya.

BEES, William 175 BORN 12 September 1871, Midsomer Norton, Somerset. DIED 20 June 1938, Coalville, Leicestershire. BURIED London Road Cemetery, Coalville. RANK Corporal.

BEESLEY, William 311 BORN 5 October 1895, Burton-on-Trent, Staffordshire. DIED 23 September 1966, Abergavenny, Monmouthshire. BURIED St Paul's Cemetery, Coventry, Warwickshire. RANK Sergeant.

BEET, Harry Churchill 170 BORN 1 April 1875, Bingham, Notts. DIED 10 January 1946, Vancouver, Canada. BURIED Mountain View Cemetery, Vancouver. RANK Captain.

BELCHER, Douglas Walter 209 BORN 15 July 1889, Surbiton, Surrey. DIED 3 June 1953, Claygate, Surrey. BURIED Holy Trinity Churchyard, Claygate. RANK Captain.

BELL, David 109 BORN 1845, Co. Down, Ireland. DIED 7 March 1920, Gillingham, Kent. BURIED Woodlands Cemetery, Gillingham. RANK Sergeant.

BELL, Donald Simpson 247 BORN 3 December 1890, Harrogate, Yorkshire. DIED 10 July 1916, in Contalmaison, Somme, France. BURIED Gordon Dump Cemetery, Albert, France.

BELL, Edward William Derrington 7 BORN 18 May 1824, Landguard Fort, Essex. DIED 10 November 1879, Belfast, Ireland. BURIED St Mary's Churchyard, Kempsey, Worcestershire. RANK Major General.

BELL, Eric Norman Frankland 244 BORN 28 August 1885, Enniskillen, N.Ireland. DIED 1 July 1916, during VC action, Somme, Thiepval, France. No known grave.

BELL, Frederick William 174 BORN 3 April 1875, Perth, Australia. DIED 28 April 1954, Bristol, Avon. BURIED Canford Cemetery, Bristol. RANK Lieutenant Colonel.

BELL, Mark Sever 113 BORN 15 May 1843, Sydney, Australia. DIED 26 June 1906, Windlesham, Surrey. BURIED All Souls' Churchyard, Ascot, Berkshire. RANK Colonel. O&D CB.

BELL-DAVIES, Richard 234 BORN 19 May 1886, Kensington, London. DIED 26 February 1966, Haslar, Hampshire. CREMATED Swaythling Crematorium, Southampton. RANK Vice Admiral. O&D CB, DSO, AFC.

BELLEW, Edward Donald 208 BORN 28 October 1882, Bombay, India. DIED 1 February 1961, Kamloops, Canada. BURIED Hillside Cemetery, Kamloops. RANK Captain.

BENNETT, Eugene Paul 260 BORN 4 June 1892, Cainscross, Gloucestershire. DIED 6 April 1970, Vincenza, Italy. CREMATED Vincenza Crematorium. RANK Captain. O&D MC.

BENT, Philip Eric 288   BORN 3 January 1891, Halifax, Nova Scotia, Canada. DIED 1 October 1917, during VC action, Polygon Wood, Belgium. No known grave. O&D DSO.

BENT, Spencer John 196   BORN 18 March 1891, Stowmarket, Suffolk. DIED 3 May 1977, Hackney, London. CREMATED West Norwood Crematorium. RANK Regimental Sergeant Major. O&D MM.

BERESFORD, Lord William Leslie de la Poer 128   BORN 20 July 1847, Mullaghbrack, Ireland. DIED 28 December 1900, Dorking, Surrey. BURIED Clonagem Churchyard, Co. Waterford, Ireland. RANK Lieutenant Colonel. O&D KCIE.

BERGIN, James 111   BORN 29 June 1845, Killbricken, Ireland. DIED 1 December 1880, Poona, India. BURIED St Patrick's Churchyard, Poona. Grave not marked.

BERRYMAN, John 15   BORN 18 July 1825, Dudley, Worcestershire. DIED 27 June 1896, Woldingham, Surrey. BURIED St Agatha's Churchyard, Woldingham. RANK Major.

BEST-DUNKLEY, Bertram 281   BORN 3 August 1890, York. DIED 5 August 1917, from wounds received during VC action, near Ypres, Belgium. BURIED Mendinghem Military Cemetery, Belgium.

BHANBHAGTA GURUNG 517   BORN September 1921, Phalbu Village, Gorkha District, Nepal. RANK Hon. Havildar.

BHANDARI RAM 503   BORN 24 July 1919, Pargna Gugeda Village, Bilaspur State, Simla Hills, India. DIED 19 May 2002, Bilaspur. RANK Subadar.

BINGHAM, the Hon. Edward Barry Stewart 242   BORN 26 July 1881, Bangor, Co. Down, Ireland. DIED 24 September 1939, London. CREMATED Golders Green Crematorium, London. RANK Rear Admiral. O&D OBE.

BIRKS, Frederick 286   BORN 16 August 1894, Buckley, Flintshire, Wales. DIED 21 September 1917. He was killed the day after his VC action whilst trying to rescue men buried by a shell, Glencorse Wood, Belgium. BURIED Perth Cemetery (China Wall), Belgium. O&D MM.

BISDEE, John Hutton 172   BORN 28 September 1869, Hutton Park, Tasmania. DIED 14 January 1930, Tranquility, Tasmania. BURIED St James' Churchyard, Tranquility. RANK Lieutenant Colonel. O&D OBE.

BISHOP, William Avery 300   BORN 8 February 1894, Ontario, Canada. DIED 11 September 1956, Palm Beach, Florida, USA. CREMATED St James's Crematorium. O&D CB, DSO and bar, MC, DFC.

BISSETT, William Davidson 353   BORN 7 August 1893, Bauchlands, Perthshire, Scotland. DIED 12 May 1971, Wrexham, Denbighshire, Wales. CREMATED Pentrebychan Crematorium, Wrexham. RANK Major.

BISSETT-SMITH, Archibald 304   BORN 19 December 1878, Aberdeenshire. DIED 10 March 1917, during VC action, Atlantic Ocean. No known grave.

BLACKBURN, Arthur Seaforth 250   BORN 25 November 1892, Adelaide, South Australia. DIED 24 November 1960, Adelaide. BURIED West Terrace AIF Cemetery, Adelaide. RANK Brigadier. O&D CMG, CBE, MC.

BLAIR, James 58   BORN 27 January 1828, Nimach, Gwalior State, India. DIED 18 January 1905, Melrose, Scotland. BURIED Trinity Churchyard, Melrose. RANK General. O&D CB.

BLAIR, Robert 65   BORN 13 March 1834, Linlithgow, West Lothian, Scotland. DIED 28 March 1859, Cawnpore, India. BURIED Old British Cemetery, Cawnpore. Grave not marked. RANK Captain.

BLAKER, Frank Gerald 464   BORN 8 May 1920, Kasauli, Punjab, India. DIED 9 July 1944, as a result of wounds received during VC action, above Taungni, Burma. BURIED Taukkyan War Cemetery, Burma. O&D MC.

BLOOMFIELD, William Anderson 261   BORN 30 January 1873, Edinburgh. DIED 12 May 1954, Ermelo, Transvaal, South Africa. BURIED Ermelo Cemetery. RANK Major.

BOGLE, Andrew Cathcart 57   BORN 20 January 1829, Glasgow. DIED 11 December 1890, Sherborne, Dorset. CREMATED Woking Crematorium, Surrey. RANK Major.

BOISRAGON, Guy Hudleston 140   BORN 5 November 1864, Kohat, India. DIED 14 July 1931, Biarritz, France. BURIED Kensal Green Cemetery, London. RANK Brigadier.

BONNER, Charles George 305   BORN 29 December 1884, Shuttington, Warwickshire. DIED 7 February 1951, Edinburgh. CREMATED Warriston Crematorium, Edinburgh. Ashes buried Aldridge, near Walsall, Staffordshire. RANK Captain. O&D DSC.

BOOTH, Anthony Clarke 127   BORN 21 April 1846, Carrington, Nottinghamshire. DIED 8 December 1899, Brierley Hill, Staffordshire. BURIED St Michael's RC Churchyard, Brierley Hill.

BOOTH, Frederick Charles 301 BORN 6 March 1890, Upper Holloway, London. DIED 14 September 1960, Brighton, Sussex. BURIED Bear Road Cemetery, Brighton. RANK Captain. O&D DCM.

BORELLA, Albert Chalmers (changed his surname to CHALMERS-BORELLA in 1939) 313 BORN 7 August 1881, Borung, Victoria, Australia. DIED 7 February 1968, Albury, Victoria. BURIED Presbyterian Cemetery, Albury. RANK Captain. O&D MM.

BORTON, Arthur Drummond 307 BORN 1 July 1883, Chevening, Kent. DIED 5 January 1933, Southwold, Suffolk. BURIED Hunton Churchyard, Kent. O&D CMG, DSO.

BOUGHEY, Stanley Henry Parry 307 BORN 9 April 1896, Ayrshire, Scotland. DIED 4 December 1917. He was killed by wounds sustained during VC action, Ramleh, Palestine. BURIED Gaza War Cemetery, Israel.

BOULGER, Abraham 68 BORN 4 September 1835, Kilcullen, Co. Kildare, Ireland. DIED 23 January 1900, Moate, Co. Westmeath, Ireland. BURIED Ballymore RC Churchyard, Co. Kildare. RANK Lieutenant Colonel

BOULTER, William Ewart 248 BORN 14 October 1892, Wigston, Leicestershire. DIED 1 June 1955, London. CREMATED Putney Vale Crematorium, London. RANK Lieutenant.

BOURCHIER, Claude Thomas 25 BORN 22 April 1831, Brayford, Devon. DIED 18 November 1877, Hove, Sussex. BURIED St Andrew's Churchyard, Buxton, Norfolk. RANK Colonel.

BOURKE, Rowland Richard Louis 366 BORN 28 November 1885, London. DIED 29 August 1958, Esquimalt, British Columbia, Canada. BURIED Royal Oak Burial Park, Victoria, British Columbia. RANK Lieutenant Commander. O&D DSO.

BOYD-ROCHFORT, George Arthur 202 BORN 1 January 1880, Co. Westmeath, Ireland. DIED 7 August 1940, Dublin. BURIED Castletown Church of Ireland Old Churchyard, Co. Westmeath, Ireland. RANK Captain.

BOYES, Duncan Gordon 106 BORN 5 November 1846, Cheltenham, Gloucestershire. DIED 26 January 1869. He committed suicide after suffering a nervous breakdown, following his court martial for breaking into the Bermuda Naval Yard without a pass., Dunedin, New Zealand. BURIED Anderson's Bay Cemetery, New Zealand.

BOYLE, Edward Courtney 231 BORN 23 March 1883, Carlisle, Cumbria. DIED 16 December 1967, Ascot, Berkshire. He was run over by a lorry at a pedestrian crossing and died of his injuries on the following day. CREMATED Woking Crematorium, Surrey. RANK Rear Admiral.

BRADBURY, Edward Kinder 192 BORN 16 August 1881, Altrincham., Cheshire. DIED 1 September 1914, during VC action at Néry, France. BURIED Néry Communal Cemetery.

BRADFORD, George Nicholson 364 BORN 23 April 1887, Darlington, Co. Durham. DIED 23 April 1918, during VC action, Zeebrugge, Belgium. BURIED Blankenberg Communal Cemetery, Belgium.

BRADFORD, Roland Boys 258 BORN 23 February 1892, Witton Park, Co. Durham. DIED 30 November 1917, in action, near Graincourt, France. BURIED Hermies British Cemetery, France. RANK Brigadier. O&D MC.

BRADLEY, Frederick Henry 175 BORN 27 September 1876, London. DIED 10 March 1943, Gwelo, Zimbabwe. BURIED Gwelo Cemetery. RANK Captain.

BRADSHAW, Joseph 28 BORN 1835, Dromkeen, Co. Limerick, Ireland. DIED 29 August 1893, St John's, Limerick. No known grave. RANK Corporal.

BRADSHAW, William 71 BORN 12 February 1830, Thurles, Co. Tipperary, Ireland. DIED 9 March 1861, Thurles. BURIED St Mary's Church of Ireland Churchyard, Thurles.

BRENNAN, Joseph Charles 90 BORN August 1836, Truro, Cornwall. DIED 24 September 1872, Folkestone, Kent. BURIED Shorncliffe Military Cemetery, Folkestone. RANK Sergeant.

BRERETON, Alexander Picton 329 BORN 13 November 1892, Alexander, Manitoba, Canada. DIED 11 June 1976, Three Hills, Alberta, Canada. BURIED Elnora Cemetery, Alberta. RANK Company Quartermaster Sergeant.

BRILLANT, Jean 328 BORN 15 March 1890, Assametquaghan, Matapadia Co., Quebec, Canada. DIED 10 August 1918, as a result of wounds sustained during VC action, Meharicourt, France. BURIED Villers-Brétonneux Military Cemetery, Fouilloy, France. O&D MC.

BRODIE, Walter Lorrain 196 BORN 28 July 1885, Edinburgh. DIED 23 August 1918, in action, Behagnies, France. BURIED Beinvillers Military Cemetery. RANK Lieutenant Colonel. O&D MC.

BRUMHEAD, Gonville 121 BORN 29 August 1845, Versailles, France. DIED 9 February 1891, Allahabad, India. BURIED New Cantonment Cemetery, Allahabad. RANK Major.

BROMLEY, Cuthbert 219   BORN 19 September 1878, Sutton Corner, Sussex. DIED 13 August 1915. He was drowned whilst returning to Gallipoli from Egypt where he had gone to recuperate, eastern Mediterranean. No known grave.

BROOKE, James Anson Otho 195   BORN 3 February 1884, Newhills, Scotland. DIED 29 October 1914, during VC action near Gheluvelt, Belgium. BURIED Zantvoorde British Cemetery, Belgium. RANK Captain (posthumous).

BROOKS, Edward 266   BORN 11 April 1833, Oakley, Buckinghamshire. DIED 26 June 1944, Oxford. BURIED Rose Hill Cemetery, Oxford.

BROOKS, Oliver 216   BORN 31 May 1889, Paulton, Somerset. DIED 25 October 1940, Windsor, Berkshire. BURIED Windsor Borough Cemetery. RANK Sergeant.

BROWN, Donald Forrester 256   BORN 23 February 1890, Dunedin, New Zealand. DIED 1 October 1916, in action, near Eaucourt L'Abbaye, France. BURIED Warlencourt British Cemetery, France.

BROWN, later BROWN-SYNGE-HUTCHINSON, Edward Douglas 172   BORN 6 March 1861, Kassouli, India. DIED 3 March 1940, Marble Arch, London. CREMATED Golders Green Crematorium. RANK Colonel. O&D CB.

BROWN, Francis David Millett 66   BORN 7 August 1837, Bhagalpur, Bengal, India. DIED 21 November 1895, Sandown, Isle of Wight. BURIED West Hill Cemetery, Winchester, Hampshire. RANK Lieutenant Colonel.

BROWN, Harry W. 268   BORN 10 May 1898, Ontario, Canada. DIED 17 August 1917, from wounds received during VC action, near Loos, France. BURIED Noeux-les-Mines Communal Cemetery, France.

BROWN, Peter 130   BORN December 1862, Sweden. DIED 11 September 1894, Cape Town, South Africa. BURIED Woltermade Cemetery, Cape Town.

BROWN, Walter Ernest 312   BORN 3 July 1885, New Norfolk, Tasmania, Australia. DIED 28 February 1942. Hours before the surrender to the Japanese at Singapore, he was seen walking towards the enemy with grenades in his hands shouting, 'No surrender for me!' He was almost certainly killed shortly afterwards, Singapore. No known grave. RANK Sergeant. O&D DCM and bar.

BROWNE, Edward Stevenson 128   BORN 23 December 1852, Cambridge. DIED 16 July 1907, Montreux, Switzerland. BURIED Clarens Cemetery, Montreux. Grave not marked. RANK Brigadier General. O&D CB.

BROWNE, Samuel James 89   BORN 3 October 1824, India. DIED 14 March 1901, Ryde, Isle of Wight. Ashes buried Town Cemetery, Ryde. RANK General. O&D GCB, KCSI.

BRUCE, William Arthur McCrae 199   BORN 15 June 1890, Edinburgh. DIED 19 December 1914, during his VC action, Givenchy, France. No known grave.

BRUNT, John Henry Cound 484   BORN 6 December 1922, Paddock Wood, Kent. DIED 10 December 1944, killed the day following VC action when his platoon HQ was shelled, near Faenza, Italy. BURIED Faenza War Cemetery. O&D MC.

BRYAN, Thomas 273   BORN 21 January 1882, Lye, Worcestershire. DIED 13 October 1945, Doncaster, Yorkshire. BURIED Arksey Cemetery, Doncaster.

BUCHAN, John Crawford 317   BORN 10 October 1892, Alloa, Clackmannan, Scotland. DIED 22 March 1918, as a result of wounds received during VC action, near Marteville, France. BURIED Roisel Communal Cemetery Extension, France.

BUCHANAN, Angus 237   BORN 11 August 1894, Coleford, Gloucestershire. DIED 1 March 1944, as a result of wounds sustained in 1917 from which he never fully recovered, Gloucester. BURIED Coleford Cemetery Churchyard. O&D MC.

BUCKINGHAM, William 204   BORN February 1886, Leicester. DIED 15 September 1916, in action, Somme, France. No known grave.

BUCKLEY, Alexander Henry 335   BORN 22 July 1891, Warren, New South Wales, Australia. DIED 1 September 1918, during VC action, Péronne, France. BURIED Péronne Communal Cemetery Extension. RANK Corporal.

BUCKLEY, Cecil William 29   BORN 7 October 1830, Location unknown. DIED 24 February 1857, Funchal, Madeira. BURIED English Cemetery, Funchal. RANK Captain.

BUCKLEY, John 48   BORN 24 May 1813, Stalybridge, Cheshire. DIED 14 July 1876, Poplar, London. BURIED Tower Hamlets Cemetery, London. Grave not marked.

BUCKLEY, Maurice Vincent (also known as SEXTON, Gerald) 342   BORN 13 April 1891, Upper

Hawthorn, Victoria, Australia. DIED 27 January 1921, after surgery following a riding accident, Victoria. BURIED Brighton Cemetery, Melbourne, Australia. O&D DCM.

BUGDEN, Patrick Joseph 288 BORN 17 March 1897, New South Wales, Australia. DIED 28 September 1917, Polygon Wood, Belgium. BURIED Glencorse Wood and then Hooge Crater Cemetery, Belgium.

BULLER, Redvers Henry (later Sir Redvers) 128 BORN 7 December 1839, Crediton, Devon. DIED 2 June 1908, Crediton. BURIED Holy Cross Churchyard, Crediton. RANK General. O&D GCB, GCMG.

BURGES, Daniel 370 BORN 1 July 1873, London. DIED 24 October 1946, Bristol. CREMATED Arnos Vale Crematorium, Bristol. O&D DSO.

BURGOYNE, Hugh Talbot 30 BORN 17 July 1833, Dublin. DIED 7 September 1870. He went down with HMS *Captain* when she foundered in a squall off Cape Finisterre, Bay of Biscay. Body not found. RANK Captain.

BURMAN, William Francis 286 BORN 30 August 1897, Stepney, London. DIED 23 October 1974, Cromer, Norfolk. CREMATED St Faith's Crematorium, Norfolk.

BURSLEM, Nathaniel Godolphin 100 BORN 2 February 1837, Limerick, Ireland. DIED July 1865, Auckland, New Zealand. No known grave. RANK Captain.

BURT, Alfred Alexander 215 BORN 3 March 1895, Port Vale, Hertfordshire. DIED 9 June 1962, Chesham, Buckinghamshire. CREMATED West Hertfordshire Crematorium. RANK Sergeant.

BURTON, Alexander Stewart 227 BORN 20 January 1893, Kyneton, Victoria, Australia. DIED 9 August 1915, during VC action, Gallipoli.

BURTON, Richard Henry 481 BORN 29 January 1923, Melton Mowbray, Leicestershire. DIED 11 July 1993, Kirriemuir, Angus, Scotland. BURIED Kirriemuir Cemetery. RANK Corporal.

BUSHELL, Christopher 319 BORN 31 October 1888, Neston, Cheshire. DIED 8 August 1918, killed leading his men in the opening attack of the last great offensive, Morlencourt, Somme, France. BURIED Querrieu British Cemetery, France. O&D DSO.

BUTLER, John Fitzhardinge Paul 197 BORN 20 December 1888, Berkeley, Gloucestershire. DIED 5 September 1916, in action, Matombo, Tanzania. BURIED Morogoro Cemetery, Tanzania. RANK Captain. O&D DSO.

BUTLER, Thomas Adair 84 BORN 12 February 1836, Soberton, Hampshire. DIED 17 May 1901, Camberley, Surrey. BURIED St Michael's Churchyard, Camberley. RANK Major.

BUTLER, William Boynton 267 BORN 20 November 1894, Leeds, Yorkshire. DIED 25 March 1972, Leeds. BURIED Hunslett Cemetery, London.

BYE, Robert James 281 BORN 12 December 1889, Glamorgan, Wales. DIED 23 August 1962, Warsop, Nottinghamshire. BURIED Warsop Cemetery. RANK Sergeant Major.

BYRNE, James 90 BORN 1822, Newtown, Co. Wicklow, Ireland. DIED 6 December 1872, Dublin. BURIED Glasnevin Cemetery, Dublin. RANK Sergeant.

BYRNE, John 20 BORN September 1832, Co. Kilkenny, Ireland. DIED 10 July 1879. He shot himself in the mouth with a revolver, Caerleon, Monmouthshire. BURIED St Woolo's Cemetery, Newport, Monmouthshire. RANK Corporal.

BYRNE, Thomas 151 BORN December 1867, St Thomas's Parish, Dublin. DIED 17 February 1944, Canterbury, Kent. BURIED West Gate Cemetery, Canterbury.

BYTHESEA, John 5 BORN 15 June 1827, Freshford, Somerset. DIED 18 May 1906, South Kensington, London. BURIED Bath Abbey Cemetery, Somerset. RANK Rear Admiral. O&D CB, CIE.

CADELL, Thomas 52 BORN 5 September 1835, Cockenzie, Scotland. DIED 6 April 1919, Edinburgh. BURIED Tranent Parish Churchyard, Edinburgh. RANK Colonel. O&D CB.

CAFE, William Martin 86 BORN 26 March 1826, London. DIED 6 August 1906, Kensington, London. BURIED Brompton Cemetery, London. RANK General.

CAFFREY, John Joseph 203 BORN 23 October 1891, Birr, Ireland. DIED 26 February 1953, Derby. BURIED Wilford Hill Cemetery, Nottingham. RANK Lance Corporal.

CAIN, Robert Henry 498 BORN 2 January 1909, Shanghai, China. DIED 2 May 1974, Crowborough, Sussex. CREMATED Worth Crematorium, Crawley, Sussex.

CAIRNS, George Albert 463 BORN 12 December 1913, Sidcup, Kent. DIED 19 March 1944, as a result of wounds received during VC action, Henu Block, Burma. BURIED Taukkyan War Cemetery, Burma.

CAIRNS, Hugh 354 BORN 4 December 1896, Ashington, Northumberland. DIED 2 November 1918, from wounds received during VC action, Valenciennes, France. BURIED Auberchicourt British Cemetery, France. O&D DCM.

CALDWELL, Thomas 315 BORN 10 February 1894, Carluke, Lanarkshire, Scotland. DIED 6 June 1969, Adelaide, South Australia. CREMATED Centennial Park Crematorium, Adelaide. RANK Company Sergeant Major.

CALVERT, Laurence 341 BORN 16 February 1892, Leeds, Yorkshire. DIED 7 July 1964, Dagenham, Essex. CREMATED South Essex Crematorium, Upminster, Essex. O&D MM.

CAMBRIDGE, Daniel 39 BORN 1820, Carrickfergus, Co. Antrim, Ireland. DIED 12 June 1882, Plumstead, London. BURIED St Nicholas Parish Churchyard, Plumstead. Grave not marked. RANK Master Gunner.

CAMERON, Aylmer Spicer 89 BORN 12 August 1833, Hampshire. DIED 10 June 1909, Alverstock, Hampshire. BURIED St Mark's Churchyard, Highcliffe, Dorset. RANK Colonel. O&D CB.

CAMERON, Donald 455 BORN 18 March 1916, Carluke, Lanarkshire, Scotland. DIED 10 April 1961, Haslar, Hampshire. CREMATED Portchester Crematorium, Hampshire. RANK Commander.

CAMPBELL, Frederick William 213 BORN 15 June 1867, Mount Forest, Ontario, Canada. DIED 19 June 1915, from wounds received during VC action, Boulogne, France. BURIED Boulogne Eastern Cemetery.

CAMPBELL, Gordon 303 BORN 6 January 1886, Croydon, Surrey. DIED 3 July 1953, Isleworth, Middlesex. BURIED All Saints Churchyard, Crondall, Hampshire. RANK Vice Admiral. O&D DSO and two bars.

CAMPBELL, John Charles 400 BORN 10 January 1894, Thurso, Scotland. DIED 26 February 1942, killed in car accident, near Halfaya Pass, Libya. BURIED Cairo War Memorial Cemetery, Egypt. RANK Major General. O&D DSO and bar, MC.

CAMPBELL, John Vaughan 256 BORN 31 October 1876, London. DIED 21 May 1944, Woodchester, Gloucestershire. CREMATED Cheltenham Crematorium, Gloucestershire. RANK Brigadier. O&D CMG, DSO.

CAMPBELL, Kenneth 404 BORN 21 April 1917, Saltcoats, Ayr, Scotland. DIED 6 April 1941, during VC action, Brest harbour, France. BURIED Brest Cemetery.

CAMPBELL, Lorne MacLaine 445 BORN 22 July 1902, The Airds, Argyllshire, Scotland. DIED 25 May 1991, The Airds. BURIED Warriston Cemetery, Edinburgh. RANK Brigadier. O&D DSO and bar, OBE, TD.

CARLESS, John Henry 305 BORN 11 November 1896, Walsall, Staffordshire. DIED 17 November 1917, during VC action, Battle of Heligoland, North Sea. BURIED at sea.

CARLIN, Patrick 86 BORN 1832, Belfast. DIED 11 May 1895, Belfast, Ireland. BURIED Friar's Bush RC Cemetery, Belfast. Grave not marked.

CARMICHAEL, John 284 BORN 1 April 1893, Airdrie, Lanarkshire. DIED 20 December 1977, Hurstmain, Glenmavis. BURIED Landward Cemetery, Airdrie. O&D MM.

CARNE, James Power 541 BORN 11 April 1906, Falmouth, Cornwall. DIED 19 April 1986, Cheltenham, Gloucestershire. CREMATED Cheltenham Crematorium. RANK Colonel. O&D DSO.

CARPENTER, Alfred Francis Blakeney 364 BORN 17 September 1881, Barnes, Surrey. DIED 27 December 1955, Lydney, Gloucestershire. CREMATED Gloucester Crematorium. RANK Vice Admiral.

CARROLL, John 278 BORN 16 August 1892, Queensland, Australia. DIED 4 October 1971, Perth, Western Australia. BURIED Karrakatta Cemetery. RANK Lance Corporal.

CARTER, Herbert Augustine 181 BORN 26 May 1874, Exeter, Devon. DIED 13 January 1916, Mwele Mdogo, Kenya. BURIED St Ercus Churchyard, St Erth, Cornwall. RANK Major.

CARTER, Nelson Victor 241 BORN 9 April 1887, Eastbourne, Sussex. DIED 30 May 1916, during VC action, Richebourg l'Avoue, France. BURIED RI Rifles Churchyard, Laventie, France.

CARTON de WIART, Adrian 246 BORN 5 May 1880, Brussels, Belgium. DIED 5 June 1963, Killinardrish, Co. Cork, Ireland. BURIED Killinardrish Church of Ireland Churchyard. RANK Lieutenant General. O&D KBE, CB, CMG, DSO.

CARTWRIGHT, George 335 BORN 9 December 1894, South Kensington, London. DIED 2 February 1978, Epping, New South Wales, Australia. CREMATED Northern Suburbs Crematorium, Sydney, Australia. RANK Captain. O&D ED.

CASSIDY, Bernard Matthew 321 BORN 17 August 1892, Canning Town, London. DIED 28 March 1918, during VC action, Arras, France. No known grave.

CASTLETON, Claude Charles 251 BORN 12 April 1893, Lowestoft, Suffolk. DIED 29 July 1916, during VC action, near Pozières, Somme, France. BURIED Pozières Military Cemetery, Somme, France.

CATES, George Edward 265 BORN 8 May 1892, Wimbledon, London. DIED 9 March 1917, as a result of wounds received during his VC action, near Bouchavesnes, France. BURIED Hem Military Cemetery. Hem-Monacu, France.

CATHER, Geoffrey St George Shillington 244 BORN 11 October 1890, Streatham, London. DIED 2 July 1916, on second consecutive day of VC action, Somme, France. No known grave.

CATOR, Harry 273 BORN 24 January 1894, Drayton, Norwich, Norfolk. DIED 7 April 1966, Norwich. BURIED Sprowston Cemetery. RANK Captain. O&D MM.

CHAFER, George William 240 BORN 16 April 1894, Bradford, Yorkshire. DIED 1 March 1966, Rotherham, Yorkshire. CREMATED Rotherham Crematorium.

CHALMERS-BORELLA, Albert, *see* Borella, Albert Chalmers

CHAMPION, James 89 BORN 1834, Hammersmith, London. DIED 4 May 1904, Hammersmith. BURIED Hammersmith Cemetery. Grave not marked. O&D MSM.

CHANNER, George Nicholas 113 BORN 7 January 1843, Allahabad, India. DIED 13 December 1905, Westward Ho!, Devon. BURIED East-the-Water Cemetery, Bideford, Devon. RANK General. O&D CB.

CHAPLIN, John Worthy 100 BORN 23 July 1840, Ewhurst Park, Hampshire. DIED 18 August 1920, Market Harborough, Leicestershire. BURIED Kibworth Harcourt Parish Churchyard, Leicestershire. RANK Colonel.

CHAPMAN, Edward Thomas 513 BORN 13 January 1920, Pontlottyn, Glamorgan, Wales. DIED 3 February 2002, New Inn, Gwent. BURIED Pentag Cemetery, New Inn. RANK Company Sergeant Major. O&D BEM.

CHARD, John Rouse Merriott 122 BORN 21 December 1847, Boxhill, Devon. DIED 1 November 1897, Hatch Beauchamp, Somerset. BURIED St John the Baptist Churchyard, Hatch Beauchamp. RANK Colonel.

CHARLTON, Edward Colquhoun 514 BORN 15 June 1920, Rowlands Mill, near Gateshead, Co. Durham. DIED 21 April 1945, as a result of wounds received during VC action, Bremervorde, Germany. BURIED Becklingen War Cemetery, Soltau, Germany.

CHASE, William St Lucien 119 BORN 2 July 1856, St Lucia, West Indies. DIED 24 June 1908, Quetta, Pakistan. BURIED English Cemetery, Quetta. RANK Colonel. O&D CB.

CHATTA SINGH 236 BORN 1886, Talsanda District, India. DIED 28 March 1961, Tilsara, India. CREMATED Tilsara. RANK Havildar. O&D PVSM.

CHAVASSE, Noel Godfrey 252, 281 BORN 9 November 1884, Oxford. DIED 4 August 1917, from wounds sustained during VC bar action, near Ypres, Belgium. BURIED Brandhoek New Military Cemetery, Belgium. O&D MC.

CHERRY, Percy Herbert 265 BORN 4 June 1895, Victoria, Australia. DIED 27 March 1917, from wounds received the day after VC action, Langnicourt, France. BURIED Quéant Road Cemetery, Buissy, France. O&D MC.

CHESHIRE, Geoffrey Leonard 389 BORN 7 September 1917, Chester, Cheshire. DIED 31 July 1992, Cavendish, Suffolk. BURIED Cavendish Churchyard, Cavendish Parish Church. RANK Group Captain. O&D OM, DSO and two bars, DFC.

CHHELU RAM 446 BORN 10 May 1905, Dhenod Village, Bhiwani Hissar District, Punjab, India. DIED 20 April 1943, during VC action, near Enfidaville, Tunisia. BURIED Sfax War Cemetery, Tunisia.

CHICKEN, George Bell 92 BORN 6 March 1838, Bishopswearmouth, Co. Durham. DIED May 1860. He was drowned, Bay of Bengal. BURIED at sea.

CHOWNE, Albert 527 BORN 19 July 1920, Sydney, Australia. DIED 25 March 1945, during VC action, between Dagua and Wewak, New Guinea. BURIED Lae War Cemetery, New Guinea. O&D MM.

CHRISTIAN, Harry 217 BORN 17 January 1892, Pennington, Lancashire. DIED 2 September 1974, Cumbria. BURIED Egremont Cemetery, Cumbria.

CHRISTIE, John Alexander 308 BORN 14 May 1895, Edmonton, London. DIED 10 September 1967, Stockport, Greater Manchester. CREMATED Stockport Crematorium.

CLAMP, William 290 BORN 28 October 1891, Lanarkshire, Scotland. DIED 9 October 1917. He was killed by a sniper very shortly after his VC action, Poelcapelle, Belgium. No known grave.

CLARE, George William Burdett 296 BORN 18 May 1889, St Ives, Huntingdonshire. DIED 29 November 1917, during VC action, Bourlon Wood, France. No known grave.

CLARKE, James 354 BORN 6 April 1894, Winsford, Cheshire. DIED 16 June 1947, Rochdale, Lancashire. BURIED Rochdale Cemetery.

CLARKE, Leo 256 BORN 1 December 1892, Waterdown, Ontario, Canada. DIED 19 October 1916, from wounds received during VC action, near Le Havre, France. BURIED Etretat Churchyard, near Le Havre.

CLARK-KENNEDY, William Hew 334 BORN 3 March 1879, Dunskey, Kirkcudbrightshire, Scotland. DIED 25 October 1961, Montreal, Canada. BURIED Mount Royal Cemetery, Montreal. O&D CMG, DSO and bar, ED.

CLEMENTS, John James 174 BORN 19 June 1872, Middelburg, South Africa. DIED 18 June 1937, Newcastle, South Africa. BURIED Town Cemetery, Newcastle. RANK Sergeant.

CLIFFORD, the Hon. Henry Hugh 20 BORN 12 September 1826, Irnham, Lincolnshire. DIED 12 April 1883, Chudleigh, Devon. BURIED Ugbrooke House, Chudleigh. RANK Major General. O&D KCMG, CB.

CLOGSTOUN, Herbert Mackworth 94 BORN 13 June 1820, Port of Spain, Trinidad. DIED 6 May 1862, Hingoli, India. BURIED Madras Cemetery. RANK Major.

CLOUTMAN, Brett Mackay (later Sir Brett) 356 BORN 7 November 1891, Muswell Hill, London. DIED 15 August 1971, Highgate, London. CREMATED Golders Green Crematorium, London. RANK Lieutenant Colonel. O&D MC.

COBBE, Alexander Stanhope 179 BORN 5 June 1870, Naini Tal, India. DIED 29 June 1931, Shambrook, Bedfordshire. BURIED St Peter's Churchyard, Shambrook. RANK General. O&D GCB, KCSI, DSO.

COCHRANE, Hugh Stewart 90 BORN 4 August 1829, Fort William, Scotland. DIED 23 April 1884, Southsea, Hampshire. BURIED Highland Road Cemetery, Southsea. RANK Colonel.

COCKBURN, Hampden Zane Churchill 173 BORN 19 November 1867, Toronto, Canada. DIED 12 July 1913, Maple Creek, Saskatchewan. BURIED St James' Cemetery, Toronto. RANK Major.

COFFEY, William 28 BORN 5 August 1829, Knocklong, Co. Limerick, Ireland. DIED 13 July 1875. He committed suicide, Sheffield, Yorkshire. BURIED Spittal Cemetery, Chesterfield, Derbyshire. RANK Sergeant. O&D DCM.

COFFIN, Clifford 281 BORN 10 February 1870, Blackheath, London. DIED 4 February 1959, Torquay, Devon. BURIED Holy Trinity Churchyard, Tunbridge Wells, Kent. RANK Major General. O&D CB, DSO and bar.

COGHILL, Nevill Josiah Aylmer 122 BORN 25 January 1852, Drumcondra, Ireland. DIED 22 January 1879, Buffalo River, South Africa. BURIED Fugitive's Drift, below Itchiane Hill, South Africa.

COGHLAN, Cornelius, *see* Coughlan, Cornelius

COLEMAN, John 38 BORN 12 July 1798, St Mary-in-the-Marsh, Romney Marsh, Kent. DIED 21 May 1858, Lucknow, India. Conflicting records indicate that he died on 4 June 1882. Burial place unknown.

COLLEY, Harold John 333 BORN 26 May 1894, Smethwick, Birmingham. DIED 25 August 1918, as a result of wounds sustained during VC action, Martinpuich, France. BURIED Mailly Wood Cemetery, France. O&D MM.

COLLIN, Joseph Henry 324 BORN 11 April 1893, Jarrow, Co. Durham. DIED 9 April 1918, during VC action, Orchard Keep, Givenchy, France. BURIED Vieille-Chapelle New Military Cemetery, France.

COLLINGS-WELLS, John Stanhope 318 BORN 19 July 1880, Caddington, Bedfordshire. DIED 27 March 1918, during VC action, Albert, France. BURIED Bouzincourt Ridge Cemetery, France. O&D DSO.

COLLINS, John 307 BORN 10 September 1880, West Hatch, Somerset. DIED 3 September 1951, Merthyr Tydfil, Mid-Glamorgan, Wales. BURIED Pant Cemetery, Merthyr Tydfil. RANK Sergeant. O&D DCM, MM.

COLLIS, James 118 BORN 9 April 1856, Cambridge. DIED 28 June 1918, Battersea, London. BURIED Wandsworth Cemetery, London.

COLTMAN, William Harold 348 BORN 17 November 1891, Rangemoor, Staffordshire. DIED 29 June 1974, Burton-on-Trent, Staffordshire. BURIED St Peter's Parish Churchyard, Burton-on-Trent. O&D DCM and bar, MM and bar.

COLUMBINE, Herbert George 318 BORN 28 November 1893, Penge, London. DIED 22 March 1918, during VC action, Hervilly Wood, France. No known grave.

COLVIN, Hugh 286 BORN 1 February 1887, Burnley, Lancashire. DIED 16 September 1962, Bangor, Co. Down, Northern Ireland. BURIED Cammoney Cemetery, Bangor. RANK Major.

COLVIN, James Morris Colquhoun 146   BORN 26 August 1870, Bijnor, Pakistan. DIED 7 December 1945, Stanway, Essex. CREMATED Ipswich Crematorium, Suffolk. RANK Colonel.

COLYER-FERGUSSON, Thomas Riversdale 281   BORN 18 February 1896, Central London. DIED 31 July 1917, during VC action, Bellewaarde, Belgium. BURIED Menin Road South Military Cemetery, Belgium.

COMBE, Robert Grierson 277   BORN 5 August 1880, Aberdeen, Scotland. DIED 3 May 1917, during VC action, south of Acheville, France. No known grave.

COMMERELL, John Edmund 41   BORN 13 January 1829, Grosvenor Square, London. DIED 21 May 1901, Hyde Park, London. BURIED Cheriton Road Cemetery, Folkestone, Kent. RANK Admiral of the Fleet. O&D GCB.

CONGREVE, Walter Norris 164   BORN 20 November 1862, Chatham, Kent. DIED 26 February 1927, Malta. BURIED at sea off Malta. RANK General. O&D KCB, MVO.

CONGREVE, William La Touche 248   BORN 22 March 1891, Burton, Cheshire. DIED 20 July 1916, during VC action, near Longueval, Somme, France. BURIED Corbie Communal Cemetery Extension, Amiens, France. O&D DSO, MC.

CONNOLLY, William 56   BORN May 1817, Liverpool, Lancashire. DIED 31 December 1891, Liverpool. BURIED Kirkdale Cemetery, Liverpool.

CONNORS, John 39   BORN October 1830, Davaugh, Listowel, Co. Kerry, Ireland. DIED 29 January 1857, Corfu. BURIED British Cemetery, Corfu Town. RANK Corporal.

CONOLLY, John Augustus 18   BORN 30 May 1829, Celbridge, Co. Dublin, Ireland. DIED 23 December 1888, Curragh, Co. Kildare, Ireland. BURIED Mount Jerome Cemetery, Dublin. RANK Lieutenant Colonel.

COOK, John 116   BORN 28 August 1843, Edinburgh. DIED 19 December 1879. He died from bullet wounds after taking part in an attack, Takht-I-Shah Massif, Afghanistan. BURIED Sherpur Cantonment Cemetery. RANK Major.

COOK, Walter 94   BORN 18 June 1834, Cripplegate, London. DIED probably 1864. He is thought to have drowned, River Ravi, Punjab, India. No known grave.

COOKE, Thomas 251   BORN 5 July 1881, Marlborough, New Zealand. DIED 25 July 1916, during VC action, Pozières, Somme, France. No known grave.

COOKSON, Edgar Christopher 232   BORN 13 December 1883, Tranmere, Cheshire. DIED 28 September 1915, during VC action, Kut-el-Amara, Mesopotamia. No known grave. O&D DSO.

COOPER, Edward 283   BORN 4 May 1896, Stockton-on-Tees, Co. Durham. DIED 19 August 1985, Stockton-on-Tees. CREMATED Teeside Crematorium, Middlesbrough. RANK Major.

COOPER, Henry 30   BORN 1825, Devonport, Devon. DIED 15 July 1893, Torpoint, Cornwall. BURIED St Anthony Churchyard, Torpoint.

COOPER, James 109   BORN September 1840, Birmingham. DIED 9 August 1889, Birmingham. BURIED Warstone Lane Cemetery, Birmingham. Grave not marked.

COPPINS, Frederick George 329   BORN 25 October 1889, London. DIED 30 March 1963, Livermore, California, USA. CREMATED Chapel of the Chimes Crematorium, Oakland, California.

CORBETT, Frederick 138   BORN 1851, Camberwell, London. DIED 25 September 1912, Essex. BURIED London Road Cemetery, Maldon, Essex. Grave not marked.

CORNWELL, John Travers 242   BORN 8 January 1900, Leyton, London. DIED 2 June 1916, from wounds received two days previously during VC action, Grimsby, Lincolnshire. BURIED Manor Park Cemetery, London

COSENS, Aubrey 509   BORN 21 May 1921, Latchford, Ontario, Canada. DIED 26 February 1945, during VC action, Mooshof, Holland. BURIED Groesbeek Canadian War Cemetery, Nijmegen, Holland.

COSGROVE, William 222   BORN 1 October 1888, Ballinookera, Co. Cork, Ireland. DIED 14 July 1936, from back injuries originally caused by machine-gun fire during VC action, London. BURIED Upper Aghada Cemetery, near Cork, Co. Cork. RANK Staff Sergeant. O&D MSM.

COSTELLO, Edmond William 145   BORN 7 August 1873, Sheikhburdin, India. DIED 7 June 1949, Eastbourne, Sussex. BURIED St Mark's Parish Churchyard, Hadlow Down, Sussex. RANK Brigadier General. O&D CMG, CVO, DSO.

COTTER, William Reginald 239   BORN March 1883, Folkestone, Kent. DIED 14 March 1916, from wounds received during VC action, Lilliers, France. BURIED Lilliers Communal Cemetery.

COUGHLAN (also known as COGHLAN), Cornelius 50   BORN 27 June 1828, Eyrecourt, Co. Galway, Ireland. DIED 14 February 1915, Westport, Co. Mayo, Ireland. BURIED Westport Old Cemetery. Grave not marked. RANK Sergeant Major.

COULSON, Gustavus Hamilton Blenkinsopp 174 BORN 1 April 1879, Wimbledon, London. DIED 18 May 1901. He was killed during VC action, Lambrechfontein, South Africa. BURIED Lambrechfontein Farm. O&D DSO.

COUNTER, Jack Thomas 326 BORN 3 November 1898, Blandford Forum, Dorset. DIED 16 September 1970, Blandford Forum. CREMATED Bournemouth Crematorium.

COURY, Gabriel George 252 BORN 13 June 1896, Liverpool. DIED 23 February 1956, Liverpool. BURIED St Peter and St Paul Churchyard, Crosby, Merseyside. RANK Captain.

COVERDALE, Charles Harry 289 BORN 21 April 1883, Manchester, Lancashire. DIED 20 November 1955, Huddersfield, Yorkshire. BURIED Edgerton Cemetery, Huddersfield. RANK Second Lieutenant. O&D MM.

COWLEY, Charles Henry 238 BORN 21 February 1872, Baghdad, Mesopotamia. DIED 25 April 1916, following his surrender to the Turks after his VC action, near Kut, Mesopotamia. He was almost certainly executed. No known grave.

COX, Christopher Augustus 265 BORN 25 December 1889, Kings Langley. Hertfordshire. DIED 28 April 1959, Kings Langley. BURIED Kings Langley Cemetery.

CRAIG, James 39 BORN 10 September 1824, Perth, Scotland. DIED 18 March 1861. He slashed his throat with a knife, Port Elizabeth, South Africa. BURIED St Mary's Cemetery, Port Elizabeth. RANK Lieutenant.

CRAIG, John Manson 306 BORN 5 March 1896, Perthshire, Scotland. DIED 19 February 1970, Crieff. CREMATED Perth Crematorium.

CRANDON, Harry George 175 BORN 12 February 1874, Wells, Somerset. DIED 2 January 1953, Swinton, Manchester. BURIED Swinton Cemetery, Manchester. RANK Corporal.

CREAGH, O'Moore (later Sir O'Moore) 117 BORN 2 April 1848, Cahirbane, Ireland. DIED 9 August 1923, South Kensington, London. BURIED East Sheen Cemetery, Surrey. RANK General. O&D GCB, GCSI.

CREAN, Thomas Joseph 176 BORN 19 April 1873, Dublin. DIED 25 March 1923, Mayfair, London. BURIED St Mary's RC Cemetery, Kensal Green, London. RANK Major. O&D DSO.

CRICHTON, James 347 BORN 15 July 1879, Carrickfergus, Co. Antrim, Ireland. DIED 22 September 1961, Takapuna, New Zealand. BURIED Waikumete Memorial Park Soldiers' Cemetery, Auckland. RANK Sergeant.

CRIMMIN, John 138 BORN 19 March 1859, Dublin. DIED 20 February 1945, Wells, Somerset. BURIED Wells Cemetery. RANK Colonel. O&D CB, CIE, VD.

CRISP, Thomas 305 BORN 28 April 1876, Lowestoft, Suffolk. DIED 15 August 1917, during VC action, off Jim Howe Bank, North Sea. No known grave. O&D DSC.

CROAK, John Bernard 328 BORN 18 May 1892, Little Bay, Newfoundland, Canada. DIED 8 August 1918, during VC action, Amiens, France. BURIED Hangard Wood British Cemetery, France.

CROSS, Arthur Henry 320 BORN 13 December 1884, Thetford, Norfolk. DIED 26 November 1965, Lambeth, London. BURIED Streatham Vale Cemetery, London. O&D MM.

CROWE, John James 325 BORN 28 December 1876, Devonport, Devon. DIED 27 February 1965, Brighton, Sussex. CREMATED Downs Crematorium, Brighton. RANK Captain.

CROWE, Joseph Petrus Hendrick 58 BORN 12 January 1826, Uitenhage, South Africa. DIED 12 April 1876, Penge, London. BURIED Old Anglican Cemetery, Uitenhage. RANK Lieutenant Colonel.

CRUICKSHANK, John Alexander 496 BORN 20 May 1920, Aberdeen, Scotland. RANK Flight Lieutenant.

CRUICKSHANK, Robert Edward 368 BORN 17 June 1888, Manitoba, Canada. DIED 30 August 1961, Blaby, Leicestershire. CREMATED Gilroes Crematorium, Leicester. RANK Major.

CRUTCHLEY, Victor Alexander Charles (later Sir Victor) 365 BORN 2 November 1893, London. DIED 24 January 1986, Bridport, Dorset. BURIED St Mary's Churchyard, Dorset. RANK Admiral. O&D KCB, DSC.

CUBITT, William George 67 BORN 19 October 1835, Calcutta, India. DIED 25 January 1903, Camberley, Surrey. BURIED St Peter's Churchyard, Frimley, Surrey. RANK Colonel. O&D DSO.

CUMMING, Arthur Edward 414 BORN 18 June 1896, Karachi, India. DIED 10 April 1971, Edinburgh, Scotland. CREMATED Warriston Crematorium, Edinburgh. RANK Brigadier. O&D OBE, MC.

CUNNINGHAM, John (Corporal) 266 BORN 22 October 1890, Thurles, Co. Tipperary, Ireland. DIED 16 April 1917, from wounds received during VC action, near Barlin, France. BURIED Barlin Communal Cemetery, France.

CUNNINGHAM, John (Private) 260   BORN 28 June 1897, Scunthorpe, Humberside. DIED 21 February 1941, from tuberculosis, Kingston-upon-Hull, Humberside. BURIED Western Cemetery, Hull.

CUNNINGHAME, William James Montgomery (later Sir William) 26   BORN 20 May 1834, Ayr, Scotland. DIED 11 November 1897, Gunton, Suffolk. BURIED Kirkmichael Churchyard, Ayr. RANK Colonel.

CURREY, William Matthew 335   BORN 19 September 1895, Wallsend, New South Wales, Australia. DIED 30 April 1948, Sydney, Australia. CREMATED Woronora Crematorium, Sydney.

CURRIE, David Vivian 492   BORN 8 July 1912, Sutherland, Saskatchewan, Canada. DIED 24 June 1986, Ottawa, Ontario, Canada. BURIED Greenwood Cemetery, Ontario. RANK Lieutenant Colonel.

CURTIS, Albert Edward 169   BORN 6 January 1866, Guildford, Surrey. DIED 18 March 1940, North Barnet, Hertfordshire. BURIED Bells Hill Cemetery, Herts. Grave not marked. RANK Sergeant.

CURTIS, Henry 33   BORN 21 December 1823, Romsey, Hampshire. DIED 23 November 1896, Portsea, Hampshire. BURIED Kingston Cemetery, Portsea.

CURTIS, Horace Augustus 351   BORN 7 March 1891, St Anthony-in-Roseland, Cornwall. DIED 1 July 1968, Redruth, Cornwall. CREMATED Penmount Crematorium, Truro, Cornwall.

CURTIS, Philip Kenneth Edward 542   BORN 7 July 1926, Devonport, Devon. DIED 23 April 1951, during VC action, Castle Hill. BURIED United Nations Memorial Cemetery, Pusan, Korea.

CUTLER, Arthur Roden 408   BORN 24 May 1916, Manly, Sydney, Australia. DIED 21 February 2002, Sydney. BURIED South Head Cemetery, Vaucluse, Sydney. O&D AK, KCMG, KCVO, CBE.

DALTON, James Langley 122   BORN December 1832, London. DIED 8 January 1887, Port Elizabeth, South Africa. BURIED Russell Road RC Cemetery, Port Elizabeth.

DALZIEL, Henry 312   BORN 18 February 1893, Irvinebank, North Queensland, Australia. DIED 24 July 1965, Brisbane, Queensland. CREMATED Mount Thompson Crematorium, Brisbane. RANK Sergeant.

DANAHER, John 132   BORN 25 June 1860, Limerick, Ireland. DIED 9 January 1919, Portsmouth, Hampshire. BURIED Milton Cemetery, Portsmouth. RANK Sergeant.

DANCOX, Frederick George 290   BORN 1879, Worcester, Worcestershire. DIED 30 November 1917, Masnières, France. No known grave.

DANIEL, Edward St John 9   BORN 17 January 1837, Clifton, Bristol. DIED 20 May 1868, Hokitika, New Zealand. BURIED Hokitika Municipal Cemetery. RANK Lieutenant.

DANIELS, Harry 205   BORN 13 December 1884, Wymondham, Norfolk. DIED 13 December 1953, Leeds, Yorkshire. CREMATED Lawnswood Crematorium, Leeds. RANK Lieutenant Colonel. O&D MC.

D'ARCY, Henry Cecil Dudgeon 128   BORN 11 August 1850, Wanganui, New Zealand. DIED August 1881. He went missing from hospital and was found dead in a cave. His death was deemed possible suicide, Arnatola Forest, South Africa. BURIED King William's Town Cemetery, Cape Province. RANK Commandant.

DARTNELL, Wilbur Taylor 234   BORN 6 April 1885, Melbourne, Australia. DIED 3 September 1915, during VC action, Maktau, Kenya. BURIED Voi Cemetery, Kenya.

DARWAN SING NEGI 198   BORN 4 March 1883, Kabartir Village, India. DIED 24 June 1950, Kafarteer Village, India. CREMATED Kafarteer Village. RANK Subadar.

DAUNT, John Charles Campbell 59   BORN 8 November 1832, Autranches, Normandy, France. DIED 15 April 1886, Bristol. BURIED Redland Green Chapel Graveyard, Bristol. RANK Colonel.

DAVEY, Philip 312   BORN 10 October 1896, Goodwood, South Australia. DIED 21 December 1953, Springbank, South Australia. BURIED AIF Cemetery, Adelaide. O&D MM.

DAVIES, James Llewellyn 281   BORN 16 March 1886, Wyndham, Ogmore Vale, Glamorgan. DIED 31 July 1917, from wounds received during VC action, near Pilckem, Belgium. BURIED Canada Farm Cemetery, Belgium.

DAVIES, John Thomas 320   BORN 29 September 1896, Tranmere, Birkenhead. DIED 28 October 1955, St Helens, Lancashire. BURIED St Helens Borough Cemetery.

DAVIES, Joseph John 250   BORN 28 April 1889, Tipton, Staffordshire. DIED 16 February 1976, Bournemouth, Dorset. CREMATED Bournemouth Crematorium. RANK Staff Sergeant.

DAVIS, Gronow 39   BORN 16 May 1828, Clifton, Bristol. DIED 18 October 1891, Clifton. BURIED Arnos Vale Cemetery, Bristol. RANK Major General.

DAVIS, James 86   BORN February 1835, Edinburgh, Scotland. DIED 2 March 1893, Edinburgh. BURIED North Merchiston Cemetery. Grave not marked.

DAWSON, James Lennox 217   BORN 25 December 1891, Tillycoultry, Central Region, Scotland. DIED 15 February 1967, Eastbourne, Sussex. CREMATED Eastbourne Crematorium. RANK Colonel.

DAY, George Fiott 41   BORN 20 June 1820, Southampton, Hampshire. DIED 18 December 1876, Weston-super-Mare, Somerset. BURIED Weston-super-Mare Cemetery. RANK Captain. O&D CB.

DAY, Sidney James 271   BORN 3 July 1891, Norwich, Norfolk. DIED 17 July 1959, Portsmouth, Hampshire. BURIED Milton Cemetery.

DAYKINS, John Brunton 352   BORN 26 March 1883, Hawick, Scotland. DIED 24 January 1933. He left his house with a gun to investigate a noise and was subsequently found lying with a bullet wound to the head, Jedburgh, Scotland. BURIED Castlewood Cemetery, Jedburgh. RANK Sergeant. O&D MM.

DEAN, Donald John 343   BORN 19 April 1897, Herne Hill, London. DIED 9 December 1985, Sittingbourne, Kent. CREMATED Charing Crematorium, Kent. RANK Colonel. O&D OBE.

DEAN, Percy Thompson 365   BORN 20 July 1877, Blackburn, Lancashire. DIED 20 March 1939, London. CREMATED Golders Green Crematorium, London. RANK Lieutenant Commander.

DEASE, Maurice James 188   BORN 28 September 1889, Gaulstown, Co. Westmeath, Ireland. DIED 23 August 1914, during VC action at Mons, Belgium. BURIED St-Symphorien Military Cemetery, Mons.

DE L'ISLE, VISCOUNT, *see* Sidney, William Philip

DE MONTMORENCY, the Hon. Raymond Harvey Lodge Joseph 151   BORN 5 February 1867, Montreal, Canada. DIED 23 February 1900. He was killed in action whilst serving with the Corps of Scouts during the 2nd Boer War, Stormberg, South Africa. BURIED Molteno Cemetery, near Dordrecht, South Africa. RANK Captain.

DEMPSEY, Denis 57   BORN 1826, Rathmichael, Bray, Co. Dublin, Ireland. DIED 10 January 1886, Toronto, Canada. BURIED St Michael's Cemetery, Toronto.

DE PASS, Frank Alexander 199   BORN 26 April 1887, Kensington, London. DIED 25 November 1914. He was shot in the head by a sniper on the day after his VC action, Festubert, France. BURIED Béthune Town Cemetery, France.

DERRICK, Thomas Currie 440   BORN 20 March 1914, Berri, Murray River, South Australia. DIED 23 May 1945, as a result of wounds received in later action at Frida Knoll, Tarakan Island, Borneo. BURIED Labuan War Cemetery, Borneo. RANK Lieutenant. O&D DCM.

DEVINE, John, *see* Divane, John

DE WIND, Edmund 317   BORN 11 December 1883, Comber, Co. Down, Ireland. DIED 21 March 1918, during VC action, near Groagie, France. No known grave.

DIAMOND, Bernard 65   BORN January 1827, Port Glenone, Co. Antrim, Ireland. DIED 25 January 1892, Masterton, New Zealand. BURIED Masterton Cemetery.

DICK-CUNYNGHAM, William Henry 117   BORN 16 June 1851, Edinburgh. DIED 7 January 1900. He died from wounds received during the Battle of Ladysmith, Ladysmith, South Africa. BURIED Ladysmith Cemetery. RANK Lieutenant Colonel.

DICKSON, Collingwood 9   BORN 20 November 1817, Valenciennes, France. DIED 28 November 1904, London. BURIED Kensal Green Cemetery, London. RANK General. O&D GCB.

DIGBY-JONES, Robert James Thomas 165   BORN 27 September 1876, Edinburgh. DIED 6 January 1900, Waggon Hill, South Africa. BURIED Ladysmith Cemetery, South Africa.

DIMMER, John Henry Stephen 196   BORN 9 October 1883, Lambeth, London. DIED 21 March 1918, in action, Marteville, France. BURIED Vadencourt British Cemetery, France. RANK Lieutenant Colonel. O&D MC.

DINESEN, Thomas 330   BORN 9 August 1892, Copenhagen, Denmark. DIED 10 March 1979, Leerbaek, Denmark. BURIED Horsholm Cemetery, Ringsted, Denmark. RANK Lieutenant.

DIVANE (also known as DEVINE), John 55   BORN November 1823, Carrabane, Co. Galway, Ireland. DIED 1 December 1888, Penzance, Cornwall. BURIED Penzance Cemetery.

DIXON, Matthew Charles 28   BORN 5 February 1821, Avranches, Brittany, France. DIED 8 January 1905, Pembury, Kent. BURIED Kensal Green Cemetery, London. RANK Major General. O&D CB.

DOBSON, Claude Congreve 374   BORN 1 January 1885, Bristol, Somerset. DIED 26 June 1940, Chatham, Kent. BURIED Woodlands Cemetery, Gillingham, Kent. RANK Rear Admiral. O&D DSO.

DOBSON, Frederick William 194   BORN 9 November 1886, Ovingham, Northumberland. DIED

13 November 1935, Newcastle upon Tyne. BURIED Ryton and Crawcrook Cemetery, Co. Durham. RANK Lance Corporal.

DONNINI, Dennis 507 BORN 17 November 1925, Easington Colliery, Co. Durham. DIED 18 January 1945, during VC action, near Roermond, Holland. BURIED Sittard War Cemetery, Limburg, Holland.

DONOHOE, Patrick 65 BORN 1820, Nenagh, Co. Tipperary, Ireland. DIED 16 August 1876, Ashbourne, Co. Meath, Ireland. BURIED Donaghmore RC Churchyard, Co. Meath.

DOOGAN, John 133 BORN March 1853, Aughrim, Ireland. DIED 24 January 1940, Folkestone, Kent. BURIED Shorncliffe Military Cemetery, Folkestone.

DORRELL, George Thomas 193 BORN 7 July 1880, Paddington, London. DIED 7 January 1971, Cobham, Surrey. CREMATED Randall's Park Crematorium, Leatherhead, Surrey. RANK Lieutenant Colonel. O&D MBE.

DOUGALL, Eric Stuart 324 BORN 13 April 1886, Tunbridge Wells, Kent. DIED 14 April 1918, killed in action four days after VC action whilst directing fire, Kemmel, Belgium. BURIED Westoutre British Cemetery, Belgium. O&D MC.

DOUGHTY-WYLIE, Charles Hotham Montagu 222 BORN 23 July 1868, Theberton, Suffolk. DIED 26 April 1915, during VC action, Gallipoli. BURIED in solitary grave at Seddul Bahr near V Beach Cemetery, Gallipoli. O&D CB CMG.

DOUGLAS, Campbell Mellis 110 BORN 5 August 1840, Grosse Island, Canada. DIED 31 December 1909, Horrington, Somerset. BURIED Wells Cemetery, Somerset. RANK Surgeon-Lieutenant-Colonel.

DOUGLAS, Henry Edward Manning 163 BORN 11 July 1875, Gillingham, Kent. DIED 14 February 1939, Droitwich, Worcestershire. BURIED Epsom Cemetery, Surrey. RANK Major General. O&D CB, CMG, DSO.

DOUGLAS-HAMILTON, Angus Falconer 214 BORN 20 August 1863, Brighton, Sussex. DIED 26 September, during VC action, Loos, France. No known grave.

DOWELL, George Dare 36 BORN 15 February 1831, Chichester, Sussex. DIED 3 August 1910, Auckland, New Zealand. BURIED Purewa Cemetery, Auckland. RANK Brevet Lieutenant Colonel.

DOWLING, William 67 BORN 1825, Thomastown, Co. Kilkenny, Ireland. DIED 17 February 1887, Liverpool, Lancashire. BURIED Liverpool RC Cemetery, Liverpool. Grave not marked. RANK Sergeant.

DOWN, John Thornton 103 BORN 2 March 1842, Fulham, London. DIED 27 April 1866, Camp Otahuhu, New Zealand. BURIED Otahuhu Old Cemetery. Grave not marked.

DOWNIE, Robert 259 BORN 12 January 1894, Glasgow. DIED 18 April 1968, Glasgow. BURIED St Kentigern's Cemetery, Glasgow. O&D MM.

DOXAT, Alexis Charles 172 BORN 9 April 1867, Surbiton, Surrey. DIED 29 November 1942, Cambridge. BURIED City Cemetery, Cambridge. RANK Major.

DOYLE, Martin 337 BORN 25 October 1894, New Ross, Co. Wexford, Ireland. DIED 20 November 1940, Dublin. BURIED Grangegorman Cemetery, Dublin. O&D MM.

DRAIN, Job Henry Charles 191 BORN 15 October 1895, Barking, Essex. DIED 26 July 1975, Barking. BURIED Rippleside Cemetery, Barking. RANK Sergeant.

DRAKE, Alfred George 203 BORN 10 December 1893, Stepney, London. DIED 23 November 1915, during VC action, near La Brique, Belgium. BURIED La Brique Military Cemetery.

DRESSER, Tom 278 BORN 21 July 1892, Pickering, Yorkshire. DIED 9 April 1982, Middlesbrough, Cleveland. BURIED Thorntree Cemetery, Middlesbrough.

DREWRY, George Leslie 219 BORN 3 November 1894, Forest Gate, London. DIED 3 August 1918, aboard HMS *William Jackson*. A block fell from the end of a derrick and struck him on the head. He died shortly afterwards, Scapa Flow, Orkney Islands. BURIED City of London Cemetery, Manor Park, London. RANK Lieutenant.

DRUMMOND, Geoffrey Heneage 367 BORN 25 January 1886, St James's Place, London. DIED 21 April 1941, Rotherhithe, London. BURIED St Peter's Church Cemetery, Buckinghamshire. RANK Lieutenant Commander.

DUFFY, James 308 BORN 17 November 1889, Gweedore, Co. Donegal, Ireland. DIED 8 April 1969, Letterkenny, Co. Donegal. BURIED Conwal Cemetery, Letterkenny.

DUFFY, Thomas 72 BORN 1806, Caulry, Co. Westmeath, Ireland. DIED 24 December 1868, Dublin. BURIED Glasnevin Cemetery, Dublin. Grave not marked.

DUGDALE, Frederic Brooks 174   BORN 21 October 1877, Burnley, Lancashire. DIED 13 November 1902; whilst hunting, his horse fell at a fence and crushed him to death, Blakemore, Gloucestershire. BURIED Longborough Churchyard, Gloucestershire.

DUNBAR-NASMITH, Sir Martin 231   BORN 1 April 1883, East Barnes, London. DIED 29 June 1965, Elgin, Grampian Region, Scotland. BURIED Holy Trinity Churchyard, Elgin. RANK Admiral. O&D KCB, KCMG.

DUNDAS, James 107   BORN 12 September 1842, Edinburgh. DIED 23 December 1879, killed by a mine whilst trying to blow up an enemy fort, Sherpur Cantonment, Afghanistan. BURIED Seah Sang Cemetery, near Sherpur, Afghanistan. RANK Captain.

DUNLAY, John 77   BORN 1831, Douglas, Co. Cork, Ireland. DIED 17 October 1890, Cork. BURIED St Joseph's Cemetery, Cork.

DUNN, Alexander Roberts 15   BORN 15 September 1833, York, Ontario, Canada. DIED 25 January 1868. He was found lying dead beside his gun during a shooting trip. An inquiry found that his death was 'purely accidental', Senafe, Ethiopia. BURIED Military Cemetery, Senafe. RANK Colonel.

DUNSIRE, Robert 215   BORN 24 November 1891, East Wemyss, Fife Region, Scotland. DIED 30 January 1916, in action, near Mazingarde, France. BURIED Mazingarde Communal Cemetery. RANK Corporal.

DUNSTAN, William 227   BORN 8 March 1895, Ballarat, East Victoria, Australia. DIED 2 March 1957, Melbourne, Australia. CREMATED Springvale Crematorium, Melbourne. RANK Lieutenant.

DUNVILLE, John Spencer 266   BORN 7 May 1896, Marylebone, London. DIED 26 June 1917, as a result of wounds sustained during VC action, near Epehy, France. BURIED Villiers-Faucon Communal Cemetery.

DURRANT, Alfred Edward 172   BORN 4 November 1864, Westminster, London. DIED 29 March 1933, Tottenham, London. BURIED Tottenham Cemetery. RANK Lance Corporal. O&D ISM.

DURRANT, Thomas Frank 420   BORN 17 October 1918, Farnborough, Kent. DIED 28 March 1942, as a result of wounds received during VC action, German military hospital, St-Nazaire, France. BURIED Escoublac-la-Baule War Cemetery near St-Nazaire.

DWYER, Edward 206   BORN 25 November 1895, Fulham, London. DIED 3 September 1916, killed in action, Somme, France. BURIED Flatiron Copse Military Cemetery, France. RANK Corporal.

DWYER, John James (later the Hon.) 288   BORN 9 March 1890, Lovett, Port Cygnet, Tasmania, Australia. DIED 17 January 1962, Bruny Island, Tasmania. BURIED Allonah Cemetery, Hobart. RANK Lieutenant.

DYNON, Denis 59   BORN September 1822, Kilmannon, Queen's Co., Ireland. DIED 16 February 1863, Dublin. No known grave.

EARDLEY, George Harold 502   BORN May 1912, Congleton, Cheshire. DIED 11 September 1991, Congleton. CREMATED Macclesfield Crematorium, Cheshire. RANK Company Sergeant Major. O&D MM.

EDMONDSON, John Hurst 398   BORN 8 October 1914, Wagga Wagga, Australia. DIED 14 April 1942, during VC action, Tobruk, Libya. BURIED Tobruk War Cemetery.

EDWARDS, Alexander 281   BORN 4 November 1885, Morayshire, Scotland. DIED 24 March 1918. He was killed in action, Bapaume, Somme, France. No known grave.

EDWARDS, Frederick Jeremiah 257   BORN 3 October 1894, Queenstown, Co. Cork, Ireland. DIED 9 March 1964, Richmond, Surrey. BURIED Richmond Cemetery, Surrey. RANK Corporal.

EDWARDS, Hughie Idwal 409   BORN 1 August 1914, Perth, Western Australia. DIED 5 August 1982, Darling Point, New South Wales. CREMATED North Suburbs Crematorium, Sydney. RANK Air Commodore. O&D KCMG, CB, DSO, OBE, DFC.

EDWARDS, Thomas 136   BORN 19 April 1863, Brill, Buckinghamshire. DIED 27 March 1952, Woodford Bridge, Essex. BURIED St Mary's Churchyard, Chigwell, Essex. Grave not marked.

EDWARDS, Wilfred 283   BORN 16 February 1894, Norwich, Norfolk. DIED 2 January 1972, Leeds, Yorkshire. BURIED Upper and Lower Wortley Cemetery, Leeds. RANK Major.

EDWARDS, William Mordaunt Marsh 138   BORN 7 May 1855, Hardingham, Norfolk. DIED 17 September 1912, Hardingham. BURIED St George's Churchyard, Hardingham. RANK Major.

EGERTON, Ernest Albert 286   BORN 10 November 1897, Longton, Staffordshire. DIED 14 February 1966, Blythe Bridge, Staffordshire. BURIED St Peter's Churchyard. RANK Sergeant.

ELCOCK, Roland Edward 351 BORN 5 June 1899, Wolverhampton, Staffordshire. DIED 6 October 1944, Dehra Dun, India. BURIED St Thomas's Churchyard, Dehra Dun. RANK Major. O&D MM.

ELLIOTT, Keith 427 BORN 25 April 1916, Apiti, New Zealand. DIED 7 October 1989, Lower Hutt, North Island, New Zealand. BURIED Paraparaumu Cemetery, Lower Hutt.

ELLIOTT-COOPER, Neville Bowes 296 BORN 22 January 1889, London. DIED 11 February 1918, as a result of wounds received during VC action whilst a prisoner of war, Hanover, Germany. BURIED Hamburg Cemetery. O&D DSO, MC.

ELPHINSTONE, Howard Craufurd 33 BORN 12 December 1829, Sunzel, near Riga, Russia. DIED 8 March 1890. He was swept overboard and drowned whilst a passenger on board a steamer to New Zealand, at sea, near Ushant, Bay of Biscay. Body never found. RANK Major General. O&D KCB (Civ), CMG, CB (Mil).

ELSTOB, Wilfrith 317 BORN 8 September 1888, Chichester, Sussex. DIED 21 March 1918, during VC action, near St Quentin, France. No known grave. O&D DSO, MC.

ELTON, Frederic Cockayne 28 BORN 23 April 1832, Whitestaunton, Somerset. DIED 24 March 1888, London. BURIED St Andrew's Parish Churchyard, Whitestaunton. RANK Lieutenant Colonel.

EMERSON, James Samuel 298 BORN 3 August 1895, Collon, Co. Louth, Ireland. DIED 6 December 1917, during VC action, near La Vacquerie, France. No known grave.

ENGLEHEART, Henry William 170 BORN 14 November 1863, Blackheath, London. DIED 9 August 1939, Datchet, Berkshire. CREMATED Woking Crematorium, Surrey. RANK Quartermaster Sergeant.

ENGLISH, William John 175 BORN 6 October 1882, Cork, Ireland. DIED 4 July 1941, at sea off Egypt. BURIED Maala Christian Cemetery, Aden, Yemen. RANK Lieutenant Colonel.

ERSKINE, John 240 BORN 13 January 1894, Dunfermline, Scotland. DIED 14 April 1917, in action, Arras, France. No known grave.

ERVINE-ANDREWS, Harold Marcus 388 BORN 29 July 1911, Keadue, Co. Cavan, Ireland. DIED 30 March 1995, Gorran, Cornwall. CREMATED Glynn Valley Crematorium, Cornwall. RANK Lieutenant Colonel.

ESMONDE, Eugene 415 BORN 1 March 1909, Thurgoland, Wortley, Yorkshire. DIED 12 February 1942, during VC action, Straits of Dover. BURIED Woodlands Cemetery, Gillingham, Kent. O&D DSO.

ESMONDE, Thomas 34 BORN 25 May 1829, Pembrokestown, Co. Waterford, Ireland. DIED 14 January 1873, Bruges, Belgium. BURIED Town Cemetery, Bruges. RANK Lieutenant Colonel.

EVANS, Arthur Walter (also known as SIMPSON, Walter) 338 BORN 8 April 1891, Everton, Liverpool. DIED 1 November 1936, Sydney, Australia. CREMATED North Suburbs Crematorium, Sydney. RANK Sergeant. O&D DCM.

EVANS, Lewis Pugh 289 BORN 3 January 1881, Abermadd, Dyfed. DIED 30 November 1962, Paddington, London. BURIED Llanbadarn Churchyard, Cardiganshire. RANK Brigadier General. O&D CB, CMG, DSO and bar.

EVANS, Samuel 28 BORN 1821, Paisley, Scotland. DIED 4 October 1901, Edinburgh. BURIED Morningside Cemetery, Edinburgh.

EVANS, William John George 251 BORN 16 February 1876, Kensington, London. DIED 28 September 1937, Annerley, London. BURIED Elmers End Cemetery, Beckenham, London.

FARMER, Donald Dickson 173 BORN 28 May 1877, Kelso, Scotland. DIED 23 December 1956, Liverpool, Lancashire. CREMATED Anfield Crematorium, Liverpool. RANK Lieutenant Colonel.

FARMER, Joseph John 133 BORN 5 May 1855, Clerkenwell, London. DIED 30 June 1930, Northwood, Middlesex. BURIED Brompton Cemetery, London. RANK Corporal. O&D MSM.

FARQUHARSON, Francis Edward Henry 84 BORN 25 March 1837, Glasgow. DIED 12 September 1875, Harberton, near Totnes, Devon. BURIED St Peter's Churchyard, Harberton. RANK Major.

FARRELL, John 15 BORN March 1826, Dublin. DIED 31 August 1865, Secunderabad, India. BURIED Secunderabad Cemetery. Grave not marked. RANK Quartermaster Sergeant.

FAULDS, William Frederick 250 BORN 19 February 1895, Cradock, Cape Province, South Africa. DIED 16 August 1950, Salisbury, Rhodesia (Harare, Zimbabwe). BURIED Pioneer Cemetery, Harare. RANK Captain. O&D MC.

FAZAL DIN 521 BORN 1 July 1921, Husain Pur, Hoshiarpur District, Punjab, India. DIED 2 March

1945, as a result of wounds received during VC action, near Pakokku, Meiktila, Burma. No known grave.

FEGEN, Edward Stephen Fogarty 396   BORN 8 October 1891, Southsea, Hampshire. DIED 5 November 1940, assumed drowned during VC action. Body not recovered. O&D SGM.

FFRENCH, Alfred Kirke 77   BORN 25 February 1835, Meerut, India. DIED 29 December 1872, Chiswick, London. BURIED Brompton Cemetery, London. RANK Captain.

FIELDING, John, *see* Williams, John.

FINCASTLE, Alexander Edward Murray, Viscount 147   BORN 22 April 1871, Portland Place, London. DIED 29 January 1962, Paddington, London. CREMATED Golders Green Crematorium, London. RANK Major. O&D DSO, MVO.

FINCH, Norman Augustus 365   BORN 26 December 1890, Handsworth, Birmingham. DIED 15 March 1966, Portsmouth, Hampshire. CREMATED Portchester Crematorium, Hampshire. RANK Lieutenant and Quartermaster. O&D MSM.

FINDLATER, George 148   BORN 15 February 1872, Forgue, Grampian. DIED 4 March 1942, Cairnhill Forglen, Grampian. BURIED Forglen Cemetery, near Turriff. RANK Pipe-Major.

FINDLAY, George de Cardonnel Elmsall 355   BORN 20 August 1889, Balloch, Dunbartonshire, Scotland. DIED 26 June 1967, Helensburgh, Renfrewshire. BURIED Kilmaranock Churchyard, Helensburgh. RANK Colonel. O&D MC and bar.

FINLAY, David 210   BORN 25 January 1893, Guardbridge, Scotland. DIED 21 January 1916, in action at Battle of Karma, Mesopotamia. No known grave. RANK Sergeant.

FIRMAN, Humphrey Osbaldston Brooke 238   BORN 24 November 1886, Kensington, London. DIED 25 April 1916, during VC action, near Kut, Mesopotamia. No known grave.

FIRTH, James 169   BORN 15 January 1874, Sheffield, Yorkshire. DIED 29 May 1921, Sheffield. BURIED Burngreave Cemetery, Sheffield.

FISHER, Frederick 207   BORN 3 August 1894, St Catherine's, Ontario, Canada. DIED 24 April 1915, during VC action, St-Julien, Belgium. No known grave.

FITZCLARENCE, Charles 160   BORN 8 May 1865, Bishopscourt, Ireland. DIED 12 November 1914. He died in action, Polygon Wood, Belgium. No known grave. RANK Brigadier General.

FITZGERALD, Richard 66   BORN December 1831, St Finbars, Cork, Ireland. DIED 1884, India. No known grave.

FITZGIBBON, Andrew 100   BORN 13 May 1845, Gujerat, India. DIED 7 March 1883, Delhi, India. BURIED Old Delhi Military Cemetery. Grave not marked. RANK Apothecary.

FITZPATRICK, Francis 130   BORN 1859, Tullycorbet, Ireland. DIED 10 July 1933, Glasgow. BURIED St Kentigern's Cemetery, Glasgow. Grave not marked.

FLAWN, Thomas 130   BORN 22 December 1857, Finedon, Northamptonshire. DIED 19 January 1925, Plumstead, Kent. BURIED Plumstead Cemetery.

FLEMING-SANDES, Arthur James Terence 216   BORN 24 June 1894, Tulse Hill Park, London. DIED 24 May 1961, Romsey, Hampshire. CREMATED Torquay Crematorium, Devon. RANK Major.

FLINN, Thomas 73   BORN August 1832, Athlone, Co. Westmeath, Ireland. DIED 10 August 1892, Athlone. BURIED Cornamagh RC Cemetery, near Athlone.

FLOWERDEW, Gordon Muriel 322   BORN 2 January 1885, Scole, Norfolk. DIED 31 March 1918, in a field hospital from wounds received during VC action, Moreuil, France. BURIED Namps-au-Val British Cemetery, France.

FOOTE, Henry Robert Bowreman 425   BORN 5 December 1904, Ishapur, Bengal, India. DIED 22 November 1993, Pulborough Hospital, Sussex. BURIED St Mary's Churchyard, West Chiltington, Sussex. RANK Major General. O&D CB, DSO.

FOOTE, John Weir 431   BORN 5 May 1904, Ontario, Canada. DIED 2 May 1988, Norwood, Ontario. BURIED St Andrew's Presbyterian Churchyard, Coburg, Ontario. RANK Major.

FORBES-ROBERTSON, James 325   BORN 7 July 1884, Strathpeffer, Ross and Cromarty, Scotland. DIED 5 August 1955, Bourton-on-the-Water, Gloucestershire. BURIED Cheltenham Borough Cemetery. RANK Brigadier General. O&D DSO and bar, MC.

FORREST, George 49   BORN 1800, Dublin. DIED 3 November 1859, Dehra Dun, India. BURIED Dehra Dun Cemetery. RANK Captain.

FORSHAW, William Thomas 226   BORN 20 April 1890, Barrow-in-Furness, Cumbria. DIED 26 May 1943, Holyport, Berkshire. BURIED Touchen End Cemetery, Bray, near Maidenhead. RANK Major.

FORSYTH, Samuel 333   BORN 3 April 1891, Wellington, New Zealand. DIED 24 August 1918, during VC action, Grevillers, France. BURIED Adanac Military Cemetery, France.

FOSBERY, George Vincent 105 BORN 1833, Stert, Wiltshire. DIED 8 May 1907, Bath, Avon. BURIED St Mary's Cemetery, Bath. RANK Colonel.

FOSS, Charles Calveley 205 BORN 8 March 1885, Kobe, Japan. DIED 9 April 1953, London. BURIED West Hill Cemetery, Hampshire. RANK Brigadier. O&D DSO.

FOSTER, Edward 266 BORN 4 February 1886, Streatham, London. DIED 22 January 1946, Tooting, London. BURIED Streatham Cemetery.

FOWLER, Edmund John 128 BORN 1861, Waterford, Ireland. DIED 26 March 1926, Colchester, Essex. BURIED Colchester Cemetery. RANK Colour Sergeant.

FRASER, Charles Crauford 93 BORN 31 August 1829, London. DIED 7 June 1895, London. BURIED Brompton Cemetery, London. RANK Lieutenant General. O&D KCB.

FRASER, Ian Edward 534 BORN 18 December 1920, Ealing, London. RANK Lieutenant Commander. O&D DSC, RD and bar.

FREEMAN, John 82 BORN 1833, Sittingbourne, Kent. DIED 1 July 1913, Hackney, London. BURIED Abney Park Cemetery, Stoke Newington, London.

FRENCH, John Alexander 432 BORN 15 July 1914, Crows Nest, Queensland, Australia. DIED 4 September 1942, during VC action, Milne Bay, New Guinea. BURIED Port Moresby War Cemetery, Papua New Guinea.

FREYBERG, Bernard Cyril 260 BORN 21 March 1889, Richmond, Surrey. DIED 4 July 1963, Windsor, Berkshire. BURIED St Martha's Churchyard, Chilworth, Surrey. RANK Lieutenant General. O&D GCMG, KCB, KBE, DSO and three bars.

FRICKLETON, Samuel 279 BORN 1 April 1891, Stirlingshire, Scotland. DIED 6 September 1971, near Wellington, New Zealand. BURIED Taita Servicemen's Cemetery. RANK Captain.

FRISBY, Cyril Hubert 344 BORN 17 September 1885, New Barnet, Hertfordshire. DIED 10 September 1961, Guildford, Surrey. BURIED Brookwood Cemetery, Woking, Surrey.

FULLER, Wilfred Dolby 205 BORN 28 July 1893, East Kirby, Nottinghamshire. DIED 22 November 1947, Frome, Somerset. BURIED Christchurch Churchyard, Frome. RANK Corporal.

FULLER, William Charles 193 BORN 13 March 1884, Laugharne, Wales. DIED 29 December 1974, Swansea. BURIED Oystermouth Cemetery, the Mumbles, Glamorgan. RANK Sergeant.

FURNESS, the Hon. Christopher 387 BORN 17 May 1912, London. DIED 24 May 1940, during VC action, near Arras, France. No known grave.

FYNN, James Henry 237 BORN 24 November 1893, Truro, Cornwall. DIED 30 March 1917, in action, near Baghdad, Mesopotamia. BURIED Baghdad. Location not known.

GABY, Alfred Edward 328 BORN 25 January 1892, Scotsdale, Tasmania, Australia. DIED 11 August 1918, shot dead by an enemy sniper three days after VC action, Villers-Bretonneux, France. BURIED Heath Cemetery, Harbonnières, France.

GAJE GHALE 436 BORN 1 August 1918, Barabak Village, Gorkha District, Nepal. DIED 28 March 2000, New Delhi. RANK Hon. Captain.

GANJU LAMA 469 BORN 22 July 1924, Sangmo, Busty, Sikkim, India. DIED 30 June 2000, Rabangla, Sikkim. RANK Hon. Captain. O&D MM.

GARDINER, George 27 BORN 1821, Gelwellen, Co. Down, Ireland. DIED 17 November 1891, Lifford, Co. Donegal, Ireland. BURIED Clouleigh Churchyard, Lifford. RANK Colour Sergeant. O&D DCM.

GARDNER, Philip John 401 BORN 25 December 1914, Sydenham, London. DIED 15 February 2003, Hove, East Sussex. CREMATED Hove Crematorium. O&D MC.

GARDNER, William 87 BORN 3 March 1821, Nemphlar, Lanarkshire, Scotland. DIED 24 October 1897, Bothwell, Lanarkshire. BURIED Bothwell Park Cemetery. RANK Sergeant. O&D MSM.

GARFORTH, Charles Ernest 190 BORN 23 October 1891, Willesden Green, London. DIED 1 July 1973, Beeston, Nottinghamshire. CREMATED Wilford Hill Crematorium, Nottingham. RANK Sergeant.

GARLAND, Donald Edward 385 BORN 28 June 1918, Ballinacor, Ireland. DIED 12 May 1940, during VC action, near Maastricht, Holland. BURIED Heverlee War Cemetery, Belgium.

GARVIN, Stephen 52 BORN 1826, Cashel, Co. Tipperary, Ireland. DIED 23 November 1874, Chesterton, Cambridgeshire. BURIED Chesterton Parish Churchyard.

GEARY, Benjamin Handley 206 BORN 29 June 1891, Marylebone, London. DIED 26 May 1976, Niagara-on-the-Lake, Canada. BURIED St Mark's Church Cemetery, Niagara-on-the-Lake. RANK Major.

GEE, Robert 296   BORN 7 May 1876, Leicester. DIED 2 August 1960, Perth, Western Australia. CREMATED Karrakata Crematorium, Perth. O&D MC.

GIAN SINGH 522   BORN 5 October 1920, Sahabpur Village, Nawashahr, Jullundur, Northern Punjab, India. DIED 6 October 1996, Nawashahr, Jullundur. CREMATED Jalandhar Cantt, near Jullundur. RANK Subadar Major.

GIBSON, Guy Penrose 451   BORN 12 August 1918, Simla, India. DIED 19 September 1944, killed when his aircraft crashed after a raid, Bergen-op-Zoom, Holland. BURIED Steenbergen-en-Kruisland RC Churchyard, Holland. O&D DSO and bar, DFC and bar.

GIFFORD, Lord Edric Frederick 112   BORN 5 July 1849, Ampney Park, Wiltshire. DIED 5 June 1911, Chichester, Sussex. BURIED Fairfield Road Cemetery, Bosham, Sussex. RANK Major.

GILL, Albert 251   BORN 8 September 1879, Birmingham. DIED 27 July 1916, during VC action, Delville Wood, Somme, France. BURIED Delville Wood Cemetery, Albert, France.

GILL, Peter 51   BORN September 1831, Dublin. DIED 24 October 1868, Morar, India. BURIED Artillery Lines Cemetery, Gwalior, India. Grave not marked. RANK Lieutenant and Barrack-Master.

GLASOCK, Horace Henry 167   BORN 16 October 1880, Islington, London. DIED 20 October 1920, Cape Town, South Africa. BURIED Maitland Road No. 4 Cemetery, Cape Town.

GOATE, William 84   BORN 12 January 1836, Fritton, Norfolk. DIED 26 October 1901, Southsea, Hampshire. BURIED Highland Road Cemetery, Southsea. Stone dedicated November 2003. RANK Corporal.

GOBAR SING NEGI 204   BORN 7 October 1893, Tehri, India. DIED 10 March 1915, during VC action, Neuve-Chapelle, France. No known grave.

GOBIND SINGH 297   BORN 7 December 1887, Damoe Village, Jodhpur, India. DIED 9 December 1942, Nagaur, Rajputana, India. CREMATED Damoe Village. RANK Jemadar.

GODLEY, Sidney Frank 190   BORN 14 August 1889, East Grinstead, Sussex. DIED 29 June 1957, Epping, Essex. BURIED St John's Churchyard, Loughton, Essex.

GOOD, Herman James 328   BORN 29 November 1887, South Bathurst, New Brunswick, Canada. DIED 18 April 1969, Bathurst. BURIED St Alban's Cemetery, Bathurst.

GOODFELLOW, Charles Augustus 94   BORN 29 November 1836, Essex. DIED 1 September 1915, Royal Leamington Spa, Warwickshire. BURIED Royal Leamington Spa Cemetery. RANK Lieutenant General. O&D CB.

GOODLAKE, Gerald Littlehales 20   BORN 14 May 1832, Wadley, Berkshire. DIED 5 April 1890, Denham, Middlesex. BURIED St Mary the Virgin Churchyard, Harefield, Middlesex. RANK Lieutenant General.

GORDON, Bernard Sidney 333   BORN 16 August 1891, Launceston, Tasmania. DIED 19 October 1963, Torquay, Queensland. CREMATED Mount Thompson Crematorium, Queensland. O&D MM.

GORDON, James Heather 409   BORN 7 March 1909, Rockingham, Western Australia. DIED 24 July 1986, Perth, Western Australia. CREMATED Karrakatta Crematorium, Perth. RANK Warrant Officer Class II.

GORDON, William Eagleson 171   BORN 4 May 1866, Bridge of Allan, Scotland. DIED 10 March 1941, London. BURIED St Alban's Churchyard, Hindhead, Surrey. RANK Colonel. O&D CBE.

GORDON, William James 141   BORN 19 May 1864, Jamaica. DIED 15 August 1922, Jamaica. BURIED Up Park Camp Military Cemetery, Jamaica. RANK Sergeant.

GORE-BROWNE, Henry George 68   BORN 30 September 1830, Newton, Roscommon, Ireland. DIED 15 November 1912, Shanklin, Isle of Wight. BURIED St Mary the Virgin Churchyard, Brook, Isle of Wight. RANK Colonel.

GORLE, Robert Vaughan 314   BORN 6 May 1896, Southsea, Hampshire. DIED 11 January 1937, of pneumonia, Durban, Natal, South Africa. BURIED Stella Wood Cemetery, Durban.

GORMAN, James 21   BORN 21 August 1834, Islington, London. DIED 18 October 1882, Spectacle Island, Sydney, Australia. BURIED Balmain Cemetery, Norton Street, Balmain, Sydney. RANK Captain of the After Guard.

GORT, John Standish Surtees Prendergast Vereker, Viscount 344   BORN 10 July 1886, Portman Square, London. DIED 31 March 1946, London. BURIED St John the Baptist Church, Penshurst, Kent. RANK Field Marshal. O&D GCB, CBE, DSO and two bars, MVO, MC.

GOSLING, William 266   BORN 15 August 1892, Wanborough, Wiltshire. DIED 12 February 1945, Wroughton, Wiltshire. BURIED St John's and St Helen's Churchyard Cemetery, Wroughton. RANK Major.

GOUGH, Charles John Stanley 50 BORN 28 January 1832, Chittagong, India. DIED 6 September 1912, Clonmel, Co. Tipperary, Ireland. BURIED St Patrick's Cemetery, Clonmel. RANK General. O&D GCB.

GOUGH, Hugh Henry 76 BORN 14 November 1833, Calcutta, India. DIED 12 May 1909, London. BURIED Kensal Green Cemetery, London. RANK General. O&D GCB.

GOUGH, John Edmund 180 BORN 25 October 1871, Muree, Pakistan. DIED 22 February 1915. He was killed in action, Estaires, France. BURIED Estaires Communal Cemetery, France. RANK Brigadier General. O&D KCB, CMG.

GOULD, Thomas William 416 BORN 28 December 1914, Dover, Kent. DIED 6 December 2001, Peterborough, Cambridgeshire. CREMATED Peterborough Crematorium.

GOURLEY, Cyril Edward 271 BORN 19 January 1893, Liverpool, Lancashire. DIED 31 January 1982, Haslemere, Surrey. BURIED Grange Cemetery, West Kirby, Wirral, Cheshire. RANK Captain. O&D MM.

GOWRIE, EARL OF, *see* Hore-Ruthven, the Hon. Alexander Gore

GRADY, Thomas 12 BORN 18 September 1831, Cheddah, Co. Galway, Ireland. DIED 18 May 1891, Drysdale, Victoria, Australia. BURIED Melbourne General Cemetery, Victoria. RANK Sergeant. O&D DCM.

GRAHAM, Gerald 34 BORN 27 June 1831, Acton, London. DIED 17 December 1899, Bideford, Devon. BURIED East-the-Water Cemetery, Bideford. RANK Lieutenant General. O&D GCB, GCMG.

GRAHAM, John Reginald Noble (later Sir Reginald) 303 BORN 17 September 1892, Calcutta, India. DIED 6 December 1980, Edinburgh. CREMATED Morton Hall Crematorium, Edinburgh. RANK Lieutenant Colonel. O&D OBE.

GRAHAM, Patrick 82 BORN 1837, Dublin, Ireland. DIED 3 June 1875, Dublin. BURIED Arbour Hill Cemetery, Dublin. Grave not marked.

GRANT, Charles James William 140 BORN 14 October 1861, Bourtie, Scotland. DIED 23 November 1932, Sidmouth, Devon. BURIED Temple Road Cemetery, Sidmouth. RANK Brevet Colonel.

GRANT, John Duncan 183 BORN 28 December 1877, Roorkee, India. DIED 20 February 1967, Tunbridge Wells, Kent. CREMATED Tunbridge Wells Crematorium. RANK Colonel. O&D CB, DSO.

GRANT, John Gilroy 335 BORN 26 August 1889, Hawera, New Zealand. DIED 25 November 1970, Auckland, New Zealand. BURIED Golders Cemetery, Waikumete, New Zealand. RANK Lieutenant.

GRANT, Peter 77 BORN 1824, Ireland. DIED 10 January 1868, Dundee, Scotland. BURIED Eastern Necropolis, Dundee. Grave not marked.

GRANT, Robert 70 BORN 1837, Harrogate, Yorkshire. DIED 7 March 1867, Islington, London. BURIED Highgate Cemetery, London.

GRATWICK, Percival Eric 429 BORN 19 October 1902, Katanning, Western Australia. DIED 25–26 October 1942, during VC action, Miteiriya Ridge, El Alamein, Egypt. BURIED El Alamein War Cemetery.

GRAY, Robert Hampton 535 BORN 2 November 1917, Trail, British Columbia, Canada. DIED 9 August 1945, during VC action, Onagawa Bay, Honshu, Japan. Body not recovered. O&D DSC.

GRAY, Thomas 385 BORN 17 May 1914, Urchfont, Wiltshire. DIED 12 May 1940, during VC action, near Maastricht, Holland. BURIED Heverlee War Cemetery, Belgium.

GRAYBURN, John Hollington 497 BORN 30 January 1918, Manora Island, Karachi Harbour, India. DIED 20 September 1944, during VC action, Lek Bridge, Arnhem, Holland. BURIED Arnhem Oosterbeek War Cemetery.

GREAVES, Fred 289 BORN 16 May 1890, Killmarsh, Derbyshire. DIED 11 June 1973, Brimington, Derbyshire. CREMATED Brimington Crematorium. RANK Sergeant.

GREEN, John Leslie 245 BORN 4 December 1888, Buckden, Cambridgeshire. DIED 1 July 1916, during VC action, Foncquevillers, France. BURIED Foncquevillers Military Cemetery.

GREEN, Patrick 56 BORN 1824, Ballinasloe, Co. Galway, Ireland. DIED 19 July 1889, Cork, Ireland. BURIED Aghada Cemetery, Co. Cork. RANK Colour Sergeant.

GREENWOOD, Harry 352 BORN 25 November 1881, Windsor, Berkshire. DIED 5 May 1948, Wimbledon, London. BURIED Putney Vale Cemetery, London. O&D DSO and bar, OBE, MC.

GREGG, Milton Fowler (later the Hon. Milton) 345 BORN 10 April 1892, Snider Mountain, King's County, New Brunswick, Canada. DIED 13 March 1978, Fredericton, New Brunswick. BURIED Snider Mountain Baptist Church Cemetery. RANK Brigadier. O&D CBE, MC and bar.

HALLIDAY, Lewis Stratford Tollemache 155   BORN 14 May 1870, Medstead, Hants. DIED 9 March 1966, Dorking, Surrey. Ashes buried Medstead Churchyard, Surrey. RANK Lieutenant General. O&D KCB.

HALLIWELL, Joel 311   BORN 29 December 1881, Middleton, Lancashire. DIED 14 June 1958, Oldham, Lancashire. BURIED Boarshaw New Cemetery, Middleton.

HALLOWES, Rupert Price 202   BORN 5 May 1881, Redhill, Surrey. DIED 1 October 1915. He was killed by a bomb which was accidentally dropped in his trench the day after his VC action, Hooge, Belgium. BURIED Bedford House Cemetery, Belgium. O&D MC.

HALTON, Albert 291   BORN 1 May 1893, Carnforth, Lancashire. DIED 24 July 1971, Westfield War Memorial Village, Lancaster. CREMATED Lancaster and Morecambe Crematorium.

HAMILTON, John Brown 287   BORN 26 August 1896, Dumbarton, Scotland. DIED 18 July 1973, East Kilbride, Scotland. CREMATED Daldowie Crematorium, Glasgow. RANK Sergeant.

HAMILTON, John Patrick 227   BORN 24 January 1896, Orange, New South Wales, Australia. DIED 27 February 1961, Sydney, Australia. BURIED Woronora Cemetery, Sydney.

HAMILTON, Thomas de Courcy 29   BORN 20 July 1825, Stranraer, Scotland. DIED 3 March 1908, Cheltenham, Gloucestershire. BURIED Cheltenham Cemetery. RANK Major General.

HAMILTON, Walter Richard Pollock 117   BORN 18 August 1856, Inistioge, Ireland. DIED 3 September 1879. He was killed during the storming of the residency, Kabul, Afghanistan. BURIED in a garden near the residency. Grave not marked.

HAMMOND, Arthur George 117   BORN 28 September 1843, Dawlish, Devon. DIED 20 April 1919, Camberley, Surrey. BURIED St Michael's Churchyard, Camberley. RANK Brigadier General. O&D KCB, DSO.

HAMPTON, Harry 171   BORN 14 December 1870, Richmond, Surrey. DIED 2 November 1922, After being struck by a train, Twickenham, Middlesex. BURIED Richmond Cemetery. RANK Colour Sergeant.

HANCOCK, Thomas 52   BORN July 1823, Kensington, London. DIED 12 March 1871. He died in a workhouse, Westminster, London. BURIED Brompton Cemetery, London. Grave not marked. RANK Corporal.

HANNA, Robert Hill 269   BORN 6 August 1887, Aughnahoory, Co. Down, Ireland. DIED 15 June 1967, Mount Lehman, British Columbia, Canada. BURIED Masonic Cemetery, British Columbia. RANK Lieutenant.

HANNAH, John 392   BORN 27 November 1921, Paisley, Scotland. DIED 9 June 1947, Markfield Sanatorium, Leicestershire. BURIED St James's Churchyard, Bristall, Leicestershire.

HANSEN, Percy Howard 228   BORN 26 October 1890, Durban, South Africa. DIED 12 February 1951, Copenhagen. BURIED Garnisons Kirkegaard, Copenhagen. RANK Brigadier. O&D DSO, MC.

HARDEN, Henry Eric 508   BORN 23 February 1912, Northfleet, Kent. DIED 23 January 1945, during VC action, near Brachterbeek, Holland. BURIED Nederweert War Cemetery, Holland.

HARDHAM, William James 173   BORN 31 July 1876, Wellington, New Zealand. DIED 13 April 1928, Wellington. BURIED Karori Soldiers' Cemetery, Wellington. RANK Captain.

HARDING, Israel 137   BORN 21 October 1833, Portsmouth, Hampshire. DIED 11 May 1917, Billingshurst, Sussex. BURIED Highland Road Cemetery, Portsmouth. RANK Chief Gunner.

HARDY, Theodore Bailey 322   BORN 20 October 1863, Exeter, Devon. DIED 18 October 1918, from wounds sustained in a later action, Rouen, France. BURIED St-Sever Cemetery Extension, Rouen. O&D DSO, MC.

HARINGTON, Hastings Edward 76   BORN 9 November 1832, Hinton Parva, Wiltshire. DIED 20 July 1861, Agra, India. BURIED Agra Cemetery. RANK Captain.

HARMAN, John Pennington 467   BORN 20 July 1914, Beckenham, Kent. DIED 9 April 1944, during VC action, Kohima, India. BURIED Kohima War Cemetery.

HARPER, John William 502   BORN 6 August 1915, Doncaster, Yorkshire. DIED 29 September 1944, during VC action, Antwerp, Belgium. BURIED Leopoldsburg War Cemetery, Belgium.

HARRIS, Thomas James 330   BORN 30 January 1892, Halling, Kent. DIED 9 August 1918, during VC action, Morlancourt, France. BURIED Dernancourt Communal Cemetery Extension, France. O&D MM.

HARRISON, Arthur Leyland 365   BORN 3 February 1886, Torquay, Devon. DIED 23 April 1918, during VC action, Zeebrugge, Belgium. No known grave.

HARRISON, John (Leading Seaman) 81   BORN 24 January 1832, Castleborough, Co. Wexford, Ireland.

DIED 27 December 1865, London. BURIED Brompton Cemetery, London. RANK Boatswain's Mate and Petty Officer. O&D MC.

HARRISON, John (Second Lieutenant) 277   BORN 2 November 1890, Kingston-upon-Hull, Yorkshire. DIED 3 May 1917, during VC action, Oppy, France. No known grave.

HART, Reginald Clare 116   BORN 11 June 1848, Co. Clare, Ireland. DIED 10 October 1931, Bournemouth, Hampshire. BURIED Netherbury Churchyard Cemetery, Dorset. RANK General. O&D GCB, KCVO.

HARTIGAN, Henry 50   BORN March 1826, Drumlea, Co. Fermanagh, Ireland. DIED 29 October 1886, Calcutta, India. BURIED Barrackpore New Cemetery, Calcutta. Grave not marked. RANK Lieutenant.

HARTLEY, Edmund Barron 130   BORN 6 May 1847, Ivybridge, Devon. DIED 20 March 1919, Ash, Hampshire. BURIED Brookwood Cemetery, Woking, Surrey. RANK Colonel. O&D CMG.

HARVEY, Francis John William 243   BORN 19 April 1873, Sydenham, London. DIED 31 May 1916, during VC action, at sea off Jutland. BURIED at sea.

HARVEY, Frederick Maurice Watson 265   BORN 1 September 1888, Meath, Ireland. DIED 24 August 1980, Calgary, Canada. BURIED Union Cemetery, Alberta. RANK Brigadier. O&D MC.

HARVEY, Jack 339   BORN 24 August 1891, Peckham, London. DIED 15 August 1940, Redhill, Surrey. BURIED Redhill Cemetery. RANK Sergeant.

HARVEY, Norman 315   BORN 6 April 1899, Newton-le-Willows, Lancashire. DIED 16 February 1942, killed in an accident while serving with the Royal Engineers, Haifa, Palestine. BURIED Khayat Beach War Cemetery, Sharon, Israel. RANK Company Quartermaster Sergeant.

HARVEY, Samuel 216   BORN 17 September 1881, Basford, Nottinghamshire. DIED 23 September 1960, Stowmarket, Suffolk. BURIED Ipswich Old Cemetery in communal grave.

HAVELOCK (later HAVELOCK-ALLAN), Henry Marsham (later Sir Henry) 69   BORN 6 August 1830, Chinsurah, India. DIED 30 December 1897. He was shot dead by Afridis in the Khyber Pass whilst riding ahead of his escort, Ali-Masjid, India. BURIED Harley Street Cemetery, Rawalpindi, India. RANK Lieutenant General. O&D GCB.

HAWKER, Lanoe George 233   BORN 30 December 1890, Longparish, Hampshire. DIED 23 November 1916, killed in a dogfight by Baron Manfred von Richthofen, near Bapaume, France. No known grave. RANK Major. O&D DSO.

HAWKES, David 84   BORN 1822, Witham, Essex. DIED 14 August 1858, Fyzabad, India. No known grave.

HAWTHORNE, Robert 61   BORN 1822, Maghera, Ireland. DIED 2 February 1879, Manchester. BURIED Ardwick Cemetery, Manchester. Grave not marked.

HAYWARD, Reginald Frederick Johnson 317   BORN 17 June 1891, East Griqualand, South Africa. DIED 17 January 1970, Chelsea, London. CREMATED Putney Vale Crematorium, London. RANK Lieutenant Colonel. O&D MC and bar, ED.

HEAPHY, Charles 103   BORN 1821, St John's Wood, London. DIED 3 August 1881, Toowong, Queensland, Australia. BURIED Toowong Cemetery.

HEATHCOTE, Alfred Spencer 53   BORN 29 March 1832, London. DIED 21 February 1912, Bowral, New South Wales, Australia. BURIED Bowral Cemetery, New South Wales. RANK Captain.

HEATON, William Edward 172   BORN 1875, Ormskirk, Lancashire. DIED 5 June 1941, Southport, Lancashire. BURIED Ormskirk Parish Churchyard. RANK Sergeant.

HEAVISIDE, Michael Wilson 277   BORN 20 October 1880, Durham City, Co. Durham. DIED 26 April 1939, after a long illness due to gas poisoning during the war, Craghead, Co. Durham. BURIED St Thomas's Churchyard, Craghead.

HEDGES, Frederick William 353   BORN 6 June 1886, Umballa, India. DIED 29 May 1954. He committed suicide by hanging himself from the banisters in his house. He had been suffering from depression for a number of years and the anniversary of the death of his son, who had died during the Second World War, had just passed, Harrogate, Yorkshire. CREMATED Stonefall Crematorium, Harrogate.

HENDERSON, Arthur 276   BORN 6 May 1893, Paisley, Scotland. DIED 24 April 1917, in action the day after VC action, Fontaine-les-Croisilles, France. BURIED Cojeul British Cemetery, St-Martin-sur-Cojeul, France. O&D MC.

HENDERSON, Edward Elers Delaval 302   BORN 2 October 1878, Simla, India. DIED 25 January 1917, as a result of wounds received during VC action, River Hai near Kut, Mesopotamia. BURIED Amara War Cemetery, Mesopotamia.

HENDERSON, George Stuart 377 BORN 5 December 1893, East Gordon, Berwickshire. DIED 24 July 1920, during VC action, near Hillah, Mesopotamia. No known grave. O&D DSO and bar, MC.

HENDERSON, Herbert Stephen 143 BORN 30 March 1870, Hillhead, Glasgow. DIED 10 August 1942, Harare, Zimbabwe. BURIED Bulawayo Town Cemetery.

HENEAGE-WALKER, Clement (later known as WALKER-HENEAGE) 91 BORN 6 March 1831, Compton Bassett, Wiltshire. DIED 9 December 1901, Compton Bassett. BURIED St Swithun's Parish Church, Compton Bassett.

HENRY, Andrew 22 BORN 1 November 1823, Woolwich, London. DIED 14 October 1870, Plymouth, Devon. BURIED Ford Park Cemetery, Plymouth. RANK Captain.

HERRING, Alfred Cecil 319 BORN 26 October 1888, Tottenham, London. DIED 10 August 1966, Weybridge, Surrey. CREMATED Woking Crematorium. RANK Major.

HEWETT, William Nathan Wrighte 18 BORN 12 August 1834, Brighton, Sussex. DIED 13 May 1888, Portsmouth, Hampshire. BURIED Highland Road Cemetery, Portsmouth. RANK Vice Admiral. O&D KCB.

HEWITSON, James 326 BORN 15 October 1892, Coniston, Lancashire. DIED 2 March 1963, Ulverston, Cumbria. BURIED Coniston Churchyard. RANK Corporal.

HEWITT, Denis George Wyldbore 282 BORN 18 December 1897, Mayfair, London. DIED 31 July 1917, shortly after VC action, near St-Julien, Ypres, Belgium. No known grave.

HEWITT, William Henry 286 BORN 19 June 1884, Ipswich, Suffolk. DIED 7 December 1966, Cheltenham, Gloucestershire. CREMATED Cheltenham Crematorium. RANK Major.

HILL, Alan Richard (later HILL-WALKER) 133 BORN 12 July 1859, Northallerton, Yorkshire. DIED 21 April 1944, Thirsk, Yorkshire. BURIED Maunby Churchyard, Thirsk. RANK Major.

HILL, Albert 250 BORN 24 May 1895, Manchester. DIED 17 February 1971, Rhode Island, USA. BURIED Highland Memorial Park, Rhode Island.

HILL, Samuel 78 BORN 1826, Glenavy, Co. Antrim, Ireland. DIED 21 February 1863, Meerut, India. BURIED St John's Cemetery, Meerut. Grave not marked.

HILLS, James (later Sir James HILLS-JOHNES) 53 BORN 20 August 1833, Neechindipur, India. DIED 3 January 1919, Dolaucothy, Carmarthenshire. BURIED Caio Churchyard, Dyfed. RANK Lieutenant General. O&D GCB.

HILL-WALKER, Alan Richard, *see* Hill, Alan Richard

HINCKLEY, George 101 BORN 22 June 1819, Liverpool, Lancashire. DIED 31 December 1904, Plymouth, Devon. BURIED Ford Park Cemetery, Plymouth. RANK Quartermaster.

HINTON, John Daniel 405 BORN 17 September 1909, Riverton, New Zealand. DIED 28 June 1997, Christchurch, New Zealand. BURIED Ruru Lawn Cemetery, Christchurch.

HIRSCH, David Philip 276 BORN 28 December 1896, Leeds, Yorkshire. DIED 23 April 1917, during VC action, near Wancourt, France. No known grave.

HITCH, Frederick 122 BORN 29 November 1856, Edmonton, London. DIED 6 January 1913, Ealing, London. BURIED St Nicholas' Churchyard, Chiswick, London.

HOBSON, Frederick 268 BORN 23 September 1873, London. DIED 18 August 1917, during VC action, Lens, France. No known grave.

HODGE, Samuel 109 BORN c. 1840, Tortola, Virgin Islands. DIED 14 January 1868, Belize. BURIED Belize City Military Cemetery. Grave not marked. RANK Lance Corporal.

HOEY, Charles Ferguson 461 BORN 29 March 1914, Duncan, Vancouver Island, British Columbia, Canada. DIED 17 February 1944, as a result of wounds received during VC action, near Arakan, Burma. BURIED Taukkyan War Cemetery, Burma. O&D MC.

HOGAN, John 198 BORN 8 April 1884, Oldham, Lancashire. DIED 6 October 1943, Oldham. BURIED Chadderton Cemetery, Oldham.

HOLBROOK, Norman Douglas 197 BORN 9 July 1888, Southsea, Hampshire. DIED 3 July 1976, Steadham Mill, Sussex. BURIED St James' Churchyard, Midhurst, Sussex. RANK Commander.

HOLIWELL, James, *see* Hollowell, James

HOLLAND, Edward James Gibson 173 BORN 2 February 1878, Ottawa, Canada. DIED 18 June 1948, Cobalt, Ontario. CREMATED St James's Crematorium, Ontario. Ashes buried Prescott, Ontario. RANK Lieutenant Colonel.

HOLLAND, John Vincent 255 BORN 19 July 1889, Athy, Co. Kildare, Ireland. DIED 27 February 1975, Hobart, Tasmania, Australia. BURIED Cornelian Bay Cemetery, Hobart.

HOLLIS, George 92 BORN October 1833, Chipping Sodbury, Gloucestershire. DIED 16 May 1879, Exwick, Devon. BURIED Exwick Cemetery.

HOLLIS, Stanley Elton 489 BORN 21 September 1912, Middlesbrough, Yorkshire. DIED 8 February 1972, Liverton Miles, Cleveland. BURIED Acklam Cemetery, Middlesbrough.

HOLLOWELL, James (also known as HOLLIWELL) 72 BORN 1823, Lambeth, London. DIED 4 April 1876, Holborn, London. BURIED Brookwood Cemetery, Woking, Surrey. Grave not marked. He is named as 'Hulloway' in the cemetery register. RANK Lance Corporal.

HOLMES, Frederick William 192 BORN 27 September 1889, Bermondsey, London. DIED 22 October 1969, Port Augusta, Australia. CREMATED Stirling North Garden Cemetery, Port Augusta. RANK Captain.

HOLMES, Joel 70 BORN 1821, Great Comershall, Yorkshire. DIED 27 July 1872, Halifax, Yorkshire. BURIED All Souls' Cemetery, Halifax. Grave not marked.

HOLMES, Thomas William 292 BORN 14 October 1898, Montreal, Canada. DIED 4 January 1950, Toronto, Canada. BURIED Greenwood Cemetery, Ontario, Canada.

HOLMES, William Edgar 350 BORN 26 June 1895, Wood Stanway, Gloucestershire. DIED 9 October 1918, during VC action, Cattenières, France. BURIED Carnières Communal Cemetery Extension, France.

HOME, Anthony Dickson 72 BORN 30 November 1826, Dunbar, Scotland. DIED 10 August 1914, Kensington, London. BURIED Highgate Cemetery, London. RANK Surgeon-General. O&D KCB.

HOME, Duncan Charles 61 BORN 10 June 1828, Jubbulpore, Central Provinces, India. DIED 1 October 1857. He was killed by the premature explosion of a mine he was laying, Malagarth, India. BURIED Bolandsharh Cemetery, India.

HONEY, Samuel Lewis 345 BORN 9 February 1894, Conn, Wellington County, Ontario, Canada. DIED 30 September 1918, as a result of wounds received during VC action, Bourlon Wood, France. BURIED Quéant Communal Cemetery, British Extension, France. O&D DCM, MM.

HOOK, Alfred Henry 126 BORN 6 August 1850, Churcham, Gloucestershire. DIED 12 March 1905, Gloucester. BURIED St Andrew's Parish Churchyard, Churcham. RANK Sergeant.

HOPE, William 34 BORN 12 April 1834, Edinburgh. DIED 17 December 1909, Chelsea, London. BURIED Brompton Cemetery, London. RANK Colonel.

HORE-RUTHVEN, the Hon. Alexander Gore Arkwright (later Earl of Gowrie) 152 BORN 6 July 1872, Clewer, Berkshire. DIED 2 May 1955, Shipton Moyne, Gloucestershire. BURIED St John the Baptist Churchyard, Shipton Moyne. RANK Brigadier General. O&D CB, GCMG, DSO and bar.

HORLOCK, Ernest George 194 BORN 24 October 1885, Alton, Hampshire. DIED 30 December 1917, at sea off Egypt. BURIED Hadra War Memorial Cemetery, Egypt. RANK Battery Sergeant Major.

HORNELL, David Ernest 495 BORN 26 January 1910, Mimico, Ontario, Canada. DIED 24 June 1944, following VC action, north of the Shetland Islands, North Atlantic. BURIED Lerwick New Cemetery, Shetland Islands.

HORSFALL, Basil Arthur 321 BORN 4 October 1887, Colombo, Ceylon. DIED 27 March 1918, during VC action, near Ablainzeville, France. No known grave.

HORWOOD, Alec George 461 BORN 6 January 1914, Deptford, London. DIED 20 January 1944, during VC action, near Kyauchaw, Burma. Body not recovered. O&D DCM.

HOUSE, William 171 BORN 7 October 1879, Thatcham, Berkshire. DIED 28 February 1912, Dover, Kent. BURIED St James' Cemetery, Dover. RANK Lance Corporal.

HOWELL, George Julian 277 BORN 23 November 1893, Sydney, New South Wales. DIED 23 December 1963, Perth, Western Australia. CREMATED Karrakatta Crematorium, Hollywood. RANK Staff Sergeant. O&D MM.

HOWSE, Neville Reginald 171 BORN 26 October 1863, Stogursey, Somerset. DIED 19 September 1930, London. BURIED Kensal Green Cemetery, London. O&D KCB, KCMG.

HUDSON, Charles Edward 369 BORN 29 May 1892, Derby. DIED 4 April 1959, St Mary's, Scilly Isles. BURIED Denbury Churchyard, Devon. RANK Major General. O&D CB, DSO and bar, MC.

HUFFAM, James Palmer 335 BORN 31 March 1897, Dunblane, Perthshire, Scotland. DIED 16 February 1968, Burnt Oak, Middlesex. CREMATED Golders Green Crematorium, London. RANK Major.

HUGHES, Matthew 32 BORN 1822, Bradford, Yorkshire. DIED 9 January 1882, Bradford. BURIED Undercliffe Cemetery, Bradford. RANK Corporal.

HUGHES, Thomas 255 BORN 10 November 1885, Coravoo, Co. Monaghan, Ireland. DIED 4 January 1942, Fencairn, Co. Monaghan. BURIED Old Bloomfield Cemetery, Co. Monaghan. RANK Corporal.

HULL, Charles 218 BORN 24 July 1890, Harrogate, Yorkshire. DIED 13 February 1953, Leeds. BURIED Woodhouse Lane Cemetery (now University of Leeds). RANK Corporal.

HULME, Alfred Clive 405 BORN 24 January 1911, Dunedin, New Zealand. DIED 2 September 1982, Tauranga, New Zealand. BURIED Dudley Cemetery near Tauranga.

HUMPSTON, Robert 29 BORN 1832, Derby. DIED 22 December 1884, Derby. BURIED Nottingham General Cemetery. Grave not marked.

HUNTER, David Ferguson 341 BORN 28 November 1891, Kingseat, Dunfermline, Scotland. DIED 14 February 1965, Dunfermline. BURIED Dunfermline Cemetery. RANK Sergeant.

HUNTER, Thomas Peck 529 BORN 6 October 1923, Aldershot, Hampshire. DIED 3 April 1945, during VC action, Argenta Gap near Ravenna, Italy. BURIED Argenta Gap War Cemetery, Ravenna, Italy.

HUTCHESON, Bellenden Seymour 339 BORN 16 December 1883, Mount Carmel, Illinois, USA. DIED 9 April 1954, Cairo, Illinois. BURIED Rosehill Cemetery, Mount Carmel. O&D MC.

HUTCHINSON, James 241 BORN 8 July 1895, Radcliffe, Lancashire. DIED 21 January 1972, Torquay, Devon. CREMATED Torquay Crematorium. RANK Corporal.

HUTT, Arthur 289 BORN 12 February 1889, Coventry, Warwickshire. DIED 14 April 1964, Coventry. CREMATED Canley Crematorium, Coventry. RANK Corporal.

IND, Alfred Ernest 176 BORN 16 September 1872, Tetbury, Gloucestershire. DIED 29 November 1916, Eccleston, Cheshire. BURIED St Mary the Virgin Churchyard, Eccleston. RANK Farrier-Sergeant.

INGHAM, Samuel, *see* Meekosha, Samuel

INGOUVILLE, George 36 BORN 7 October 1826, St Saviour, Jersey. DIED 13 January 1869. Drowned at sea. Body never found.

INGRAM, George Mawby 349 BORN 18 March 1889, Bendigo, Victoria, Australia. DIED 30 June 1961, Hastings, Victoria. BURIED Frankston Cemetery, Victoria. O&D MM.

INKSON, Edgar Thomas 167 BORN 5 April 1872, Naini Tal, India. DIED 19 February 1947, Chichester, West Sussex. Ashes buried Brookwood Cemetery, Surrey. RANK Colonel. O&D DSO.

INNES, James John McLeod 83 BORN 5 February 1830, Baghalpur, Bengal, India. DIED 13 December 1907, Cambridge. BURIED City Cemetery, Cambridge. RANK Lieutenant General. O&D CB.

INSALL, Gilbert Stuart Martin 234 BORN 14 May 1894, Paris. DIED 17 February 1972, Monk's Hill, Scrooby, Yorkshire. CREMATED Rose Hill Crematorium, Doncaster. RANK Group Captain. O&D MC.

INWOOD, Reginald Roy 285 BORN 14 July 1890, Renmark, North Adelaide, South Australia. DIED 23 October 1971, St Peter's, Adelaide. BURIED AIF Cemetery, Adelaide. RANK Sergeant.

IRWIN, Charles 78 BORN 1824, Manorhamilton, Co. Leitrim, Ireland. DIED 8 April 1873, Newton Butler, Co. Fermanagh, Ireland. BURIED St Mark's Church of Ireland Churchyard, Agfhadrumsee, Co. Fermanagh.

ISHAR SINGH 376 BORN 30 December 1895, Nenwan, Hoshiarpur District, Punjab, India. DIED 2 December 1963, Nenwan. CREMATED Penam Village, Hoshiarpur District. RANK Captain.

JACKA, Albert 223 BORN 10 January 1893, Layard, Australia. DIED 17 January 1932, Melbourne, Australia. BURIED St Kilda Cemetery, Melbourne. RANK Captain. O&D MC and bar.

JACKMAN, James Joseph Bernard 401 BORN 19 March 1916, Glenageary, Co. Dublin. DIED 25 November 1941, killed the day after VC action, El Duda near Tobruk. BURIED Tobruk War Cemetery, Libya.

JACKSON, Harold 318 BORN 31 May 1892, Kirton, Lincolnshire. DIED 24 August 1918, in action, Thiepval, Somme, France. BURIED AIF Burial Ground, Flers, France.

JACKSON, Norman Cyril 485 BORN 8 April 1919, Ealing, London. DIED 26 March 1994, Hampton Hill, Middlesex. BURIED Percy Road Cemetery, Twickenham, Middlesex. RANK Warrant Officer.

JACKSON, Thomas Norman 345 BORN 11 February 1897, Swinton, Yorkshire. DIED 27 September 1918, during VC action, near Graincourt, France. BURIED Sanders Keep Military Cemetery, France.

JACKSON, William 241 BORN 13 September 1897, Gunbar, New South Wales, Australia. DIED 5 August 1959, Melbourne, Australia. CREMATED Springvale Crematorium, Melbourne.

JAMES, Manley Angell 317 BORN 12 July 1896, Odiham, Hampshire. DIED 23 September 1975,

Westbury on Trym, Bristol. CREMATED Canford Crematorium, Bristol. RANK Brigadier. O&D DSO, MC, MBE.

JAMES, Walter Herbert 226 BORN 13 November 1888, Ladywood, Birmingham. DIED 15 August 1958, Kensington, London. CREMATED West London Crematorium. RANK Major.

JAMIESON, David Auldgo 491 BORN 1 October 1920, Thornham, Norfolk. DIED 5 May 2001, Burnham Market, Norfolk. BURIED Burnham Norton Churchyard. RANK Major. O&D CVO.

JARRATT, George 277 BORN 22 July 1891, Kennington, London. DIED 3 May 1917, during VC action, near Pelves, France. No known grave.

JARRETT, Hanson Chambers Taylor 93 BORN 22 March 1839, Madras, India. DIED 11 April 1891, Saugor, India. BURIED Saugor New Cemetery. RANK Colonel.

JARVIS, Charles Alfred 190 BORN 29 March 1881, Fraserburgh, Scotland. DIED 19 November 1948, Dundee. BURIED St Monance Cemetery, Fife, Scotland.

JEE, Joseph 71 BORN 9 February 1819, Hartshill, Warwickshire. DIED 17 March 1899, Queniborough, Leicestershire. BURIED Ratcliffe Roman Catholic College Cemetery, Queniborough. RANK Deputy Surgeon-General. O&D CB.

JEFFERSON, Francis Arthur 477 BORN 18 August 1921, Ulverston, Lancashire. DIED 4 September 1982. Took his own life whilst suffering from depression after his VC was stolen, Oldham, Lancashire. CREMATED Overdale Crematorium, Bolton, Lancashire. RANK Lance Corporal.

JEFFRIES, Clarence Smith 291 BORN 26 October 1894, Newcastle, New South Wales, Australia. DIED 12 October 1917, during VC action, Hillside Farm, Passchendaele, Belgium. BURIED Tyne Cot Cemetery, Belgium.

JENNINGS, Edward 76 BORN 1820, Ballinrobe, Co. Mayo, Ireland. DIED 10 May 1889, North Shields, Northumberland. BURIED Preston Cemetery, North Shields.

JENSEN, Joergen Christian 265 BORN 15 January 1891, Loegstoer, Aalborg, Denmark. DIED 31 May 1922, as a result of wartime wounds, Adelaide, South Australia. BURIED West Terrace AIF Cemetery, Adelaide.

JEROME, Henry Edward 90 BORN 28 February 1830, Antigua, West Indies. DIED 25 February 1901, Bath, Somerset. BURIED Lansdown Cemetery, Bath. RANK Major General.

JERRARD, Alan 358 BORN 3 December 1897, Lewisham, London. DIED 14 May 1968, Lyme Regis, Dorset. CREMATED Exeter and Devon Crematorium, Exeter. RANK Flight Lieutenant.

JOHNSON, Dudley Graham 355 BORN 13 February 1884, Bourton-on-the-Water, Gloucestershire. DIED 21 December 1975, Fleet, Hampshire. BURIED Christ Church Churchyard, Church Crookham, Hampshire. RANK Major General. O&D CB, DSO and bar, MC.

JOHNSON, Frederick Henry 214 BORN 15 August 1890, Streatham, London. DIED 26 November 1917, in action, Cambrai, France. No known grave. RANK Major.

JOHNSON, James Bulmer 314 BORN 31 December 1889, Widdrington, Northumberland. DIED 23 March 1943, Plymouth, Devon. CREMATED Efford Crematorium, Plymouth.

JOHNSON, William Henry 348 BORN 15 October 1890, Worksop, Nottinghamshire. DIED 25 April 1945, Arnold, Nottinghamshire. BURIED Redhill Cemetery, Nottingham. O&D MM.

JOHNSTON, Robert 162 BORN 13 August 1872, Laputa, Ireland. DIED 24 March 1950, Kilkenny, Ireland. BURIED St Mary's Churchyard, Inistiogne, Ireland. RANK Major.

JOHNSTON, William Henry 193 BORN 21 December 1879, Leith, Scotland. DIED 8 June 1915, in action, Ypres, Belgium. BURIED Perth Cemetery, Zillebeke, Belgium. RANK Major.

JOHNSTONE, William (enlisted and served as John) 5 BORN 6 August 1823, Hanover, Germany. DIED 20 August 1857. BURIED at sea in the St Vincent Passage.

JONES, Alfred Stowell 50 BORN 24 January 1832, Liverpool, Lancashire. DIED 29 May 1920, Finchampstead, Berkshire. BURIED St James Churchyard, Finchampstead. RANK Lieutenant Colonel.

JONES, David 255 BORN 10 January 1891, Liverpool. DIED 7 October 1916, in action at Battle for Transloy Ridges, Somme, France. BURIED Bancourt British Cemetery, France.

JONES, Henry Mitchell 33 BORN 11 February 1831, Dublin. DIED 18 December 1916, Eastbourne, Sussex. BURIED Ocklynge Old Cemetery, Eastbourne.

JONES, Herbert 550 BORN 14 May 1940, Putney, London. DIED 28 May 1982, during VC action, on the slopes of Darwin Hill, Falkland Islands. BURIED Blue Beach War Cemetery, Port San Carlos, Falkland Islands. O&D OBE.

JONES, Loftus William 243 BORN 13 November 1879, Petersfield, Hampshire. DIED 31 May 1916, during VC action, at sea off Jutland. BURIED Kviberg Cemetery, Gothenburg, Sweden.

JONES, Richard Basil Brandram 239 BORN 30 April 1897, Brockley, London. DIED 21 May 1916, during VC action, near Vimy, France. No known grave.

JONES, Robert 126 BORN 19 August 1857, Tynewydd, Gwent. DIED 6 September 1898. He committed suicide, Madley, Hereford. BURIED St Peter's Churchyard, Peterchurch, Hereford.

JONES, Thomas Alfred 257 BORN 25 December 1880, Runcorn, Cheshire. DIED 30 January 1956, Runcorn. BURIED Runcorn Cemetery. O&D DCM.

JONES, William 126 BORN 1839, Evesham, Worcestershire. DIED 15 April 1913, Ardwick, Manchester. BURIED Philips Park Cemetery, Manchester.

JOTHAM, Eustace 217 BORN 28 November 1883, Kidderminster, Worcestershire. DIED 7 January 1915, during VC action, Spina Khaisora, India. BURIED Miranshar Cemetery.

JOYNT, William Donovan 332 BORN 19 March 1889, Elsterwick, Melbourne, Australia. DIED 5 May 1986, Windsor, Melbourne. BURIED Brighton Lawn Cemetery, Victoria. RANK Lieutenant Colonel.

JUDSON, Reginald Stanley 334 BORN 29 September 1881, Wharehine, New Zealand. DIED 26 August 1972, Auckland, New Zealand. BURIED Walkumete Cemetery, Auckland. RANK Major. O&D DCM, MM.

KAEBLE, Joseph 311 BORN 5 May 1893, Quebec, Canada. DIED 9 June 1918, during VC action, Neuville-Vitasse, France. BURIED Wanquentin Communal Cemetery Extension, France. O&D MM.

KAMAL RAM 476 BORN 17 December 1924, Bhalupura Village, Karauli State, India. DIED 1 July 1982, Bholupura. CREMATED Sawai Madhopur, Rajasthan, India. RANK Hon. Major.

KARAMJEET SINGH JUDGE 524 BORN 25 May 1923, Kapurthala State, India. DIED 18 March 1945, during VC action, Myingyan, near Meiktila, Burma. CREMATED at unknown location.

KARANBAHADUR RANA 357 BORN 20 December 1898, Litung, Baghlung District, Nepal. DIED 6 August 1973, Litung. BURIED Bharse Gulmi, Litung.

KAVANAGH, Thomas Henry 74 BORN 15 July 1821, Mullingar, Co. Westmeath, Ireland. DIED 13 November 1882, Gibraltar. BURIED North Front Cemetery, Gibraltar.

KEATINGE, Richard Harte 89 BORN 17 June 1825, Dublin, Ireland. DIED 24 May 1904, Horsham, Sussex. BURIED Hills Street Cemetery, Horsham. RANK Lieutenant General. O&D CSI.

KELLAWAY, Joseph 30 BORN 1 September 1824, Kingston, Dorset. DIED 2 October 1880, Chatham, Kent. BURIED Maidstone Road Cemetery, Chatham. RANK Chief Boatswain.

KELLIHER, Richard 438 BORN 1 September 1910, Ballybeggan, Tralee, Ireland. DIED 28 January 1963, Melbourne, Australia. BURIED Springvale Lawn Cemetery, Melbourne.

KELLS, Robert 66 BORN 7 April 1832, Meerut, India. DIED 14 April 1905, Lambeth, London. BURIED Lambeth Cemetery, London. Grave not marked. RANK Sergeant. O&D RVM.

KELLY, Henry 259 BORN 10 July 1887, Manchester. DIED 18 January 1960, Lancashire. BURIED Southern Cemetery, Manchester. RANK Major. O&D MC and bar.

KENEALLY, William Stephen 220 BORN 26 December 1886, Wexford, Ireland. DIED 29 June 1915, in action during Battle of Gully Ravine, Gallipoli. BURIED Lancashire Landing Cemetery, Gallipoli. RANK Sergeant.

KENNA, Edward 528 BORN 6 July 1919, Hamilton, Western Victoria, Australia.

KENNA, Paul Aloysius 151 BORN 16 August 1862, Liverpool, Lancashire. DIED 30 August 1915. He was killed by a sniper, Gallipoli, Turkey. BURIED Lala Baba Cemetery, Gallipoli. RANK Brigadier General. O&D DSO.

KENNEALLY, John Patrick (real name Leslie Robinson) 448 BORN 15 March 1921, Balsall Heath, Birmingham. DIED 27 September 2000, Rochford, Worcestershire. BURIED St Michael's and All Angels Churchyard, Rochford. RANK Company Quartermaster Sergeant

KENNEDY, Charles Thomas 173 BORN 6 January 1876, Edinburgh. DIED 24 April 1907, Edinburgh. BURIED North Merchiston Cemetery, Edinburgh.

KENNY, Henry Edward 214 BORN 27 July 1888, Hackney, London. DIED 6 May 1979. Chertsey, Surrey. CREMATED Woking Crematorium. RANK Sergeant.

KENNY, James 78 BORN 1824, Dublin. DIED 2 October 1862, Mooltan, India. BURIED Mooltan Cemetery. Grave not marked.

KENNY, Thomas 203 BORN 4 April 1882, South Wingate, Co. Durham. DIED 29 November 1948, Co. Durham. BURIED Wheatley Hill Cemetery, Co. Durham. RANK Lance Sergeant.

KENNY, Thomas James Bede 273 BORN 29 September 1896, Sydney, New South Wales, Australia. DIED 15 April 1953, Sydney. BURIED Botany Cemetery, Matraville, Sydney. RANK Corporal.

KENNY, William 195   BORN 24 August 1880, Drogheda, Ireland. DIED 10 January 1936,
Hammersmith, London. BURIED Brookwood Cemetery, Woking. RANK Drum-Major.

KENNY, William David 376   BORN 1 February 1899, Saintfield, Co. Down, Ireland. DIED 2 January
1920, during VC action, near Kot Kai, North-West Frontier, India. BURIED Jandola Cemetery,
Pakistan.

KER, Allan Ebenezer 318   BORN 5 March 1883, Edinburgh, Scotland. DIED 12 September 1958,
Hampstead, London. BURIED West Hampstead Cemetery. RANK Major.

KERR, George Fraser 345   BORN 8 June 1895, Deseronto, Ontario, Canada. DIED 8 December 1929,
overcome by carbon monoxide fumes while sitting in his car waiting for the engine to warm up,
Toronto. BURIED Mount Pleasant Cemetery, Toronto. RANK Captain. O&D MC and bar, MM.

KERR, John Chipman 257   BORN 11 January 1887, Fox River, Nova Scotia, Canada. DIED
19 February 1963, Port Moody, British Columbia, Canada. BURIED Mountain View Cemetery,
Vancouver.

KERR, William Alexander 56   BORN 18 July 1831, Melrose, Scotland. DIED 21 May 1919, Folkestone,
Kent. BURIED Cheriton Road Cemetery, Folkestone. RANK Captain.

KEYES, Geoffrey Charles Tasker 398   BORN 18 May 1917, Aberdour, Scotland. DIED 18 November
1941, during VC action, Sidi Rafa, Libya. BURIED Benghazi War Cemetery, Libya. O&D MC.

KEYSOR, Leonard Maurice 227   BORN 3 November 1885, Paddington, London. DIED 12 October
1951, Paddington. CREMATED Golders Green Crematorium, London. RANK Lieutenant.

KEYWORTH, Leonard James 212   BORN 12 April 1893, Lincoln. DIED 19 October 1915, from wounds
received in action, Noux-les-Mines, France. BURIED Abbeville Communal Cemetery, France.
RANK Corporal.

KHUDADAD KHAN 195   BORN 26 October 1888, Chakawl, India. DIED 8 March 1971, Rukhan Tehsil
Village, near Chakawl, Pakistan. BURIED Rukhan Village Cemetery. RANK Subadar.

KIBBY, William Henry 428   BORN 15 April 1903, Winlaton, Co. Durham. DIED 31 October 1942,
during VC action, Miteiriya Ridge, El Alamein, Egypt. BURIED El Alamein War Cemetery.

KILBY, Arthur Forbes Gordon 214   BORN 3 February 1885, East Hayes, Gloucestershire. DIED
25 September 1915, during VC action, near Cuinchy, France. BURIED Arras Road Cemetery, Loos,
France. O&D MC.

KINGSBURY, Bruce Steel 432   BORN 8 January 1918, Armadale, Melbourne, Australia. DIED
29 August 1942, during VC action, Isurava, New Guinea. BURIED Port Moresby War Cemetery,
Papua New Guinea.

KINROSS, Cecil John 292   BORN 13 July 1897, Clackmannan, Scotland. DIED 21 June 1957, Lougheed,
Alberta, Canada. BURIED Lougheed Cemetery.

KIRBY, Frank Howard 170   BORN 12 November 1871, Thame, Oxon. DIED 8 July 1956, Sidcup, Kent.
CREMATED Streatham Vale Crematorium. RANK Lieutenant Colonel. O&D CBE, DCM.

KIRK, James 355   BORN 27 January 1897, Cheadle Hulme, Cheshire. DIED 4 November 1918, during
VC action, Oise Canal near Ors, France. BURIED Ors Communal Cemetery, France.

KIRK, John 51   BORN July 1827, Liverpool, Lancashire. DIED 31 August 1865, Liverpool. BURIED
Liverpool Cemetery.

KNIGHT, Alfred Joseph 287   BORN 24 August 1888, Ladywood, Birmingham. DIED 4 December 1960,
Edgbaston, Birmingham. BURIED Oscott College Road Cemetery. RANK Second Lieutenant.
O&D MBE.

KNIGHT, Arthur George 313   BORN 26 June 1886, Haywards Heath, Sussex. DIED 3 September 1918,
in a field hospital from wounds received during VC action, Hendescourt, France. BURIED
Dominion Cemetery, France. RANK Sergeant.

KNIGHT, Henry James 172   BORN 5 November 1878, Yeovil, Somerset. DIED 24 November 1955,
Winterbourne Anderson, Dorset. CREMATED Bournemouth Crematorium, Dorset. RANK Captain.

KNOWLAND, George Arthur 516   BORN 16 August 1922, Catford, Kent. DIED 31 January 1945,
during VC action, near Kangaw, west of Mandalay, Burma. BURIED Taukkyan War Cemetery,
Burma.

KNOX, Cecil Leonard 319   BORN 9 May 1889, Nuneaton, Warwickshire. DIED 4 February 1943, from
injuries sustained during a motorcycle accident, Nuneaton. CREMATED Gilroes Crematorium,
Leicester. RANK Major.

KNOX, John Simpson 8   BORN 30 September 1828, Calton, Glasgow. DIED 8 January 1897,
Cheltenham, Gloucestershire. BURIED Cheltenham Cemetery. RANK Brevet Major.

KONOWAL, Filip 269 BORN 15 September 1886, Podolsky, Ukraine, Russia. DIED 3 June 1959, Ontario, Canada. BURIED Notre Dame de Lourdes Cemetery, Ontario.

KULBIR THAPA 202 BORN 15 December 1889, Nigalpani, Palpa District, Nepal. DIED 3 October 1956, Nigalpani. No known grave. RANK Havildar.

LACHHIMAN GURUNG 524 BORN 30 December 1916, Dawakhani Village, Chitwan District, Western Nepal. RANK Hon. Havildar.

LAFONE, Alexander Malins 307 BORN 19 August 1870, Waterloo, Liverpool. DIED 27 October 1917, during VC action, near Beersheba, Palestine. BURIED Beersheba War Cemetery, Israel.

LAIDLAW, Daniel Logan 214 BORN 26 July 1875, Little Swinton, Northumberland. DIED 2 June 1950, Shoresdean, Borders Region. BURIED Norham Churchyard, Northumberland. Stone dedicated 2002. RANK Sergeant-Piper.

LALA 236 BORN 20 April 1876, Parol, Kangra District, India. DIED 23 March 1927, Parol. CREMATED Parol. RANK Jemadar.

LALBAHADUR THAPA 443 BORN February 1906, Somsa Village, Baghlung, Western Nepal. DIED 20 October 1968, Paklihawa, Nepal. BURIED Paklihawa Camp Cemetery, Nepal. RANK Subadar Major. O&D OBI.

LAMBERT, George 57 BORN 18 December 1819, Market Hill, Co. Armagh, Ireland. DIED 10 February 1860, Sheffield, Yorkshire. BURIED Wardsend Cemetery, Sheffield. RANK Lieutenant and Adjutant.

LANE, Thomas 100 BORN May 1836, Cork, Ireland. DIED 12 April 1889, Kimberley, South Africa. BURIED Gladstone Cemetery, Kimberley.

LASCELLES, Arthur Moore 297 BORN 12 October 1880, Streatham, London. DIED 7 November 1918, in action, Fontaine, France. BURIED Dourlers Communal Cemetery Extension, France. O&D MC.

LASSEN, Anders Frederik Emil Victor Schau 530 BORN 22 September 1920, South Zealand, Denmark. DIED 9 April 1945, during VC action, north shore of Lake Comacchio, Italy. BURIED Argenta Gap War Cemetery, Ravenna, Italy. O&D MC and 2 bars.

LAUDER, David Ross 228 BORN 21 January 1894, East Glentire, Airdrie, Scotland. DIED 4 June 1972, Cranhill, Glasgow. CREMATED Daldowie Crematorium.

LAUGHNAN, Thomas 76 BORN August 1824, Kilmadaugh, Co. Galway, Ireland. DIED 23 July 1864, Co. Galway. No known grave.

LAURENT, Harry John 341 BORN 15 April 1895, Tarata, Taranaki, New Zealand. DIED 9 December 1987, Hastings, New Zealand. CREMATED Hawera Crematorium, Taraniki. RANK Lieutenant Colonel.

LAWRENCE, Brian Turner Tom 171 BORN 9 November 1873, Bewdley, Worcestershire. DIED 7 June 1949, Nakuru, Kenya. CREMATED Nakuru Crematorium. RANK Lieutenant Colonel.

LAWRENCE, Samuel Hill 67 BORN 22 January 1831, Cork, Ireland. DIED 17 June 1868, Montevideo, Uruguay. BURIED British Cemetery, Montevideo. RANK Major.

LAWSON, Edward 148 BORN 11 April 1873, Newcastle upon Tyne. DIED 2 July 1955, Walker, Tyne and Wear. BURIED Heaton Cemetery, Newcastle upon Tyne.

LEACH, Edward Pemberton 116 BORN 2 April 1847, Londonderry, Ireland. DIED 27 April 1913, Cadenabbia, Italy. BURIED Grienze Churchyard, near Cadenabbia. RANK General. O&D KCB, KCVO.

LEACH, James Edgar 198 BORN 27 July 1892, North Shields, Northumberland. DIED 15 August 1958, Shepherds Bush, London. CREMATED Mortlake Crematorium, Surrey. RANK Captain.

LEAK, John 251 BORN 1896, Portsmouth, Hampshire. DIED 20 October 1972, Adelaide, South Australia. BURIED Stirling District Cemetery, Adelaide.

LEAKEY, Nigel Gray 403 BORN 1 January 1913, Kiganjo, Kenya. DIED 19 May 1941, during VC action, near Billate River, Abyssinia. No known grave.

LEARMONTH, Okill Massey 268 BORN 22 February 1894, Quebec City, Canada. DIED 19 August 1917, of wounds received during VC action, Loos, France. BURIED Noeux-les-Mines Communal Cemetery, France. O&D MC.

LEAROYD, Roderick Alastair Brook 391 BORN 5 February 1913, Folkestone, Kent. DIED 24 January 1996, Rustington, Sussex. CREMATED Worthing Crematorium, Sussex. RANK Wing Commander.

LEET, William Knox 128 BORN 3 November 1833, Dalkey, Ireland. DIED 29 June 1898, Great Chart, Kent. BURIED St Mary the Virgin Churchyard, Great Chart. RANK Major General. O&D CB.

LEITCH, Peter 34   BORN 1820, Orwell, Kinross, Scotland. DIED 6 December 1892, Fulham, London. BURIED Hammersmith Cemetery, London. Grave not marked.

LEITH, James Edgar 90   BORN 26 May 1826, Glenkindie, Aberdeenshire, Scotland. DIED 13 May 1869, Hyde Park, London. BURIED Towie Churchyard, near Glenkindie. RANK Major.

LENDRIM, William James (also known as LENDRUM) 27   BORN 1 January 1830, Ireland. DIED 28 November 1891, Camberley, Surrey. BURIED Royal Military Academy Cemetery, Camberley. RANK Sergeant Major.

LENNOX, Wilbraham Oates 26   BORN 4 August 1830, Goodwood, Sussex. DIED 7 February 1897, London. BURIED Lewes Road Cemetery, Brighton. RANK Lieutenant General. O&D KCB.

LENON, Edmund Henry 100   BORN 26 August 1838, Mortlake, Surrey. DIED 15 April 1893, Lambeth, London. BURIED Kensal Green Cemetery, London. Grave not marked. RANK Lieutenant Colonel.

LE PATOUREL, Herbert Wallace 434   BORN 20 June 1916, Guernsey, Channel Islands. DIED 4 September 1979, Chewton Mendip, Somerset. CREMATED South Bristol Crematorium, Bristol. RANK Brigadier.

LE QUESNE, Ferdinand Simeon 139   BORN 25 December 1863, Jersey. DIED 14 April 1950, Bristol, Avon. BURIED Canford Cemetery, Bristol. RANK Lieutenant Colonel.

LESTER, Frank 350   BORN 18 February 1896, Huyton, Liverpool, Lancashire. DIED 12 October 1918, during VC action, Neuvilly, France. BURIED Neuvilly Communal Cemetery Extension, France.

LEWIS, Hubert William 260   BORN 1 May 1896, Milford Haven, Dyfed, Wales. DIED 22 February 1977, Milford Haven. BURIED St Katherine's Cemetery, Milford Haven.

LEWIS, Leonard Allan 342   BORN 28 February 1895, Whitney-on-Wye, Herefordshire. DIED 21 September 1918, during VC action, Rossnoy, France. BURIED Lempire, France, by Australian troops. Grave later lost.

LIDDELL, Ian Oswald 514   BORN 19 October 1919, Shanghai, China. DIED 21 April 1945, killed after VC action by a sniper, near Rothenburg, Germany. BURIED Becklingen War Cemetery, Soltau, Germany.

LIDDELL, John Aiden 233   BORN 3 August 1888, Newcastle-upon-Tyne. DIED 31 August 1915, from wounds received during VC action, La Panne, Belgium. BURIED Basingstoke Old Cemetery, Hampshire. O&D MC.

LINTON, John Wallace 381   BORN 15 October 1905, Malpas, Monmouthshire, Wales. DIED 17 March 1943, aboard HM Submarine *Turbulent* after striking a mine, off Maddelina harbour, Sardinia, Italy. Body not recovered. O&D DSO, DSC.

LISLE-PHILLIPPS, Everard Aloysius 50   BORN 28 May 1835, Coleorton, Leics. DIED 18 September 1857, during VC action at Delhi, India. BURIED Old Delhi Military Cemetery. Grave not marked.

LISTER, Joseph 291   BORN 19 October 1886, Salford, Lancashire. DIED 19 January 1963, Reddish Hospital, Stockport, Cheshire. BURIED Willow Grove Cemetery, Reddish.

LLOYD, Owen Edward Pennefather 142   BORN 1 January 1854, Co. Roscommon, Ireland. DIED 5 July 1941, St Leonards-on-Sea, Sussex. BURIED Kensal Green Cemetery, London. RANK Major General. O&D KCB.

LODGE, Isaac 168   BORN 6 May 1866, Great Canfield, Essex. DIED 18 June 1923, Hyde Park, London. BURIED Hendon Park Cemetery, London. RANK Bombardier.

LOOSEMORE, Arnold 283   BORN 7 June 1896, Sharrow, Yorkshire. DIED 10 April 1924, as a result of tuberculosis, Stannington, near Sheffield. BURIED Ecclesall Churchyard, Sheffield. RANK Sergeant. O&D DCM.

LORD, David Samuel Anthony 499   BORN 18 October 1913, Cork, Ireland. DIED 19 September 1944, during VC action, north-west of Arnhem, Holland. BURIED Arnhem Oosterbeek War Cemetery, Holland. O&D DFC.

LOUDOUN-SHAND, Stewart Walker 245   BORN 8 October 1879, Ceylon. DIED 1 July 1916, during VC action, Fricourt, Somme, France. BURIED Norfolk Cemetery, Bécourt, France.

LOWERSON, Albert David 336   BORN 2 August 1896, Myrtleford, Victoria, Australia. DIED 15 December 1945, Myrtleford. BURIED Myrtleford Cemetery.

LOYD-LINDSAY, Robert James (later Lord Wantage) 8   BORN 17 April 1832, Balcarres, Fife, Scotland. DIED 10 June 1901, Lockinge, Berkshire. BURIED in vault at Ardington Church, Wantage, Oxfordshire. RANK Brigadier General. O&D KCB.

LUCAS, Charles Davis 5   BORN 19 February 1834, Drumargole, Co. Armagh, Ireland. DIED 7 August

1914, Great Culverden, Kent. BURIED St Lawrence's Churchyard, Mereworth, Kent. RANK Rear Admiral.

LUCAS, John 99 BORN 1826, Clashganny, Ireland. DIED 4 March 1892, Dublin. BURIED St James Churchyard, Dublin. Grave not marked. RANK Sergeant Major.

LUKE, Frederick 192 BORN 29 September 1895, Lockerley, Hampshire. DIED 12 March 1983, Glasgow. CREMATED Linn Crematorium, Glasgow. RANK Sergeant.

LUMLEY, Charles 39 BORN 1824, Forres, Morayshire, Scotland. DIED 17 October 1858. He committed suicide, Brecknock, Powys. BURIED Brecon Cathedral Churchyard, Powys. RANK Major.

LUMSDEN, Frederick William 266 BORN 14 December 1872, Fyzabad, India. DIED 4 June 1918. He was shot through the head by a sniper, Blairvill, near Arras, France. BURIED Berles New Military Cemetery, Berles-au-Bois, France. RANK Brigadier General. O&D CB, DSO and three bars.

LYALL, Graham Thomson 346 BORN 8 March 1892, Manchester, Lancashire. DIED 28 November 1941, killed in action, Mersa Matruh, Egypt. BURIED Halfaya Sollum War Cemetery, Egypt. RANK Colonel.

LYELL, Charles Anthony, the Lord 446 BORN 14 June 1913, Cadogan Gardens, London. DIED 27 April 1943, during VC action, Dj Bou Arada, Tunisia. BURIED Massicault War Cemetery, Tunisia.

LYNN, John 209 BORN 1887, Forest Hill, London. DIED 2 May 1915, during VC action, Wieltje, Belgium. O&D DCM.

LYONS, John 33 BORN 1824, Carlow, Ireland. DIED 20 April 1867, Naas, Co. Kildare, Ireland. Burial place unknown. RANK Corporal.

LYSONS, Henry 128 BORN 13 July 1858, Morden, Surrey. DIED 24 July 1907, Marylebone, London. BURIED St Peter's Churchyard, Rodmarton, Gloucestershire. RANK Colonel. O&D CB.

LYSTER, Harry Hammon 91 BORN 24 December 1830, Blackrock, Co. Dublin, Ireland. DIED 1 February 1922, London. BURIED St James the Less Churchyard, Stubbing, Berkshire. RANK Lieutenant General. O&D CB.

McARTHUR, Thomas, *see* Arthur, Thomas

McAULAY, John 295 BORN 27 December 1888, Fife, Scotland. DIED 14 January 1956, Burnside, Glasgow. BURIED New Eastwood Cemetery, Glasgow. O&D DCM.

McBEAN, William 85 BORN 1 January 1818, Inverness, Scotland. DIED 23 June 1878, Shooters Hill, London. BURIED Grange Cemetery, Edinburgh. RANK Major General.

McBEATH, Robert Gordon 294 BORN 22 December 1898, Fraserburgh, Caithness, Scotland. DIED 9 October 1922. He was shot dead whilst serving with the Canadian Police, Vancouver, Canada. CREMATED Mountain View Crematorium, Vancouver.

McCARTHY, Lawrence Dominic 332 BORN 21 January 1892, York, Western Australia. DIED 25 May 1975, Heidelberg, Victoria, Australia. CREMATED Springvale Crematorium, Melbourne.

McCORRIE, Charles (also known as McCURRY) 35 BORN 1830, Killead, Co. Antrim, Ireland. DIED 8 April 1857, Malta. BURIED Msida Bastion Cemetery, Valletta, Malta. Grave not marked.

McCREA, John Frederick 130 BORN 2 April 1854, St Peter Port, Guernsey. DIED 16 July 1894, Kokstad, South Africa. BURIED Kokstad Cemetery, East Griqualand, Cape Province. RANK Surgeon-Major.

McCUDDEN, James Thomas Byford 300 BORN 28 March 1895, Gillingham, Kent. DIED 9 July 1918. He was killed in a flying accident on his way to take over his new squadron, Marquise, France. BURIED Wavans British Cemetery, France. RANK Major. O&D DSO and bar, MC and bar, MM.

McCURRY, Charles, *see* McCorrie, Charles

McDERMOND, John 22 BORN 1832, Glasgow. DIED 22 July 1868, Glasgow. BURIED Woodside Cemetery, Paisley, Glasgow. Grave not marked.

MacDONALD, Henry 28 BORN 28 May 1823, Inverness, Scotland. DIED 15 February 1893, Glasgow. BURIED Western Necropolis, Glasgow. RANK Hon. Captain.

McDONELL, William Fraser 57 BORN 17 December 1829, Cheltenham, Gloucestershire. DIED 31 July 1894, Cheltenham. BURIED St Peter's Churchyard, Leckenham, Gloucestershire.

McDOUGALL, John 100 BORN 1839, Edinburgh, Scotland. DIED 10 March 1869, Edinburgh. BURIED Old Calton Cemetery, Edinburgh.

McDOUGALL, Stanley Robert 321 BORN 23 July 1890, Hobart, Tasmania, Australia. DIED 7 July 1968, Scottsdale, Tasmania. CREMATED Norwood Crematorium, Mitchell, Canberra. O&D MM.

MacDOWELL, Thain Wendell 273 BORN 16 September 1890, Quebec, Canada. DIED 27 March 1960, Nassau, Bahamas. BURIED Oakland Cemetery. RANK Colonel. O&D DSO.

McFADZEAN, William Frederick 245 BORN 9 October 1895, Lurgan, Co. Armagh, Ireland. DIED 1 July 1916, during VC action, Thiepval, Somme, France. No known grave.

McGAW, Samuel 113 BORN 1838, Kirkmichael, Scotland. DIED 22 July 1878. He dropped dead from sunstroke on arrival in Larnaca, Cyprus. BURIED British Cemetery, Kyrenia, Cyprus. RANK Sergeant.

McGEE, Lewis 289 BORN 13 May 1888, Tasmania, Australia. DIED 13 October 1917. He was shot in the head during an attack nine days after his VC action, Passchendaele, Belgium. BURIED Tyne Cot Cemetery, Belgium.

McGOVERN, John 53 BORN 16 May 1825, Templeport, Co. Cavan, Ireland. DIED 22 November 1888, Hamilton, Ontario, Canada. BURIED Holy Sepulchre Cemetery, Hamilton.

McGREGOR, David Stuart 315 BORN 16 October 1895, Edinburgh, Scotland. DIED 22 October 1918, during VC action, near Hoogemolen, Belgium. BURIED Staceghem Communal Cemetery, Belgium.

McGREGOR, John 347 BORN 11 February 1889, Cawdor, Nairn, Scotland. DIED 9 June 1952, Powell River, British Columbia, Canada. BURIED Cranberry Lake Cemetery, Powell River. RANK Lieutenant Colonel. O&D MC and bar, DCM, ED.

McGREGOR, Roderick 29 BORN 1822, Dunain, near Inverness, Scotland. DIED 9 August 1888, Buntait, Urquhart, Inverness. BURIED St Mary's Churchyard, Drumnadrochit, Highland Region.

McGUFFIE, Louis 313 BORN 15 March 1893, Wigtown, Galloway, Scotland. DIED 4 October 1918, killed by a shell a few days after his VC action, Wytschaete, Belgium. BURIED Zantvoorde British Cemetery, Belgium.

McGUIRE, James 63 BORN 1827, Enniskillen, Co. Fermanagh, Ireland. DIED 22 December 1862, Lisnaskea, Co. Fermanagh, Ireland. BURIED Donagh Cemetery, Lisnaskea. Grave not marked.

McHALE, Patrick 73 BORN 1826, Killala, Co. Mayo, Ireland. DIED 26 October 1866, Shorncliffe, Kent. BURIED Shorncliffe Military Cemetery.

McINNES, Hugh 76 BORN October 1835, Anderston, Glasgow. DIED 7 December 1879, Glasgow. BURIED Dalbeth Cemetery, Glasgow. Grave not marked.

McINTOSH, George Imlach 282 BORN 22 April 1897, Banffshire, Scotland. DIED 20 June 1960, Aberdeen, Scotland. BURIED New Cemetery, Banff. RANK Flight Sergeant.

MacINTYRE, David Lowe 333 BORN 18 June 1895, Portnahaven, Isle of Islay, Scotland. DIED 31 July 1967, Edinburgh. CREMATED Warriston Crematorium, Edinburgh. RANK Major General. O&D CB.

MACINTYRE, Donald 111 BORN 12 September 1831, Kincraig, Scotland. DIED 15 April 1903, Fortrose, Scotland. BURIED Rosmarkie Churchyard, near Fortrose. RANK Major General.

McIVER, Hugh 333 BORN 21 June 1890, Kilbarchan, Renfrewshire, Scotland. DIED 2 September 1918, killed during an attack on a machine-gun post, Courcelles, France. BURIED Vracourt Copse Cemetery, France. O&D MM and bar.

MACKAY, David 78 BORN 23 November 1831, Howe, Caithness, Scotland. DIED 18 November 1880, Lesmahagow, Lanarkshire, Scotland. BURIED Lesmahagow Cemetery.

McKAY, Ian 551 BORN 7 May 1953, Wortley, Yorkshire. DIED 12 June 1982, during VC action, on the slopes of Mount Longdon, Falkland Islands. BURIED Aldershot Military Cemetery, Hampshire.

MACKAY, John Frederick 170 BORN 21 July 1873, Edinburgh. DIED 9 January 1930, Nice, France. BURIED Cimetière de Caucade, Nice. RANK Lieutenant Colonel.

McKEAN, George Burdon 310 BORN 4 July 1888, Bishop Auckland, Co. Durham. DIED 26 November 1926, in a dreadful accident when a circular saw disintegrated in a sawmill he owned, Potter's Bar, Hertfordshire. BURIED Brighton Extra-Mural Cemetery, Sussex. RANK Captain. O&D MC, MM.

McKECHNIE, James 8 BORN June 1826, Paisley, Renfrewshire, Scotland. DIED 5 July 1886, Glasgow. BURIED Eastern Necropolis, Glasgow. Grave not marked.

McKENNA, Edward 102 BORN 15 February 1827, Leeds, Yorkshirehire. DIED 8 June 1908, Palmerston North, New Zealand. BURIED Terrace End Cemetery, Palmerston North. RANK Ensign.

McKENZIE, Albert Edward 366 BORN 23 October 1898, Bermondsey, London. DIED 3 November 1918. Having made a near total recovery from wounds sustained during VC action, died of influenza during epidemic, Chatham, Kent. BURIED Camberwell Cemetery, London.

MAGNER, Michael 111   BORN 21 June 1840, Co. Fermanagh, Ireland. DIED 6 February 1897, Melbourne, Australia. BURIED Melbourne General Cemetery. RANK Corporal.

MAHONEY, Patrick 70   BORN 1827, Waterford, Ireland. DIED 30 October 1857, Lucknow, India. No known grave.

MAHONY, John Keefer 477   BORN 30 June 1911, New Westminster, British Columbia, Canada. DIED 16 December 1990, London, Ontario. CREMATED Mount Pleasant Crematorium, London, Ontario.

MAILLARD, William Job 153   BORN 10 March 1863, Banwell, Somerset. DIED 10 September 1903, Bournemouth, Dorset. BURIED Wimborne Road Cemetery, Bournemouth. RANK Staff Surgeon.

MALCOLM, Hugh Gordon 433   BORN 2 May 1917, Dundee, Scotland. DIED 4 December 1942, during VC action, near Chouigui, Tunisia. BURIED Beja War Cemetery, Tunisia.

MALCOLMSON, John Grant 98   BORN 9 February 1835, Muchrach, Scotland. DIED 14 August 1902, London. BURIED Kensal Green Cemetery, London. RANK Captain. O&D MVO.

MALING, George Allen 203   BORN 6 October 1888, Sunderland, Co. Durham. DIED 9 July 1929, Lee, London. BURIED Chislehurst Cemetery, Kent. RANK Captain.

MALLESON, Wilfred St Aubyn 220   BORN 17 September 1896, Kirkee, India. DIED 21 July 1975, St Clement, Cornwall. CREMATED Penmount Crematorium, Truro, Cornwall. RANK Captain.

MALONE, Joseph 15   BORN 11 January 1833, Eccles, Manchester. DIED 28 June 1883, Pinetown, Natal, South Africa. BURIED St Andrew's Churchyard, Pinetown. RANK Captain and Riding Master.

MANGLES, Ross Lowis 57   BORN 14 April 1833, Calcutta, India. DIED 28 February 1905, Pirbright, Surrey. BURIED Brookwood Cemetery, Surrey.

MANLEY, William George Nicholas 103   BORN 17 December 1831, Dublin, Ireland. DIED 16 November 1901, Cheltenham, Gloucestershire. BURIED Cheltenham Cemetery. RANK Surgeon-General.

MANNERS-SMITH, John 140   BORN 30 August 1864, Lahore, Pakistan. DIED 6 January 1920, London. BURIED Kensal Green Cemetery, London. RANK Lieutenant Colonel. O&D CIE, CVO.

MANNOCK, Edward 358   BORN 24 May 1887, Ballincollig, Co. Cork, Ireland. DIED 26 July 1918, Having shot down an enemy aircraft whilst flying with a new member of the squadron, he was hit by ground fire. His aircraft caught fire and crashed behind German lines, near Lillers, France. No known grave.

MANSEL-JONES, Conwyn 169   BORN 14 June 1871, Beddington, Surrey. DIED 29 May 1942, Brockenhurst, Hampshire. BURIED St Nicholas' Churchyard, Brockenhurst. O&D CMG, DSO.

MANSER, Leslie Thomas 422   BORN 11 May 1922, New Delhi, India. DIED 31 May 1942, during VC action near Bree, Belgium. BURIED Heverlee War Cemetery, Belgium.

MANTLE, Jack Foreman 392   BORN 12 April 1917, Wandsworth, London. DIED 4 July 1940, during VC action, on HMS *Foylebank*. BURIED Portland Royal Naval Cemetery, Dorset.

MARINER, William (enlisted as William Wignall) 211   BORN 29 May 1882, Chorley, Lancashire. DIED 1 July 1916, killed in action, Loos, France. No known grave.

MARLING, Sir Percival Scrope 136   BORN 6 March 1861, Stroud, Gloucestershire. DIED 29 May 1936, Stroud. BURIED All Saints Church, Selsley, Stroud. RANK Colonel. O&D CB.

MARSHALL, James Neville 355   BORN 12 June 1887, Stretford, Manchester. DIED 4 November 1918, during VC action, Sambre–Oise Canal near Ors, France. BURIED Ors Communal Cemetery, France. O&D MC and bar.

MARSHALL, William Thomas 134   BORN 5 December 1854, Newark, Nottinghamshire. DIED 11 September 1920, Kirkcaldy, Scotland. BURIED Bennochy Road Cemetery, Kirkcaldy. RANK Lieutenant Colonel and Quartermaster.

MARTIN, Cyril Gordon 206   BORN 19 December 1891, Foochow, China. DIED 14 August 1980, Woolwich, London. CREMATED Eltham Crematorium, London. RANK Brigadier. O&D CBE, DSO.

MARTINEAU, Horace Robert 162   BORN 31 October 1874, Bayswater, London. DIED 7 April 1916, Dunedin, New Zealand. BURIED Andersons Bay Soldiers' Cemetery, Dunedin. RANK Lieutenant.

MARTIN-LEAKE, Arthur 176, 195   BORN 4 April 1874, Standen, Hertfordshire. DIED 22 June 1953, Ware, Hertfordshire. Ashes buried St John the Evangelist Churchyard, Ware. RANK Lieutenant Colonel.

MASTERS, Richard George 324   BORN 23 March 1877, Southport, Lancashire. DIED 4 April 1963, Southport. BURIED St Cuthbert's Parish Churchyard, Southport.

MASTERSON, James Edward Ignatius 166   BORN 20 June 1862, place unknown. DIED 24 December 1935, Waterlooville, Hampshire. BURIED Hulbert Road Cemetery, Waterlooville. RANK Major.

MAUDE, Francis Cornwallis 71 BORN 28 October 1828, London. DIED 19 October 1900, Windsor, Berkshire. BURIED Windsor Borough Cemetery. RANK Colonel. O&D CB.

MAUDE, Frederick Francis 39 BORN 20 December 1821, Lisnadill, Co. Armagh, Ireland. DIED 20 June 1897, Torquay, Devon. BURIED Brompton Cemetery, London. RANK General. O&D GCB.

MAUFE, Thomas Harold Broadbent 278 BORN 6 May 1898, Ilkley, Yorkshire. DIED 28 March 1942. He was killed during mortar practice whilst serving in the Home Guard, Ilkley. BURIED Ilkley Cemetery. RANK Captain.

MAXWELL, Francis Aylmer 168 BORN 7 September 1871, Guildford, Surrey. DIED 21 September 1917. He was killed in action whilst commanding 27th Infantry Brigade, Ypres, Belgium. BURIED Ypres Reservoir Cemetery. RANK Brigadier General. O&D CSI, DSO and bar.

MAXWELL, Joseph 349 BORN 10 February 1896, Sydney, New South Wales, Australia. DIED 6 July 1967, Matraville, New South Wales. CREMATED Eastern Suburbs Crematorium, Botany Bay, Sydney. O&D MC and bar, DCM.

MAY, Henry 195 BORN 29 July 1885, Glasgow. DIED 26 July 1941, Glasgow. BURIED Riddrie Park Cemetery, Glasgow. RANK Lieutenant.

MAYGAR, Leslie Cecil 175 BORN 26 May 1874, Kilmore, Australia. DIED 17 November 1917. Killed in action at the Battle of Beersheba, Israel. BURIED Beersheba War Cemetery. RANK Lieutenant Colonel. O&D DSO, VD.

MAYO, Arthur 83 BORN 18 May 1840, Oxford. DIED 18 May 1920, Boscombe, Dorset. BURIED East Cemetery, Boscombe.

MAYSON, Tom Fletcher 282 BORN 3 November 1893, Silecroft, Cumbria. DIED 21 February 1958, Barrow-in-Furness, Lancashire. BURIED at Mary's Churchyard, Whicham, near Silecroft.

MEEKOSHA, Samuel (in 1939 changed to INGHAM by deed poll) 203 BORN 16 September 1893, Leeds, Yorkshire. DIED 8 December 1950, Oakdale, Gwent, Wales. CREMATED Glyntaff Crematorium, Pontypridd. RANK Major.

MEIKLE, John 327 BORN 11 September 1898, Kirkintilloch, Dunbartonshire, Scotland. DIED 20 July 1918, during VC action, near Marfaux, France. BURIED Marfaux British Cemetery. O&D MM.

MEIKLEJOHN, Matthew Fontaine Maury 162 BORN 27 November 1870, Clapham, London. DIED 4 July 1913. His horse bolted in Hyde Park, and he turned it towards some railings to avoid a group of children. He was badly thrown and died a week later, Middlesex Hospital, London. BURIED Brookwood Cemetery, Woking, Surrey. RANK Major.

MELLISH, Edward Noel 239 BORN 24 December 1880, Barnet. Hertfordshire. DIED 8 July 1962, South Petherton, Somerset. CREMATED Weymouth Crematorium, Dorset. O&D MC.

MELLISS, Charles John 154 BORN 12 September 1862, Mhow, India. DIED 6 June 1936, Camberley, Surrey. BURIED St Peter's Churchyard, Frimley, Surrey. RANK Major General. O&D KCB, KCMG.

MELVILL, Teignmouth 126 BORN 8 September 1842, Marylebone, London. DIED 22 January 1879, Buffalo River, South Africa. BURIED Fugitive's Drift, below Itchiane Hill, South Africa.

MELVIN, Charles 303 BORN 2 May 1885, Montrose, Scotland. DIED 17 July 1941, Kirriemuir, Tayside Region, Scotland. BURIED Kirriemuir Cemetery.

MERRIFIELD, William 348 BORN 9 October 1890, Brentwood, Essex. DIED 8 August 1943, Toronto, Canada. BURIED West Korah Cemetery, Sault-Ste-Marie, Ontario. O&D MM.

MERRITT, Charles Cecil Ingersoll 430 BORN 10 November 1908, Vancouver, Canada. DIED 12 July 2000, Vancouver. BURIED Ocean View Memorial Park, Burnaby, Vancouver.

METCALF, William Henry 339 BORN 29 January 1885, Waite, Maine, USA. DIED 8 August 1968, South Portland, Maine. BURIED Bayside Cemetery, Eastport, Maine. O&D MM.

MEYNELL, Godfrey 378 BORN 20 May 1904, Meynell Langley, Derbyshire. DIED 29 September 1935, during VC action, near Mohmand, North-West Frontier, India. BURIED Guides Cemetery, Mardan, North-West Frontier. O&D MC.

MIDDLETON, Rawdon Hume 423 BORN 22 July 1916, Waverley, Sydney, Australia. DIED 29 November 1942, during VC action when his aircraft crashed at sea, near Dymchurch, Kent. BURIED St John's Churchyard, Mildenhall, Suffolk. RANK Pilot Officer (posthumous).

MIERS, Anthony Cecil Capel 418 BORN 11 November 1906, Birchwood, Inverness, Scotland. DIED 30 June 1985, Inverness. BURIED Tomnahurich Cemetery, Inverness. RANK Rear Admiral. O&D KBE, CB, DSO and bar.

MILBANKE, John Peniston (later Sir John) 165 BORN 9 October 1872, London. DIED 21 August 1915, killed in action, Gallipoli, Turkey. No known grave. RANK Lieutenant Colonel.

GREGG, William 311   BORN 27 January 1890, Heanor, Derbyshire. DIED 9 August 1969, Heanor. CREMATED Heanor Crematorium. RANK Company Sergeant Major. O&D DCM, MM.

GRENFELL, Francis Octavus 191   BORN 4 September 1880, Hatchlands, Surrey. DIED 24 May 1915, in action, Hooge, Belgium. BURIED Vlamertinghe Military Cemetery, near Ypres.

GRIBBLE, Julian Royds 319   BORN 5 January 1897, London. DIED 25 November 1918, while a prisoner of war, Kessel, Germany. BURIED Niederzehren Cemetery, Kessel.

GRIEVE, John 15   BORN 3 May 1821, Musselburgh, Midlothian, Scotland. DIED 1 December 1873, Inveresk, Midlothian. BURIED St Michael's Churchyard, Inveresk. Stone erected 2003. RANK Lieutenant and Adjutant.

GRIEVE, Robert Cuthbert 279   BORN 19 June 1889, Melbourne, Victoria, Australia. DIED 4 October 1957, Melbourne. BURIED Springvale Cemetery, Melbourne.

GRIFFITHS, William 110   BORN 1841, Co. Roscommon, Ireland. DIED 22 January 1879. He was killed during the Battle of Isandlwana, Isandlwana, South Africa. His body was recovered five months later still wearing his VC. Grave not marked.

GRIMBALDESTON, William Henry 284   BORN 19 September 1889, Blackburn, Lancashire. DIED 13 August 1959, Blackburn. CREMATED Pleasington Crematorium, Blackburn.

GRIMSHAW, John Elisha 219   BORN 23 January 1893, Abram, Lancashire. DIED 20 July 1980, Isleworth, Middlesex. CREMATED South West Middlesex Crematorium, Hanworth. RANK Lieutenant Colonel.

GRISTOCK, George 388   BORN 14 January 1905, Pretoria, South Africa. DIED 16 June 1940, as a result of wounds received during VC action, Brighton. BURIED Bear Road Cemetery, Brighton.

GROGAN, George William St George 327   BORN 1 September 1875, St Andrews, Fifeshire, Scotland. DIED 3 January 1962, Sunningdale, Berkshire. CREMATED Woking Crematorium, Surrey. O&D CB, CMG, DSO and bar.

GUISE, John Christopher (later Sir John) 77   BORN 27 July 1826, Highnam, Gloucestershire. DIED 5 February 1895, Gorey, Co. Wexford, Ireland. BURIED Gorey Churchyard. RANK Lieutenant General. O&D CB.

GUNN, George Ward 399   BORN 26 July 1912, Muggleswick, Co. Durham. DIED 21 November 1941, during VC action, near Sidi Rezegh Airfield, Libya. BURIED Knightsbridge War Cemetery, Acroma, Libya. O&D MC.

GURNEY, Arthur Stanley 428   BORN 15 December 1908, Murchison Goldfields, Western Australia. DIED 22 July 1942, during VC action, Tel-el-Eisa, Egypt. BURIED El Alamein War Cemetery, Egypt.

GUY, Basil John Douglas 155   BORN 9 May 1882, Bishop Auckland, Co. Durham. DIED 28 December 1956, Lambeth, London. BURIED St Michael's and All Angels Churchyard, Pirbright, Surrey. RANK Commander. O&D DSO.

HACKETT, Thomas Bernard 78   BORN 15 June 1836, Riverstown, Co. Tipperary, Ireland. DIED 5 October 1880. He was killed by the explosion of his own gun, Arrabeg, Offaly, Ireland. BURIED Lockeen Churchyard, Co. Tipperary. RANK Lieutenant Colonel.

HACKETT, William 240   BORN 11 June 1873, Nottingham. DIED 27 June 1916, during VC action, near Givenchy, France. No known grave.

HAINE, Reginald Leonard 276   BORN 10 July 1896, Wandsworth, London. DIED 12 June 1982, Lambeth, London. CREMATED Chichester Crematorium, Sussex. RANK Lieutenant Colonel. O&D MC and bar.

HALE, Thomas Egerton 39   BORN 24 September 1832, Nantwich, Cheshire. DIED 25 December 1909, Nantwich. BURIED Acton Parish Churchyard, near Nantwich. RANK Lieutenant Colonel. O&D CB.

HALL, Arthur Charles 336   BORN 11 August 1896, Granville, New South Wales, Australia. DIED 25 February 1978, New South Wales. BURIED St Matthew's Anglican Churchyard, Coolabah, New South Wales. RANK Lieutenant.

HALL, Frederick William 208   BORN 21 February 1885, Kilkenny, Ireland. DIED 24 April 1915, during VC action, Poelcappelle, Belgium. No known grave.

HALL, William 79   BORN 25 April 1829, Nova Scotia, Canada. DIED 25 August 1904, Avonport, Nova Scotia. BURIED Hantsport Baptist Church Cemetery, Nova Scotia. RANK Quartermaster and Petty Officer.

McKENZIE, Hugh McDonald 293   BORN 5 December 1885, Liverpool, Lancashire. DIED 30 October 1917, during VC action, Meescheele Spur, Belgium. No known grave. O&D DCM.

MACKENZIE, James 199   BORN 2 April 1884, West Glen, Scotland. DIED 19 December 1914. He was shot through the heart by a sniper a few hours after his VC action, Rouges Bancs, France. No known grave.

MACKENZIE, John 153   BORN 22 November 1871, Contin, Scotland. DIED 17 May 1915. He was killed in action, Béthune, France. BURIED Guards Cemetery, Cuinchy, France. RANK Major.

MACKEY, John Bernard 533   BORN 16 May 1922, Leichhardt, Sydney, Australia. DIED 12 May 1945, during VC action, Tarakan Island off the coast of North Borneo. BURIED Labuan War Cemetery, Borneo.

MACKINTOSH, Donald 275   BORN 7 February 1896, Glasgow, Scotland. DIED 11 April 1917, during VC action, near Fampoux, France. BURIED Brown's Copse Cemetery, France.

MACLEAN, Hector Lachlan Stewart 148   BORN 13 September 1897, Bannu, Pakistan. DIED 17 August 1897, Nawa Kili, Pakistan. BURIED St Alban's Churchyard, Mardan, Pakistan.

McLEOD, Alan Arnett 357   BORN 20 April 1899, Manitoba, Canada. DIED 6 November 1918, from influenza during the epidemic, Winnipeg, Canada. BURIED Winnipeg Presbyterian Cemetery.

McMANUS, Peter 72   BORN March 1829, Tynan, Co. Armagh, Ireland. DIED 27 April 1859, Allahabad, India. No known grave. RANK Sergeant.

McMASTER, Valentine Munbee 71   BORN 16 May 1834, Trichinopoly, India. DIED 22 January 1872, Belfast. BURIED City Cemetery, Belfast, Northern Ireland. RANK Surgeon.

McNAIR, Eric Archibald 239   BORN 16 June 1894, Calcutta. DIED 12 August 1918, from chronic dysentery, Genoa, Italy. BURIED Staglieno Commonwealth War Graves Cemetery, Genoa. RANK Captain.

McNALLY, William 369   BORN 16 December 1894, Murton, Co. Durham. DIED 5 January 1976, Murton. CREMATED Tyne and Wear Crematorium, Sunderland. O&D MM.

McNAMARA, Frank Hubert 298   BORN 4 April 1896, Victoria, Australia. DIED 2 November 1961, Gerrards Cross, Buckinghamshire. BURIED St Joseph's Priory, Gerrards Cross. RANK Air Vice Marshal. O&D CB, CBE.

McNAMARA, John 340   BORN 28 October 1887, Preston, Lancashire. DIED 16 October 1918, killed in action, Solesmes, France. BURIED Romeries Cemetery Extension, France.

McNEILL, John Carstairs 103   BORN 28 March 1831, Isle of Colonsay, Scotland. DIED 25 May 1904, St James's Palace, London. BURIED in family chapel at Oronsay Priory, Isle of Colonsay. RANK Major General. O&D GCVO, KCB, KCMG.

McNESS, Frederick 257   BORN 22 January 1892, Bramley, Yorkshire. DIED 4 May 1958. He took his own life whilst 'balance of mind disturbed', Boscombe, Dorset. CREMATED Bournemouth Crematorium. No memorial. RANK Sergeant.

MACPHERSON, Herbert Taylor 71   BORN 22 January 1827, Ardersier, Inverness-shire, Scotland. DIED 20 October 1886, Prome, Burma. BURIED Yay Way Cemetery, North Okalapa, Noka, Myanmar. Grave not marked. RANK Major General. O&D GCB, KCSI.

McPHERSON, Stewart 72   BORN 1822, Culross, Dunfermline, Scotland. DIED 7 December 1892, Culross. BURIED Culross Abbey Cemetery.

McPHIE, James 351   BORN 18 December 1894, Edinburgh, Scotland. DIED 14 October 1918, during VC action, Canal de la Sensée near Aubencheul-au-Bac, France. BURIED Naves Communal Cemetery Extension, France.

McQUIRT, Bernard 83   BORN 1829, Lurgan, Co. Armagh, Ireland. DIED 5 October 1888, Belfast. BURIED City Cemetery, Belfast.

McREADY-DIARMID, Allastair Malcolm Cluny 296   BORN 21 March 1888, Southgate, London. DIED 1 December 1917, during VC action, Moeuvres, France. No known grave.

MACTIER, Robert 336   BORN 17 May 1890, Tatura, Victoria, Australia. DIED 1 September 1918, during VC action, Péronne, France. BURIED Hem Farm Cemetery, Hem-Monacu, France.

McWHEENEY, William 12   BORN 1830, Bangor, Co. Down, Ireland. DIED 17 May 1866, Dover, Kent. BURIED St James's Cemetery, Dover.

MADDEN, Ambrose 18   BORN 1820, Cork. DIED 1 January 1863, Jamaica. BURIED Up Park Military Cemetery, Jamaica. RANK Lieutenant.

MAGENNIS, James Joseph 534   BORN 27 October 1919, Belfast, Northern Ireland. DIED 11 February 1986, Halifax, Yorkshire. CREMATED Nab Wood Crematorium, Shipley, Yorkshire.

MILES, Francis George 352   BORN 9 July 1896, Clearwell, Gloucestershire. DIED 8 November 1961, Clearwell. BURIED St Peter's Parish Churchyard, Clearwell.

MILLAR, Duncan 94   BORN June 1831, Kilmarnock, Scotland. DIED 15 July 1881, Glasgow. BURIED St Kentigern's Cemetery, Glasgow.

MILLER, Frederick 22   BORN 10 November 1831, Radway-under-Edge Hill, Warwickshire. DIED 17 February 1874, Cape Town, South Africa. BURIED Ossuary Garden of Remembrance, Observatory, Cape Town. RANK Lieutenant Colonel.

MILLER, James 251   BORN 13 March 1890, Houghton, Lancashire. DIED 31 July 1916, from wounds received during VC action, near Bazentin-le-Petit, Somme. BURIED Dartmoor Cemetery, Albert, France.

MILLER, James William 73   BORN 1820, Glasgow. DIED 12 June 1892, Simla, India. BURIED Simla Churchyard. Grave not marked. RANK Hon. Lieutenant.

MILLS, Walter 272   BORN 20 June 1894, Oldham, Lancashire. DIED 11 December 1917. He was killed by gas poisoning shortly after his VC action, Givenchy, France. BURIED Gorre British Cemetery, France.

MILNE, William Johnstone 274   BORN 21 December 1891, Lanarkshire, Scotland. DIED 9 April 1917, from wounds received during VC action, near Vimy, France. No known grave.

MINER, Herbert Garnet Bedford 329   BORN 24 June 1891, Cedar Springs, Ontario, Canada. DIED 8 August 1918, during VC action, Demuin, France. BURIED Crouy British Cemetery, Somme, France.

MIR DAST 208   BORN 3 December 1874, Tirah, India. DIED 19 January 1945, Peshawar, Pakistan. BURIED Warsak Road Cemetery, Pakistan. RANK Subadar. O&D IOM.

MITCHELL, Coulson Norman 350   BORN 11 December 1889, Winnipeg, Manitoba, Canada. DIED 17 November 1978, Mount Royal, Quebec, Canada. BURIED Field of Honour Cemetery, Pointe Claire, Mount Royal, Quebec. RANK Lieutenant Colonel. O&D MC.

MITCHELL, George Allan 473   BORN 30 August 1911, Highgate, London. DIED 24 January 1944, during VC action, Damiano Ridge, Italy. BURIED Minturno War Cemetery, Italy.

MITCHELL, Samuel 104   BORN 8 September 1841, Woburn, Bedfordshire. DIED 16 March 1894, Hokitika, New Zealand. BURIED on hillside near Ross, New Zealand.

MOFFAT, Martin Joseph 314   BORN 15 April 1882, Sligo, Ireland. DIED 5 January 1946. He drowned in the sea; there was nothing to show how he entered the water, but there were suggestions that it could have been suicide as he had just lost his job as constable, Rosses Point, Sligo. BURIED Sligo Town Cemetery.

MOLYNEUX, John 291   BORN 22 November 1890, St Helens, Lancashire. DIED 25 March 1972, St Helens. CREMATED St Helens Crematorium.

MONAGHAN, Thomas 93   BORN 18 April 1833, Abergavenny, Wales. DIED 10 November 1895, Woolwich, London. BURIED Woolwich Cemetery. RANK Sergeant Major.

MONGER, George 79   BORN 3 March 1840, Woodmancott, Hampshire. DIED 9 August 1887, St Leonards-on-Sea, Sussex. BURIED Hastings Borough Cemetery, Sussex.

MOON, Rupert Vance 278   BORN 14 August 1892, Victoria, Australia. DIED 28 February 1986, Whittington, Victoria. BURIED Mount Duneed Cemetery, Victoria. RANK Captain.

MOOR, George Raymond Dallas 226   BORN 22 October 1896, Melbourne, Australia. DIED 3 November 1918, from influenza during the epidemic, Mouveaux, France. BURIED Y Farm Military Cemetery, Bois-Grenier, France. RANK Lieutenant. O&D MC and bar.

MOORE, Arthur Thomas 98   BORN 20 September 1830, Co. Louth, Ireland. DIED 25 April 1923, Dublin. BURIED Mount Jerome Cemetery, Dublin. RANK Major General. O&D CB.

MOORE, Hans Garrett 114   BORN 31 March 1834, Richmond Barracks, Dublin, Ireland. DIED 7 October 1889. He was drowned during a tremendous gale, Lough Derg, Ireland. BURIED Mount Jerome Cemetery, Dublin. RANK Colonel. O&D CB.

MOORE, Montague Shadworth Seymour 284   BORN 9 October 1896, Bournemouth, Dorset. DIED 12 September 1966, Nyeri, Kenya. CREMATED Langata Crematorium, Nairobi, Kenya. RANK Major.

MORLEY, Samuel 87   BORN December 1829, Radcliffe on Trent, Nottinghamshire. DIED 16 June 1888, Nottingham. BURIED General Cemetery, Nottingham.

MORRELL, Thomas, *see* Young, Thomas

MORROW, Robert 206   BORN 7 September 1891, Sessia, Ireland. DIED 26 April 1915, from wounds received in action, St-Jean, Belgium. BURIED White House Cemetery, St-Jean.